MBO
UPDATED

BOOKS BY PAUL MALI

MANAGING BY OBJECTIVES

HOW TO MANAGE BY OBJECTIVES

IMPROVING TOTAL PRODUCTIVITY

MANAGEMENT HANDBOOK

WRITING AND WORD PROCESSING

MBO UPDATED: A HANDBOOK OF PRACTICES AND
TECHNIQUES FOR MANAGING BY OBJECTIVES

MBO
UPDATED

A HANDBOOK OF PRACTICES
AND TECHNIQUES FOR
MANAGING BY OBJECTIVES

PAUL MALI, PhD, CMC

Graduate School of Business,
University of Hartford, and
Paul Mali & Associates,
Management Consultants

A Wiley-Interscience Publication
JOHN WILEY & SONS
New York • Chichester • Brisbane • Toronto • Singapore

Library of Congress Cataloging in Publication Data:
Mali, Paul.
  MBO updated.

  Includes index.
  1. Management by objectives. I. Title.
HD30.65.M35   1986   658.4'012   85-20381
ISBN 0-471-82987-0

Printed in the United States of America

10 9 8 7 6 5 4 3 2 1

Excellence is getting results
you are committed to
rather than just whatever happens.

Preface

A great deal of experience has been accumulated with the practice of managing by objectives (MBO) over the years. Some of it is bad. Much of it is good. The practice of MBO itself has changed with experience. It has changed because companies, like society, are finding that they must change to deal with the new turbulent forces of our age. These forces are such that we feel our management processes must continually be fine tuned to adjust for a new static, a new set of demands, a new challenge. MBO must change too.

WHY THIS HANDBOOK?

MBO Updated is primarily a guide and reference book. It is a tool to be used by managerial practitioners in the day-to-day work of their organizations. Like a tool, it should never be more than a short reach away. It does not address in depth all functions that make a company run. But it does provide sufficient breadth of coverage for most practitioners of MBO. The more frequently it is used, the more useful it becomes. This MBO book aims to achieve four objectives:

1.   To update the practice of MBO since its inception in the 1960s and 1970s. I have collected and documented within these covers the latest MBO practices of organizations. These practices and the guidelines presented are useful for solving productivity and performance problems now faced and those to come. Eight of ten companies in the United States now practice MBO. The seasoned practitioner will find old and proven material here but also new tips and new ways to use MBO. (Readers who are acquainted with the basic elements of MBO might want to skip the first few chapters and move to those chapters that deal directly with managerial issues and concerns.) The practitioner will see how MBO has been modified to meet contemporary issues. This book serves as an operating guide for those who wish to introduce productivity improvement into their organizations using the latest MBO skills and proven strategies.

2.   To provide a complete reference guide for the practice of MBO for managers who are moving into or upward in management. Firms that practice MBO will find this handbook an efficient way to get new managers and supervisors oriented and indoctrinated into MBO practice. Study of the handbook is an easy way for them to catch up with their managerial colleagues.

3.   To foster clearer communications and understanding of MBO principles, concepts, and practices by providing definitions and explanations of terms, expressions, techniques and procedures, illustrations, and examples. The MBO field is loaded with ideas and concepts that need defining and clarifying. This book documents proven techniques and practices.

4.   To suggest practical guidelines for the solution of "real world" problems for middle and lower management personnel. A reference guidebook should always be close by for use when a problem emerges.

WHO WILL FIND THIS HANDBOOK USEFUL?

This handbook will be of great help to the following:

1.   Managerial practitioners at any level of the organization who are responsible for productivity and results in their companies, departments, or groups. The handbook contains appli-

cations from strategic planning to motivation of employees. The handbook gives special emphasis to understanding and doing.

2. Personnel who have been recently appointed to a managerial position or have been promoted to a higher managerial position and need to upgrade and update to newly acquired responsibilities. The handbook is loaded with "how to" techniques for the effective start in a new endeavor.

3. Students of management in university or other educational institutions. They will find the handbook an invaluable resource for real world application of what they learn about in their academic studies and research. MBA students will gain an overview of MBO practices to complement their MBA degrees.

4. Training directors. They will find the handbook an excellent resource for their management development programs. The handbook can aid in content and substance of management issues, case studies, group interactions, and problem solutions.

5. Public and university librarians. They will find the handbook an indispensable reference for the multitude of questions about management topics raised by the general public, special groups, community associations, and students.

6. Administrators in government and trade associations. They will find descriptions of many techniques and practices employed in the private sector which are useful to the public sector. These practices are seldom directly applicable, but with thought and modification they can be adapted to public organizations.

WHAT IS DIFFERENT ABOUT THIS HANDBOOK?

This handbook contains several innovative features not found in other available MBO literature.

1. *Projected Trends to the Twenty-first Century.* A realistic look at what is emerging, the attitudes and skills needed, and how MBO will fit in the new futuristic scenarios.

2. *Organized View of MBO Management Practices.* A pinnacle view of MBO as practiced by top, middle, and lower management within the responsibilities of functions, programs, projects, and departments.

3. *Comparative Performance of MBO Practicing Corporations.* Statistical and graphic comparisons as averages of MBO-practicing firms versus total U.S. businesses.

4. *MBO Theory.* A conceptual framework based on foundation theories that explains meaningfully why MBO works.

5. *MBO Strategies.*   Five successful models of MBO practice.

6. *Japanese MBO.*   An in-depth description of the practice
of MBO in Japan, with contrasts between the American and the
Japanese practice.

7. *MBO Applications.*   How MBO can be used and made
effective in the following areas: business plans, strategic planning, program and project management, engineering, resource
management, and performance appraisals.

8. *Case Histories.*   In-depth descriptions of five organizations, both private and public, showing the current status of the
art of MBO.

9. *MBO of the Future.*   Where is MBO going? What is its
future? A description of what's new about MBO. Predictions up
to 2050 AD.

SOURCES OF INFORMATION

The material for this book has been drawn from several sources:

1. *Research Surveys.*   Two major surveys were conducted
for this handbook, the first to answer the question, "Who is
practicing MBO?" and the second to find out what MBO process
is used and its unique features. Results of these surveys are
reported here.

2. *Interviews with Key Management Personnel.*   Key management personnel responsible for the overseeing of the MBO
process in their firms were interviewed to collect an internal
view. All were positive about the practice of MBO but were
quick to add that a modified MBO prevailed in their companies.

3. *Case Histories.*   An entire chapter is devoted to in-depth
practices of MBO by a spectrum of organizations ranging from a
company ranking 14 in Fortune 500 corporations to a major city
in the United States.

4. *Consulting Experience and Work Assignments.*   A management consultant has an advantage not found in other types of
work. Instead of remaining with one company and its set of
problems, a consultant goes to many companies and confronts a
wide diversity of problems. The following is a list of clients from
which experience has been gained:

(a)   Industrial and manufacturing. AMF Cuno,
Bellofram, Bolton-Emerson, Celanese, Combus-
tion Engineering, Emhart, General Electric, General Dynamics, International Business Machines,

Ingersol Rand, Kimberly-Clark, Mallory Battery, McDonnell Douglas, Otis Elevator, Ralston Purina, Scharr Industries, Sun Oil, Sylvania Electric, United Technologies, Westinghouse, Beatrice Foods, Hanes, Boise Cascade, R. J. Reynolds, Pratt & Whitney, EBASCO, Alcan Aluminum, Foster Pumps, United States Steel.

(b) Business and retail. A. C. Nielson, Benton & Bowles, Gino's, Glenmore Distillers, Holiday Inns, Kyanize Paint, Sambo's, S. New England Eggs, Winkleman's Department Chain.

(c) Publishing. Caron International, McGraw-Hill, R. R. Donnelly & Sons, John Wiley & Sons.

(d) Health care and social agencies. Charlette Hungerford Hospital, Child Welfare League of America, Cystic Fibrosis, Evangelical Methodist Hospital, Public Health Institute of Connecticut, St. Joseph's Manor, Waterford Country School, Yale Medical Center.

(e) Utilities, banks, and insurance. Aetna Life & Casualty, Connecticut Bank & Trust, Government Employees Insurance, Groton Utilities, Hartford Insurance Group, Hartford National Bank, Holyoke Mutual Fire Insurance, Northeast Utilities, Southern New England Telephone, State Street Bank of Boston, United Illuminating.

(f) Professional firms. Arthur Young, Booz, Allen & Hamilton; Dalton, Dalton & Little; Frank Brown & Co.; James O'Rice Associates; Management Center of Cambridge; Peat, Marwick & Mitchell; Stone & Webster Engineering; Cygna Energy; Canadian Comprehensive Auditing Foundation; American Productivity Center; Productivity Inc.

(g) Public administration and government. Connecticut Correction Department, Connecticut Research Commission, City of Newport, Department of Consumer Protection (Connecticut), Norfolk Naval Shipyard, State of Connecticut, State of Wisconsin, State of Rhode Island, Town of Groton, Town of Newington, Town of Windsor.

(h) Educational institutions. Lee Public School System, Prince Community College, State of New Jersey Educational Department, State University of New York, South Central Community College,

University of Connecticut, University of Hartford, University of Maine.

(i)   Trade associations.   Hartford Chamber of Commerce, Hartford Jaycees, industrial management clubs, New Haven Jaycees, Springfield Chamber of Commerce.

5.   *Personal Experience and Prior Publications.*   I have been a manager and director of a major corporation whose principal responsibility was the development and overseeing of the corporate MBO process. Two books have emerged from that experience: *Managing By Objectives* and *How To Manage By Objectives*.

A WORD ABOUT MANAGEMENT PROCESSES OR TECHNIQUES

The era of the casual manager who uses trial-and-error methods until the work is completed began disappearing about a decade ago. Casual performance results in waste of resources, heavy expenditure of time, and low levels of performance. To compete in the 1980s and on into the future, efficient processes that accomplish productivity gains are needed. More attention must be given to implementation or to the utilization lag between "knowing" and "doing." Accordingly, many processes and techniques are presented in this text in a concrete and practical fashion, with suggestions for implementation. However, rigid guidelines for behavior, which stifle individual thinking and innovation, are *not* presented. My intention is to show how managers can move away from the casual approach to work planning, measuring, and doing that can be reviewed, evaluated, and improved. A method of productivity improvement is successful when its processes are recorded, examined, scrutinized, appraised, and adopted as a procedure until a better method is developed. The adage "practice makes perfect" is not always right. Practice with feedback, review, analysis, and change can make perfect.

The processes described in this handbook are intended to encourage managers to think about their own procedures and to develop what ultimately are the best ones for the job at hand. Any process suggested here would probably have to be modified to be used effectively in the unique setting of an organization. Many authors tend to concentrate heavily on the development of new knowledge, without suggesting how to implement it. This has resulted in a utilization lag. The new concepts and information presented in this handbook are accompanied by descriptions of specific processes. Thus many processes are included in this book.

PAUL MALI

New London, Connecticut
January 1986

Acknowledgments

This handbook is the collaborative effort of many people in the management field. Much appreciation is extended to the many clients in the United States, Canada, England, Japan, and Brazil who afforded me the opportunity to see and help their MBO processes. They have been my richest sources of information—hundreds and hundreds of organizations, all different, yet having some degree of commonality because of the MBO process. Special thanks go to Michael J. Hamilton, my editor at John Wiley & Sons, who urged the project originally and even provided motivators from time to time to get the work done. Also my thanks to Mary Daniello, senior production supervisor at John Wiley & Sons, who moved the edited manuscript to the printing stage. Sandra Ash should be cited not only for typing the manuscript but for her patience in deciphering the "Mali hieroglyphics" in pencil form.

P.M.

Contents

PART 2   THEORY, PRINCIPLES, STRATEGIES, AND BENEFITS OF MBO

PART 3   MBO PRACTICES AND PROCESSES

PART 4   MBO APPLICATIONS

PART 5   FUTURE OF MBO

MBO
UPDATED

The Challenge
for MBO

Managing in the past has been principally concerned with getting things done. Managing in the future adds another dimension to this process. What prevents me from getting things done? Why do things change from what I expect?

The chapter in Part 1 discusses reasons that prevent managers from getting things done. It examines the events and processes taking place in the management world that pose special challenges for MBO. It describes the changes occurring on the road to the 21st century in markets, business, and governments and the changes in the skills and competencies needed by individual managers.

1

MANAGING ON THE BUMPY ROAD TO THE 21st CENTURY

IN THIS CHAPTER

EMERGING CHALLENGES
HIDDEN PRACTICES OF MANAGERS
INDICATORS OF MANAGERS IN TROUBLE
WHY MANAGERS BECOME INCOMPETENT
AGENDA NEEDS FOR MANAGERS

The year 2000 AD is just around the corner. From the standpoint of long-range planning, it is already here. As decisions made in the 1940s affected what happened in the 1960s, and decisions made in the 1960s affected what happened in the 1980s, so decisions made in the 1980s will affect what occurs when the new century arrives. Changes since the 1940s have been phenomenal! The products that have evolved since then show that growth has been exponential. Companies today are organized and committed to develop new products far into the future. Some examples of technologic and life-style changes that have occurred since 1940 are illustrated in Table 1.1.

No one will deny that our world has experienced more changes in the past 40 years than in the preceding 400 years. We must be prepared to lift our sights even further, however, as changes in the next 20 years will be greater than those of the past 200 years. The rapid expansion will continue. But new demands emerge every day, and we must be prepared for the demands of

TABLE 1.1   Evolution of Technology Since 1940

1940	1960	1980
Radio	Stereo equipment	Quadraphonic equipment
Propeller aircraft	Turbojet	High-speed jet
"Mom and pop" grocery store	Supermarket	Shopping mall
Disk audio recorder	Tape audio recorder	Video cassette recorder
TV receiver	Cable TV	Home movie TV
Gas oven	Electric oven	Microwave oven
Oil burner water heater	Electric water heater	Solar panel water heater
Analog computer	Digital computer	Portable home computer

the future. We prepare by inquiring, probing, analyzing, proposing, and deciding.

The purpose of this first chapter is to:

1.   Describe briefly the major issues and concerns managers will face on the road to the 21st century. The turbulent times we live in have posed new ones. Others are extensions of issues and concerns of the past.
2.   Reveal the hidden practices of managers. We must realize that the real world of management differs from the ideal.
3.   Enumerate indicators that a manager is in trouble.
4.   Give reasons why competent managers become incompetent.
5.   Describe the needs of managers as they move toward the 21st century.

EMERGING CHALLENGES

Rarely has there been a time when the practice of management has been more demanding, more challenging, more stressful than it is today. Current issues and concerns, and those emerging, indicate that individual managers as well as organizations will go down a bumpy road to the 21st century. Throughout the first half of this century, America dominated the world economy. At present, the western world and the developing countries are the key. In the future, it will be the total world, and the developing countries will be the significant component in the mix. Social and cultural differences among nations are fast disappearing. We will soon dress alike, talk alike, eat alike, and think alike. This may be comforting, disquieting, exciting, or dismaying. In any event, it will create managerial challenges and problems.

We are all well aware of some of our current problems: problems of the economy, profitability, consumerism, political and governmental conflicts, ecology, depletion of resources, environmental pollution, ethics, civil protest, terrorism, and many others. The problems vary in intensity and are often overwhelming. More and as yet unknown problems are sure to come. They will be transnational or globular. The following list of trends and statistics gives an idea of future challenges:

1. *The World Adds 200,000 People per Day.* The United Nations predicts that the world's population in 2000 AD is estimated greater than 8 billion. Today it is 4.5 billion. The growth rate will be 200,000 people per day, so that 15 years later the population will have doubled to 16 billion. More people will be living on this earth at one time than have lived throughout all history.

2. *The World Is Divided Between "Haves" and "Have Nots."* Of the 4.5 billion people now living, 700 million have an income of less than $50/year. These people live on the edge of starvation. A group three times this size, 2.5 billion, have food every day but not much more. These "have-nots" represent a large market for products and services, but they are poor and politically unstable. They are beginning to demand their share, and thus are a threat and a challenge.

3. *Megalopolis and Regional Super Governments Are Here.* Problems and growth do not respect political boundaries. Nationwide in the United States there are 80,000 separate and distinct units of government. New York State alone has 2362 separate taxing jurisdictions—57 counties, 62 cities, 557 villages, 755 school districts, and 931 towns. Many of these entities are failing to solve their internal problems. The regional approach, often called the systems approach, is a valid and necessary approach to solving super level and interdisciplinary problems. The historic axiom is still valid: "The whole is a result of its parts." If the parts have problems, so will the whole.

4. *More Managers and Supervisors Are Needed in a Service Economy.* The United States has become a service economy since 1956, when the number of blue-collar workers was at parity with the number of white-collar workers. Today white-collar workers occupy 65 percent of the labor market; in five years the figure will be 75 percent. White-collar workers are programmers, teachers, secretaries, bureaucrats, lawyers, bankers, technicians. John Naisbitt, in his book *Megatrends*, identifies the transition from farmer to laborer to clerk. Productivity declines in a service economy because of its labor-intensive nature, which is difficult to mechanize. Service work demands more supervision than does manufacturing or agriculture, which means that more managers and supervisors are required. If the future increase is a mere 1 percent of the labor force, close to 1 million more managers and supervisors will be needed. If we add to this number replacements for the tens of thousands who retire, die, or leave management, it is easy to see a massive shortage of capable managers and supervisors within the next decade.

5. *Internationalization of Business Continues.* Business plans are on a multinational scale. Increased productivity is experienced from transna-

tional cooperatives and collaborations. Global markets have given challenging problems to multinational companies. In 1904 the Ford Motor Company incorporated and established one subsidiary in Canada. Today Ford manufactures and assembles its products in 20 countries and sells them in about 185 countries and territories. Of every 100 cars Ford manufactures, 68 are sold in North America, 22 in Europe, and 10 in the rest of the world.

Two most important observations can be made from this brief statistical "megalook" into the future: The future will be even more complex than today, and resources will be limited or will run out. Complexity and scarcity are the two big challenges of the future. Few will disagree with this.

A closer look at what appears to be emerging on the road to the 21st century reveals 15 specific issues:

1. Fast growing world competition (the majority of world corporations are foreign based).
2. Transnational collaborations to control markets (nations are uniting for personal gain).
3. Volatile economy (cyclical swings of inflation and recession).
4. Energy dependence on high costs (unshaken connection with cost acceleration).
5. Quality deterioration (quality is a key competitive factor).
6. Burgeoning government bureaucracy (huge growth in government spending).
7. Productivity decline (other countries have exceeded the U.S. pace).
8. Product maturation (declining entrepreneurial investments and activity).
9. Fast changing society (experience and past guidelines are of little use in the future).
10. Effects of organizational strategies (everyone is countermoving from anticipated moves).
11. Casual managers as cause of mediocrity (old-style management is on its way out).
12. Growth of robotization (150,000 robots are now in use in the world, 80,000 in Japan alone).
13. Information mismanagement (a horrendous flow of information needs managing).
14. Office of the future (place of work for growing knowledge workers).
15. Decline in motivation to work (people want more time off).

Each of these issues is now taken up in more detail.

Fast Growing World Competition

In the 1960s the United States moved more and more into an international economy, in which McDonald's hamburgers were sold in Tokyo, Boeing 707s in Thailand, shoe machinery in Italy, Bic pens in Brazil, and Xerox machines in India. At that time, three quarters of the world's corporations were American based. Americans were playing the global game, and they achieved substantial success.

In the 1980s a reversal occurred. America lost its number 1 position. Two thirds of the world's corporations became foreign based. Foreign management has now caught up with American management. The Saudis sell oil, the Japanese Nikons, the Germans Volkswagens, the Spanish shoes, the Philippinos low-cost garments, the Brazilians coffee, and the Canadians shopping malls. In world markets America has slipped its domination from three quarters to one third. Foreign competitors are now operating formidably in the United States. Taiwan, Korea, Brazil, Mexico, and other so-called lesser developed countries now provide more than 50 percent of our imports and consume less than 40 percent of our exports. The United States is suddenly part of one gigantic world market. American companies must now accept the challenge of catch-up competition from all over the world. They must deal with highly organized and well-coordinated "foreign states." Foreign countries have developed political business collaborations which blur distinctions among political, social, religious, and economic factors and which have subsidies and countervailing duties. These collaborations heighten the impact of international disputes and resolutions. This means politics affects business and business affects politics.

Emerging Transnational Collaborations

Countries are banding together into transnational confederations. World politics is interwoven with business. OPEC (Organization of Petroleum Exporting Countries) is an outstanding example of an oil collaboration. This cartel controls price, supply, and production. This in turn supports political programs of host countries. Multinational corporations who need world markets to survive and grow with their huge annual sales will participate in business with host countries. General Motors and Toyota join together to market a car for world use. R.J. Reynolds and the Chinese government sign a contract to manufacture and distribute cigarettes on a world-wide scale. India, Mexico, and other countries have policies that investment capital can no longer come from multinationals but only from sources within the country. These multinational corporations provide technology, marketing, taxes, and profit sharing, while host countries provide capital investment, manufacturing, employees, and management. These transnational confederates are also political-business partners achieving multifaceted goals: economic, political, social, and religious. By the year 2000 AD, 70 percent of the world's population will be concentrated in eight nations: China, India, Pakistan, Bangladesh, Indonesia, Brazil, Mexico, and Nigeria (in descending order). These countries present vast opportunities for consumer outlets. They have low labor rates but most are financially and politically unstable.

Volatile Economy

Runaway inflation is, from a manager's point of view, runaway costs. Inflation destroys people's savings, wrecks pensions and retirement incomes, retards progress, and gives accounting a deceptive meaning. It also erodes the purchasing power of money, drives up interest rates, and causes uncertainty about the future. It affects greatly those on fixed incomes such as the poor, the elderly, the disabled, and the retired. Inflation followed quickly by recession is now called stagflation. We have moved into a stagflation-ridden world.

The inflation rate in England is 20 percent, in Brazil 80 percent, in South Africa 120 percent, and in Israel 180 percent. In the United States, from 1950 to 1956 the average rate of inflation was 3 percent. From 1965 to 1970 it picked up to 4 percent. From 1970 to 1975 it reached 10 percent. After declining somewhat, in 1980 it reached almost 20 percent. At this writing, it is between 3 and 4 percent and dropping with periods of recession. This pattern of irregularity of the rate indicates an unstable economy. The real danger of stagflation is not what it is but its unpredictability. Managers must now project inflationary effects in their forecasting, while looking for recession possibilities. This enhances risk. The future becomes more uncertain than ever before.

Energy Dependence

At the present time the United States is energy dependent. We cannot run our industrial economy efficiently with energy from our own sources. This means that any drastic cutoff in oil, gas, or other energy sources for whatever reason, be it war, politics, or policies, will require a painful adjustment in our life-style as well as in our company operations. We are roughly 50 percent dependent on outside energy sources, while our internal consumer demands for energy are increasing at a rate of 10 percent per year. This suggests we are moving toward an energy crisis. It also suggests waits to get gas, shrinking home size, smaller cars, continued price increases, brownouts, waits for production runs, radical cutbacks in lighting, and lighter and smaller materials will continue for some time to come. Energy dependence is worldwide. Management in any spot on planet Earth must now take into account the effect of energy costs on the buying and selling of products, services, and materials. There is no debate about the need for energy conservation and for development of new energy sources. In the meantime, however, managers must cope with the challenge of managing with high energy costs and depleting resources.

Quality Deterioration

Before World War II, "made in Japan" signified cheap, shoddy, and short-lived products. Today, the same words represent products of quality, reliability, and long life. In contrast, "made in the United States" before World War II meant quality, reliability, and long life. Does this image hold today? In the 1940s, the United States was a pacesetter in more than 33 industries, which gave rise to the internationalization of American corporations. In the 1980s, the United States is a pacesetter in only three industries—aerospace, agriculture, and computers. Boeing still makes the best commercial aircraft in the world, and International Harvester and John Deere Company produce the most reliable farm equipment. IBM and other American computers sell worldwide. Why did we lose pacesetting leadership in the other industries?

We are just waking up to the fact that quality has deteriorated in American products. Many companies are running to turn the clock back. Quality specialists are being given more clout. Vendors are required to supply better parts or lose business. Workers are being formed into quality circles to search for ways to improve quality. Will the turnaround be quick enough? Meanwhile, our foreign purchases are increasing; they comprise 28 percent of our autos, 30 percent of our sporting and athletic goods, 34 percent of our microwave ovens, 90 percent of our CB radios and motorcycles, and 100 percent of our video cassette recorders. Quality improvement looms as a major challenge of the day.

Burgeoning Government Bureaucracy

It took 185 years, from 1776 to 1961, for the federal budget to reach $100 billion. It took ten years, from 1961 to 1971, for it to reach $200 billion. In four more years it had reached $300 billion. In another three years, from 1975 to 1978, the budget reached $400 billion. And from 1977 to 1978, only one year, it expanded to $500 billion. The budget escalation has been exponential! Today the budget expands unpredictably as the national debt expands. The national debt in 1900 was $1.2 billion. In 1935, it was $29 billion. In 1955, $258 billion. In 1975, $533 billion. In 1980, it rose to $880 billion. In 1984, it reached $1.2 trillion.

At this writing, the national debt has arrived at over $1.4 trillion. The interest on the national debt alone is over $140 billion/year! A quick calculation shows it took the national debt 55 years, from 1900 to 1955, to expand from $1 billion to $250 billion, but such an expansion occurred in only three years in the 1970s. If the mushrooming continues, the national debt will reach $2 trillion by 1986. A mushrooming national debt stimulates limitless taxation and deficit spending which, in turn, burdens future generations. It destroys the frugality principle in living styles. It sanctions a cost of government that is a disincentive to work, saving, and investment.

The root causes of this burgeoning growth of both budget and national debt are many. Inflation is one. Skyrocketing costs is another. Borrowing is a third. Increased rules, regulations, and governance is a significant fourth. But the biggest is the growth of services and programs, with the staffs and bureaucrats to support them. The welfare system greatly affects the getting and holding of jobs by means of welfare check handouts, food stamps, unemployment compensation, and subsidized housing. This encourages the weak to become weaker, creates a false sense of security, cements dependence for many future generations, and creates a welfare state that forces the nonproductive to exploit the productive.

Burgeoning government bureaucracy greatly hampers the free enterprise system. It replaces freedoms with regulations and assures spiraling taxation that discourages capital formation. When General Motors first started, few or no federal laws pertained to it. Today it is under the jurisdiction of 20 different federal laws and the supporting agencies. In a typical year the U.S. Congress churns out 400 new laws, while federal agencies churn out 7500 new rules and codes. Government grows each year, posing a critical challenge for management. Burgeoning bureaucracy runs up debt and a set of obligations in taxpayers' names. It erodes initiative and individualism, the basis of entrepreneurship.

Productivity Decline

The U.S. productivity rate has been steadily declining since 1950. Five countries—Japan, West Germany, France, Italy, and Canada—will surpass the United States in productivity in absolute terms in the late 1980s if the current trend continues. The United States, which used to enjoy a pace-setting position in productivity, has fallen behind. Declining productivity diminishes needed profits, requires capital investment for efficiency and effectiveness, spurs unemployment, blocks growth to higher living standards, and hinders scientific and technological innovations.

The real struggle for productivity is within the firm. When productivity is low and the company is inefficient in translating its resources, the company must cope in one of four ways. First, it can pass the drop in productivity to its customers in the form of price increases. How long can a firm do this in the face of foreign competition? Second, it can expect some employees to work harder than the unproductive employees to make up the deficiency. But how long are productive employees willing to do this? Third, it can buy basic parts, subassemblies, or the total product from highly productive sources and merely attach the company's label and image to it. Many companies already do this. How long will it be before the supplier becomes the competitor? Fourth and last, it can convert casual and uninformed managers into productivity managers who have attitudes of improvement, ways of measuring productivity, and strategies for improving the productivity of the firm. This present-day issue is of critical concern.

Product Maturation Results in Business Maturation!

Products are maturing! Most products in the market today have been in existence for some time. To illustrate, few or no changes have occurred in the following products since World War II: circuit breakers, toilet equipment, garments, mass transportation, and lamps. In the case of products in which changes have occurred, such as computers, video entertainment equipment, electronic mail equipment, and word processors, high-growth companies have emerged. These companies are the growing sector of our economy.

When products mature, businesses mature! After having an initial growth period derived from an advantage of product, service, or distribution, a company tends to settle down to management of assets, resources, and employees. The original entrepreneurial spirit begins to wane. The surge of creativity needed to extend products and markets is no longer there. This is not necessarily bad. It is only bad, and even a disaster, if competitors recover the initial entrepreneurial thrust and move their business to new levels of growth, or if a new company steps in.

Competitive products catch up in both quantity and quality when a company relies on mature products. World competitors have learned how to produce the same products with higher quality and lower costs. The mature company needs new technological breakthroughs so that products may be extended for new growth. Corporations that survive the turbulent 1980s will be those with new technological thrusts. Probably 90 percent of the products sold in the next decade do not exist today. The corollary is that 90 percent of the corporations of the next decade will differ from the corporations of today. The new challenge is to reinstitute the entrepreneurial spirit and reestablish creativity.

Fast Changing Society

No one will deny that the world has experienced more changes in the last 100 years than in the preceding 1000 years. And if the exponential trend continues into the future, we can expect as much change in the next 20 years as has occurred in the last 200 years. In other words, the year 2005 AD will be as different from 1985 as 1985 is different from 1785.

The changes have been exciting! New products, new corporations, new leisure activities, higher standards of living, increased benefits, different life-styles. But let's not stop here. In this fast changing period, we have experienced some major economic problems. We have had seven recessions since World War II. During the same period we have tried, with no lasting success, three different economic philosophies: Keynesian, neoclassical, and supply side. The stock market has been down more than it has been up. Bankruptcies in the United States, according to Dun & Bradstreet, increased from 7919 in 1979 to 25,346 in 1982, a 320 percent increase.

Productivity has steadily declined, from 3.5 percent after World War II to 1.9 percent in 1980. At this writing, it has risen to 3.0 percent. During the same period, our decision making has oscillated between many dichotomies: government versus private business, capitalistic system versus socialistic system, labor versus management, interests of the state versus interests of the individual, minorities versus majorities, importers versus exporters, defense spending versus social spending, and the "haves" versus the "have nots." Great changes, both positive and negative, among these dichotomies indicate we're in a fast changing, volatile society in which success experiences of the past provide few guidelines for the future. In fact, the future isn't anymore what it used to be. We must say goodbye to traditional practices of history! The fast changing society undermines policies, breeds obsolescence, instigates veneer-type decision making, and devastates product life cycles. The new row of challenges ahead of us indicates *new attitudes, new points of view, new approaches* will be the order of the day for managerial practitioners.

Effects of Organizational Strategies

Most businesses, like armies, are very much aware that they can perish for want of the right strategy. They know they must outthink, outplan, outdecide, and outmaneuver competitors. Organizations that have done this successfully have a competitive advantage; they "squeeze out" more than they are "squeezed in" by the competition. To be successful, the company must understand what is happening in the industry. Then it decides which of the competitive niches available it should attempt to dominate. A strategy is developed on how to compete and how to win.

Businesses have played this game in the past and for the most part have played it well. But a new strategic game has emerged, that of developing strategies to deal with traditional noncompetitors as well as competitors. Companies must now interpret and react to decisions generated by so-called noncompeting organizations. No company thinks it is competing against the U.S. government. But the U.S. government's strategies to solve its problems, whether these be matters of inflation, recession, social spending, defense, or air pollution, generate ripples that affect corporate strategy in the marketplace. U.S. government regulations demand compliance in a variety of areas. Compliance cost American industries and businesses $100 billion in 1980 alone, an amount roughly equal to the total net profits of all U.S. corporations for the same year. Foreign government strategies for stimulating economic growth, by subsidizing loans and supporting low interest rates, will generate ripples that affect noncompetitive businesses in other countries. At this writing, the Japanese government is granting 3.5 percent interest loans for starting a new business. This is bound to affect many businesses already operating in Japan as well as in other countries. Unions of noncompetitor organizations that are experiencing special difficulties will have wide effects. Such was the case with the airline controllers' strike, which caused changes in strategies for coffee delivery, tourist travel, and executive conferences in Chicago. Those who develop strategies for the bumpy road to the 21st century must consider the innovative and sophisticated strategies of noncompeting organizations. The challenge is to play a much more global strategic game than in the past.

Casual Managers as Causes of Mediocrity

The casual managers of today were at one time the ambitious, aggressive managers of yesterday. They successfully met the challenges of yesterday. But somewhere on the way to the executive suite, they got comfortable. They achieved a safe niche and a good salary with lots of benefits. Now they are interested only in keeping the boat from rocking. The need to struggle, to stretch, to survive, to compete, to learn, motivations and enthusiasm, all have gone. And there they sit, mediocre at the top, the middle, the bottom, intending to sit it out until retirement. When they do move, they move casually, getting the job done in the course of time. They encourage solutions to problems, doing little or nothing about changing the conditions that produce the problems. The casual manager is mediocre in performance, and therefore is a marked person. This manager will not survive the turbulent challenges lying ahead.

Interest in casual management has developed from the basic question: "What about managerial productivity?" Management salaries are estimated at $250 billion (20 percent of the gross national product). Benefits are $150 billion (11 percent of the GNP). Together they comprise $400 billion, or 31 percent of the GNP. An improvement in managerial productivity of any percentage point would result in a huge improvement in productivity. In most companies, roughly 10 percent of employees are in management. One percent are in top management. And one tenth of one percent hold policy-level positions. If the work force is estimated at 90 million people, 9 million are in management. If the conservative estimate of 40 percent of these are assumed to be casual managers, their removal could generate a savings of $160 billion in salaries and benefits. Casual management is an expensive problem for business. The enemy is within! Unfortunately, the problem goes beyond salaries and benefits. A major challenge of our turbulent times is to find ways to convert casual managers to productivity managers. If this is not possible, the casual managers should be screened out of leadership positions in organizations and retired early. Casual managers dislike the MBO process. It demands a formal approach for getting results within a specific time. MBO changes the casual manager into a deliberate one.

Growth of Robotization

A robot revolution is sweeping the world. Estimates of the number of robots now in use vary, but a figure of more than 150,000 seems to be generally acceptable, Japan leading with 80,000 and adding 350 more per month.

Those using robots seem to be moving into a science-fiction era. Robot devices are performing such tasks as welding, painting, lifting, assembling, screening, checking, and inspecting. In some companies, robots are making robots! In Japan, robots are expected to clean, do laundry, serve tea, and aid in the care of handicapped persons. A malfunctioning robot has already killed a person in Japan.

Most robots are mere mechanical arms that can perform simple repetitive jobs. The cost of their operation is as low as $5.50/hour. In American terminology they may be better classified as mechanized processes or automated machines. The fact remains that the use of automated machines, or simply "automation," has been steadily growing in business and industry. New technologies have spurred the applications. Some of these technologies are lasers, fiber optics, communication satellites, packet switching, microprocessors, computer-aided design, computer-aided manufacturing, and word processing. In Japan, a project to be completed by 1990 is the automated factory. The name is MUM, an acronym for methodology for unmanned manufacture. The specifications are:

Objective	Total automation for batch manufacturing; assembly of 2000 different automotive parts into 50 different products
Processes	Forging, casting, welding, heat treating, painting
Costs	More than $500 million for a 250,000 square foot plant
Personnel	Total required to run plant, 10

In the past, automation was thought of as the cause of unemployment. It was more the cause of job transitions. But today, improvement in productivity has been ascribed to automation. Controversial as automation may be, we are moving into a digital world. Computer graphics, CAD/CAM, cybernation, and numerical programmed control are the exciting managerial challenges of the future. They have more potential to increase productivity than any development since electricity. Many managers still do not move with these developments. These managers will be dropouts on the road to the 21st century. The robot movement is not opening a way to retirement from work but a way of movement into the huge challenge of doing work that now is undone.

Information Mismanagement

One of the many skills of an effective managerial practitioner is having available the right kind of information in the right form with the right facts before he or she makes a decision. Poor decisions arise more from lack of information than from any other single factor. Since the advent of the information explosion there is no dearth of information. American offices daily spew out nearly 750 million pages of computer printouts, 300 million photocopies, and 100 million letters. Senior programmers stagger under the weight of printouts containing up to 3000 pages. Once these are delivered, only a few more hours are needed to generate another few thousand pages, if desired. Horrendous volumes of mostly obsolete, greatly imperfect, somewhat incomplete, and partly valuable information already exist. If good decision making is based on information substance rather than form and file, a better job of managing information must be done. Certified, valid information is needed. Also needed is an automatic eraser of old information when it is replaced by new.

The larger the organization, the more it tends to pay attention to proliferation of information form and file rather than to management of information substance and fact. Most organizations follow a dangerous assumption that management has current knowledge about a situation when, in fact, it knows only the history of its experience.

Office of the Future

The majority of 90 million American workers earn their livelihood in the office. The United States has become a nation of professional and service workers. In 1984, 65 percent of the work force (58 million) was classified as white-collar workers. By 1990, this number will reach 60 million. Historically the office was the place for management, administrators, and secretaries. Today and on toward the 21st century, it will be the work place for the majority of working Americans, both management and nonmanagement. The same thing will happen in other countries.

The office has seldom been a focus of concern. The number of white-collar workers steadily trickling into office work, however, calls for productivity increases in the office. In one corporation, white-collar productivity over two decades has increased a mere 4 percent, as against an 80 percent increase for factory workers. The record shows millions of dollars are spent on machinery and automation in the factory, but little for improving the output of the office. White-collar workers have traditionally been less productive than blue-collar workers because of the nature of the work. It is nonrepetitive, demands thought and group interaction, and the processes are unique. Information is continually changing, and often key decisions are made by nonmanagement personnel. Quantifying and improving productivity in the office will not be easy. An army of devices and technologies is becoming available to help, such as word processors, electronic mail, control work stations, video teleconferencing, facsimile switching, and telephonic reproductions.

The greatest observable aspect of this growing emphasis on office work is that the work involves the functions and responsibilities of management but that the workers are nonmanagers. How skillful are these workers in executing the processes of management? Will productivity in the office be directly determined by the skill of white-collar workers and the equipment they have? This is another managerial challenge.

Decline in Motivation to Work

In 1950, it took seven Japanese or three German workers to match one American worker's industrial output. In 1980, two Japanese or 1.3 Germans do as well. By 1990, if productivity rates continue as they are, three Americans will be equivalent to one Japanese and to 0.7 German. Japanese workers are not concerned about American workers, since they know the latter do not work long hours or work intensely. They are instead concerned about Korean workers, who work four times as hard as they do. Since World War II, American workers have arrived at the highest level of affluence they have ever achieved. Electronic entertainment, higher education, travel, and social interplay are available on a scale never before experienced.

It appears that most American workers want to work less; leisure time motivates them more than other goals. Job benefits, the fastest growing components in the employee compensation package, have now reached 25 to 40 percent of the wage dollar. Especially noticeable is the increased number of holidays—up to 30/year in some cases. If the trend continues and the number of holidays increases to 52/year, the 32-hour work week has arrived. Finding employees who are willing to work as hard as their counterparts of the previous two decades will be difficult. The challenge of management is to find new and innovative ways to reverse the decline in motivation for work among employees.

HIDDEN PRACTICES OF MANAGERS

The real world of management is not orderly, well defined, or clear as to its goals, objectives, strategies, work processes, problems, or decision making. It is a jungle of ideas, methods, techniques, and divergent ways that often result in duplication, omissions, and conflicts. Textbook principles on organizations, authority, command, and policies are more a set of assumptions than tested principles. The real world of management is loaded with complexities, confusion, variance, scarcities, conflicts, unproven alternatives, company politics, trial and error, frustration, stress, disappointment, insatiable wants, and imperfect information. The real world of management contains upheavals from sudden quitting of key people, redirections from the failure of a plan, realignments because of conflicts in personalities, and canceled designs and product developments from new market vibrations. These and other sudden changes force managers into role playing as in Greek tragedies, in which actors wore masks. The masks suggest the script role that must be played before an audience. But behind the masks are the real managers with their real selves attempting to resolve their dichotomous situation.

This section lists some of the hidden practices of the management world. The list suggests that there are two worlds in management—the world that is and the world we would like, the hidden world and the imagined world of assumptions. The list is not intended to be comprehensive, but rather to give insight into this hidden world and to convince that it is there.

1. *Managers Live With Silent Threats.* Managers are reluctant to fire unwanted employees because of threats of recrimination. These threats are often unwritten and nonverbalized. Managers know that employees have several avenues they can take if recrimination is to be instituted: (1) court suits with extensive litigation if legal rights have been violated; (2) EEOC hearings with possible heavy fines if discrimination practices can be shown; (3) "strike calls" or slowdowns from unions with grievances; and (4) appeal to top management, resulting in uneasy accountability with the bosses. Managers retain mediocre and unwanted employees to avoid these potential threats and thus ensure self-preservation. But managers prefer to rid themselves of mediocre and unwanted employees. As time goes on they begin to accept these conditions. At the age of 40, the pull of a pension, seniority, and vested interest in the job becomes stronger than the desire to get rid of unwanted employees. This pull stiffens until the manager is frozen to the job along with mediocre employees.

2. *Getting Something Done Right Often Means Doing It Yourself.* Getting things done and done right through other people is fundamental to management everywhere. Getting things done through others is common; getting things done "right" through others is not. Consequently, managers find themselves doing the work over or doing it themselves from the beginning when doing it right is imperative. Managers have mediocre employees as a legacy, for reasons of faulty selection, hiring, or transfer, poor training, and development, or interest mismatched with the job.

3. *Authority Seldom Equals Responsibilities.* Managers almost never have authority equal to their responsibility. They are expected to act on and be responsible for more duties than indicated in their job description, organization chart, or memorandum of authorization. Additionally, managers often depend on the actions and decisions of people who cannot be influenced or controlled. Seldom is a company run "by the book." If such a book were written, it would be out of date before it could be printed and handed out. Consequently, managers find themselves meeting specific expectations for which there is no well-established personal authority. The organization chart is only a broad indicator of expectations, like plans for building a house.

4. *White-Collar Crime Is Tolerated.* Managers find themselves in unwilling involvement with white-collar crimes, sometimes generated by upper levels of management but more frequently by subordinates in the form of expense account cheating or take home of company products and materials. Managers would like to keep expenses and use of company equipment, supplies, and products honest and low. Prosecution and punishment cause personal pain and are costly to procedures. The manager desires to have a trust environment without need for elaborate and costly regulations,

checkers, paperwork, and controllers. This cost is higher than the cost of the crime.

5. *Compromise Is a Way of Life.* Managers practice cooperation and compromise to avoid the insecure finality of win–lose judgments. The older the manager, the greater the insecurity and the greater the use of compromise. Few indeed avoid the compromise trail to work on winning all the way. They give in or sell part of the battle to others, as half winning is better than not winning at all. It's more comfortable too! Few have the tough mindedness to set down what is wanted and go after it with vigor and tireless perseverance, going over the obstacles and never quitting so long as there remains a single chance of arriving. Compromise is a high managerial cost. It often is a last resort.

6. *Giving In to Labor Unions Keeps Costs Down.* Managers give in to unions because strikes are costly in terms of money, time, turnover, and image. To take a strike is to assume "all-the-way costs" that often bring a firm to the point of disaster. Managers know that unions work, and work well. They are an adversary force that buys benefits for its members. An "all-the-way" confrontation with this force is avoided by giving in to the unions and passing on increased costs to customers in the form of price increases. Customer withdrawal is far less costly than a strike.

7. *Role Playing Is Necessary.* Managers are expected to show no feelings from imprisoned frustrations, anxieties, and hostilities, even to the point of emotional exhaustion. Their behavior is marked by outward calm and poise. They give many signals that convey they are in control and all is being managed. But underneath may lie a quiet desperation that at any moment can cause a leap toward a job in a different company or a transfer to another section. Resumés are often kept updated for that leap. Until then there is orderly restraint, quiet hope, and never-failing expectations for a better situation.

8. *Signals of Being Overworked and Underpaid Are Common.* Managers give signals of working long hours, handling enormous burdens, and having pivotal responsibilities. Some even advertise the sacrifices they make for the good of the company, sacrifices little appreciated by superior officers or subordinate employees. The fact is, however, most managers work a full day but not an overly long one. When quitting time comes, except for those sudden emergencies which no one can control, they leave the office with a sense of accomplishment. They have time for family, friends, neighbors, hobbies, vacations, and even entertainment. They are well paid.

9. *Decision Making Sometimes Doesn't Proceed From Good Judgment.* Managers act and behave as if their decisions are the basis for their firm to move ahead. They impress with their great individual performance. Some will even boast they can run every job in the company better than the person in charge. Decision making is often a solo experience, but good judgment arises from a collective process. Good judgment results from many minds being brought to bear on the problems, policies, and direction. Good judgment is the knitting of bits of wisdom and experiences from many brains.

Unless this collectivism is made to happen, decision making will not show good judgment.

10. *Good Human Relations and Individual Motivation Often Take a Back Seat.* Managers get things done through people by using a variety of methods. They start with good human relations and individual motivation. If these don't work they resort to the powers of coercion and to sanctions, by threatening exposure or cutting off benefits. The latter method, in the short run, is very effective in producing desirable behavior. Managers are tempted to use it on a regular basis and many do.

11. *Autocrats Operate in the Team Participative Process.* Managers make up their mind early on important matters requiring decisions and use the participative process to gain support and affirmation. This is a submergence of the authoritarian principle. Others are manipulated in a participative game play. Subordinates do not help the boss make up his or her mind. They are merely informed and made to "feel" as if they are part of a decision-making team. This process is great for the managerial ego but poor for good judgment and team building.

12. *Plans Fail Partly Because of Premature Visibility.* Managers are frustrated to the hilt with the high plan failure they experience. They give their plans high visibility and generally "toot" their horn about what they're going to do . They don't keep quiet about it. Unfortunately, strategies and detailed information on how these will be accomplished are also revealed. These fall into the hands of adversaries or competitors, who can then construct obstacles to ensure failure or compromise. Managers often blame the planning process or lack of resources. The real culprits go unnoticed.

13. *First Directions Are Not Always the Best Directions.* Managers engage too often in split-second decisions, decide on jet-propelled procedures and fast-moving processes. They fail to see that first impressions of performance are often wrong, that first solutions to a problem are often not the best. They fail to see that first starters are not always the first to come in. This kind of managerial practice can cost a company its future. It spreads chaos. Managers need to assess performance in a variety of situations, to assess a variety of solutions before adopting the best. They need to give the slow starters a look, as these often finish first.

14. *Substitute for Excellence.* Managers have in common with employees reasons for staying in their job—making a living, having security, the prospect of a good pension and extensive benefits. They also share reasons for their advancement and promotion—not making waves, longevity, loyalty, and devotion. They ignore the sure and quick road to the top: excellence. Few there be on this road. This is the reason few are at the top.

INDICATORS OF MANAGERS IN TROUBLE

An indicator is a signal, a vibration sensed by the manager. It is not conclusive proof. Its pressure alerts the receiver to the possibility of difficulty. To the manager, an indicator is important as a sign of trouble. The 22 attributes that follow are indicators of poor management skills. Indicators are valuable because we can then establish objectives and supporting action plans in terms of these indicators. These indicators help us know that what we are doing is right. Monitoring the indicators serves to reveal whether we are deeper in trouble or improving.

Attribute	Behavior
Possesses inadequate knowledge	Low level and vague understanding of product information and product technology
Lacks skills for competitiveness	Overlooks business enterprise operating in free market with continuous adversaries, opposers, and competitors
Ignores productivity	Lacks ability to measure and manage together components of people and work
Hesitates to take risk	Lacks stamina to move with innovations in face of uncertainty
Generates excessive waste	Misplaces resources
Mishandles crises	Uses easy answers rather than searching for lasting solutions
Makes frequent mistakes	Accepts too much pressure with shallow skills
Misses schedules	Omits coordinating time connectives of work components
Gives foggy directions	Plans without specific and attainable expectations
Misjudges priorities	Misinterprets critical from trivial
Practices neglect	Pays little attention to unfilled critical needs
Allows delays	Backlogs work to point of never catching up
Cuts costs indiscriminately	Trades future cost performance for today's urgencies
Spends too much time in meetings	Fails to manage time as resource
Avoids hard work	Dodges rigorous challenges that give stress and discomfort
Tolerates worker mediocrity	Possesses little ability to get performance improvement

Attribute	Behavior
Allows conflicts to become hostilities	Possesses little ability to resolve disagreements
Lacks flexibility	Follows well-entrenched behavior patterns
Refrains from and inhibits development	Rests on past accomplishments, stagnating, and falling into obsolescence

WHY MANAGERS BECOME INCOMPETENT

Some managers are good. A few are really great. Most do the job. They meet but do not exceed performance expectations. Unfortunately, many are borderline. There are those who are marginal or unsatisfactory performers. The factors that produce incompetence are many and varied, and each operates to a different degree. Often several operate together. Overall, the decline and eventual failure of a firm begins when firm management practices factors of incompetence. The firm that needs government to bail it out in the form of free handouts or tax breaks becomes dependent, and incompetence factors soon take root. Handouts and tax subsidies are not "free," they are exploited from the productive. The firm that prospers when the business cycle favors its products or services but is in trouble when the cycle changes is the firm that becomes unstable. Business cycle swings raise havoc with the inflexible. The firm that plunders its employees by withholding deserved pay increases, or exploits its customers by raising prices to remain solvent, is on the road toward total incompetence.

A firm begins to fail when it abandons a fundamental idea, the idea that the firm must look to itself, examine itself, and depend on itself, on its own skills, innovations, new directions, and resources. There exists a kind of unofficial "managerial welfare." We see millions of people dependent on welfare, but we don't easily see the hundreds of thousands of firms who depend on and need the handouts, the breaks, the special favors in order to survive. These firms are guided by incompetent management. They practice the factors of incompetence.

Operating a business is tough. Making several key decisions often at the same time is enormously difficult. Risks enter in because of lack of information. Every company runs into trouble and complications with these decisions. They often bring about crises. The term "crisis" suggests a major difficulty that could lead to bankruptcy or failure. Many consider the crisis a sudden difficulty. It is not. It is merely a materialization of a difficulty long in the making, usually the result of months or years of delay in facing up to solving problems completely and permanently. Many managers put off problem solving for one of two reasons: The manager lacks the courage and "guts" to do what has to be done or is incompetent or not skillful enough to bring to bear on the problem what is needed for its solution. These types of managers are in trouble.

Five general causes produce managerial incompetence: managerial obsolescence, burnout, high tolerance for mediocrity, casual approach to managing, and dilution of effort.

Managerial Obsolescence

Managers do become obsolete! Equipment and machines become obsolete because newer machines are more effective, efficient, and versatile. Similarly, managers become obsolete because newer managers are more effective, efficient, and versatile. Obsolescence in machines is easily seen; obsolescence in managers is not. Many managers who go to the office, look effective, attend meetings, and act and behave like managers in fact are obsolete. This is not to say they are "stupid" or "nonfunctional." They simply have failed to keep abreast of new knowledge and to acquire new skills to perform their job in a manner acceptable by current standards. They use practices that were effective and efficient in the past and do not realize that better practices and procedures are now available. These managers have lost their managerial value, even though their compensation and benefits are high.

Managerial obsolescence seldom occurs abruptly. It is a slow, creeping process, like "hardening of the arteries." Its measurement is nearly impossible. Estimates of the number of obsolescent managers vary from 5 to as high as 50 percent of the total managers in an organization.

The causes of managerial obsolescence are many, some major, some minor. They operate in multiples rather than singles. Often they have little to do with the company or the individual, more to do with the profession or the society. The major causes are:

1. Complacency and satisfaction with present conditions. Managers who enjoy success are reluctant to change methods and skills.
2. Failure to keep abreast of changing managerial developments and to learn new skills. Managers simply do not wish to find the time or the opportunity to understand and learn new techniques available for possible use.
3. Functioning in a new position after a promotion without first achieving the needed competency level.
4. Inability to keep up with technological developments. Management and technology overlap considerably.
5. Basic lack of ability. The manager has never really developed as a manager.

The causes of managerial obsolescence are so entrenched that they do not lend themselves easily to elimination. A few things can be done to prevent or minimize their effects:

1. Acquire the attitude that this condition affects all managers.
2. Establish performance expectancy factors and revise them periodically for currency and effectiveness.
3. Measure actual performance against expected performance.
4. Institute training and development programs for new skills and techniques.
5. Encourage managers to be active in their profession through meetings, books, magazines, and conferences.
6. Offer faster job rotation and more job enrichment.
7. Encourage managers to pursue advanced educational programs, research, and writing.

Burnout

Burnout is a state of extreme fatigue or frustration in failure brought about by intense devotion and dedication to a project, task, or objective. The intense effort failed to produce the expected results. The performance requirements for completing a committed plan were significant and sufficient, but conditions prevented the plan's success. The result is severe disappointment for the participants. Managers get into trouble because this disappointment eats away, producing burnout. The disappointment results in diminished vitality, energy, and ability to function. The phenomenon of burnout is more one of degree than of existence or nonexistence. That is, disappointments in failing to reach small or large achievements take their toll over time in the form of reduced performance and increased mistakes.

Burnout, like managerial obsolescence, does not occur overnight. It sets in over a period of weeks, months, and even years. Here are a few causes:

1. Sustaining over a long period the pressure and stress needed to accomplish something and experiencing failure or defeat.
2. Reaching for levels of attainment that are not feasible, practical, or realistic.
3. Being overanxious for professional acceptance and recognition by peers and superiors.
4. Having excessive feelings of insecurity and fear of losing a job or of failing to move up in the organization as expected.
5. Having established routines and procedures affected by fast changing conditions or volatile situations.

Minimizing or eliminating burnout is not easy, since discounting failure is not easy. Here are a few things that can help minimize burnout:

1. Set realistic and attainable expectations in goals and objectives.
2. Break up large-scale achievements into smaller plateaus or progress milestones.
3. Experience a series of successes by mixing formidable challenges with easily attainable challenges.
4. Prevent long sustained high pressure for accomplishment by scheduling shorter low-pressure or low-stress accomplishments.
5. Set up routines or procedures in which attainment can be experienced on a regular basis.
6. Control fast changing situations.

High Tolerance for Mediocrity

The managers who do not face up to their responsibility to exact from their employees high performance and to get rid of people who cannot meet this performance level are managers who allow a personal practice of mediocrity. Mediocrity is not unacceptable performance; that's "dead wood." Mediocrity is performance at the low end of the acceptable region. It is just barely doing the job. One who tolerates mediocrity is simply indifferent to potential performance. But mediocrity is like a disease; it contaminates and spreads. Mediocrity tolerated in one subordinate eventually infects all subordinates. The most tragic aspect of mediocrity is its contaminating effect on managers themselves. Persons who tolerate mediocrity in subordinates develop the equal tendency to tolerate it in themselves.

All companies tolerate mediocrity to some degree. Some reasons are:

1. Shortage of qualified personnel, forcing a manager to prefer a mediocre employee to none or to a potential employee who is worse than mediocre.
2. Insufficient funds and resources for upgrading, updating, and developing skills of employees.
3. Practice of seniority and tenure within union ranks or job longevity. Seniority grants preferential treatment to long-service employees, and managers tend to overlook weaknesses.
4. Game playing with the performance appraisal system. The intent of performance appraisal systems is to identify good and bad performance and to feed back results to employees for reinforcement or correction. When this is not done, employees are confused.

Several things can be done to remove the practice of tolerating mediocrity:

1. Formal and deliberate "performance stretch" (MBO helps considerably).

2. Preemployment training to bring employees to the needed competence level.

3. System of backups for every key job. This includes training and development for backup personnel.

4. Institution of incentive/recognition programs for achievement awards.

5. Institution of a management accountability program to expect and ensure managerial performance in all key areas.

6. Creation of an atmosphere and attitude that job security rests with skills and ability rather than with tenure and seniority.

Casual Approach to Managing

Competition in the marketplace is sometimes viewed as a "game" to be played with fun and delight. The players are managers. The people are buyers. There are even business games for sale in which players can experience a win or loss—make money or go bankrupt. When the game is over, life continues. This view of competition as a lot of fun has encouraged an attitude that win or lose, things continue as they are. If you don't win one day, you may the next. This view fosters a lackadaisical approach to management. It encourages a casual attitude toward getting results. This view is myopic and dangerous. Competitive life is not like this.

Another view is that competition is "economic war," that the marketplace is a battlefield in which strategies are developed and moves and countermoves are made to win the battle. In this view, victory means capturing the market for a product even if the company is destroyed or driven bankrupt in the process. This view is a frightening one, posing managers as military commanders waging economic war with their competitive opponents. Winning means survival. Without a win, things will not continue as they are. Although this view is frightening, it is real, sobering, and accurate. This view motivates. More, it disrupts the comfortable, safe niche of the "game" approach in management. It demands that managers develop their style and process. It alerts management to the fact that getting results must be a deliberate, formal, and intense effort. It requires getting rid of trial-and-error methods, reaction approaches, emulation of a predecessor, or fire drill approaches.

Strategic planning and strategic managing result from the view that competition is indeed an economic war that must be waged. Casual approaches succeed in an organization when the business cycle favors or is "in tune" with the products and services of the company. In this case, the company succeeds in spite of itself. But when the business cycle turns, the firm experiences difficulties and managers fall into trouble. The hallmark of a professional manager is the ability to develop and apply whatever strategies are needed for existing business conditions. Such a manager is able to change strategy when conditions change. This handbook is devoted to managers who wish to develop the needed strategies for getting results in their organization. MBO as a strategy looms high on the list.

Dilution of Effort

Innovations and change occur in organizations with such rapidity that managers do not have time to complete orientation and adjustment to them. Changes ofen carry with them problems that compound at a fast rate. Managers attempt to keep pace with this tempo of complexity by stretching wider and wider their scope of activities. Managers compress within hours or days the work that formerly took weeks or months. Today's manager must give time and attention to many more items and a wider spectrum of activities. In an attempt to avoid running afoul and to bring order and progress to intricate and interweaving demands, managers spread their time and energy across the entire spectrum. Managers literally spread themselves thin over many responsibilities. They end up doing many things but doing none of them well. Dilution of effort occurs, and even more dilution appears to be the prospect for managers in the future.

Managers need to face the spectrum of demands made on them, to sort them, and then to concentrate on the few high payoff items. They need to deploy limited resources where these resources count most. They cannot commit themselves to every important demand that comes down the pike, since resources for handling these ever-increasing demands simply do not exist. Managers must develop a sense of focus and concentrate on those demands that will yield the results needed. Here are a few things that can help minimize dilution of effort:

1. Having a formal and deliberate practice of setting and following priorities.
2. Establishing and reaching for formal and accountable goals and objectives.
3. Selecting and pursuing high payoff opportunities and rejecting nominal or low payoff ones.
4. Practicing efficient management by getting the most for the least.

AGENDA NEEDS FOR MANAGERS

The emerging challenges to management, the hidden practices of the management world, the indicators of managers in trouble, and why managers become incompetent as described in the previous sections, show why it is imperative that managers examine their orientation, knowledge, and skills for present-day applicability. If we derive from the 15 challenges described in the first section of this chapter what a manager's needs will be on the way to the 21st century with regard to orientation, knowledge, and skills, the results might be those seen in Table 1.2.

TABLE 1.2   Emerging Issues and What Managers Will Need to Cope With Them

Trends	Orientation	Needs of Manager Knowledge	Skills
Fast growing world competition	International market	Competitiveness	Strategic decision making
Transnational collaborations	National governments	Political/ business collaborations	Participation, negotiation
Volatile economy	Changes in the economy	Flexible planning	Risk taking
Energy dependence	Conservation	Efficiency	Resource handling
Quality deterioration	Customers	Quality control	Errorless decisions
Burgeoning government bureaucracy	Free enterprise system	Regulation reduction	Entrepreneurship
Productivity decline	Work processes	Measurement efficiency	Productivity scorekeeping
Product maturation	New products	Expanding technology	Innovativeness
Fast changing society	Changes	Miniplanning	Flexible style
Effects of organizational strategies	Global issues	Ripple effects of noncompetitors	Strategic decision making
Casual managers as cause of mediocrity	Managerial productivity	Higher performance	Time utilization
Growth of robotization	Automation	High technology	Computerized design and manufacturing
Information mismanagement	Information	Information processing	Validation
Office of the future	White-collar workers	Employees in management	Employee participation
Decline in motivation	Motivation to work	Human resources	Generation of motivators

This book is designed to cover these aspects of orientation, knowledge, and skills, with special emphasis on skills. MBO is both substance and process. That is, it is the conceptual framework and vehicle by means of which the issues and concerns covered in this chapter can be managed effectively and efficiently on the road to the 21st century.

SUMMARY

The year 2000 AD is just around the corner. Managers need a perspective to the 21st century. Much of what we do today will affect our managing into the future. The statistics cited in this chapter give a sense of what's happening.

Fifteen specific issues and concerns are described. These affect managers everywhere, and will be decisive in management performance.

Managers must face up to the reality that their world has two aspects: the world that is and the world as it should be, the hidden world of management practices and the imagined world of assumptions. The 15 hidden management practices cited, such as living with threats, tolerating white-collar crime, compromising, and giving in to labor unions, give some idea of the disparity of these two worlds.

Indicators of managers in trouble include inadequate knowledge, lack of concern about productivity, mishandling of crises, allowance of delays, and avoidance of hard work. Indicators are signals, not proof. To managers these signals are important, because they reveal whether the managers are in trouble. These indicators are forerunners of incompetence. Managers become incompetent because of obsolescence, burnout, and casual approach to management, among other reasons. Finally, the chapter describes agenda needs for managers on their way to the 21st century. These needs are derived from the challenges emerging and the individual problems of managers.

BIBLIOGRAPHY

Business Week Editors, "The Breakdown of U.S. Innovation." *Business Week*, February 16, 1976.

Cetron, Marvin, and O'Toole, Thomas, *Encounters with the Future: Forecast into the 21st Century*. New York: McGraw-Hill, 1982.

Drucker, Peter F., *Age of Discontinuity: Guidelines to Our Changing Society*. New York: Harper & Row, 1968.

Drucker, Peter F., *Managing in Turbulent Times*. New York: Harper & Row, 1980.

Drucker, Peter F., *The Changing World of the Executive*. New York: Time Books, 1982.

Freudenberger, Herbert J., *Burn Out*. New York: Bantam Books, 1980.

Heilbroner, Robert L., and Lester Thurow, *Five Economic Challenges*. Englewood Cliffs, NJ: Prentice-Hall, 1981, Chapters 1 and 5.

Naisbitt, John, *Megatrends*. New York: Warner Books, 1982.

Toffler, Alvin, *The Third Wave*. New York: Bantam Books, 1980.

PART 2

Theory, Principles, Strategies, and Benefits of MBO

While some management personnel regard MBO as a recent discovery, it has in fact been around for some time. There is a critical need to identify and formalize the principles, the theory, and the strategic models that operate to give MBO its character. The four chapters in this section describe the foundations and fundamentals of MBO. These chapters set the framework for the entire handbook. Benefits of the practice of MBO are also completely described in this section. Readers who are "seasoned MBO practitioners" and have a thorough grasp of MBO fundamentals may want to skip this section and go on to the next.

2

PINNACLE VIEW
OF MBO

The practice of managing by objectives (MBO) is widespread and pervasive in private and public organizations throughout the world. The setting of goals and establishment of objectives with supporting plans appear to be common practices. Ask anyone in any organization, "Do you set or follow a prescribed set of objectives?" and the answer inevitably is "Yes," even though methods vary. The exact practice of MBO from firm to firm must vary, since each firm is unique.

This chapter provides a basis for understanding the differences. More specifically:

1. MBO is defined. The definition is a distillation of the definition of at least nine experts with their special views and emphasis.
2. MBO is contrasted with traditional management. This helps us understand the differences between MBO and the historic way of managing.

3. A pinnacle view of MBO is provided, that is, the total picture with the major levels of management and their responsibilities.
4. Who is practicing MBO? We briefly look at some of the excellent companies.
5. What makes a high-performing enterprise is discussed. After all, this is the hope and expectation of MBO, to produce high performance.
6. A brief history of MBO development is given, as found in the literature.

WHAT IS MBO?

Throughout the history of human performance, many statements made by many people have given rise to the basic idea and philosophy of MBO. For example, Moses had "ten goals" on stone tablets that were targets for the Hebrews (Exodus 20). Solomon, the wise man of old, once said, "Better is the end of a thing than the beginning thereof" (Ecclesiastes 7:8). Solomon suggested it is results that count. King Arthur and the Knights of the Round Table rode into the fields at the beginning of each month and told the serfs which fields to plough and what was expected. At the end of the month they rode out again, and rewarded the serfs with grain or punished them by cutting off their head.

In more recent times, the MBO idea and philosophy have been applied to management. Many persons have seen and experienced certain concerns and issues in management and have defined MBO in terms of these. Table 2.1 shows the variations in definitions.

TABLE 2.1 Concerns and Issues of Management and Related Definitions of MBO

Managerial Concerns and Issues	Author	Definition
Directing	Peter Drucker	MBO is directing each job toward the objectives of the whole business.
System performance	George S. Odiorne	MBO is a process whereby the superior and subordinate managers of an organization jointly identify its common goals, define each individual's major areas of responsibility in terms of results expected of him and use these measures as guides for operating the unit and assessing the contribution of each of its members.

TABLE 2.1 *(Continued)*

Managerial Concerns and Issues	Author	Definition
Getting results	Dale D. McConkey	MBO is management by results as an approach to management planning and evaluation in which specific targets for a year or for some other length of time are established for each manager, on the basis of the results which each must achieve if the overall objectives of the company are to be realized.
Strategic planning with employee satisfaction	Paul Mali	MBO is a strategy of planning and getting results in the direction that management wishes and needs to take while meeting the goals and satisfaction of its participants.
Performance and development	John W. Humble	MBO is a system that integrates the company's goals of profit and growth with the manager's needs to contribute and develop himself personally.
Motivation	Charles W. Hughes	MBO makes company goals known to the employees and provides opportunities for employees to participate meaningfully in meeting these objectives. In a way that gives employees a chance for identifying personal goals, the motivation to work that results will achieve company goals as well as personal goals.
Behavior	Karl Albrecht	MBO is a pattern of behavior of a manager in guiding the firm into the future through the efforts of people.
System overview of management	Anthony P. Raia	MBO is a philosophy of management which reflects proactive rather than a reactive way of managing. MBO is also a process consisting of a series of interdependent and interrelated steps. MBO is a system of management designed to facilitate planning and organizational control, organizing and assigning tasks, problem-solving, decision-making, motivation, self-control and other important management functions.

TABLE 2.1   (*Continued*)

Managerial Concerns and Issues	Author	Definition
Method	W.J. Reddin	MBO is a powerful management tool and may even be considered a method of managing.
Productivity	Paul Mali	MBO is a six-step interrelated and interdependent process—identify potential productivity areas, quantify productivity level desired, specify a measurable productivity objective, develop a plan for attaining objectives, control with time milestones of progress, and evaluate productivity reached.

The definitions in the table are many and varied. Each has special emphasis, depending on the view of the author. A distillation of the ten views finds MBO described in six categories, each with certain features:

1. MBO is a strategy.
   - (a) A series of unique competitive maneuvers for arriving at results.
   - (b) A process for collaborative decision making.
   - (c) A method for "how to" manage in a given situation with competitors in the same situation.
2. MBO is a process of planning and control.
   - (a) A way to give future directions to complex organizations.
   - (b) An approach for predicting and making future events happen.
   - (c) A method that allows for advance thinking and planning.
3. MBO is a participation process leading to a commitment.
   - (a) Agreed to by managers responsible for the accomplishment.
   - (b) Agreed to by those who must contribute resources and time in support of the accomplishment.
   - (c) Agreed to by those who must accomplish actions to ensure accomplishments.
4. MBO is a performance and evaluation system for getting results.
   - (a) Engenders teamwork through collaboration and participation.
   - (b) Links individuals with the total organization.
   - (c) Provides means of measuring and evaluating performance.
5. MBO is an attitude.
   - (a) Views management's mission as change and improvement.

    (b)   Views managing as proactive and not reactive.

    (c)   Views managerial behavior as a life-style of performance stretches.

  6. MBO is a time-oriented process for getting results.

    (a)   Views results as to be achieved over a critical time period.

    (b)   Views time as a factor in productivity.

    (c)   Views results that occur after time expectations as a managerial shortcoming.

MBO can be any one or a combination of the six views just described. The MBO definition followed in this text attempts to reflect all six views: MBO is a strategy, a process of planning and control, a process of participation, a system for getting results, a managerial attitude, and a process of time control. The definition that follows embraces all of these:

> MBO is a participative system of managing in which managers look ahead for improvements, think strategically, set performance stretch objectives at the beginning of a time period, develop action and supporting plans, and ensure accountability for results at the end of the time period.

This definition was easily understood by the top management of companies listed in *Business Week*'s excellent companies, *Fortune*'s best-managed corporations, and *Dun's Review* annual best-managed organizations. The response of these managers to this definition was favorable. More will be said about this later in this chapter under the heading "Who Is Practicing MBO?."

Six major ideas are inherent in the MBO concept: strategic planning, total management, setting of objectives, individual motivation, measurement of results, and time.

Strategic Planning Process

The strategic planning process in corporate planning begins with strategic thinking. Strategic thinking means looking far ahead in a timetable to plan the blending of activities and operations of individual managers needed to achieve long- and short-range results in the context of problems, competition, constraint, opportunities, and opposing forces. It is a deliberate coordination of resources with the calendar so that individual managers can be signaled to propose, act, and accomplish at designated times. Achievement of a 10 percent reduction in operating costs by all departments within three operating quarters is an example of a timetable of strategic planning. Complete development of ventilator fans, model B, within six months to increase market share is another example of a timetable of strategic coordination.

Total Management

Total management refers to a formalized effort to involve and coordinate the contributions of each manager toward a common goal. A management system is created within the organization that brings together competences in the form of people and equipment for handling the organization's functions and purposes or subfunctions and subpurposes. A hospital needs an internal management system to utilize and coordinate to the fullest the contributions of physicians, nurses, laboratory equipment, lab technicians, operating rooms, dietitians, pharmacists, and supervisors. Similarly, an educational institution needs an internal management system to utilize and coordinate the contributions of faculty, administrators, laboratories, computer equipment, accountants, classrooms, lecture halls, and clerks. A missile manufacturer requires a management system to coordinate metallurgists, stress analysts, computers, fluid dynamicists, electronic controls, fuel, meters, mechanical and heat transfer equipment, and control engineers. Management by objectives creates a management system for connecting the role and contribution of each manager for achieving large-scale accomplishments.

Setting of Objectives

A clear statement of purpose expressed as objectives is the most outstanding measure of effective management. It answers the question, "What results can we expect?" Objectives are accomplishments planned and expected to be completed within a time period. They are targets. They are results. They represent solutions to problems. They represent opportunities to be seized. A general objective might be to improve sales, lower costs, create new markets, or reduce absenteeism. Specific objectives might be achievement of a net profit—net worth ratio of 6.25 percent. Reduction of employee absenteeism from 12 to 6 percent is an example of a personnel management objective for a government agency. An increase in customer inquiries from 10,000/year to 15,000/year is an example of an advertising objective for an individual salesman. A 50 percent reduction of material waste is an example of a cost improvement objective for a foreman in a machine shop. The setting of objectives and their pursuit through action steps leading to results is the heart and core of MBO.

Individual Motivation

Individual motivation refers to personal involvement and participation in the objective-setting process action planning, progress review and problem solving. Involvement tends to generate a desire and willingness to achieve. MBO is a motivational strategy, since commitments and accomplishments lead to a high degree of individual satisfaction. The unit restaurant manager of a large, scattered franchise chain is highly motivated when allowed to participate in all aspects of his or her unit's operations, such as payroll, overhead, hiring, customer relations, advertising, and maintenance. A pipe-welding supervisor is motivated when allowed to participate in the many segments of the total welding job, such as pipe weld design, welding equipment acquisition, inspection, training, qualification, and weld stress analysis. MBO promotes desirable behavior through motivation.

Measurement of Results

Measurement is needed in management to know what has been accomplished. It is needed to know if work has been completed or how it is progressing. The same is true of athletics, when players need to know their score to sense their progress. Good athletes become good only through scorekeeping. The inclusion of measurement dimensions within objective statements allows scorekeeping of progress and completion. The machinist who grinds ten flange faces on a pipe per day uses measurement to evaluate the work. The manager who analyzes budget performance of contracting vendors needs measurement to make the analysis within a responsive time period to correct for overruns. The president who makes a decision to enter a new market with new products and commits his or her organization to additional personnel, increased plant capacity, and capital expenditure must use measures to achieve a set of results within an expected time period. Finally, profit itself is a measurement. It is the bottom line of the plus and minus measures along the way. Progress can only be measured in terms of what one is trying to make progress toward. Some professionals who do creative and nonquantified work have difficulty in planning measures of results. For this group a collection of indicators could serve as a basis of measurement.

Time

Time is a basic measure applied to every objective. MBO is not simply getting results, but getting results within a time period. The units for measuring a result can vary widely, depending on the type of activity involved in the objective. For example, in a high-volume production line, output may be measured on a daily basis, whereas in the space program, results may be measured over a five-year period. The time unit is set so that progress toward an objective can be measured for review and control. With a time schedule, an objective can be broken down into milestones of progress. This provides natural points for progress reviews.

MBO CONTRASTED WITH TRADITIONAL MANAGEMENT

Many areas in the practice of MBO are the same as those in management. However, there are many differences. Management methods of the past included: 1) domination; (2) emulation of a predecessor; (3) management by reaction; (4) management by exception; (5) trial and error; (6) hunch; and (7) paternalism. The differences with MBO are obvious. It is these differences that give MBO an edge over traditional management in creating a system for getting results. For example, managerial processes have often been thought of as parts of an iceberg. One often hears in management circles about the "management iceberg." This analogy is used to show that 90 percent of what traditional management does is informal and out of sight. Only 10 percent is formal and above the surface. This traditional view indicates that the "what" of management is visible and open. The "who," "where," "when," and "why," however, are submerged and difficult to trace. In traditional management, these are a part of in-process managing. In contrast, in MBO the what, who, where, how, when, and why of managing must be visible and open in advance of actual practice. In the iceberg analogy, MBO requires 90 percent of the managerial processes to be open, visible, and formal well before implementation (Figure 2.1).

Another important difference between traditional management and MBO is in systems. MBO tends to create a dynamic network in which the connection between and among management personnel relates to directions, results, schedules, and communications, whereas in traditional management the system created is more static, and authority, positions, delegation, and control are the principal features (Figure 2.2). Table 2.2 illustrates some of the other differences between MBO and traditional management.

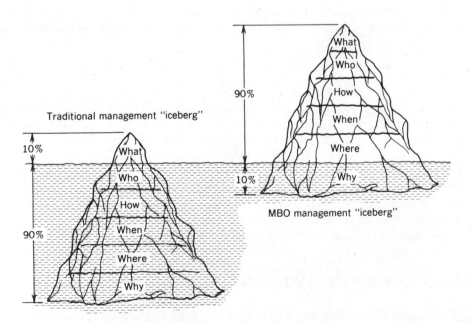

FIGURE 2.1   MBO lifts the iceberg to give visibility to the managerial processes.

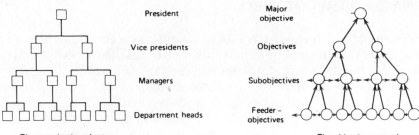

The organization chart   The objective network

FIGURE 2.2 MBO creates a management system.

TABLE 2.2 Contrasts Between Traditional Management and MBO

Traditional Management	MBO
Boss sets goals and delegates responsibility	Boss and subordinate set goals mutually
Planning, organizing, staffing, directing, and controlling interwoven with in-process planning	Processes of management executed in planning period (sophisticated planning); everything is laid out before activity begins
Evaluation at the end of implementation	Evaluation during planning period, during operation, and at end
Accountability centralized	Accountability decentralized
Decision making done with nebulous alternatives	Decision making done with alternatives listed in priority array; consequences of alternatives clear
Focus is on activities	Focus is on results and achievements
Problem solving has past orientation	Problem solving has future orientation
Management system coordinated with people	Management system coordinated through objectives and people
Leadership by personality and charm	Leadership by style, process, and goals
Improvements a random process (luck factor high)	Improvements a way of life (central sense of mission)
Objectives generated from top management	Objectives generated from all levels of management
Forms and rules are basis of control of human resources	Strategic annual plans are basis of control of human resources
Only few management persons interact	Entire organization interacts
System aimed primarily at operations or productions	System aimed at all functions and departments, including operations and productions
Employee participation is source of ideas and solutions	Participative management style allows shared decision making
Problem solving during implementation	Problem solving as much as possible during planning
Responsibility for planning with top management	Responsibility for planning with every manager
Day-to-day managing	Results-to-results managing

PINNACLE VIEW OF MBO

The practice of management is complex. Complexity stems from the need to pull together the efforts of hundreds and often thousands of people and the capacities of highly technical facilities and special equipment in many different locations, and to make the best use of millions of borrowed dollars toward a predetermined set of goals and expectations. The practice of management involves the tailoring of technology to do a business with customers, selection from a vast array of alternative products or services, and making of compromises and tradeoffs to accommodate varying demands from stockholders, employees, unions, government, and the public. The name of the game is "management of complexity." Those who do an excellent job of managing complexity are those who seem to have a total view of management.

With MBO the situation is no different. Those who manage well with MBO manage with a pinnacle view of the total process and its practices, as exemplified in Figure 2.3. Levels of management are connected with the practices of management. This total MBO view in an organization reveals four basic practices: (1) planning practices (Figure 2.4); (2) preparation practices (Figure 2.5); (3) performance practices (Figure 2.6); and (4) evaluation practices (Figure 2.7). These are described briefly here.

Planning Practices

Planning practices include thinking ahead, creating expectations, devising activities, and diagramming courses of action. Planning is deciding in advance, with the best information available, what is to be done, how it is to be done, who will do it, and when. The existence of various types of plans suggests strategies. Planned strategies are to incorporate priorities of time, approaches, and techniques; objectives; and resource support. Yet the one common ingredient in all plans is performance expectations. Flexibility and adaptability are achieved in plans through contingency thinking and building of options to allow for new choices and new decision making when new factors emerge. Planning, thinking, and analysis are vital and basic to all the other fundamental management practices.

Preparation Practices

Arranging and ensuring the availability of the employees, facilities, tools, money, materials, supplies, and vendors necessary to complete devised plans comprise preparation practices. These practices bridge planning and performance. Responsive and time arrangements of skills and resources can make a critical difference in execution of plans. Preparation requires knowing what is to be achieved, breaking down the work into packages, giving the packages to qualified and responsible personnel, and assuring that facilities, materials, machines, supplies, tools, workers, and vendors are

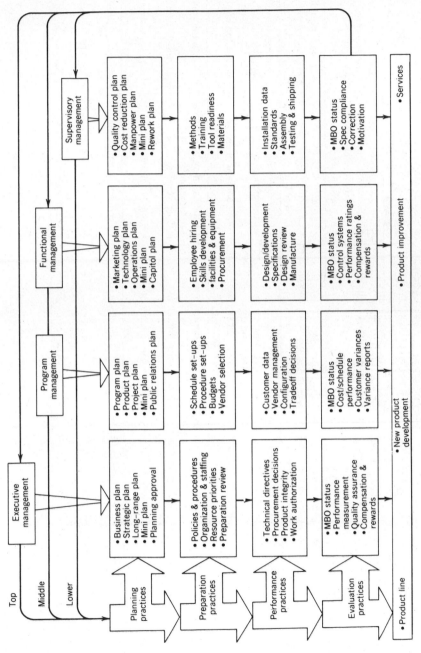

FIGURE 2.3 Pinnacle view of MBO practices in an organization.

41

	Executive Management	Program Management	Functional Management	Supervisory Management
Business Plan	• Stockholders requirements • CEO's guidelines • Mission payoff	• Financial expectation • Validation of guidelines • Direct process	• Technological assumptions • Validation of guidelines • Integration of business & technology	• Guideline awareness • Validation of guidelines • Data support
Strategic Plan	• Assumptions & options • Survey of strategies • Selection of strategies	• Forecasts • Competitive analysis • Market data	• Trends • Capacity • Productivity	• Tactical procedures • Data & information • Supportive ideas
Managing by Objectives	• Overall objectives • Integration of plans • Approval of objectives	• Prime objectives • Coordination of departments • Review of support objectives	• Department objectives • Participation • Validation of objectives	• Performance objectives • Participation • Validation of objectives
Program Plan	• Assignment of business targets • Setting of priorities • Allocation of resources	• Establishment of budgets • Establishment of schedules • Establishment of standards	• Establishment of technical requirements • Cost formation • Time requirements	• Data & information • Technical participation • Support validation
Department Plans	• Assignment of business targets • Technology advancement • Review and approval	• Guidelines for costs • Guidelines for performance • Guidelines for schedules	• Technical commitments • Timing by job level • Pareto's law	• Resources support • Quality control support • Planning feedback

FIGURE 2.4 Planning practices.

	Executive Management	Program Management	Functional Management	Supervisory Management
Organization	• Set policies • Establish structures • Assign programs & projects	• Set up programs & projects • Establish working groups • Identify vendors	• Assign responsibilities • Set up performance standards • Conduct coordination meetings	• Define work packages • Assign responsibilities • Clarify authorities
Schedules	• Set priorities • Establish baselines • Approve budgets and schedules	• Establish master schedules • Develop configurations • Establish program breakdown structure	• Establish time/work requirements • Establish time standards • Get budget information	• Establish working schedules • Establish work/package priorities • Agree on delivery dates
Manpower	• Requisition personnel • Set up hiring incentives • Approve personnel	• Define man-hour requirements • Prepare orientation & training • Manpower placement	• Make up skills inventory • Write job descriptions • Hire & place	• Set up performance standards • Set up training process • Set up record systems
Facilities	• Coordinate facilities • Validate capacity utilization • Approve facility use	• Support capital plan • Support facility need • Support procurement	• Assure capital equipment availability • Procure equipment • Compile documentation	• Acquire tools • Set up maintenance programs • Review equipment effectiveness

FIGURE 2.5 Preparation practices.

	Executive Management	Program Management	Functional Management	Supervisory Management
Design Development	• Set up guidelines for proposals • Make policies • Make bid decisions	• Set up program requirements • Assure communications • Approve design concept	• Make technical analysis • Do conceptual design • Carry out design reviews	• Complete work orders • Support design effort • Test reviews
Procurement Process	• Make make/buy decisions • Decide on legal constraints • Decide on authority limits	• Coordinate requirements • Manage vendors • Review vendor results	• Decide on specs • Select vendors • Integrate results	• Issue purchase orders • Certify vendors • Carry out vendor inspection
Product Integrity	• Make policies • Approve standards • Review quality control	• Approve technical data to user • Audit quality control • Act as customer liaison	• Assure product reliability • Assure quality • Assure spec compliance	• Check skill certification • Check safety certification • Check maintainability
Authorization & Accomplishment	• Establish authority • Review results • Sign off	• Make tradeoff decisions • Issue work orders • Approve work schedules	• Procure • Manufacture & assemble • Test & ship	• Do performance reviews • Do resource-use reviews • Complete work packages

FIGURE 2.6 Performance practices.

	Executive Management	Program Management	Functional Management	Supervisory Management
MBO Status	• Conduct MBO reviews • Assure results • Issue MBO summaries	• Identify MBO variances • Correct MBO status • Report MBO status	• Identify MBO variances • Correct MBO status • Report MBO status	• Identify MBO variances • Correct MBO variance • Report MBO status
Cost/Schedule Performance Measurement	• Make financial review • Assure profit targets • Issue new authorizations	• Review programs • Make cost/schedule reviews • Approve corrective plans	• Correct cost overruns • Correct delays • Issue budget reports	• Complete rework • Expedite deliveries • Assure compliance
Product Quality Measurement	• Approve variance reports • Review customer satsisfaction • Complete authorizations	• Assure customer requirements • Approve reports • Release documentation	• Make audit for compliance • Resolve customer complaints • Document	• Correct deficiencies • Correct customer complaints • Supply data
Personnel Evaluation	• Do performance reviews • Correction & development • Give compensation & rewards	• Make evaluations to functional management • Document • Make recommendations	• Rate employee performance • Rate development programs • Give compensation & rewards	• Rate employee performance • Rate individual development • Give compensation & rewards

FIGURE 2.7 Evaluation practices.

available and committed when the work package is to be started. Preparation practices develop and release the capability in people and the capacity in physical assets. In many ways, utilization of capacity is a measure of the effectiveness of preparation practices.

Performance Practices

Performance practices ensure the effective and efficient carrying out of tasks called for in the plans. Getting things done is a deliberate process. Those who define the process, develop it, and make it efficient can deliver profound results. The process requires conception and development of designs, clear understanding of plans, decisions about whether to buy or make parts, and assembly and testing of hardware. It requires communication and negotiation of requirements and tradeoffs with customers. It requires hard work, perseverance, and coordination of various tasks within a work sequence. It requires correction of unfavorable results at the time these results begin to emerge.

Evaluation Practices

Evaluation practices include measuring, assessing, and appraising results accomplished, comparing these with expectations, and making corrections, if necessary. Comparing actual performance with plans, analyzing the variances found, and identifying how to correct and pull in the performance differences require measurement and evaluations of MBO completion status, cost/schedule performance, product integrity, worker appraisal, financial results, and competitive analysis. Effective evaluation is a well-organized system designed to keep all levels of management informed on status and what to do to correct or adjust. For evaluation, performance indicators that signal progress or deviation from progress are built into the work process.

WHO IS PRACTICING MBO?

MBO is practiced successfully in the United States, England, Canada, Japan, Germany, France, Italy, Brazil, Mexico, India, and other countries. MBO is practiced in large and small, private and public organizations and in religious and social areas. There is no question that MBO is popular. Since its practice varies from organization to organization, specific and accurate identification of who uses it is difficult. Even the MBO titles vary. Some names used for MBO are: management by objectives, management by results, management by objectives and results, management by goals, managing by objectives, goal setting, managing for results, work planning for objectives, productivity by objectives, managing with accountability, objectives strategies and tactics, organizational objectives and mission, and goals and objectives. Even though the terms tend to suggest varying elements of programs, systems, and practices, they describe the same process.

The MBO philosophy and concept of each is the same: Each manager should have goals arrived at through participation, plans to achieve them, and a way of evaluating results. George Odiorne estimated that eight of ten U.S. businesses are managed by objectives. In a paper presented at the International MBO Seminar in Bowling Green, Ohio, August 21 to 22, 1978, entitled "Applying MBO—Changes in the Organization," Jim Tarter reported that between 40 and 50 percent of the Fortune 500 corporations have planning and control systems that meet the basic characteristics of an MBO process. In a major study by the National Industrial Conference Board Study No. 212 covering 147 companies of various sizes and in various industries, 122 of these companies (82 percent) reported practicing MBO for each of their major functions and departments.

In a study conducted for this book, eight companies singled out by *Business Week* as being the best-managed companies in 1982 (Table 2.3), four singled out by *Fortune* as being the best-managed companies in 1981 (Table 2.4), and ten singled out by *Dun's Review* as being excellent corporations from 1975 to 1980 (Table 2.5) were surveyed as to the extent of MBO used in them. When asked the question, "Do you practice MBO in your firm?," most responded affirmatively. The survey suggested the following definition of MBO:

> *MBO is a participative system of managing in which managers look ahead for improvements, think strategically, set performance stretch objectives at a beginning period, develop supporting plans, and give accountability for results at the end of the period.*

The results of the survey are tabulated in Tables 2.3, 2.4, and 2.5. Seventy-five of *Business Week*'s best-managed corporations practiced MBO, 75 percent of *Fortune*'s, and 65 percent of *Dun's Review*. The others practice MBO partially. Few companies said they did not use it at all! The percentages are significant, since these corporations are the cream of the crop. They are the excellent corporations! These tables also show the uses made of MBO. These uses and other responses made by these high-performing companies will be taken up in later chapters. In summary, one might infer that 70 to 80 percent of businesses and corporations practice MBO in some way or another. Since there are over 17 million businesses in the United States and over 2.5 million registered corporations, one can surmise from statistical inference that most set objectives in an annual cycle in some way.

TABLE 2.3 MBO Practice by *Business Week's* Best-Managed Companies of 1981

	IBM	3M	Johnson & Johnson	Texas Instruments	Dana	Emerson Electric	Hewlett Packard	Digital Equipment	Total	Percentage
MBO practice										
Yes	x	x	x	x		x	x		6	75
No									0	0
Partially					x			x	2	25
Length of time										
Under 3 years									0	0
4–6 years								x	1	13
7–10 years	x		x		x				3	38
10 years and over		x		x		x	x		4	50
Primary uses										
Strategic planning				x	x			x	3	38
Operational planning		x		x	x		x	x	5	63
Performance appraisal	x	x	x	x		x	x	x	7	88
Productivity		x	x	x	x			x	5	63
Motivation		x	x		x				3	38
Measures of effectiveness										
Before, after sales, profits, performance	x	x	x	x	x	x	x		7	88
Reactions from management	x		x	x				x	4	50
Reactions from employees							x		1	13

TABLE 2.4   MBO Practice by *Fortune*'s Best-Managed Corporations of 1981

	GE	IBM	Exxon	Emerson Eleric	Total	Percentage
MBO practice						
Yes	x	x		x	3	75
No					0	0
Partially			x		1	25
Length of time						
Under 3 years					0	0
4–6 years					0	0
7–10 years		x	x		2	50
10 years and over	x			x	2	50
Primary uses						
Strategic planning	x				1	25
Operational planning	x		x		2	50
Performance appraisal	x	x		x	3	75
Productivity			x		1	25
Motivation			x		1	25
Measures of effectiveness						
Before, after sales, profits, performance	x			x	2	50
Reactions from management	x	x	x		3	75
Reactions from employees					0	0

ARE MBO COMPANIES HIGH-PERFORMANCE ENTERPRISES?

Management is big business from any perspective. Sales run into trillions of dollars, and profits run into billions. Even management compensation is highly significant. Managerial salaries in 1983 were at an all-time high, estimated at $250 billion, which is roughly 20 percent of the gross national product. Benefits for management are another $150 billion. The total for both is about $400 billion, roughly 35 percent of the GNP.

Statistical estimates of corporate and managerial performance are impressive! A key question to be answered here is, "Are MBO-practicing companies high-performing enterprises?" Does an MBO corporate planning process make the difference between normal performance and superperformance?

No organization can depend on individual genius; the supply is always too scarce. But an organization can depend on being able to take normally performing managers and through teamwork and the planning process receive superperformance. In fact, the purpose of organization is to allow ordinary managers to do extraordinary things.

TABLE 2.5   MBO Practice by *Dun's Review* Excellent Companies of 1975–1980

	MBO Practice			Length of Time (yr)				Strategic Planning
	Yes	No	Partially	<3	4–6	7–10	10 & over	
American Standard	x				x			
Gannett	x				x			
Intel	x					x		
Perkin-Elmer			x				x	x
Standard Oil (Indiana)			x		x			x
American Broadcasting Co.		x						
Digital Equipment			x		x			x
Raytheon	x						x	x
Revlon			x				x	
Union Pacific			x				x	x
Boeing			x				x	x
Caterpillar Tractor	x						x	
Continental Bank	x					x		
General Electric	x						x	x
Schlumberger	x					x		x
Beatrice Foods	x				x			
Emerson Electric	x						x	
General Motors			x				x	x
Halliburton			x	x				x
Ralston Purina	x						x	
Bendix	x				x			
Bank of America	x					x		
Phillip Morris	x					x		x
IBM	x					x		
Merrill Lynch	x				x			
Hewlett Packard	x						x	
Total	17	1	8	1	7	5	11	11
Percentage	65	4	31	4	29	21	46	42

A comparative glance at the performance of companies that practice and do not practice MBO reveals that MBO does give a corporate planning process that's decisive. MBO-practicing enterprises *are* high-performing enterprises! Those who responded in the MBO survey as practicing MBO are identified as best-managed corporations.

Corporate scoreboards are shown in Tables 2.6 through 2.10 and performance ratios are graphically illustrated in Figures 2.8 through 2.11. These clearly differentiate the superperformers from the normal performers. The companies and performance measures shown in the tables and figures are as follows:

1. *Organizations.*

    (a)   Total U.S. businesses and corporations as reported by the U.S.

| | Primary Uses | | | Measures of Effectiveness | | |
Operational Planning	Performance Appraisal	Productivity	Motivation	Before, After Sales, Profits, & Performance	Reactions From Management	Reactions From Employees
x	x			x	x	
x	x			x		
x					x	
x	x			x	x	
x	x	x	x	x		x
x	x	x		x	x	
x				x	x	
	x					x
x	x			x	x	
x				x		
x	x	x	x	x		
x	x		x		x	
x	x			x	x	
x	x			x		
x	x		x	x		
	x			x		
x	x	x		x		
x	x	x	x	x	x	
x	x		x			
x	x		x	x		
			x			
				x		
	x				x	
x	x			x	x	
x	x					x
20	20	5	8	18	11	3
77	77	19	31	69	42	12

Department of Commerce in the *Annual Statistical Abstracts*, "Business Enterprise" chapters, 1965 to 1983 (Table 2.6).

(b) The 500 largest corporations in the United States as reported by *Fortune* magazine in the annual "500 Corporation Directory," 1965 to 1983 (Table 2.7).

(c) The chief executive officer's best-managed corporations as reported in *Fortune* magazine, May 1981, in a major survey of the 500 CEOs of the *Fortune 500* corporations. The four best-managed corporations according to these CEOs are General Electric, IBM, Exxon, and Emerson Electric (Table 2.8).

(d) *Business Week*'s excellent corporations as reported in *Business Week*, 21 July 1981, in a major study of corporations. The excellent corporations are IBM, Procter & Gamble, 3M, Johnson & Johnson, Texas Instruments, Dana, Emerson Electric, Hewlett-Packard, Digital Equipment, and McDonald's. Procter & Gamble and McDonald's are not included as they refused to participate in the survey conducted for this handbook (Table 2.9).

(e)   *Dun's* annual five best-managed companies as reported in *Dun's Review*, 1975 to 1980. The selected corporations during this period are American Standard, Gannett, Intel, Perkin-Elmer, Standard Oil of Indiana, American Broadcasting Co., Digital Equipment, Raytheon, Revlon, Union Pacific, Boeing, Caterpillar Tractor, Continental Bank, General Electric, Schlumberger, Beatrice Foods, Emerson Electric, General Motors, Halliburton, Ralston Purina, Bendix, Bank of America, Phillip Morris, IBM, Merrill Lynch, and Hewlett Packard (Table 2.10).

2. *Performance Ratios.*   Statistical averages used to aggregate individual corporations into each of the categories:

(a)   Percent profitability.   Ratio of net income to total sales through the period 1965 to 1983.

(b)   Percent productivity.   Ratio of net income to total investors' equity through the period 1965 to 1983 (the familiar output/input ratio).

(c)   Profit contribution.   Net income per employee through the period 1965 to 1983.

(d)   Organizational efficiency.   Total sales per employee over the period 1965 to 1983.

Figures 2.8 through 2.11 show that the best U.S. corporations, almost all of which use MBO, are superior to total U.S. businesses and corporations and the 500 largest U.S. corporations.

TABLE 2.6   Aggregate Performance of All U.S. Businesses and Corporations, 1965 Through 1983

	1965	1970	1975	1980	1983
Sales ($ billions)	1,469	2,082	3,685	7,159	8,200
Profits ($ billions)	111	109	196	302	340
Employees (millions)	51.1	61.3	63.6	74.7	79.0
Assets ($ billions)	1,724	2,635	4,287	7,617	8,500
Percent profitability	7.5	5.2	5.3	4.2	4.2
Percent productivity	6.4	4.1	4.5	3.9	4.0
Profit contribution	2,172	1,778	3,081	4,042	4,303
Organizational efficiency	28,747	33,964	57,940	95,836	103,797

Source: U.S. Department of Commerce, *Annual Statistical Abstracts*, 1965 to 1983.

TABLE 2.7 Performance of 500 Largest U.S. Corporations, 1965 Through 1983

	1965	1970	1975	1980	1983
Sales ($ billions)	298	464	865	1,650	1,686
Profits ($ billions)	20.0	21.7	379	81.2	68.8
Employees (millions)	11.3	14.6	14.1	15.9	14.1
Percent return on total investment	11.8	9.5	51.2	21.1	21.2
Percent profitability	6.7	3.9	4.3	4.9	4.1
Percent productivity	11.8	9.5	51.2	21.1	21.2
Profit contribution	1,769	1,486	2,684	5,107	4,879
Organizational efficiency	24,141	31,780	61,347	103,792	117,131

Source: *Fortune* magazine, "500 Corporate Directory," 1965 to 1983.

TABLE 2.8 Performance of Four Best-Managed U.S. Corporations[a] According to *Fortune 500* CEOs, 1965 Through 1983

	1965	1970	1975	1980	1983
Sales ($ billions)	5.38	8.36	18.48	39.33	39.75
Profits ($ billions)	.473	.678	1.29	2.74	3.20
Employees (millions)	.195	.208	.209	.242	.229
Percent return on total investment	17.5	14.7	42.1	36.9	26.9
Percent profitability	8.8	8.1	7.9	7.7	8.9
Percent productivity	17.5	14.7	42.1	36.9	26.9
Profit contribution	2,427	3,253	6,187	11,331	13,981
Organizational efficiency	27,603	40,116	88,607	162,650	173,675

[a]Four corporations are Emerson Electric, Exxon, General Electric, and IBM.
Source: *Fortune* magazine, May 1981.

TABLE 2.9 Performance of *Business Week*'s Excellent U.S. Corporations,[a] 1965 Through 1983

	1965	1970	1975	1980	1983
Sales ($ billions)	.893	1.81	3.14	6.53	9.14
Profits ($ billions)	.100	.210	.348	.713	.991
Employees (millions)	.056	.069	.073	.099	.105
Percent return on total investment	17.2	22.8	66.9	31.7	148.3
Percent profitability	11.1	11.6	11.0	10.9	10.8
Percent productivity	17.2	22.8	66.9	31.7	18.5
Profit contribution	1,798	3,052	4,792	7,229	9,411
Organizational efficiency	16,060	26,316	43,239	66,209	86,799

[a]Corporations are Dana, Digital Equipment, Emerson Electric, Hewlett-Packard, IBM, Johnson & Johnson, 3M, and Texas Instruments.
Source: *Business Week*, July 21, 1981.

TABLE 2.10 Performance of *Dun's Review* Best Managed U.S. Companies, 1965 Through 1983

	1965	1970	1975	1980	1983
Sales ($ billions)	2.88	3.35	5.7	10.6	12.5
Profits ($ billions)	.255	.174	.340	.630	.880
Employees (millions)	.102	.115	.106	.124	.112
Percent return on total investment	15.4	13.9	49.9	37.5	30.6
Percent profitability	8.8	5.2	5.9	5.9	7.0
Percent productivity	15.4	13.9	49.9	37.5	30.6
Profit Contribution	2,497	1,514	3,201	5,072	7,892
Organizational efficiency	28,207	29,155	53,672	85,328	112,107

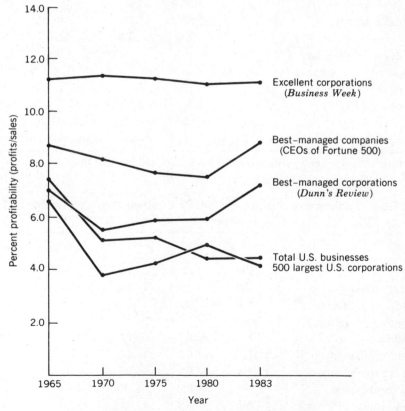

FIGURE 2.8 Profitability through the years.

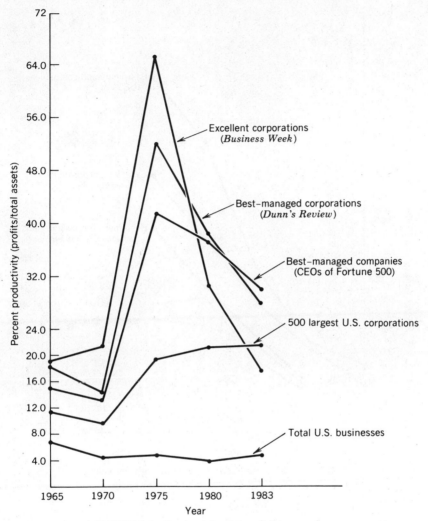

FIGURE 2.9 Productivity through the years.

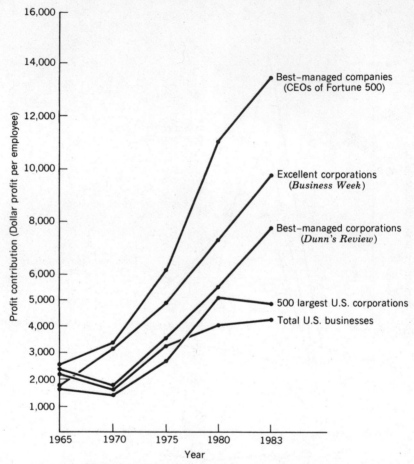

FIGURE 2.10 Profit contribution through the years.

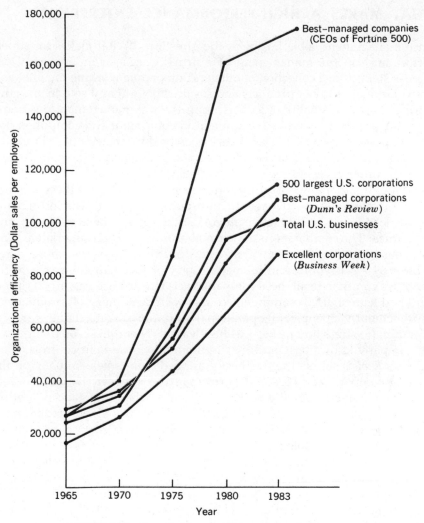

FIGURE 2.11 Organizational efficiency through the years.

WHAT MAKES A HIGH-PERFORMANCE ENTERPRISE?

Since management is big business, the question, "What makes for super-performance in the management of a firm?," begs for an answer. Does success stem from a collection of outstanding people working together as a team? From an array of products and services bought and sold in an active market? From the quality of leadership in the top management positions? From the acquisition and use of automated equipment and computers that predict performance and control variances of diverse activities? From the skillful use of zero-based budgeting, matrix management, strategic management, or other excellent tools such as these?

Although superlative organizations use a fair number of these modern business techniques, what makes them superlative is a combination of many things: leadership, thinking, teamwork, strategies, practices, tools, and techniques. The combinations are termed attributes. Each superlative company has found combinations that work for it in a high-performing way.

Business Week reported in its major study of excellent companies eight attributes common to all these companies: (1) bias toward action; (2) simple form and lean staff; (3) continued contact with customers; (4) productivity improvement via people; (5) operational autonomy to encourage entrepreneurship; (6) stress on one key business value; (7) emphasis on doing what the company knows best; and (8) simultaneous loose-tight controls.

Dun's Review selects the five best-managed companies annually on the basis of company earnings and performance. However, Dun's also analyzes the companies for the attributes that give them outstanding performance. From the period 1975 to 1980, 16 attributes were identified from the best-managed companies. These are (1) sophisticated financial astuteness, (2) unsurpassed technology, (3) management innovations, (4) emphasis on corporate growth and productivity, (5) market acumen, (6) strategic competitive planning, (7) management depth, (8) swiftness to new markets, (9) employment of management fundamentals, (10) mastery of planning, (11) long-range capital commitments, (12) aggressive pursuit of objectives and goals, (13) focus and control on the company as a business, (14) strong leadership, (15) corporate individualism, and (16) diversification and mixed acquisitions.

The National Industrial Conference Board, in a study of 147 companies of various sizes and industries, found that certain industries use more management practices, attributes, and tools than others. The attributes of each company varied. The compiled study revealed five management processes in widespread use: (1) electronic data processing, (2) managing by objectives, (3) management information systems, (4) organization development, and (5) direct costing.

In the study by *Fortune* magazine, chief executives of the Fortune 500 companies were asked to name the best-managed companies in the 500 list. What is significant about this survey is that the chief executive officers did the evaluation. Four companies emerged—General Electric, IBM, Exxon, and Emerson Electric. The attributes cited most by these CEOs were (1) constant pursuit of improvement, (2) productivity management, (3) worker motivation, (4) effective business strategies, (5) entrepreneurial spirit, (6) managing for inflation, (7) intensive planning, and (8) setting of tough objectives.

Many other studies purport to identify what makes an excellent company. Each extracts attributes as causes for success. Space does not permit reporting all these studies. If a summary of all of these attributes from various studies could be made, the following would probably be found as contributing to high performance:

1. *Firm Makes Management Fundamentals Work Effectively.* These fundamentals are effective problem solving, mastery in the planning process, persuasive communication, financial astuteness, orientation of the organization as a business, motivation of employees, quick resolution of conflicts, evaluation for correction, setting and maintenance of standards for quality and performance, right decisions when needed, development and maintenance of a competitive edge, and simultaneous loose-tight controls.

2. *Firm Has Attitudes Needed During Given Periods.* These attitudes are pursuit of improvement as a way of life, planning made with a global perspective, customer acquisition and retention given high priority, competition seen as more than a game, employee participation in commitments actively sought, flexibility to move with changing situations, creation of a climate for personal development and skills, and getting results as a prime responsibility.

3. *Firm Practices Efficiency Management.* Aspects of efficient management are scorekeeping for productivity improvement, resource conservation and control, lean and flexible organization, encouragement of employee involvement in productivity improvement, and capital commitments for automated processes.

4. *Firm Makes Skillful Use of Management Techniques, Tools, and Processes.* These techniques, tools, and processes are strategic competitive planning and managing, negotiation skills for agreements and consensus, quality assurance, management information systems, zero-based budgeting, time management, computer-aided decision making, and aggressive pursuit of objectives that transcend past performance.

5. *Firm Pursuing Innovations as a Way of Life.* These innovations include entrepreneurial "spirit" practiced by leaders, substantial innovations within a needed time frame, research and development as continuous functions, development of a technological edge, formal pursuit of new products, and entrepreneurial outlook in decision making.

The studies conducted by *Business Week, Dun's Review, Fortune* magazine, and the Industrial Conference Board all seem to be in rough agreement on the 15 concerns of the future and the skills that are now and will be needed, as described in the first chapter of this book.

Returning now to the question asked at the beginning of this section, "What makes a high performance enterprise?," one can answer that it is not the adoption and emulation of the attributes, techniques, and tools of another company. Rather, it is the development of unique combinations of attitudes, techniques, and tools that work well for the organization. All excellent corporations discussed in this chapter will be found to have quite different managements.

RECENT HISTORY OF MBO DEVELOPMENT

As we look for the origins of MBO, we find that the technique has developed through history in the form of practices, philosophy, statements, and articles. Table 2.11 lists key contributions of individuals since 1954 (any deletions are unintentional).

TABLE 2.11   Recent History in MBO Development

Publication Date	Author	Book Title	Key Contributions
1954	Peter F. Drucker	*Practice of Management*	First use of MBO title; urged objectives be set for every key result of managers
1960	Douglas M. McGregor	*Human Side of Enterprise*	Theory x, theory y; participation process between supervisor and subordinate; integrating individual goals with those of the firm
1961	Edward C. Schleh	*Management by Results*	Results approach in management; planning for results; delegation by results; management objectives
1964	Richard H. Schaffer	*Managing by Total Objectives*	Pursuing total objectives in managing total enterprise
1964	Peter F. Drucker	*Managing for Results*	Entrepreneurial responsibilities connected with performance results; focuses MBO in opportunities
1965	Charles L. Hughes	*Goal Setting*	Goal-setting processes; goals for motivation; creating goal-oriented organizations
1965	Dale D. McConkey	*How to Manage by Results*	How to set up MBO as a results program; translating responsibilities to results; case histories

TABLE 2.11 (*Continued*)

Publication Date	Author	Book Title	Key Contributions
1965	George S. Odiorne	*Management by Objectives*	First use of MBO in book title; systems approach to MBO; gave MBO a "movement" effect
1966	Raymond F. Valentine	*Performance Objectives for Managers*	Managerial efficiency through setting of performance objectives; objectives by levels; quantification of objectives
1966	J.D. Batten	*Beyond Management by Objectives*	Use of motivation to implement MBO; integration of human resources into MBO
1966	Ernest C. Miller	*Objectives and Standards*	Integration of planning and control using objectives and performance standards; research report of company's use of objectives and standards
1968	Walter S. Wikstrom	*Management by and with Objectives*	Practices of companies implementing MBO; appraisal by results
1969	George S. Odiorne	*Management Decisions by Objectives*	Use of MBO in the problem-solving decision-making process
1970	John W. Humble	*Management by Objectives in Action*	MBO as a system; case experiences of MBO in British organizations
1970	George L. Morrisey	*Management by Objectives and Results*	MOR: connecting objectives with results; roles and missions in MBO
1970	George S. Odiorne	*Training by Objectives*	Use of MBO in training and development function
1971	W.J. Reddin	*Effective Management by Objectives*	Use of effectiveness areas in MBO; team implementation of MBO; 3-D method of MBO
1971	Glenn H. Varney	*Management by Objectives*	Performance improvement cycles; individual performance planning
1972	Paul Mali	*Managing by Objectives*	MBO as a strategic planning process in a series of time-connected phases; operational planning; validation of objectives; trouble-shooting charts

TABLE 2.11   (*Continued*)

Publication Date	Author	Book Title	Key Contributions
1972	John W. Humble	*How To Manage by Objectives*	Pitfalls of MBO; MBO practices; improvement analysis checklists
1972	Arthur C. Beck, Ellis D. Hillmar	*Practical Approach to Organizational Development Through MBO*	Use of MBO for organizational development; MBO/R as an intervention in organizations
1973	Stephen J. Carroll, Jr., Henry L. Tosi	*Management by Objectives: Application and Research*	Research study of MBO practices; guidelines for designing and implementing an MBO system
1974	Anthony P. Raia	*Managing by Objecitves*	Systematic approach for implementing MBO in an organization
1975	Dale D. McConkey	*MBO for Nonprofit Organizations*	Application of MBO in wide variety of nonprofit organizations
1978	Paul Mali	*Improving Total Productivity: MBO Strategies for Business, Government, and Non-Profit Organizations*	First application of MBO to productivity problems; use of MBO as a productivity measure; managing productivity by objectives
1978	William Giegold	*MBO: A Self-Instructional Approach*	Self-instructions for strategic planning; MBO process and performance appraisal
1978	Karl Albrecht	*Successful Management by Objectives*	Guidelines for making MBO practices effective and successful; MBO as a behavior pattern for managers
1979	George S. Odiorne	*MBO II*	Update of growth and refinements of MBO since first book
1982	Charles R. MacDonald	*MBO Can Work!*	Innovative approach to MBO—management by contract (way to harmonize goals of managers with subordinates and total organization
1983	James L. Riggs, Glenn H. Felix	*Productivity by Objectives*	MBO as a productivity process and measure for achieving goals and objectives
1986	Paul Mali	*MBO Updated*	First handbook on MBO state of art; updating and integrating of MBO productivity practices with corporate planning process

SUMMARY

This chapter describes the difficulty in defining MBO. Ten different experts all present slightly different definitions, due to their individual emphasis and view. The following definition is suggested:

> *MBO is a participative system of managing in which managers look ahead for improvements, think strategically, set performance stretch objectives at the beginning of a period, develop action and supporting plans, and ensure accountability for results at the end of the period.*

Six major components in a definitive sequence shake out as areas of concern in the MBO process: (1) strategic planning; (2) total management; (3) setting of objectives; (4) individual motivation; (5) measurements of results; and (6) time.

A checklist of comparisons of MBO and traditional management is presented. The single most important difference is that MBO requires a rather complete plan of management up front during planning periods, whereas traditional managing relies on in-process planning.

A pinnacle view of MBO is provided in this chapter. Several charts and illustrations show levels of management and their functions in four basic phases of MBO: (1) planning practices; (2) preparation practices; (3) performance practices; and (4) evaluation practices. What makes a high performance company is also covered. Since business is big business, it is essential to have some careful notion as to what makes for superperformance in a company. Several studies have been reported, and five basic criteria seem to summarize most: (1) making management fundamentals work effectively in the firm; (2) having needed attitudes during given periods of time; (3) practicing efficiency management; (4) using special management techniques, tools, and processes skillfully; and (5) pursuing innovations as a way of life.

Finally, this chapter outlines who is practicing MBO. No accurate figure is possible, since concepts and philosophies of MBO vary from firm to firm. General estimates indicate that 70 to 80 percent of all companies practice MBO in some form. Forty to fifty percent of the Fortune 500 corporations practice MBO, and from 65 to 80 percent of the excellent companies such as *Business Week*'s ten best-managed companies, *Fortune*'s four best-managed companies, and *Dun's Review* ten excellent corporations practice MBO in some way. A recent history of MBO development as traced through the book literature is also included. Starting with Peter Drucker in 1954 down through 1985, contributors are identified in the MBO movement.

BIBLIOGRAPHY

Albrecht, Karl, *Successful Management by Objectives*. Englewood Cliffs, NJ: Prentice-Hall, 1978, p. 20.

Batten, J.D., *Beyond Management by Objectives*. New York: American Management Association, 1966.

Beck, Arthur C. and Hillman, Ellis D., *Practical Approach to Organization Development Through MBO*. Reading, MA: Addison-Wesley, 1972.

Business Week Editors, "Corporate Scoreboard." *Business Week*, March 15, 1982, p. 69.

Carroll, Stephen J. and Tosi, Henry L., *Management by Objectives: Applications and Research*. New York: McMillan, 1973.

Drucker, Peter F., *The Practices of Management*. New York: Harper and Brothers, 1954, p. 121.

Drucker, Peter F., *Managing for Results*. New York: Harper & Row, 1964.

Felix, Glenn H. and Riggs, James L., *Productivity by Objectives*. Englewood Cliffs, NJ: Prentice-Hall, 1983.

Fortune magazine Editors, "C.E.O.'s Pick the Best Managed Companies." *Fortune*, May 4, 1981, p. 133.

Fortune magazine Editors, "The Largest U.S. Industrial Corporations." *Fortune*, May 3, 1982.

Giegold, William, *MBO: A Self-Instructional Approach*. New York: McGraw-Hill, 1978.

Hughes, Charles L., *Goal Setting*. New York: American Management Association, 1965, p. 29.

Humble, John W., *Management by Objectives in Action*. New York: McGraw-Hill, 1970, p. 21.

Ludlow, Hope T., "Management Techniques in the Management Marketplace." Conference Board Record, New York, May 1973, pp. 55–60.

MacDonald, Charles R., *MBO Can Work!* New York: McGraw-Hill, 1982.

Mali, Paul, *Managing by Objectives*. New York: Wiley, 1972, p. 1.

Mali, Paul, *Improving Total Productivity*. New York: Wiley, 1978.

McConkey, Dale D., *How to Manage by Results*. New York: American Management Association, 1965, pp. 88–95.

McConkey, Dale D., *MBO for Nonprofit Organizations*. New York: American Management Association, 1975.

McGregor, Douglas M., *Human Side of Enterprise*. New York: McGraw-Hill, 1960.

Miller, Ernest C., *Objectives and Standards*. New York: American Management Association, 1966.

Morrisey, George L., *Management by Objectives and Results*. Reading, MA: Addison-Wesley, 1970.

Odiorne, George S., *Management by Objectives*. New York: Pitman Publishing, 1965, pp. 122–126.

Odiorne, George S., *Management Decisions by Objectives*. Englewood Cliffs, NJ: Prentice-Hall, 1969.

Odiorne, George S., *Training by Objectives*. New York: McMillan, 1970.

Odiorne, George S., *MBO II*. New York: Pitman Publishing, 1979.

Raia, Anthony P., *Managing by Objectives*. Glenview, IL: Scott, Foresman & Co., 1974, pp. 11–12.

Reddin, W.J., *Effective Management by Objectives*. New York: McGraw-Hill, 1971.

Schaffer, Richard H., *Managing by Total Objectives*. New York: McGraw-Hill, 1964.

Schleh, Edward C., *Management by Results*. New York: McGraw-Hill, 1961.

U.S. Department of Commerce, *Business Statistics—1979–1982*. Washington, D.C.: U.S. Department of Commerce.

Valentine, Raymond F., *Performance Objectives for Managers*. New York: American Management Association, 1966.

Varney, Glenn H., *Management by Objectives*. Chicago: Dartnell Corp., 1971.

Wikstrom, Walter S., *Management by and with Objectives*. New York: American Management Association, 1968.

3

MBO THEORY, PRINCIPLES, AND BENEFITS

IN THIS CHAPTER

REASONS FOR USING MBO
MANAGEMENT THEORY
MBO OPERATING PRINCIPLES
WHAT MAKES MBO WORK?
BENEFITS FROM MBO

Management is one of the greatest and most effective forces known for leading and altering human history. Its practice has brought about profound achievements through the ages—domestication of animals, development of codes and standards for human behavior, rapid intercontinental transportation, affluence for millions of people, generation of nuclear energy, radio and television transmission that allows information to reach millions at once, space travel, and computerization of information. The list of achievements is never ending. Rarely has a discipline emerged to assume such a pivotal point of influence and change. The achievements have been possible because management exists to execute a purpose or a mission. Management is the process of making decisions with and about people, methods, money, tools, materials, and time for the purpose of attaining predetermined goals. The substance of management is action and reaction to make things better. The deepest satisfaction of a successful management group is to leave a project, program, product, or service better than they found it. The deepest frustration and dissatisfaction is to leave it worse.

This chapter discusses the theory, principles, and benefits of MBO for the firm and for managerial practitioners. More specifically, it (1) gives reasons for using MBO; (2) describes MBO theory and where it fits in the "jungle of management theory," which gives a feel for the conceptual framework of MBO; (3) presents 20 MBO operating principles, which give insight to MBO practice; (4) discusses what makes MBO work; and (5) gives the uses and benefits from managing by objectives. Forty special benefits are identified for the company, for the manager, and for the employee.

REASONS FOR USING MBO

MBO exists to further the management movement in the business world. It accomplishes many things for the company in which it is used. Eight important and prime targets of MBO are (1) perpetuation of the enterprise, (2) increase in the firm's profit performance, (3) satisfaction of stockholders, (4) satisfaction of customers, (5) setting of directions for growth, (6) satisfaction of employees, (7) advancement of the technology of the firm, and (8) community contribution of the firm. These goals, the degree of company commitment to them, and measures to evaluate their achievement are shown in Figure 3.1.

Perpetuation of the Enterprise

The work of MBO management is to make the firm grow, shrink, expand, change, but *never terminate*! A first duty of MBO management is to assure the firm's survivability. Although maximization of profit is a desirable goal, it is not as critical as avoidance of losses, losses that will bring the firm to an end. Bankruptcy is the most obvious measure of ineffective performance. Management must invest time and effort in developing its own replacements, and these in turn will assume the responsibilities of perpetuating the firm. People may come and go, but the firm continues. MBO helps to perpetuate the enterprise.

Increase in Profit Performance

Profit performance is by far the most critical responsibility of MBO management. In many ways it is the measure of how well other responsibilities are executed. Profit results are needed for both the investors of the firm and the economy of which the firm is a part. Profits support government, health, education, labor markets, and the community life-style in general. The work of MBO management is the sale of goods and services at prices the market is able and willing to pay. If management is efficient and effective, customers will buy products at a price greater than the costs incurred to produce them. The difference is profit. Increasing a company's profit performance in an ethical manner is an on-going critical responsibility of management. MBO helps to increase profit performance.

Targets of MBO	Some Evaluative Measures	Degree of Company Commitment
• Community contribution	• Taxes; employment levels; grants; affirmative action plans; giving policies; executive participation; service	
• Advancement of technology	• Research reports; R&D budgets; new product introduction; patents granted; feasibility reports; professional presentation	
• Satisfaction of employees	• Turnover; morale; absenteeism; benefits ratio; incentives; grievance rate; strike ratio; suggestion submittal rate	
• Satisfaction of customers	• Repeat order rate; complaint ratio; return ratios; defective reports; inventory levels; delivery slippage reports	
• Satisfaction of stockholders	• Price per share; dividend distribution; equity growth; earnings yield; preference dividend/preference share ratio	
• Setting of directions for growth	• Mission statements; business plan; objective statements; long-range plan; operational plan; strategic plan	
• Increase in profit performance	• Profits; return on investment; productivity; operating costs; price/earnings ratio; sales per employee; value added per employee	
• Perpetuation of the enterprise	• Breakeven points; cash flow; equity; liabilities; current ratio; bad debt losses; capacity utilization; debt/equity ratio; sales growth	

FIGURE 3.1 Targets of MBO with evaluative measures.

Satisfaction of Stockholders

Owners of companies, by virtue of their investment of time, money, and skill, are entitled both legally and morally to a realistic, reasonable, and continuing return on their investment. The work of MBO management makes certain that at all times and under all circumstances owners get this return. It also ensures that owners are able to take pride in their firm, its people, its products and services, and its management. It follows that management has a legal duty to the stockholders to not personally profit at their expense. MBO helps to satisfy stockholders.

Satisfaction of Customers

To start a business is to find a customer. To be in business is to hold on to customers. The essence of business, therefore, is repeat business; the satisfied customer keeps buying, which perpetuates the firm. Customers have the right to expect and receive from a company a well-crafted product, promptness in service, and reliability of product or service. Satisfied customers themselves represent assets built up over time. MBO helps to satisfy customers.

Setting of Directions for Growth

The directive responsibility of MBO management nearly always occupies the forefront of executive attention. This prime duty involves initiation of plans, operation of programs, making of decisions, evaluation, and control within a coordinated system that delivers results. Executives who grasp the reins and give directions for growth of the firm assume work burdens of analysis and stress not often found in our society. This responsibility alone can prove the downfall of a firm or an executive, and often does both. The work of giving directions for growth of a firm requires accurate assessments of where the firm is and sophisticated planning strategies for where it should go. It requires special actions and reactions toward competitor adversaries to assure a growth position in the market. MBO helps to give progressive directions to the firm.

Satisfaction of Employees

The work of MBO management is to provide employment policies and practices that offer employees from top to bottom rewarding and satisfying experiences. Each job must be satisfying, rather than being just a step in the promotion ladder to a satisfying job. Rewards should include more than just a higher salary and more financial benefits. They should include the excitement of the challenge of innovations, the recognition of important achievements, the sense of independence and personal discretion, and the satisfaction of personal participation in decision making. This satisfaction must permeate all levels, from executives to managers to supervisors to bottom-level employees. Satisfied employees have job security based on individual performance, individual initiative, and individual achievement of objectives that the employees helped to establish. MBO helps to satisfy employees.

Advancement of the Technology of the Organization

Technology is the knowledge of ways of doing things. It is a body of formal information that comprises the concepts, principles, processes, methods, and techniques that an organization exploits to develop products and services. Thus we have machine technology, food processing technology, electronic technology, and hundreds of others. As companies grow and use to the limit the technology on which they are based, their potential for new products and services diminishes. The work of MBO management must expand the abilities of the firm with new knowledge and new information. This requires a policy of substantial investment of company funds in advancement of technology through research and development. This in turn necessitates a policy of motivating technical personnel to adopt as a central sense of mission technological monitoring that will lead to new products and services. MBO helps to advance the technology of the firm.

Community Contribution

The work of MBO management often turns the company toward the community of which it is a part. This attention to the outside, such as to government, labor markets, health services, educational institutions, or social agencies, is to examine the nature of the relationship between the company and the community, and the importance of cooperation and contribution. The relationship requires mutual development and help in areas of values, people, services, policies, and resources. Profit making of a firm is crucial for the community, as it is the basis for taxes, employment, charity, and affirmative action. The work of management individually and collectively helps others to be better citizens, better neighbors, and better human beings. It perpetuates a democratic society. MBO helps the company contribute to the community.

MANAGEMENT THEORY

The reader is undoubtedly aware that there is a good deal of controversy over management theory, let alone MBO theory. The reason is that the phenomenon of management is very complex. The complexity stems from the interaction and overlapping that exist among technology, sociology, economics, and business. Where one ends and the other begins is difficult to trace. A theory is an explanation of the how and why of a complex phenomenon. Thus management theory is an attempt to explain the management phenomenon. MBO theory is an attempt to explain the MBO phenomenon. This section describes one MBO theory and where it fits into management theory.

Foundation Theories of Management Thought

Five foundation theories or schools of management thought have evolved over the years as views of the management phenomenon. Each school claims to be the theoretical framework that explains how management works.

1. *Economic School.* This view describes management in terms of creation of free markets for the buying and selling of goods among free people who struggle to meet their basic material needs. The manager performs in such a way that the greatest amount of profit can be realized by the company. Basic ideas in the economic school are competing, demand supplying, producing, marketing, pricing, costing, capital investing, legislating, and budgeting. Some theorists of this school are Adam Smith, Henry George, and John Stuart Mill.

2. *Process School.* This view describes management in terms of the functions performed in an organization by a manager. These functions are variously stated but basically are planning, scheduling, organizing, staffing, job designing, supervising, controlling, and auditing. The process school emphasizes progressive movement from one point to another until an act is completed. Some theorists of this school are Henry Fayal, Frank Gilbreth, and Henry Gault.

3. *Systems School.* This view describes management in terms of systems and totalities. The manager sees all variables in the environment as mutually dependent and interactive. Management is the movement of individuals into and out of a system, the interaction of individuals with the environment, and the interaction of individuals with each other. Organizations are open, adaptive, and contrived systems developed to execute some kind of purpose. Basic ideas in the systems school are networking, programming, automating, optimizing, interfacing, simulating, and life cycling. Some theorists of this school are Kenneth Boulding, D.C. Phillips, F.E. Kast, and J.E. Rosenzweig.

4. *Quantitative School.* This view describes management in terms of mathematical models, statistical processes, computer applications, and scientific processes. Proponents of this school are greatly concerned with decision making and to a large degree with measurement and scorekeeping. Problem solving is an immediate application of this approach. Since the heart and core of management work is problem solving, this school of thought is most attractive. Basic ideas in the quantitative school are breakeven analysis, linear programming, queuing, modeling, probability analysis, sampling, correlating, differentiating, averaging, and integrating. Some

theorists of this school are Charles Babbage, C.W. Churchman, and J. W. Forrester.

5. *Behavioral School.* This view describes management as concerned with human behavior. It contends that because management entails getting things done with people, the effective manager must understand the importance of factors such as needs, drives, learning, motivation, perception, leadership, personality, work groups, participation, interaction, and development. The behavioral school of thought is still in its infancy. Some theorists of this school are Hugo Munsterberg, Elton Mayo, Abraham Maslow, and Fred Hertzberg.

These schools of thought are currently in vogue. Each has taken a position in explaining the management phenomenon. Each has important concepts to contribute to management. Yet each has important weaknesses, and these give reason for the existence of other views. Each school of thought grows, changes, and diminishes as new elements are added and old elements are removed.

MBO theory is eclectic. It synthesizes elements from each of the schools. It recognizes that there is no one best way to handle changing situations. There is no one best way to plan, to lead, to organize a group, to control activities. Each situation must be considered for itself. Therefore MBO is a synthesis of needed management elements from the five foundation schools of thought. MBO is based on these foundation theories, but it includes only those elements and practices that will best handle a situation emerging from external or internal environments. In MBO, a variety of sources provide what is needed to manage a particular situation. When the situation changes, a new synthesis is formed. This synthesis is a strategy when considered in a time cycle (Figure 3.2).

MBO strategies vary from year to year because new selections and syntheses are made owing to new situations. Table 3.1 lists the key points to MBO theory.

MBO OPERATING PRINCIPLES

The practice of MBO is based on a systematic and sensitive kind of thinking, perceiving, analyzing, synthesizing, and decision making. The operating principles described in this section give insight into MBO thought. They are intended to provide guides for MBO practice and thinking. They are not intended to be fundamental truths based on extensive research. They imply how a manager ought to act in a certain predictable manner. Readers who are effective in the practice of MBO will sense that they practice these principles. Readers who are not effective in MBO practice will sense the absence of these principles.

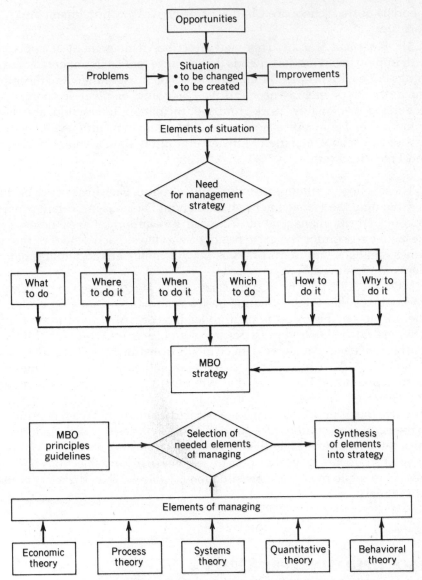

FIGURE 3.2 MBO synthesizes elements from foundation theories.

TABLE 3.1 Key Points of MBO Theory

Theoretical Assumptions	MBO Theory
Management thought and substance emerge from a variety of sources.	MBO uses many sources for its practice. MBO selects elements from economic, process, systems, quantitative, and behavioral theory.
There is no one best way to manage changing situations.	MBO manages changes in a natural way. At the beginning of a time period, a strategy is formulated that best fits the situation at hand or the situation to be created. A new strategy is developed at a new time period.
The prime work of a manager is sizing up a situation and selecting a course of action.	MBO is a course of action for a situation. A manager is required to select objectives that fit a situation with plans for implementing the objective.
Managing requires full use of all resources of the firm.	MBO stretches performance regularly. It gives managers opportunity to fully utilize intellectual and creative potential.
People want an opportunity to achieve or to know they contribute to achievement.	MBO is achievement directed. Managers seek progress and achievement through objectives and measurable milestones.
People are highly motivated to work hard if rewards and satisfaction are connected with the work.	MBO builds in motivators in the work. Managers and employees participate in formulating objectives and the processes of implementing them.
Managers engage in many common problems but use many different means to solve these problems.	MBO is unique to problem and problem solver. A manager sets up an MBO strategy to fit skills, knowledge, and resources.
There is no universal method or system for planning and controlling. Because of competition, no universal method is desired.	MBO is both strategic thinking and strategic planning. A manager sets up a strategic plan as a course of action and also to have a better course of action than competitive counterparts.
Leadership style is superior when it fits the tasks and factors of the situation.	MBO is a style. A manager who is committed to an MBO plan lives the style necessary to accomplish the plan.
Managers find themselves continually negotiating and trading off benefits with results.	MBO is a negotiated agreement. A manager gives visibility to the compromises necessary in a plan and proceeds with that understanding.

TABLE 3.2   MBO Principles Synthesize Elements From the Five Basic Schools of Management Thought

MBO Principles	Economic Theory (Money)	Process Theory (Functions)	Systems Theory (Input/Output)	Quantitative Theory (Measurement)	Behavioral Theory (People)
Improvement	Changes	Planning			Learning
Expectation		Forecasting			Perceiving
Achievement	Profit	Procedures	Projects	Measuring	
Strategic thinking	Competing	Planning	Environmental interaction	Risk	
Targeting	Marketing	Controlling		Decision making	
Risk taking	Marketing	Forecasting		Probability	Leading
Linking		Organization	Network		Participating
Performance stretch		Capacity planning	Potential		Motivating
Accountability	Profit	Controlling		Measuring	Commitment
Scorekeeping	Productivity		Optimizing	Data collecting	
Motivation	Rewards				Coincidence of needs
Required effort		Activity		Measuring	
Appropriate activity		Controlling		Measuring	
Prioritizing	Competing	Controlling			Leading
Participation	Benefits			Decision making	
Elasticity		Scheduling	Coordinating		Interacting
Feedback and feedforward		Controlling		Measuring	
Commitment			Interlocking	Measuring	Pledges
Futuristic control	Projections	Controlling		Modes	
Programming results		Organization	Information		

Table 3.2 summarizes the principles of MBO and their relationship to the five schools of management thought.

Principle of Improvement

Even though the future of an organization is uncertain, managers must act and react to make it better than it has been in the past.

The mission of MBO management is improvement. Managers must act and react to make things better than they found them. It is tragic to live and be gratified with mediocrity when we can achieve excellence. Managers must look into the future, visualize changes that could be made, and act to implement these changes. To pursue improvement is to pursue change. This is the pursuit of excellence! Opportunities to set and pursue objectives are opportunities to make the firm better than it was in the past. Managers must adopt as a personal mission leaving their jobs better than they found them.

Principle of Expectation

People tend to expend more effort and better thinking toward reaching goals when the probability of receiving a reward from the goal is known in advance and the reward is expected.

To state an objective is to state an expectation. Allowing the value or importance of an objective to be seen in advance tends to elicit the type of behavior needed for accomplishment of the objective. This is like a self-fulfilling prophecy, a future event that tends to happen because someone stated it formally. Value and benefit are seen in the expectation. These set in motion thinking, efforts, and forces which work to make them happen. Formal statement of the goal of leading the industry in sales volume makes the goal more likely to be accomplished than if it is not stated at all. The goal must be thought about before it can happen at all. Future results occur from causes generated and directed in the present.

Principle of Achievement

Great achievements are more likely to happen when they are first "thought up" and then broken down and pursued in smaller interrelated progressive steps.

There is "magic" to thinking big. This is how big achievements have come about. There are no limits on the size of achievements that can be thought up. But those who fulfill them are those who break them down into smaller but interrelated accomplishments. Thus large-scale acts can be achieved when short-term resources are focused and directed toward them. Any large goal can be broken down into a number of smaller subgoals that will almost certainly be less overwhelming. The function of MBO management begins whenever the work to be accomplished is too much for one person or one organization. In the case of a person, some of the work is delegated to an assistant. Similarly, when the work and the achievement are too great for one organization or one department, the work can be broken down into small, easily handled steps, which will greatly increase the prospect of completing it. Objectives should be strategically set for both long-range large accomplishments and short-range annual results, and a strong connection set up between the two.

Principle of Strategic Thinking

Decisions for future action are more likely to be found effective when many courses of action are considered with their respective opportunities, competitiveness, risk, assumptions, constraints, and payoffs.

Strategic thinking is thinking about the future with competitors in mind and devising strategies to outmaneuver these competitors to meet this future. It is devising many strategies but selecting the best way. Strategic planning looks at a chain of cause-and-effect consequences over time to see if a manager is going to make it. Strategic thinking goes beyond this. It decides on the desired future effect and formulates present-day causes to make it happen. Objective setting and strategic thinking go hand in hand. One creates the future, the other juxtaposes the organization relative to competitors in that future. Strategic planning starts with strategic thinking.

Principle of Targeting

The greater the focus of efforts and resources of a future-specific accomplishment on a time scale, the greater the likelihood of reaching this accomplishment.

The difference between the achiever and the nonachiever lies in the secret of focus. The achiever says no to the trivial and yes to the critically important. The achiever tells the urgent to wait until the critically important is finished! Normally an organization tends to spread its time, effort, and resources across a large spectrum of possibilities. This often means doing many things but not necessarily doing them well. When an organization proceeds to sort, select, give priority to, and concentrate on what is needed, the likelihood increases that what is needed will get done. An organization that has ten objectives all with equal priority ignores the principle of targeting and assumes that all the objectives have equal benefits. Commitment to an objective is commitment to a specific targeted accomplishment.

Principle of Risk Taking

The greater the departure from present ways into an uncertain future, the greater the risk of error, mistakes, and resistance.

To avoid errors, mistakes, and resistance is to avoid progress and to stay static. Risk is always present when pursuing some future event or expected value. To reach this value means taking risks. It means the possibility of failure. Thus a concerted effort should be made to set objectives so as to optimize expected value and minimize risk of failure. Pursuing few objectives with high payoff but low risk is far better than pursuing many objectives with moderate payoff but high risk. Plan completion tends to vary inversely with complexity, uncertainty, and longevity.

Principle of Linking

The more linking of commitments in advance among managers and their resources, the more likely a management system emerges and is prepared to move the enterprise in a prescribed direction.

An organization exists to unify effort toward some given end. Unity of effort means acting together in unison. It is a natural propensity for functions, departments, and persons to extol their individuality and move in separate ways. Blending and interlocking among functions, departments, and persons require cooperation, tradeoffs, and compromise. Setting objectives in a participative process in advance of doing work gives visibility to the state of coordination in an MBO management system. Unity of managerial action is more likely when there is pursuit of common objectives. Work tasks that are arranged, sequenced, and timed are more likely to be completed than tasks that are disorganized and nonsequenced and have arbitrary completion times.

Principle of Performance Stretch

The more managers tolerate mediocrity in subordinates, the more they tolerate it in themselves.

When the personal mission of a manager results in higher levels of performance, the overall improvement mission of MBO is achieved. Organizational improvement is the sum total of improvements resulting from individual managers reaching for higher levels of performance. When a manager does not urge surbordinates to stretch for higher levels of performance, he or she tends to not stretch either. When many managers do this, the firm becomes mediocre. Performance stretch should be a continuous process of all managers. Setting objectives allows for continuous practice of stretch, since new objectives are stretches from previous ones.

Principle of Accountability

Accountability for results is more likely to happen when employees understand, participate in, and are held responsible for what is to be done and what resources will be used.

Traditional accountability means explaining the reason what, how, and why responsibilities were discharged or executed in the manner they were. Since resource use and costs have become critical, a new view has emerged. The new concept of accountability is giving reasons on what, how, when, where, and why during the planning phase, before commitments and well in advance of doing the work. This means the management process to be used has high visibility. MBO management must now sell both what is to be done and how it will be done. The setting of objectives, development of support plans, and identification of ways to evaluate results, done during the planning phase, provide an easy way to meet the accountability demanded of top management, funding sources, customers, and taxpayers.

Principle of Scorekeeping

Productivity is more likely to improve when expected results are measured and made greater in the same time frame that expected resource use is measured and made less.

Productivity is more for less. It is the ratio of output to input compared over a period of time. Productivity can be intensified when a scorekeeping index is developed as a set point. Changes in either performance or resource use within a time period will disturb this set point. Keeping score with the changes enables managers to see the effects of a decision on the productivity set point. Building measures into objective statements facilitates predicting, managing, and evaluating for productivity improvements.

Principle of Motivation

The greater the alignment of employee expectancies (needs) with employer expectancies (objectives), the greater the motivation to accomplish both.

Employees work primarily for themselves and only secondarily for their employer. They work to meet their needs and personal goals. When these needs and goals are closely aligned to employer needs and goals, motivation to accomplish both increases. This alignment is termed "needs coincidence." The closer the alignment, the more intense the motivation. Motivation for increased results, performance, or productivity can be heightened when situations are created to encourage coincidence. When superior and subordinates agree jointly in a give-and-take process on a set of objectives, motivation is enhanced.

Principle of Required Effort

The amount of effort required in getting results must be commensurate with the results expected.

Any given set of results requires a minimum effort level. Unless that effort level is attained, the results will not be realized. Determining the effort level is as important as deciding on the results. Support plans and activities in completing a set of objectives are measures of the level of effort required to complete the objectives. When a set of objectives is not reached, too often the quality and scope of the objectives are blamed. Little is said about the required level of effort not being expended.

Principle of Appropriate Activity

Activity will expand to keep busy the number of people allocated in an organization. As people are added, activity will grow. As people are reduced, activity will shrink.

Activity is essential in getting the job done. But there are two problems with activity. First, activity doers have a tendency to engage in activity for its own sake. Those responsible for activities tend to perpetuate them to maintain and justify their jobs. The more people involved in activities, the more work they will find to do. Second, disconnected activity for a specific direction is liable to lead almost anywhere. If the activity is brought to an end, the end point is usually a position not sought, desired, or needed. The setting of objectives requires that supporting action plans or activity plans be made. The activities proposed must be connected and aimed at the attainment of the objectives. When the objectives are completed, the activities come to an end.

Principle of Prioritizing

Priorities in getting things done are assigned in direct proportion to personal preferences and may or may not be relevant to high payoff for the organization.

Most people get things done by giving priority to those that are familiar and to which personal skills apply, those with high urgency, those that scream the loudest, or those that yield the greatest personal return. This means that objectives with high payoff for the organization may not get the attention needed and may often be neglected. Priority assignments from a spectrum of possible objectives should be made on the basis of high payoff for both the organization and the individual.

Principle of Participation

Productivity increases rapidly when employees participate in the decisions affecting it and when expected benefits are shared with those who produce them.

Participation for the sake of participation does not work. Allowing people to be listened to, to submit ideas, or even to help with the solution of problems helps somewhat but does not generate the intense motivation needed for outstanding results. Personal commitment to work hard for a task, a project, or the company increases when the person is allowed to share in the benefits of the task, the project, or the company. The allowance of participation in decision making and sharing of the benefits achieved are what generate intense motivation. An objective is more likely to be achieved when those committed to it participate in its formation.

Principle of Elasticity

Results tend to increase when the same amount of work is achieved in a shorter period of time—when work is pitted against deadlines.

Since work is elastic and time is not, work can be stretched to fit the time set for its completion. Managers must play the clock, since work will be stretched to meet hidden or unknown reasons. Time deadlines signal individuals and departments when to start and when to finish. They also signal coordination and collaboration with others who must contribute to the work. Setting objectives with a time strategy allows signals for start-stop, coordination, and collaboration.

Principle of Feedback and Feedforward

The quicker the difference between actual and planned performance is fed back to managers, the quicker adjustments can be made to assure performance as intended.

Managers need to be informed on progress being made in work. This allows them to assess and regulate the activities needed for expected milestones to make sure that what is happening is intended to happen. Evaluating and checking actual performance against planned performance provides information feedback that affirms original decisions or suggests needed changes. With every formal set of objectives is a status-reporting system designed to keep all levels of management informed on developments and results that may affect originally set objectives. The greater the solving of operating problems in the planning process, the less the likelihood of experiencing these problems in operations.

Principle of Commitment

Setting expectations as commitments is more likely to set up an interlocking process for the enterprise.

Most people engage in activities on the basis of duty, cooperation, support, loyalty, or recompense. These bases are not strong enough to support a process in which the enterprise and many people will move in a prescribed direction. Commitment, a strong pledge that is binding, locks individual managers and their plans together for a period of time to achieve objectives. With this view objectives are commitments.

Principle of System Control

Control over a newly developed situation increases rapidly when key points of control are identified and managed in advance.

To control a system, a manager must be able to take at least as many distinct actions or as great a variety of countermeasures as the observed system exhibits. To control a new system to be created by a plan, key control points must be identified in the plan. As the plan is implemented and the new system emerges, the key control points must be managed if the entire system is to be controlled.

Principle of Programming Results

When a manager is faced with both highly organized tasks and disorganized tasks, the former will take precedence over the latter.

Information and tasks fall into one of two categories: programmed or nonprogrammed, that is to say, organized or disorganized. Nonprogrammed or disorganized information is usually avoided by managers. Programmed and organized information usually receives immediate attention. MBO planning gives managers highly programmed and organized information in advance, which makes managing and getting results easier.

WHAT MAKES MBO WORK?

Managers have distinct motives that impel them to action. These motives are basic and natural, they are part of the makeup of a manager. Four of these motives are distinguishable from many others. They seem to be unique to managerial people who get things done—who need to get things done. The four are (1) urge to achieve, (2) need to move toward excellence, (3) desire to contribute, and (4) need for identity. They are the basis of why MBO works.

Urge to Achieve

Purposeful activity that follows a course of action to some end is compatible with the deep human urge for growth, development, and life. The will to work hard to achieve something significant gives meaning and importance to living. This does not refer to achievement for its own sake; this has little meaning. Rather it refers to progressive achievement, the progressive reaching of higher levels. Achievement in the work situation must not be a mere possibility but a realistic certainty, if economic life is to be meaningful, stimulating, and fulfilling.

Many organizations have understood this basic human need and have set standards of accomplishment far beyond realistic expectancy, believing that the formidable challenge will spur people to work harder. More often than not, this does not work. If an individual works very hard, accomplishes a great deal, but never quite reaches the formidable goal, he or she takes the attitude, "What's the use?" The standard that can never be attained loses all meaning. For example, the general manager of a paper mill company set a goal of 15 percent cost reduction every year for the production manager. In light of the cost of materials, supplies, labor, and overhead, this was an almost impossible goal. In the first year, the production manager achieved about 10 percent cost reduction. Although actually this was a good job, it did not meet the general manager's expectancy. The next year the goal was again set at 15 percent cost reduction. By the middle of the year the impossibility of ever reaching this goal became apparent, and discouragement set in. Three months later the production manager quit and the general manager had to find a replacement. The general manager soon discovered that the replacement was not nearly as good as the previous person. In fact, the production manager who left turned out be be extremely effective and successful in another firm. It had been the general manager's notion that an extremely high goal would spur performance, but most of us need the satisfaction of achievement, and an impossible goal makes it very difficult to experience this. The urge to achieve must be matched with achievements! What is MBO's place here?

- MBO is a process for selecting an opportunity for achievement from among many alternatives.
- MBO provides an opportunity for individuals to reach never-ending pinnacles.
- MBO motivates toward achieving something significant and important, which gives meaning to life.

Need to Move Toward Excellence

No large plan is ever completed—only stages are completed. The reason for this is that almost everything undergoes change. The changing nature of change spins off changes, so that excellence always lies just ahead but is never reached. Purposeful activity that follows a course of action to an end where disorder is changed to order, the unfinished to the finished, disorganization to organization is activity that moves us toward excellence.

A look at the historical development of a product, say refrigeration, illustrates this. The first stage of refrigeration was the spring house. This was a house built over a cool spring where food could be kept cool. Then came the ice box. Food and ice were placed in the same box. The next stage was the electric refrigerator, in which cooling was achieved by an electric heat pump. Then came the freezer, in which food could be kept frozen for many months. The new stage of development is the long-life package. This allows food to be frozen for many years with no deterioration. Have we finally arrived at the end stage of product development? No. The move toward excellence occurs in stages; the final stage is never reached. How does MBO fit in with the need for excellence?

- MBO is a progressive process that moves individuals and enterprises toward higher stages of development.
- MBO requires cycles of performance stretches in progressive stages.
- MBO in its practice requires a mission of improvement.

Desire to Contribute

Economic life without productive work is meaningless, dull, and sterile. Engaging in purposeful activity is in the nature of humans. Purposeful work provides satisfaction, especially when directed toward a common good. This common good may be manifested in many ways, such as taxes for government or salaries for raising employees' standards of living. Humans experience great satisfaction when they know they are contributing to this common good. Great drives are generated when opportunities are available for contribution.

In a major study of 5000 small companies, the entrepreneurial founders of the companies were asked for their prime motives for starting the business. One of the top five motives was the desire to contribute to the community and to others. This contribution was achieved in one way by giving people jobs, providing for employee security, and helping individuals toward an economic position and gain. The desire to contribute must be matched with a channel for making this contribution. MBO can be this channel.

- MBO gives people an opportunity to contribute to a common goal.
- MBO provides a process for directing purpose to any desired end.
- MBO requires a package of results to meet some kind of need.

Need for Identity

People are embarked on a quest for identity. Everyone desires distinction and recognition through the use of personal creative powers and talents. This quest never ends, because the conditions by which identity and "whoness" are realized are constantly changing. We are identified in many complex ways, but chiefly by the results of our thinking, creating, and decision making. Since economic life is a major opportunity to express our thinking, creativity, and decision making, we are most likely to realize our identity in the economic setting.

Everyone is known by name, address, family relationships, and employment. But uniqueness and recognition of individual identity depend on personal achievement and on *the contribution made to the human family*. Thus Edison is known for his electric lamp, Einstein for the theory of relativity, Sikorsky for helicopters, and Krock for McDonald's hamburgers. The need for meaningful identity can be matched with a process, MBO, that encourages uniqueness and accomplishment in the work world.

- MBO opens the way for use of the creative powers of an individual.
- MBO provides individual hallmarks in the work world for others to see and admire.
- MBO releases the stored human potential to individual performance through personal challenge.

BENEFITS FROM MBO

The number of organizations that reportedly have adopted the strategy of managing by objectives is now in the thousands and continues to grow, with ever-widening claims of greater and more favorable results. These organizations formulate what objectives they wish to achieve, organize resources and programs to reach these objectives, identify the barriers to reaching them, and push toward success with intense effort. With this kind of approach, results do not just happen. Rather money, time, and effort are heavily committed to plans, programs, and actions designed to obtain results, which often can mean success or failure of the enterprise or the individual manager responsible. Experience of successful results has in turn stimulated interest in refining and sharpening MBO to obtain even better results. Furthermore, the users of this strategy not only extol the merits of its applications for survival and growth but also claim improvements and often complete elimination of troublesome organizational conditions. Some of the benefits reported by organizations are the following: (1) improvements in the job of managing, (2) improvements in profit attainment, (3) accurate performance appraisals, (4) heightened motivation to achieve, (5) management development, and (6) coordinated teamwork with organizational clarity. Table 3.3 summarizes the benefits of the practice of MBO.

Improvements in Job of Managing

By far the most frequently mentioned benefit of MBO is improvement in the job of managing itself. A high degree of clarity is brought to the normal management functions of planning, preparing, performing, and evaluation. Managers are much more likely to achieve whatever they set out to achieve because targets are better defined, strategies are clearly seen, and implementation is easier.

When Honeywell Corporation decided to make MBO a corporate-wide philosophy for all its profit centers, it brought precision of thinking, planning, activating, coordinating, and controlling to its managers. The concept gave them a sense of focus and concentration. They experienced MBO as a total approach to the task of management. They did not regard the concept as a program, a staff activity, or a panacea for an immediate problem; rather it was the heart and core of *managing* the organization. Honeywell continues to use MBO after several decades. One Honeywell executive reported that formerly, managing in Honeywell was unpredictable, almost a game of chance. With the advent of MBO, all managers knew just what was expected of them and how their performance was measured. Job descriptions and job specifications were clarified; instead of generalized duties that could be performed in a number of acceptable ways, specific job results were set forth and performance levels defined. For many managers this changed the job of managing from a trial-and-error method to one involving precise directions, relevant activities, and needed results.

The 3M Company, another great user of MBO, noted the strong tendency of executives and managers in their operation to assume that the important goals of a unit were well known and understood. The degree to which this is or is not true often makes the difference between mediocre and outstanding accomplishments. By adopting the MBO approach for all levels of supervision, 3M achieved a clarity of vision about the mission and results of the units. The 3M Company noted that this way of managing tended to eliminate the "political" atmosphere, that is, the need to try to guess what the boss wants and how far to go in an attempt to please him or her. At the 3M Company, MBO also eliminated the confusion in directions that formerly ensued when there was a turnover in management at a high level.

Improvements in Profit Attainment

The major purpose of a profit plan is to reach a predetermined profit objective through a systematic and deliberate organization of all efforts and resources in the enterprise. Hence a profit plan must include the objective, the means for reaching it, and provisions for making adjustments when changes occur. This basic description of profit planning fits precisely the concept of MBO. The major distinction between traditional profit-planning activities and the more effective MBO approach lies in personal involvement and commitment. The traditional approach is largely fiscal, with projections and budgets set by staff functions. The MBO approach is motivational; profit objectives are set and agreed on through participation and commitment of managers.

Like all companies, United Air Lines must make a profit to survive as a business and to fulfill its obligations to the public, to its stockholders, and to its employees. The effort of every unit is directed toward profit making. Department and division heads down to the section level participate in setting individual performance goals and plans of action for meeting the company's overall profit objectives. These individual performance goals are directed toward profit making with specific targets in passenger sales, cargo

TABLE 3.3 Benefits of MBO to the Company, to Managers, and to Employees

Benefits to Company	Benefits to Managers	Benefits to Employees
Better decision making in planning because of high visibility of individual plans	Aid in defining job and expectations of a manager	Improved attitude toward work through prospects of challenge and innovation
Clarification of organizational mission, goals, and expectations	Accountability established before work commences	Raised confidence in leadership and management
Planning forced into every level and department	Minimization of managerial frustrations by means of greater self-direction and control	Raised morale with feeling of participation and accomplishment
Increased achievement of large-scale results	Work done when needed in a specific period of time	Clearer information for appraisal of performance for promotions, compensation, and benefits
Creation of expectations for improvement on continuous basis	Gains employees' respect	Better work accomplishment, which enhances job security, longevity, and satisfaction
Efficient use of scarce resources	Simplification of tasks for smoother operation by minimization of operational problems	Development of pride in company that knows what it is doing and where it is going
Greater productivity through built-in measures in planning and control	Leverage for promotion, compensation, and benefits	Clarification of responsibilities and accountability
Better coordination with other departments, which fosters teamwork and interlocking	Persuasive for top management decisions for allocation of scarce resources	

Clearer information on performance appraisals for managers

Heightened motivation for managers and supervisors, as drive for accomplishment is seen by top management

Better financial performance

Linking of long-range targets with annual budget system

Provision of structure for repetition of desirable programs and rejection of undesirable ones

Source of useful information for salary and incentive bonus plan administration

Better prediction of promotability of managers in succession planning

Better connections of continuous programs with new goals and objectives

Clearer information for setting priorities on high payoff opportunities

Provision of leadership opportunity through goal-achievement cycles

Development of insights into impact and consequences of proposed decisions

Clarification of communications between levels, departments, and bosses

Enhanced development of manager through challenge-stretch-learning cycles

Heightened motivation to improve performance through participation and prospects of recognition

Opportunity to participate in management decision making while in non-managerial position

Confidence to assume self-responsibility

sales, air mail, air freight, agency sales, convention sales, reduced costs of advertising, turnover, purchasing, operations, and services.

The Otis Elevator Company, which operates in the United States through the medium of ten districts or zones, conducts each of these zones as though it were a separate elevator company. Each zone operates on an individual profit-and-loss basis. Each zone is expected to set cost reduction objectives by the cooperative effort of all who are in the position to influence cost and expense. The president of Otis Elevator reports that through this procedure, with use of MBO, the firm has realized a 30 percent reduction in construction costs. In the opinion of this president, the most important single obligation of managers is to determine what should be considered par for their unit and then devote their efforts to developing an organization that will reach or exceed this par.

To make profits happen, all efforts must be organized to meet a timed set of profit objectives. This does not mean some people and some efforts, but all people and all efforts, within a prescribed period to time. This requires involvement and commitment from people who are a part of the process.

Accurate Performance Appraisals

The process of defining qualitatively and quantitatively areas of responsibility results not only in a more comfortable feeling among personnel, but also in establishment of accurate criteria for evaluation and appraisal of performance. When each member of management, down to and including first-line supervisors, has a clear understanding of what his or her responsibilities are, how they will be measured, and when they are to be accomplished, accountability for executing these responsibilities is intensified. Performance is judged more accurately, since it is based on specific accomplishments within a period of time and not on subjective or generalized opinions. MBO provides an objective measuring instrument for evaluating actual performance against expected performance. When the concept is well developed within an organization, the practice of self-evaluation and self-accountability becomes possible. An incumbent is in the position to evaluate the results of his or her own performance, since requirements are clear, specific, and measurable. Willingness of managers to appraise and evaluate subordinates is also improved with MBO.

At the Plastic Products and Resin Division of Monsanto Company, managers had to be wheedled and cajoled into conducting performance appraisals. Many regarded this task as a staff activity rather than as part of their own regular duties. As a result, managers completed performance appraisals only after they had done everything else for which they were accountable. With implementation of MBO, a new realization developed throughout the organization—that there is a direct relationship between achievement and rewards. The evaluation of performance is to justify both. Performance appraisal not only has moved closer to line activity but also has greater appeal to line managers as a measure of performance.

With the installation of MBO at the Colt Heating and Ventilation

Company, several troublesome problems were eliminated. The concept defined the company's organizational structure by eliminating unclear areas of responsibility. A simplified job improvement plan was instituted, job descriptions were rewritten and clarified, and performance standards were made more relevant and specific to the organization. This reduced the amount of time needed for performance appraisals, which allowed the company to devote only 25 percent of its time to job review, that is, to looking backward, and 75 percent to looking forward.

State Farm Insurance Companies has consciously steered away from traditional personality-factor appraisals and management-skills ratings simply because it believes these approaches tend to lead both appraisal and appraiser into confusion. This confusion stems from use of indefinite terms, vagueness as to what is desired, and difficulty in assessing behavior in the directions intended. State Farm found that appraisal of persons at the middle and upper levels of management was very difficult, because they possessed complex and difficult personality patterns as well as a wide variety of managerial skills. The management performance guide based on the concept of MBO shifted the appraisal approach to "results-oriented," "objective-oriented," or "accomplishment-oriented." The major emphasis now is on the establishment of job-centered objectives within a future period of time.

Use of the concept of MBO in appraisal work has a clarifying effect on important work and ensures accountability for its completion within a period of time.

Heightened Motivation to Achieve

It is an excellent idea for subordinates to participate and have a voice along with their superiors in setting departmental or organizational objectives. It gives them an opportunity to contribute their ideas, which heightens their sense of worth, self-recognition, and motivation. When participation is offered deliberately and systematically, motivation and enthusiasm can be intensified. This, in turn, tends to stimulate further participation in improvements, since the individuals know that their ideas, efforts, and contributions may have a significant impact on the organization. Employees' sense of participation and belonging, recognition of their own worth, and feelings of accomplishment form a potent motivational base on which the company can rely to help it reach its goals. The more clearly subordinates perceive how their contributions fit into the flow process of intermediate results leading to ultimate results, the more heightened will be their motivation.

At the Grand Union company, motivation is encouraged through decentralizing authority and spreading responsibility. As the president put it, "Along with profit sharing as a motivating tool goes problem sharing. We have found the latter just about as important in building and maintaining the spirit of belonging."

The chairman of the board of the Bridgeport Brass Company stated that the biggest single factor in the success of any organization is getting the people employed in the enterprise *united* in the purpose of making it a success. At Bridgeport Brass, a sense of belonging and participation in achieving common goals is encouraged by all managers on all levels.

General Electric conducted a study on how to increase motivation in its plants, focusing on how to improve the productive motivation of workers. A pilot study was undertaken to assess several job-related factors, such as cycle time, size of group, training, and task repetitiveness. The study showed that participation in decisions by employees and responsibility for their own work resulted in a high degree of productive motivation. Attitudes and motivation for getting the work out were unmistakably better for those individuals permitted to use their own discretion and set their own work objectives.

Management Development

Management development is still another benefit resulting from the practice of MBO. The MBO strategy is a kind of self-discipline. A person must think about what he or she is going to do the following year. The kinds of activities, schedules, and resources that are required to get a particular job done must be personally spelled out. This training is a great help in the development of individuals as managers. Insufficient skills and development needs can be easily pinpointed.

The Royal Naval Supply and Transport Service, a worldwide supply and transport organization, believes the involvement factor is a strong motivation for managerial development and morale. By getting managers to suggest ways in which performance in their area of responsibility can be improved as well as to suggest the actions they will take, the dates by which they will accomplish their task, and the standards by which their performance can be judged, the company encourages the managers to become psychologically involved in self-development.

Organization development through MBO at the St. Regis Paper Company was used to establish good management practice that could be used throughout the company. The *Guidelines for Managing at St. Regis* grew out of this activity and was extended to all divisions. The establishment of the guidelines was thought of as an organizational and management development program. MBO concepts are readily apparent in many of the guidelines.

MBO allows development to take place informally, naturally, and simultaneously. That is, the individual manager acquires knowledge and skills on the job as by-products of meeting performance requirements. This is a key need in the area of management development. We need more and more to shift learning experiences from the classroom to the real world of the job, where most of the problems and challenges are found. We need more and more to shift to the individual the burden of pursuing self-development and self-education. Opportunities for learning and for change, and chances for experimenting, are natural ingredients in the objective-setting process.

Coordinated Teamwork with Organizational Clarity

Historically, several methods have been used to find, place, and fit individuals within the organization as members of a team. One method has been the interview process, in which team "fitness" is assessed through depth interviews to discover values, backgrounds, and interests. Another is psychological testing for identification of different traits or temperaments, to forecast compatibility for a group or project. Still another is temporary placement within a section or group as a trial or test of behavior for permanent placement. These methods have their virtues and their vices. They are largely behavioral and require assessment of personality, attitudes, and traits, assessments that are difficult to make.

MBO provides an alternative for getting individuals coordinated into a unity of action. This is accomplished by aligning and interlocking individual manager's plans within the enterprise without too much concern over personality assessment and trait evaluation. Essentially this means that teamwork on each organizational level and between levels is achieved by blending individual plans and pursuits. Pursuit of joint objectives is evidence that coordination and interlocking between two or more individuals, two or more departments, or two or more functions has taken place. The evaluation of the performance of joint objectives is still further evidence that coordination and teamwork were practiced to some degree.

The General Mills Corporation made what appeared to be a minor change in its approach to handling MBO yet proved to be of great importance in obtaining organizational coordination. At the top of the organization, the setting of specific job-related objectives seemed to be an easy task; at lower levels, it was hard to relate goals to the upper levels. The company thought the difficulty might be overcome if the objective-setting process could be tied to the manager's organizational position guide. This guide listed accountabilities by position and level. After some juggling and experimenting, objectives were set for most accountabilities, and General Mills experienced an organizational unity and coordinated teamwork that had not existed formerly. The spread downward and upward through the organization brought a closer and more workable control of operations.

The president of the Minneapolis-Moline Company believes that the building and retaining of a management team require careful determination of where the company is heading, the establishment of areas for individual initiative, an opportunity for cross-pollination of ideas, and the development of a system of built-in checks and balances for organizational control. His policy, an MBO approach, is centralized planning and control in conjunction with decentralized authority and responsibility. As a result, this firm's president views large corporations with many autonomous divisions as multiplications of well-coordinated medium-sized companies.

Summary of Benefits

An organization is never really sure whether it is working to its maximum potential. It is never sure whether the allocated scarce resources are being utilized and coordinated where they count most for the enterprise. Guessing is rampant! Misfits and poorly placed personnel are everywhere. Judgment is risky and uncertain because of faulty and insufficient information, direction, and coordination. MBO is positively centered on blending plans of action for getting results. Implementation of the strategy tends to identify early the misfits and redundancy in the organization. This brings about definition and clarity to operating teamwork. For the company, it changes the acquisition of results from a low probability to a high expectancy.

SUMMARY

The practice of MBO is widespread and pervasive in private and public organizations throughout the world. The setting of goals and establishment of supporting plans appear to be practices common to most of these, but not all define and practice MBO in the same way. Nonetheless, the reasons for use of MBO have common grounds. This chapter identifies eight targets or goals of MBO.

MBO theory is complex. It is eclectic, that is, it is a selection and synthesis of managerial elements from five foundation schools of thought: economic theory, process theory, systems theory, quantitative theory, and behavioral theory. The selection and synthesis are based on the situation at hand or the situation to be created.

The 20 guidelines to MBO thinking, its operating principles, as outlined in this chapter are improvement, expectation, achievement, strategic thinking, targeting, risk taking, performance stretch, linking, account-ability, scorekeeping, motivation, required effort, appropriate activity, prioritizing, participation, elasticity, feedback and feedforward, commit-ment, system control, and programming results. What makes MBO work well is explained by four distinct and fundamental motives of human beings. These motives provide the "fire power" for MBO to work and work well. They are (1) the urge to achieve, (2) the need to move toward excellence, (3) the desire to contribute, and (4) the need for identity.

The benefits of the practice of MBO are many and varied. Forty distinct benefits are identified here and are placed in one of three major categories: benefits for the company, benefits for managers, and benefits for employees. Benefits are summarized as:

- Improvements in the job of managing
- Improvements in profit attainment
- Accurate performance appraisal
- Heightened motivation to achieve
- Management development
- Coordinated teamwork with organizational clarity

MBO not only has high merit for application in an organization, but also eliminates many troublesome problems that plague management.

BIBLIOGRAPHY

Albrecht, Karl, *Successful Management by Objectives*. Englewood Cliffs, NJ: Prentice-Hall, 1978, p. 20.

Drucker, Peter F., *The Practice of Management*. New York: Harper and Brothers, 1954, p. 121.

Hughes, Charles L., *Goal Setting*. New York: American Management Association, 1965, p. 22.

Humble, John W., *How to Manage by Objectives*. New York: American Management Association, 1972, p. 4.

Mali, Paul, *Managing by Objectives*. New York: Wiley, 1972, p. 1.

Mali, Paul, *Management Handbook*. New York: Wiley, 1981, Chs. 1 and 2.

McConkey, Dale D., *How to Manage by Results*. New York: American Management Association, 1965, pp. 15, 88–95.

National Industrial Conference Board, *Managing by and with Objectives*. Research Study No. 212, 1968, pp. 21–26.

Odiorne, George S., *Management by Objectives*. New York: Pitman Publishing, 1965, p. 55.

O'Shea, J.J., "Colt Heating & Ventilation Limited." In John W. Humble, Ed., *Management by Objectives in Action*. New York: McGraw-Hill, 1970, pp. 30–47.

Peterson, LeRoy, A., "Establishing Objectives." In H.B. Maynard, Ed., *Top Management Handbook*. New York: McGraw-Hill, 1960, pp. 181–199.

Raia, Anthony P., *Managing by Objectives*. Glenview, IL: Scott, Foresman, 1974, p. 11.

Reddin, W.J., *Effective Management by Objectives*. New York: McGraw-Hill, 1971, p. 11.

Shield, Lansing P., "Directing the Attainment of Objectives." In H.B. Maynard, Ed., *Top Management Handbook*. New York: McGraw-Hill, 1960, pp. 302–316.

4

GOAL AND OBJECTIVE
SETTING IN MBO

Every mission or goal adopted by a manager is an urge to move in a certain direction. Every objective formed and committed to by a manager is a prediction for results to be accomplished in that same direction. Mission adopters, goal setters, and objective formers look ahead for a set of results, formalize them into a set of expectations, and arrange conditions, resources, and activities to make their predictions come true. When these predictions or expectations are shared with the members of an organization for analysis, modifications, validation, and acceptance, a management team emerges with a sense of direction and a set of unified commitments.

The responsibility of management is to establish missions, plot directions, form commitments for results, and develop supporting plans. Top management assures that all managers of the team engage in this process of looking ahead.

This chapter describes the role of mission, goals, objectives, and results in the MBO process. The specific sections cover (1) what missions, goals, and objectives are and where they come from, (2) guidelines for setting and writing goals and objectives, and (3) sample goals and objectives. This chapter is important, because it focuses on the central idea of MBO—objectives and the objective-setting process.

DEFINITIONS: MISSION, GOALS, OBJECTIVES, AND RESULTS

To have a mission is to exist and be alive. To pursue goals is to move in a certain direction, to be active. To reach for objectives is to transcend and improve. To experience results is to see contributions and to be satisfied and fulfilled. The four elements of mission, goals, objectives, and results are the basic elements of the MBO process. They are interrelated sequentially, as seen in Figure 4.1.

Goals emerge from mission. Objectives are formulated from goals. Action plans implement objectives. Results are the end products of plans. This is the heart and core of thinking through the MBO process. It is the heart and core of managing. Each one of these elements is discussed here.

MISSION

Mission is an organization's reason for existence. It is the broad identification of a company with products or services in a market. An organization comes into existence to occupy a role in the business market and to carry out some definite intent. This is the why of its organization, the reason for its being. Determining the business it is in is a determination of the role of the firm in the market in the eyes of the customer. A mission is a role that has

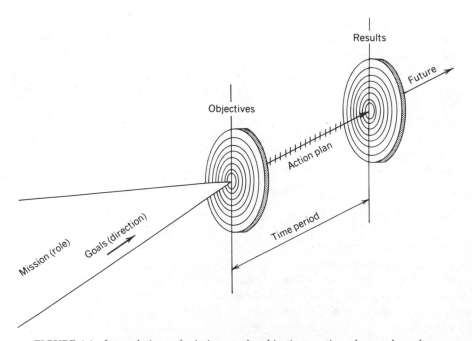

FIGURE 4.1   Interrelations of mission, goals, objectives, action plan, and results.

been played by a firm for a long time. The role has become well known to customers, competitors, clients, government, and the market community. A mission identity can be referred to as a "company image." Such an image emerges when a company deals with customers over a long period of time. The image gives continuing assurance to customers about the purpose of the organization. In fact, the answer to the question, "What is our business?," is a statement or expression of the company's mission. When employees of an organization know the mission or mission identity, they are better able to participate in the thinking, support, and skills needed by the organization. "What is our business?," "What is our mission?," and "What is our mission identity," must be managed in the same way as goals, objectives, and results, since one gives direction to the other. A ladder has a mission. Leaning the ladder on a building to be painted is a goal. The rungs on the ladder are the objectives. Painting the building is the result.

Defining the mission of a business is the starting point for charting goals. It is also the starting point for strategic planning and program collaborations. Two general approaches are used to conceptualize the nature of a business or its mission. One is to define the business in terms of resource capabilities, such as capital assets, facilities, equipment, site location, money assets, technological ability, and even skills of employees. Thus a business may be defined as "manufacture of microcircuitry." This suggests manufacturing facilities with skilled employees capable of doing skilled micro work.

The second approach is to conceptualize the business in the eyes of the customer or client in terms of a program, product, or service. This approach is how markets are served. Thus, "provision of data and word processors for high-technology research" is a market-oriented mission.

Most define their business in terms of the second approach. I believe that a combination of the two is more effective, greater emphasis being given to the second approach. This combination serves to produce goals for the major functions of the organization. The major functions, such as marketing, finance, engineering, production, and quality control, have a good basis for development of goals and formulation of objectives. Table 4.1 illustrates the combination approach.

To formulate effective mission statements using the combination approach, the following factors need to be carefully analyzed:

1. *Resource Use.*
    (a)   Facility used and capacity not used.
    (b)   Equipment used and capacity not used.
    (c)   Skills used and capacity not used.
    (d)   Superlatives in facility, equipment, and skills.
    (e)   Technology used and annexation of new technologies.
    (f)   Present cost behavior and potential for change.

2. *Market Use.*

    (a) Customer groups served and their buying behavior.
    (b) Customer functions served and their nature.
    (c) Market share.
    (d) Uniqueness of product.
    (e) Present pricing behavior and potential for change.
    (f) Market needs and degree of fulfillment.

GOALS

Goals are the organization's move in a certain direction. They are guidelines toward which planning, effort, and energy are directed. Goals are a statement that suggests action. They are the desired end conditions. Mission is the role of the firm in the market, but goals are the movement it takes through market complexities to reach customers. Goals emerge as a result of a need, a problem, an opportunity from the mission that stirs movement of the enterprise toward it. Identification of mission and establishment of goals start the MBO planning process in an organization. These are musts for top management or the chief executive officer. They are also vital for department heads or others who have a destiny or a direction to move. Table 4.2 shows examples of missions and goals of businesses.

Goals tend to be fuzzy and general. A manager may say, "Let's expand our product line to incorporate the new technologies." Another might say, "We need to set up a manufacturing operation on the European continent to

TABLE 4.1   Approaches to Definition of Company Mission

Resource Use Approach	Market Use Approach	Combination of Resource and Market Use Approach
Manufacture of microcircuitry	Provision of low-price circuits for video phones	Manufacture of lowest priced microcircuitry for home video phones
Assembly of electronic components into systems	Provision of data and word processors for high-technology research	Formulation of electronic systems for data and word processors in high-technology research
Construction and fabrication of large metal and concrete components	Provision of custom-built additions to nuclear power plants	Construction of custom-built metal and concrete additions to nuclear power plants in worldwide installations

TABLE 4.2   Examples of Missions and Goals of Businesses

Business	Mission	Goals
American Airlines	To transport people to major cities in the United States	To transport people efficiently, safely, and comfortably to reachable locations in the airline network
Metropolitan Life Insurance	To provide financial security against unplanned disasters	To predict and provide financial security for corporation employees against unplanned disasters from sickness and accidents
New York Times	To inform readers on latest events and items of interest	To deliver information efficiently and inexpensively on current events and items of readers' interest
Harvard University	To provide knowledge, skills, and behavioral change	To provide facilities, environment, and faculty conducive to knowledge, skills, and behavioral change for a worldwide clientele
Mayo Clinic	To diagnose and treat the sick	To provide facilities and medical analysts for the unusually sick and to render diagnosis and treatment

serve our European customers." Still another might say, "We need to improve the productivity of the corporate administrative staff." In each of these examples, the statement is general and vague. A variety of conditions can satisfy the suggested goal. But the goal does serve as a starting point. It does suggest an action to be taken and thus becomes a useful communications tool. It triggers thinking, analysis, involvement, evaluation, and even controversy. It encourages managers to start thinking about the future and the direction that needs to be taken toward that future. The most difficult part of a vague and generalized goal statement is its acceptance as a basis for development of a specific objective. Nonetheless, goal statements are useful in the mission-goals-objectives-results sequence.

After goals are selected, they are reviewed continuously, since goals change. This review considers relevance, appropriateness, and practicality.

A source for the development of goals in addition to the mission statement is an internal organizational need, that is, the need to solve a general issue, problem, or frustration within the firm. This provides an opportunity for functional managers to develop goals within the mission statement alongside top management. The process is illustrated in Table 4.3.

TABLE 4.3   General Process for Selecting Goals or Objectives

Organizational	Choices to Solve Problem	Why Choice Needed	Goal Areas
Losing money	Sales improvement Cost reduction Price increases Capital expense reduction	Enterprise doesn't just want to make money; it must make as much as it can	Profitability
High losses and huge wastes	New methods Better work practices Capital equipment investment Improvement in worker effectiveness	Enterprise doesn't just want to get the work out; it must get the work out efficiently	Productivity
Products not selling	Product improvement Improvement in product competitiveness Product development New product introductions	Enterprise doesn't just want to enter markets with products; it must have steady stream of new and better products	Entrepreneurial
Dissatisfied employees	New policies Improvement in quality of work life Elimination of bad practices Job redesign	Enterprise doesn't just want employees; it wants employees who work hard and stay	Morale
Reject rate high	Institution of quality standards Employees matched with jobs Training for proficiency Set up of quality assurance procedures	Enterprise doesn't just want to produce products on time; it must do this with few or no rejects	Quality
Schedule slippage	Efficiency training Installation of schedule system Increase in capacity System of expediting	Enterprise doesn't just want to deliver products; it must deliver to meet customer expectations	Scheduling

aware, through observation and study, of the many complex factors within and without the organization that exert pressure and thus create needs. Examples of these pressures are:

Pressures From Within Organization	Pressures From Organization's Environment
Low sales growth	Excessive pollution
Excessive order backlog	High taxes

Pressures From Within Organization	Pressures From Organization's Environment
Loss of key customers	Poor site location
High accident rate	Inhibiting laws
High waste and spoilage	Government interference
Excessive repairs	High regulations
Interdepartmental disputes	Compliance audits
High corrective work	Court suits
Low inventory	Poor public image
Low return on investment	Rumors in community
Rivalries	Poor labor market
High overhead	Unskilled manpower
Excessive turnover	Theft and vandalism
Loose quality control	Political unrest
High costs	Poor water supply
High material handling costs	High energy costs
High absenteeism	Sewage backups
Continuous errors	Poor law enforcement
High reject rate	High unemployment costs
	Low economic development

These pressures stir managers to select and set goals. The goals set the general direction to be followed by members of the organization. Guidelines for goal management are shown in Table 4.4.

TABLE 4.4   Guidelines in Goal Management

Goal awareness	Unless an organization knows its goals, it will not be able to achieve them.
Goal expectation	Goals represent the final consequence of a series of planned actions.
Goal priorities	No organization or individual can do everything at once. Some goals must have preeminence over others. Goals help clarify priorities.
Goal changes	Conditions from which goals are set are constantly changing, which means goals need to be reviewed, revised, and reselected.
Goal continuity	Goals never come to an end, since new ones are established while old ones are being completed.

TABLE 4.4 *(Continued)*

Goal coincidence	Organizations get more results and employees are more satisfied when there is a reasonable degree of coincidence between personal and organizational goals.
Goal levels	Goals can exist at a number of levels and across department structure, but the most important goals exist at the top, since it gives direction to the entire organization.
Goal seeking	The goals a person or organization seeks tell a great deal about what the person or organization is or what it will become. Goals lead the individual or organization into the future.
Goal setting	Goals are set in an iterative process between people and the organization, various options and alternatives being tried. The final goals adopted are the best "fit" for all concerned. The process starts with people.
Goal processes	Goals as ends determine the means. The processes used to complete goals are selected and developed in terms of the goals.
Goal communication	Goals are an expression of the people in an organization; goals inform about where they want to go and what they want to become.
Goal motivation	Goals stimulate the will to accomplish. Organizational goals are completed by employees when they participate in setting them up in accord with their personal goals.
Goal effectiveness	Goals well stated are at least half the solution to reaching them.
Goal transcendence	Goals that offer opportunities to change perpetuation of the past will move an organization from one state of being to another.
Goal unity	Goals are synthesized between the organization and individuals through agreement or direction, work design, responsibility, delegation, and control processes. Goals promote a person's sense of unity and solidarity with other people.
Goal leadership	Goal leadership is helping individuals find and set personal goals through the context of organizational goals.
Goal power	There is power in doing. There is no power in talking. Goals help doers by clarifying directions, expectations, and outcomes. Goals help a person resolve problems.
Goal attainment	Large-scale accomplishments are achieved by achievement of a series of small scale tasks within realistic time ranges.

102

TABLE 4.4   (*Continued*)

Goal opportunity	Every goal selected, committed to, and pursued means the door is closed to another goal. Goals selected must have high payoff.
Goal mistakes	Choice of the wrong goals can generate huge mistakes that can prove costly or threaten survivability.
Goal measurement	Casual managers do not want measurements in goals, since these demand and challenge performance. The casual approach gives reason for avoidance of measurements and concealment of accountability.
Goal setting skills	The more frequent goal setting and goal achievement are practiced, the more skillful will the process become.
Goal confidence	Goals set for low levels of performance mean managers who are unsure and unwilling to handle challenges. Goals set for high levels of performance mean managers who are confident and willing to handle challenges.
Goal resources	Goal-setting commitments in an organization will set in motion the resources needed to achieve the goals.
Goal perspective	Goal setting is a forward-looking process that diagrams a course of action into the future. A goal is not meeting an awaited future; a goal is creating a future.

Sample Goals

Managers take for granted that their organization knows its goals. They often assume what the goals are. The assumptions are misleading in many cases. The first step in MBO thinking is to formalize the direction of the company by defining and clearly stating its goals. The following are examples of goals in seven fields of human effort and in U.S. organizations and businesses.

1. *Business Goals.*
    (a) Perpetuate the enterprise and ensure its survivability in spite of effective competitors, unplanned losses, and ineffective performance of the firm's employees.
    (b) Increase profit performance through design and production of quality products and services at prices customers are willing to pay.
    (c) Satisfy stockholders and owners of the enterprise with a reasonable, realistic, and continuing return on investment.
    (d) Satisfy customers by meeting and often exceeding their expectations of promptness, craftsmanship, and reliability for value paid.

(e)   Give directions to the firm with actions and reactions toward competitors that assure a growth position in the market.

(f)   Satisfy employees with policies, procedures, and work practices that yield rewarding experiences, benefits, and financial gain and a healthy work place.

(g)   Improve productivity by reducing operating costs, waste of human resources and materials, and duplication of duties while enhancing performance and accomplishments through self-contained and self-regulated work processes.

(h)   Advance the technology of the enterprise through research and new knowledge, information, and competence in order to expand the technological base on which innovations of products and services can be made.

(i)   Improve the quality of work life through achieving as high a degree of self-contained production or automation as possible in order to reduce boring, unfulfilling, and monotonous work for employees.

(j)   Search out and develop new options in energy utilization or alternatives that will lead to a reduction in energy dependence and high operating costs.

(k)   Expand the capacity and flexibility of the enterprise through skill and organizational development to meet the demands of changing markets.

(l)   Assure resources availability for the firm by establishing supplier relationships and pursuing options for substitution or replacement.

(m)   Develop and maintain a positive public image through appropriate communication media or corporate contributions and role in the community.

(n)   Communicate clearly and persuasively to stockholders, customers, employees, and the community through effective and efficient media and publications.

(o)   Contribute to the community by sharing expertise and resources in programs and services for making citizens better neighbors and more effective human beings.

2. *Government Goals.*

(a)   Perpetuate constitutional democracy by proposing, electing, and removing representatives for all people to form a just government to act on their behalf.

(b)   Protect and ensure the rights and freedoms of individuals, enterprises, and institutions according to the articles and amendments of the Constitution through an effective, efficient, and equitable system of justice.

(c) Satisfy citizens with laws, policies, procedures, programs, and services that promote their welfare, security, advancement, and happiness.

(d) Protect natural resources, the environment, and personal and public property through prevention, reduction, and elimination of waste, crime, and crime-supported activities and conditions.

(e) Ensure equal opportunity and treatment of all citizens regardless of race, age, nationality, sex, or religion.

(f) Protect and defend citizens against foreign threats, forces, or takeovers through a strong and capable military organization, allies, and deterrent activities.

(g) Uphold the right and the practice through a system of education to receive as much enlightenment for all citizens to their maximum potential and capability.

(h) Stimulate progress and improve the quality of living within the limits imposed by legal and social constraints by granting as much creative freedom to individuals, groups, and enterprises as possible.

(i) Give directions to the economy by proposing, regulating, strengthening, fixing, and protecting the monetary system of trade, commerce, and transportation between suppliers and consumers.

(j) Provide aid in disasters by maintaining policies, practices, resources, and assistance that will meet and control emergencies.

(k) Expand tax base capacity through innovations, development, expansion, and productivity of material resources, manufacturing, new technology, and capital development.

(l) Cooperate and collaborate with other governments for mutual protection, security, trade, enterprises, and benefits.

(m) Improve productivity of managed resources and public funds by reducing operating costs and waste of resources and materials while enhancing performance and accomplishments.

(n) Promote advances in science and technology by stimulating research programs, supporting activities, and provide funding and leadership where needed.

(o) Acquire national self-sufficiency and independence in the areas of natural resources, agriculture, energy, technology, and manufacturing.

3. *Health-Care Goals.*

(a) Perpetuate care and concern for the sick through policies, practices, institutions, agencies, facilities, and treatment centers.

(b)   Satisfy patients by meeting and often exceeding their health care needs in sickness and injury with effective diagnosis, treatment, convalescence, and rehabilitation.

(c)   Expand the competence, capacity, and skills of qualified health-care practitioners and staff through continued development and expansion of knowledge in medicine, nursing, health administration, and health technologies.

(d)   Expand health-care capacity and flexibility through capital improvements of the health-care facility to accommodate increased demands for better and more effective health care.

(e)   Reduce the cost of health care for each patient through novel and innovative practices, such as outpatient visits rather than overnight stays, without diminishing the quality of patient care.

(f)   Advance preventive medicine through community and public education programs on preventive measures and self-help health practices.

(g)   Provide equal opportunity through federal, state, and local programs for health care for the ill and injured in spite of age, nationality, race, or socioeconomic factors.

(h)   Continue formal programs and activities that keep costs to patients as low as possible through public giving, state funds, federal grants, fund-raising projects, and corporate gifts.

(i)   Reduce potential for error, incompetence, and misjudgment through validation of procedures, checks and balances, tight controls, rigorous training for certification, and continuing education.

(j)   Satisfy employees with competitive salaries, reasonable demands on time, good fringe benefits, and a pleasant work environment.

(k)   Promote computerized information, computerized storage and retrieval of medical records, treatment alternatives, and efficient and effective practices and procedures for decision making.

(l)   Expand opportunities for participation in patient health and care through community volunteer services of time and skills.

4. *Educational Goals.*

(a)   Motivate students toward lifelong learning through effective use of the lasting values of challenge, accomplishment, participation, recognition, quality, creativity, and progress.

(b)   Promote mastery of basic skills in reading, writing, speaking, listening, analyzing, and quantifying for strengthening of communications and sound decision making.

(c)   Provide students with a fund of knowledge, concepts, and information in science, math, economics, arts, literature, philosophy, and language to form a foundation for the development of skills for earning a living.

(d) Develop skills and confidence of students to define problems, analyze and create information for alternatives, and select choices.

(e) Stimulate intellectual curiosity so that students raise questions about problems and experiences and seek answers through faculty, books, media, people, and personal experimentation.

(f) Give competence in life-style behavior for understanding, accepting, and contributing toward responsibilities and expectations of family members and society.

(g) Develop moral and ethical attitudes and behavior to enable individuals to be useful in a changing society and to respect the rights of people, personal and public property, and cultural differences.

(h) Foster understanding of economic principles that will lead to sound use of money.

(i) Give equal opportunity through programs and services for individuals to develop to their full potential regardless of differences in ability, interest, talents, gifts, and rate of learning.

(j) Expand competence, capacity, and flexibility of faculty to teach curriculum content so that they keep pace with and even lead societal needs.

(k) Promote physical, social, and emotional health through understanding and application of sound principles and useful practices.

(l) Satisfy taxpayers or funding sources by meeting and often exceeding their expectations of educational effectiveness, administrative efficiency, and notable progress for value paid.

(m) Graduate students who reasonably reflect the models of educational behavior designed in a curriculum that meets national, state, and local standards.

(n) Employ qualified, competent, and exemplary teachers to conduct effective learning processes for students.

(o) Upgrade and update the curriculum, equipment, and facilities on a continuous basis in order for the classroom to have scholastic relevancy and to be a microcosm of real-world challenges and problems.

(p) Perpetuate the institution and ensure its survivability in spite of rising costs, diminishing supply of students, competitive success of other institutions, and constraining demands of government and taxpayers.

(q)   Foster healthy and sound societal and ethical values despite the confusing and often contradictory moral issues and opinions of the times.

5.   *Religious Goals.*

(a)   Promote reverence for God through the development of a God-centered life-style of understanding and living.

(b)   Enhance the development of the spiritual nature of human existence along with the emotional, physical, intellectual, and social.

(c)   Foster understanding of holy scriptures and the plan of salvation in order for humans to pursue the mystery, enigma, and concept of a future life.

(d)   Stimulate curiosity over the mysteries of life and the nature of humans in order for individuals to arrive at a meaningful self-concept in the context of present-day expectations.

(e)   Motivate humans for love toward other humans through understanding of the purpose of existence and the ultimate aim and development of the human family.

(f)   Provide counsel and guidelines for those with questions about or problems dealing with difficulties in life situations in the home, marriage, family, job, and community.

(g)   Promote moral and ethical tenets of faith and righteousness for individuals in order for them to know and have standards of right and wrong.

(h)   Preach faith and hope continuously and effectively to give strength and courage to despairing individuals.

(i)   Preserve the varieties of human experiences and historical information to provide the human family with options and choices in future decision making.

(j)   Give direction to programs and services intended to help those in spiritual, physical, and social need.

(k)   Give knowledge, concepts, and information about scriptures; examples of faith; and principles of righteousness to the young for effective indoctrination to a God-centered life.

(l)   Preserve, support, and nurture those traditional values that heighten the goodness of humans and discourage and diminish those new values that heighten the depravity of humans.

(m)   Encourage financial contributions and funding for supporting programs, services, and the help needed in a religious grouping.

(n)   Develop ambitions and skills among pastors, elders, evangelists, and ministers for effective performance of services such as marriages, funerals, last rites, services, religious studies, and fellowships.

6. *Social Goals.*

   (a) Perpetuate concern for social illnesses such as alcoholism, other drug addiction, and divorce through policies, practices, programs, institutions, agencies, facilities, and treatment centers.

   (b) Satisfy public needs by meeting and often exceeding the need for help in problems and frustrations from marriage, family, job, and the community.

   (c) Advance preventive social medicine through community and public education, programs of information, preventive measures, and self-help social betterment practices.

   (d) Employ qualified and competent professional staff in public agencies to ensure high-quality services to the socially ill.

   (e) Upgrade and update existing public programs and services with new information, latest effective techniques, innovative procedures, and recent research.

   (f) Cooperate and collaborate with other agencies for mutual sharing of resources, programs, and services.

   (g) Expand opportunities for involvement and participation in social care and concern in policy making, resource provisions, need determination, and agency funding.

   (h) Continue to secure financial and other forms of support for public agencies through high program performance of social care, helpful assistance to other agencies in need, and proposal of novel changes and innovative programs.

   (i) Improve productivity of managed resources and public funds by reducing operating costs and waste of resources and materials, while enhancing performance and accomplishments.

   (j) Provide effective and proficient management in program planning, budgeting, operating, and evaluating.

7. *Individual Goals.*

   (a) Develop and sustain a reverence for God who has created life, given provisions for sustaining it, and given the opportunity for its continuance in a future time.

   (b) Perpetuate the gift of life and ensure survival through acquisition of water, food, clothing, shelter, and security.

   (c) Maintain mental, physical, and emotional health in order to proceed with and improve life's endowments.

   (d) Have the opportunity to marry, raise a family, and establish a home in order to attain fulfillment and happiness through the family experience.

   (e) Have the opportunity to join a group or groups for participation, companionship, social interchange, human fellowship, and interactive love.

(f)   Use creative freedom to develop and pursue ideas or values that enable attainment of the highest possible level of self-fulfillment and achievement.

(g)   Develop a life-style that permits leisure time through routinization of responsibilities, familiarity with and control of work and environment, and avoidance of activities that lead to frustration and chaos.

(h)   Recognize and act on responsibilities and expectations as a member of the human family and citizen of a country.

(i)   Develop the skills and abilities to find, hold, and advance in a job that provides a level of income sufficient for a wide variety of changing needs and values.

(j)   Acquire materials, equipment, and objects that help to make life easy, comfortable, and enjoyable.

(k)   Acquire the knowledge, wisdom, and experience to handle and make effective decisions about problems and challenges encountered in the home, job, and community.

(l)   Develop the skills and proficiency for communicating with others with ease, understanding, and clarity.

(m)   Travel to distant lands to enrich and appreciate values and life-styles of other cultures.

(n)   Attain a level of dignity through social recognition of personal contribution and worth in the job, home, and community.

(o)   Have the opportunity and courage to produce or strive for change for the betterment of others or to leave life better than it was found.

(p)   Increase money reserves to a level sufficient for maintenance of life-style and health needs in later life or in retirement.

Goals of Organizations

Organization	Goal
Academy of International Business	To foster education and advance professional standards in the field of international business
Academy of Management Review	To publish theory-, concept-, and review-type articles
Accreditation Board for Engineering and Technology, Inc.	To accredit college programs in engineering and engineering technology in the United States
Adult Education Association of the United States of America	To increase lifelong learning opportunities for all people and to build a strong adult education movement

Organization	Goal
The Advertising Council	To promote voluntary citizen actions to help solve national problems
American Association for the Advancement of Science	To further the work of scientists, to facilitate cooperation among them, to foster scientific freedom and responsibility, to improve the effectiveness of science in the promotion of human welfare, and to increase public understanding and appreciation of the importance and promise of the methods of science in human progress
American Association of Cost Engineers	To promote and advance the science and art of cost engineering through educational forums, standardization of terminology, encouragement of inclusion of cost engineering instruction in engineering curricula, and cooperation with other organizations
American Association of School Administrators	To develop educational leaders, initiate and support favorable laws, promote programs and activities that focus on leadership, and cultivate a favorable climate
American Bankers Association	To enhance the ability of America's banks and bankers to serve the needs and desires of the American public
American Business Women's Association	To promote the professional, educational, cultural, and social advancement of business women
American Economic Association	To encourage economic research, to issue publications on economic subjects, and to encourage freedom of economic discussion
American Federation of Labor and Congress of Industrial Organizations	To advocate policies favorable to members
American Federation of Small Business	To comment and lobby on issues of interest to small business people

Organization	Goal
American Health Care Association	To promote high standards of professional care and enactment of favorable laws, to inform and educate the public and health care professionals, and to unite and organize licensed health care facilities and associations
American Library Association	To promote and improve library service and librarianship
American Management Association	To provide quality programs, products, and services to the managerial process
American Production and Inventory Control Society, Inc.	To operate for research and educational purposes in the profession of production and inventory control
Associated General Contractors of America	To gain and maintain control of the labor force, provide leadership in legislative matters, and help members manage their businesses in the construction industry
Association of Governing Boards of Universities and Colleges	To help the members of college and university boards fulfill their roles and meet their responsibilities
Future Business Leaders of America/ Phi Beta Kappa	To develop the business skills and character of high school and college business students
Minority Business Information Institute, Inc.	To provide a specialized center for minority economic development
National Association of Home Builders	To make possible ownership of well-designed, well-constructed, and well-located homes under the free enterprise system for every American family
National Association of Regional Councils	To promote cooperation among local governments
National Center for Productivity and Quality of Working Life	To improve productivity and the quality of working life
National Music Council	To promote discussion and interchange of information about musical affairs and problems in American culture

Organization	Goal
New England Association of Schools and Colleges, Inc.	To advance the cause of education in the colleges and schools of New England and other geographical areas
University of Southern California College of Continuing Education	To provide training and skill development for increased productivity

Connecticut General Life Insurance Company

1. Institute new structured insurance programs for high risk surgeons. (innovation)
2. Institute a new 24-hour claim center phone for people unable to call during normal business hours. (innovation)
3. Decrease time to process all review claims by 20 percent during the next 12-month period. (productivity)
4. Buy 60-day option on municipal bonds for the city of Nashville (site of the World's Fair). (financial resources)
5. Initiate rotating job program that would require all in the company except executive officers to change jobs every four years. (innovation, worker performance, and attitudes)
6. Raise rates and reduce internal costs for a combined net saving of 15 percent in the next year. (profitability)

Pratt and Whitney, Division of United Technologies

1. Market an engine that will consume 15 percent less fuel, to be used on aircraft that will carry 150 to 200 people. (market standing, innovation)
2. Make new turbine disks for stages 1 through 5 on new military engines by HIP process, which will reduce machine scrap of raw material by 25 percent. (productivity)
3. Enter into agreement with Chinese titanium dealers to purchase 30 percent of all titanium they mine for the next five years, to create a stockpile of this precious metal for the future. (physical and financial resources)
4. Consolidate responsibilities in quality assurance by eliminating 10 percent of all middle managers. (managerial performance and development)
5. Increase cash awards by 33 percent for employee incentive and cost-reduction plans in the hope of increasing savings in these areas. (worker performance and attitudes)

6. Increase grants by 10 percent to development programs for minority and inner city youth, a corporate assistance goal. (social responsibility)

7. Increase sales by 40 percent of fuel-savings kits for use in existing in-flight engines, items that are guaranteed profit items. (profitability)

Connecticut State Government, Department of Motor Vehicles

1. Start drive-in service for renewal of licenses and registrations. (innovation)

2. Streamline procedure for handling transfer of title requests to decrease average time for processing by 10 percent. (productivity)

3. Increase yearly passenger vehicle registration fee by 20 percent. (physical/financial resources, solvency)

4. Generate names of candidates for new supervisory positions needed due to expansion of department. (managerial development and performance)

5. Reduce mandatory overtime required of each worker for each month by 50 percent. (solvency, worker attitudes)

6. Produce two new films for use by state schools that show evils of driving while diverted with distractions. (social responsibility)

American Medical Association

1. Announce support for development of mass production techniques for interferon (based on organization-sponsored testing of the drug for safety and effectiveness). (innovation)

2. Increase donations in net dollars during annual dinner dance by 12.5 percent. (profitability and/or financial resources)

3. Establish a series of forums around the nation to discuss euthanasia. (social responsibility)

4. Devise new method for the evaluation of physicians who wish to become residents at hospitals. (managerial performance and development)

5. Survey surgeons at major hospitals across the nation to determine needed innovations and main problems in carrying out required duties. (worker performance and attitude)

American Diabetes Association

1. Aid in the marketing of a new artificial pancreas unit by allowing members to attend demonstration of it in service. (innovation)

2. Increase membership in the New England chapter by 5 percent/year for the next three years. (productivity)

3. Increase intake through subscriptions to *Diabetes Forecast* magazine, a 50 percent net profit item, by 10 percent over the next six-month period. (financial resources)
4. Allow for more stability by having chapter presidents serve two years instead of one. (manager performance and development)
5. Expand HOTLINE service for answering questions concerning diabetes to 15 new metropolitan areas in the coming six months. (social responsibility, distribution of information)

Boston University Educational Institution

1. Introduce certain courses to be taught from 6:00 a.m. to 8:00 a.m. for people who wish to take courses and are unavailable at any other time of the day. (innovation)
2. Eliminate school deficits through consolidation and cutbacks within the next nine months. (profitability)
3. Increase combined hours for lecture and research required of tenured professors for each 18-month period by 10 percent, and increase salaries the like amount. (instructor performance, productivity, development)
4. Send athletes in major sports throughout the greater Boston area to hold clinics for underprivileged and handicapped children. (social responsibility)
5. Increase expectations for this year's alumni fund drive by 20 percent; acquire five townhouses in the school area for use as student housing in the coming school years. (physical and financial resources)
6. Develop and introduce 12 new programs in the colleges of the school. (student development)

OBJECTIVES

A goal is not an objective. Goals form the basis of objectives. When results to be accomplished are specified in specific measurable terms within a goal area, an objective emerges. The goal is more general, more directional, than the objective. The goal sets the direction of the firm. The objective sets the results to be achieved in that direction. Objectives are events, performance attainments, or accomplishments that are planned and expected to happen within the directions set by goals. They serve as targets for action to be taken today so that results are obtained tomorrow. Managers must see that even though the future of their organization is uncertain, they must act and react to make the organization better than it has been in the past. Objectives are statements of this view.

More specifically, objectives are end results achievable within a certain period of time. Improvements, problem-solving, seizing a new opportunity, eliminating a frustration, and starting an entrepreneurial innovation are guidelines for setting objectives within the direction of a goal as the goal fits within the mission of the business.

"Improve profits" is a goal that sets a direction; "achieve 30 percent return on investments before taxes for next year" is an objective that gives results expected within a specific period of time. "Care for the sick" is another goal that sets a direction; "reduce the infectious disease rate from 15 to 10 percent in region I in six months" is an objective that gives desired results within a specific period of time.

Throughout the history of management, the area of objectives has been the most neglected area of managerial activities. Today, managers everywhere will quickly show their lists of formalized objectives for a future period. There is no scarcity of objectives among managers. A careful examination of these objectives, however, reveals a wide variety of deficiencies. Some are platitudes, such as "improve efficiency." Others cover an illusively broad range, such as "experience continuous business growth." Still others deal with nebulous activities, such as "improve communication." Broad generalities have increasingly crept in, with language used in such a way that a variety of meanings are implied. Because of the language in which they are phrased, these generalities can be manipulated to mislead and misinform, to twist and distort their real intent. Inherent in these generalities is a range of possibilities that cannot be refuted or rejected, yet nothing in them gives specific direction. Such generalities, lacking in specificity but accepted by all, are called "motherhoods." Motherhoods have a tendency to creep into statements of objectives because they *sound good*, are *readily acceptable*, and offer a *comfortable distance and range*. Although motherhoods are an acceptable part of day-to-day management language and are often found with goals, they should not be permitted in a statement of objectives. Some examples of motherhoods follow.

Improve managerial effectiveness	Achieve greatest efficiency
Increase profits	Attain highest quality possible
Increased share of market	Continue existing management
Render better customer service	Improve delivery time
Improve economic conditions	Complete study of new program
Lower production costs	Streamline procedures
Achieve technological leadership	Complete planning for future requirements
Maintain good labor relations	Cooperate in maintaining equipment

Decrease delay time	Increase sales volume
Communicate with other depart- ments	Provide more timely assistance
Develop cost awareness	Maintain morale and attitudes

The lack of specificity in a motherhood renders the statement of objectives unmeasurable. Further, an objective that does not have measurable points is difficult to control and achieve. Managers tend to use motherhoods either because they are uncertain about possible goals or because they lack the information necessary to pin down exactly what is required. The following guidelines are useful in eliminating motherhoods in statements of objectives.

Avoid	Use
Oversimplifications	Words that indicate how much
Sensational terms	Terms that can be proved or demon- strated
Understated or overstated words	Precise terms designating actions that can be controlled and measured
Opinions subject to change	Terms that lend themselves to clarifica-
Exaggerations	tion by percentages, ratios, numbers,
Inexactness	averages, index numbers, correlations,
Idealistic terms	and standard deviations
Terms that have a range of meanings	

Objectives must be quantified when relevant and feasible. The more concrete the information a supervisor can build into his or her objective statement, the more likely it is that a real meeting of minds will be achieved among those involved. The situation might be compared with a football game: In football there is no ambiguity as to where the goal posts are and in what direction the teams should travel. The field is marked so that each player can measure whether he is moving toward the objective or away from it. This quantified precision brings clarity and meaning to football play. When management personnel do not know specifically where they are heading and how good a job they are doing, their results become divergent and their work inefficient.

The specificity of results—"how much"—is just as important as the type or kind of results. The measurable points built into the written formal statement of an objective specify both the quantity of results expected and the period of time in which they are to be achieved. Quantification of motherhoods translates them to conditions that must exist when a job is well done. To the greatest extent possible, objectives should be quantified. Following is a list of performance indicators or yardsticks by means of which objectives can be quantified.

1. *Profit.* Sales/costs ratio; sales growth rates and profiles; actual costs/budget ratio; overhead cost levels and drift ratios; net profit as percentage of sales; percentage of increase in dividends; sales/cost proportion trends and levels; frequency and size of sales orders; cost of transportation as percentage of sales level and order size; mean deviations from standard costs; variable cost rates and levels for sales order sizes and levels; percentage of return on investments; percentage of share of actual and potential markets; current assets/current liabilities ratio; accounts receivable trends, rates and collectibility ratios; cost of employee recruitment and placement; direct/indirect labor ratio; marginal cost trends and ratios; profit/total assets ratio; debt/equity ratio; sales per employee; net operating income; debt/total assets ratio; dividend rates.

2. *Productivity and Schedules.*   Cost per unit; inventory correlates with sales levels; actual costs/standard cost ratio; back-order profiles and rates; back-order correlates with inventory levels; frequency and range of missed delivery dates; percentage of deadlines met; percentage of performance variance against budgets; set-up time rates and profiles; machine hours per product correlated with process types; percentage of utilization of labor capacity; output/input correlates between equipment utilization and labor capacity; percentage of projects completed against forecasts; equipment depreciation and obsolescence trends; downtime of equipment; percentage of time in raw materials inventory; experienced production personnel/new personnel ratio; farmed-out work/in-company production ratio; output per unit of labor input; delay in work completion behind schedule; frequency rates for rescheduling; overshipments.

3. *Efficiency.*   Percentage of error in filling orders; defect correction ratio; percentage of scrap and waste; mean and range of equipment downtime; damage claims as percentage of sales levels and orders; percentage of unit cost in material handling; overshipment and undershipment ratios; percentage of utilization of capital equipment; percentage of utilization of available floor space; inventory/assets ratio; traffic intensity ratios; task time completion rates; percentage of hand motions; queue ratios; percentage of items delivered as promised; inventory turnover; percentage of rework; percentage of set-up and preparation time; frequency of depletion of safety stock; demand time/supply time ratio; minimum lead time reorder levels; net sales/inventory ratio; stockouts to desired service levels; utilization of floor space.

4. *Manpower Management.* Quits and mobility flow rates; before and after training scores; absenteeism ratio; weed-out and screening profile rates; percentage of implementation of performance appraisal recommendations; percentage implemented with placement planning charts; accident frequency profiles and rates; supervisory appointment rate from presupervisory selection and training; health profile trends and rates; total suggestions submitted and percentage implemented; employee transfer request profiles and rates; grievance generation and settlement ratios; average tardiness trends and rates; number and settlement of disciplinary cases; percentage of time allowances for personal needs; number of promotions within; overtime deterioration ratios; recruitment and placement costs; percentage of completed development experiences; percentages of error; additions of staff per repetitive program; employee turnover; number of disciplinary cases.

5. *Quality.* Percent rejects internal; percent rejects external; number of complaints from customers by categories; number of deficiencies in quality control audits; actual/standard performance ratio; number of standards in key areas; warranty costs; cost of rework; number of deficiencies in vendor and supplier audits; scrap percentage rates; amount of repeat business; delays from rework; errors in filling orders; damage claims; number of inspectors; unacceptable reasons for variation.

6. *Marketing.* Sales increase; market penetration; share of market; timeliness of trend forecasts; actual performance/sales forecast ratio; sales to sales budgets; number of needs fulfillment to user requirements; new product development per time unit; product improvements per time unit; customer complaints; cost of sales; cost of distribution; size of orders.

7. *Innovations.* Patents; number of proposals submitted; number of feasibility studies accepted; number of new products; number of product changes; percent product maturation; number of technological features over competing products; number of processes computerized; technical personnel/nontechnical personnel ratio; number of employee suggestions submitted; number of employee suggestions accepted.

Various methods can be used to connect general goals with specific objectives. But the most effective connecting occurs when a key measurement or indicator forms the basis of results within a goal. Table 4.5 illustrates this point.

TABLE 4.5   Connecting Goals With Objectives

Mission Identity (Goals)	Area of Results (Subgoals)	Key Measurements (Indicators)	Objectives (Performance Expectations)
To provide cost-effective use of resources	Rework (reduce rework)	Cost of rework; number of customer complaints	Reduce cost of rework 30 percent by January 1; achieve two-day complaint-handling process by end of year
To protect homes from unplanned electrical surges	Circuit breakers (redesign circuit breakers)	Number of innovations for competitive edge; competitive cost	Achieve a speed of closure of 5 seconds with new materials by January 1; reduce weight of closure cradle 20 percent in new materials design by January 1
To protect person and property	Crime (control and reduce crime)	Number of street muggings; number of auto thefts	Reduce street muggings in county 30 percent by January 1; achieve 95 percent car locking in parking areas by January 1
To improve profits	Costs (reduce costs)	Sales/costs ratio	Improve sales/costs ratio 15% with same sales volume by July 1
To improve efficiency of organization	Value added (increase value-added rate)	Amount of value added per employee	Increase value-added rate 5% in Division A by January 1
To introduce new products	R&D feasibility studies (achieve marketable products	Ratio of feasible ideas to marketable opportunities	Achieve 10:1 feasibility/marketable ideas for R&D department by January 1
To establish performance standards	All key jobs (increase number of jobs completed)	Number of jobs completed	Achieve 10 percent completion rate for each quarter in establishing standards of performance

Process of Formulating an Objective

The following list shows some of the traditional major areas of results that top management uses to get better results within its mission.

1. *Return on Investment (ROI).*   Increasing the rate or percentage of profit or interest returned to the enterprise as a result of undertaking an investment or capital commitment at some early period of time.

2. *Profitability.*   Increasing the ratio of sales dollars to operating costs.

3. *Sales Volume.*   Increasing the amount of disposed of or sold products, services, or merchandise in an existing or created market.

4. *Cost Benefit.*   Maintaining minimal expense in the selection and deployment of resources, equipment, materials, methods, and manpower.

5. *Schedule.*   Meeting a predetermined time program that projects events, operations, arrivals, and departures. A sense of pace is structured and reached.

6. *Feasibility.*   Capable of being done or effected in a practical way.

7. *Customer Effects.*   Avoiding situations that would retard patronage.

8. *Competitive Advantage.*   Avoiding acts that would favor a rival selling goods and services in the same market.

9. *Employee Morale.*   Creating a climate and mood conducive to willing and dependable performance.

10. *Union Unrest.*   Avoiding actions disruptive to collective bargaining efforts.

11. *Community Image.*   Avoiding acts that give the company an unpleasant appearance in the eyes of the community.

12. *Legislative Actions.*   Avoiding practices that might provoke legal action to retard or stop competition and growth.

13. *Cash Position.*   Creating a favorable and necessary situation in which turnover of capital follows a cycle from cash to assets to receivables and back to cash, in sufficient time for the enterprise's use.

14. *Opportunities for Improvement.*   Exploiting uniquely timed situations for market growth and diversification.

15. *Quality Requirements.*   Avoiding acts aimed at reducing the ability of a product or service to satisfy its specified design.

16. *Safety Needs.*   Avoiding activities that are unsafe and areas where safety standards are minimal.

17. *Tax Benefits.*   Avoiding acts that exceed the statute of limitations and bring about tax increases.

The actual process of formulating objectives varies from firm to firm, which has led analysts to believe that a great deal of confusion exists. I do not share this view. The variety of approaches only constitutes the variety of processes used to bring these commitments about in the face of markets, customers, employees, unions, stockholders, and government. The variety of approaches is nothing more than a variety of strategies. The next chapter will deal with some of these different strategies. Mark McConkie of the University of Colorado, in his analysis, attempted to clarify the goal-setting process by analyzing the works of 39 leading MBO experts. His findings are reproduced here, with permission, in Table 4.6.

TABLE 4.6 How Experts[a]View the MBO Goal-Setting Process[b]

In the Goal-Setting Process, MBO Should Include the Following Features:	Drucker	Schleh	McGregor	Likert	Schaffer	Huse	Hughes	Odiorne	McConkey	Valentine	Miller	Wikstrom	Howell	Scanlan	Tosi & Carroll	Ivancevich
Top management sets goals, subordinates agree							•									
Subordinates set goals, subordinates agree	•		•	•				•			•					•
Superiors and subordinates jointly set goals					•				•	•				•	•	
MBO is adaptable: degree of goal-setting participation varies with each organization				•					•	•			•		•	
Some combination of the above as a joint goal-setting venture	•					•			•					•	•	
No description of goal-setting procedures given																
Goals & Objectives Should:																
Be defined in terms of measurable results	•	•	•	•	•	•	•	•	•	•	•	•	•	•	•	•
Be specific	•	•	•	•	•	•	•	•	•	•	•	•	•	•	•	•
Always be "verifiable" and be quantifiable whenever possible	•	•		•		•	•	•		•	•	•	•	•		
Include target date for completion	•	•	•	•		•			•	•	•	•		•	•	•
Be in writing		•		•				•	•							
Be reviewed two to four times per year		•														
Be reviewed "periodically"			•	•	•	•		•	•	•	•	•	•		•	•
Have priority weightings	•	•					•	•	•	•	•			•		
Have an accompanying action plan			•	•	•	•	•		•	•		•		•		
Set maximum cost/resource factors						•	•		•	•						•
Be flexible; change as needed		•		•		•			•			•	•		•	
Integrate individual and organizational goals	•	•	•	•	•	•	•	•	•	•	•	•	•	•	•	•

[a]While Kirchoff qualifies as an expert in terms of the criteria used here, his work is not referred to in this table because it makes no attempt to define or describe MBO.

[b]Symbol • indicates that experts agree MBO should include feature.

122

Sloan & Schrieber	Levinson	Morrisey	Reddin	Lasagna	Chartrand	Koontz	Lahti	Schuster	Varney	Carvalho	Humble	Mali	Mahler	Kleber	Knezevich	Beck & Hillman	Brady	White	Raia	Shetty & Carlisle	McConkie	Number of Responses	Percentage in Agreement
						•	•	•		•	•								•			2	5%
•	•	•							•				•	•									
			•		•				•			•	•		•	•						11	29%
			•	•	•							•	•				•		•			13	34%
												•						•				1	3%
•	•		•	•	•	•	•	•	•	•		•	•		•	•	•	•	•	•	•	37	97%
•	•		•	•	•	•	•	•	•	•		•	•		•	•	•	•	•	•	•	37	97%
•		•	•	•		•			•	•	•	•	•	•				•	•	•	•	26	68%
•		•	•	•	•	•	•					•	•	•	•			•	•	•	•	27	71%
•		•	•			•	•					•						•	•	•	•	14	37%
•		•				•	•														•	5	14%
•	•	•	•		•	•	•	•	•	•		•	•	•		•		•	•	•	•	31	82%
	•	•			•				•			•		•	•	•		•			•	19	50%
•	•	•			•		•	•	•			•	•		•	•		•			•	21	55%
	•	•	•						•			•	•			•	•	•			•	15	40%
		•	•	•	•	•	•		•		•	•	•	•	•			•	•	•	•	25	66%
•	•	•	•	•	•	•	•	•	•			•	•	•	•	•		•	•	•	•	36	94%

123

TABLE 4.7   Nine Guidelines for Objective-Setting Process

Guideline	Total Number of Responses	Percentage of Authorities in Agreement
Goals and objectives should be specific	37	97
Goals and objectives should be defined in terms of measurable results	37	97
Individual goals should be linked to overall organization goals.	36	94
Objectives should be reviewed "period-ically	31	82
Time period for goal accomplishment should be specified.	27	71
Wherever possible, indicator of results should be quantifiable; otherwise, it should at least be verifiable.	26	68
Objectives should be flexible and changed as conditions warrant.	25	66
Objectives should include plan of action for accomplishing results.	21	55
Objectives should be assigned priorities.	19	50

To summarize the results in Table 4.6, nine objective-setting guidelines seem to constitute the backbone of MBO goal-setting processes. The MBO authorities also agreed on high levels of subordinate involvement in the objective-setting processes, although differences exist as to the form that involvement should take. Also the experts gave evidence that MBO leads to increased specificity, which helps improve overall planning (Table 4.7).

Guidelines for Writing Objectives

Managers and administrators have tended to regard the setting of objectives as a relatively simple process. This perception is deceptive. Formalizing a statement of objectives requires precision of thinking, prediction, and work measurement not usually found in the planning process. It also requires making commitments involving others. Many managers are not accustomed to such practices. Many firms report that objectives/statements are often fuzzy collections of commitments that result in misunderstandings and misinterpretations. Many are ambiguous, or they incorporate ways to escape the commitment. The words carry different meanings for different people, depending on where or when they are used and who uses them. The following ten points are useful guidelines for writing objectives.

1.   *Objectives Must Be Specific and Verifiable.*   The heart of an objective is the results predicted to be accomplished, but accomplishment cannot be determined unless measurement parameters are built in to the objectives.

2. *Objectives Must Achieve Single-ended Results.* The tendency to achieve several possibilities within an objective should be discouraged. Multiple directions confuse the focus and allocation of resources.

3. *Objectives Must Be Set Against Deadlines.* Deadlines are set so that the result occurs when the organization needs it. An objective that is achieved beyond its time limit automatically loses its productivity, because time as a resource has been lost. All objectives must be time oriented.

4. *Objectives Must Be Attainable.* Challenges are necessary for improvement, but a challenge must be within the range of performance capability and resource availability.

5. *Objectives Must Be Responsive to the Needs of the Organization.* Improvement comes about when innovative opportunities are deliberately sought and exploited in the context of the needs of the organization. Greatest results are a leap forward in performance with the same resources, or the same performance with considerable reduction in resources.

6. *Objectives Must Motivate Those Who Will Achieve Them.* Motivational processes, such as participation, must be used in the formation of the objective. In an article on ways to kill MBO, McConkey wrote: "Instead of getting subordinates involved in their commitments, write the objectives yourself and hand them out to each subordinate."

7. *Objectives Must Be Supportable by the Organization.* Targets must coincide with availability of resources, facilities, skills, and equipment. This supports the idea that greatest results occur when the total organization commits its resources and its processes. Support is assured when objectives have accompanying strategic and operational plans.

8. *Objectives Must Be Controllable.* Targets must be reducible into milestones of progress to allow for control and correction. Specific objectives easily lend themselves to divisibility.

9. *Objectives Must Have Assigned Accountability.* An organizational unit, identified by name, must be accountable for an agreed-on objective and its required action. Specific individuals, by name and position, are part of the ultimate accountability.

10. *Objectives Must Be Evaluative and Validated.* The results sought in an objective must be communicated in terms that are understood by the people who will authorize the go-ahead. A tentative evaluation of results must be given to these sources before there is authorization to proceed. A validation must be made before this authorization is pursued.

A statement of objective should not be a one-way commitment but rather a circular, two-way, flowing interchange of intentions among the many people who are involved. The selection of words is critical, since words—even commonplace words and phrases—carry different meanings for different people, depending on where or when the words are used and who uses them. There are many language barriers in the management-business-technical world. Words such as "total systems," "input," "indicator," "promotion," "supervisor," and hundreds of others pose interpretive problems in meaning and usage. One person, on the basis of experience and education, may use these terms to mean something quite different from what the listener, on the basis of a different background, understands. A statement of objectives, since it is to be communicated to several people, should be aimed at these specific people. Formalization of the statement carries with it the implication that all who are involved agree to the essence of the objective and the content of the statement. It is impossible to obtain agreement if the words used are vague, ambiguous, or misleading. In actuality, the meanings of words overlap and carry emotional connotations; they may be provocative, biased, attitudinal, and complex. A statement of objectives cannot be structured and worded ignoring the fact that people of diverse backgrounds are involved. The statement must relate to those involved in terms of how they feel and what they think. To ignore this fact is to ignore the two-way communication that is necessary in obtaining commitment.

Advantages of Quantified Objectives

There are many advantages to quantifying objectives in the objective-setting process. First, quantified objectives define and clarify the elements of expected results better than any verbal description could. They provide a better configuration of what is expected. "To improve morale" is a motherhood and a verbalized expectancy, but "to improve morale by reducing the monthly number of grievances from 10 to 5" is a quantified objective and a specific target. A second advantage of quantified objectives is their built-in measurement of effectiveness. The measurement of progress toward an end result is difficult, if not impossible, with qualitative statements. Using a measurement to describe a future result also provides a way of measuring the activities that will make it happen. Management can see the relationships among data, resources, and skills needed to deal with different situations. Reduction of the number of grievances from 10 to 5 suggests the relationship of several skills and activities, such as handling people, knowing the labor contract, and being able to nip trouble in the bud.

A third advantage of quantified objectives is that they can be enlarged or reduced for progressive performance stretches. This is hardly possible with verbal descriptions. To improve morale by reducing the number of grievances from 10 to 5 for the first year implies a second-year effort to reduce the number perhaps from 5 to 3. Reducing costs 10 percent the first year suggests a further reduction in subsequent years. Quantification gives the statement an intrinsic manipulative value; that is, results can be manipulated as to both direction and the speed at which they are achieved.

A fourth advantage of quantified objectives is that they offer a means of keeping unknowns and uncertainties at a given level. The quantitative feature helps visualize the effects the results will have on other areas. To reduce the number of grievances from 10 to 5 implies the need for a sharper and better level of supervision. If training is necessary, how much will it cost? When can it be conducted? What will the program consist of? Quantitative statements tend to make unknowns more knowable.

A fifth advantage of quantified objectives is that quality and value can be incorporated in them. The argument that measurable objectives prevent individual judgment about value, priority, and subjective criteria does not hold. Payoff for the individual or the company can be computed using a weighted factor with respect to value and other subjective criteria.

Example:

Objective 1 contributes eight times more to goal A than does objective 2, but both contribute equally to goal B. The contribution C of the two objectives to the two goals can be expressed as

$$C_{1A} = 8 \qquad C_{1B} = 5$$
$$C_{2A} = 1 \qquad C_{2B} = 5$$

The value V of each objective is the sum of the products of the contributions and value of the respective goals (G).
The value of objective 1 is

$$V_1 = C_{1A}G_A + C_{1B}G_B$$
$$V_1 = (8)(5) + (5)(1) = 45$$

The value for objective 2 is

$$V_2 = C_{2A}G_A + C_{2B}G_B$$
$$V_2 = (1)(5) + (5)(1) = 10$$

The accomplishment of objective 1 is thus 4.5 times more valuable to the organization than is the accomplishment of objective 2. Thus subjective value can be included into an objective appraisal with weighted factors.

When quantification of the objective is not possible, activity indices can and should be used to give confidence and high probability that desired results will be reached. These activity indices should be used with care, however, vague and irrelevant statements being avoided. These indices are a type of yardstick for measuring results of an objective; however, meaningful application of this technique is challenging. More will be said on quantifying objectives in Chapter 8 on productivity.

The quantification of objectives also has limitations and disadvantages. Numbers are tricky. They may suggest a precision that does not exist, or they may oversimplify. Mathematics, statistics, and other quantifying techniques are not generally known by the average person. The liquidity ratio of current assets to current liabilities is an excellent quantified measure to use in an objective statement. This assumes, however, that everyone involved understands this measure, which often is not the case. Those who do not understand may regard the statement as impractical, or perhaps too theoretical. It may also be argued that quantification of human judgment is not possible. The mechanical procedure offered by numbers is no substitute for an intuitive, mature, and experiential decision. Experiential decision making should not be thrown out the window. Rather it should be complemented by numerical methods.

Another limitation is the impossibility of quantifying certain areas of behavior and leadership that are known to be critical. Such leadership qualities as sincerity, open-mindedness, character, impartiality, and tactfulness are important agents in achievement of results. It may be argued that behavioral and leadership skills are not results to be targeted but resources and activities necessary to reach results. Many supervisors, however, do target these qualities in their objectives/programs. In this case they are at best feeder objectives, and acquisition of the quality should be assessed with use of some type of performance indicator. For example, acquisition of a skill can be measured with before- and after-examination scores.

These limitations are significant but do not outweigh the advantages and benefits offered by objectives quantification. Statements of objectives must be formulated carefully with built-in measures.

Number of Objectives

The number of objectives to be pursued during a coming period varies from company to company, for several reasons. First, the scope of each company's objectives varies. A chemical company may set objectives for its profit centers and major departments for five years; a restaurant chain may set the same kind of objectives but limit the time to one year. The time required for accomplishment of a given set of results varies among companies because the importance of the results varies.

Second, the nature of the job varies from company to company. Different product lines, types of markets, available resources, and company size cause corresponding differences in the number and type of responsibilities the chief executive, functional staff, managers, and supervisors must manage within their organization. The president of a business that employs 500 has a job somewhat different from the president of a company that employs 40,000. A company that deals in defense products has a different set of responsibilities from one that deals in consumer goods. Finally, the importance of achieving the objective varies from company to company. Most companies will agree that there are seven key result areas for which objectives should be specified:

1. Profitability and growth.
2. Market position and penetration.
3. Productivity.

4. Product leadership.
5. Employee morale, development, and attitudes.
6. Physical and financial resources.
7. Public responsibility.

Few companies will agree on the importance attached to each of the key areas within a given period of time. A pharmaceutical firm that has polluted a river for ten years and is now concerned with possible litigation from the government and the community will place a greater emphasis on public responsibility within the next few years. A trucking firm that has experienced wildcat strikes and excessive labor grievances will give greater weight to improving employee attitudes, morale, and satisfaction. A small tool manufacturer that has experienced a decline in defense contracts must give a great deal of attention to market position and product leadership. The number of objectives to be pursued will be unique to each company because each business differs in the type and number of improvements that must be made within a period of time.

Some MBO practices have suggested the following rule to determine a proper number of objectives: No position should have more than five objectives; departments should have no more than six and major functions no more than eight. The beginning practitioner of MBO tends to adopt a great number of objectives, thus violating the MBO rule of crawling before walking and walking before running. Working toward too many only dilutes effort by spreading resources too thin. The number of objectives selected should be kept small but significant in terms of results for the enterprise and the individual.

Sample Objectives That Are Measurable

This section provides sample objectives for an entire organization. These objectives are developed singly or jointly for interlocking and coordination. It also provides sample functional objectives. The functions are finance, marketing, research and engineering, production, and personnel.

1. *Objectives for Overall Organization.*
    (a) Achieve a 15 percent return on investment within four operating quarters.
    (b) Reduce cost during the current operating year 24 percent of approved budgets, prorated 6 percent per quarter.
    (c) Maintain a current asset/current debt ratio of not less than 3.0 for the next fiscal year.
    (d) Achieve a net profit average of at least 7 percent of sales and 11 percent of net worth.

    (e)   Increase market position for nondefense items from 15 percent to 30 percent; maintain market position for defense items at current levels.

    (f)   Achieve a product line mix in which 80 percent of sales is made by no more than 20 percent of R&D customers.

    (g)   Complete a management control reporting system of all operating divisions by April 1.

    (h)   Complete an operating and financial strategy statement for reaching objectives within two months for presentation to the Board of Directors at the May meeting.

    (i)   Obtain from research efforts two accepted improvements per month for ten consecutive months to raise sales of product K 15 percent.

    (j)   Reduce plant operating costs to $0.54/100 units produced by January 1.

    (k)   Develop technological capability to introduce two new products in market sector BB at end of three-year profit plan.

    (l)   Reduce capital expenditures, class B, from $350,000 to $150,000 during the coming biennial.

2. *Finance Objectives.*

    (a)   Reduce by two days the six-day time lag in preparation of division cost reduction reports using an agreed-on follow-through system.

    (b)   Achieve an average age of accounts receivable not to exceed 25 days.

    (c)   Restrict bad debt losses to less than 3 percent of reporting nondefense sales by end of first quarter.

    (d)   Improve margin by 15 percent with same revenues but 30 percent reduction in costs by end of year.

    (e)   Increase by 15 percent the working cash needed by the firm in each of three banks at the end of the year by holding inventory levels at 80 percent capacity.

    (f)   Complete training of three replacements for agreed-upon key positions in the accounting section by next June.

    (g)   Complete study and construct index of expense trends for all departments for the past five years and project anticipated expense of future at annual intervals. Set 10 percent reduction targets from these projected expense trends.

    (h)   Collect ten suggested cost-reduction ideas per month from each of six operating managers for months of July through December.

    (i)   Complete write-up and acceptance of company cost-reduction manual and distribute to all members of management within two months.

- (j) Install five suggestion boxes in five company locations to collect employee suggestions for cost reduction in job procedures.
- (k) Collect from six operating managers long-distance telephone call analyses and recommendations for control of number, type, and cost of calls by beginning of next quarter.
- (l) Reduce dollar value of cost of returned material credits from an average of $20,000/month in the preceding year to $15,000/month in the coming year.
- (m) Reduce current debt/tangible net worth position to 35 percent for proposed creditor portfolio.
- (n) Reduce fixed assets to a level not to exceed three quarters of tangible net worth in the next two years.
- (o) Improve profits/payroll margin from 5 percent to 10 percent within the next four profit-sharing quarters.

3. *Marketing Objectives.*
   - (a) Implement proposed system B for processing and expediting the filling of back orders at the rate of ten per month until 90 percent of back orders are filled. Reinstate system A when back-order level is reached.
   - (b) Increase sales revenues of a new product 15 percent within 12 months by concentrating existing expense levels of promotions in New England.
   - (c) Increase merchandise total turnover merchandise inventory in store from four to six within the current fiscal year.
   - (d) Hold sales expenses in the coming year to 5 percent of total sales while increasing sales manpower 10 percent.
   - (e) Secure 100 percent distribution in markets D, E, and F of district 3.
   - (f) Convince three wholesalers to introduce new merchandising under a prearranged monthly schedule.
   - (g) Increase occupancy ratio in hotel rooms from a yearly mean of 65 percent to 85 percent while maintaining the rate structure.
   - (h) Complete training program A for all district representatives to assure their readiness to distribute product Y at the first of the year.
   - (i) Reduce average handling time of customer statements by 10 percent.
   - (j) Complete painting of ten trucks with new advertising campaign within one month.
   - (k) Complete 75 percent of follow-up calls to new inquiries within three days of initial inquiry.
   - (l) Reduce number of customer complaints on commercial business from 22 percent to 10 percent of orders billed. Dollars of

settlement should not exceed 5 percent of total commercial billing.

(m) Improve sales per employee to $25,000 during the next five-year profit plan.

(n) Change percentage of sales to consumer, industry, and government from 20, 28, and 52 percent to 30, 35, and 35 percent, respectively.

(o) Complete a strategy statement within three months for giving two new segments of the market, brand X to be introduced next season.

4. *Research and Engineering Objectives.*

(a) Decrease research effort ratio of feasible marketing ideas to actual marketing products from 10 to 5 within the coming fiscal year.

(b) Complete design and development of a new prototype in 14 months within a cost of $140,000 without farm-out work to vendors.

(c) Complete product design specification for product M within the budgetary period.

(d) Supply three new products to marketing within the coming fiscal year with forecasted sales of not less than $1.5 million.

(e) Get approval from three departments of production, plans for customer, costs, and schedule within three months.

(f) Complete PERT layout for contract B within the prebudgetary planning schedule.

(g) Complete value analysis job plan for three engineering sections during operating quarter.

(h) Increase diversification program with development and introduction of five new products within the small-product line.

(i) Complete literature and patent search by end of year for five patentable ideas useful in entering new markets K, L, and M.

(j) Reduce research investment payout time from three to two years.

(k) Improve research know-how in section B by increasing Ph.D hires by 20 percent.

(l) Reduce the R&D budget as percent of net sales from 4.5 to 3.5 in the next five-year profit plan while maintaining services and new product development.

(m) Maintain lead competitor's position in market with four new product introductions in the next five-year profit plan.

5. *Production Objectives.*

(a) Reduce frequency of lost-time injuries from 21 million to 6 million man-hours within six months of installation of new safety awareness program.

(b) Maintain overtime hours at the level of 5 percent of scheduled hours while completing emergency work program A.

(c) Reduce cost of pump and engineer repairs from $10,000/year/mechanic to $5,000/year/mechanic.

(d) Maintain once-a-day contact with all subordinates at their work stations and hold a once-a-month work appraisal meeting in office with all subordinates.

(e) Complete construction of 5000-square-foot two-story approved addition to existing plan within cost of $5000 by spring of next year.

(f) Master ten techniques in work simplification as related to machine shop operations through a six-month monthly cost-reduction meeting for machine-shop supervisors.

(g) Reduce clerical labor costs in three departments by $50,000 with the installation of a data processing system whose leasing and operational costs are not to exceed 50 percent of the projected savings.

(h) Reduce weld rejects of Hy-80 steels from 6 percent to 3 percent of all plates in assembly S.

(i) Maintain total heat losses at 5 percent of total heat transferred when changing from system A to system B.

(j) Deliver 16 units/day for less than $45.00/unit to shipping point B.

(k) Reduce inventory lead time from three weeks to two weeks while maintaining customer services.

(l) Reduce obsolete items and all adjustments to inventory to 6 percent of commercial sales dollars.

(m) Complete master schedule of sales and inventories for fiscal year 19XX to reduce stock-out frequency rate to $2\frac{1}{2}$.

(n) Complete by next year a vendor rating system to maintain price, delivery schedule, and reliability at or below an index established for the past five-year record.

(o) Achieve for the machine shop a process layout by 19XX to reduce material-handling costs to 22 percent of manufactured costs.

6. *Personnel Objectives.*

(a) Select five candidates in the third quartile from 25 trainees successfully completing supervisory training, these candidates to be temporarily appointed for six months at the new division.

(b) Reduce cost of recruiting each engineer from $450 to $250 while meeting requisition totals and dates.

(c)   Complete preparations for labor negotiations by apprising all management personnel of needed contract changes; hold bimonthly meetings for discussions and conduct two simulated labor bargaining sessions to gain insights on strategy.

(d)   At a cost not to exceed $15,000, conduct a sampling survey of the company's hiring image in three adjacent labor markets.

(e)   Complete for distribution at the end of month X a 20-page ten-topic industrial-relations policy manual for newly hired employees.

(f)   Decrease termination rate of clerical employees from 25 percent to 15 percent.

(g)   Increase outside correspondence answered from 25 percent to 75 percent within 24 hours.

(h)   Read 12 new books in management by the end of a year at the rate of one per month.

(i)   Complete a course in statistics within the next semester with a grade of B or better.

(j)   Set up and validate five standards of qualifications for new hourly employees.

(k)   Complete within three months an attitude survey of labor-management relations among all employees within a cost of $1800.

(l)   Reduce frequency of grievances by the end of the year from an annual average of 35 to 20.

(m)   Complete planning, organization, and installation of an employee suggestion system at the start of next year's cost-reduction program.

(n)   Complete training by December 19XX of 600 supervisors in two-day seminars on managing by objectives.

(o)   Reduce absenteeism record for next year from 8 percent to 5 percent.

ACTION PLANS AND RESULTS

Results are the outcome or consequence of proceeding with selected goals and objectives. Results are the end or product of a process or plan. From a managerial standpoint, they are the desired condition to be created in the enterprise whether they be increased profits, improved productivity, greater sales, higher quality products, or improved morale. Translation of objectives into results requires an action plan, that is, a program of activities and efforts that will implement objectives. How simple or complex the action plan will be is determined by the simplicity or complexity of the objectives. In either event, action plans bridge objectives and results. Action plans unite established and agreed-on objectives with pursued results and final results.

Action plans give directions for the myriad steps that must be taken by members of management and various departments. They lay out a route, almost like a map, that must be followed to ensure accomplishment of the objective. To find the correct or most efficient route, several may have to be considered. Evaluation and judgment are very important here, since a poor or ineffective action plan can fault or frustrate accomplishment of objectives. In fact, my experience is that failures to reach objectives results more often from faulty action plans than from faulty objectives. An action plan is the means through which two distinct processes are unified—establishment of objectives and pursuit of objectives. The action plan gives a clear understanding to both manager and employee of what must be done to achieve the agreed-on objective. It also gives understanding and allows agreement among managers, as it links managers both vertically and horizontally. This organizational linking of managers is accomplished first through setting of objectives and later through individual action plans. A good action plan shows what the employee will do, what the manager will do, and the role that other managers will have in the plan. This sharing of individual plans and communicating what each person will be doing enhances the validity of the overall plan and makes clear the need for joint efforts. Managers do a good job of sharing with one another what objectives they are trying to achieve, but they fall short on informing others where interaction is needed as the activity of the action plan progresses.

Several later chapters in this book deal with the development of action plans and the validation of these plans in detail to suit the objectives to be pursued. Here only a series of steps with selected criteria are given to show what is needed to lay out an action plan for an objective.

STEP 1.   Consider results in an objective as a target.   Having clear targets tends to generate an effective action plan strategy. The action plan becomes an objective-seeking plan as a form of self-fulfillment. Targeting suggests the needed behavior toward the predetermined objectives. Targets that are objectives or objectives broken down and assigned to each member of the team must be visible to all members. This visibility creates the mental processes needed to generate elements of an action plan strategy.

STEP 2.   Identify assumptions in the situation of the action plan.   An assumption is defined as the best estimate of the impact that external or internal factors may have on the ability to complete a plan and get desired results. Assumptions make the action plan possible and realistic. The formulation of assumptions through fact finding and analysis means identifying events, people, decisions, and equipment that most likely will affect the plan. The assumptions are recorded and continuously tracked for validity. A good approach to setting up assumptions is to identify the forces that will aid the completion of an objective and the forces that will delay or defeat its completion.

STEP 3.   Lay out and sequence required activities into work packages. This involves the laying out and sequencing into a program of the work processes, methods, techniques, procedures, equipment, facilities, manpower, skills, and other resources that are needed for reaching an objective. This is programming—formulating two or more steps or actions into a program sequence that, when followed, will lead to completion of an objective. These steps or phases should be sufficiently detailed into workable units or work packages to be delegated to others. In a later chapter, work break-down structure and work packages are described in detail as units in an action plan. Suffice it to say here that the work to be done should be broken down and subdivided until it reaches a task level that can be performed by departments or individual workers. Two or more work packages that require similar types of effort should be grouped together to conserve resources and gain accountability from one source.

STEP 4.   Set up action plan schedule.   Work packages or work units in steps should be assigned according to time sequence and priority. Time sequencing is the arrangement of starting and ending times for each unit as the units relate to each other. Prioritizing is the recognition of which units are critical in the sequence and which require special focus and attention. More will be said about scheduling in the chapter on time scheduling. Here it should be emphasized that no matter how complex the work packages, the sequencing, and the timing, a clear path must be laid out that shows how an objective will be accomplished at a prescribed period of time.

STEP 5.   Gain agreement and support.   Elements of an action plan often relate to other departments and managers whose support and cooperation are vital to the success of the plan. This relationship requires conferring with these other managers and departments for agreement, collaboration, and support when needed. How much support and cooperation are needed depend on the objective. Some objectives require very little, some a great deal. The "political" overtones, both internal and external, should not be overlooked in programming action plans, for every plan will have allies and opponents.

STEP 6.   Identify and develop contingencies to the action plan.   Every plan has its obstacles, obstacles that will prevent achievement of objectives despite all efforts. Since obstacles are inevitable, they must be sought and identified. Finally, contingency actions to deal with these obstacles must be devised.

SUMMARY

Every mission or goal is an urge to move in a certain direction. Every objective formed and committed to by a manager is a prediction for results to be accomplished in the same direction. Mission and goals are two pieces of the same pie. When written they define what the nature of the business is and in what direction it is moving. To choose goals wisely one must understand the pressures or concerns the firm is experiencing and the options or alternatives that are available to the firm. MBO leadership is knowing these concerns and pressures and getting others to select alternatives that meet them while satisfying individual goals. Many principles help in selecting, defining, and committing an organization to goals. This chapter identifies 25 of them. Sample goals from seven major areas of human effort and institutions are given. These major areas are (1) business, (2) government, (3) health care, (4) education, (5) religion, (6) society, and (7) individuals. Sample goals of typical organizations in the United States were also included in this chapter.

How goals were made to work through measurement is also a subject of this chapter. Objectives arise from goals that have been made measurable. Many managers state objectives in general expressions, termed "motherhoods." Motherhoods lack specificity for evaluating and appraising what was accomplished. Building in performance indicators in objective statements allows managerial practitioners to see clearly what is expected of them. A comprehensive list of performance indicators or yardsticks is given in this chapter along with how they bridge goals and objectives.

The process of formulating and writing an objective is an important one. The practitioner must clearly know the key areas of responsibilities that will help the firm move in the direction specified in its mission. Nine objective-setting guidelines seem to constitute the backbone of the MBO goal-setting process. Since participation in the goal-setting process is important, five subordinate involvement practices are also identified here. Ten major guidelines are given for writing objectives effectively. They are summarized as follows:

1. Objectives must be specific and verifiable.
2. Objectives must achieve single-ended results.
3. Objectives must be set against deadlines.
4. Objectives must be attainable.
5. Objectives must be opportunistic.
6. Objectives must stimulate the motivation of those who will achieve them.
7. Objectives must be supportable by the organization.
8. Objectives must be controllable.
9. Objectives must have assigned accountability.
10. Objectives must be evaluative.

Finally, sample objectives were included in the areas of the overall organization, finance, marketing, production, and personnel.

BIBLIOGRAPHY

Carroll, Stephen, Jr., and Tosi, Henry L., *Management By Objectives*. New York: Macmillan, 1974.

Drucker, Peter F., *Management: Tasks · Responsibilities · Practices*. New York: Harper & Row, 1973.

Follett, Robert, *How To Keep Score in Business*. Chicago: Follett, 1978.

Hughes, Charles L., *Goal Setting*. New York: American Management Association, 1965.

Mali, Paul, *Managing By Objectives*. New York: Wiley, 1972.

McConkie, Mark L., "A Clarification of the Goal-Setting and Appraisal Processes in MBO." *Academy of Management Review*, January 1979, pp. 29–40.

President's Commission on National Goals, *Goals for Americans*. Englewood Cliffs, NJ: Prentice-Hall, 1960.

5

MBO STRATEGIES

IN THIS CHAPTER

STRATEGIES OF MBO PRACTICES
GENERAL MBO
INDIVIDUAL MBO
SUPERVISORY MBO
GROUP MBO
ORGANIZATION MBO

MBO practitioners vary on how they use MBO in their life-style and in their company. Any comparison of practitioners reveals a wide spectrum of differences. Each has taken the MBO concepts and principles and adapted them uniquely for personal and company purposes. Roy Gentiles, president and chief executive officer of Alcan Aluminum Corporation, calls his MBO program an "integrated communications system for managing." It really is a modified MBO process. This program is described in detail in Chapter 18 on case histories.

Five MBO strategies seem to be the most commonly used. This chapter identifies and clarifies these strategies. Each has been reduced to its essential elements. Even the examples that illustrate the strategies are simple, perhaps even simplistic. The strategies have been broken down into steps to provide for clearer understanding and ease of implementation for readers. I have found that most management personnel suffer from the inability to make things work rather than from ignorance of how things work. Like the famous expression of old, "In theory we can, in practice we don't." Paper solutions are easy. Making them work is a formidable task. Describing the strategies in steps helps intuitive grasp of the implementation process. The steps are not a rigid procedure to be followed, but rather a general roadway from start to finish. The practitioner will make whatever adjustments are needed to fit his or her unique situation.

STRATEGIES OF MBO PRACTICES

The development and use of strategies is essentially an art. It is very similar to the art of leadership. Elements that make a leader are unique to the person and the situation. The strategist also has a unique and artful approach to strategies. The five most common MBO strategies practiced by companies, and their fundamental principles, are as follows:

Strategy	Fundamental Principle
General MBO	Manager sets up planning procedure in series of time phases for getting results expected of him or her and the unit.
Individual MBO	Individual identifies major areas of responsibilities, sets results in that context, and joins them with objectives or expectations to be achieved by the company in a coming period.
Supervisory MBO	Supervisor and subordinate jointly identify common objectives to be achieved in a coming period.
Group MBO	Members of an existing team, through interaction and participation, collaborate in concerns and develop common objectives to be achieved in a coming period.
Organization MBO	All management personnel of the organization, through a process of participation, iteration, and optimization by levels, collaboratively arrive at common objectives to be achieved in a coming period.

These strategies can be varied to fit MBO into unique and changing situations of the firm. Each strategy will carry different amounts and degrees of effectiveness and efficiency for the firm that adopts it. The relationship between collaboration and commitment to results and achievement of results is shown in Figure 5.1. In spite of the many strategies that prevail due to changes in consumers, products, markets, services, technology, trends, competition, and values, some common elements emerge. It is these common elements that shape the future direction and nature of the enterprise or department depending on where the strategy is applied. Strategy here is not intended to mean the long-range effect of complex factors on the business. Rather, strategy means the pattern or mix of managerial elements brought together for achieving goals or objectives needed within a period of time

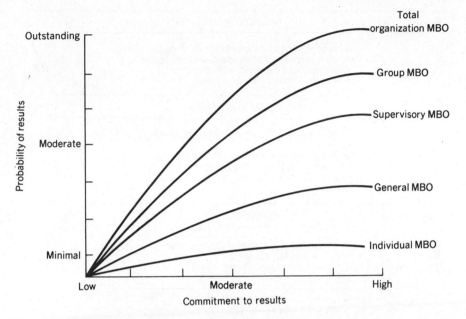

FIGURE 5.1   Relation of collaboration and commitment to results.

with a given situation. In this context, strategy is concerned with visualizing in the most simplified form, the complexities of the real world while considering the conflicts and problems which emerge in the process. MBO strategies are a visual perception of the way of setting a managerial roadway to get to a point of accomplishment. The five most powerful elements common to most strategies are shown in Figure 5.2 and are described in greater detail in this and other chapters of the book.

GENERAL MBO

Everyone plans. That is, everyone looks ahead to some future time and determines what is to be done and how to do it. Most planning, however, is informal, within the mind, and lacks commitment. In many ways, informal planning defines the casual performer. There is need to make planning deliberate. General MBO serves this need. It is based on the following principle:

> *General MBO is a process whereby a manager sets up a planning procedure in a series of time phases for joining the results expected of him or her and the unit with the total results expected of the firm.*

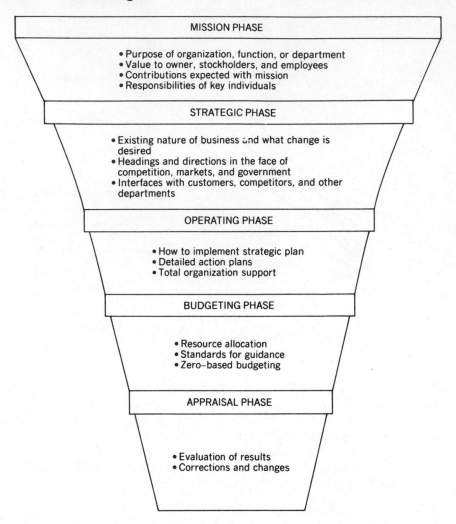

FIGURE 5.2   Common elements in MBO strategy.

General MBO is used for several reasons:

1.   To make planning thought formal and deliberate.   This means making planning thought a formal process by writing it down, sharing it with others, referring to it frequently, reviewing it often for guidance and direction, and having a perspective of what should be completed and when.

2.   To achieve large results through small steps or phases.   Large accomplishments are broken down into smaller phases. These phases are executed in a certain order. The phases are additive and integrative. When all phases are completed, the large accomplishment is completed.

3.   To gauge results in a time perspective.   The calendar or schedule has the unique ability of signaling practitioners when certain features of a plan should be started and when other features should be completed. A completed plan generates many signals which give the practitioner the direction to take and the decision to be made.

4.   To give clarity to many parts that must be connected.   A plan is a future accomplishment. But it has an overall perspective, in which people, resources, materials, and methods are pulled together for the overall results. Omissions or duplications are spotted with an overall plan.

Six Steps in the General MBO Process

The six steps in the general MBO process are demonstrated in Figure 5.3 and discussed here.

1.   *Situation Analysis (Where Are We Now?).*   Past and present events are analyzed to estimate the likelihood of their future recurrence. Analysis indicates the type of event that may occur if past and present trends are diminishing. This step identifies developing issues and problems that need change, correction, or managing.

2.   *Improvement Analysis (Why We Ought to Change).*   Each issue is analyzed to determine the consequences of not dealing with it, correcting it, or managing it. This step forms the rationale of why we must eliminate the problems, grasp the new opportunities, and proceed with improvements.

3.   *Setting Goals and Objectives (Where We Want to Go).*   Expectations that are to be achieved on a short- and long-term basis are established. Objectives are the end results of an organization, department, or group. Objectives indicate the events that will emerge in making the future.

4.   *Development of Operational Plans (How We Get There).*   Operational plans are carefully thought-out specific plans of implementation. They arrange in sequence and priority the activities needed to accomplish an objective. These activities are the tasks and actions best suited and arranged for reaching end results. The time requirements for the activities indicated in programming are established. These time requirements are sequenced from start and stop baselines and signal the coordination and cooperation of large groups of people with resources and skills. Methods of performing work are agreed on and set down. These methods create a uniform way for everyone to reach in unison the set of expectations in the formalized objectives. The resources such as money, people, space, capacity, inventory, equipment, and time needed to reach a set of expectations are allocated. This budgeting in the planning process ensures that resources are not only available but stand ready for use in the plan.

5.   *Validation of Plans (Confidence That We Will Get There).*   The implementation of the plan is analyzed for potential problems. This analysis deliberately searches for where trouble may occur or how barriers may emerge to

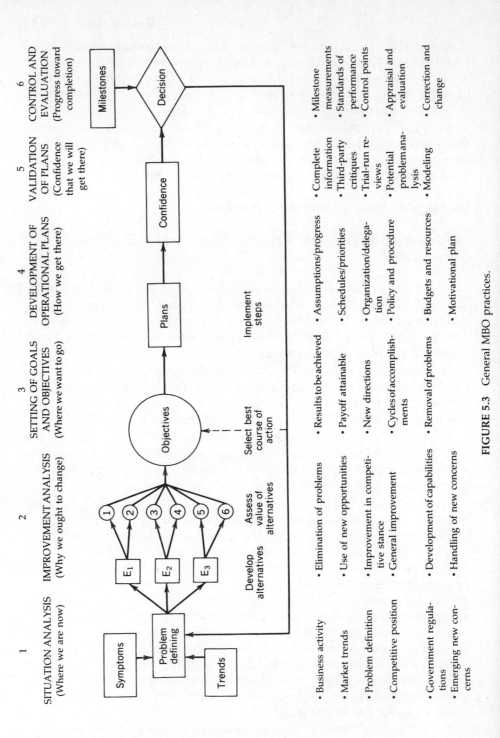

FIGURE 5.3 General MBO practices.

frustrate the plan. Analysis modifies the plan to circumvent barriers or eliminate trouble spots.

6. *Control and Evaluation (Progress Toward Completion).*   The purpose of control is to keep activities and efforts on a prescribed course. Managers keep themselves informed on progress being made by comparing actual progress with planned progress at control points. These control points are called milestones. This step establishes milestones for the appraisal of quantity, quality, time, costs, and progress.

Table 5.1 shows how the general MBO process is used.

INDIVIDUAL MBO

Not everyone does organizational planning. Many do individual planning, because organizational constraints or colleagues and managers who don't want to be involved preclude organizational planning. Not all organizations are convinced of the usefulness of MBO. Often individuals make personal plans for organizing and completing their work. Individual MBO serves the need for individual planning. It is based on the following principle:

> *Individual MBO is a process whereby an individual identifies major areas of responsibilities, sets results in that context, and joins them with objectives or expectations to be achieved by the company in a coming period.*

There are several reasons for use of individual MBO.

1. *To Provide a Focus on High-Payoff Responsibilities.*   Conscientious managers tend to do everything that is demanded of them. As a result, they dilute their efforts. Individual MBO helps managers separate high-payoff concerns from low-payoff concerns.

2. *To Provide a Personalized System for Self-Motivation.*   People who have bosses able to motivate them are most fortunate. What about those who do not? Self-motivation is one answer. Individual MBO provides a personalized system that generates self-motivation for the individual who practices it.

3. *To Better Control Time.*   Poor time management with shifting priorities causes response to urgent demands rather than to important demands. Individual MBO provides control over allocation of time over a wide range of varying expectations.

4. *To Encourage an Individualized Life-Style.*   MBO has far-reaching value, especially outside the firm. Its basic concepts and practices can be applied in a variety of circumstances in responsibilities or expectations outside the planning process of an enterprise. Individual MBO can be used in the family, church, recreation, and neighborhood projects, among others.

TABLE 5.1 Use of General MBO Process in Engineering Department With Low Product Development

Step 1: Situation Analysis (Where We Are Now)	Step 2: Improvement Analysis (Why We Ought to Change)	Step 3: Setting of Goals and Objectives (Where We Want to Go)	Step 4: Development of Operational Plans (How We Get There)	Step 5: Validation of Plans (Confidence We Will Get There)	Step 6: Control and Evaluation (Progress Toward Completion)
Competition formidable Long-term projects never completed Excessive plan errors Insufficient product development Excessive engineering turnover	Long-term projects basis of future survival and growth of company Competition stiffening from overseas	Offer ten new products or product improvements to marketing for adoption within next five years	Set up project management Create closer liaison with customers and Institute PERT[a] system Set up six-month productivity measures and standards	Staff validation meeting Six-month trial review Potential problem analysis every three months for for one year	Monthly staff meetings Reports from customer visits PERT system operation Two new products per year

[a] PERT, an acronym that suggests a time control procedure. The letters represent Program Evaluation Review Technique.

5. *To Unfold the Stored Potential Within a Human Being.*   Mediocrity is practiced primarily by individuals. Mediocrity is not unacceptable performance but rather performance of low quality. Performance improves when potential is unfolded. There is need to unfold the human potential. Individual MBO provides for an opportunity for individuals to stretch their performance. When practiced over a long period of time with annual cycles, it helps the person experience significant growth because potential is continuously released.

6. *To Encourage High Risk Taking for High-Payoff Opportunities.*   Taking high risks for low payoff should be avoided. A process is needed to separate high payoff from low payoff. Individual MBO gives some direction for the amount of risk taking that is worthwhile.

Eight Steps in the Individual MBO Process

The eight steps in individual MBO are illustrated in Figure 5.4 and discussed here.

1. *Situation Analysis (What Must Be Done Now).*   Demands, problems, responsibilities, and expectations are analyzed. The analysis identifies the total demands a manager faces. Any attempt to handle all of them would result in dilution of effort.

2. *Payoff Analysis (Why I Ought to Concentrate).*   All of the demands placed on managers do not have equal or high payoff. In fact, most demands have low payoff. Managers must analyze each demand to see if it presents a new opportunity, a problem solution, or great value. They must arrange demands from high payoff to low payoff.

3. *Focusing of Effort (Which Demands Have Highest Payoff?).*   In this step, high-payoff demands are selected for concentration. Trivial demands must be dropped or postponed for another time. This step requires application of the Pareto rule, that is, pursuit of 20% of high-payoff demands.

4. *Setting of Goals and Objectives (Where I Want to Go).*   High-payoff items are written up as objectives to be completed on a short-term or long-term basis. Objectives are formally written in statements for review and evaluation.

5. *Stretching of Performance (How I Stretch Performance).*   Many of today's leading behavioral scientists believe that the average individual functions at not more than 10 to 20 percent of latent potential. A 5 to 15 percent performance stretch within each objective statement would help unfold this inherent potential. In this step the manager reaches for the highest payoff possible by stretching results.

6. *Development of Operational Plans (How I Get There).*   Operational plans are carefully thought-out specific plans of implementation that arrange in sequence and priority the activities needed to accomplish an objective. These activities are the tasks or actions best suited for reaching results.

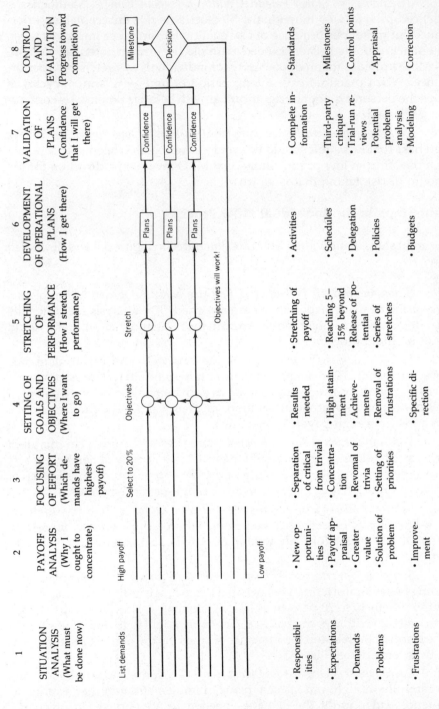

FIGURE 5.4 Individual MBO process.

1	2	3	4	5	6	7	8
SITUATION ANALYSIS (What must be done now)	PAYOFF ANALYSIS (Why I ought to concentrate)	FOCUSING OF EFFORT (Which demands have highest payoff)	SETTING OF GOALS AND OBJECTIVES (Where I want to go)	STRETCHING OF PERFORMANCE (How I stretch performance)	DEVELOPMENT OF OPERATIONAL PLANS (How I get there)	VALIDATION OF PLANS (Confidence that I will get there)	CONTROL AND EVALUATION (Progress toward completion)

List demands

High payoff

Low payoff

Select to 20%

Objectives

Stretch

Objectives will work!

Milestone

Decision

Plans Plans Plans

Confidence Confidence Confidence

- Responsibilities
- Expectations
- Demands
- Problems
- Frustrations

- New opportunities
- Payoff appraisal
- Greater value
- Solution of problem
- Improvement

- Separation of critical from trivial
- Concentration
- Removal of trivia
- Setting of priorities

- Results needed
- High attainment
- Achievements
- Removal of frustrations
- Specific direction

- Stretching of payoff
- Reaching 5–15% beyond
- Release of potential
- Series of stretches

- Activities
- Schedules
- Delegation
- Policies
- Budgets

- Complete information
- Third-party critique
- Trial-run reviews
- Potential problem analysis
- Modeling

- Standards
- Milestones
- Control points
- Appraisal
- Correction

Operational plans also establish the time requirements for the tasks to be completed. Time baselines signal start, stop, and coordination. This step requires that every objective have a supporting plan.

7. *Validation of Plans (Confidence That I Will Get There).* Problems will always emerge in the implementation of a plan. No one can foresee exactly the trouble spots or the barriers that may emerge to frustrate a plan. This step allows for analysis of potential trouble spots. If problems are revealed, plans are modified to circumvent or solve the problems.

8. *Control and Evaluation (Progress Toward Completion).* Control keeps activities and efforts on a prescribed course. Managers inform themselves about progress by comparing actual accomplishments with planned accomplishments at control points. These control points are called milestones. In this step, milestones are established for the appraisal of quantity, quality, time, costs, and progress.

Table 5.2 illustrates how the individual MBO process is used.

SUPERVISORY MBO

The lowest level of collaborative planning is between a manager and one subordinate. This is the lowest level of teamwork, since the smallest team consists of at least two members. When a manager comes together with a subordinate to set objectives, the two really are forming a team. Even this smallest form of teamwork must have direction and purpose. Supervisory MBO serves this need. It is based on the following principle:

> *Supervisory MBO is a process whereby supervisor and subordinate jointly identify common objectives to be achieved in a coming period.*

There are several reasons for use of supervisory MBO.

1. *To Allow for Participation in the Commitment Process.* The word "commitment" suggests a pledge or dedication in any kind of pursuit. When two people collaborate and participate, each influencing what the pursuit shall be, the emerging commitment involves both. Supervisory MBO allows a subordinate to participate with his or her supervisor in the formation of objectives and in the locations of implementation. Because of this participation and formation, both feel committed to expected results.

2. *To Clarify Communications Between Supervisor and Subordinate.* Too often a subordinate engages in and completes work that he or she thinks is expected by the supervisor, only to discover the supervisor expected something else. Supervisory MBO is a communication process. Agreed-on directions and operating plans are put in writing so that subordinates can refer to and review them.

TABLE 5.2   Use of Individual MBO Process by Salesperson

Step 1: Situation Analysis (What Must Be Done Now)	Step 2: Payoff Analysis (Why I Ought To Concentrate)	Step 3: Focusing of Effort (Which Demands Have Highest Payoff?)	Step 4: Setting of Goals and Objectives (Where I Want to Go)	Step 5: Stretching of Performance (How I Stretch Performance)	Step 6: Development of Operational Plans (How I Get There)	Step 7: Validation of Plans (Confidence That I Will Get There)	Step 8: Control and Evaluation (Progress Toward Completion)
Attend meetings	Increase sales	Increase sales	Increase sales to 15M by Jan. 1	Increase sales to 16M by Jan. 1	Develop new brochure	Present plan at sales meeting	Attain sales of $4000/quarter
Write reports	Handle complaints	Handle complaints	Reduce customer complaints from ten to six per month	Reduce customer complaints from ten to five per month	Add new product feature	Try out plan in one area	Eliminate five complaints per month
Increase sales	Penetrate new areas	Penetrate new areas	Sell to five new clients in three new areas by July 1	Sell to six new clients in three new areas by July 1	Follow up plan	Make potential problem analysis with sales group	Add two clients per month
Handle complaints	Write reports				Improve Q/C at shipping		
Remove old items	Attend meetings				Call customers at receipt		
Assist others	Assist others				Use substitute plan		
Develop new form	Develop new form				Analyze competition		
Attend seminars	Attend seminars				Telephone plan		
Penetrate new areas	Remove old items				New package promotion		
	Review file						

3. *To Set up a Basis for Performance Evaluation.* All supervisors have the responsibility of evaluating the performance of their subordinates. Traditionally this evaluation has been fraught with problems, such as misunderstanding of what is expected, disappointment in the turn out of results, and disruption with changing priorities. Supervisory MBO clarifies at the beginning of a time period what is expected and to what extent; it builds in priorities to be followed.

4. *To Motivate Individuals for Higher Levels of Performance.* Supervisors can take one of two general approaches to motivating employees. One is to assign work, stand back and look at the total situation, and then determine how best to motivate the people to do the work within the situation. A second approach is to build into the work motivators based on the situation and the work and then to assign the work to people. In the second approach, it is the work that motivates. Supervisory MBO allows motivators to be built into objectives and the locations of implementation.

5. *To Collaborate for Greater Results.* MBO is a results-oriented way of managing. Getting results is its main thrust. Results can be obtained in several ways. The greater the working collaboration and commitment, the more likely the desired results will occur. Collaboration facilitates communication, clarifies expectations, and brings closer coordination. This in turn strengthens the smallest team in an organization, the supervisor and his or her subordinate.

6. *To Minimize Disparity between Boss and Subordinate.* Employees work primarily for themselves and only secondarily for their employer. Their desires and personal needs do not usually fall within the framework of company needs. An employee goes to work for a company with a set of expectations that may or may not coincide with the set of expectations the company has for this employee. Usually a disparity exists between the two. The wider the disparity, the more minimal the results. The smaller the disparity, the more maximal the results (Figure 5.5).

Five Steps in the Supervisory MBO Process

The five steps in supervisory MBO are illustrated in Figure 5.6 and discussed here.

1. *Collaboration of Supervisor and Subordinate (What Must Be Done and Why).* Supervisor and subordinate mutually analyze demands, the situation, and their responsibilities and determine what must be done and why. This step establishes the organization's expectations. Both a general and a specific assessment is made of the situation to uncover problems and opportunities. This occurs at a formal and deliberate meeting and interview, not a cursory happenstance meeting. The supervisor and subordinate's collaboration may take anywhere from four hours to three days. Guidelines from the organization are formalized by both.

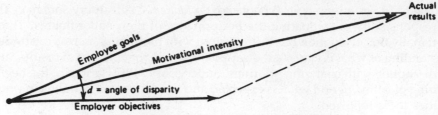

Case I: close alignment; high results; strong motivation

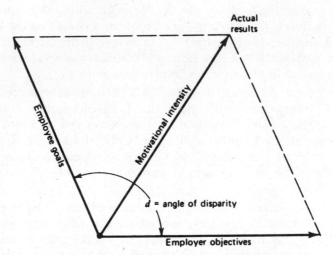

Case II: wide alignment; moderate results; moderate motivation

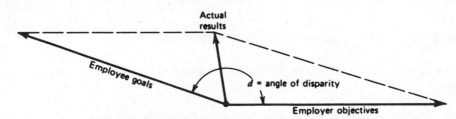

Case III: very wide alignment; poor results; weak motivation

FIGURE 5.5 Motivational intensity caused by employer and employee disparity.

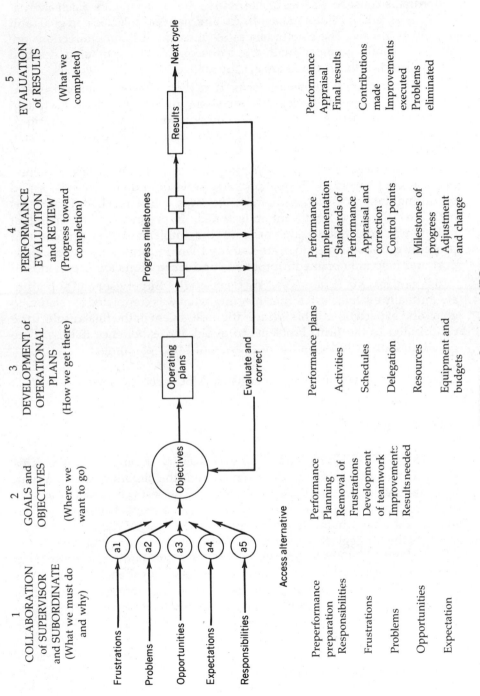

FIGURE 5.6 Supervisory MBO process.

153

2. *Setting of Goals and Objectives (Where We Want to Go).*   Supervisor and subordinate consider a series of alternative directions to take. Each alternative is assessed for value and payoff. An alternative is selected and goals and objectives are set. The consequences of pursuing the same directions are discussed and compared with the consequences of pursuing selected alternative directions. Goals are set mutually.

3. *Development of Operational Plans (How We Get There).*   Supervisor and subordinate together develop specific steps toward objectives. Each step constitutes an action item for implementation. Schedules, priorities, resources, preparations, equipment, and budgets are organized for reaching objectives.

4. *Performance and Evaluation (Progress Toward Completion).*   Action plans are implemented. Evaluation by supervisor and employee is carried on during the process to assure that objectives will be reached. Progress is noted by them at significant milestones. If progress is not noted at milestones, adjustments are made in the implementation process and procedure. Periodic meetings are held by them to ascertain progress. Support and help are obtained if problems and frustrations are experienced.

5. *Evaluation of Results (What We Completed).*   Supervisor and subordinate mutually evaluate in a formal meeting what was completed in relation to goals and expectations. This is a specific assessment of the final results to be contributed to the firm. Problems to avoid and experience that help are noted and are included in the next cycle of MBO planning.

Table 5.3 illustrates how the supervisory MBO process is used.

GROUP MBO

Some MBO practitioners tend to approach every situation with the same general management approach. Even though the situations are different, they employ the same approach consistently. The best way to handle a given situation, however, is to select a suitable specific strategy. Each situation has mixed and quite unique economic and social factors. When the situation changes the strategy should change. Some situations are best handled by one individual. Others are best managed by both supervisor and subordinate. There also comes a time when the group as a whole is best able to deal with the needs of a situation. Here the manager brings together his or her team, section, or department of individuals who have relevant responsibilities and interests. The emphasis is on the group as a work team, in contrast to individuals, and the group includes the "boss." Group members share what they perceive to be their responsibilities. Objectives are established on a group basis. New York City Transit illustrates the workings of group MBO. Its case history is given in Chapter 18.

TABLE 5.3 Use of Supervisory MBO Process

Step 1: Collaboration (What Must Be Done and Why)	Step 2: Setting of Goals and Objectives (Where We Want to Go)	Step 3: Development of Operational Plans (How We Get There)	Step 4: Performance and Evaluation (Progress Toward Completion)	Step 5: Evaluation of Results (What We Completed)
Schedule Slippage Backlog excessive High grievance rate Loss of key customers Turnover excessive High overhead	*Reduce Schedule Slippage* Alternatives Lengthen delivery dates Set up master schedule Add more personnel Objective Complete computerized master schedule to reduce slippage from three to 0 weeks by January 1	*Action Plan* Redesign flow process for PERT[a] schedule Computerize customer orders, in-process manufacturing, inventory, and delivery lead time Use traveler form for expediting	Redesign flow process by April 1 Set up computer system by September 1 Have traveler form completed by November 1	Schedule slippage reduced from two weeks to 0 weeks Quoted delivery dates to customers are met

[a]PERT, an acronym for a time control procedure. The letters represent Program Evaluation Review Technique.

Group MBO is based on the following principle:

> *Group MBO is a process whereby members of an existing team or group, through interaction and participation, collaboratively join together for concerns and develop common objectives to be achieved in a coming period.*

The Group MBO process is used for several reasons.

1. *To Solve Problems Collectively.*   Every manager is required to solve problems. The effectiveness and efficiency of problem solving are enhanced when several people or members of a group come together and apply skills needed for the solution. Group thinking in problem definition and alternatives is better than individual thinking. Additionally, the group needs to collaborate on both the solution to the problem and the goals and directions needed to leave behind the situation causing the problem. Collaboration can solve emerging problems on a continuing basis.

2. *To Build the Group into a Team.*   Very little can be expected from employees who say, "Don't ask me—I only work here." Obviously these employees have been left out. They don't know where they are or where they're going. A difficulty of other MBO strategies is that they strengthen individuals in their performance but frequently do not help much with teamwork, that is, to individuals contributing as members of a group. Group MBO balances the pursuit of a task and a set of results with cooperation with others. It ensures that all responsibilities are covered and that overlaps are minimized. It contributes to "esprit de corps" in a group or department.

3. *To Reallocate Limited Resources.*   Most groups have limited resources for accomplishing their goals. Often high-performing individuals complete a task or a goal with some resources to spare. Group MBO encourages the allocation of any extra resources to critical areas. Better resource allocation is possible with group participation.

4. *To Improve the Quality of Decision Making.*   It has often been said that 50 percent of the effort needed to arrive at a decision goes into defining what kind of decision is needed. Determining this has been known as the diagnosis of a situation. In group MBO, all members of the group participate in clearly determining the kind of decision to be made. This is far better than individuals doing it alone.

5. *To Resolve Conflicts.*   At the root of interpersonal conflict is frustration. Frustration can emerge when a person tries to satisfy a need or reach a goal. Too often the frustration is caused by other individuals striving to reach their own goals. Group MBO brings together individuals for the identification of these frustrations and determination of how conflicts can be kept to a minimum or eliminated entirely.

Six Steps in the Group MBO Process

The six steps in group MBO are illustrated in Figure 5.7 and discussed here.

1. *Gathering of Information and Conduct of Group Dialogue (What's Happening).* Information is collected prior to initiation of group work. All persons should be aware of the meeting objectives and its time limits. Problems are identified by supervisors, managers, and members of the group. New opportunities and new developments are collected for group discussion. Each member of the group is expected to participate in the identification of difficulties, frustrations, problems, or opportunities. Group members discuss what is happening and share pertinent information and thinking. Important ground rules are established regarding how issues and disagreements will be handled, to minimize misunderstanding and communication breakdown.

2. *Collaborative Diagnosis (Causes and Possible Alternatives).* Group participation begins, to diagnose the meaning of the information shared and disruptive difficulties. With "straight talk and honest behavioral reactions," group members communicate effectively and get to the heart of the causes of difficulties and frustrations. Jumping to quick answers or conclusions is discouraged. Disagreements among participants can actually help produce creative solutions. People who disagree should be viewed as sources of ideas and not as troublemakers. The person who wins an argument may not have the best solution. Group members identify the causes of difficulties and suggest alternative courses of action. Brainstorming is an ongoing process during this step. All responsibilities are identified and covered.

3. *Group Goal Setting (What Direction Should We Take?).* Alternatives that are reviewed, prioritized, and selected are stated as goals and objectives. These are constructed by group members. An objective-setting format or procedure collects the group's agreement as to goal statements, general time requirements, and resources to be used. Group participation and interaction center primarily on the goals but leave specifics to the fourth step of group MBO. Participants allow their ideas to fit the format, which permits documentation. The group may undergo a struggle in trying to get consensus on the statement of objectives. If all fails, the group votes, postpones decisions, or delegates to the boss. Once a goal or objective is decided on it is owned by the group and not the individual.

4. *Delegation of Team Member Responsibilities (How Work Will Be Done).* Team members identify responsibilities and support areas needed to accomplish the mission, the goals, and the objectives. Each team member, by delegation and assignment, develops specific plans for the role and responsibility for his or her contribution to the group's goals and objectives. Team members experiencing difficulties ask other members of the group for ideas, help, and support.

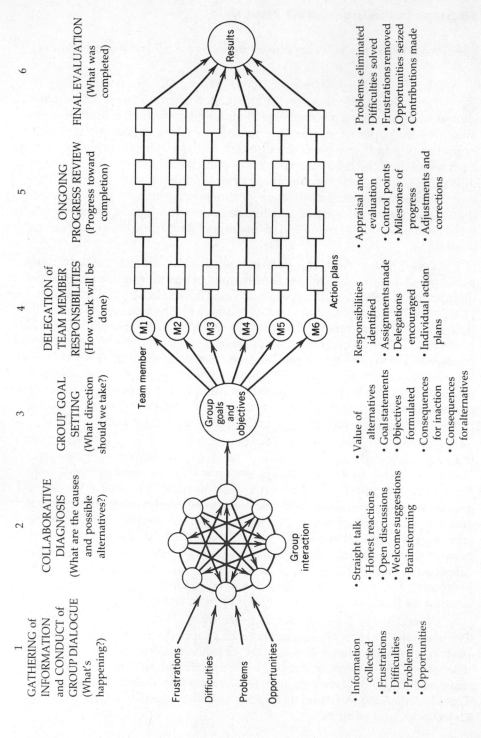

FIGURE 5.7 Group MBO process.

1	2	3	4	5	6
GATHERING of INFORMATION and CONDUCT of GROUP DIALOGUE (What's happening?)	COLLABORATIVE DIAGNOSIS (What are the causes and possible alternatives?)	GROUP GOAL SETTING (What direction should we take?)	DELEGATION of TEAM MEMBER RESPONSIBILITIES (How will work be done)	ONGOING PROGRESS REVIEW (Progress toward completion)	FINAL EVALUATION (What was completed)

Frustrations
Difficulties
Problems
Opportunities

Group interaction

Group goals and objectives

Team member

M1
M2
M3
M4
M5
M6

Action plans

Results

• Information collected
• Frustrations
• Difficulties
• Problems
• Opportunities

• Straight talk
• Honest reactions
• Open discussions
• Welcome suggestions
• Brainstorming

• Value of alternatives
• Goal statements
• Objectives formulated
• Consequences for inaction
• Consequences for alternatives

• Responsibilities identified
• Assignments made
• Delegations encouraged
• Individual action plans

• Appraisal and evaluation
• Control points
• Milestones of progress
• Adjustments and corrections

• Problems eliminated
• Difficulties solved
• Frustrations removed
• Opportunities seized
• Contributions made

5.   *Ongoing Progress Reviews (Progress Toward Completion).*   Group participants come together on a regular basis to evaluate their progress toward reaching goals. If they are solving problems, the progress sessions are intended to determine problem elimination. Group participants discuss effectiveness, efficiency, and productivity of the work conduct as agreed on.

6.   *Final Evaluation (What Was Completed).*   Group participants make final evaluations and appraisals with respect to the original frustrations, difficulties, problems, or opportunities that activated the group. They engage in dialogue to see how to extrapolate learning and results into the future or into other groups. This is sharing of information.

Tables 5.4 and 5.5 illustrate how group MBO is used.

ORGANIZATION MBO

The fifth and final strategy suggested is one in which all managers and supervisors in the organization are involved and expected to submit short- and long-range plans for their responsibilities. This strategy is the most productive of all the strategies, since it vitalizes and makes the entire organization work. Organization MBO is a systematic way of executing a series of decisions to arrive at a unified agreement in the organization. Lack of organization is much too common in business and government. Many are reluctant to admit it.

Organization MBO reaches for agreement among many people. It is a strategy for bringing "system" into the process of decision making. Organization MBO, itself, requires planning, since each organization must learn how this technique fits its needs and character. Planning is divided into two phases: strategic planning by top management and operational planning by lower levels of management, which supports and implements the strategic plan. Organization MBO is based on the following principle:

> *Organization MBO is a process whereby all managerial personnel of an organization, through a process of participation, iteration, and optimization by levels, collaboratively arrive at common objectives to be achieved in a coming period.*

There are several reasons for use of organization MBO.

1.   *To Get All Managers to go in the Same Direction.*   Organization MBO is an excellent way to get an entire organization aligned, unified, and heading in the same direction. Most organizations are disjointed, fragmented, and moving in different directions. This is a significant cause of organizational inefficiency. Nonalignment of managers on an organizationwide basis produces disunity. Organization MBO creates alignment and unity by both levels and periods of time. It creates a management system that supports

TABLE 5.4 Use of Group MBO Process in Public Works Department of a Local Government

Step 1: Gathering of Information and Conduct of Group Dialogue (What's Happening)	Step 2: Collaborative Diagnosis (Causes and Possible Alternatives)	Step 3: Group Goal Setting (What Direction Should We Take?)	Step 4: Delegation of Team Member Responsibilities (How Work Will Be Done)	Step 5: Ongoing Progress Review (Progress Toward Completion)	Step 6: Final Evaluation (What Was Completed)
Accidents increasing Many pothole complaints Icy streets hazardous Water pocket accumulation Dirt roads need completion Road markings need repainting	Budgets too tight Not enough personnel No system of priorities Lack of accountability in department	Complete MBO program with priorities and accountability by January 1 Organize maintenance schedule into preventive and emergency sections by March 1 Institute street improvement program by March 1	Program budget to be completed by assistant manager Maintenance schedule to be completed by foreman Street improvement program to be completed by street engineer	Program budget reviewed and approved by town manager, mayor, and town council Preventive maintenance completed in slack periods; emergency maintenance completed after storms 100% of street development completed in four years	Program budget operating Preventive and emergency maintenance completed when needed 25% street development completed per year

TABLE 5.5 Group Objectives and Budgets for Streets and Highways

MBO Program Budget Program Summary BF-8 New	Department of Public Works	Division of Highway	Activity Roadways	Account No. 311

Department/Division Mission Statement: *To maintain all town roads and water courses in a safe and efficient condition and to provide highway equipment and personnel to other town departments*

Program Title	Percent of Department Time	Program Resources				Total
		Personal Services	*Supplies, Service & Maintenance, Repairs*	*Grants & Contracts*	*Capital Outlay*	
Street maintenance To preserve and improve the safety of existing roads (safety engineer)	27	$ 80,927	$11,847	$ 49,809	—	$142,583
Street drainage To assure safe travel on roadways and reduce road maintenance (maintenance crew)	14	42,000	25,249	26,733	3,900	97,882
Street construction To promote development (planner)	9	25,991	1,849	15,500	—	43,340
Support services To supply equipment and manpower to other town agencies	19	56,525	1,849	—	540	58,914
Water courses To maintain and improve natural brooks and streams (maintenance crew)	6	15,981	6,849	—	—	22,830

TABLE 5.5 *(Continued)*

Program Title	Percent of Department Time	Personal Services	Supplies, Service & Maintenance, Repairs	Grants & Contracts	Capital Outlay	Total
			Program Resources			
Leaf removal To protect road drainage system and maintain safe travel (maintenance crew)	8	21,875	1,849	14,000	—	37,724
Street sweeping To preserve and enhance the attractiveness and safety of town roads (maintenance crew)	2	5,145	1,849	8,000	—	14,994
Refuse removal To collect street rubbish; Christmas trees; clean up, townwide by town council (garbage removers)	2	6,125	1,849	—	—	7,974
Storm control (Account 313) To make roads safe during and after storms (safety engineer)	9	25,994	—	20,770	—	46,764
Traffic control and information To install and maintain signs, signals, and road markings to assure safe travel (signal electrician)	4	11,500	20,959	—	—	32,459
Total	100%	$292,063	$74,149	$134,812	$4,440	$505,464

and responds to top management leadership directions. Long-range planning done at the top is termed "strategic planning," and implementation planning accomplished at lower levels is termed "operational planning."

2. *To Experience the "Quantum Jump" in Results.*   "Synergism" is a term that suggests the total is more than the sum of its parts. One plus one equals three is an example of synergism. For a company to experience synergism means that it is truly organized. Such organization is accomplished by the alignment and coordination of the objectives of the managers. Effective coordination of expected results and efficient coordination of resource uses bring about synergism. Organization MBO makes this coordination work.

3. *To Better Manage Complexities.*   What makes a process, procedure, or task complex is the large number of components involved, their interaction with each other, and the start-stop timing of each of the components. Since organizations have a bright future with regard to growing complexity, the need to unify components is high. Organization MBO sets up a scheme for signaling the start-stop of action plans in a unified format for the entire organization.

4. *To Improve Organizational Productivity.*   Productivity is influenced by three factors: performance, resource use, and a combination of these. Attainment of a high level of productivity in an organization requires management of these three factors. Organization MBO allows productivity objectives to be set for the entire organization with commitments as to performance, resource use, and combinations of the two from every manager in the firm. Organization MBO gives visibility to this commitment during the planning phase.

5. *To Better Utilize Resources.*   Resources are scarce! They will always be scarce. People, facilities, equipment, materials, money, and time are often wasted because of idleness, redundancy, and poor allocation. Organization MBO gives visibility to the utilization of resources in a priority array before there is commitment. Managers commit to use of resources in collaboration with other managers for the best and total use for the enterprise. Organizational MBO balances efforts and resources of the organization.

Making Organization MBO Work!

Once a strategic plan is developed by top managers, guidelines are issued to key managers in lower levels. (Strategic planning will be taken up in detail in another chapter.) Each manager of a division, department, program or project proceeds to submit his or her group or supervisory MBO to top management for coordination, integration, and agreement. An iterative method is used by top management to search and decide on the greatest number of outcomes that maximize resources and effort. This method entails a series of successive approximation steps, and these steps often must be scrutinized several levels up in the organization before even the early ones are finalized. Managers should not expect to complete elements

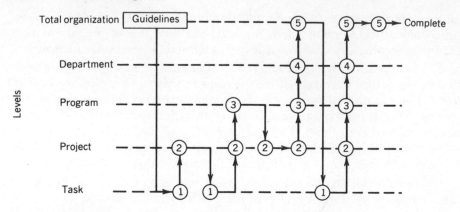

FIGURE 5.8 Iteration of individual plans for operational plans.

in their operational plan until all steps have been exposed, explored, and agreed on at all levels. This is shown diagrammatically in Figure 5.8.

The operational plan becomes a "format" that generates common data across programs, projects, departments, functions, and major levels of the organization. The objectives stated within the operational plan must contain measurable outcomes and be flexible to permit continual revisions. Furthermore, the specificity of each objective changes as the organizational level changes. A primary objective is basically intended to satisfy a departmental goal, a secondary objective to satisfy a program objective, and a tertiary objective to satisfy a project or task objective. These basic relationships are shown in Figure 5.9. Both the strategic and operational plan formats are supported with additional documentation and information that may not be included in the specific plans.

The amount of time needed to complete the participation, iteration, and optimization processes within the levels of an organization can be prodigious. Obviously, the greater the number of levels the greater the time needed. For a corporation with 25,000 employees, as much as six months may be needed in advance of an operating year. For a major complex organization such as a state government, the time requirement may be as high as 18 months. The following illustrates how organization MBO may be divided into a schedule for its development:

April–July	President develops guidelines for the coming year
July	Guidelines issued to all key departments
August	MBO documents developed by key departments; they include plans and budgets
September	MBO documents reviewed by higher levels and returned for adjustments
October	Controller integrates all budgets and delivers them to president for review

November   President returns MBO package to all levels to
                 incorporate changes

December   President delivers MBO plan to Board of
                 Directors for review and approval

December   Last changes made by Board

January 1   Plan and budgetary year begin

The organization MBO format is backed up by and supported with lots of information that is not included in the plan. The information is available if requested by any of the managers who review and validate the plans. Each division head, program manager, department head, director, or vice president distills summary information into the basic element of the plan. These basic elements are described in Figures 5.10 and 5.11.

The primary "product" of the organization MBO plan is a briefly written, eight-section format that all divisions, departments, programs, and projects develop for the operational year (Figure 5.10). This format is summarized as follows:

1. *Mission or Mission Identity*.   This section describes the general purpose and goals for which the organization or unit exists. The mission or mission identity is usually a long-term general direction for which general results are desired and expected. The mission is expressed for both the overall organization and its major functions. This section should include:

   (a)   Brief statement of goals of the firm; a five-year view.

   (b)   Statement of previous goals and reasons for changes.

2. *Information and Assumptions*.   This section collects the information needed to serve as guidelines for planning. Information could be from such areas as the marketplace, government, legislation, competition, environment, and customer. This section should include:

   (a)   Implications from a two- to five-year forecast analysis and trend.

   (b)   Assumptions made for planning to move ahead.

   (c)   Competitive edge analysis: list of competitors and their offerings.

   (d)   Customer goals and needs.

   (e)   Spare capacity or capabilities available but not used.

3. *Programs or Areas of Results*.   This section identifies the programs, projects, or areas of results pursued by an organized group of people. Functions can be termed programs. They are a group of related outcomes, outputs, or expected results. The related outcomes, whether they be products, services, programs, or projects, contribute to a larger outcome, such as mission. This section should include:

   (a)   Brief description of programs, projects, or areas of results.

   (b)   List of programs used in the past or potential programs for the future.

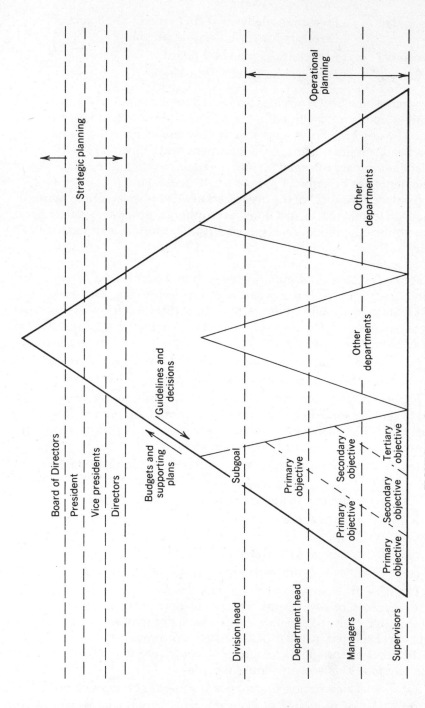

FIGURE 5.9 Organization MBO developed by all levels.

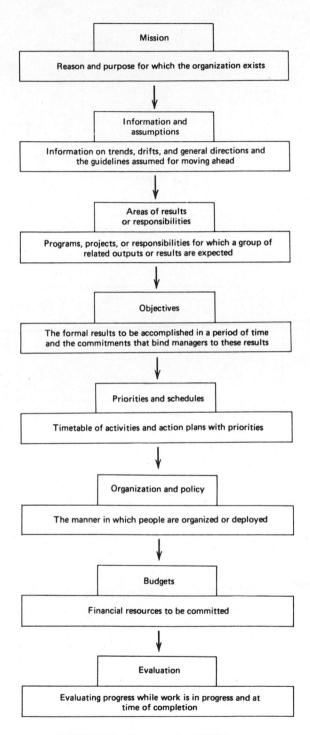

FIGURE 5.10 Organization MBO format.

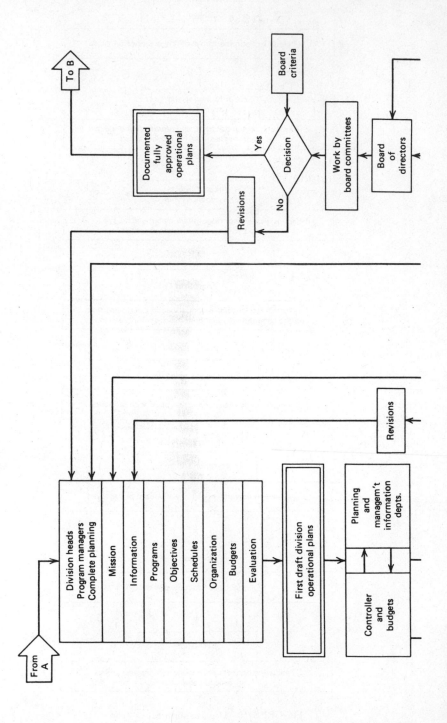

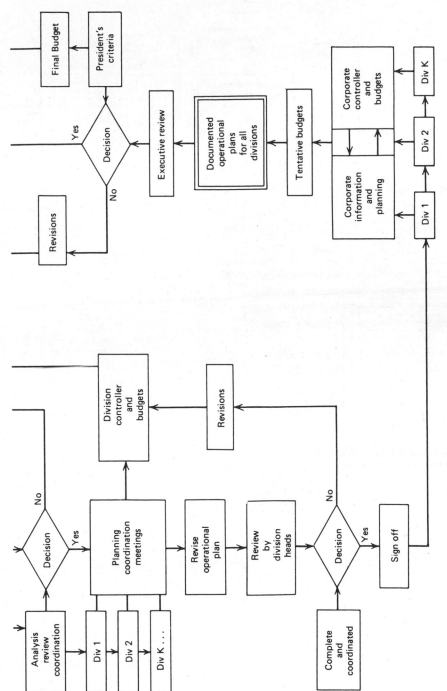

FIGURE 5.11 Illustration of a cycle of events in organization MBO planning for a large multidivision corporation.

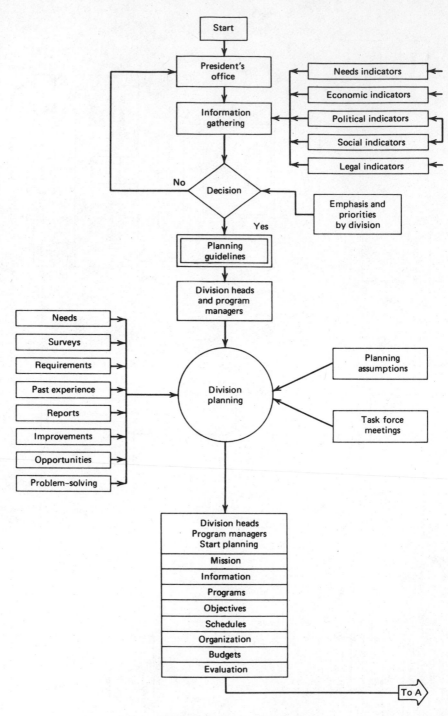

FIGURE 5.11 *(continued)*

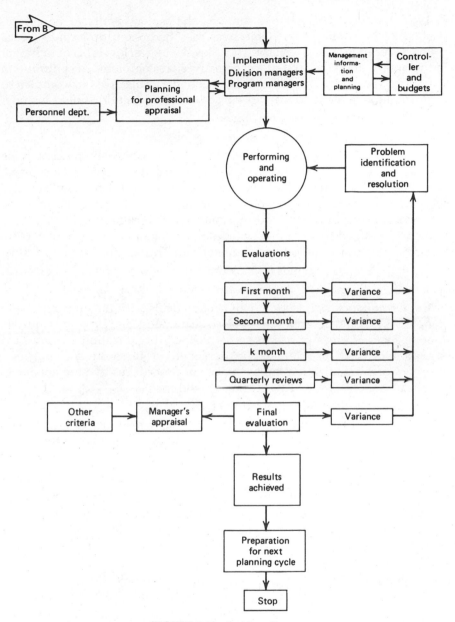

FIGURE 5.11 *(continued)*

4. *Objectives.* This section contains the major results to be accomplished in the coming year. Objectives may be broken down into levels: primary, secondary, and tertiary. These levels suggest levels of commitment in the organization. When tertiary objectives are completed, a contribution is made to a secondary objective. When secondary objectives are completed, a contribution is made to primary objectives. This section should include:

(a) List of primary objectives.

(b) List of secondary and tertiary objectives.

5. *Priorities, Schedules, and Activities.* This section helps determine when and how various objectives are to be accomplished. Action plans, activities, and tasks are identified and described. The schedule "signals" what comes first, when, and who does what. More important, the schedule selected should allow for monitoring, control, and evaluation. (Readers who want an amplified treatment of schedules are asked to read Chapter 14 on managing high-technology and engineering.) This section should include:

(a) List of activities and actions needed to complete an objective.

(b) Timetable of activities and actions, with priorities.

6. *Organization and Policy.* This section deals with the effective use of people. As mission describes the goals to be pursued, and programs indicate the subgoals or areas of results to be reached, organization indicates the structure of how people will be deployed in function and purpose. Furthermore, organization implies policy or procedures that are needed to carry out the objectives. This section should include:

(a) Up-to-date organization chart.

(b) Position summaries indicating major responsibilities.

(c) Statement of organizational changes needed to carry out the plan for the coming year.

(d) Brief description of new policies that are needed or old policies needing change or removal.

7. *Budgets.* This section describes the financial resources to be committed to the operational plan. These are the estimated but valid costs to be entailed in completing primary and secondary objectives. This section should include:

(a) Estimated budget allocations for each objective.

(b) Total budget estimate to implement the operational plan.

8. *Evaluation.* Planning for results also means planning for evaluating the results. Evaluating work performance in progress requires comparing actual performance with expected performance. This section describes how evaluation will be conducted so that variances are collected and conveyed to those who can execute a correction. This section should include:

(a) Milestones of progress dates that connect objectives with results, and evaluative measures at these dates.

(b) Monthly or quarterly self-monitoring control points.

Example: *Insurance Company*

1. *Mission.*   To provide prompt and accurate service to policyholders.
2. *Information and Assumptions.*
    (a)   Adoption of no-fault laws will occur in ten additional states.
    (b)   High mandatory deductibles will be moderate in numbers for next two years.
    (c)   Competitors using efficiency factors for new selling thrust.
3. *Programs.*
    (a)   Reduction of complaints in claims processing.
    (b)   Manpower utilization improvement.
4. *Objectives.*
    (a)   Reduce claims processing time from ten days to six days by January 1.
    (b)   Improve utilization of manpower by reaching 4% productivity increase per year without lowering quality of service.
5. *Schedule.*

Activities	Schedule
Redesign claims processing	⊢——⊣
Set up productivity standards	⊢—⊣
Organize special task force	⊢———⊣
Trial and validation	⊢—⊣
Implementation and feedback	⊢————————⊣

6. *Organization.*   A special task committee will be set up to spearhead efforts. No change in organization or policy is required.
7. *Budgets.*

	1978 Actual	1979 Estimated	1980 No Change	1980 Change	1980 Total
Surveys and analyses	36,000	36,500	36,800	(4,200)	$32,600
Trial and test	0	11,600	11,800	0	$11,800

8. *Evaluation.*   Quarterly milestones as follows:
    (a)   Claims processing time: One-day reduction achievement at quarterly dates.
    (b)   Productivity: 1 percent improvement at quarterly dates.

Example: *Manufacturing Company*

1. *Mission.* To improve profitability of division with better cost management.
2. *Information.*
   (a) Competitors have reduced prices 8 percent in all product lines.
   (b) No new materials availability expected in the next five years.
   (c) Cost savings must center on ways of managing instead of new designs.
3. *Program.* Cost reduction.
4. *Objectives.* Achieve 12 percent reduction of operating costs during coming year for all department heads.
5. *Schedule.*

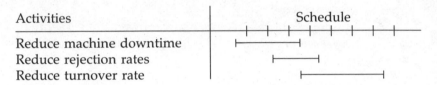

Activities	Schedule
Reduce machine downtime	
Reduce rejection rates	
Reduce turnover rate	

6. *Organization.* Set up new department called "Methods Improvement."
7. *Budgets.*

Expenses	1978 Actual	1979 Estimated	1980 Estimated
Preventive maintenance	0	10,000	15,000
Error reduction training	0	3,000	5,000
Process analysis	0	20,000	30,000
Job enlargement	0	15,000	20,000

8. *Evaluation.*
   (a) Monthly milestones of 1 percent per month achievable by all departments.
   (b) Monthly meetings to correct variances.

Example: *City Government*

1. *Mission.* To protect person and property.
2. *Information.*
   (a) Citizens' complaints increased 35% in six months.
   (b) Muggings and auto theft continued as council agenda items.
   (c) Secondary effects of primary crime increasing.
3. *Program.* Reduction of crime.

4. *Objective.*   Reduce street muggings 28 percent within radius of two miles by January 1.

5. *Schedule.*

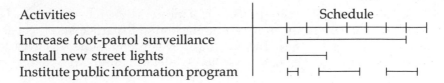

Activities	Schedule
Increase foot-patrol surveillance	
Install new street lights	
Institute public information program	

6. *Organization.*   Institute new full-time crime coordinator reporting directly to mayor.

7. *Budgets.*

	1980 Estimated	1980 Actual	1980 Estimated
Foot-patrol surveillance	300,000		
Installation of new street lights	150,000		
Institution of public information program	10,000		

8. *Evaluation.*   Quarterly milestones of progress at 7 percent at milestone dates.

SUMMARY

MBO practitioners vary on how they use MBO in their life-style and in their company. There is a wide spectrum of differences. Five strategies have emerged that are the most common. This chapter identifies and describes these as follows:

1. *General MBO.*   General MBO is a process whereby a manager sets up a planning procedure in a series of time phases for joining the results expected of him or her and the department with the total results expected of the firm. There are six steps in the general MBO process: situation analysis, improvement analysis, setting of goals and objectives, development of operational plans, validation of plans, and control and evaluation.

2. *Individual MBO.*   Individual MBO is a process whereby an individual identifies major areas of responsibilities, sets results in that context, and joins them with objectives or expectations to be achieved by the company in a coming period. There are eight steps in individual MBO: situation analysis, payoff analysis, focusing of effort, setting of goals and objectives, stretching of performance, development of operational plans, validation of plans, and control and evaluation.

3. *Supervisory MBO.*   Supervisory MBO is a process whereby supervisor and subordinate jointly identify common objectives to be achieved in a

coming period. There are five steps in the supervisory MBO process: collaboration of supervisor and subordinate, setting of goals and objectives, development of operational plans, performance and evaluation, and evaluation of results.

4. *Group MBO.* Group MBO is a process whereby members of an existing team or group, through interaction and participation, collaboratively join together for concerns and develop common objectives to be achieved in a coming period. There are six steps in group MBO: gathering of information, collaborative diagnosis, group goal setting, delegation of team member responsibilities, ongoing progress reviews, and final evaluation.

5. *Organization MBO.* Organization MBO is a process whereby all managerial personnel of an organization, through a process of participation, iteration, and optimization by levels, collaboratively arrive at common objectives to be achieved in a coming period. Organization MBO has a format in which eight basic elements make up the plan: mission, information and assumptions, areas of results or responsibilities, objectives, priorities and schedules, organization and policy, budgets, and evaluation.

BIBLIOGRAPHY

Ansoff, H.L., *Corporate Strategy.* New York: McGraw-Hill, 1965.

Branch, M.C., *The Corporate Planning Process.* New York: American Management Association, 1962.

Drucker, Peter F., *The Practice of Management.* New York: Harper & Row, 1954.

Drucker, Peter F., *Managing for Results.* New York: Harper & Row, 1964.

Ewing, D.W., *The Human Side of Planning.* New York: Macmillan, 1969.

Ferrell, R.W., *Customer-Oriented Planning.* New York: American Management Association, 1968.

Granger, C.H., "How To Set Company Objectives." *Management Review*, Vol. 59, July 1970, pp. 64–68.

Granger, C.H., "The Hierarchy of Objectives." *Harvard Business Review*, Vol. 42, No. 3, May–June 1974, pp. 212–216.

Green, Edward J., *Workbook for Corporate Planning.* New York: American Management Association, 1974.

Humphrey, A.S., "Getting Management Commitment to Planning a New Approach." *Long Range Planning*, Vol. 7, No. 1, February 1974, pp. 43–46.

Jones, H., *Preparing Company Plans.* New York: Halsted, 1974.

Kastens, Merritt, *Long-Range Planning for Your Business*, New York: American Management Association, 1976.

Mace, M.L., "The President and Corporate Planning." *Harvard Business Review*, Vol. 43, No. 1, January–February 1965, pp. 320–326.

Mali, Paul, *Managing by Objectives.* New York: Wiley, 1972.

Odiorne, George, *Management by Objectives.* New York: Pitman, 1965.

Schleh, Edward, *Management Tactician.* New York: McGraw-Hill, 1974.

Vancil, Richard F., and Lorange, Peter, "Strategic Planning in Diversified Companies." *Harvard Business Review*, Vol. 53, No. 1, January–February 1975, pp. 186–190.

PART 3

MBO Practices and Processes

To be successful, MBO practitioners have to learn to fit MBO into organizational and corporate practices and processes. MBO becomes a life-style, without formal procedures and techniques. This MBO life-style helps the manager with normal responsibilities and decision making. The six chapters in this section describe the use of MBO in the normal responsibilities and expectations of managerial work. They cover such basic responsibilities as problem solving, cost improvement, productivity improvement, efficiency, and motivation, and also making MBO workable in the enterprise.

6

USING MBO IN THE PROBLEM-SOLVING PROCESS

IN THIS CHAPTER

HOW MBO HELPS DEFINE PROBLEMS
MANAGERIAL SOLUTIONS TO PROBLEMS ARE "POSSIBILITIES"
MANAGERIAL ATTITUDES THAT HELP IN PROBLEM SOLVING
WHAT MAKES A PROBLEM WORTH SOLVING?
SIX STEPS TO RATIONAL PROBLEM SOLVING

Managers create problems when they set and strive to complete objectives. Objective setting means improvement, improvement means change, and change creates new problems as the new displaces the old. Management thus can be regarded as the creative destruction of existing situations to bring about improvement! Managers need to apply a systematic approach to getting problems resolved efficiently, especially in the implementation of objectives. Such a systematic approach is illustrated in Figure 6.1. The skills a manager uses are mostly attitudes, mental processes, strategies, techniques, analysis, and decision making.

Much of the information people need to solve problems is within them. People fail to make use of information they already have. Why don't they use it? Largely because they are creatures of habit. Problem solving requires keeping the mind open for new meanings. Some solutions appear suddenly, but usually the best solutions appear after much thought and analysis. Problem solvers must keep their mind open for new combinations and new insights. This chapter gives insight to skills needed. It examines the nature of decisions, steps in problem solving, attitudes needed, and the impact of the action during implementation.

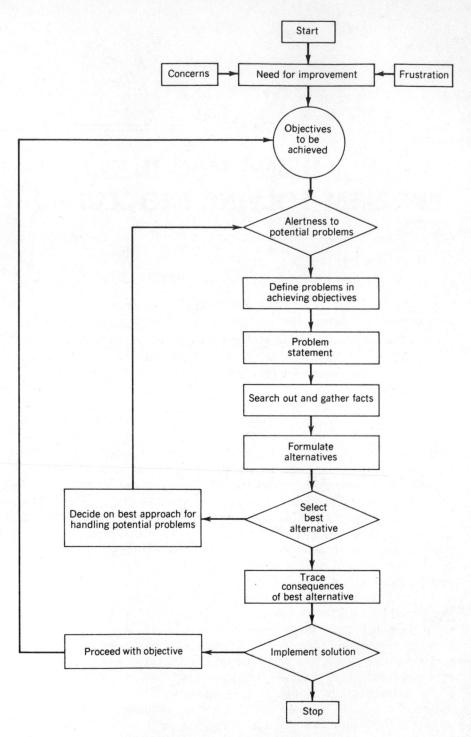

FIGURE 6.1 The problem-solving process.

HOW MBO HELPS DEFINE PROBLEMS

Managerial problems are complex. They are in reality complexes—groups of problems put under one heading for convenience of reference. When we say "personnel problems," "productivity problems," or "quality control problems," we use a category of reference as though we have defined the problems and know exactly the type of individual who will be asked to help solve them. But this easy-definition easy-category approach can cause more problems than it solves, since it implies that problems have been defined. They haven't. The category approach can be useful, however, for raising questions, making analyses, and evaluating the difficulties from which problems arise. The following are types of problems:

Low profits	Backlogs	Conflicts
High costs	Rejects	Poor morale
Loss of key customers	High pollution	High accident rate
Missed schedules	Defects	Faulty attitudes
Waste and spoilage	Excessive repairs	Rivalries
Budget variance	Rework	Noncooperation
High downtime	High pilferage	Low morale
Low productivity	Duplication	Hostility
Diagreements	Maturing of products	Obsolete inventory
Low sales	High overhead	Excessive turnover

In management, a problem can be defined as the difference between a desired set of conditions and the actual set of conditions. This does not mean that both desired and actual conditions are clearly known. Often the problem is complicated exactly because these are not known accurately. A large part of the manager's problem definition is analyzing, measuring, and evaluating causal factors and their interrelationships, as shown in Figure 6.2.

The setting of objectives and measurement of performance toward these objectives helps managers focus on the difference. This directs attention to any deficiency requiring corrective action. It helps define the problem that needs a solution. A decision is first and foremost a choice. Having alternatives available to remove deficiencies makes choice easier. MBO helps minimize deficiences by establishing a relationship or connection between cause and effect, by clarifying expectations and the deviations from these expectations. The more precise and specific the expectation, the more readily a deviation from it can be recognized. MBO helps identify the corrective action needed to remove the deviation by identifying in advance and in the planning context the activities needed to restore the direction to a goal or objective.

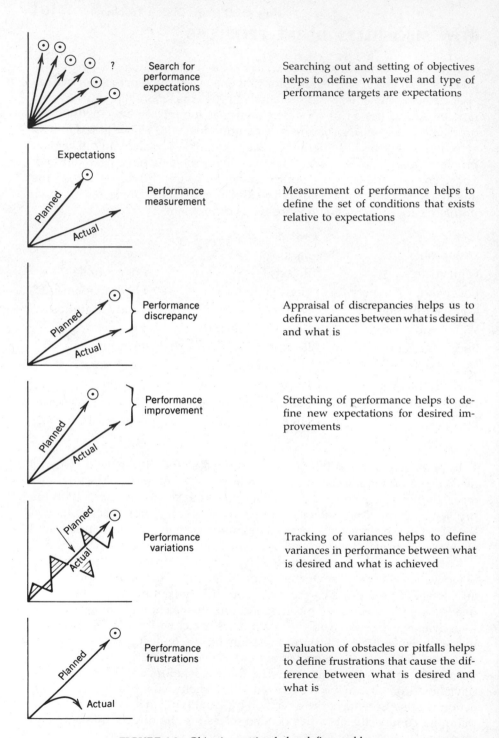

Search for performance expectations		Searching out and setting of objectives helps to define what level and type of performance targets are expectations
Performance measurement		Measurement of performance helps to define the set of conditions that exists relative to expectations
Performance discrepancy		Appraisal of discrepancies helps us to define variances between what is desired and what is
Performance improvement		Stretching of performance helps to define new expectations for desired improvements
Performance variations		Tracking of variances helps to define variances in performance between what is desired and what is achieved
Performance frustrations		Evaluation of obstacles or pitfalls helps to define frustrations that cause the difference between what is desired and what is

FIGURE 6.2 Objective setting helps define problems.

MANAGERIAL SOLUTIONS TO PROBLEMS ARE "POSSIBILITIES"

Only in mathematical problems are answers exact, specific, complete, and perfect. In management answers to problems rarely are exact. Most are a cluster of possibilities. Managers continually have expectations of the way things ought to be. These expectations suggest many possibilities or alternatives. Even after the manager has selected one possibility, he or she is uneasy, wondering whether a different selection would have been better. Selection of a possibility does not mean elimination of a problem. The possibility must be tried. More often than not, trying out the possibility may only reduce the performance discrepancy, measurable variance, or frustration but may not eliminate it. The choice of possibility, therefore, is an intermediate step between problem definition and its elimination.

Problem analysis and choice of problem solution are the basis of decision analysis. Problem solution in general eliminates or solves something in the past. Problem solution relative to implementation of objectives eliminates or solves something that will emerge in the future. "Open end" thinking, in which a range of possibilities are considered, does improve on the quality of a final decision. This is illustrated as follows:

Solution Principle	Examples
Selecting the best possibility from among many good possibilities	Hiring a prospect from among many good candidates
Selecting the most critical trouble from among many troubles	Replacing a piece of equipment that breaks down more often than other faulty equipment
Selecting the highest payoff proposal from among many proposals	Deciding for cost effectiveness from among cost avoidance, cost reduction, and cost control
Selecting the solution easiest to live with from among many difficult to live with	Settling a strike and accepting proposed terms for a contract
Selecting the greatest concern from among many concerns	Meeting a customer's schedule even though overtime and extra people are needed
Selecting the most critical item of frustration from among many frustrating items	Accepting low morale of employees and stockholders to raise morale of customers

The "solution principle" is a cluster of alternatives that give a number of possible courses of action. The decision maker thus can choose the best course of action among many courses of action. This means a manager should never decide on a single course of action unless he has considered several possibilities. Often the search for the "best" possible alternative can be a waste of effort as well as time, and simply selecting one "good" alternative will suffice for the problem.

MANAGERIAL ATTITUDES THAT HELP IN PROBLEM SOLVING

Problem solving begins with the attitude of the problem solver, rather than with the problem-solving process itself. The right kinds of attitudes and perceptions of the entire situation by managers and supervisors can bring about a positive approach in the selection and execution of the solution. Additionally, attitudes can actually prevent managers from being good problem solvers, which means managers can become part of the very problem they are trying to solve. I'm sure the reader has often heard the old saying, "Are you part of the problem or part of the solution?"

The following attitudes represent positive views possessed by managers and supervisors who are effective and efficient in handling all kinds of problems. Each view is summarized with a guideline attitude that will help managers in attitude adjustment.

1.   Managers must accept problem solving as a way of life!   Problems always exist when people, equipment, resources, and money are brought together, coordinated, and directed toward a set of objectives. Anyone who hates facing and solving problems should stay away from management. Problem solving is the heart and core of a manager's job. Instead of avoiding problems, the manager should develop the skills to handle them efficiently. Managers must prepare for and expect problems. Problem solving is the job.

> *Guideline Attitude: When facing problems, do not complain about them but develop the skills to solve them.*

2.   Managers must plan to face problems when they set objectives. Setting objectives means improvement. Improvement means change. Change means new problems, which will emerge as existing situations are replaced with the new. As managers pressure for change and improvement, they create new problems. This is inevitable. Setting objectives for improvement and innovation means creating and reaching for problems. If the problems that will be generated by striving for the objective will exceed the value of the objective, the objective-setter may want to select another objective.

> *Guideline Attitude: When setting an objective, define the problems that will emerge and assess whether pursuit of the objective is worth it!*

3.   Managers often face "batches " of problems rather than individual ones.   Problems usually do not emerge one at a time. They do not file by in a single line for the manager to handle one at a time. More often than not they come in "batches" at a fast rate and without warning. Managers often face the decision of which problem to work on first, which to tackle second, and so forth. Often they must work on several problems simultaneously. They need special skills for this.

> *Guideline Attitude: When batches of problems emerge, have a system of priorities that can guide the order of problem solving according to payoff and time.*

4.   Managers must view problems as signs of something out of control.   The effectiveness of a manager is how well he or she keeps a situation under control. A single problem is an indication that something is wrong. Many problems are a strong indication that the situation is going out of control and needs to be analyzed and restructured. Batches of problems occurring without warning show that the situation is already out of control. The number, types, and levels of problems are a strong measure of how well a manager is managing.

> *Guideline Attitude: When a problem emerges, use it to determine whether it signals a situation well managed and under control.*

5.   Managers should view problems as opportunities.   The prime mission of a manager is improvement. A problem is an indication that something is not working well and needs to be changed. Since managers welcome improvement, which requires change, a problem is an opportunity for how, where, and when this improvement or change can be defined and proposed for the organization. Additionally, does the solution of the problem help the company? Does it open up a marketing opportunity? Does solving a customer problem become an opportunity to reach new customers?

> *Guideline Attitude: When a problem emerges, try to use its solution as a new opportunity to introduce an innovation or improvement.*

6.   Managers must solve causes rather than symptoms of problems. When problems emerge, there is usually pressure and stress to take care of them immediately and completely. Hence the tendency is to move with dispatch, without taking the time to differentiate symptoms from causes. This results in poor problem definition. Consequently, symptoms are worked on while causes remain untouched. In many ways, this is the reason why problems are perpetuated rather than solved once and for all. They reappear because they have not been defined in the first place. Managers must develop the ability to define problems and the skills to solve them.

General Attitude: When a problem emerges, take the time to define it completely and accurately.

7.   Managers should possess humility in solving problems.   Some managers think, "Since I don't know how to solve this problem, there isn't any solution. I can't solve it, so no one else can." These managers perceive themselves as superthinkers and supersolvers; others are subthinkers and subsolvers. Humility of mind in a manager is a must, since no one manager can handle effectively all the varied challenges that may arise.

Guideline Attitude: When solutions to problems do not appear, consult with others.

WHAT MAKES A PROBLEM WORTH SOLVING?

Few people like problems. Hence the natural tendency in problem solving is to pick the first solution that comes to mind and "run with it." The first solution may not be the best solution. The first solution may not even be worth the effort. In fact, the problem may not be worth solving. Before a problem is to be solved, the solver should raise questions: "Is it worth solving?," "What benefits will accrue to me, to others, or to the organization?," "How long will it take to solve the problem?," "How tightly coupled is the problem to performance implementation?". Several guidelines can be used to guide the answers to these questions. These guidelines are:

1.   The payoff must be greater than the cost.   Every problem-solving effort incurs a cost. Every problem unsolved is in itself a cost. The cost could be time wasted, material expended, or effort that did not complete a task. The cost could be the "ripples" or secondary effects that occur if the problem is allowed to exist. The payoff or benefits accrued from a solution, when proposed, must be greater than the cost of solving the problem or greater than the effects caused by the problem if allowed to exist. The benefits or payoff can be for the manager, the department, or the organization. Benefits can be the elimination of the consequences of not solving and getting rid of the problem.

2.   The solution must help complete an objective.   Setting of objectives is but a fraction of the effort needed in achieving results. Most of the effort involved in completing objectives goes to solving the myriad of problems encountered along the way. Problems can form obstacles for the pursuit and completion of objectives. A problem is well worth solving when an important objective is completed. When obstacles have been removed, if not permanently at least temporarily, work can then move ahead progressively.

3.   Problem elimination must improve productivity.   Effectiveness and efficiency are highly influenced by the existence of problems. The more

problems, the less effectiveness and efficiency; the less problems, the more effectiveness and efficiency. By definition, productivity is the ratio of effectiveness to efficiency. Any effort to improve effectiveness and efficiency is an effort to enhance productivity. Solving problems that hinder productivity is well worth the effort.

4. Solutions must improve human relations and morale. For many people, the work world is no fun at all. Employees put up with annoyances, disruptions, and inefficiencies. These adversely affect morale and human relations. Improvement in the quality of work life, now a strong movement in human relations, should be a key consideration when solutions are developed and proposed for problems. Problem solving that gives consideration to improving human relations and morale is well worth the effort.

5. Solutions must yield "opportunity value" of time. Time is now an important company resource. Managing and controlling it are prime responsibilities of all managers. Time is important not so much because of its cost but because of its "opportunity value," that is, the opportunity it presents for completing a task or implementing a decision. A problem is well worth solving if its solution enhances ability to seize the opportunity value of time that may never again be available. Solution is worth every effort if that opportunity value will lead to an invention of innovation.

SIX STEPS TO RATIONAL PROBLEM SOLVING

Problem solving is one of management's chief preoccupations. There are always too many problems. They are very demanding. They involve many people. Solutions are costly. No matter where a manager is performing in the organization, problem solving is his or her heart and core activity. The following principles should help managers in viewing and approaching problems:

1. Prepare for and expect problems.
2. Don't waste time trying to solve problems for which there are no solutions.
3. Gather valid and sufficient information and facts before attempting problem solving.
4. Don't use a solution to a problem that will only create bigger problems.
5. Always have alternatives before making a decision.
6. Don't confuse urgent problems with important problems.
7. Consider first nonpeople-type solutions.
8. Don't judge the importance of a problem solely on familiarity.
9. Most problems can be broken up into subproblems.

10. Always focus on critical and high-payoff areas.
11. Don't assume you always have the skills to solve a problem.
12. The quality of alternatives increases with quantity.
13. Problem solving is costly and should be approached with this fact in mind.
14. There are many possible solutions to a problem but only one is best for the situation.
15. The setting of objectives always creates new problems.
16. Problems emerge at inopportune times.
17. Emerging problems are signs of change or something out of control.
18. The more skillful the problem solver, the less time required to deal with a problem.
19. First solutions to problems are not always the best solutions.
20. Forethought in problem solving always minimizes the need for afterthought.

The MBO practitioner must have top-flight skills to solve problems, since problems represent the prime obstacles to achievement of objectives. The MBO practitioner must apply a systematic and sequential series of steps with rational judgments in order to handle and eliminate problems. This kind of sequential thinking can be thought of as a problem-solving process. The process is summarized in Table 6.1 and described in detail in the following sections.

TABLE 6.1   The Problem-Solving Process

Sequential Steps	Attitudes	Techniques for Implementation[a]
Be alert to potential problems	Accept emerging problems when objectives are set	Alertness checklist technique
Define problems	Separate problems from symptoms	Questioning analysis Effect-cause analysis
Gather information	Have minimal information to act	Factors of the situation technique Checking assumptions
Generate alternatives as solutions	Formulate several attractive alternatives	Creativity techniques Value analysis
Decide on best solution	Separate best alternative from others	Decision-making matrix Selection comparison technique
Evaluate consequences of decision	Always trace consequences before acting	Cause-effect diagrams Third-party reviews Delphi technique

[a] See text for descriptions of techniques.

Virtually every effective MBO practitioner follows a well-developed series of steps in the decision-making process. There may be different emphases or intensities in these steps, or even different steps, but the rational thinking process is the same.

First Step: Managers Need to Be Alert to Emerging Problems

MBO practitioners need to be alert and sensitive to the possibility of problems developing as a consequence of the setting, coordination, and implementation of objectives. If they can develop alertness and awareness during the planning and setting of objectives phases, problems or potential disruptions can be resolved long before they get a firm start. Problems are nipped in the bud. If, for example, two major objectives by two high-level managers will conflict when implemented, the managers should settle the points of conflict before settling on the objectives.

The skillful problem solver should make every attempt to prevent problems from emerging in the first place. This approach puts less strain on the organization, the people, and the managers. This means predicting where problems will emerge. Prediction is not always simple. The following techniques help managers develop the skill for this type of prediction.

Alertness Checklist Technique

The following checklist of situational conditions is a guide to where problems are likely to emerge when objectives are being considered. The presence of any of these "alert-sensitivity" conditions signals the need for action to control and minimize their effects on the generation of problems. This checklist guide in answering the question, "What could go wrong?"

Tight deadlines

Objectives unattainable

New, complex, or unfamiliar process or equipment to be used

New employee without sufficient skills or experience

Changed priorities

Objectives not understood

No alternatives

More than one person involved

Bottleneck exists

Two or more objectives set and not coordinated

No backup of key people

Sequence of elements critical

Rising costs

Production rate slowdown

Excessive handling

Labor unrest emerging

Idle time with no abatement

Red tape in process

Errors and poor skills that produced them

Excessive rework

Objectives not measurable

Repetition of past problems

Potential Problem Analysis

Potential problems are inherent in any new venture. They can be predicted from present known experience. Potential problem analysis, as a technique,

TABLE 6.2 Example of Potential Problem Analysis

Objective to be reached	Improve productivity in welding tie-bars to 100 welds per week using newly purchased semiautomatic equipment	
Potential problems	Welders not using equipment correctly	Equipment not functioning as expected
Percent likelihood	90 percent	60 percent
Likely causes	Nonfamiliarization, inadequate skills, no instruction books	All equipment not installed equipment damaged, poor quality check
Planning action to prevent problems	Deliver equipment in advance, give factory skill training, send books in advance	Deliver equipment early, have standby equipment, recheck quality on site

is the analysis of a situation for present deviations that may cause future problems. A prescribed plan should be loaded with these future problems. Potential problem analysis is the identification of problems that could prevent the completion of future objectives. It forsees the preventive actions needed. Table 6.2 illustrates the analysis.

Second Step: Managers Must Define Problems Before Solving Them

Problems do not emerge well defined and ready for a solution. They do not come in packages all ready for the solver. They emerge as situations that are complex, filled with conflicts, heavy with obscurity, uncertain as to outcome, changing in nature, and disruptive in impact. Most managers are eager to solve these problems, since they often view early and quick solutions as good solutions. This eagerness to move before a problem has been identified and defined accounts for inefficiencies, ineffectiveness, frustration, and the reemergence of the same problems at a later time. The second step in the problem-solving rational process is to disentangle the problem from the situation so that it may be viewed clearly and completely. Distinguishing between the problem situation and the problem itself is the first effort. This is problem definition, or diagnosis. Diagnosis makes clear the exact nature of the trouble or difficulty that is to be resolved. The following techniques are useful.

Questioning Analysis Technique

Asking questions is the ABC of analysis and diagnosis. Asking all kinds of questions is likely to lead to all kinds of information and even answers. A carefully worded question is already half the answer. A vague question elicits a vague answer. Figure 6.3 illustrates seven questions that aid in diagnosis.

Types of Questions	Purpose	Question Format
"What" questions 	To define situation To identify nature of situation To consider alternatives	What has happened? What are you doing? What would happen if I stopped?
"Why" questions 	To find causes To determine motives To elicit explanations	Why are you dissatisfied? Why did he go? Why must it be this way?
"How" questions 	To describe process To identify steps To establish limits	How does it work? How can it be done? How far does it go?
"Which" questions 	To compare To select To evaluate	Which is the better plan? Which of the men answered? Which fact is important?
"Where" questions 	To identify place To predict outcome To locate source	Where is the machine? Where will we be if we lose? Where did you get your information?

FIGURE 6.3 Questioning analysis technique.

Types of Questions	Purpose	Question Format
"When" questions	To establish time To elicit decision To mark event	When did they leave? When shall I stop? When did it happen?
"Who" questions	To identify person To separate people To pry for information	Who is he? Who works for him? Who did you see there?

FIGURE 6.3   *(continued)*

Effect-Cause Analysis

Every event is an effect. Things don't just happen without reason. For every effect, there is a cause. Working from effect to cause is always worked backward in time to uncover the roots and basic reasons why the effect exists. Finding the cause of a present-day symptom is an excellent way to define the problem. This suggests that the anatomy of a problem is an effect-cause combination. Too often problems are defined by merely stating their symptoms. This is shortsighted. Accurate identification of an effect and its cause is to define the problem in such a way that possible solutions can be perceived. A problem solution is basically an eliminator of a cause producing an effect. Every cause has an eliminator that will erase, oppose, or remove it. A multiplicity of effects implies a multiplicity of causes and in turn a multiplicity of eliminators. The following are typical effects in management situations:

Excessive backlog	Low inventory
High accident rate	Low profits
Schedule slippage	High overhead
High waste and spoilage	Sales volume off
Excessive pollution	High costs
Excessive repairs	Low morale
Loss of customers	High downtime
Rivalries	High absenteeism

Low sales growth   Overtime deterioration
High pilferage   Excessive returns
Much corrective work   Ineffective advertising
High rejection rate

The following are typical causes producing effects in management situations:

Negative attitudes   Poor products
Low motivation   Lack of coordination
Seasonal influences   High wage rates
Inadequate safety practices   No shipping instructions
Shrinking economy   Wrong materials
Poor organization   Insufficient communications
Strikes   Lack of skills
No standards   No preventive effort
Poor method or process   Not enough controls
Faulty equipment   Weather conditions
Mismatched job and employee   Insufficient records
Bad layout   Too much quality

Matching effects with causes half solves the problem. What remains to be done is to find eliminators of the causes. The sequence, therefore, is identification of the effects, matching of the causes that produce them, and searching out of eliminators to remove the causes.

Third Step: Managers Must Gather Facts and Information

Problem solvers are often ignorant of the facts of a problem they are to solve. Gathering of facts and information concerning the problem is important for both understanding of the basis of the problem and development of alternatives for its solution. Most managers can only produce a few facts when solving a problem, because seldom are they well informed when something goes wrong. Much of the information retained belongs in the category of what is desired, what is pleasant, or what is reported. Memory is tricky. But memory plays an important role in the problem-solving process. The problem solver must rely on witnesses' observations and their retention of information. Two techniques are described here to improve the ability to gather facts and information in the problem-solving process.

Factors of the Situation Technique

Solving problems demands correct facts and information about the problem and the situation. Much of the difficulty of problem solving lies in the impossibility of getting all the facts together, assuring they are accurate, and ascribing the right meaning to them in the situation. Getting correct facts can be thought of as having four parts.

1. *Collecting Facts.*   Research, questioning, interviews, meetings, conferences, written statements, quotations, studies, surveys, questionnaires, incidents, observations, hearings, reports, books, magazines, newspapers.

2. *Determining Sufficiency of Facts.*   Counting, measuring, evaluating, computing, assessing, comparing, checking, testing, validating, simulating, reviewing, reenacting.

3. *Ascertaining Correctness of Facts.*   Verifying with others, third-party reviews, double-checking deviation, rechecking variance, comparing with experience, comparing with standards, trial and experiment.

4. *Determining Meaning of Facts.*   Complies with rules, fits expectations, follows procedure, completes forms, meets policies, carries out decisions, achieves objectives, performs to standards, relieves bottlenecks, releases resources.

Checking Assumptions Technique

Assumptions are forecasts or predictions based on fragmentary information. They are temporary guesses regarding the probable development of events that may affect a decision or a solution to a problem. Assumptions cannot have high accuracy because they deal with the future. Most decisions, if not all, are based on incomplete, imperfect, and changing information, information that is often poor. Lead-time requirements in planning and decision making are such that managers must go ahead with whatever information is available regardless of its quality. With the rapid rate of change in our highly technological society, the little reliable information available soon becomes unreliable.

Checking of assumptions is an important technique for assuring that the facts and information used in making the assumptions are reliable. The technique can be described in four steps.

1. *Formalization of Assumption Making.*   Methods: written statements; including assumptions as formal step in planning; collecting them in a form; including them as part of planning documents; including them as part of problem solution.

2. *Agreement on Assumptions.*   Methods: third-party reviews; verifying with others; presenting to groups with feedback interaction; verification conferences.

3. *Updating of Assumptions.*   Methods: continuing collection of information; checking and double-checking of new information with assumptions; responsiveness checks.

4. *Validation of Assumptions.* Methods: assigning probabilities to each assumption; collecting new information and noting if probability of event occurring increases or decreases; watching trend for increasing or decreasing probability (assumptions whose probability of occurrence increases when new information is collected tend to be valid; those whose probability decreases tend to be invalid and should be changed).

Fourth Step: Managers Must Generate Alternatives With Creative Techniques

A manager should produce a second solution after he or she has found the first. Rarely is there ever one exact answer or solution to one well-defined problem. In management, a family of solutions is more often the case. This is a range of alternatives, each with its own particular set of advantages and disadvantages that may give different degrees of benefit to each alternative. The fact that each alternative will have different degrees of effectiveness and benefit is a good reason always to generate several alternatives, in order to have as many good alternatives as possible.

Quantity alone does not guarantee the best choice will be made. But quantity does give a range of benefits to choose from. Furthermore, the mental activity needed to develop and produce more than one solution forces the problem solver to think the problem through and attack it from several angles. Thinking up alternatives means thinking creatively. The creative manager is the manager who is able to see many possible solutions to a given problem. Several techniques that can help managers develop the skill for generating alternatives are described here.

Brainstorming Technique

Brainstorming, either on an individual basis or with a group, is a way of stimulating the mind to be uninhibited in generating ideas. Brainstorming is similar to a bull session. The principle to be followed is suspension of judgment; conclusions are not arrived at quickly. As a technique, brainstorming can quickly provide a large number of alternatives in a short time. The technique attacks the problem with a storm of possibilities, new, different, crazy, and wild. The technique is as follows:

1. State the problem and be sure all understand it.
2. Rule out negative thinking and evaluation of ideas, and suspend judgment about the merit of each idea.
3. Ask everyone to reach for any kind of idea, no matter how irrelevant or impractical it may seem.
4. List the ideas and encourage hitchhiking for more ideas.
5. Evaluate the relevancy and practicality of the ideas on the list.

A brainstorming worksheet is seen in Figure 6.4.

Checklist Technique

Stimulating the mind is the key to generating alternatives. A checklist of questions can often provoke a new point of view. Each question is a self-

---

For the purposes of this activity, the brainstorming sessions consist of only three steps:

1. Information gathering on the problem and background.
2. Fifteen-minute idea-generating period.
3. Ten-minute idea-categorizing period.

You may select a problem from your own work environment or you can brainstorm on the problem given with this worksheet. Make certain everyone understands the problem before you begin to generate ideas. Plan to have a chalkboard, flip chart, or some other visual means for recording ideas.

1. Write a statement of the problem for which you will use brainstorming to develop alternative solutions.

2. "Reach out" and "stretch for" ideas, ways, new methods, novel approaches, by freewheeling for the unusual. Write the results of your brainstorming session.

3. Evaluate into categories the ideas collected, considering payoff, practicality, and relevancy.

FIGURE 6.4   Brainstorming worksheet.

question, that is, the individual is then forced to answer the question posed. Responses are then collected and examined for their own worth and practicality. It is important to note that these mental activities take time. The anxious and the impatient will lose out on the "treasure" that is buried deeply.

Alec Osborn's famous list of questions is reproduced here.

- *Put to Other Uses?* New ways to use as is? Other uses if modified?
- *Adapt?* What else is like this? What other idea does this suggest? Does past offer parallel? What could I copy? Whom could I emulate?
- *Modify?* New twist? Change meaning, color, motion, sound, odor, form, shape? Other changes?
- *Magnify?* What to add? More time? Greater frequency? Stronger? Higher? Longer? Thicker? Extra value? Plus ingredient? Duplicate? Multiply? Exaggerate?
- *Minify?* What to subtract? Smaller? Condensed? Miniature? Lower? Shorter? Lighter? Omit? Streamline? Split up? Understate?
- *Substitute?* Who else instead? What else instead? Other ingredient? Other material? Other process? Other power? Other place? Other approach? Other tone of voice?
- *Rearrange?* Interchange components? Other pattern? Other layout? Other sequence? Transpose cause and effect? Change pace? Change schedule?
- *Reverse?* Transpose positive and negative? How about opposites? Turn it backward? Turn it upside down? Reverse roles? Change shoes? Turn tables? Turn other cheek?
- *Combine?* How about a blend, an alloy, an assortment, an ensemble? Combine units? Combine purposes? Combine appeals? Combine ideas?

Problem-Solving Log Technique

Managerial work is seldom a concentration in one area, at one time, on one problem. The work rotates over several areas during varying times with many problems. Quite often a useful and effective alternative would emerge in the mind if time were sufficient. Too often, however, the first alternative is adopted as the solution because time is short. The problem-solving log technique is a longer term individual record-keeping technique in which problems are logged in, alternatives are collected as they emerge, and the best alternative is selected after much consideration. The basic idea of the problem-solving log technique is allowing time for collection of several alternatives. It discourages use of the first alternative that emerges. Table 6.3 gives an example of this technique.

TABLE 6.3   Problem-Solving Log Technique

Problem	Date	Alternatives (Possibilities)	Solution (What I Decided to Do)	Comments (Did It Work?)
Department Backlog too high	9/3			
		Add personnel	_____	_____
	9/3	Automate procedures	_____	_____
	9/3	Give priorities to work	_____	_____
	9/15	Schedule overtime	_____	_____
	9/30	_____	_____	_____
		_____	_____	_____

The basic idea of the problem-solving log is for managers to take a break when they are stuck, to allow time to pass to rethink and reanalyze. This is especially important when alternatives to the problem do not emerge.

Consultative Technique

Problems are often new to the problem solver but "old hat" for other problem solvers in other companies. In this technique the environment is explored; what others are doing or have done is investigated. Sometimes the problem had been solved years ago only to reemerge in recent times. Few people record problems and their solutions; these are just part of the human experience. Talking about the problem with someone can be a powerful feedback to detection of important points and details. The consultative technique is the approach of consulting with others who have been faced with similar problems, to collect ideas for the solution. The consultative technique seldom uncovers an exact solution to an exact problem. But it can lead to useful ideas that with some modification will solve the problem. A variation on what someone else has done might be the exact solution sought. Here are some sources useful for the consultative technique:

1. Counterparts in private companies.
2. Counterparts in the public sector.
3. Counterparts in private companies in other countries.
4. Related books, handbooks, and reference manuals.
5. Articles in trade journals, magazines, special reports.
6. Seminars, conferences, special meetings where participation is encouraged.
7. Professional consultants with related experience.

Other Techniques

The following is a brief list of additional creative techniques useful for generating alternatives:

1. *Synectics.* This is similar to brainstorming except the problem is not defined or given to the group. The group, through interaction and mental activities, arrives at the problem during the group discussion. At the beginning only the leader may be aware of the problem.

2. *Idea Matrix.* In this procedure, a few ideas that have been gathered are listed in a downward or across array or in a matrix. Seeing an idea in combination with other ideas, either vertical or lateral, may stimulate more ideas.

3. *Gordon Technique.* This is also similar to brainstorming except it attacks the underlying concept of the problem, the product, or the concern. The underlying concept or function is explored at length to collect ideas. For example, designers of electric razors will find their underlying concept is cutting. By exploring all aspects of cutting, they will collect new ideas.

4. *Daydreaming.* This technique encourages uninterrupted daydreaming about the problem. A sheet of paper is presented with one question: "If I had my way and every possible resource at my disposal, how could I solve this problem?" Getting an entire group involved could produce some interesting alternatives.

Value Analysis

Value analysis is an organized effort directed at analyzing the functions of systems, equipment procedures, designs, and supplies for the purpose of achieving the required functions at the lowest overall cost consistent with requirements for performance, reliability, and maintainability. The investigative benefit of value analysis for generating alternatives is inestimable. Value analysis goes deep into the purpose of the product, its function and the features that support its function and examines overdesign. Value analysis as a tool for cost reduction is described in detail in this book in Chapter 7 on cost performance improvement using MBO. The creative aspects of this technique lie in the intense and analytical questioning process that generates ideas for changes and improvements.

Fifth Step: Managers Must Select the Best Alternative

Painstaking effort and analysis have gone into the process up to this point. The challenge now is to evaluate the alternatives to find the best few. This means the alternatives must be weighed in terms of value, payoff, or utility—the utility of a gamble. One of the chief differences between an objective program that produces outstanding results and one that produces mediocre results lies in the utility or payoff weight that is assigned to the various alternatives. Two techniques are described here on how to select the best alternative from among many alternatives.

Decision-Making Matrix Techniques

To determine which alternative has the greatest payoff, we need decision criteria or standards for action. These are measures for weighing utility. They are guidelines by which an alternative is judged as to its value in and applicability to the situation. The weight that is assigned to each alternative on the basis of a standard for action is a vernier or degree of priority. A payoff matrix or decision-making matrix is a useful way to represent how weights will be allocated to each standard of action, as illustrated in Table 6.4. The matrix in this table is a grid on which alternatives are placed with the standards in an adjacent position. Finding the alternative that best meets all necessary standards is the process of optimizing. A numerical ranking procedure, probability assignments, or percentages can be used as the vernier for assessing how well the alternative meets the standard for action. A ranking procedure was used in Table 6.4, which thus illustrates a ranking matrix. Alternatives are assigned rank numbers on the basis of how well they meet utility standards. The step-by-step procedure for developing the best ranking from the decision matrix is as follows:

STEP 1.   Select the standards for action that constitute greatest utility in the situation or problem at hand.

STEP 2.   Using a numerical ranking sequence, weigh each alternative in order of utility for each columnar standard, 1 for greatest utility, 2 for next greatest, and so on.

STEP 3.   Continue the process of ranking each of the alternatives by columns until all standards have been covered.

STEP 4.   If standards are to be given differences in value, rank the standards across in order of importance and multiply the cell value by this weight.

STEP 5.   Add horizontally the cell values to arrive at the total score in the total score column.

STEP 6.   Select the lowest rank number in the total score column as the alternative that best meets all criteria.

The best selection of alternatives is enhanced when the decision to find the best is connected to the problem and guided.

Selection Comparison Technique

A decision based on a simple choice—"this" or "that"—can be reached with swift speed, high accuracy, and great effectiveness. But far more often the

TABLE 6.4 Decision-Making Matrix Technique for Situational Problem: Production Department Unable to Meet Production Quota

Effects (Symptoms)	Causes (Conditional Forces)	Eliminators (Improvement Alternatives)	Decision Matrix Standards to Decide[a]				Total Rank Across	Best Alternative (Objectives to Be Completed)
			Customer Effects	Sales Volume	Union Unrest	Feasibility		
Backlog excessive	Machine idleness and downtime high	Use preventive maintenance program	3	2	2	3	10	Second objective: Set up of preventive maintenance program
Schedule slippage	Unsequenced ordering of parts	PERT[b] ordering of parts from vendors	2	1	5	1	9	First objective: PERT ordering of parts from vendors
High overhead	Excessive travel expense	Set up travel expense control	6	7	6	6	25	
Turnover excessive	Low motivation	Design jobs for job enrichment	5	5	4	5	19	
High grievance rate	Contract violations by supervision	Train supervisors in labor contract	7	6	1	4	18	
Loss of key customers	Product breakdown disrupts customers' operations	Improve design reliability	1	3	7	7	18	
Reject rate high	Careless errors among employees	Motivate and train employees	4	4	3	2	13	

[a]Rank order, probabilities, or percentages can be used for assessing alternatives against the decision standard within the column. Here the rank-order method is used. A wide range of standards is available.

[b]PERT, an acronym for a time control procedure. Letters represent Program Evaluation Review Technique.

decision is based on a whole complex of circumstances or factors that yield values in a broad range. The decision maker is often faced with a whole list of alternatives of which all or most appear attractive. The selection comparison technique is an analysis of all alternatives done by comparing two alternatives at a time from a large list of alternatives. A standard or criterion is selected and two alternatives are judged as to which best meets the criterion. Table 6.5 illustrates the following example:

STEP 1.   List alternatives (John, Helen, Harry, Robert, Dan, Frank).

STEP 2.   Decide on standard or standards to be used for selection (high verbal articulation in meetings and aggressive follow-up).

STEP 3.   Compare each item with every other item, two at a time. (John and Helen, John and Harry, John and Robert, John and Dan, John and Frank. Then Helen and Harry, Helen and Robert, and so on.)

STEP 4.   Within each pair, decide who best meets the standard and record that judgment with a tally mark.

STEP 5.   Add the tally marks across; the alternative with the most tally marks is the best decision.

Sixth Step: Managers Must See Consequences of the Selection

At this point in the problem-solving process, the best alternative has been selected as the best solution to the problem. Traditionally this is the final action prior to implementation. But a final caveat is: Look before leaping. New questions should be raised before the solution is implemented: "What could go wrong?" "What is the impact?" What new problems could emerge?" "Are secondary problems worse than the primary problems?" "What serious consequences could develop that could make our decision backfire?" Ignoring such questions is to ignore the impact of the decision.

TABLE 6.5   Illustration of Selection Comparison Technique

Employees to Be Placed in New Sales Job	Standards		Total Tally	Best Selection
	Articulate in Meetings	Aggressive in Follow-up		
John	11	11	4	
Helen	111		3	
Harry	11	111	5	
Robert	111	11	5	
Dan	11111	11111	10	*
Frank	1	111	4	

Sometimes picking the lesser of two alternatives may be wiser, since this alternative generates fewer secondary problems than the best alternative. Jumping to conclusions must be prevented. The decision maker and problem solver should look at this possibility. Several techniques are suggested for this.

Cause—Effect Diagrams

The cause—effect diagram is a "picture" that relates future possible effects from implementation of the alternative. In every effect there are likely to be interrelated causes. The cause—effect diagram is also termed a "decision tree." Making a decision is more than selecting a course of action, it is foreseeing the impact the effects of the decision will have on the situation to which it is directed. The decision tree or cause—effect diagram helps to anticipate faults that may occur in a proposed set of objectives or a decision before implementation. The tree is made up of a series of nodes and branches. Each branch represents an alternative course of action. The nodes represent the chance events or problems that may occur as a result of selecting that course of action. Figure 6.5 illustrates this. Variation of the cause—effect diagram is seen in the troubleshooter's guide to solving ware-

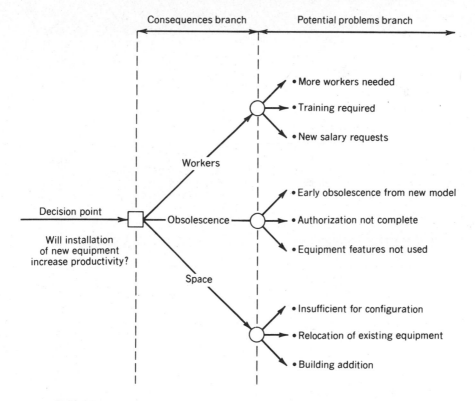

FIGURE 6.5   Cause—effect diagram for viewing consequences of action.

house problems described by Howard Way and Edward Smykay at Rutgers University in their article, "Who's Minding the Storage," published in the *Management Review* (Figure 6.6). The enormous impact of cause−effect relationships in objective-setting processes and in the ultimate commitments of the enterprise makes their analysis worthwhile. Solving problems by working from cause to effect is always working into the future. Causes are the producers of effects. Regarded in this light, they can be improvement forecasts. Every time a person says, "What would happen if we tried . . .?," he or she is thinking and forecasting from cause to effect. Conversely, working from effect to cause is working backward in time. Every time the question , "Why did this happen?," is asked, a person is thinking and analyzing from effect to cause. Managerial analysis and problem solving follow this logical procedure. It is unfortunate that most managerial time is devoted to the past, that is, to analyzing from effect to cause, thereby resulting only in unmaking the past. A 180-degree shift in orientation offers

CAUSE	EFFECT	Inventory variance	Overstocking	Obsolete inventory	Increased inventory costs	Increase in back orders	Customer service failures	Lost customers	Negative balances	Compound errors	Mysterious overages	Loss in asset accounts	Production down time	Emergency production runs	Excessive overtime	High labor turnover	High training costs		
Receive wrong part number																			
Issue wrong part number																			
Report wrong part number																			
Record wrong weight																			
Report wrong weight																			
Use wrong unit of measure																			
Applied wrong unit of measure																			
Issue wrong pack count																			
Report wrong pack count																			
Miscount inventory																			
Mislocate inventory																			
Lose document																			
Fail to post document																			
Post wrong quantity																			
Post to wrong record																			
Fail to update file																			
Update wrong file																			
Update file out of order																			
Lose file																			
Keypunch error																			
Data transmittal error																			
Faulty program logic																			
Component failure																			

FIGURE 6.6 Troubleshooter's guide to solving warehouse problems (*Source:* Howard Way, Jr. and Edward W. Smykay, "Who's Minding the Storage?," *Management Review*, August 1980, pp. 14−22.)

the opportunity to devote cause–effect analysis to improvement forecasts. Using cause–effect reasoning in the present provides a good basis for selection of objectives for the future. The following principles help in the development of a cause–effect perspective.

Principle 1. A single cause can generate an ever-widening chain of primary effects. These primary effects become causes of secondary effects.

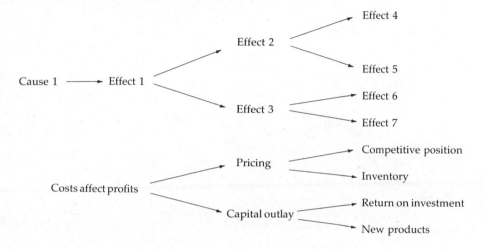

Principle 2. A cause–effect relationship can be interchanged when directed to a new objective or a new situation.

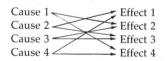

$$\text{Cause} \rightleftharpoons \text{Effect}$$
$$\text{Sales} - \text{costs} = \text{profits}$$
$$\text{Sales} - \text{profits} = \text{costs}$$

Principle 3. When there are several optional causes producing variable effects, cause–effect relationships can be selected and directed toward an objective.

Principle 4.   A cause constraint occurs when causes hold back the completion of a desired effect.

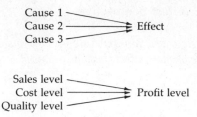

Principle 5.   An effect constraint occurs when causes hold back the completion of a desired cause.

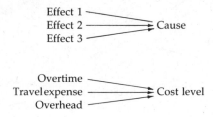

Third-Party Review

Another technique useful for tracing the consequences of implementation of best alternatives is the third-party review. This means having one or more individuals "run through" or "dry run" the impact of implementing an objective or an alternative for a solution. The third-party review is guided by the following criteria:

1. *Completeness.*   Have all consequences been considered?
2. *Attainability.*   Would the solution be attainable in the time specified?
3. *Support.* Have the backing and support of key people been obtained?
4. *Payoff.*   Is the value of the solution greater than the new emergent problems?
5. *Feasibility.*   Is it capable of being done in a practical way?
6. *Quality.*   Does it increase the quality feature?
7. *Safety.*   Does it create hazards?
8. *Morale.*   Is it disruptive to worker morale?

A "fresh" group of noncommitted individuals would perform better for a third-party review than an existing committed group. The aim is to see weaknesses and deficiencies in the implementation of a proposed solution.

Delphi Technique

The Delphi technique is useful in the decision-making process when a large group of people are involved. It is useful in getting consensus of considered opinions and well-thought-out ideas. Writing down ideas and responding to questionnaires helps people think a problem through, which helps avoid "off the top of the head" responses.

At its best, a group decision is a balanced decision that takes into account differing viewpoints and the interaction of individuals. This technique is useful for long-range planning when no immediate decision is needed or when it is inconvenient for group members to meet together. The technique was designed by Norman Dalkey at the Rand Corporation and has been used in universities, government, and industry.

The Delphi technique has three main elements:

1. Group members do not meet face to face.
2. Carefully designed questionnaires covering the plan idea or problem are used.
3. Periodically the information from the questionnaires is summarized and fed back to the respondents.

The following are the steps for the Delphi technique.

STEP 1. Design and distribute to a group of respondents who are anonymous to one another a questionnaire to obtain information on a topic or problem.

STEP 2. Have respondents independently answer the questionnaire and return it.

STEP 3. Summarize all responses and prepare a feedback report on the results of the first questionnaire.

STEP 4. Design a second questionnaire to probe more deeply into the problem and distribute this *with* the feedback report to the respondents.

STEP 5. Have respondents independently evaluate the report and then respond to the second set of questions. They return the questionnaire along with their individual priority vote on the ideas generated so far in the report.

STEP 6. Summarize the results, develop a final report, and distribute it to the respondents.

SUMMARY

Managers create problems when they set objectives and strive to complete them. They need to apply a systematic type of thinking to prying out the problems that will emerge in the practice of MBO. This will allow managers to "picture" the decision-making process and the consequences of implementing the decision. MBO helps define problems by helping managers develop and examine this overall picture with use of its processes and interacting details. The most important first component in problem solving in the MBO context is the attitudes of the practitioner. Several attitudes are identified and described in this chapter. They are:

- Managers must accept problem solving as a way of life.
- Managers must plan to face problems when they set objectives.
- Managers will often face batches of problems rather than individual ones.
- Managers must view problems as signs of something out of control.
- Managers should view problems as opportunities.
- Managers should possess humility in solving problems.

Guidelines for developing these attitudes are suggested in this chapter. Problem solving as a rational thinking process is also presented, and six major steps are identified. Techniques are suggested on how to execute each step. The steps are:

1. Be alert to potential problems.
2. Define the problem.
3. Gather problem information.
4. Generate solution alternatives.
5. Decide on the best solution.
6. Evaluate the consequences of the decision.

Problem solving will always be the heart and core of management. The development of skills in handling problems can be a decisive factor in effective implementation of MBO.

BIBLIOGRAPHY

Bierman, Harold, Jr., et al., *Quantitative Analysis for Business Decisions*. Homewood, IL: Richard D. Irwin, 1981.

DeBono, Edward, *New Think*. New York: Basic Books, 1967.

Fallon, Carlos, *Value Analysis*. New York: Wiley-Interscience, 1971.

Hauser, Ralph I., "Problem Solving." In P. Mali, Ed., *Management Handbook*. New York: Wiley, 1981.

Hodnet, Edward, *The Art of Problem Solving*. New York: Harper & Row, 1955.

Kepner, Charles H., and Tregoe, Benjamin B., *The Rational Manager*. New York: McGraw-Hill, 1965.

Mager, R.F., and Pipe, Peter, *Analyzing Performance Problems*. New York: Pitman, 1970.

Maier, Norman R., *Problem-Solving Discussions and Conferences*. New York: McGraw-Hill, 1963.

Mali, Paul, *Managing by Objectives*. New York: Wiley, 1972.

Miles, Lawrence, *Techniques of Value Analysis and Engineering*. New York: McGraw-Hill, 1961.

Odiorne, G., *Management Decision by Objectives*. Englewood Cliffs, NJ: Prentice-Hall, 1968.

Osborn, Alex F., *Applied Imagination*. New York: Scribner's, 1953.

Parnes, Sidney J., and Briordi, Angelo M., "Creativity in Action." In P. Mali, Ed., *Management Handbook*. New York: Wiley, 1981.

Way, Howard, Jr. and Smykay, Edward W., "Who's Minding the Storage," *Management Review*, August 1980, pp. 14–22.

7

COST IMPROVEMENT
WITH MBO

IN THIS CHAPTER

WHY COST IMPROVEMENT IS IMPORTANT
SIX APPROACHES TO COST IMPROVEMENT
HOW TO START A COST-IMPROVEMENT EFFORT

Cost performance improvement is a major responsibility for every member of the management team, and in fact for all members of the organization, from board chairman to employees. It is a positive approach to a continuous problem of all organizations, that of reducing and keeping costs down through efficient and effective management. The best approach in executing this cost performance responsibility lies in understanding the importance of cost improvement and then choosing the best techniques for bringing it about. Management has the principal responsibility, since it controls the myriad of decisions that have a direct or indirect impact on costs.

The reasons that cost reduction efforts often are not effective are many.

- Cost performance improvement competes with other problems for managers' time, and therefore effort toward it is diluted.
- Cost managing with use of traditional budgeting approaches is not making progress. The traditional budgeting system washes away any incremental improvements made by cost reductions.
- Cost performance skills and competence are not normally available in personnel. Many see cost performance as a complex accounting process. Lack of education and training engenders fear.

- Efforts at cost performance improvement tend to give management personnel the feeling of being criticized for present practices. They want to avoid visibility of poor performance.
- Cost performance policies and procedures are weak or loosely defined and executed.
- Cost performance improvement generally creates unrest with the union because of its change implication. This may create new and unwanted problems for managers.

This chapter centers on making cost improvement a deliberate and realizable attainment for managers and supervisors. Several topics are included: (1) Why cost improvement is important; (2) six approaches to improving cost performance: cost planning with zero-based budgeting (ZBB), cost attitudes, cost avoidance, cost reduction, cost control, and cost effectiveness, and several techniques to implement each approach; and (3) how to start a cost improvement effort.

WHY COST IMPROVEMENT IS IMPORTANT

Costs are rising. Competition is growing keener. Resources are becoming more and more scarce. These are not events, they are trends. The future projection of these trends is up. Stagflation continues, and periodically it goes out of control. Many companies escape the cost-price squeeze threatened by increasing prices by passing the increase on to consumers. This is the history of inflation and recession. Cost performance improvement must be a continuous function involving the active participation of the whole organization. The effort must be defined with top management support. The following are reasons why cost performance improvement must be a way of life for supervisors and employees.

1. *Job Security and Longevity.*   Job security may be strong when economic cycles favor the firm. The passing on of increased costs to customers may be an ongoing and unobjectionable practice. But what happens when economic cycles turn against the firm? When increased costs cannot be passed on? The firm struggles to survive, and this in turn threatens job security of both management and employees. Cost performance cannot be an accident. It must result from good and effective supervision. This, more than any other factor, ensures job security and longevity.

2. *Competition.*   Because inflation causes price increases, customers are becoming more anxious to get the best prices. If a competitor is able to exercise better cost performance, and thus offer lower prices, the threat of survival emerges. In cost management, it is not one company rivaling another; it is rather the skill of one supervisor against that of a rival supervisor. Cost performance is not a matter of choice for any company in

our free-enterprise system. It is the type of performance that keeps the free-enterprise system in force. The ability to reduce prices through cost improvement provides a competitive edge that is difficult to beat.

3. *Improved Potential for Rewards.* Every employee looks forward to improving his or her financial rewards and benefits in an organization. No one wants to remain at an existing level of remuneration. Cost performance improvement broadens the base for better wages, salaries, fringe benefits, vacations, insurance, and holidays. After all, increased rewards are only possible when direct costs are held at levels that allow surpluses to be allocated within the organization. Cost improvement makes possible wage increases to employees while they are still enjoying the same "bottom line."

4. *Better Working Conditions and Quality of Work Life.* Employees every-where look forward to better working conditions, which improve the quality of their work life. Improvements range from equipment designed to make work easier to facilities that foster health, safety, and comfort. Money invested in equipment, tools, and facilities must necessarily come from the profits made by the enterprise. Cost performance's major mission is to improve profitability so as to give a reasonable return on investment for stockholders. When profits are high enough, the potential for their use to better the quality of work life is assured.

5. *Job Satisfaction and Personal Pride.* Waste, rework, rejects, failures, errors, and delays are factors used by workers to measure whether their knowledge and skills have been proficiently applied in the work process. These factors are cost expenditures. Each drains the resources of people, time, and material, which can seriously affect jobs and the company. Of necessity, cost improvement means elimination or reduction of these factors. When these cost factors are controlled and even reduced, job satisfaction and personal pride are enhanced. In other words, gains from cost improvement enhance morale. When these cost factors continue to prevail and even increase, worker satisfaction and sense of contribution are seriously damaged. Outstanding work means work at the lowest possible costs.

6. *Contributions to Government, Health, and Community.* Profit performance by an enterprise is crucial for many groups. The principal one is the stockholders, who loan money to the enterprise for an expected rate of return. Other groups also depend on profits. High profits mean higher taxes to be used by government, health programs, education, welfare programs, and the community in general. Cost improvement is a must for these groups. Cost improvement delights shareholders by making possible increased dividends, while it also contributes to the tax base that must be used to support life-styles.

7. *Base for Future Expansion.* The mission of research and development is to develop new products and services to be sold in the years ahead. This mission is expensive. It is also vital. Without it the enterprise drifts along and even begins to sink, as products mature and become obsolete. Cost

improvement provides retained earnings for investment in research and development programs, which in turn provide new products and services for continuing the profitability of the firm. Cost improvement builds a base for future expansion.

SIX APPROACHES TO COST IMPROVEMENT

Cost improvement is a deliberate, systematic, planned effort with year-in and year-out consistency. Last-ditch cost cutting and slashing are desperate one-shot attempts by panicked management to make up for lack of foresight and planning. Cost improvement is the planning of better cost performance into the job itself. The cost-reduction pattern is built into the work plan in such a way that the manager controls and reduces costs as he or she completes the technical and functional aspects of the job. Six approaches to improving cost performance are suggested:

1. *Cost Attitude Improvement.* The development of understanding among employees that every move they make has an impact on costs, and that these moves must be made with cost performance in mind.
2. *Cost Planning and Budgeting.* The development of short-range operational plans that cover one fiscal period. These plans target the cost performance desired and needed.
3. *Cost Avoidance.* The removal or elimination of a cost item anticipated and budgeted but not needed.
4. *Cost Reduction.* The performance of work so efficiently that costs incurred remain below allowable standards or approved budgets.
5. *Cost Control.* The performance of work in a way that meets and holds to cost standards or expected cost performance levels.
6. *Cost Effectiveness.* The expenditure of funds for an item not budgeted or anticipated but which reduces costs in other areas.

For each of these approaches there are techniques a practitioner can use for improving cost performance. No one approach or technique can stand alone. Cost improvement is successful only when equal vigor and attention are given to all six approaches. The six approaches and some implementing techniques are illustrated in Figure 7.1 and are described briefly in the next sections.

Cost Attitude Improvement

Many management personnel view cost improvement as a program or a response to a directive or as a cooperative effort with departments of accounting and budgeting. This is a false and misleading view. Cost improvement should be a way of life, an attitude. Its core is the acceptance of

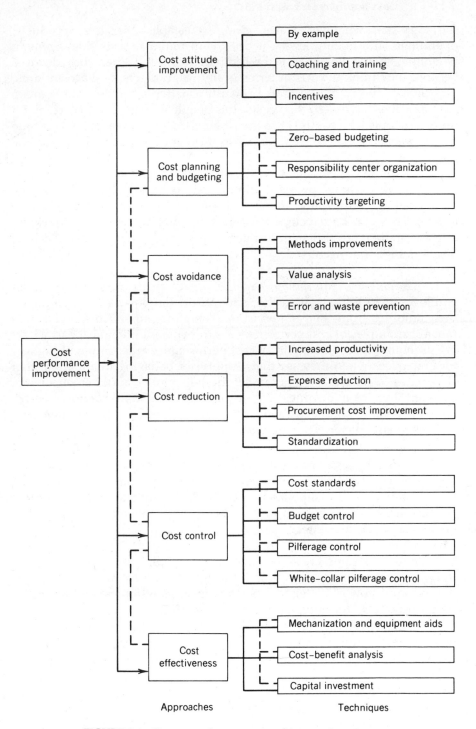

Approaches   Techniques

FIGURE 7.1 Six approaches to cost performance improvement.

the idea that whatever a firm does to establish services, products, operations, and quality levels, it does with minimal costs. Management personnel should not need to be reminded of this. When they do, it is because they think of costs in terms of figures, budgets, and accountants. They ignore the fact that costs are primarily a matter of people. Every move a person makes has an effect on costs. It is people who generate costs, and it must be people who control or reduce them. It is for this reason that attitude development is a first step, first for the supervisor and later for the employee.

Cost attitude development begins with cost consciousness. To be cost conscious is to have predispositions and natural inclinations for the identification, control, and reduction of costs. *These predispositions can be learned*. They can be developed within employees. Three techniques are effective in their development: supervisory example, supervisory coaching and training, and incentives.

1. *Learning by Supervisory Example.* The greatest influence in an employee's work life is his or her supervisor. Employees learn and align their attitudes from their supervisors. Therefore supervisors themselves must be examples of cost performance improvement. The most earthshaking pronouncement in support of cost performance fades into nothingness for employees when they see their supervisor behaving in a manner that accelerates costs. Supervisors can set the tone and do much to encourage cost-performance-mindedness by displaying attitudes, behavior, and actions in behalf of sound cost performance. Employees will take their cues from their supervisor. They will learn by example.

2. *Learning Through Supervisory Coaching and Training.* Generally employees do not have the skills and techniques most effective for cost improvement. They can learn these skills through a day-to-day coaching relationship with the supervisor—coaching that urges, prompts, leads, instructs, corrects, disciplines, and trains; coaching that makes the poor cost performer better, the better cost performer best, and the best cost performer superlative.

Training programs are also useful in developing cost consciousness. In-house seminars and courses can be designed to give an understanding of the why and how of better cost performance. Newsletters and brochures sent periodically to employees serve as reminders of cost performance efforts. Intensive and more sophisticated cost accounting or cost management courses in the academic sphere can also help to provide the skills and techniques for cost performance.

3. *Learning Through Incentives.* Cost performance improves rapidly when its benefits are shared with those who produce it. Suggestion systems provide an opportunity for employees to participate in improving cost performance. Each suggestion that is accepted and implemented earns the contributor an award. This alone makes the system worthwhile. More important than the monetary incentive, however, is the fact that a sugges-

tion plan offers the development of cost consciousness and attitudes that are wanted in the seeker of new ideas. Incentives, both monetary and laudatory, can create a state of mind in an employee that can be a powerful determinant of attitude development and change. In other words, an employee who continually seeks new ways to improve cost performance because of incentives of personal gain will eventually develop the frame of mind to do this automatically and naturally.

The following is a list of cost improvement attitudes supervisors must build in to the work situation for both themselves and their employees:

1. Cost performance improvement must be deliberately made to happen; it will not happen randomly.
2. Cost control and reduction are responsibilities of every employee, with management providing the lead.
3. Cost reduction and effectiveness improvement must be a way and style of economic life. The need for role playing or special assignments to reduce costs indicates the lack of such a way of life.
4. Costs are usually thought of in terms of facts, figures, and accountants, but they are primarily a matter of people working and performing efficiently.
5. Cost-reducing patterns must be built into the work plan itself rather than being implemented after the work is completed.
6. The mission of cost improvement is generic to the managerial function.
7. It is not the cost performance of individual employees that counts, but the total cost performance of all employees.
8. In the final analysis of whether cost reduction efforts have worked, the only real measurement is the resultant savings.
9. Cost performance improvement must ensure that quality is maintained or improved.
10. It is management's job to see that the right climate exists for the production of new ideas for working efficiently.

Cost Planning and Budgeting

A budget is often described as a short-range operational plan. It is developed on the basis of short-term objectives of the organization. Yet its structure, design, and philosophy should fit in the long-range plan of the organization. Each budget should be a milestone marking the accomplishment of short-term objectives as a step forward in the achievement of the long-term objectives. Coordination between short-range and long-range objectives should similarly require coordination between short-range and long-range budgeting. Insistence on well-defined objectives can eliminate many of the problems associated with cost planning and budgeting. Connecting financial resources to be used with objectives to be achieved is the integration of MBO with budgeting.

- If an MBO objective is established, it should be funded by an associated budget.
- If an MBO budget is established, it should be related to an associated MBO objective.
- If an MBO budget is established, it should be committed after consideration of competitors.
- If a strategic MBO budget is established, it should be to outmaneuver competitors.

Cost planning identifies the costs allowable for achieving an MBO objective. Budgeting identifies the control structure required for holding costs to the plan. Three techniques for effective cost planning and budgeting are briefly described here.

Zero-Based Planning and Budgeting—a Rising Star!

MBO satisfies the new demand for accountability. The MBO process requires that commitments to the past cease. The perpetuation of programs because of their historical value must be analyzed in terms of current critical priorities. Spending will not be allowed on the basis of a past decision but on an agreed-on level of expectations of needs and results. Traditional line-item budgeting, which tends to perpetuate commitments that have origins in the past, is a prevalent practice in both private and public organizations. It uses the past level of expenditures as a base and concentrates on projected increases or decreases from that base. Historical data are related to the budget year. Such a procedure leads to examination of only a small portion of the overall budget, the increases or decreases, rather than to a close scrutiny of every facet of it. This means budget analysis concentrates on justifying increases only. This traditional approach is based on the assumption that every function being performed is effective and essential. It provides an "institutionalized framework" for perpetuating past commitments. In many cases the past is 20, 30, or 40 years ago. The assumptions were valid for priorities and concerns that existed at that time. They may not be valid in terms of new priorities and concerns. Previous methods for performing tasks may have become inefficient, outdated, or unnecessary. Funding and decision-making top management personnel are asking how many of the existing functions and programs can be eliminated to provide funds for new and vital programs. This is not to say that all existing projects, programs, and commitments do not have value, but that limited resources must be allocated to new concerns and priorities.

Budgeting traditionally has been a tool for control. When integrated with

MBO, it becomes a tool for planning and control. When put on a zero-based reference, it becomes the basis of planning, control, and decision making. There is a striking parallel between traditional budgeting and zero-based budgeting with MBO, as shown in Table 7.1.

Zero-based budgeting is a new formal process that does not carry over past commitments or perpetuate a base budget that has been "institutionalized." The process starts with a zero base or a zero datum and requires each program or functional manager to demonstrate precisely and convincingly the need for the function, department, program, or project under his or her supervision, before funds are provided. The manager must delineate the results that will be delivered if funding and support are given. Distinct units of work or projects are analyzed, ranked in order of priority, and set up under a program cost center. The program cost center has identified goals or missions. These units of work have been variously termed "work packages," such as used in Program Evaluation Review Technique (PERT) scheduling networks, or "achievement packages," such as used in MBO systems, or what Peter Pyhrr refers to as "decision packages." A decision package is a document that contains all the information needed by funding sources to approve or disapprove it for budget entry. The decision package is definitive enough for managers to evaluate its benefits in comparison with

TABLE 7.1 Traditional Budgeting Compared With Zero-Based Budgeting

Criterion	Traditional Budgeting	Zero-Based Budgeting With MBO
Objectives	Understood though not directly expressed	Clearly and precisely expressed
Purpose	Planning and control	Planning, control, motivating, coordinating, and synthesizing
Scheme	Future is extension of past	Future is created from what's needed but guided by present and past strategic thinking
Structure	Quantitative	Quantitative and qualitative
Style	Delegative	Participative
Allocation	Dividing assigned total to program	Establishing total program needs, then dividing resources
Time	Short range	Short range and long range
Emphasis	Financial	Results, methods, activities, financial
Accountability	During and after performance	Before, during, and after performance
Format	Simple	Comprehensive
Decision making	Consequences known after fact	Consequences known before fact
Pattern of organization	Functional and personnel	Decentralized cost centers

other packages. The information in a decision package will vary from organization to organization but generally will contain the following information and will be classified under a program cost center whose mission or goals are clearly delineated:

1. Objectives to be pursued.
2. Measures of effectiveness and efficiency.
3. Alternative courses of action and the reason for selecting a certain course.
4. Benefits when the objective is achieved.
5. Consequences if the objective is not pursued or an existing activity is eliminated.
6. Costs.
7. Time schedule.

The preparation of the decision packages themselves is similar in many respects to the objective-setting process. A form that helps in the collection of needed information is illustrated in Figure 7.2.

The following illustrates a decision package in zero-based planning and budgeting.

Example: *Name of Decision Package: Reduction in Muggings*

Program Cost Center: Police precinct
Goal of Center: Reduce crime in 30 block area

1. *Objective.* Reduce muggings 20 percent in the 30 blocks while reducing costs 10 percent by January 1.
2. *Measurement.*
   (a)   Before

$$PI = \frac{80 \text{ to } 70 \text{ muggings}}{8 \text{ officers (4 patrol cars)}} = \frac{1.25 \text{ muggings}}{\text{officer}}$$

   (b)   After

$$PI = \frac{70 \text{ to } 56 \text{ muggings}}{6 \text{ officers (patrolmen)}} = \frac{2.33 \text{ muggings}}{\text{officer}}$$

3. *Courses of Action.*
   (a)   Increase number of patrol car surveillances.
   (b)   Set up foot-officer surveillance.
   (c)   Install new street lights for better illumination.
   (d)   Institute awareness program through TV, radio, and newspapers.

DECISION PACKAGE FORM

Project _____ Prepared by _____ Dept. _____ Date_____

Decision unit _____   Approved by _____

Objective to be accomplished:	Resources required	Current year (actual)	Budget year
	Personnel		
Results measurements:	Labor costs		
	Indirect costs		
Courses of action:	Travel costs		
	Contingency experiences		
	Totals		

Benefits or results expected:		
	Potential problems	Contingency actions
Consequences if objective not completed:		

FIGURE 7.2   Decision package form.

Best course of action: Foot-officer surveillance is the most effective way to pursue muggers through off-street alleyways.

4. *Benefits.*
    (a) Reduction in mugging rate.
    (b) Rehabilitation more likely for young mugger than for older hardened criminal.
    (c) Contribution toward safer street.
    (d) Avoidance of potentential loss of life.
5. *Consequences if Not Done.*
    (a) Mugging rate increase.
    (b) Nonapprehended mugger encouraged to continue.
    (c) Refusal of people to walk and shop will affect sales tax potential.
    (d) Accidental killings more likely.

6. *Costs.*   Costs reduced from $96,000 to $72,000.
7. *Schedule.*   To be fully operational by January 1.

The decision packages are aggregated under each program cost center and ranked in value and benefit to the organization. A manager can then determine the benefits at a certain level of expenditure to meet existing or new priorities. The consequences of not carrying out the activities at these levels can also be viewed. Table 7.2 illustrates benefits analysis for different decision packages. The analysis follows the analysis described in previous chapters discussing MBO principles.

A mosquito-control program under a health department cost center of a town may have as many as six decision packages, all dealing with mosquito control but on different levels. The first level may be a $10,000 budget covering 50 acres and benefiting 62 families. The second level may be $24,000 covering 120 acres and benefiting 155 families. The third level may be $42,000 covering 320 acres and benefiting 489 families. Thus the decision package array continues, providing for the decision maker the amount of benefits possible with different levels of expenditure. The value of zero-based planning and budgeting is in its potential for canceling old commitments that have little or marginal value for the new and promising opportunities and prospects that give the organization a chance for improvement. Additionally, it puts the decision maker in the position of "shopping" for the "best buy" of benefits with a given level of expenditure.

Zero-based planning and budgeting as a process sharpens accountability. It puts managers in the position of accounting for how resources will be

TABLE 7.2   Benefits Analysis

Program Cost Center	Decision Packages	Level of Costs	Bigger Benefits	Quicker Benefits	Related Benefits	Long-Range Benefits	Best Decision
A	DP-1	C_1		Benefit costs			
	DP-2	C_2		or			
	DP-3	C_3		benefit ranking			
	DP-4	C_4					
	DP-5	C_5					
B	DP-1	C_1		Benefit costs			
	DP-2	C_2		or			
	DP-3	C_3		benefit ranking			
	DP-4	C_4					
	DP-5	C_5					
⋮	⋮	⋮					

TABLE 7.3   Comparison Between Traditional Line-Item
Budgeting and New Zero-Based Program Budgeting

	Traditional Line-Item Budgeting	Zero-Based Program Budgeting
Program	A	A
Last year	$350,000	0
Proposed changes	10%	Total number of decision packages for the coming year
Proposed budget	$385,000	$325,000

consumed and for the benefits that will be derived in advance of decisions and actual implementation. This is good planning. It puts the funder, taxpayer, customer, or client in the "shopper's seat" to buy desired results from a large array of possibilities. This means that boards of directors, boards of education, and city and town councils can make reasonable and responsible decisions regarding how to set up and allocate a limited budget toward a wide range of priorities. A comparison between traditional line-item budgeting and the new zero-based budgeting is shown in Table 7.3. The zero-based budgeting process gives decision makers many advantages:

1. A better view of the consequences of not pursuing an objective, what will happen if another alternative is selected.
2. A clearer view of the benefits if an objective is pursued. Motives for the effort are clearly delineated.
3. A better view of where budget cuts can be made to align costs with existing funds.
4. A better view of how to eliminate low-priority functions, activities, and programs and provide funds for new an vital projects. It is like asking, "If the budget were cut 10 percent, what effect would there be?" Or, "If the budget were increased 10 percent, what benefits would accrue?"
5. A better view of how to balance decisions in terms of risk, cost, service, and multiple requirements of multiple departments and groups.
6. A better view of how costs are consolidated into cost centers for control, forecasting, and productivity measurement.
7. A better view of where to institute changes of flexibility and applications of funding based on service demands that have recently emerged.

8. A better view of how iteration between many levels of an organization is taking place for coordination and optimization of the entire organization.

9. A better view of supporting documentation that clarifies evaluation and accountability of results and expenditures.

The Southern California Edison Company began experimenting with zero-based planning and budgeting in 1974. The problems of fuel shortages, rising prices, and reduced sales pointed to projected earnings substantially below 1974 goals. Consequently, department managers were directed to submit estimates of activities that could be reduced. But this caused an arbitrariness of "crash" reductions that proved inflexible. The company tested the zero-based process and found it to be enlightening. In 1975 the zero-based process was extended to the entire company and the results were:

- Personnel reductions saved 9 percent of the budget.
- Decision packages gave a better way to set priorities.
- Permanent dollar savings were significant.
- Planning and budgeting improved in areas of responsibility.
- Surveillance by senior management over proposed activities was better for the coming budgetary year.

Zero-based planning and budgeting is not the total answer for handling the problems of an accounting and budgeting system, but it comes close. The decision package concept allows for both planning and productivity and the inclusion of these plans in the resource allocations of a budget. What more could one ask?

Responsibility Center Organization

A responsibility center is a formal activity in an organization in which costs or concerns are collected, tabulated, measured for results, and reported for accountability and decision making. Traditionally, responsibility centers are budget centers that follow functional organization charts. The advantage of this traditional scheme is that it allows assignment of cost responsibility to recognizable functional heads. But the approach has a serious drawback: Operation performance or results are reported somewhere other than the budget center. In other words, budget reporting and performance reporting are separated by both location and level. This traditional approach fits the organization to the accountability system. A need exists to fit the accounting system to the organization. The accounting process from a responsibility center should aggregate at that center all the information, data, figures, statistics, performance results, benefits, resource uses, and expenses that are needed to give responsibility reports. Collecting information in these centers engenders more effective responsibility reports. Several types of responsibility centers have emerged in both public and private organizations.

1. *Cost Centers.* A recognizable and definable activity within the organization, in which *costs* are collected and assigned. These cost centers may be established for a machine, a group of machines, a process, several activities, a project, or a system. They may be established with individuals, a group, or a collection of groups. A responsibility center may have a number of cost centers. All cost information is collected, accumulated, and controlled from these centers.

2. *Profit Centers.* A recognizable and definable activity within the organization, in which *sales revenue data* and *costs* are collected and assigned. Profit centers are established to give profit responsibility to lower levels, divisions, or product managers who need to make decisions in short time periods. Profit motive is also assigned to these centers to motivate the manager, especially if there is bonus participation. Profit centers may have a number of cost centers and sales centers.

3. *Productivity Centers.* A recognizable and definable activity within the organization, in which *performance data* and *costs* are collected and assigned. Collection of both performance and cost data in the same responsibility center makes measurement and tracking of productivity easier and more effective. Most organizations experience difficulty in the measurement of productivity because of the separation and diffusion of the parameters needed for its measurement. Productivity centers should collect performance data for the measurement of productivity.

4. *Investment Center.* A recognizable and definable activity within the organization, in which *information* and *data* are collected and assigned in order to measure and track return on investment. This is a profit center with separate capital, investment considerations, and calculations. The rate of return in investment centers is carefully monitored for cost effectiveness. Better management is possible when top management can compare increases or decreases in rates of return from differences in the investment bases. This comparison includes varying depreciation methods, different inventory valuations, and comparative value of purchased with leased equipment.

Productivity Targeting

Productivity targeting is the direction of thinking, planning, efforts, activities, resources, and equipment to recognized and predetermined productivity objectives. It is a planning and behavior strategy that enables an individual to acquire the skills and abilities to organize for productivity achievements. The strategy is based on the MBO principle of targeting: The greater the focus of efforts and resources on a future specific accomplishment on a time scale, the greater the likelihood of reaching the accomplishment. The strategy of productivity targeting is briefly as follows:

STEP 1.   Develop the need for productivity awareness. Productivity awareness gives shape and perspective to what must be done. It provides the "why" for setting of productivity targets.

STEP 2.   Set productivity targets. Transform a lack of direction and a vague mission into a solid purpose and a specific thing to do.

STEP 3.   Establish for each target a plan of action. Transform an established target into a pursued objective by setting up an action plan with scheduling, budgeting, and resource allocation.

STEP 4.   Break down large targets into smaller ones. A main, complex productivity target can be achieved by orderly sequencing of smaller subsidiary targets.

STEP 5.   Provide a way to measure whether each target has been hit. Build into each target the means to determine whether the target has been accomplished. This means can be the [actual productivity measurement] of the target pursued.

STEP 6.   Be alert to diversionary target traps. These are obstacles and barriers that prevent the reaching or building of the target. Contingency action plans help to circumvent obstacles.

Productivity targeting as a strategy is a cost improvement planning effort. More will be said on productivity and efficiency in Chapters 8 and 9 of this handbook.

Cost Avoidance

The removal or elimination of an anticipated and budgeted cost item should be a prime effort in improvement of cost performance. Avoidance of the expenditure completely before it commences is most attractive. Avoidance does not mean elimination of the work, the function, or the expectation. It means a new process, a new way, a new product, or a new approach has been discovered that will allow avoiding the expenditure. If an anticipated delivery would cost $12,000 per month FOB dock in a new program in which the budget has been approved, but a new supplier is located who is willing to absorb delivery costs, the approach used for cost performance improvement is cost avoidance. The cost avoidance effort centers on planned expenditures. It is cost reduction before the work begins. It is more "preventive cost expenditures," a kind of validation that should be applied to plans, budgets, and strategies. The essential difference between cost avoidance and cost reduction is that the former avoids costs before work begins and the latter reduces costs while work is being completed. Three techniques of implementing cost avoidance are briefly described here. These techniques are equally applicable to the cost reduction approach described in the next section.

Methods and Systems Improvement

Better methods and more efficient systems mean avoided costs or lower costs. The methods improvement supervisor has the attitude "there must be a better way." Methods improvement, a form of work simplification, is a common-sense step-by-step technique of studying and analyzing work to find easier and better ways of doing it. It also applies to a systematic analysis of materials, parts, and supplies to determine the necessity of using them, their adequacy, the availability of lower cost substitutes, or the possibility of avoiding the costs completely. It has one vital principle: Every detail of a job should be examined for wasted or excessive energy, materials, time, or motion. There are six steps to this technique:

STEP 1. Select the job, operation, process, or product to be improved. Look for problems: high rework; missed schedules; excessive paperwork; excessive backlog; excessive pollution; high accident rates; high waste; excessive repairs; too much corrective work; high turnover; high machine downtime; high absenteeism.

Look for areas of improvement: loss of key customers; increased rivalries; excessive resistance; unbalanced inventory; dilution of effort; high overhead; loose quality control; increasing costs; excessive transfer requests; high material handling time.

Look for new opportunities: in an old production system; in an old product line; low profits; lowered sales volume; low morale; poor public image; unexplored materials; traditional methods; unchanged designs and process layouts; forms.

STEP 2. Chart the job, operation, or process to be improved. Use symbols to graphically represent the procedures for work or flow of work. The flowchart is a road map and serves as a communication device of the present work situation (see Figure 7.3).

STEP 3. Question the details of time, sequence, and methods for improvement. Four fundamental questions for work improvement are: Eliminate? Combine? Simplify? Rearrange? Work improvement requires an open mind. The complacent individual with a closed mind is a major obstacle to simplification of work. Self-imposed limitations on thinking prevent the emergence of alternatives or options for simplifying work. In methods improvement or work simplification, nothing is taken for granted. There are many ways to do any operation, and methods improvement is an attempt to find the best cost performance way. The methods improvement supervisor consults those concerned with the process,

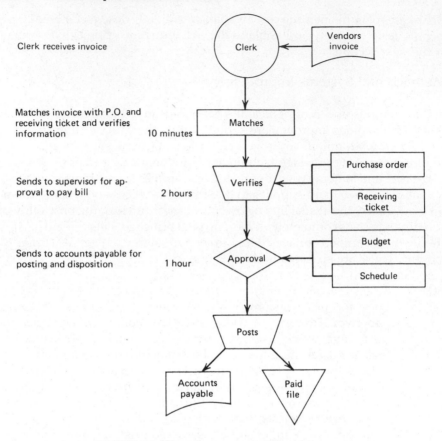

FIGURE 7.3   Flow chart representation of a process.

those who are intimately acquainted with its details, and makes them members of the cost-improvement team. To facilitate the skills for conducting methods improvement, a series of methods improvement actions can be taken to avoid or reduce costs:

1.   *Design Action Checklist.*   Can the design or parts of the design be eliminated, combined, simplified, or rearranged by loosening tolerances, reducing weight, reducing size, heat treating, reducing lengths, reducing vibration and number of parts, reducing visual requirements, eliminating extras, redesigning for standardization, achieving greater interchangeability, redesigning dangling parts, specifying minimum material, designing for smaller grasping area, chamfering mating parts, reducing finishing requirements, redesigning to permit symmetrical parts?

2.   *Materials Action Checklist.*   Can the materials or purchased stock be eliminated, combined, simplified, or rearranged by substituting another material, using new material available,

using scrap or rejects, changing size and weight, using stronger materials, changing size received, reducing packaging specs, changing quantities shipped, changing packaging material, making rather than buying, buying rather than making, buying supplier's standard sizes, asking supplier to do work on material, standardizing forms or patterns, changing finish specifications, reducing incoming quality requirements?

3. *Methods Action Checklist.* Can the method of doing work be eliminated, combined, simplified, or rearranged by reassigning work to lower paid worker; labeling parts for training; using lowest body member possible; performing in a rhythmic sequence; removing regrasp; locating tools in a proper work location; reducing bending, turning, walking, and kneeling; changing procedure from difficult to easy; employing part-time help during peaks; using a weight count; using symmetrical hand motions; eliminating going to the same place more than once; keeping stock close to work; using better light; reducing number of parts moved; setting up procedures for random work?

4. *Equipment Action Checklist.* Can the equipment, tools, and machinery of the workplace be eliminated, combined, simplified, or rearranged by using multipurpose jigs, reducing clamps, using automatic feeds on machines, color-coding tools and equipment, changing physical process arrangement, using simply operated machines, using foot pedals, changing to semiautomatic, using power tools, locating pins or stops, using combination tools, having enough space for handling, using hoists for lifting, picking up more than one at a time, using extension on controls, using positioning devices?

5. *Sequence Action Checklist.* Can the sequence of procedure or product be eliminated, combined, simplified, or rearranged by changing order of performance, changing people in the process, performing two operations simultaneously, performing operations in another department, omitting operations, using multi-spindle setups, reversing order, dividing one operation into two, combining two operations into one, dispatching material from one place, reducing number of steps, introducing labor-handling equipment, combining machinery or tools, doing work while parts are in transit, minimizing number or controls, arranging steps in best order?

STEP 4. Rechart the improved or simplified job, operation, or process. Once a process, procedure, or work layout has been improved to get the most practical results in the shortest period of time with the least amount of effort at the lowest cost, rechart the work layout with its changes. The changes proposed must be clearly seen in the overall process. The "new ripples" it generates must be clearly established in the layout. In other words, the secondary problems cannot be greater than the solutions to the primary problems. The new work layout must be attainable and useful.

STEP 5.   Evaluate and compare the differences before and after.   The proposed improvement in cost performance must be measured in sufficient detail to clearly justify its implementation. It must be valid, useful, timely, and practical. The cost savings must be clearly visible when the proposed plan is compared with the present situation. Figure 7.4 shows a form useful in evaluating the differences between the two.

STEP 6.   Apply the new method if it really does avoid or reduce costs.   This step is the selling and persuasive step. In it the savings from the new proposal are combined with an action plan to persuade top management and the affected departments to adopt the new method. This step should not be minimized. There is always resistance to change by those who wish to protect their own innovations. To ask people to abandon long-time commitments that they have personally instituted is a challenge of the greatest proportions. Many excellent proposals have been denied because they were not presented to show that the benefits accrued to both the company and the affected departments.

An example of these steps in methods improvement is shown in Figure 7.5. Methods improvement practitioners, as they improve methods, begin to develop systems. They assure that all the parts and steps in a process not only are done simply and with the least cost but are also connected and work together for a common purpose. A well-defined system working efficiently

Work process elements	Present		Proposed		Difference	
	No.	Time	No.	Time	No.	Time
◯ Operation						
⇨ Transportation						
Inspection						
◻ Delay						
▽ Storage						
Total operation and time						
Total distance						

FIGURE 7.4   Evaluating the difference in a process layout.

Flow Process Chart

	600 Assemblies	Present		Proposed		Difference	
Summary		No.	Time	No.	Time	No.	Time
○	Operations	7	304.8	7	700	–	234.8
⇨	Transportation	10	4.2	4	.5	6	3.7
□	Inspections	–		1		–	+1
D	Delays	–		2		+2	
▽	Storages	3	v	1	v	v	–2
	Totals	20	309	15	705	–5	238.5
	Distances traveled	417 Ft		80 Ft		337 Ft.	

No. _____
Page _____
Of _____

(min/lot)

Job _____ Assemble slab—wooden pencil _____

Follow the   ☐ Product   ☐ Man
             ☐ Material ☐ Form

Chart begins ___ Slabs in storeroom ___
Chart ends ___ Assembled and clamped ___
Chartered by ___ P.O.E.   Date 9/29 ___

Details of proposal method	Operation	Transport	Inspection	Delay	Storage	Distance in feet	Quantity	Time Est.	Notes
1. Stores in storeroom	○	⇨	□	D	▽				
2. To slotter-groover by hand truck	○	⇨	□	D	▽	25	1200	.25	Finished stock thinner one box contains 1200 four — stock slabs (2400) (pencils)
3. Slot cut in bottom and four grooves in top	●	⇨	□	D	▽		1200	30.00	One pass thru tandem set machines
4. To lead laying machine (one-half lot — see 9)	○	⇨	□	D	▽	25	600	.13	Hand truck
5. Wait for lead layer	○	⇨	□	D	▽		600	v	Stock delay between lots all four-groove run before starting next size
6. Loaded in machine magazine	●	⇨	□	D	▽		600	–	Loaded during machine operation
7. Lead layed in slab	●	⇨	□	D	▽			20.00	Push bar mach. pushes slabs from bottom of mag. under lead hopper
8. Inspected for full leads, moved to topper (see 12)	○	⇨	□	D	▽				Inspected by machine tender on steel bench slide on way to topper during machine time
	○	⇨	□	D	▽				
9. To glue-topper (one-half lot see 4)	○	⇨	□	D	▽	30	600	.15	Hand Truck
10. Wait for glue topper	○	⇨	□	D	▽		600		Refer 5
11. Loaded in glue machine magazine	●	⇨	□	D	▽		600	2.40	Glue-topper loads 25 slabs at time into mag. = 24 loads @ .10 min/load
12. Glued	●	⇨	□	D	▽		600		Push bar mach. pushes slab over glue wheel into topping position
13. Topped and turned	●	⇨	□	D	▽		600	11.60	Topper places glued slab on leaded slab and turns on edge
14. Assembled slabs clamped by topper	●	⇨	□	D	▽		600	6.00	Topper clamps unit of 25 assem. slabs = 24 units (Topper paced by layer)
	○	⇨	□	D	▽				
	○	⇨	□	D	▽				

FIGURE 7.5   Flow process chart for assembling pencil slabs.

and effectively formerly was a system that was carefully improved over several cycles. In methods-improvement analysis, careful consideration should be given to formation of a system that leans heavily on cost avoidance. The following are examples of systems that, when properly designed and managed, avoid costs: inventory control system; employment system; accounts receivable system; performance appraisal system; data processing system; expense control system; forecasting system; management information system; materials handling system.

Several criteria are useful in ascertaining whether a system is operating effectively and efficiently:

1.   The system must be formally defined with a written purpose, policy, set of procedures, and expected results.
2.   The system must operate with minimal time, people, and resources and maximal performance, productivity, and profitability.
3.   The system must have a built-in feedback of information for checking if results are as expected or whether corrections must be made.
4.   The system must not be more complex than the abilities of the people who must work in the system.
5.   The system must have milestones of progress to allow quick recognition whether milestone expectations have been realized, so that corrections can be made in time.
6.   The system must not cost as much as or more than the results it is delivering within an amortized period of time.
7.   The system must be understood by those who will operate it.

Value Analysis

Value analysis is an organized effort directed at analyzing the functions of systems, equipment, and supplies for the purpose of achieving these functions at the lowest overall cost but at a level consistent with requirements for performance, reliability, and maintainability. Value analysis helps identify unnecessary costs throughout the product or process cycle. It is also used to analyze activities. The scope of value analysis falls into three areas: (1) design value engineering, in which functional designs, design guides, standards, and specs and design reviews are examined for cost improvements; (2) procurement value analysis, in which procurement practices and purchases with suppliers and vendors are examined for cost improvement; and (3) administrative value analysis, in which systems, procedures, policies, processes, and activities are examined for cost improvement.

Value analysis is analysis in great depth. Whereas wasteful or unneeded practices are easily detected and eliminated, functional ineffectiveness and inefficiencies are not so easily detected and eliminated. Value analysis goes deep into the purpose of the product, its function, the features that support its functions, and its design. It separates the overall function of a part,

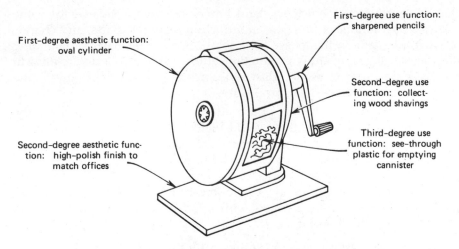

First-degree use function:
sharpened pencils

First-degree aesthetic function:
oval cylinder

Second-degree use
function: collect-
ing wood shavings

Second-degree aesthetic function: high-polish finish to
match offices

Third-degree use
function: see-through
plastic for emptying
cannister

FIGURE 7.6   Cost broken down by function in pencil sharpener.

product, or process into the use function and the aesthetic function. Each is important. But for decision making the two need to be separated, so that costs can be weighed against use and aesthetic values. Use and aesthetic functions can be further divided into first-, second-, and third-degree functions. Again this clarifies for the decision maker how cost is allocated in the various functions of a product and how value can be matched with these functions. Figure 7.6 illustrates this with a pencil sharpener.

The guiding principles of value analysis are as follows:

1. The value and usefulness of the product, process, or procedure must be worth its price or cost.
2. All features of the product, process, or procedure must be needed.
3. All usable parts or steps must be made or taken by the lowest cost method.
4. The design includes materials and processes with the least cost that best meet the function.
5. The design includes materials and processes that are standardized for the industry.
6. The design includes materials and processes that several vendors can supply under competitive bidding.

Value analysis determines whether each feature of the designed product or process is worth the value and is paying for itself. It starts with a job plan analysis. The essential phases in the analysis are:

1. *Information Collection Phase.* In this phase a product, service, process, or procedure is selected that is high in cost, is loaded with problems

that are obstacles for efficiency, and has never been evaluated for value analysis. Definitions of function, subfunction, features, parts, and characteristics are made in this phase. The total costs are established, including life-cycle costs and quantity production. Information is collected relative to trouble spots, grievances, and difficulties people are experiencing with the product, service, process, or procedure.

2.   *Analysis Phase.*   In this phase attempts are made to aggregate the information into a format that would yield the greatest return for value analysis effort. For example, problems are classified from large to small savings benefits and from large to small difficulties. Products are organized from the most difficult to produce to the easiest to produce. Processes are organized from the complex flow to the simple flow. Assumptions underlying present practices are clarified with intensive questions. Examples of questions are shown in Figure 7.7.

3.   *Creativity Phase.*   This phase allows for the creative process to begin, a process that will yield ideas for changes and improvements. The questioning process of phase 2 is continued in this phase, since questioning is a form of thinking that leads to creativity—penetrating questions spark ideas for improvement. Several creativity techniques can help:

- Brainstorming: Generating a multitude of ideas that could be further developed.
- Use of Checklists: Aiding the mind by reviewing lists of thought-provoking ideas that help illustrate variations.
- Consultation: Consulting with others who can bring a fresh approach to an old system.
- Comparison: Comparing and evaluating the ideas of others for solutions.

4.   *Evaluation Phase.*   In this phase the ideas and proposals developed in the previous phase are analyzed and screened. The ideas are reviewed to determine their value and worth. A set of criteria or standards is selected to help in the evaluation of ideas. A rough approximation of potential savings is developed in this phase.

5.   *Planning Phase.*   This is the development phase. Ideas that have value and worth are developed and detailed as to costs, sales potential, productivity, and resource conservation. A definitive plan results. Costs are reviewed and savings are calculated formally for top-management review.

6.   *Reporting Phase.*   In this phase a report is made to top management. The report is a proposal that attempts to persuade management to approve and implement the proposed idea. This can be the hardest phase of all since skepticism and resistance to change will inevitably be encountered.

WHAT?

1. Is it necessary?
2. Do you know exactly what you are doing?
3. Is there some other way of getting the same results?
4. Is it being done because some other job is not right?
5. Is any equipment used less than 50% of the time?
6. Are we using the most up-to-date tools?
7. Are we providing more quality than required?

WHERE?

1. Can the "do" be performed in a fixture or holding device?
2. Is the "do" performed in the most convenient location?
3. Can your vendor or supplier do it cheaper or quicker?
4. Are materials and tools located within grasp efficiency?
5. Is the work space laid out according to the best sequence of motions?
6. Is space being taken by obsolete materials and supplies?

WHEN?

1. Can the "do" be performed on several objects at once?
2. Can the "do" be reversed?
3. Can two parts be picked up at the same time?
4. Can the sequence of the operation be rearranged?
5. Can we have tools, blueprints, job instructions brought out to machine ahead of time?
6. Will better planning reduce set-up time?

WHO?

1. Are both hands performing "do" details?
2. Do you leave it to the employee, how to do?
3. Do you have the faster or more careful employee doing?
4. Do you need the best-trained employee to do the easiest job?
5. Is the operator trained to do the job efficiently?
6. Can someone on an off-shift or lunch period provide set-up work?

HOW?

1. Will simple mechanical aids be helpful?
2. Are parts designed for easy performance of the "do" details?
3. Will a foot-pedal-operated device assist the hands?
4. Can parts be slid rather than picked up?
5. Has the process or procedure been analyzed to see whether steps can be omitted?
6. Can the sequence be changed, shifted, or rearranged?

FIGURE 7.7 Examples of questions asked in the value analysis technique.

The major difference of value analysis compared with the many other techniques of cost performance improvement is its in-depth analysis of design, development, and testing. Consequently more time is needed for the development of skills to implement the technique.

A very important development in the value analysis technique is activity value analysis (AVA). This is in-depth evaluation of every group activity to find, assess, and eliminate activities that have minimal or casual value in the group (Figure 7.8). AVA may also be used in departments with many groups or on an individual basis. Steps in AVA are as follows:

STEP 1.   Define and list the activities, functions, and services produced in a group, section, or department. Identify the individual end product and value of each contribution (or consequences of not doing it), with its associated costs. Summarize the total costs of all activities.

STEP 2.   Examine the relevant value and priority of the activities, functions, and services compared with their costs. Rank them from most valuable to least valuable.

STEP 3.   Assess the activities to determine if they are traditional, habitual, or prerogative driven for very little reason. This requires an exchange of ideas and judgments between the generator of services and the receiver of services.

STEP 4.   Sift out activities that can be eliminated without affecting the current mode of doing work, current expectations, and needed services to other departments.

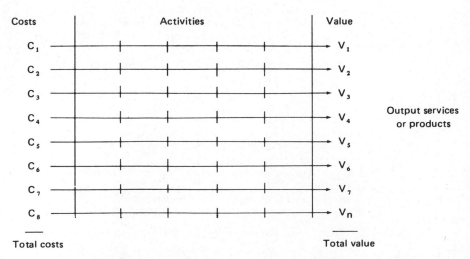

FIGURE 7.8   Value/cost identification in a cost center.

STEP 5. Identify the costs that are saved by proposing changes with reductions or eliminations.

STEP 6. Submit proposals to top management for the reduction or elimination of the activities for cost avoidance or cost reduction by the affected manager.

Waste Prevention

Cost performance improvement begins with the recognition of waste and its stoppage before it occurs or its prevention from recurring. Waste occurs for many reasons. The principal ones are:

1. *Lack of or Poor Planning.* Plans that have been poorly contrived, are without detail, are uncoordinated, and are nonvalidated inevitably produce waste. The principal waste is time.

2. *Errors.* Employees who are poorly trained, without skills, and with minimal experience commit errors that inevitably cause waste.

3. *Poor Work Attitudes.* Employees who do not care, are sloppy in work habits, or have no system of accountability cause waste.

4. *Faulty and Obsolete Equipment.* Equipment that is faulty, in need of repair, or obsolete for needed operations causes waste. Rapid change in technology renders existing equipment ineffective or insufficient.

5. *Stress and Pressure of Diminishing Time.* Rushing work to meet a schedule or working under terrific pressure is bound to cause waste. Error and rework are the first effects, but waste is the second and lasting effect.

The cost performance practitioner will view waste as a misplaced resource, a mismanaged asset, and will exert every effort to control, reduce, and prevent it. Several techniques are directly applicable to waste prevention, each acting to eliminate the causes of waste just described. These are worth mentioning even briefly.

1. *Improve on Operational Planning.* Each plan should be carefully reviewed to assure that waste prevention has been considered in the planning of work.

2. *Conduct Training.* Formal and informal training are a must for employees to assure that they have the skills for the job. Training ensures the competence necessary for accuracy.

3. *Develop Attitudes for Good Work.* Employees must have the attitude that doing it right the first time is a personal and important responsibility.

4. *Replace or Repair Defective Equipment.* Maintenance of equipment is a responsibility most management personnel have accepted. But in waste prevention, preventive maintenance is a must.

5. *Make Schedules Realistic and Attainable.*   The value of a challenge cannot be refuted. However, if rework, rejects, and waste result, it is better to relieve the pressure and allow the employee to do it right the first time.

Waste is often ignored because facts about it are lacking. When facts and measurements are available, something can be done about the waste problem. Figure 7.9 shows a checklist of wastes that can easily be prevented.

Waste of Time

- Not investigating immediately when repairs are needed.
- Failing to get workers started on time and working to quitting time.
- Allowing workers to kill time by talking, visiting, and socializing.
- Having too many people employed.
- Failing to get workers to do more work than they do.
- Not having the tools and equipment to do the job.
- Scheduling overtime that could have been avoided.
- Failing to make instructions clear to workers.

Waste of Materials

- Allowing materials to be spoiled through poor training.
- Failing to explain monetary value of materials to workers.
- Allowing work to be spoiled by employees with poor eyesight or health.
- Using material unsuited to the work.
- Using more expensive materials than needed.
- Getting defective work from an employee who did it for correction.
- Ordering more materials than needed.
- Allowing spoilage due to poor storage of materials.

Waste of Equipment

- Failing to keep equipment in good condition.
- Being ignorant of the capability and uses of equipment.
- Using large machines for small work and vice versa.
- Not cooperating with the maintenance department on care of equipment.
- Ordering repair of machinery that should be scrapped and replaced.
- Failing to listen to workers' complaints about equipment.
- Allowing "shoe string" repairs.
- Not keeping informed on latest equipment.

Waste of Labor

- Failing to use the best worker for the job.
- Enforcing discipline too strictly or too laxly.
- Failing to correct a worker immediately after an error.
- Failing to question workers on time accountability.
- Giving incomplete orders to do a job.
- Not giving enough attention to jobs that are complex.
- Failing to train an understudy.
- Allowing poor housekeeping that interferes with people.

FIGURE 7.9 Checklist for easily preventable wastes.

Cost Reduction

It's an accepted fact that one dollar saved in the manufacture, purchase, or consumption of raw materials is approximately equal to the profit on ten dollars in sales. This means that increased profits result from either of two efforts: increasing sales while holding costs level or holding sales level while decreasing costs. Cost reduction is a planned approach to reducing expenses, wastes, and costs without damage to product quality or customer service expectation. Cost reduction is not an accounting function. Accounting may provide the facts and figures that form the basis of cost reduction efforts, but these efforts lie most directly on those who generate them. The individuals who make the greatest cost decisions should be the ones most involved in cost reduction efforts. People such as top managers, purchasing agents, supervisors, and engineers are cost determiners. Therefore they should lead the cost reduction efforts. People such as accounting clerks, research analysts, data processing administrators, and inventory managers should be a part of, but not necessarily leaders of, the effort.

Three techniques are briefly described here as ways to implement cost reduction. The reader is reminded that the techniques for cost avoidance are equally applicable to cost reduction.

Expenditure Reduction

The fastest and most direct way to reduce costs is to reduce expenditures. Those who make decisions to incur expenditures are in the best position to hold and even reduce costs. The danger here is the possibility of reducing or affecting performance in some way. Cost reduction requires a careful assessment of the value of reduced costs against the value of reduced performance. When the value of reducing costs is greater than the value of reducing performance, a decision to favor reduced costs should be made. When the value of not reducing performance is greater than the value of reducing costs, a decision to favor performance should be made.

A checklist for areas attractive for expenditure reduction follows. It should be remembered that reduction occurs when the cost savings outweigh the costs of reduced performance.

1. Reduce costs by laying off mediocre employees or employees not carrying their weight; by not replacing employees who have retired, quit, transferred, or left for any reason; by eliminating general pay increases and providing increases on the basis of performance and contributions; and by eliminating overtime, holiday work, and extra time.
2. Reduce operating budgets by making across-the-board cuts, by eliminating nonessential budget items, and by eliminating or deferring budget items with low priority.
3. Replace employees who leave with employees who are less expensive in terms of salary and benefits—students, moonlighters,

retirees, and handicapped workers; hire part-time workers during peak periods; and hire military retirees who have good and relevant experience.

4. Reduce advertising expense through reducing the costs for institutional, image-generating, and awareness types of advertisements. These ads serve to generate a general awareness and reaction from the market.

5. Reduce commissions expense for selling of products and services, particularly to repeat customers or to long-time customers of the firm.

6. Reduce computer expense through reducing lease time or downtime of the computer. Spare capacity available could be sold or reallocated under lease or rental agreements.

7. Reduce energy resource expense through reducing use of electricity, fuel, and water.

8. Reduce telephone expense through reducing number of telephones, length of time on telephone, special telephone services not needed, and special telephone units. Eliminate personal toll calls.

9. Reduce paper reproducing and filing expense through reducing number of copies, using cheaper paper, decreasing distribution and purging old files.

10. Reduce traveling expense by limiting trips, using closer suppliers and distributors, holding conferences by telephone, and giving minimal travel allowances.

11. Reduce tax expense through better reporting of taxable but depreciated assets, using tax shelters, and taking advantage of government tax incentives.

12. Reduce equipment expense by returning unused equipment, tables, chairs, typewriters, cabinets, tools, fixtures, and gauges.

13. Reduce operating expenses by reporting leaky valves, escaping gas, faulty equipment, arching switches, and machines running idle.

14. Reduce accident expense by removing hazards, using safe containers, avoiding poor housekeeping, and establishing safe practices and procedures.

Productivity Improvement

The most effective way to reduce costs is through improved productivity. Reducing costs by reducing expenditures is bound to hurt performance, which may or may not hurt productivity. But reducing costs through greater productivity assures that both performance and costs are considered in any decision to change either. Chapter 8 in this handbook covers improving productivity, and includes the many techniques and processes available for reducing costs. The following are a few of these techniques: work-focus productivity generator; work-flow productivity increaser; resource-accountability clarifier; time-scheduling productivity multiplier; productivity tracker; cost-productivity allocator; and productivity-effectiveness planner. Each of these techniques requires decisions that will reduce costs only after the effects of the technique on performance are known. This prevents driving costs down for the sake of costs alone. For example, productivity improvement for cost reduction is better effected when employees are upgraded in their skills and abilities.

Procurement Cost Improvement

The procurement function in an enterprise has become a critical cost performance function, since thousands and even millions of dollars are committed by it. Inefficiency, ineffectiveness, or poor cost performance in procurement can be multiplied manyfold to generate unwanted or unneeded costs. The potential for savings is so great that procurement cost improvement must be an ongoing effort. The procurement function refers to all departments that in some way determine what to buy, where to buy, the time to buy, the quantity to be bought, the quality to be bought, and the price to pay; arrange for transportation, expediting, and follow up; receive what was bought; or process invoices for payment and disbursement of cash. Often all departments of an enterprise are involved in these activities. The efficiency and effectiveness of these departments affect operating costs in many ways.

Good management of the procurement-cost function entails at least a policy statement from top management expressing attitude and general guidelines; formalizing responsibilities for the activities and accountability of results; spelling out the relationship between the purchasing and other departments; and establishing suppliers in such a way that the enterprise is favored in cost relationships, public image, proprietary information, contractual agreements, and business ethics with regard to conflicts of interest, gifts, and allowable entertainment. A purchasing manual is a must to set up cost-handling practices for internal personnel and external suppliers.

The following are practices that, when properly instituted, can bring about cost reduction:

1. *Competitive Bidding.*   Competitive bids should be solicited when purchases exceed certain dollar limits. Invitations should be sent only to acceptable suppliers who understand the bidding process.

2. *Value Analysis.*   A deliberate and formal effort should be made to combat the problems of cost reduction by the examination of value and the price of the value to the customer.

3. *Quantity Buying.*   A network of acceptable suppliers who provide discounts or other cost savings incentives for volume or quantity buying should be established. Annual blanket orders can be set up for price protection and quantity discounts.

4. *Frequent Use of Blanket Purchase Orders.* Blanket purchase orders should be used with known and reliable vendors, if prices can be agreed on at the beginning of a period and a blanket order issued for the entire period. Vendors welcome the prospect of long-range selling, and buyers gain with fixed prices for volume buying under inflationary price escalation.

5. *Special Discounts for On-Time Payments.* Discounts of 2, 3, or 5 percent should be taken for on-time payments. Suppliers who provide these incentives should be sought and used if they meet purchasing qualifications. On-time payment discounts can add up to considerable savings on an annual basis: As much as 36¢ of expenses goes for the use of suppliers, and this money can be saved with discounts.

6. *Return of Unused Purchases.* Overbuying is more a practice than an exception. Many suppliers will allow return of unused purchases for credit. Return prevents unused supplies and materials from being wasted.

7. *Quality-Purchase Analysis.* Over-quality buying is an expensive practice. Assessing the needed quality level and buying to match that level can frequently result in reduced costs.

8. *Reclaim of Materials for Resale.* Resale programs can be developed whereby scrap and reject materials can be salvaged and sold to other vendors.

9. *Negotiated Trade Discounts.* Trade discounts at higher than traditional rates can be obtained through price negotiations. These negotiations of price reductions are tradeoffs to the customer if the customer will allow delivery to suit the supplier.

Standardization

Standardization is a process in which a wide variety of unique items and specialties are reduced to a few basic models and types. The process encourages efficiency and economics in handling, storing, ordering, and producing. When a company reviews the 1500 items it carries in stock and available for purchase and finds it can eliminate 800 of them with little impact on sales volume, that effort is an example of standardization, and can result in large savings. The following steps can bring about standardization:

STEP 1. Make a list of items such as inventories, materials, projects, stocks, services, programs and so on, now being developed or purchased for a company. Each item should be described as to why it is unique.

STEP 2. Arrange the items in decreasing order of importance and payoff for sales, costs, or customer needs.

STEP 3. Classify the items into three categories. In Category A are those that can not be altered in any way, since they are vital and have high payoff; in Category B are items that can be combined in such a way that a standard can be used with some options; and in Category C are items that can be eliminated entirely, since they contribute very little.

Standardization programs are intended to root out unneeded inventories. They can bring direct savings.

Cost Control

There comes a time in the operations of an enterprise when neither cost avoidance nor cost redirection can prevail, a time when an expected cost will occur and only an effort to hold it to a certain level is feasible. In this situation, a cost-control system is needed to measure actual costs and report the costs against certain levels of expectation. The cost-control system must collect cost data that reflect the actual conditions by product, by operations, and by department. It must be set up on a real-time basis; that is, reports from the system should be delivered to cost performance practitioners in time for them to execute corrective action. Cost variances from the system are brought to the attention of management so that planning and operating decisions can be made. The cost-control system must be useful in controlling costs and should quickly identify problem areas or unprofitable products or services. The data contained in the cost records should be periodically reconciled with the data in the general account books of the enterprise.

Cost Standards

Where costs must be held to certain levels, cost standards should be developed and introduced into the cost-control system. A cost standard should be set for each item to be controlled. Actual expenditures per unit of time can then be compared against these standards. Standards can be set up under a task-performance analysis, in which information is collected to form the basis of the standards. Such information includes present costs, past costs, average costs over any given period, cost changes and trends, backup documentation for proposal estimates, measures of the effectiveness of cost reduction efforts, and an index of groups' cost performance to motivate cost consciousness and cost reduction. The following are examples of cost standards:

- Cost of pump and engine repair material does not exceed $3500/year/machine.
- Total pipeline maintenance cost is less than $315/year/mile of pipe maintained.
- Cost of gasket supplies is less than $100/year.
- Total fuel loss is less than 1 percent of total barrels.

- Operating overtime hours are less than 3 percent of scheduled hours worked.
- Weld rejects are less than 5 percent of radiographed welds accepted.

Budgetary Control

Budgets are plans for allocation of resources. They represent blueprints of a projected plan of action. Thus work-force budgets, financial budgets, capital budgets, materials budgets, purchases budgets, inventory budgets, and cost-of-materials-used budgets are all designed to provide direct control over precious resources. But budget preparation procedures do not usually allow plenty of time for information gathering. Budgets are formed with insufficient information, poor information, obsolete information, changing information, all under limited time. Furthermore, a budget once formulated is seldom scrutinized to assure that it meets the cost performance needed. In fact, the uncertainty of information and the commitment implication of a budget tend to force managers to build up or pad the budget for "personal safety" reasons. Additionally, personnel who plan budgets are generally not skillful in cost performance improvement. Thus budgets provide store-houses of possibilities for improvement of cost performance.

Budgets for the operation of a department, section, facility, or plant are usually set up before the actual operation is started. The budgets can be formulated on the basis of history, estimates, or standards. Actual variances can be acted on for control and reduction.

The following are suggestions for improving budgeting procedures for good cost performance:

1. Budget formation should follow a deliberate and efficient procedure.
2. Information used in budgets should be valid for the use intended.
3. Budget allocations should be realistic and alterable.
4. Reporting variance should be in a frame for correcting the variances.
5. Variances should be reported to those who are generating them.
6. Budgets should be sufficiently detailed to specify intention.
7. Budgets should have supporting information for justification.
8. Budgets, objectives, and goals should be well connected.
9. The formats of budgets should have a strong relevance to expected performance.
10. Errors in budget formation and implementation should be fed back to those responsible for them as an effort to prevent future errors.

Pilferage Control

The record shows that of every three people who work for a company, one will never steal, a second will steal at every available chance, and a third will steal if the opportunity arises and he or she feels able to get away with it. Thus two of every three employees are potential problems in security. American industry pays 6.5 percent of gross annual sales for pilferage. The cost practitioner must accept the fact that internal security is a must. A person's reasons for stealing from the company vary from a need to support extravagant living or pay unforeseen expenses to a feeling that he or she must make up for insufficient compensation by the company. The practitioner must set up a system of internal checks that will stop pilferage. The following guidelines may be useful:

1. Treat the cash register and the handling of cash with great respect. Follow an operating manual's procedure for cash control, deposits, tapes, safe control, and reports.
2. Set up a stock and inventory system of spread control in which one person checks the work, deposits, inventory, and so forth of another.
3. Keep accurate records as described in the operating manual. Money or stock should be checked by a senior employee.
4. Practice the surprise audit and be sure everyone knows it. Plan frequent surprise audits of various critical areas in which opportunity for defalcation may be high.
5. Look at recorded percentages to detect leaks of cash, costs, supplies, materials, and tools. The more locked doors, the less leakage.

White-Collar Pilferage Control

White-collar crimes have now developed into a significant cost drainer for American industries. As the number of white-collar workers grows because of increased white-collar jobs such as computer programming, accounting, administration, engineering, teaching, office work, and so on, this cost drain will increase. Blue-collar pilferage centers on materials, tools, supplies, products, and inventories. White-collar pilferage centers on items such as:

1. *Use of Company Time.*   The prime pilferage of white-collar workers from a company is use of company time to engage in and complete personal work, activities, or commitments. The work can range from completing political and community activities to running a small business or enterprise on the side—all while on a company payroll.
2. *Unauthorized Personal Toll Calls.*   Telephone bills include both charges made on behalf of the company and charges made for personal needs. The extent of toll call abuse is nearly impossible to determine, as this activity is subversive and quiet.
3. *Unauthorized Use of Company Equipment.*   Unless it is a company policy to permit employees to use company equipment, unauthorized equipment use constitutes a form of pilferage. Paper-reproducing ma-

chines, company cars, photographic equipment, and special tools are examples of company equipment that is used for personal ends.

4. *Pocketing of Money From Sales of Company Products.*   Employees are often given special discounts on the purchase of company products. Resale of these products at listed prices can be a legitimate and acceptable activity. But the stealing of company products and resale at reduced prices not only hurts the company's cost performance record but leads the employee to the arena of out-and-out crime.

White-collar pilferage is difficult to control, since many of the people involved are executives and management personnel. Getting employees to sign "no conflict-of-interest" statements before employment is one approach to the problem. Giving visibility to policies that prohibit pilferage is another. Use of security guards at the entrances and exits of the company is still another. Special investigators with a focused surveillance are useful in determining the length and breadth of pilferage. Special training for supervisors to spot irregularities is also useful. The problem continues to grow, significantly affecting cost performance.

Cost Effectiveness

This approach allows the expenditure of funds not budgeted or planned, for the purpose of reducing costs in other areas or departments. In other words, sometimes a company has to spend money to save money. The anticipated savings represent an attractive and significant return for the invested money. The return cannot be minimal or marginal; it must be at least as attractive as the return on money invested outside the firm. Top management must agree that feeding profits back into the firm is the best investment opportunity they can decide on.

Capital Investments

Because capital expenditure generally involve large sums of money with more or less permanent commitments, decisions concerning them must have a positive effect on the economic health of the firm. An ill-advised decision concerning capital additions frequently cannot be revised. It could shake the financial stability of the firm or even bring the company to a point where its survivability is in doubt. On the other hand, a well-advised decision to commit a capital expenditure for reducing costs can put the firm in a solid state of profitability for a long time to come. Both the timing of capital expenditures and the amount of funds to be invested in new plants or equipment involve serious policy decisions concerning the consistency of the cash flow of the firm and its existing financial burdens. Although this chapter does not deal with these issues, they should not be ignored by the cost performance practitioner. Ideas on the subject must be developed formally and in considerable detail. Any proposal for a capital expenditure will entail the collaboration of at least the accounting department and probably others. A cost-effectiveness proposal should include the following:

1. Description of the idea as a project.
2. Reasons and values of the idea for cost reduction.
3. Facts and figures collected.
4. Advantages and disadvantages of the project.
5. Evaluation of investment worth and subsequent savings.
6. Outline of financial requirements.
7. Brief plan for launching the project with objectives, schedules, and procedures.

Cost–Benefit Analysis

This technique evaluates, during a planning period, the benefits that might be expected from a decision to go ahead with the purchase of equipment, the value of pursuing a project, or the expected return from the start of a program. It is a systematic analysis of the major costs and benefits involved in various patterns of expenditure and resource allocation. This implies that before being approved a budget should undergo analysis to ensure that maximum benefit is obtained by the planned expenditure. The cost–benefit analysis looks at options or alternatives that might give other beneficial effects. If the organization has been restructured into cost centers to which budgets are allocated and performance measures are aggregated, a cost–benefit analysis can be made between and among cost centers. Through this process improvements in productivity, tradeoffs, and compromises can be made.

In many ways, cost–benefit analysis is priority setting with use of two parameters: costs and benefits. Decisions to adopt any one option are based on several reviews of the available options. The general approach to cost–benefit analysis is illustrated in Table 7.4.

In this analysis, probability of occurrence is the risk factor, the degree of uncertainty in realizing the benefits. One can see that the highest potential benefit with the least cost is not necessarily the option to select, since the

TABLE 7.4   Cost–Benefits Analysis

Ventures (Equipment, Projects, or Programs)	Costs	Potential Benefits	Benefits Analysis		
			Probability of Occurrence	Expected Benefits	Expected Savings
Option A	$4000	$6000	.40	$2400	1600
Option B	1000	4000	.60	2400	1400
Option C	2000	4000	.90	2400	1600
Option D	3000	4500	.75	3375	375

probability of occurrence is not very attractive. In cost–benefit analysis, cost and benefits are measured against the confidence and probability of occurrence.

Equipment Aids and Mechanization

When an organization conducts its operation so that labor and labor-connected services are primary, the organization is said to be labor intensive. Cost effectiveness through mechanization may be pursued in labor-intensive situations by examining where equipment, equipment aids, or equipment handling processes can be brought in to complement labor or to replace labor. In either event, a savings is possible but a cost expenditure is required. As in any cost-effectiveness proposal, the savings must exceed expenditures.

HOW TO START A COST-IMPROVEMENT EFFORT

Cost performance improvement in itself is not a new idea, but an *organized approach* for improving the cost performance of management and nonmanagement personnel may be a new idea for many managers and their company. Only when cost-improvement activities are aimed at definite targets in a companywide approach are there productive results. The sending of letters or memos from the president to employees asking them to save on costs is too casual an approach, and gets few or no results. Nor does reliance on the accounting department. True, the department will provide the data and basis for planning of the cost-improvement effort, but it is a fallacy to think that the effort begins and ends in the company's ledgers.

Cost performance improvement can happen only when it is a planned, long-range, companywide activity on every level of all organizational functions, an organized method of reducing waste of time, labor power, materials, and expenses in all departments without affecting the product, quality, or profitable sales and contracts. This organized approach results in improved return on investment through greater profit volume. A total cost improvement program can be introduced into a company with use of the following steps. Figure 7.10 gives a specific example.

STEP 1.   Secure support of top management.
  (a)   Cost improvement effort is directed from top management.
  (b)   Participation by all top personnel must be a personal commitment.
  (c)   Policy and scope of effort are formally defined and announced.
  (d)   Top management takes the lead and gives an example of the effort.

COST PERFORMANCE IMPROVEMENT

Division: Central   Department: Plastics

Originator: Harvey Small   Date: 3/10/85   Approved: P. A. Beck   Date: 3/15/85

Type: Confidence:
- ☐ Cost Avoidance   - ☒ Valid and immediate
- ☒ Cost Reduction   - ☐ Valid but long range
- ☐ Cost Control   - ☐ Non-valid, needs work
- ☐ Cost Effectiveness

Previous Method	Proposed Method
Description:	Description:
a) At the plastics dept., acrylic plastic is cut by four knife jigs, each having 20 rotor knives and one bit knife.	a) Recent evaluation indicates total number of knives not needed.
b) Knife jig system in operation over 30 years.	b) Suggest using new knife jigs, each having 8 rotor knives and 2-bit knives. (Number reduces from 84 to 40)
c) Knives purchased for these jigs come from various domestic suppliers and are purchased 4 times per year.	c) Located source in England that can be shown knives are equal or better in quality for 40 to 50 percent less if purchased for annual quantity.

Previous Method Costs:

Labor	$ 4,500
Materials	64,000
Other	————
Total	$68,500

Proposed Method Costs:

Labor	$ 2,500
Materials	37,000
Other	————
Total	$39,500

Summary:

Savings per year	$29,000
Cost to implement change	400
Net Savings per year	$28,600

Time to write off ___none___ year(s)   Approved by: __/S/ Operations Mgr.__

Follow Up

Date	Remarks	Date	Remarks

FIGURE 7.10   Cost performance improvement.

STEP 2.   Develop a plan.

   (a)   Cost targets, cost objectives, and goals are set by all departments.

   (b)   Defined savings are allocated in departments and set up in a schedule.

   (c)   Accountability for savings is related to all key managers.

   (d)   A system is defined for collecting, analyzing, and reporting savings.

STEP 3.   Organize the effort.

   (a)   A coordinator is selected to provide centrality and continuity.

   (b)   All departments are represented in committee meetings held weekly.

   (c)   The coordinator is needler, analyzer, worrier, and stimulator.

   (d)   Committee meetings are a forum to direct the entire program.

   (e)   The coordinator issues a weekly memo of minutes of meetings to all management.

STEP 4.   Promote the program.

   (a)   Communications consist of memos, newsletters, booklets, reports, and meetings.

   (b)   Contests and competition are set up between departments and contributors.

   (c)   Training programs and seminars are conducted.

   (d)   Boss-subordinate interviews discuss and enlist participation.

STEP 5.   Develop a system for collecting ideas for improvement.

   (a)   Cost performance improvement forms are given to all managers and employees.

   (b)   A cost improvement committee is the vehicle for collecting ideas.

   (c)   An employee suggestion system with incentives is set up.

   (d)   Department staff has brainstorming sessions for new ideas.

   (e)   Audits and outside consultants are used.

   (f)   Vendors, suppliers, salespeople, and outside presentations are used.

   (g)   Visitations and conferences with neighboring companies are organized.

   (h)   Magazines, books, competitor practices, and trade meetings are used.

STEP 6.   Develop a system for analyzing and implementing ideas.

   (a)   Proposals are classified by savings, by confidence, by immediacy.

(b)   Committee recommends proposals to line management.

(c)   Priority agreements are made with line management.

(d)   Changes are recommended to originators.

STEP 7.   Develop a system for reporting results.

(a)   Accounting personnel set up a collection of results.

(b)   Scorekeeping results are given to committee and overall company.

(c)   Recognition is given to departments and to contributors.

(d)   Implications and suggestions to improve the effort are made.

Example: *Cost Reduction Program in Small Wholesaling Firm of 30 Employees (Table 7.5)*

System of Collecting Ideas

An employee suggestion system is designed to reward employees who submit ideas to improve service to customers; lower the cost of storage, maintenance, and handling of supplies; improve safety or working conditions; or protect property and equipment. All nonsupervisory employees are eligible to participate, and awards of up to $1000 in U.S. savings bonds may be made. Ideas that result in a neater, more efficient, safer, or healthier work area may win awards of not less than $25. There is no limit to the number of suggestions that may be submitted and the number of awards given. Joint suggestions are allowed, each member sharing the award. Awards are given on the basis of 10 percent of the savings accrued within a 12-month period.

Analysis of Implementation of One Idea

1.   *Suggestion by Employee.*   Standardize office supplies and reduce idle storage of supplies in desks and cabinets.

2.   *Analysis.*   During a six-month period, purchasing included 18 different kinds of paper clips, 34 different types of pencils, 16 different types of ballpoint pens, 19 different types of erasers, 8 different types of staples, and 18 different types of plain paper pads. Employees in general think that different types are stocked because of departmental preferences, but standardization is most welcome.

3.   *Organization and Schedule.*   A committee with office manager presiding is formed to consider how best to standardize and set up inventory and purchasing targets. The suggestions are: reduce inventory by 25 percent and reduce ordering and purchasing costs by 25 percent, reduction to take place within six months with monthly reports and feedback to all employees; institute purchasing control system and competitive supply bids; institute inventory control system.

TABLE 7.5 Summary of Cost Performance Improvement in Small Wholesaling Firm

Division: Central		Depts.: All		Period Beginning: 2/1/85		Period Ending: 4/15/85		
Date Submitted	Operation	Title of Cost Improvement Item	Type[a]	Confidence	Estimated Annual Savings	Date Savings to Begin	Estimated Cost	Net Savings	Project Needed
2/15/85	Engineering	Substitute locally made tools	CR	Valid	$ 9,500	2/15/85	$ 500	$ 9,000	No
3/20/85	Engineering	Relocate LP gas shortage rack	CR	Valid	1,500	3/30/85	700	800	No
3/20/85	Operations	Reprocess & reclaim scrap	CE	Nonvalid	30,000	5/15/85	10,000	20,000	Yes
3/15/85	Operations	New materials handling process	CR	Valid	8,000	3/20/85	2,000	6,000	No
3/25/85	Purchasing	Quantity purchase of Stock # 3	CR	Valid	40,000	4/1/85	30,000	10,000	No
					$89,000		$43,200	$45,800	

[a] CR, cost reduction; CE, cost effectiveness.

252

4. *Promotion.* Suggestions are made to alternate a series of motivational posters at six bulletin board locations throughout the period; have a display table in the lunch room showing costs and varieties of supplies; provide a biweekly chart of progress to supervisors and to bulletin boards on results of program.

5. *Results of Program.* Standardization at this firm reduced inventory 40 percent, reduced ordering costs 51 percent, and reduced purchasing costs 25 percent.

Six Steps for Individual Cost Performance Improvement

1. Pick a task to improve. Select a high cost area never worked on before.
2. Get the facts for doing the task. Collect information on quality, errors, rework.
3. Ask why the task is done that way. Question alternate ways of doing the work.
4. Work out an easier, simpler, and less costly way. The selected way must yield savings.
5. Have a plan for implementation. Set an objective and detail the steps to reach it.
6. Get a decision to move ahead. Sell the plan and get the approval.

Indicators of Cost Improvement Progress

1. Resultant savings on a continuous basis.
2. Reduction in operating budgets.
3. Reduction in personnel and improvement in productivity.
4. Reduction in resource expenses.
5. Reduction in travel expenses.
6. Reduction in manufacturing unit costs.
7. Reduction in overhead costs.
8. Reduction in repair parts turnover.
9. Improvement on equipment downtime.
10. Reduction of scrap record.
11. Percent increase in suggestion awards.
12. Improved performance appraisals.
13. Reduction in number of rejects and rework.
14. Reduction in unit cost of materials handling.
15. Reduction of number of errors in filling orders.
16. Reduction in number of customer complaints.
17. Increased sales and contract awards.

18. Improved return on capital investment.
19. Improved profits as percentage of sales.
20. Improved disbursement of profits.

SUMMARY

Cost performance improvement is not a program or an overnight excursion in cost cutting, nor is it a project with a start-stop cycle. It is more a work life-style that continues as long as work continues. It starts with attitude and an understanding of why the life-style is necessary. It then incorporates approaches, techniques, and skills for practicing it. Six approaches are explained in this chapter: cost attitude improvement, cost planning and budgeting, cost avoidance, cost reduction, cost control, and cost effectiveness. Techniques are suggested for each of these approaches, which are interrelated. Getting started with these approaches and techniques is also explained. Cost performance improvement must be a responsibility for every employee, but management personnel must exert the leadership.

BIBLIOGRAPHY

Mali, Paul, *Improving Total Productivity*. New York: Wiley, 1978.

Miles, Lawrence D., *Techniques of Value Analysis*. New York: McGraw-Hill, 1961.

Pyhrr, Peter A., *Zero-Base Budgeting*. New York: Wiley, 1973.

Staley, John D., *The Cost-Minded Manager*. New York: American Management Association, 1961.

Stettler, Howard F., *Systems Based Independent Audits*. Englewood Cliffs, NJ.: Prentice-Hall, 1971,

Tec, Leon, *Targets*. New York: Harper & Row, 1980.

Welsch, Glenn A., *Budgeting: Profit Planning and Control*. Englewood Cliffs, NJ: Prentice-Hall, 1971.

8

PRODUCTIVITY IMPROVEMENT WITH MBO

IN THIS CHAPTER

WHAT IS PRODUCTIVITY?
MAJOR CAUSES OF PRODUCTIVITY DECLINE
MEASUREMENT: THE PRODUCTIVITY BREAKTHROUGH
MANAGING TO IMPROVE PRODUCTIVITY
MANAGING PRODUCTIVITY BY OBJECTIVES (MPBO)
ORGANIZATION STRATEGIES FOR PRODUCTIVITY IMPROVEMENT
PRACTICES FOR IMPROVING PRODUCTIVITY

The era of the casual manager has been disappearing for a decade or more. This type of manager wastes resources, expends large amounts of time, and executes commitments on a trial-and-error basis. We've moved into an era in which managers must clearly and deliberately define the results wanted, allocate carefully the resources needed, set up an effective and efficient work process, and provide the day-to-day surveillance and control needed for accomplishment of the intended results. We've moved into an era in which productivity is managed.

This chapter describes the nature of productivity, its concept, causes of its decline in an organization, and ways to measure it. The strategy of managing productivity by objectives (MPBO) is explained, along with seven techniques for improving productivity. Productivity strategies, practices, and standards are also covered.

WHAT IS PRODUCTIVITY?

Productivity is not production! It is not pushing steel out the front door as fast as possible without regard for safety and quality. Nor is productivity performance, or results. Production, performance, and results are only components of a productivity effort. Most people associate the concept of productivity with production and manufacturing, because in these functions it is most visible, tangible, and measurable. Productivity management is not usually formal, because managers generally have vague understanding about it. Few see it as a tool. Employees view productivity as a management benefit, not an employee benefit. Workers have little understanding about how productivity can help them, and in fact usually regard any effort to promote productivity as harmful to them. Productivity data of the past and present are important. But plans for future productivity are more important. Productivity is affected by many factors in the work process, some controllable, some uncontrollable; some critical, some trivial; some predictable, some unpredictable; some long range, some short range. Managing productivity means managing these factors. Productivity and quality of work life are inseparable. Managing productivity means managing them both.

The concept and definition of organizational productivity must be broad enough to include all of its components. Therefore:

> *Productivity is the measure of how well resources are brought together in an organization and utilized to accomplish a set of results. Productivity is reaching the highest level of performance with the least expenditure of resources. Simply stated: Productivity is getting more for less.*

This definition has two parts. The first part is a set of results, or performance. This part refers to effectiveness in reaching a mission or a planned achievement or a needed value, without regard to the costs incurred on the way. A Fleetwood Cadillac can be used to deliver a small package three blocks away and can therefore be effective in that mission, but its use obviously is a gross misallocation of resources. Effectiveness standards refer to achievement of results regardless of cost or when cost is not a critical problem. The whole productivity question starts with what must be accomplished. Profits, patient care, budget performance, sales volume, highways completed, student enrollments, production quotas, and program completions are examples of accomplishments. Accomplishment of a set of results is by far the most important focus of the productivity concept, because without a set of results there is no productivity. The focus on a set of results for productivity closely follows concepts of MBO and is described later in this chapter as MPBO.

The second part of the productivity definition implies consumption of resources, without which achievements are not likely to happen and productivity cannot exist. This second part of the concept specifies the number, type, and level of resources needed. Productivity requires resources such as plant capacity, personnel, costs, raw materials, facilities, capital, technology, budgets, supplies, and information. How well these resources are brought together and how much of them is expended refers to efficiency in achieving results. High productivity suggests minimum use of resources. Efficiency implies attainment of a level or range of results that is acceptable but not necessarily desirable. There is no virtue in delivering a package three blocks away on foot, incurring no cost and using minimal resources, if in the process the package arrives too late and the individual needing the package has left. The delivery is efficient but not effective.

George Kuper, former acting executive director of the National Commission on Productivity and Work Quality, thinks of productivity as a combination of effectiveness and efficiency. To determine productivity one must ask both whether the desired result was achieved (the effectiveness question) and what resources were consumed to achieve it (the efficiency question). Therefore *productivity is a combination of effectiveness and efficiency!* Effectiveness relates to performance, efficiency to resource utilization. How well resources are brought together and utilized is indicated by comparing the magnitude or volume of results, often called output (effectiveness), with the magnitude and volume of the resources, often called input (efficiency). This ratio becomes an index of the definition and measurement of productivity:

$$\text{Productivity index (PI)} = \frac{\text{output obtained}}{\text{input expended}} = \frac{\text{performance achieved}}{\text{resources consumed}} = \frac{\text{effectiveness}}{\text{efficiency}}$$

A basic prerequisite for productivity improvement in an organization is that both the output (performance achievement) and the input (resources consumed) be measurable while maintaining a level of quality. If performance and resources cannot be measured, the work processes must be rearranged so that measurement is possible. Figure 8.1, on page 258, shows the differences between a goal, a performance objective, a performance standard, and a productivity objective.

MAJOR CAUSES OF PRODUCTIVITY DECLINE

1. *Inability to Measure Subsequent Stretching Performance of White-Collar Workers.* Shocking wastes of resources result from our inability to measure, evaluate, and manage the productivity of a growing white-collar work force. White-collar workers make up the bulk of a growing employment force in the service industries, knowledge jobs, health-care fields, educational institutions, government services, human-services work, research, and the like. At this writing, the labor force is 55% white collar and the trend

Goal: Reduce rework.

Performance objective: Reduce rework from $40,000 to $20,000 by January 1.

Performance standard: Performance is satisfactory when rework is not greater than $20,000 per year.

Productivity objective: Reduce rework from $40,000 to $20,000 with a new process that costs $2000 (PI = $20,000/2000 = 10) by January 1.

$$\text{Productivity/quality index (PQI)} = \frac{\text{output obtained}}{\text{input expended}} \times \text{quality factor}$$

$$\text{PQI} = \frac{\text{performance (output)}}{\text{resource use (input)}} \times \text{quality factor} = \frac{\text{effectiveness in work results}}{\text{efficiency in completing work}} \times \frac{\text{Adherence to}}{\text{quality standards}}$$

Example:

$$\text{PQI} = \frac{40 \text{ work packages}}{10 \text{ weeks}} \times 1 = 4 \text{ work packages per week (quality factor} = 1)$$

FIGURE 8.1 Differences between goal, performance objective, performance standard, and productivity objective.

is up. White-collar employees have no tradition of having their work evaluated for productivity. Managers in knowledge jobs are not trained to measure and manage productivity.

2. *Benefits Awarded Without Equivalent in Productivity.* Spiraling inflation results from the giving of rewards and benefits without receipt of the equivalent in productivity and accountability. When wage increases, cost-of-living increments, compensation benefits, and automatic labor-contract handouts are given without corresponding increases in productivity, the net difference is, by definition, inflation. Inflation plagues us because costs rise faster than productivity and prices are increased to equalize the difference.

3. *Delays from Inefficiency in the Organization.* Delays and time lags result from diffused authority and inefficiency in complex superorganizations. Processes and skills that bring about large projects with large complexities have brought with them lagging reaction time, authority dilution, and diffused accountability. Harlan Cleveland described it as "interlaced webs of tension in which control is loose, power diffused, and centers of decision plural."

4. *Push for Organizational Growth Instead of Productivity Growth.* Costs soar from organizational expansion that reduces growth. As an organization grows and expands, the need for additional staff becomes inevitable. Increased hiring results in higher costs, high resource use, wasted time, and burdening paperwork. Productivity declines if this type of resource use is

continued in the traditional way. Management has traditionally pushed for organizational growth. We now know this means soaring costs. What we really want is productivity growth.

5. *Low Motivation Among Employees.*   Low motivation prevails among a rising number of workers. As workers and their families achieve relatively high incomes and standards of living, they assume a life-style and attitudes characteristic of affluence. This affluence, however, has affected the traditional reasons people work. Long-standing motivators do not seem as effective as in the past.

6. *Delays Caused by Material Shortages.*   Late product deliveries are caused by scarcity of key materials: Steel, copper, energy, paper, plastics, and glass. It takes considerable time for these materials to be delivered. The delays affect productivity. In many cases managers must pay sharply higher prices for materials needed in a shorter time frame for their operations.

7. *Unresolved and Ignored Conflicts and Frustrations.*   Unresolved human conflicts and difficulties in cooperation result in organizational ineffectiveness. Organizations are driving managers, supervisors, and employees to set goals and try to accomplish them. This is good! However, in the setting of goals and working toward their completion, disparities, lack of coordination, and conflicts inevitably develop. Conflicts vary from minor differences of opinion to intensive discord. When they are severe, unity of action is seriously disrupted and productivity is affected.

8. *Inhibiting Antiquated Laws and Increased Litigation.*   Management options and prerogatives for productivity are constrained by increasing legislative intrusions and by antiquated laws. Social legislation, environmental controls, safety regulations, price and wage controls, and labor-management bargaining constraints have brought about "legalized" participative management. Many of the goals legislation tries to achieve are worthwhile. But when the laws and legal constraints enforcing these goals are at best marginal in value, or are obsolete, damage is done. Many of the laws were set up originally to solve problems in a different economic era, under different conditions. Many are now obsolete.

9. *Dissatisfied Workers Doing Boring Work.*   Dissatisfying and boring work results from specialized and restrictive work processes. For many people, work is no fun at all. Specialization and division of work processes into small steps to gain efficiency also bring tedium and boredom. Work used to be back breaking for millions of workers; now it is mind tormenting. Dissatisfied people find all kinds of reasons to avoid work, and productivity is affected.

10. *Decreased Product and Service Innovations.*   New opportunities and innovations are declining from the impact of rapid technological change and high costs. When technology changes because of an innovation, expensive equipment purchases for the original work process become obsolete. Amortization usually takes years. Rapid technology change generates stress on

amortization, cost, time, people, and buildings. Paradoxically, research and development (R & D) is the function that brought about the technological innovation. R & D usually gets squeezed because it has long-range, rather than short-range, value to an organization.

11. *Demand for Leisure Time Reducing Productive Hours.*   Time commitments are disrupted by the increasing demand of workers for leisure time. Social scientists predict that we are moving toward a world of less work and more leisure time. Automation is one cause. The means to purchase pleasure is second. Riva Poor states that it is critical that we locate, explore, and utilize time innovations such as the four-day workweek in order to bolster the productivity that has been basic in improving the quality of our lives.

12. *Workers Failing to Keep up With Knowledge.*   Knowledge of working people becomes obsolete because of their inability to keep pace with accelerating information. The swift-moving current of information, knowledge, and skills makes it difficult for practitioners to keep up with new developments in their field. They are caught up in the ambiguous position of having to help bring about knowledge advancement while being inevitably affected by it.

Causes of Productivity Decline Among Blue-Collar (Hardware) Workers and White-Collar (Knowledge) Workers

Characteristics of the white-collar and the blue-collar work force are compared in Table 8.1.

In 1956, the number of white-collar workers in the United States was at parity with the number of blue-collar workers. Since that time, the first group has grown to be the largest segment of the American workforce. By the end of the decade, 60 percent of the workforce will be white-collar

TABLE 8.1   Characteristics of White-Collar and Blue-Collar Workers

White-Collar Worker	Blue-Collar Worker
Works with information and people	Works with hardware and physical things
Service and process oriented	Equipment and machinery oriented
Professional (college)	Nonprofessional (vocational)
Output not easily measured and inventory not possible	Output easily measured and inventoried
Work completed anywhere	Goes to place of work
Needs skill, time, information and decisions for productivity	Needs equipment and tools for productivity
Loyal to profession	Loyal to union
Wants acceptable monetary rewards in fulfilling work	Wants monetary rewards in acceptable work
Compensation exempt	Compensation nonexempt
Productivity not forcible, since work not visible and intangible	Productivity forcible, since work visible and tangible

workers. This group consists of management personnel, engineers, lawyers, medical doctors, nurses, supervisors, public administrators, government workers, social workers, computer analysts, self-employed workers, sales workers, data programmers, quality-control staff, designers, draftsmen, and research and development staff.

The productivity of white-collar workers ranges between 50 and 60 percent, when the management approach is casual and informal and productivity is not measured. When scorekeeping and formal management methods are used, 90 percent is possible.

Checklist of Causes of Poor Productivity: White-Collar Workers

- Attitudes unsupportive of productivity vigor
- Casual approaches to completing work
- Lack of measure for scorekeeping
- Objectives or targets hazy or nonexistent
- Only a few key individuals committed to productivity targets
- Annual cycle of performance stretching nonexistent
- Effort for productivity not distinguishable from other efforts
- Resource use not integrated in performance centers
- Accountability for productivity nonexistent
- Time not viewed as costly resource
- Individuals not trained for expected performance before they start work
- Performance standards hazy or nonexistent
- Wage increases and benefits given without productivity justification
- Formal evaluation of productivity nonexistent or interval greater than annually
- No system of personnel backup for key individuals
- Actual and formal research and development effort in organization
- Employees not allowed to participate in changes and decisions affecting their job
- No esprit de corps in working climate
- No formal methods for collecting ideas, changes, and innovations for problem solving and improvements
- No "firing up" of employees for productivity
- No formal productivity plans integrated in other organizational plans

Checklist of Causes of Poor Productivity: Blue-Collar Workers

- Late starts and early quits of employees
- Slow work pace
- Lack of work policies

- Delays of materials and tools
- Low machine operator work load
- Too high or too low incentive earnings
- No formal ways to improve
- Use of an ineffective method
- Two man setups
- Many breakdowns
- Outmoded technology
- Faulty machines and equipment
- Errors on drawings
- Lack of job standards
- Unawareness of job standards
- Too high or too low worker/supervisor ratio
- Missed shipping dates
- Too many end-product variations
- High worker turnover
- High cost of scrap and rework
- Award of benefits without equal performance
- Productivity ignorance in management
- Lack of productivity planning
- Incorrect parts at assembly operations
- Unawareness of resources to be used before work commences
- Status reporting system not self-correcting
- Inaccurate time accounting
- Low machine uptime
- High in-process inventories
- Resource accountability disconnected from performance accountability

MEASUREMENT: THE PRODUCTIVITY BREAKTHROUGH

Clearly, "how much happened?" is just as important as "what happened?." Productivity gains imply a measure of change from "what was" to "what's desired." Gains cannot be appreciated without knowledge of why and how to keep score. Management of productivity with measurement is a major breakthrough for productivity improvement. Several techniques are now available for measuring productivity. They are briefly stated here and described in detail in a later section of this chapter.

1. *Measurement Using Productivity Ratios.* The productivity ratio is divided into five categories: (a) overall indexes; (b) objective ratios; (c) cost ratios; (d) work-standards ratios; and (e) time-standard ratios.

2. *Measurement Using Management by Objectives.*   The productivity ratio is expressed as a measure of effectiveness and efficiency and is used in the MBO work process from start to finish. There is (a) MBO measure, (b) MBO productivity, and (c) MBO as a process.

3. *Measurement Using Factors That Affect Productivity.*   The productivity ratio is expressed with these factors. There is (a) total factor productivity, (b) quality factor productivity, (c) value-added factor productivity, and (d) base-year factor productivity.

4. *Measurement Using Productivity Checklist Indicators.*   The productivity ratio is expressed indirectly as times completed in relation to total items expected.

5. *Measurement Using Productivity Audits.*   The productivity ratio is applied to the total organization as a measure of whether expected standards have been met.

6. *Measurement Using Productivity Set Points.*   Several ratios of different functions in an organization are summed up into one set point. Changes in this set point are tracked and controlled.

Why Keeping Score Is Important!

Productivity scorekeeping is important because jobs are lost, promotions are won, raises are given, dividends are distributed, incentives are made, plans are established, products are expanded, tools are purchased, companies are merged, corporations are bought and sold, all on the basis of productivity scores. Good scores are wanted in productivity even if they don't reflect the true productivity status. A good status is all that is needed. Specific reasons why keeping score for productivity is important are as follows:

1. It reveals the quality of decisions made by management.
2. It scores the level and amount of effectiveness and efficiency that prevail in a work process.
3. It assures that a ripple effect through many departments can be controlled and minimized.
4. It facilitates tracing consumption of scarce resources.
5. It aids greatly in justifying the purchase of high-cost equipment and capital investment.
6. It allows evaluation of the fumbling, the looseness, and the casualness of how employees and managers work.
7. It gives a measure of spare capacity of a department, a company, or even individuals.
8. It provides data and information for planning of alternative strategies and actions for improvement and gains in a coming period.
9. It helps dispense rewards in terms of contributions.
10. It signals the need for corrective action in a work situation.

Why Keeping Score Is Difficult!

Businesses are complex! How work is carried out in business is complex. Productivity in many ways is a measure of how well everything works together—people, objectives, methods, materials, and money. This complexity makes productivity scorekeeping formidable. Specific reasons are:

1.   Much of a complete work process is submerged and out of sight. It is difficult to measure what can't be seen. (The complete work process must be made visible, defined, and evaluated.)

2.   Productivity is often measured after the work is in process. This makes exact measurement difficult. (Scorekeeping control points must be built in when work is designed.)

3.   Language and terms in management are difficult to quantify. Economics, morale, and quality are examples of such terms. (Indirect measures can be useful in evaluating these terms.)

4.   Activity is often measured as accomplishment. The two are confused. Increasing effectiveness, communicating often, and providing assistance are activities, but increased profits, decreased time, and lower costs are accomplishments.

5.   The history of productivity measurement is at the macro level. In the past, measurement skill has resided in the economist, not the manager. (Measures of productivity for managers need to be developed, and managers need to be trained in their use.)

Ways to Measure Productivity

What is needed for productivity measurement is not a standard set of methods created by experts and imposed on the organization but rather individualized methods suited to the special circumstances of the organization—measures for self-observation, self-analysis, self-scoring, and self-reporting. Ten methods of scoring are as follows.

Productivity Ratio

The productivity ratio is the ratio of performance output over the resources used to complete the output (input).

$$\text{Productivity} = \frac{\text{performance output}}{\text{resource use}}$$

Example:

$$\text{Productivity} = \frac{\$30.0 \text{ million sales}}{1000 \text{ employees}} = \$30,000 \text{ sales/employee}$$

Figure 8.2 shows some typical ratios in an organization.

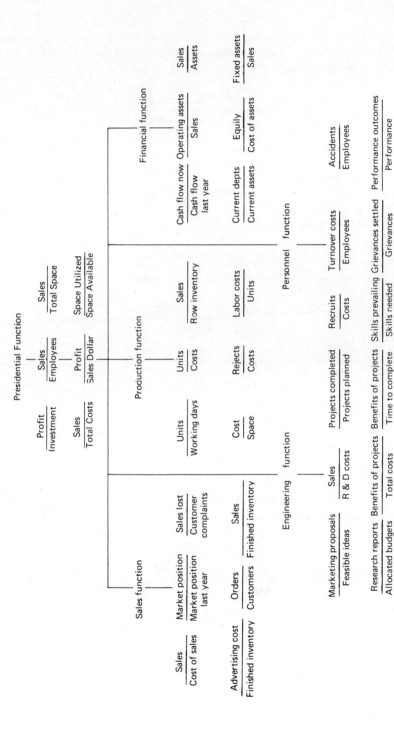

FIGURE 8.2 Productivity index applied to functions in an organization.

MBO Measure

MBO is a process for managing. The essence of the process is setting of objectives (expectations) and evaluation of how well the objectives were achieved (actual output).

$$\text{MBO measure} = \frac{\text{actual output}}{\text{expected output}}$$

Example:

$$\text{MBO measure} = \frac{8 \text{ work packages completed}}{10 \text{ work packages planned}} = 80\%$$

Typical MBO measures are:

$$\frac{\text{Actual sales performance}}{\text{Forecasted sales performance}}$$

$$\frac{\text{Budget performance}}{\text{Authorized budget}}$$

$$\frac{\text{Projects completed}}{\text{Projects planned}}$$

$$\frac{\text{Quits}}{\text{Expected quits}}$$

MBO Productivity

MBO productivity incorporates the MBO measure into the basic productivity index of output over input.

$$\text{MBO productivity} = \frac{\dfrac{\text{Quantity produced}}{\text{Quantity expected}}}{\dfrac{\text{Resources consumed}}{\text{Resources planned}}} = \frac{\dfrac{Qp}{Qe}}{\dfrac{Rc}{Rp}}$$

Example:

$$\text{MBO productivity} = \frac{\dfrac{24 \text{ work packages produced}}{20 \text{ work packages expected}}}{\dfrac{4 \text{ actual weeks}}{5 \text{ planned weeks}}} = 1.5$$

Typical MBO productivity measures are:

$$\frac{\text{Actual production units}}{\text{Planned production units}}$$

$$\frac{\text{Acutal rework time}}{\text{Budgeted time for rework}}$$

$$\frac{\text{Number of benefits realized}}{\text{Number of benefits expected}}$$

$$\frac{\text{Costs incurred}}{\text{Authorized budget}}$$

Total-Factor Productivity

Total-factor productivity incorporates all of the resource inputs needed to deliver an output.

$$\text{Total-factor productivity} = \frac{\text{performance output}}{\text{labor} + \text{capital} + \text{resources} + \text{miscellaneous (input)}}$$

Example:

Performance output, sales:	$1,000,000
Resource use	
Purchases:	$ 80,000
Materials:	300,000
Depreciation:	20,000
Salaries:	300,000
Capital investment:	100,000
Total input:	$ 800,000

$$\text{Total-factor productivity} = \frac{\$1,000,000 \text{ performance output}}{\$800,000 \text{ resources used}} = 1.25$$

Quality-Factor Productivity*

Quality-factor productivity allows for measurement of both productivity and quality simultaneously. It is the productivity index multiplied by the quality factor. The quality factor represents the standard to be met in the productivity process. The quality factor is the weighting factor in the numeric computation.

---

* Quality-factor weighting can be used for all ten productivity measures.

$$\text{Quality-factor productivity} = \frac{\text{quantity produced}}{\text{quantity expected}} \times \text{quality factor}$$

Example 1: *Use of Quality Factor by Levels*

2 = above standards, 1 = met standards, 0.5 = below standards

$$\text{Quality-factor productivity} = \frac{9 \text{ work packages produced}}{10 \text{ work packages expected}} \times 2 = 1.8$$

Example 2: *Use of Quality Factor by Indicators*

Indicators	Observations
Errors	_____
Customer satisfaction	X
Schedule	_____
Rework completed	X
Aesthetics	X
Safety	X
Value	X
Improved	X

$$\text{Quality factor} = \frac{6 \text{ observed}}{8 \text{ expected}} = 0.75$$

$$\text{Quality-factor productivity} = \frac{9 \text{ work packages produced}}{10 \text{ work packages expected}} \times 0.75 = 0.68$$

Other Examples:

$$\frac{\dfrac{\text{Value added through labor}}{\text{Salary, dollars}} \times \text{quality factor}}{\text{Base period ratio}}$$

$$\frac{\dfrac{\text{Value added through labor}}{\text{General supplies, dollars}} \times \text{quality factor}}{\text{Base period ratio}}$$

where

$$\text{Quality factor} = \frac{\text{annual scrap budget}}{\text{annualized monthly production scrap}}$$

The value added will be based on standard hours. The standard hours will be indexed to reflect changes due to process improvement, and so on.

$$\frac{\text{Percent overtime base year}}{\text{Percent overtime current year}}$$

$$\frac{\dfrac{\text{Lines of orders shipped on time}}{\text{total lines}} \times \text{quality factor}}{\text{Base period, percent}}$$

where quality factor reflects frequency of shipping errors.

$$\frac{\text{Actual hours reported}}{\text{Available payroll hours}}$$

This is often referred to as utilization.

$$\frac{\text{Absenteeism, base period}}{\text{Absenteeism, current ratio}}$$

$$\frac{\text{Standard hours utilized}}{\text{Actual hours utilized}}$$

This will be indexed for changes in standards often referred to as efficiency.

$$\frac{\dfrac{\text{Dollars late}}{\text{Total dollars shipped}}}{\text{Base period, percent}}$$

$$\frac{\text{Chemical processing quality level, current period}}{\text{Chemical processing quality level, base period}}$$

The quality level is determined by the percent of batches of the product that are approved by quality assurance without rework.

$$\frac{\dfrac{\text{Cost savings by engineering, dollars}}{\text{Engineering salaries, dollars}}}{\text{Base period ratio}}$$

$$\frac{\dfrac{\text{Standard hours utilized}}{\text{Indirect labor hours}}}{\text{Base period ratio}}$$

$$\frac{\dfrac{\text{Rework hours, base period}}{\text{Total standard hours, base period}}}{\text{Ratio for current period}}$$

Value-Added Factor Productivity

Value added is the difference between the price of materials and services purchased to make a product and the product's final selling price.

$$\text{Value added} = \text{selling price} - \text{production purchases}$$

$$\text{Total value added} = \text{total sales} - \text{total production purchases}$$

$$\text{Value added} = \$1,000,000 - \$600,000 = \$400,000$$

$$\text{Value-added productivity} = \frac{\text{total performance output}}{\text{total purchases input}}$$

Example 1:

$$\text{Value-added productivity} = \frac{\$1,000,000 \text{ sales}}{\$600,000 \text{ purchases}} = 1.67$$

Example 2:

$$\text{Value-added productivity} = \frac{\text{value added}}{\text{total employees}} = \frac{\$400,000}{20}$$

$$= \$20,000/\text{employee}$$

Base-Year Factor Productivity

Base-year productivity is a measure of the changes in productivity from a reference base year.

$$\text{Base-year productivity} = \frac{\text{productivity, current year}}{\text{productivity, base year}} \times 100$$

$$\text{Base-year productivity} = \frac{\dfrac{\text{performance, current year}}{\text{resources used, current year}}}{\dfrac{\text{performance, base year}}{\text{resources used, base year}}} \times 100$$

Example:

$$\text{Base-year productivity} = \frac{\dfrac{\text{hours lost per year, current year}}{\text{average number of employees, current year}}}{\dfrac{\text{hours lost per year, base year}}{\text{average number of employees, base year}}}$$

$$\text{Base-year productivity} = \frac{\dfrac{200 \text{ hours}}{80 \text{ employees}}}{\dfrac{420 \text{ hours}}{81 \text{ employees}}} = \frac{2.25}{5.18} = 48\% \text{ improvement}$$

Productivity Checklist Indicators

Evaluations, or "judged actions," made with checklist indicators can indirectly measure productivity by specifying the actions needed for performance effectiveness and resource efficiency. This assessment is qualitative. The productivity index is calculated as follows:

$$\text{Productivity index (PI)} = \frac{\text{checklist indicators completed}}{\text{total indicators}}$$

Example: *Mental Health Worker for Children*

Responsibilities That Yield High Productivity	Observed in Worker
Sets example of behavior wanted.	X
Helps children learn desirable health habits.	X
Enriches care environment for social opportunities.	
Cooperates and assists in other programs.	X
Involves children in meaningful routine work.	X
Teaches safety habits.	
Develops self-control traits.	X
Encourages children to try.	X
Gives children choices.	X
Continually seeks causes of behavior.	X
Disciplines as necessary.	
Puts child's best interests first.	X
Avoids condescending manner.	X
Radiates infectious attitude of enthusiasm.	X
Helps children be accepted by group.	X

$$\text{PI} = \frac{12 \text{ indicators observed in worker}}{15 \text{ required responsibilities}} = 80\%$$

Productivity Audits

Productivity audits arise from management's need to have specific information on the level and progress of productivity in the organization so that

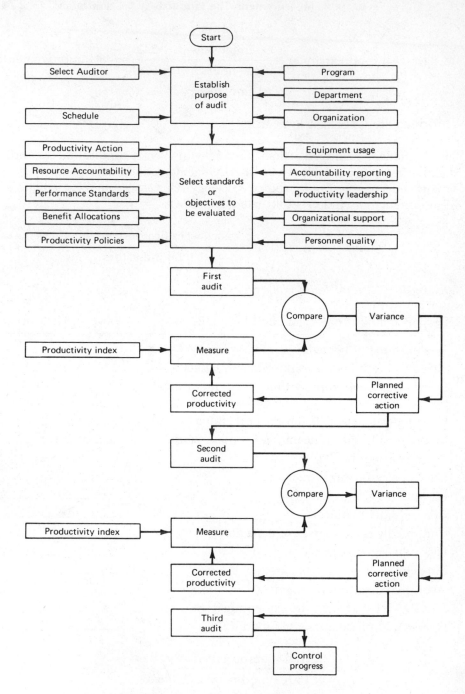

FIGURE 8.3 Productivity audit process.

necessary action can be taken. A productivity audit is really a measure of productivity vigor over time. Figure 8.3 illustrates the productivity audit process.

The productivity audit attempts to quantify how well an organization, a function, or a program meets the expectancies of each standard (Table 8.2).

Productivity Set Point

"Bottom line" is a phrase often used to suggest the final results of financial accounting of a firm or organization. The bottom line is a target set up during planning toward which all efforts during operating and control are directed. The bottom line is really a financial synthesis of the results to be attained by all departments and managers.

The "productivity set point" is similar to the bottom line. Productivity set points are targets set up during productivity planning. All efforts during operating and control are directed toward reaching these targets. Productivity set points are a synthesis of the productivity expectations of departments and managers in an organization. The measurement format for set points follows a matrix. Tables 8.3, 8.4, 8.5, and 8.6, on the following pages, show examples of matrices for sales productivity, top management productivity, operations productivity, and engineering productivity.

TABLE 8.2 Productivity Audit: Productivity Vigor Changes in Olympic Manufacturing Company

Standards	First-Year Point Rating			Third-Year Point Rating			Productivity Improvement (%)
	Maximum	Minimum	Actual	Maximum	Minimum	Actual	
Productivity actions	150	120	20	150	120	120	500
Resources accountability	75	50	30	75	50	40	33
Performance standards	100	75	20	100	75	80	300
Benefit allocations	125	100	20	125	100	80	300
Productivity policies	100	75	10	100	75	80	700
Equipment usage	150	110	80	150	110	120	50
Accountability reporting	50	35	10	50	35	40	300
Productivity leadership	125	100	20	125	100	100	400
Organizational support	50	35	20	50	35	40	100
Personnel quality	75	50	40	75	50	65	63
Total	1000	750	240	1000	750	765	218

TABLE 8.3 Sales Productivity Matrix

Productivity Concerns	Sales	Customer Satisfaction	Quality	· · ·
Scorekeeping ratios	$\dfrac{\text{Sales}}{\text{Budget}}$	$\dfrac{\text{Repeat orders}}{\text{Total orders}}$	$\dfrac{\text{Accepted orders}}{\text{Total orders}}$	· · ·
Actual measures	950	0.70	0.90	
Expected measures	1000	0.90	0.95	
Percent efficient	0.95	0.78	0.94	
Manager's weights	3	1	2	
Weighted efficiency	2.85	0.78	1.88	Productivity $\longrightarrow$ set point = 5.5

TABLE 8.4 Top Management Productivity Matrix

Productivity Concerns	Return on Investment	Profitability	Organization Efficiency	· · ·
Scorekeeping ratios	$\dfrac{\text{Profits}}{\text{Capital}}$	$\dfrac{\text{Sales}}{\text{Costs}}$	$\dfrac{\text{Value added}}{\text{Employees}}$	· · ·
Actual measures				
Expected measures				
Percent efficient				
Manager's weights				
Weighted efficiency				Productivity set point =

TABLE 8.5   Operations Productivity Matrix

Productivity Concerns	Production	Schedule	Quality	· · ·
Scorekeeping ratios	Volume / Costs	Delays / Schedule	Rework / Units	· · ·
Actual measures				
Expected measures				
Percent efficient				
Manager's weights				
Weighted efficiency				Productivity set point =

TABLE 8.6   Engineering Productivity Matrix

Productivity Concerns	Designs	Customer Requests	Improvements	· · ·
Scorekeeping ratios	Accepted designs / Proposals	Work packages / Time	Projects completed / Projects planned	· · ·
Actual measures				
Expected measures				
Percent efficient				
Manager's weight				
Weighted efficiency				Productivity set point =

Example: Objective Setting Through Ratio Measurements

The Hartford Insurance Group* is a multinational operation, managing both its domestic business and ITT's international insurance operations. The Hartford is a major property-casualty insurance company, with a growing life insurance division and real estate investments. The Hartford does not appear on any *Fortune* listing. Its parent company, ITT, is twenty-first on the Fortune 500 list. The Hartford's productivity has been compared with the

---

* Special acknowledgment is given here to Marc Gerritt at the Hartford Insurance Group for information supplied for this example.

TABLE 8.7 Comparative Performance of Selected Insurance Companies

Assets (000's)		Revenues (000's)		Net Income (000's)		Stockholder's Equity (000's)		Number of Employees	
Aetna	$35,752,700	Aetna	$13,318,000	Aetna	$561,000	Aetna	$3,281,100	INA	40,155
Travelers	21,637,986	Travelers	8,790,092	Travelers	362,739	Travelers	2,643,125	Aetna	39,100
Hartford	11,680,309	INA	5,255,000	INA	292,738	Continental	2,122,756	Loews	29,400
INA	10,604,000	Hartford	4,629,655	Hartford	287,955	Hartford	2,020,118	Travelers	29,339
Loews	9,125,112	Loews	4,535,098	AIG	284,699	INA	1,841,585	Transamerica	29,000
Transamerica	8,887,023	Transamerica	4,384,055	Continental	269,192	AIG	1,592,411	Hartford	23,000
Lincoln	8,470,373	Continental	3,419,046	Transamerica	244,979	Transamerica	1,485,482	Continental	22,649
Continental	8,215,970	USF&G	2,709,475	USF&G	223,101	USF&G	1,324,018	AIG	21,500
AIG	6,899,756	Lincoln	2,692,911	Loews	206,099	Lincoln	1,311,817	Lincoln	14,570
USF&G	4,247,339	AIG	2,252,945	Lincoln	175,697	Loews	1,194,589	Reliance	9,500
Reliance	2,681,239	Reliance	1,350,933	Reliance	92,904	Reliance	359,013	USF&G	8,650

TABLE 8.8 Comparative Productivity Measures of Selected Insurance Companies

Revenues/Assets		Net Income/Assets		Net Income/Revenues		Net Income/ Stockholder's Equity		Revenues/Employee		Net Income/Employee	
USF&G	.53	USF&G	.053	AIG	.105	Reliance	.259	Aetna	$340,600	USF&G	$25,792
Reliance	.50	AIG	.041	USF&G	.099	AIG	.179	Travelers	299,604	Aetna	14,363
Loews	.50	Reliance	.035	Continental	.079	Loews	.173	USF&G	260,456	AIG	13,242
INA	.49	Continental	.032	Reliance	.069	Aetna	.171	Hartford	201,289	Hartford	12,520
Transamerica	.42	INA	.028	Lincoln	.065	USF&G	.169	Lincoln	184,825	Travelers	12,364
Continental	.40	Transamerica	.028	Hartford	.062	Transamerica	.165	Loews	154,255	Lincoln	12,059
Travelers	.40	Hartford	.025	Transamerica	.056	INA	.159	Transamerica	151,174	Continental	11,885
Hartford	.40	Loews	.023	INA	.056	Hartford	.143	Continental	150,958	Reliance	9,779
AIG	.39	Lincoln	.021	Loews	.045	Travelers	.137	Reliance	142,203	Transamerica	8,448
Aetna	.37	Travelers	.017	Aetna	.042	Lincoln	.134	INA	130,868	INA	7,290
Lincoln	.32	Aetna	.016	Travelers	.041	Continental	.127	AIG	126,022	Loews	7,010

productivity of companies with similar operations. Ten companies have been selected: Aetna, Travelers, INA, Loews, Transamerica, Lincoln, Continental, AIG, USF&G, and Reliance. Six financially based productivity ratios have been chosen to assess corporate productivity: revenues/assets; net income/assets; net income/revenues; net income/stockholder's equity; revenues/employee; net income/employee. Table 8.7 is a ranking of the 11 companies by assets, revenues, net income, stockholder's equity, and number of employees. Table 8.8 ranks the companies on the chosen productivity ratios. Averaging the productivity ratios from Table 8.8 yields the following: revenues/assets .44, net income/assets .029, net income/revenues .057, net income/stockholder's equity .165, revenues/employee $194,750, and net income/employee $12,250.

The most obvious aspect of the productivity ranking is that most of the companies are high in some ratios and low in others. The Hartford was about the middle in all ratios, ranking no higher than fourth and no lower than eighth. From the average rank of each ratio, the Hartford's overall productivity rank is fourth, behind USF&G, Reliance, and AIG.

Because of the variations in rank, "stretch groups" of the five most productive companies in each category are established. Averaging the productivity measures of the top five performers in each category yields the following: revenues/assets .50, net income/assets .038, net income/revenues .083, net income/stockholder's equity .190, revenues/employee $257,354, and net income/employee $15,656. For the Hartford to match the averages of the companies comprising the "stretch performance list," it would need to achieve the percentage increases shown in Table 8.9.

For the Hartford to equal performance of companies on the stretch list it would need to follow the objectives outlined as follows. The rate of the Hartford's asset growth makes it appear unreasonable to bring asset ratios up to the stretch group performance within a short time. Hence a three-year time frame is set for productivity improvement. Objectives are set to prevent the further deterioration of asset ratios, which has been the trend over the past two years.

TABLE 8.9   Stretch Performance

Productivity Measure	Hartford	Stretch Group	Percent Increase Required
Revenues/assets	.40	.50	25
Net income/assets	.025	.038	52
Net income/revenues	.062	.083	34
Net income/stockholder's equity	.143	.190	33
Revenues/employees	$201,289	$257,354	28
Net income/employee	$12,520	$15,656	25

1. *Revenues/Assets.*
    (a) Objective.   Improve revenues/assets ratio to .43 in three years by increasing revenue growth from 1978 to 1980 from an average of 11 percent annual growth to 20 percent annual growth, while maintaining growth of assets at 16.5 percent annually.
    (b) Actions.   Since asset growth appears to be a constant, and restriction of asset growth does not seem desirable, increase revenues by (1) capturing more large commercial property-casualty accounts through discounts and competitive bidding, (2) increasing group life-health insurance revenues by expanding group sales through more aggressive advertising and marketing, (3) introducing new life-health and property-casualty products that offer high value to customers, (4) improving revenues from cash by converting cash to short-term interest-bearing assets, (5) improving customer service to attract more business, and (6) increasing production capacity for life-health business through use of automated support, to allow acceptance of additional business.

2. *Net Income/Assets.*
    (a) Objective.   Improve net income/assets ratio to 0.27 in three years by increasing net income at an annual rate of 20 percent rather than the 1978 to 1980 rate of 7.5 percent, while assets continue to increase at 16.5 percent annually.
    (b) Actions.   (1) Reduce expenses through automation and training, to hold staff growth; (2) improve underwriting results by reducing losses through more careful analysis of accounts and improved loss control services; (3) reduce personal lines business, and increase more profitable commercial lines business, to increase operating income; (4) review claim payment practices to reduce unwarranted payments; (5) annually review lease/buy decisions on real estate and equipment to minimize expenses for given tax and money rates; (6) develop alternative marketing methods, such as direct sales, with lower expense requirements.

3. *Net Income/Revenues.*
    (a) Objective.   Maintain net income/revenues ratio at .062 over the next three years by increasing both at a 20% annual rate.

4. *Net Income Stockholder's Equity.*
    (a) Objective.   Increase net income/stockholder's equity ratio from current .143 to .186 in three years by increasing the rate of net income growth from 7.5% annually to 20% annually, while stockholder's equity grows at the 1978 to 1980 rate of 9.8% annually.

5. *Revenues/Employee and Net Income/Employee.*

    (a) Objective. Increase net income/employee from $12,520 to $15,656 and revenues/employee from $201,289 to $252,354 in three years by increasing both net income and revenues at a 20% annual rate while holding employee growth to a maximum 11.4% annual rate.

    (b) Actions. Use automation and improved methods to restrict employee growth.

The performance measures of the Hartford Insurance Group of ITT will decline if current trends are not improved: Assets grow steadily, revenues grow at a slower rate, and net income fluctuates on the basis of market conditions.

Growth in revenues and net income requires that the Hartford abandon its policy of maintaining but not expanding its market share. Expansion of market share can most easily be done in the life insurance market, where the Hartford is not currently a major factor.

MANAGING TO IMPROVE PRODUCTIVITY

Productivity is a comparative ratio of performance output relative to resource input. Measurement of this ratio at some point is measurement of the existing level and vigor of productivity. But the improvement of productivity means the making of decisions both in planning and operations such that this ratio becomes larger. The larger the ratio, the greater the productivity. The smaller the ratio, the less the productivity. Thus the ratio can be improved by changing performance output (the numerator), resource input (the denominator), or both.

$$\text{Productivity} = \frac{\text{performance output}}{\text{resource use}}$$

Productivity increases when the net difference between these two factors becomes greater from any one of five managerial decisions. These decisions are described in the following example:

$$\text{Productivity index} = \frac{\text{results}}{\text{resources}} = \frac{\text{sales}}{\text{employees}} = \frac{\$600,000}{10}$$

$$= \$60,000/\text{employee}$$

1. *Improve Productivity by Managing Effectively.*

    Principle: Increase performance while holding resource use (costs) the same.

This approach concentrates on improvement of performance while costs are held to a limited amount. This is a most useful approach when the business cycle is beginning to recover or to expand.

$$\text{Productivity index} = \frac{\text{sales (up)}}{\text{employees (hold)}} = \frac{\$700,000}{10} = \$70,000/\text{employee}$$

2. *Improve Productivity by Managing Efficiently.*

   Principle: Hold performance the same while reducing resources (costs).

This approach concentrates on reduction of costs while performance is held to previous levels. This is a most useful approach when the business cycle is beginning to decline into a recession.

$$\text{Productivity index} = \frac{\text{sales (hold)}}{\text{employees (down)}} = \frac{\$600,000}{8} = \$75,000/\text{employee}$$

3. *Improve Productivity by Managing Effectively (Performance) and Efficiently (Costs).*

   Principle: Increase performance while at the same time reducing resource input (costs).

Managing effectively and efficiently at the same time is the true definition of productivity—getting more for less. This is the most attractive of all the approaches, but tends to be idealistic. Yet this is the ultimate measure of the productivity manager.

$$\text{Productivity index} = \frac{\text{sales (up)}}{\text{employees (down)}} = \frac{\$630,000}{9} = \$70,000/\text{employee}$$

4. *Improve Productivity by Managing Real Growth.*

   Principle: Increase both performance and resource use (costs) but by lesser amounts.

Managing for real growth is managing productivity. This approach concentrates on increasing both performance and resource use but in dispropor-tionate amounts. Performance increases at a faster rate than costs. This is a most useful approach when the business cycle is expanding at a fast rate.

$$\text{Productivity index} = \frac{\text{sales (up)}}{\text{employees (up)}} = \frac{\$900,000}{12} = \$75,000/\text{employee}$$

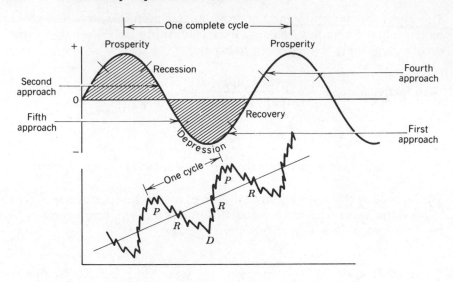

FIGURE 8.4 Managing productivity at different phases of the business cycle.

5. *Improve Productivity by Managing Economic Slow-up.*

Principle: Decrease both performance and resource use (costs) but by lesser amounts.

Managing during times of economic slow-up can result in productivity improvement as costs drop at a faster rate than drops in performance. This approach is most useful when the business cycle is undergoing recession and depression.

$$\text{Productivity index} = \frac{\text{sales (down)}}{\text{employees (down)}} = \frac{\$525,000}{7} = \$75,000/\text{employee}$$

Selection of the most appropriate approach for the improvement of productivity at different phases of the business cycle is illustrated in Figure 8.4.

MANAGING PRODUCTIVITY BY OBJECTIVES (MPBO)

Managing productivity by objectives (MPBO) is an adaptation of MBO. All of the principles, guidelines, and practices described in this handbook apply. MBO can be thought of as measurement by objectives, and productivity closely follows a measurement concept. MPBO is a six-step process, but does not exclude additional steps. These additional steps are incorporated in one or more of the following main steps:

1. Identify potential productivity areas.
2. Quantify productivity level desired.
3. Specify a measurable productivity objective.
4. Develop a plan for attaining objectives.
5. Control with milestones of progress.
6. Evaluate productivity reached.

The flow diagram in Figure 8.5 shows that all steps are sequentially related. How MPBO is applied is shown in two examples: the supervisor and the public administrator.

The Supervisor

STEP 1. Identify productivity area.
   (a) Responsibility: welding production.
   (b) Performance: weld 40 plates, 50 assemblies weekly with no more than two plate rejects (5%).
   (c) Resources: two workers, welding machine, 40 hours/week

STEP 2. Quantify productivity.
   (a) Before:

$$PI = \frac{40 \text{ plates}}{2 \text{ workers}} = \frac{20 \text{ plates}}{1 \text{ worker}} = \frac{2 \text{ rejects}}{40 \text{ plates}} = 0.05 \text{ (5\%) reject rate}$$

   (b) After:

$$PI = \frac{60 \text{ plates}}{2 \text{ workers}} = \frac{30 \text{ plates}}{1 \text{ worker}} = \frac{2 \text{ rejects}}{60 \text{ plates}} = 0.03 \text{ (3\%) reject rate}$$

STEP 3. Specify productivity objective: Achieve 60 plate-welding results weekly, 30 plates/worker, with no more than two plate rejects (3%) by January 1.

STEP 4. Develop a plan: Install new semiautomatic welding machine, and provide 80 hours training for welders.

STEP 5. Control with milestones of progress.

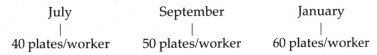

July	September	January
|	|	|
40 plates/worker	50 plates/worker	60 plates/worker

STEP 6. Evaluate productivity: By January 1, 60 plates are welded in 40 hours (50% productivity improvement), while a two-plate rejection rate is maintained (40% quality improvement).

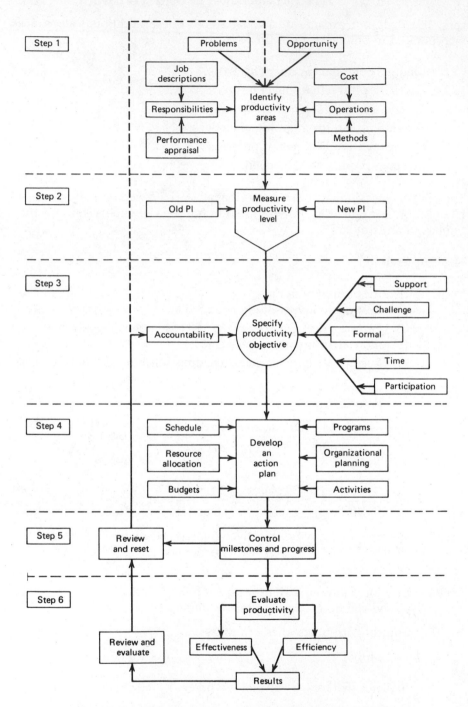

FIGURE 8.5 The strategy of managing productivity by objectives.

The Public Administrator

STEP 1. Identify productivity area.
   (a) Responsibility: Maintain clean streets.
   (b) Performance: 20 streets swept once a week with no visible paper debris.
   (c) Resources: Five workers, one machine, 14 hours/week.

STEP 2. Quantify productivity.
   (a) Before:

$$PI = \frac{20 \text{ streets}}{14 \text{ hours}} = \frac{1.5 \text{ streets}}{1 \text{ hour}}$$

   (b) After:

$$PI = \frac{40 \text{ streets}}{10 \text{ hours}} = \frac{4 \text{ streets}}{1 \text{ hour}}$$

STEP 3. Specify productivity objective: Reduce time to clean all 450 streets in town from 300 hours to 100 hours (4 streets/hour) by September 1.

STEP 4. Develop a plan: Organize into a team approach—two paper pickers, one manual sweeper, one machine sweeper, one follow-up and inspector.

STEP 5. Control with milestones of progress.

March	May	July	September
1.5 streets/hour	2 streets/hour	3 streets/hour	4 streets/hour

STEP 6. Evaluate productivity: By September 1450 streets are cleaned within 100 hours (160% productivity improvement).

ORGANIZATION STRATEGIES FOR PRODUCTIVITY IMPROVEMENT

Strategies are comprehensive plans resulting from decisions on how best to reach objectives with resources now available or available in the future. They are planned maneuvers to get a set of results. Management strategies are comprehensive practices intended to achieve certain goals and objectives of the enterprise.

Conventional Approach	Strategic Approach
Impulsive and in-process decision making	Formal and advanced planning and decision making
Total, "do everything," approach	"Key factor actions" approach

Conventional Approach	Strategic Approach
Search for all alternatives	Search for key alternatives
Use of all resources to an end	Use of significant and vital few resources to an end
Gains useful primarily for short run	Gains useful for both short and long runs
Fixed view of processes, procedures, and policies	Progressive view of processes, procedures, and policies
Little information on competitors other than their presence	"Game plan" for moves and countermoves of external and internal decisions

Managing productivity is selecting strategies that are superior to competitors.

Table 8.10 shows a productivity strategy matrix for comparing a firm with its competitors.

Five general strategies are now recognized as means organizations can use to formally attempt to bring about productivity improvement. These strategies, briefly described here with their methods of implementation, have been compiled from observations and work conducted over the years with well over 100 major U.S. corporations. They are as follows:

1. *Total Management Strategy.* This strategy requires that all managers and supervisors in a company, from top to bottom levels, give productivity improvement high priority in their extensive list of responsibilities. This strategy is a total management effort. All management personnel are expected to deliver results; no one is exempt. Productivity results are expected through a time schedule of commitments. Methods of implementing this strategy are:

    (a) Managing productivity by objectives (MPBO). Each manager and supervisor is expected to plan for productivity improvement by determining where improvement is possible, setting objec-

TABLE 8.10   Managing Productivity Is Managing Competitive Strategies

	What firm is doing	What firm is not doing
What competitors are doing	Common strategies	Competitive catch-up
What competitors are not doing	Competitive edge	New strategies not used

tives, and then developing plans for attaining these objectives. The plans are set at the beginning of the year. How well the productivity objectives have been completed is evaluated at the end of the year. This process is continued each year until a high level of productivity is attained by all managers and supervisors.

(b) Productivity mindedness through coaching.   A model of desirable attitudes and work practice is developed for all levels of management. Each manager and supervisor is aware of and trained for this model. Each manager and supervisor, starting at the highest level and working down to employees, coaches his or her subordinates on a daily and weekly basis on ways and means of getting productivity. Additionally, the desirable attitudes and work practices are incorporated into new employee orientation programs, training programs, and employee newsletters. All management personnel become productivity minded with all subordinates, reminding them of its value, need, method, and realization.

(c) Performance appraisal incentive-reward systems.   Appraisal systems are designed that incorporate incentive rewards based on productivity performance. Each employee is formally appraised in terms of productivity accomplishments. Wage increases, bonuses, vacations, or time off are given to those who increase their productivity.

(d) Time-management.   Since time is now recognized as a critical resource, managers and supervisors are given time-management skills, skills for getting more done in less time or at least getting the job done in the budgeted time. Scheduling skills and time control and utilization techniques are employed by all managers and supervisors with subordinates' work package and work assignments.

(e) Quality of work life and human relations managing.   Managers and supervisors analyze their work situation to find and eliminate impediments to employee productivity. Jobs, positions, and work stations are arranged to incorporate motivators, human behaviors, and job enrichment factors for producing employee satisfaction and thus promoting productivity. The discretionary content of jobs is expanded to increase motivation toward productivity.

2. *Top Management Strategy.*   This strategy requires the participation of only the executive or top management members of the organization. People at this level discuss and gain agreement on the ways and means of improving productivity of the firm. Decision making in this case is not participated in by all management members. Support is given, however, by ranks. Methods of implementing this strategy are:

(a) Investment capital purchases for mechanization.   Top management studies and analyzes where investment capital outlays can be made in work processes for improved mechanization or automation. Analysis of equipment use with modernization or automation for productivity improvement is given high priority. Equipment and facility aids are especially considered when work processes are labor intensive.

(1) CAD/CAM.   CAD/CAM is an abbreviation for computer-aided design/computer-aided manufacturing. Computers are integrated into the production process to improve productivity. CAD/CAM systems store, retrieve, manipulate, and display numerical data with unsurpassed speed and accuracy. They also improve product and manufacturing quality. CAD/CAM systems require heavy capital outlays. Productivity benefit studies are a must.

(2) Robotics.   Traditionally, robots have been used to do assorted nasty jobs for reasons of safety, health, and morale. With advances in computer technology, however, robots can now be programmed to perform a wide variety of tasks for productivity. Robot stations can integrate as many as 20 operations, and the speed, accuracy, and quality far surpass the human equivalents. This new technology is attractive, but robots have high price tags.

(3) Automation.   The difference between automation and mechanization lies in feedback, the concept of self-correction. Automated systems are self-correcting. What make mechanized systems automated are applications of numerical control: microprocessor control, minicomputer control, and large-scale computer control. Complex automated equipment is extremely expensive. Payoff periods are short. Automated projects must be carefully justified. Safety is easy, but quality and productivity are not.

(b) Work policies.   Top management discusses, collaborates, and agrees and then sets productivity policies on hiring, employment, job benefits, overhead, commitments, insurance, facility use, retirement, customer relations, discipline standards, performance standards, and many other work practices. Tight controls are enacted on job benefits. Policies are instituted to control where productivity is being lost.

(c) Productivity audits.   Formally conducted productivity audits are conducted by each member of top management to meet previously agreed-on standards of productivity performance. These audits are similar to financial audits, program audits, and operation audits. The standards are developed and agreed on by the executives. The audit determines whether functional units, departments, or programs are utilizing their resources effectively and efficiently.

(d) Incentive programs for employees.   Special employee benefit programs, such as profit-sharing, bonus plans, thrift plans, stock participation plans, and productivity sharing plans, are set up by top management to get the participation of all employees in improving productivity. Wage incentives are applied to jobs that easily lend themselves to work that can be measured and evaluated for productivity increases.

(e) Union/management agreements.   This method invites bargaining for productivity gains between a union and management within a firm. Productivity gain clauses are spelled out in detail in the labor contracts. Results are shared between employees and the company. A union management committee measures, evaluates, and agrees on the distribution of the gains.

(f) Organizational development.   Top management analyzes functions, departments, programs, projects, and line/staff relationships to determine how efficient the organization is for reaching higher levels of productivity. Top management questions traditional organizational relationships and institutes new forms of relationships to meet new complexities.

3. *Task Force Strategy.*   This strategy requires the participation of a special task force or of committee representatives of the various departments of the organization. The representatives come from various management levels. They are selected on the basis of special skills, interests, or motivation they can bring to the committee. The task force basically is an examining group with authority only to recommend. Methods of implementing this strategy are:

(a) Special projects for improvement.   The task force examines a variety of "trouble spots," "bottlenecks," or "opportunities" with a view toward change and betterment. A project or program is recommended that will bring about the changes desired. Example projects are cost reduction, waste control, energy use reduction, and labor cost reduction. The task force studies, analyzes, evaluates, and recommends to top management *what to do* to solve the problem.

(b) Activity value analysis.   This is value analysis applied to the total activities of the firm. The task force spearheads a program for encouraging managers to examine the wide variety of activities conducted in the course of work commitments. Value analysis techniques are applied to these activities to ascertain their value in terms of the cost of maintaining them.

(c) Productivity-benefit analysis.   The task force conducts special studies of options or alternative ventures that may be pursued to achieve a special benefit in some future time. Investigation of options involves assessment of resource costs and gains in cost reduction, time, or productivity. Priority setting is often a benefit of this type of analysis.

4. *Expert-Consultant Strategy*.   This strategy requires the participation of experts educated and trained to improve productivity of work processes. These individuals understand and are capable of setting up standards and evaluating how well these standards are achieved. The consultants can be *internally employed* as a part of the firm or *contracted externally*. The internal consultants are located in a special department within the firm. They are the professionals who study and analyze work operations with the view to improve productivity. The external consultants come from consulting firms who specialized in certain processes and operations of businesses. Their skills are often decisive in bringing about productivity improvements. Methods of implementing this strategy are many and varied. Only a few will be briefly described.

(a)   Work simplification.   This is an organized approach for simplifying a work process, work station, or work responsibilities. The analysis focuses on making the work process less expensive, less error prone, less complex, and with fewer operating points. The work flow is defined from start to finish. It is then analyzed for ways to improve it. A new work-flow process is developed incorporating the improvements. A comparative analysis is made between the old and the new to calculate changes in productivity. Time and motion studies as well as work sampling are frequently incorporated into work simplification.

(b)   Work distribution analysis.   Work responsibilities have a tendency to become diffused and duplicated in complex organizations. The work distribution analysis is an organized approach to match work load with work accountability. It gives a graphic picture of how resources (workers) are assigned to duties or work responsibilities. The matrix resulting from this analysis makes visible the total situation, thus allowing changes to be made for productivity improvement.

(c)   Equipment aids.   Equipment aids are attractive applications for labor-intensive jobs. Equipment can reduce time and resources needed and increase work performance. Expert consultants are often knowledgeable about equipment that can be used in certain applications of a work process. These experts also perform 1investment capital analysis to determine the value of productivity gains in relation to the cost for developing these gains.

(d)   Training.   Understanding and managing productivity appear to be simple. They are deceptively simple. Productivity, in itself, is a measurement concept with which many managers have not come to grips. Expert consultants who have had experience in setting up measurement processes and ways to evaluate productivity may be useful in imparting knowledge, skills, and know-how about productivity to managers and firms lacking

these. Training programs, seminars, and special courses conducted for management practitioners are invaluable for bringing
about a catch-up process.

5. *Eclectic Modeling Strategy.* The strategies already described are seldom pursued individually. Most companies select combinations of them
that are useful or critical to the organization at a particular time. At another
time a different combination may be more useful. The eclectic modeling
strategy is an organized approach in which one, two or more of the other
four strategies are combined for application to a unique situation prevailing
in a firm. When the situation changes, the techniques change with it. Use of
the eclectic modeling strategy requires knowledge of all the other strategies
and some understanding of their effectiveness for certain situations. The
eclectic approach requires the development and validation of a model useful
for one and only one firm. A different model is required for a different firm.
If two companies are using the eclectic modeling strategy and experiencing
productivity improvements, they are using different models. Each has
developed its unique model and has refined it to a high level of utilization. A
matrix for guiding the development of a model for a given productivity
situation with many dimensions is illustrated in Table 8.11. The matrix is an
"oversimplification" of a complex set of variables. Admittedly, the assignment of most effective (ME) and effective (E) is at best a cautious guideline.
The manager who is intimately acquainted with a productivity situation or
frustration is most able to assess which strategy and techniques would best
serve.

Seven Techniques to Improve Productivity

Hiring "brains" was formerly the one way for a manager or supervisor to get
things done. With the challenge of complexity, we now see that intelligence
is only a first quality. Other qualities are needed—energy, perseverance,
ability, calm, collaboration, agreeableness, and others! Managers and supervisors must even enjoy, to some degree, complexity and constant change, or
they won't survive. Further, they must have skills for dealing with day-to-
day complexities that affect productivity. They must be able to sense the
emergence of problems, to "cut through" to and identify the causes, and
then to muster enough resources and energy to solve the problems.

Seven techniques to aid in managing complexity for greater productivity
are now suggested and briefly illustrated. The names assigned to them,
although apparent jargon, are intended to convey the process of end results
as a managerial strategy.

Work-Focus Productivity Generator

Managers and supervisors who give equal time, energy, and resources to
each demand find that they begin to spread themselves thin. Their produc-

TABLE 8.11 Selection Matrix for Eclectic Modeling

Strategies	Productivity Situations and Frustrations → Spiraling Costs	Compensation and Benefits Disconnected from Productivity	Measuring and Evaluating White-Collar Workers	Outdated Practices and Processes	Rapid Technological Changes	Inhibition Effects of Laws and Regulations	Poor Attitudes and Understanding	Vague Accountability for Resource Use	Uncoordinated Organization	Low Motivation for Productivity	Delays and Late Deliveries	Lack of Standards and Expectations	Lack of Productivity Leadership
MPBO	ME		ME					ME	E			ME	ME
Coaching							ME						E
Performance appraisals		E					E	E				E	
Time management											ME		
QWL and Human relations (Total Management)										E			

	Item	1	2	3	4	5	6	7	8	9	10	11	12
Top Management	Investment capital					ME							
	Work policies				E							E	E
	Audits			E			ME					E	E
	Incentive programs		ME								ME		
	Union/Management agreements		E								E		
	Organization									ME			
Task Force	Special projects	E				E							
	Activity value analysis	E								E	E		
	Production—Benefits analysis	E				E							
	Work simplification	E		E	ME								
Expert Consultants	Work distribution								E				
	Equipment aids					E					E		
	Training					E		E					
Eclectic modeling	Select and Combine												

ME = Most Effective
E = Effective

293

tivity tends to drop because dilution of effort occurs. The work-focus productivity generator is a management technique based on Pareto's law that forces a manager to sort, select, and concentrate on a critical few demands among the trivial many. The ratio of the vital few to the trivial many has been estimated at 20/80 (the 20/80 percent rule). Several organizations have found this estimate to be true. Twenty percent of a bank's customers account for 80 percent of the dollars invested; 20 percent of hospital patients have 80 percent of the medical need; 20 percent of inventory accounts for 80 percent of sales.

The technique works as follows: (1) List all the demands and responsibilities faced by a manager; (2) arrange the list in order of importance; (3) select the top 20 percent as the critical few; (4) write demands as productivity targets; and (5) stretch productivity targets 5 to 15 percent. The entire process of the work-focus productivity generator is illustrated in Figure 8.6.

Work-Flow Productivity Increaser

In this technique, a work process is viewed in an organized way that forces a series of questions that may lead to improvements in productivity.

1. *Better Service.*   Can you deliver better and more effective results?
2. *Less Expensive.*   Can you deliver existing results at less cost?
3. *Faster.*   Can you deliver existing results at the same cost faster?
4. *Fewer Errors.*   Can you deliver existing results at the same cost with fewer errors?
5. *Less Paper and Fewer Records.*   Can you deliver existing results with less paper and fewer records?

The *work-flow productivity increaser* describes in detail the work elements that must be performed from a beginning decision to a concluding evaluation. The technique works as follows: (1) Describe a work-flow process from start to finish; (2) analyze for work-flow improvements; (3) develop an improved network-flow process; (4) make a comparative analysis; (5) validate the estimated savings; and (6) set productivity objectives and implement new work-flow procesess. The procedure for the entire technique is illustrated in Figure 8.7.

Resource-Accountability Clarifier

When responsibility assignments are diffused, accountability is nebulous. When matching of the work load with the work force is fuzzy, effectiveness and efficiency are uncertain. The clarifier provides an overview of how specific resources, particularly personnel, have been allocated to achieve certain performance objectives. The technique works as follows: (1) Establish a matrix of performance objectives versus resource allocations; (2) iden-

Example: *The Psychotherapist*

Step 1. List the demands and responsibilities.

- Perform administrative duties.
- Participate in agency planning session.
- Conduct individual and group psychotherapy.
- Perform routine tests.
- Provide surveillance of child-care workers' activities.
- Assist in developing agency programs.
- Evaluate test results and complete treatment plans.
- Write progress reports.
- Make referrals.
- Recommend routine expenditures.

Step 2. Arrange list in order of importance.

- Evaluate test results and complete treatment plans.
- Conduct individual and group psychotherapy.
- Write progress reports.
- Provide surveillance of child-care workers' activities.
- Assist in developing agency programs.
- Perform routine tests.
- Make referrals.
- Recommend routine expenditures.
- Participate in agency's planning session.
- Perform administrative duties.

Step 3. Select the critical few (20%).

- Evaluate test results and complete treatment plans.
- Conduct individual and group psychotherapy.

Step 4. Write demands as productivity targets.

- Complete ten treatment plans for an admission rate of five clients/month (productivity index = 10/5 = 2).
- Complete eight therapeutic individual and group sessions per week (productivity index = 8/5 = 1.6).

Step 5. Stretch productivity targets (5 to 15%).

- Complete 12 treatment plans for an admission rate of five clients/month (Productivity index = 12/5 = 2.4).
- Complete ten therapeutic individual and group sessions per week (productivity index = 10/5 = 2).

FIGURE 8.6 Procedure for work-focus productivity generator.

tify activities needed to reach performance objectives; and (3) analyze to clarify how resources are assigned to objectives. The entire process is illustrated in Figure 8.8.

Time-Scheduling Productivity Multiplier

Increasing complexity in organizations puts managers in a race against time. This is often due to the elasticity of work. That is, personnel have a tendency

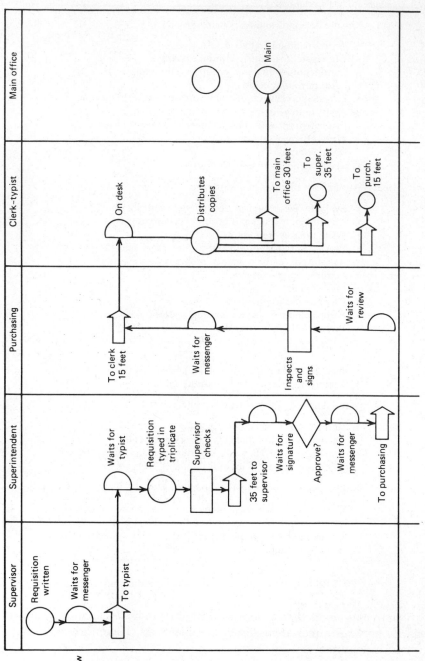

Old
work - flow
process

Supervisor	Superintendent	Purchasing	Clerk-typist	Main office

Supervisor: Requisition written → Waits for messenger → To typist

Superintendent: Waits for typist → Requisition typed in triplicate → Supervisor checks → 35 feet to supervisor → Waits for signature → Approve? → Waits for messenger → To purchasing

Purchasing: To clerk 15 feet → Waits for messenger → Inspects and signs → Waits for review

Clerk-typist: On desk → Distributes copies → To main office 30 feet → To super. 35 feet → To purch. 15 feet

Main office: Main

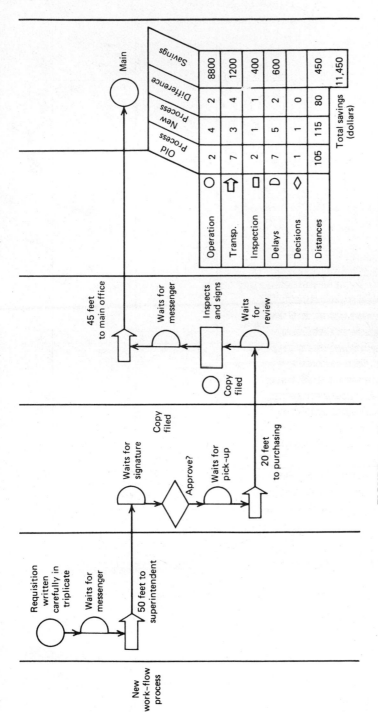

		Old Process	New Process	Difference	Savings
Operation	○	2	4	2	8800
Transp.	⇧	7	3	4	1200
Inspection	▢	2	1	1	400
Delays	D	7	5	2	600
Decisions	◇	1	1	0	
Distances		105	115	80	450

Total savings 11,450
(dollars)

FIGURE 8.7 The process of requisitioning of tools in a FIRM.

Resource Accountability Clarifier

Performance Objectives (Annual)

Weekly Resource Allocation	Increase Sales Revenues 15%		Expand Territorial Coverage to 60%		Reduce Customer Complaints from 50 to 20		Hold Travel Expense to 6% of Billing		Total
Frank Thomas Sales Manager	Sales planning	−4	Sales planning	−4	Interviewing clients	−3	Dept. meetings	−3	
	Customer conferences	8	Customer conferences	−14	Follow-up	−1	Expense reports	−1	
	Sales proposals	−2	Sales proposals	−4	*Sufficient attention?*				
	Sales reports	−4							
too much time!									
Hours	18		22		4		4		48
Joseph Sully Sales Representative	Telephone calls	−3	Telephone calls	−2	Quality checks	−3	Department meetings	−3	
	Customer contacts	−12	Customer contacts	−9			Expense reports	−2	
	Corres-pondence	−1	Corres-pondence	−1	*too little time!*		*Isn't there a system for handling?*		
	Travel	−7	Travel	−2					
	Sales reports	−1	Sales reports	−2					
Hours	24		16		3		5		48
Harry Bane Sales Representative	Telephone calls	−2	Telephone calls	−1	Quality checks	−3	Dept. meetings	−3	
	Customer contacts	−10	Customer contacts	−9			Expense reports	−2	
	Corres-pondence	−2	Corres-pondence	−2					
	Travel	−9	Travel	−2					
	Sales reports	−1	Sales reports	−2					
Hours	24		16		3		5		48
Mary Clark Administrative	Processing orders	−7	Assembling proposals	−6	Interviewing clients	−5	Checking office expenses	−5	
	Preparing reports	−3	Handling calls	−4	Checking	−2			
			Correspondence	−6	*her job?*				
			Take dictation	−2					
Hours	10		18		7		5		40
Helen Case Steno Pool	Take dictation	−2	Take dictation	−2			Errands	10	
	Typing	12	Typing	−5			Filing	2	
	Handling calls	−3	Handling calls	−1					
	Filing	1	Filing	−2					
Hours	18		10				12		40
Total Hours	94		82		17		31		224

Total allocation profile

125 100 75 50 25 0

Expected

Actual

FIGURE 8.8   Field sales office analysis.

to stretch their work commitments to their own good rather than to organizational plans. Many will recognize this as Parkinson's law. If a deadline for completion of a task is extended, the individuals responsible for completing the task will pace themselves to the deadline.

The time-scheduling productivity multiplier is a technique for "playing the clock." Deadlines are changed to increase productivity. The basic principle of the process is: *When performance is held at a given level, productivity increases as an inverse function of time.* Figures 8.9 and 8.10 illustrate this.

Productivity Tracker

One of the significant characteristics of complex organizations is that no two accomplishments or performance outputs are ever exactly alike, even with the same people, processes, or materials. Resources are never consumed in exactly the same manner and amounts, although the variations may be small. When variations are small, changes in productivity can often be ignored; when they are great, however, productivity is critically affected. Wide fluctuations in productivity cannot be ignored.

The productivity tracker is a graphic time comparison of the actual productivity measured and evaluated in a work process and the desired or targeted productivity. Actual productivity is observed, tracked, and controlled under limits. The productivity tracker technique works as follows: (1) Plot productivity (PI) on a time matrix toward an objective; (2) set the control limits; (3) plot actual productivity; and (4) evaluate for corrective actions. The productivity tracker is illustrated in Figure 8.11.

Cost-Productivity Allocator

This is a technique for the reallocation of costs to improve productivity. It works against traditional, across-the-board percentage cuts, which remove the good with the bad. The cost-productivity allocator allows costs to be cut where performance is marginal and costs to rise where high performance

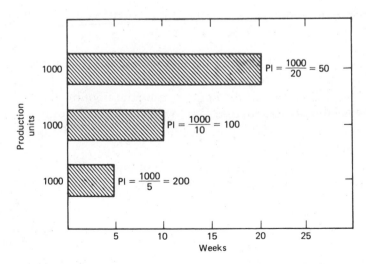

FIGURE 8.9 Productivity increases with shortening deadlines.

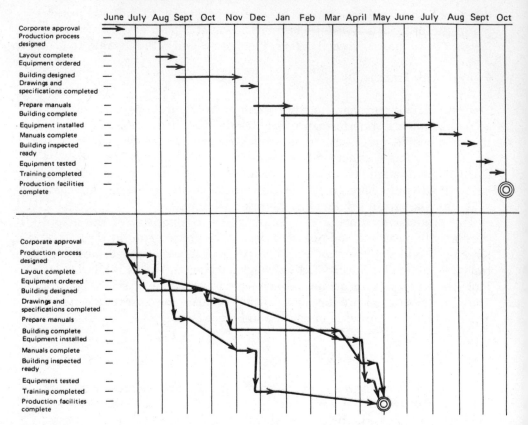

FIGURE 8.10   Scheduling process for pencil tab manufacturing facility.

can be realized. Before this technique is described, some definitions are in order:

- *Cost Avoidance.*   Removing or eliminating a cost item that has been anticipated and budgeted for but not expended.
- *Cost Reduction.*   Reducing or decreasing the amount of a cost item that has been budgeted for and is in a process of expenditure.
- *Cost Control.*   Spending but holding the amount of a cost item to a budget standard.
- *Cost Effectiveness.*   Increasing the spending allocated in a budget because it will affect performance improvement or reduce costs in the long run.

In any array of cost items, these four cost concepts are roughly related in the percentage distribution shown in Figure 8.12.

The cost-productivity allocator technique is as follows: (1) List the cost demands in a budget or cost array; (2) arrange the list in order of greatest

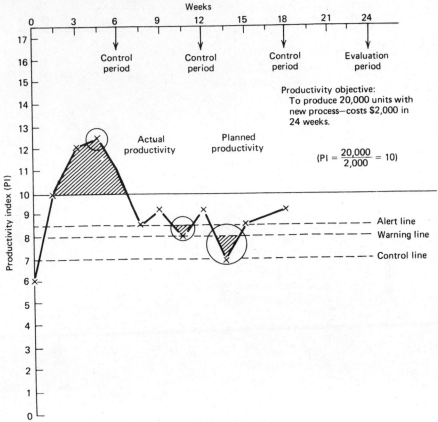

FIGURE 8.11 Control of production in manufacturing plant.

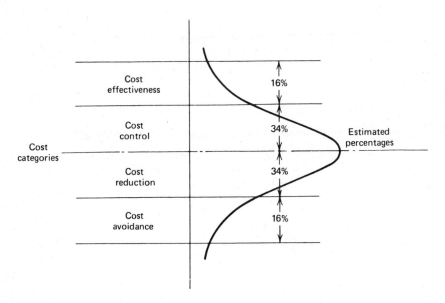

FIGURE 8.12 Cost–productivity curve.

Example: Field Sales Office

Step 1.   List the cost demands.

- Travel expense
- Office decor and posters
- New telephone contact program
- Rental
- Salaries
- Utilities
- Supplies and materials
- Advertising promotion
- Client luncheons
- Janitorial expense
- New sales proposal process
- Information and subscription service
- Printing expense

Step 2.   Arrange in order of benefit.

- New telephone contact program
- New sales proposal process
- Advertising promotion
- Salaries
- Travel expense
- Rental
- Utilities
- Janitorial expense
- Supplies and materials
- Printing expense
- Office decor and posters
- Information and subscription service
- Client luncheons

Step 3.   Categorize according to cost-productivity curve.

Step 4.   Redistribute savings (R).

• New telephone contact program • New sales proposal process • Advertising promotion • Salaries	Cost effectiveness
• Travel expense • Special taxes • Rental • Utilities • Janitorial expense	Cost control
R → Supplies and materials R → Printing expense	Cost reduction
R → Office decor and posters R → Information and subscription service R → Client luncheons	Cost avoidance

FIGURE 8.13   Procedure for cost-productivity allocator.

benefit to least benefit; (3) separate the demands according to the cost-productivity curve; and (4) redistribute savings to cost effectiveness items. The technique is illustrated in Figure 8.13.

Productivity-Effectiveness Planner

This method evaluates, during the planning period, the benefits that might be expected from a decision to go ahead with a program, project, function, or the organization itself. It is a systematic analysis approximating the major costs and benefits involved in various patterns of resource allocation. The *productivity-effectiveness analysis* requires that options or alternatives are available that might give other beneficial effects. If the organization has been structured into cost centers, and if budgets are allocated to these centers and performance measures are also aggregated, a productivity-benefit analysis can be made between and among cost centers. Through this process, productivity tradeoffs can be made. The general approach to productivity-effectiveness planning is illustrated in Table 8.12.

When dollar figures are not available but quality items are, an alternate approach is to use a checklist of these items. Resources are items of commitment. Benefits are items of gain. Probability of occurrence items are risk factors. This approach is shown in Table 8.13 in which, for purposes of illustration, the items are assumed to be at parity. In actual cases they probably are not equal and a weighting method should be used.

TABLE 8.12 Productivity-Effectiveness Planning

			Benefits Analysis		
Ventures	Costs (C)	Potential Benefits	Probability of Occurrence	Expected Benefits (B)	Productivity P = B/C
Option A	$4000	$6000	.80	$4800	1.20
Option B	1000	4000	.95	3800	3.80
Option C	2000	4000	.95	3800	1.90
Option D	3000	4500	.75	3375	1.13

TABLE 8.13 Productivity-Effectiveness Planning

			Benefits Analysis		
Ventures	Resources (R)	Potential Benefits	Probability of Occurrence	Expected Benefits (B)	Productivity P = B/R
	(items)				
Option A	30	20 ×	.70	14.0	0.47
Option B	24	22 ×	.85	18.7	0.78
Option C	14	20 ×	.90	18.0	1.28
Option D	32	26 ×	.80	20.8	0.65

PRACTICES FOR IMPROVING PRODUCTIVITY

Productivity Actions

1. Key individuals commit their work to and manage their work against well-defined, properly stated, and precisely measurable productivity objectives and goals. The objectives are written and open for review.
2. Productivity objectives are consistent with missions, statements, and other objectives of the organization.
3. Productivity objectives are set at levels similar to or greater than previous levels.
4. Productivity effort unique and distinguishes it from other efforts needed and practiced in the organization.
5. Productivity progress toward meeting of performance-cost milestones can be assessed for early detection and correction of problems.

Resource Accountability

1. Resources are aggregated and accounted for in budgets located at well-organized cost centers, which have as their mission achievement of plans and objectives.
2. Time is viewed as a critical resource and its management is clearly linked to priority systems, schedules, and avoidance of work on trivia.
3. Through a budgeting information system, cost centers account for resource use and waste, regardless of where resources are consumed or where waste is found.
4. Use of resources aggregated and approved follows an annual datum or zero-based format.
5. Cost centers are closely aligned with the functional authority of the organization structure.

Performance Standards

1. Individuals are aware of their performance expectancies before they start work and are trained for these.
2. Performance standards are clearly defined, attainable, accurate, and measurable.
3. Individuals are aware of the amount of resources they are to use in completing performance standards.
4. Individuals have controls on the amount of resources they are to use in completing performance standards.
5. Performance measures are made and aggregated within cost centers.
6. Productivity is measured with resource use and performance results at cost centers.

Benefit Allocations

1. Costs of benefits are precisely identified and connected in cost centers.
2. Rewards and benefits are connected with and allocated according to performance and productivity data.
3. Increased benefits are given only with increased productivity.
4. The benefits to be achieved for each program, project, or plan are clearly articulated.
5. Planned benefit allocations accompany planned productivity improvement.
6. Productivity is a decision-making criterion in negotiations and tradeoffs.

Productivity Policies

1. A productivity mission statement has been issued, actively pursued, and given high priority by top management.
2. Managers must submit formal productivity plans to be integrated into an overall productivity plan.
3. Productivity results are formally evaluated once a year.
4. Gains resulting from increased productivity are shared with those responsible for the increase.
5. Productivity improvement is practiced within all cost centers or departments of the organization.

Equipment Use and Technology

1. Equipment purchases are justified on the basis of data showing productivity improvement or savings from use of the equipment.
2. Planned equipment use shows choice of best available equipment options for productivity.
3. Technological innovation and the use of technological aids are visible practices.
4. Equipment purchase, use, and expenditures are controlled and reported through cost centers.
5. Short-range tradeoff benefits should not incapacitate long-range benefit expectations.

Accountability Reporting

1. A status-reporting system gives accountability sources information on total variances from an established plan of productivity improvement.

2. Required and expected productivity is delegated and traceable to a specific person in the organization.
3. Observed productivity is in fact the same as reported productivity.
4. The status-reporting system is self-correcting through feedback to workers.
5. A formal annual report is submitted to top management on productivity progress.

Productivity Leadership

1. Leaders operate and manage in a research–action manner for productivity improvements.
2. Leaders "tune-up" the organizational search for ways to improve.
3. Employees share a high level of esprit de corps.
4. Leaders operate a system that seeks and channels work-improvement innovations from workers.
5. Leaders allow high clashes in productivity ideas but low clashes in interpersonal relations.
6. Competition is encouraged for results but not among personalities.
7. Leaders delegate work responsibilities accompanied by accountability.
8. Leaders conduct and make use of periodic productivity audits.

Organizational Support

1. The power structure is recognizable and close to that of the formal organization. All unnecessary or marginal functions are eliminated.
2. Decision making is delegated to the most critical point of productivity action or to the cost centers where the work is accomplished and the impact is greatest.
3. There is balanced effort from all significant units.
4. Employees are allowed to participate in decisions affecting their own and related jobs.
5. Research and development is a formal and deliberate effort in the organization.

Manpower Quality

1. Individuals are open and expressively positive for productivity improvement.

2. Self-renewal, obsolescence, and low performance are personal concerns.
3. Orientation, training, and coaching for abilities and skills for productivity are given to workers.
4. A personnel backup system is in place so productivity does not suffer when turnover occurs.
5. Productivity skills are a prime criterion in the recruitment, selection, and hiring of personnel.

Policies and Guidelines

1. First-line supervisors have an "open-door" policy in dealing with employees.
2. Production is slow enough so that the job can be done right the first time.
3. Part-time workers are used during busy periods.
4. Mediocre employees are terminated.
5. Work simplification skills are given to all supervisors.
6. Overqualified individuals are not hired.
7. Employees are appraised in accordance with performance appraisal system.
8. Flow charts are made of decisions to be made, tracing their impact.
9. Successful practices are identified and their use reinforced.
10. Overtime is used to accommodate for insufficient personnel.
11. Deadlines are advanced in work assignments.
12. First-line supervisors are trained in labor contract administration.
13. Secretaries and typists use word processors.
14. Employees are given time to inspect their own work after they complete it.
15. A written procedure is established for a complex activity that is performed frequently.
16. For every key job there is an identified backup who is trained and ready.
17. Job descriptions are written for every key job, giving productivity guidelines.
18. Managers maintain a list of things to do and update their priorities each morning.
19. Time management skills are taught to all white-collar workers.
20. Participative teams are set up between labor and management in areas of mutual interest.
21. White-collar employees are given technical writing training.

Sample Job Descriptions With Productivity Responsibilities

JOB DESCRIPTION
With Productivity Guidelines
(PI = Productivity Index)

JOB TITLE: Purchasing Agent

SECTION: Purchasing Department   NUMBER IN JOB: 8
DATE: April 19xx
DEPARTMENT: Materials Control   REPORTS TO: Purchasing
                                                              Director
BASIC FUNCTION: Procurement and delivery of materials and supplies
                              to meet the requirements of all departments

---

Duties	Productivity Evaluative Measures
1. Develop new sources of supply and methods of procurement.	1. Develop 10 new sources of supply out of 15 potential sources. $$PI = \frac{10}{15} = \frac{2 \text{ sources developed}}{3 \text{ sources considered}}$$
2. Make recommendations regarding substitution of lower cost materials.	2. Achievement acceptance of three of five recommendations for substitution of lower-cost materials. $$PI = \frac{3 \text{ substitutions accepted}}{5 \text{ substitutions suggested}}$$
3. Attend meetings of appropriate organizations in the field to establish and maintain contacts.	3. Attend seven of ten meetings held during the course of the year. $$PI = \frac{7 \text{ meetings attended}}{10 \text{ meetings held}}$$
4. Confer with key vendors and potential vendors to keep in direct contact with supply conditions.	4. Devote 35% of available time to vendors and potential vendors.
5. Visit vendor plants and, with maturity and judgment, represent the company favorably in such contacts.	5. Visit 50% of vendor plants, on a rotating basis, every quarter.
6. After briefing with purchase order details, make prompt reports to purchasing director on request and participate on short notice in conferences with vice president-materials and others on all major transactions.	6. Response time to requests from purchasing director two days or less.

JOB DESCRIPTION
With Productivity Guidelines
(PI = Productivity Index)

JOB TITLE: Personnel Administrator

SECTION: Employee Relations   NUMBER IN JOB: 2
DATE: June 19xx

DEPARTMENT: Industrial Relations
REPORTS TO: Manager of Employee Relations

BASIC FUNCTION: Administration of employee relations programs and policies and employee counseling for effective utilization of human resources

Duties	Productivity Evaluative Measures
1. Recruit, select, and hire personnel for various departments.	1. Fill each vacancy within 30 working days. $PI = 30$ days/vacancy Turnover in first year due to performance no more than two out of possible 50 hired. $PI = \dfrac{2 \text{ terminations}}{50 \text{ persons hired}} = 4\%$ Average cost/hire not to exceed \$365. $PI = \$365$/hire
2. Administer and complete employee relations problem-solving projects assigned by vice president of industrial relations.	2. Complete and submit at least five reports out of possible six special projects attempted during the year. $PI = \dfrac{5 \text{ completed reports}}{6 \text{ projects}} = 0.83$ completion rate
3. Counsel exempt employee relative to status, benefits, and work conditions.	3. Elapsed time between notification of status change and counseling not more than one working day. $PI = 1$ day/status change

Duties	Productivity Evaluative Measures
4. Administer affirmative action program for recruiting and hiring.	4. Increase number of minorities in management positions from 25 to 30 by end of current year.

$$PI = \frac{5 \text{ new minority hires}}{25 \text{ current minority mgmt. personnel}}$$

$$= 20\% \text{ increase}$$

two hired within year to have officer potential within three years

$$PI = \frac{2 \text{ officers}}{3 \text{ years}} = \frac{18 \text{ months}}{1 \text{ officer}}$$

5. Prepare and develop employee relations administrative manual.

5. Complete employment selections within two months. Number of sections returned for errors or incompleteness, none.

$$PI = \frac{0 \text{ errors}}{1 \text{ completed section}}$$

$$= 100\%$$

JOB DESCRIPTION
With Productivity Guidelines
(PI = Productivity Index)

JOB TITLE: Manager of Employee Relations

SECTION: Employee Relations   NUMBER IN JOB: 1
DATE: April 19xx

DEPARTMENT: Industrial Relations   REPORTS TO: Vice President

BASIC FUNCTION: Administration of employee and labor-relations program and policies to ensure effective utilization of all
human resources

Duties	Productivity Evaluative Measures
1. Assist and advise vice president on active union issues and union organization drives, and stimulate corrective or preventive programs.	1. Reduce present annual turnover of 145 employees by 116 at home facility by assessing, developing, and implementing corrective program. $$PI = \frac{116}{145} = 80\%$$
2. Develop and assist in developing contract language and negotiation strategies for all labor contracts.	2. Complete negotiation strategies checklist of 26 items for home facility with no more than two incomplete/repeat items by 12/30/xx. $$PI = \frac{2\,\text{incomplete items}}{26\,\text{checklist items}}$$ $= 7.6\%$ repeat rate
3. Implement, audit, and monitor labor relation programs and policies for all facilities.	3. Assess attendance policies of all facilities and develop and implement new or modified attendance policies by 6/30/xx. $$PI = \frac{4\,\text{new or modified}\ \text{attendance policies}}{4\,\text{present}\ \text{attendance policies}}$$ $= 100\%$ new or modified policy implementation

Duties	Productivity Evaluative Measures
4. Monitor home-products group contract application, grievance handling, and arbitration.	4. Review and resolve ten grievances/week for facilities management.
	$$PI = \frac{10 \text{ grievances/week}}{5 \text{ work days/week}}$$
	$$= 2 \text{ grievances/day}$$
5. Negotiate home-products group labor contracts.	5. Successfully negotiate two of three labor agreements that expire during fiscal 19xx.
	$$PI = \frac{2}{3} = 66\% \text{ success rate}$$
6. Administer and monitor as appropriate OSHA procedures and programs.	6. Ensure that eight of nine comany facilities are adequately informed of and pass compliance with affecting OSHA procedures.
	$$PI = \frac{8 \text{ facilities pass compliance}}{9 \text{ total facilities}}$$
	$$= 89\%$$
7. Assist in developing, monitoring, and auditing affirmative action program for all facilities.	7. On receipt of affirmative action plans by 12/30/xx, audit all nine plans within three months.
	$$PI = \frac{9 \text{ plans}}{3 \text{ months}} = \frac{3 \text{ affirmative action plans}}{\text{month}}$$

JOB DESCRIPTION
With Productivity Guidelines
(PI = Productivity Index)

JOB TITLE: Regional Controller

SECTION: NUMBER IN JOB: 14   DATE: March 19xx

DEPARTMENT: Accounting   REPORTS TO: Regional Manager

BASIC FUNCTION: Plan development, control assurance, and reporting of profitability for enterprise to top management and owners

Duties	Productivity Evaluative Measures
1. Prepare annual regional profit plans from overall regional goals and objectives.	1. Develop profit plan anticipating minimum sales of $500,000/month and total expenses of no more than $100,000/month. $$PI = \dfrac{\dfrac{100,000}{\text{gross profits}}}{\dfrac{500,000}{\text{total sales}}} = 0.20\% \text{ gross contribution}$$
2. Assist other regional department managers as necessary in preparation of their departmental budgets.	2. Complete eight departmental budgets within 21 days. $$PI = \dfrac{8\,\text{budgets}}{21\,\text{days}} = 0.38\,\text{budgets/days}$$
3. Continuously monitor all aspects, costs, and revenues of regional operations in accordance with plan. Anticipates significant deviations from plan.	3. Establish plan that total costs will be no more than $300,000/month for entire region comprising eight districts. $$PI = \dfrac{\dfrac{300,000}{\text{total cost}}}{8\,\text{districts}} = 37,500\,\text{max. cost/district}$$

Duties	Productivity Evaluative Measures
4. Review all significant customer proposals for proper pricing in accordance with corporate and regional policy.	4. Review all customer proposals priced at $25,000 or more to ensure minimum mark-up factor of cost-to-manufacture/list price of 1.9.

$$PI = \frac{95,000 \text{ total price}}{50,000 \text{ cost to manufacture}}$$

$$= 1.9 \text{ mark-up factor}$$

5. Supervise and perform as necessary regional finance accounting functions not performed at corporate level, including but not limited to processing of invoices and (travel) expense reports for payment.	5. Process 40 expense reports and 200 agent invoices per week with help of three clerks.

$$PI = \frac{240 \text{ accounts}}{3 \text{ persons}}$$

$$= 80 \text{ accounts/person/week}$$

JOB DESCRIPTION
With Productivity Guidelines
(PI = Productivity Index)

JOB TITLE: Public Relations Director

SECTION: NUMBER IN JOB: 1   DATE: 5/22/xx

DEPARTMENT: Public Relations   REPORTS TO: President

BASIC FUNCTION: Effective use of communications to achieve a most favorable impression or image for the enterprise with customers, suppliers, stockholders, employees, financial community, and the general public

---

Duties	Productivity Evaluative Measures
1. Create favorable company identification among consumers and the general public.	1. Resolve all complaints within two weeks from date of receipt. $$PI = \frac{4 \text{ complaints}}{2 \text{ weeks}}$$ $$= 2 \text{ complaints/week}$$ Achieve administrative performance to keep complaints fewer than 100/year. $$PI = \frac{52 \text{ weeks}}{100 \text{ complaints}} = 52\%$$
2. Promote relations with radio and TV networks, periodical and newspaper publishers, and other related organizations.	2. Produce 12 radio commercials in 12 months. $$PI = \frac{12 \text{ commercials}}{12 \text{ months}}$$ $$= 1 \text{ commercial/month}$$
3. Promote relations with community associations, civic leaders, social or fraternal clubs, and commercial associations affiliated with local communities.	3. Maintain personal contact with ten local community groups per week. $$PI = \frac{10 \text{ contacts}}{1 \text{ week}} = 2 \text{ contacts/week}$$
4. Establish and operate appropriate public relations services, such as film library, photographic services, speakers' bureau, and guided plant tours.	4. Conduct guided plant tours in 12 months. $$PI = \frac{24 \text{ tours}}{12 \text{ months}} = 2 \text{ tours/month}$$

Duties	Productivity Evaluative Measures

5. Prepare and publish company newspaper.

6. Arrange for appropriate outside services by public relations firms, subject to final management approval

7. Assure that public relations efforts are being provided and executed in all designated marketing areas.

5. Prepare and publish 24 editions of company newspaper in 12 months, with even frequency.

$$PI = \frac{24\,\text{editions}}{12\,\text{months}} = 2\,\text{editions/month}$$

6. Achieve administrative performance so that outside PR firm involvement consumes no more than 5% of annual PR budget.

$$PI = \frac{\$5,000\,\text{outside}}{\$100,000\,\text{budget}} = 5\%$$

7. Issue weekly reports to the 2 marketing managers and request feedback.

$$PI = \frac{2\,\text{reports}}{1\,\text{week}}$$

JOB DESCRIPTION
With Productivity Guidelines
(PI = Productivity Index)

JOB TITLE: Marketing Staff Assistant

SECTION: Distributor   NUMBER IN JOB: 3   DATE: June 19xx

DEPARTMENT: Marketing   REPORTS TO: Manager of Distribution

BASIC FUNCTION: Receiving, quoting, and processing distributor orders for all systems and spare parts; following through with all necessary interactions with other departments

---

Duties	Productivity Evaluative Measures
1. Receive and process distributor quotations and orders for distribution to accounting, purchasing, and engineering departments as required.	1. Complete five telephone system quotes within average of 15 days. $$PI = \frac{5 \text{ quotes}}{15 \text{ days}} = \frac{1}{3 \text{ days}}$$ Completely process 1200 telephone system and spare part orders with no more than 1% error. $$PI = \frac{1200 \text{ orders}}{240 \text{ work days}} = \frac{5 \text{ orders}}{1 \text{ work day}}$$
2. Organize information and prepare distributor sales input for manager's monthly letter.	2. Complete monthly distributor sales input report. $$PI = \frac{1 \text{ report}}{1 \text{ month}}$$
3. Prepare and maintain records and control shipping data for distributor information.	3. Record distributor order input in order input file log: distributor name and purchase order number, material, shipping schedule, price. $$PI = \frac{5 \text{ orders recorded}}{1 \text{ day}}$$
4. Contact distributors frequently by written correspondence and by telephone.	4. Receive and process 1200 telephone orders and order acknowledgments: 100 received, 100 acknowledged monthly. $$PI = \frac{200 \text{ orders}}{1 \text{ month}} = \frac{10 \text{ orders}}{1 \text{ day}}$$

Duties	Productivity Evaluative Measures
5. Make entries in job order log and prepare monthly report of distributor order input.	5. Record distributor orders and process monthly order input report. $$PI = \frac{100 \text{ orders \& input record}}{1 \text{ month}}$$
6. Prepare marketing bulletins and sales training material for transmittal to distributors.	6. Complete and process marketing information bulletins and sales training material. $$PI = \frac{5 \text{ training materials}}{1 \text{ month}}$$

JOB DESCRIPTION
With Productivity Guidelines
(PI = Productivity Index)

JOB TITLE: Supervisor

SECTION: Production Control   NUMBER IN JOB: 8
DATE: July 19xx

DEPARTMENT: Manufacturing   REPORTS TO: Manager of
Production Control

BASIC FUNCTION: Planning, direction, and control of flow of work through all phases of manufacturing, assembly, and testing while coordinating activities of engineering, quality assurance, sales, and other departments to meet customer requirements of performance, cost, and established schedules

Duties	Productivity Evaluative Measures
1. Schedule and coordinate detail parts inventory resolving problems of expediting.	1. Achieve a finished detail parts inventory so that 85% of the monthly unit requirements are at final assembly the first week of each month. (a) Establish PERT chart showing critical items and centers. (b) Use five expediters to follow an average of 1000 problems per month. $$PI = \frac{1000}{5} = \frac{200 \text{ problem parts}}{\text{expediter}}$$
2. Advise all production supervisors of their scheduled work loads on a daily and weekly basis so that labor-hour requirements may be accurately scheduled.	2. For all metal-cuttting departments: Ensure that efficiency does not fall below 0.94. For all supporting departments, assembly and test departments: Ensure that efficiency does not fall below 0.89.
3. Direct the surveillance of all manufacturing and supporting departments for all rework inventories to assure that corrections are properly made to avoid repetition of rework schedule.	3. Achieve a minimum rework charge so that 3% of the total rework load is not duplicated. $$PI = \frac{6 \text{ duplicate rework hours}}{200 \text{ total rework hours}}$$ $$= 0.03$$

Duties	Productivity Evaluative Measures

4. Coordinate effort with purchasing personnel regarding vendor items requirement to ensure timely deliveries to meet in-plant fabrication and shipment to schedule. Police the processing of customer-rejected materials through all quality assurance, inspection, and manufacturing phases to assure earliest possible delivery.

5. Maintain surveillance of status and progress of production-control programs of quality cost and schedule objectives.

4. Maintain a purchase parts inventory so that the total vendor past-due status does not exceed 10 percent for the first month past due, 5 percent for the second month past due, and 1 percent for the third month past due.

5. Accumulate monthly cost-performance reports according to productivity categories; review actual performance in terms of cost, quality, and schedule, with plans and budget previously determined. Cost guidelines: actual performance must be within ± 0.02 of budget. Quality guidelines yield must be at least 90 percent on all manufacturing lots. Schedule performance no past due conditions allowed to exist.

JOB DESCRIPTION
With Productivity Guidelines
(PI = Productivity Index)

JOB TITLE: Bank Teller

SECTION: NUMBER IN JOB: 8   DATE: Nov. 19xx

DEPARTMENT: Banking Services   REPORTS TO: Head Teller

BASIC FUNCTION: Provision of wide variety of full-service banking
needs and selling of bank services to customers, under general supervision; operation of a variety of
machines and equipment relative to teller duties

Duties	Productivity Evaluative Measures
1. Set up teller station with adequate cash, forms, and supplies, taking no more than 20 minutes before opening.	1. $$PI = \frac{1 \text{ daily setup}}{20 \text{ min.}} = \frac{20 \text{ min./setup}}{\text{day}}$$
2. Perform no less than 500 deposits or payment operations per six-hour shift.	2. $$PI = \frac{500 \text{ cash receipt transactions}}{6 \text{ hours}}$$ $$= 83 \text{ transactions/hour}$$
3a. Perform no less than 100 check cashings or process withdrawals per six-hour shift.	3a. $$PI = \frac{100 \text{ cash payment transactions}}{6 \text{ hours}}$$ $$= 16 \text{ transactions/hour}$$
b. Have no more than three erroneously processed withdrawals per 20-day work period.	b. $$PI = \frac{3 \text{ process errors}}{12,000 \text{ cash payment transactions}}$$ $$= 0.00025 \text{ error rate}$$
4. Answer or redirect all customer inquiries, displaying no displeasure.	4. $$PI = \frac{\text{all satisfied customers}}{\text{all customer inquiries}}$$ $$= 100\% \text{ happiness rate}$$
5. Promote additional banking services to at least 25% of customers passing through teller line and selling services to 10% of these.	5. $$PI = \frac{1 \text{ service sold}}{3 \text{ services promoted}} = 0.33$$

Duties	Productivity Evaluative Measures
6. Contact computer center for balances and hold in relation to #3 transactions in no more than 3 minutes per transaction.	6. $$PI = \frac{1 \text{ contact transaction}}{3 \text{ min.}}$$
7. Balance daily transactions and prepare daily transactions report, keeping overages and shortages to less than 2 occurrences (over \$20) per 60-day work period.	7. $$PI = \frac{2 \text{ over and short occurrences}}{60 \text{ balance days}}$$ $$= \frac{1 \text{ occurrence}}{30 \text{ days}}$$
8. Daily verification and process of night deposits or mail deposits in conjunction with balancing in less than 30 minutes, in no more than 45 minutes for every immediately preceding nonbanking day.	8. $$PI = \frac{1 \text{ night deposit verification process}}{45 \text{ min. (no. of nonbanking days)}}$$ $$= \frac{1 \text{ verification process}}{45 \text{ min.}}$$

JOB DESCRIPTION
With Productivity Guidelines
(PI = Productivity Index)

JOB TITLE: Senior Analyst/Programmer

SECTION: Computer Facility   NUMBER IN JOB: 20
DATE: Oct. 19xx

DEPARTMENT: Data Processing   REPORTS TO: Manager of Computer Facilities

BASIC FUNCTION: Conduct of system feasibility studies and provision of computer programming support to all departments

---

Duties	Productivity Evaluative Measures
1. Perform feasibility and cost benefit studies and evaluates existing systems and procedures.	1. Complete costing of all projects within 21 days of receipt; complete all projects within +10 percent and −30 percent of original estimates.
2. Maintains accurate project control and accounting (PCRS) data; assist project leader (supervisor) in status reporting and associated administrative duties as assigned.	2. Weekly PCRS and machine allocation listings will be reviewed by each supervisor to ensure that tolerance limits of PDS and machine time are met for each project.
3. Prepare JCL at all levels for all functions; evaluate existing job JCL and optimize if necessary or recommend changes to supervisor or responsible programmer/ analyst.	3. Supervisor monitors monthly listing of jobs and results that are distributed by the data center to each administrator; jobs are broken down by programmer's initials.
4. Debug moderate to complex technical problems requiring understanding and effective use of ABEND dumps; decipher logic flow in trouble shooting and problem solving.	4. Problems encountered in testing should not jeopardize overall standards of 90 percent of DPSRs completed on time and 98 percent submitted without rejections or major restrictions.
5. Evaluate and resolve operational difficulties encountered while executing programs in a production environment.	5. Answer 80 percent of error referrals within five working days and 95 percent within ten days; accurate logs are kept by a referral unit and each supervisor.

SUMMARY

The growing complexity of today's technological society in the context of shrinking resources, high energy costs, and mushrooming population makes the case for management of productivity stronger and more urgent than ever. Pressures from most segments of our society are growing so fast that breakthroughs in productivity are unnecessary if our standard of living and the quality of work life are to continue to improve.

This chapter probes some of the issues and concerns related to managing productivity. It provides the view, the approach, the tools, and the techniques to bring about its improvement.

BIBLIOGRAPHY

Adam, Everett E., Hershauer, James C., and Ruch, William, A., *Productivity and Quality: Measurement As a Basis for Improvement*. Englewood Cliffs, NJ: Prentice-Hall, 1981.

Cleveland, Harlan, *The Future Executive*. New York: Harper & Row, 1972, pp. 11−17.

Computervision, *The CAD/CAM Handbook*. Computervision Corporation, Bedford, 1980.

Davis, Hiram, *Productivity Accounting*. Philadelphia: University of Pennsylvania, Wharton School, Reprint Edition, 1978.

Eilon, Samuel, Gold, Bela, and Soeson, Judith, *Applied Productivity Analysis for Industry*. New York: Pergamon, 1976.

Glaser, Edward M., *Productivity Gains Through Worklife Improvement*. New York: American Management Association, 1979.

Gregerman, Ira B., *Knowledge Worker Productivity*. New York: American Management Association, 1981.

Harrison, Jared F., *Improving Performance and Productivity*. Reading, MA: Addison-Wesley, 1978.

Hinrichs, John R., *Practical Management for Productivity*. New York: Litton, 1978.

Hughes Aircraft Company, *R & D Productivity*. Culver City, CA: Hughes Aircraft Company, 1978.

Kuper, George, "Productivity: A National Concern." In *Productivity in Policing*. New York: Police Foundation, 1975, pp. 1−3. (The Police Foundation was established by the Ford Foundation.)

Lindberg, Roy A., and Cohn, Theodore. *Operations Auditing*. New York: American Management Association, 1972.

Mali, Paul, *Managing by Objectives*. New York: Wiley, 1972.

Mali, Paul, *Improving Total Productivity*. New York: Wiley, 1978.

Mali, Paul, *Management Handbook*. New York: Wiley, 1981.

Moore, Brian E., and Ross, Timothy L., *The Scanlon Way to Improved Productivity*. New York: Wiley, 1978.

Nolan, Robert E., Young, Richard T., DiSylvester, Ben C., *Improving Productivity Through Advanced Office Controls*. New York: American Management Association, 1980.

Norman, R.G., and Bahiri, S., *Productivity Measurment and Incentives*. London: Butterworth, 1972.

O'Toole, James, *Work and the Quality of Life: Resource Papers for Work in America*. Cambridge, MA: MIT Press, 1974.

Rosow, Jerome M., Ed., *Productivity Prospects for Growth*. Nw York: D. Van Nostrand, 1981.

Ross, Joel E., *Productivity, People and Profits*. Reston, VA: Prentice-Hall, 1981.

Scharf, Alan D., "More Pareto's Law." In *Industrial Business Management*. Saskatoon, Saskatchewan: Saskatchewan Research Council, January 1974.

Sibson, Robert E., *Increasing Employee Productivity*. New York: American Management Association, 1976.

Siegel, Irving H., *Company Productivity: Measurement for Improvement*. Kalamazoo, MI: UpJohn Institute, 1980.

Sloma, Richard S., *How to Measure Managerial Performance*. New York: Macmillan, 1980.

Sutermeister, Robert A., *People and Productivity*. New York: McGraw-Hill, 1976.

Vough, Clair F., *Productivity, a Practical Program for Improving Efficiency*. New York: American Management Association, 1979.

Washnis, George J., *Productivity Improvement Handbook for State and Local Government*. New York: Wiley, 1979.

Westwick, C.A., *How to Use Management Ratios*. New York: Wiley, 1976.

9
EFFICIENCY MANAGEMENT WITH QUANTITATIVE MBO

IN THIS CHAPTER

PRACTICING EFFICIENCY MANAGEMENT
TECHNIQUES FOR MEASURING EFFICIENCY

An organization that is termed "efficient" is producing a desired effect with little waste. It is achieving its pursued goals and objectives with few or no mistakes, failures, mishaps, or misjudgments. It is getting the greatest possible value from the least expenditure possible. Efficiency can also mean having enough flexibility to switch goals and objectives in midstream because of changing economic and governmental conditions and restraints, and doing so at little cost.

Efficiency assessment of organizations is greatly complicated, because organizations themselves are tremendously complex. Assessing how well labor, materials, components, equipment, purchases, services, money, information, and decision making are mixed together to achieve a stated purpose is one of the greatest challenges of modern management. Although the bottom line measures business performance rather than management performance, the two are interrelated. Initiation of a score card for business often provides a way for management to keep score. The two components are so interrelated that gains in one sector of the organization can be offset by losses of management in another sector.

This chapter provides guidelines that indicate "levels" and "states" of efficiency. The key to these indications is measurement. Quantitative techniques are essential. Some of these are suggested for several of the major functions of an organization. Overall scorekeeping and measurement can be divided into four categories:

1. Performance of capital, appropriations, and returns.
2. Performance of people, goals, and results.
3. Performance of innovations, sales, and markets.
4. Performance of planning, strategies, and growth.

"How much is the result?" is just as important as "What is the result?" In many ways, managing by objectives is measuring by objectives.

PRACTICING EFFICIENCY MANAGEMENT

The word "efficiency" is seldom used in management. In any ten management books, only one, if any, will have the word "efficiency" in the index. Only one, if any, deals with this issue as a management concern in a significant way. This is a shortcoming of management experts, because practitioners on the firing line want to act and react efficiently. A major use for MBO is to infuse efficiency into the management process. Efficiency in management must be dealt with openly and deliberately, since it permeates management practice so intensely and pervasively. If efficiency means getting a desired effect with little or no waste, inefficiency means getting a desired or undesired effect with a great deal of waste. Expressions such as "casual performance," "rework schedules," "plan failures," "skills obsolescence," "ineffective effort," and "mediocre employee" all deal with efficiency issues. The heart and core of these issues is "how much," "how little," "how many," "how few."

Effectiveness relates to whether goals or objectives are achieved. Efficiency relates to how well or how much of a resource, such as time or effort, is utilized in the pursuit of goals and performance of activities. The two concepts of efficiency and effectiveness comprise the fundamental measurement of productivity, as described in the previous chapter. Effectiveness is related to performance output and efficiency is related to resource input.

Efficiency implies attainment of a range of acceptable results with minimum costs. Efficiency focuses on the best methods, procedures, or processes for performing in the least wasteful manner. Efficiency is related to effectiveness as shown diagrammatically in Figure 9.1. The effectiveness standard is a benchmark or reference point to measure waste or degree of acceptable performance. Efficiency is the input in the productivity ratio. This was explained in the previous chapter on productivity. Efficiency can be calculated as follows:

$$\text{Efficiency (E)} = \frac{\text{effectiveness (P)}}{\text{productivity index (PI)}}$$

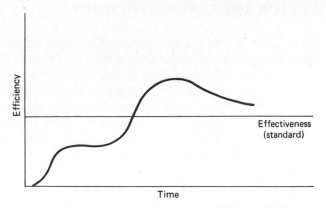

FIGURE 9.1 Relationships of efficiency to effectiveness.

Example:

A company with a productivity index of $20,000 in sales per employee is planning to increase its sales performance from $10 million to $12 million by becoming more efficient. The predicted efficiency is:

$$E = \frac{P}{PI} = \frac{\$12,000,000}{\$20,000} = 600 \text{ employees}$$

600 employees is the required manpower level for delivering the new planned sales level.

Efficiency as applied to organizations and functions in an organization is a relative rather than an absolute concept, that is, a function is efficient relative to itself over a period of time or relative to the same function in another organization. Efficiency cannot be judged without comparison. For the comparison, quantitative measures are needed, such as relative rank order, points on a grading scale such as 1 to 10, ratio differences, or numbers that indicate how much or simply current position. Exxon is number 1 in the Fortune 500 list because of its measured position of sales and profitability relative to those of the 499 other companies on the list; New York City Transit is the largest transit system in the world because of the size of its routes and the number of passengers transported compared with other transit systems. Grant's department store chain, one of the largest and oldest such chains in the United States, went bankrupt because its measured profitability was unacceptable to both stockholders and creditors. Hanes Hosiery, manufacturer of women's stockings, has long been noted for its efficient operation. The company consistently makes over 30 percent on net investment per year and sales have steadily been expanding at a rate greater than 6 percent per year for more than ten years.

TECHNIQUES FOR MEASURING EFFICIENCY

Efficiency measures are not exact. They give only relative indications. Having relative figures, however, is better than having no figures. The remainder of this chapter provides measures and suggested forms for assessing in a comparative manner the efficiency of functions in organizations and the efficiency of processes in managerial decision making. The measures and forms are organized into the following areas: (1) planning and profitability; (2) organization; (3) marketing; (4) budgeting and controls; (5) quality; (6) production; (7) data processing; (8) staffing; and (9) motivating.

Planning and Profitability

Key Areas of Planning	Typical Practices	Indicators for Tracking and Evaluating
Strategic and operational planning	MBO documents	Long- and short-range plans annually formalized toward goals; top management and key people involved and committed
Planning process	Planning process manual; training conducted	All plans follow series of process elements that assure and measure results, time, costs, responsibility, change, and how results will be achieved; key people trained to these elements
Responsibility improvement	MBO documents	All key decision makers submit annual plans for responsibility improvement and innovation
Budgets	Budget reports	Plans and budgets approved jointly; quarterly reviews
Integrative planning	MBO documents	System for linking and integrating plans by departments and levels
Employee participation	MBO documents	System for collecting ideas for improvements from employees and considering them in planning

Key Areas of Planning	Typical Practices	Indicators for Tracking and Evaluating
Accountability	Quarterly progress reports	Key decision makers explain variances from previous plans and previous periods
Flexibility	Mini plans and formal plan changes	System for handling important changes without abandoning plan
Achievement	MBO documents	Results of plans of previous periods
Value	MBO documents	Worth of plan clearly judged with its costs

Measures of Profitability

$$\text{Profits} = \text{sales} - \text{costs} \qquad \text{Profits} = \text{gains} - \text{losses}$$

$$\text{Profitability} = \frac{\text{sales}}{\text{costs}} \qquad \text{Profitability} = \frac{\text{gains} - \text{losses}}{\text{investments}}$$

Measures of Planning Efficiency

$$\frac{\text{No. of projects completed}}{\text{No. of projects planned}} \qquad \frac{\text{No. of objectives set}}{\text{No. of objectives completed}} \qquad \frac{\text{No. of work packages completed}}{\text{No. of work packages planned}}$$

$$\frac{\text{No. of improvements implemented}}{\text{Improvements/plan} \times \text{number of plans}} \qquad \frac{\text{Improvement value}}{\text{No. of plans}} \qquad \frac{\text{No. of plan errors}}{\text{No. of plans}}$$

$$\frac{\text{No. of plans}}{\text{No. of supervisors}} \qquad \frac{\text{No. of proposals accepted}}{\text{No. of feasible proposals}} \qquad \frac{\text{No. of delays}}{\text{Scheduled time}}$$

Corporate Directions with Goal Setting

Planned outcome and actual outcome are always different. The course of corporate directions can be plotted to show the amount of deviation between planned direction and actual direction (Figure 9.2). MBO is more effective when changes are made in both planning and organization to minimize the deviation. Corporate direction is provided by the Board of Directors and its committees. The Board provides guidelines for improvement and growth. This is briefly described in Figures 9.3, 9.4, and 9.5.

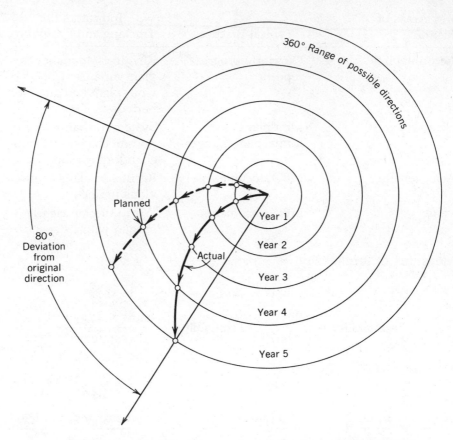

FIGURE 9.2 Deviation between planned direction and actual outcome.

Trustees responsible to the owners of an enterprise to keep a balance of interests among stockholders, employees, customers, and the public.

Responsibilities	Duties	Measures of Effectiveness
1. Determine general direction and goals and guide firm toward accomplishment	(a) Participate in goal formation (b) Revise goals when conditions change (c) Assure objectives of managers supportive of goals	Statement of goals issued, communicated to management, and kept current
2. Establish legal structure for the firm	(a) Select and operate legal structure (b) Arbitrate disputes among owners, staff, and government (c) Issue transfer, and register legal matters of the firm	Establish by-laws that control problems of litigation and fiduciary matters and provide protection for owners
3. Employ competent and remove incompetent executives	(a) Select, hire, and fix compensation (b) Establish responsibilities and evaluate work (c) Delegate authority to execute decisions	Annual statement of profitability and reports of growth and productivity
4. Advise on broad policies for the entire organization	(a) Advise on planning and policies for products, acquisitions, and new directions (b) Arbitrate contracts (c) Surveil compliance to policies	Policy manual and compliance audit
5. Approve budget and financial directions of firm	(a) Establish and approve budgets (b) Approve working capital and capital investments (c) Authorize plans, programs, and services (d) Provide payments to owners	Reasonable return on investment to owners and reasonable compensation to employees
6. General audit of the firm	(a) Establish audit criteria to protect owners (b) Conduct periodic audits (c) Strengthen and improve organizational weaknesses	Audit report with recommendations for improvement
7. Participate in community activities	(a) Provide leadership in community (b) Show accountability to public for stewardship (c) Relate services of company to community	Issue special reports periodically, issue public releases, and occupy community roles

Measures for evaluating board's ineffectiveness:
  (a) Members rubber stamp presidents' decision.
  (b) Members do not do "homework" before Board meetings.
  (c) Members are derelict in fiduciary obligation to owners.
  (d) Members never attend meetings and are only interested in personal gain.
  (e) Members have conflict of interest.
  (f) Members are not paid for services.
  (g) Members accept atmosphere of no criticism.

FIGURE 9.3 Functions of the Board of Directors and its committees.

Ways to Grow	Reasons for Growth		Guidelines for Managing Growth
Expansion	(a)	Expansion must fill an unfulfilled need in the market	1. Growth effort must be guided by an entrepreneurial manager.
	(b)	Expansion gives opportunity for utilizing unutilized potential and capacity	2. A special team with entrepreneurial qualities guides the coordination for growth
	(c)	Expansion is easily accomplished since competition doesn't exist	3. Management practices and styles can be integrated to existing management system
	(d)	Expansion is the quickest way for higher levels of profitability	4. Long-range plans should be established with annual milestones of progress
Acquisitions	(a)	The acquisition provides diversification for higher levels of profitability	5. Growth plans must be compatible with operation plans
	(b)	The acquisition gives priority to supplied critical materials	6. The way to grow must be reasonable in cost with an attractive rate of return
	(c)	The acquisition expands the distribution network to new areas and customers	7. The way to grow must not generate secondary problems that erase benefits of solving problems
	(d)	The acquisition has products and facilities not easily developed	8. The way to grow must not dilute or lessen management control of operations
Mergers	(a)	The merger will fill a gap with existing products or markets or extend existing products to new markets	9. Planning for compatibility is a must for pay scales, benefits, policies, and practices
	(b)	The merger will add specialized processes not easily available	
	(c)	The merger will provide unique Research & Development capability	
	(d)	The merger will utilize excellent management available in existing company	
Contracting	(a)	The contract is an opportunity for profits on a one-shot basis	
	(b)	The contract will result in mutual benefits for solicited or unsolicited new customers	
	(c)	The contract will help develop the firm's technology in a new area	
	(d)	The contract requires lending management without continuing commitments	

FIGURE 9.4 Guidelines for company growth.

Listed below are eight functions pertinent to a management situation. Please check the appropriate box under each function, indicating where, in your opinion, it should be included in a program for improving the management of the company.

1. Technology Functions
   - ☐ Understanding product terms and processes
   - ☐ Measurements (metric, etc.)
   - ☐ Exploiting opportunities in industry
   - ☐ Getting greatest value from support services
   - ☐ Other _____

2. Purpose Function
   - ☐ Developing formal long-range directions
   - ☐ Forecasting relevant trends and movements
   - ☐ Developing objectives for annual improvements
   - ☐ Developing plans for getting results
   - ☐ Other _____

3. Marketing Function
   - ☐ Developing customer-oriented organization
   - ☐ Making a buy-sell analysis in distribution business
   - ☐ Collecting intelligence on competitors
   - ☐ Developing a competitive edge
   - ☐ Other _____

4. Operations Function
   - ☐ Handling time in order-search-delivery processes
   - ☐ Understanding inventory control systems
   - ☐ Master planning for space utilization
   - ☐ Knowing how to coordinate dispersions
   - ☐ Other _____

5. Financial Function
   - ☐ Understanding financial statements
   - ☐ Using ratios for forecasting and decision-making
   - ☐ Calculating cash flow
   - ☐ Making cost-benefit analysis (or profitability)
   - ☐ Other _____

6. People Function
   - ☐ Understanding and motivating employees
   - ☐ Leadership skills for productivity improvement
   - ☐ Changing worker attitudes and morale
   - ☐ Appraising and rewarding employees
   - ☐ Other _____

7. Legal Function
   - ☐ Knowing the legal framework for managing
   - ☐ Labor contract administration
   - ☐ Handling OSHA requirements
   - ☐ Recent legislation that restrains managing
   - ☐ Other _____

8. Organization Function
   - ☐ Clarifying communications-authority relationship
   - ☐ Developing employees for higher positions
   - ☐ Setting up training programs for skills improvement
   - ☐ Placement planning analysis
   - ☐ Other _____

List, in order of difficulty, the three most difficult problems that you continually face: (If you do not have any, indicate none.)

1.

2.

3.

Name _____ Tel. No. _____

Location _____

FIGURE 9.5 Management improvement analysis.

Profit Planning Worksheets

Successful managers hit profit targets more often than their unsuccessful colleagues because they plan their profits and keep their operations and activities pointed in that direction. Once their MBO plan has been developed, they never lose sight of their prime objective—to finish the year with a profit. Profit improvement is profit planning. Figures 9.6, 9.7, 9.8, and 9.9 are aids in this direction.

MBO Planning Calendar

The planning process can start and stop at any convenient time of the year. Each organization must find what works for it. The most crucial point is to have a planning process with an associated calendar. The calendar should be given to all members of the planning process to ensure that signals are provided for all members to execute the action items in the process. Figure 9.10 is an example of a typical planning calendar.

Plan Evaluation

MBO planning is not without its faults or weaknesses. The existence of an MBO plan does not guarantee results. Evaluating an MBO plan for format, essentials, and confidence factors aids greatly in ensuring successful implementation of the plan. Figure 9.11 is an example of a plan evaluation. Plan evaluation is greatly enhanced when an operations analysis and audit is conducted during the planning phase. This is illustrated in Figure 9.12.

Payoff Matrix

A payoff matrix is a grid or chart that indicates the greatest payoff possible from a series of attractive alternatives. On it expected value is ranked against guiding standards. Each alternative is ranked for each guiding standard (Table 9.1).

CONTRIBUTIONS FOR
PROFITS IMPROVEMENT

	Profits Last Year	Profits Next Year	Total Profit Contribution
Sales improvement	$ _____	$ _____	$ _____
Cost performance improvement	_____	_____	_____
Price margin improvement	_____	_____	_____
Capital investment improvement	_____	_____	_____
Totals	$ _____	$ _____	$ _____

PROFIT RATIO TESTS

	Historical Ratios			Annual Plan	Long-range Projections	
	19xx	19xx	19xx	19xx	19xx	19xx
Sales Ratios:						
Percent Growth	____	____	____	____	____	____
Sales/Division	____	____	____	____	____	____
Market Share	____	____	____	____	____	____
Profit Ratios:						
Profit/Sales	____	____	____	____	____	____
Sales/Investment	____	____	____	____	____	____
Profit Equity	____	____	____	____	____	____
Earnings/Share	____	____	____	____	____	____
Solvency Ratios:						
Assets/Liabilities	____	____	____	____	____	____
Liabilities/Worth	____	____	____	____	____	____
Current L/Fixed L	____	____	____	____	____	____
Efficiency Ratios:						
Costs/Sales	____	____	____	____	____	____
Sales/Employee	____	____	____	____	____	____
Costs/Square Foot	____	____	____	____	____	____
Capacity utilization	____	____	____	____	____	____

FIGURE 9.6 Forms for analyzing profit improvement.

BUDGETED INCOME STATEMENT

Planned sales (F & I)	$ _____	
Less sales costs	_____	
Gross margin	_____	$ _____
Operating costs (F & I)	$ _____	
Direct labor	$ _____	
Direct material	_____	
Total direct contribution	_____	$ _____
Mf'g overhead (F & I)	$ _____	
Adm't overhead (F & I)	_____	
General overhead (F & I)	_____	
Total overhead	_____	$ _____
Estimated operating profits		$ _____

BUDGETED BALANCE SHEET

Current Assets:		
Cash	$ _____	
Accounts receivable	_____	
Raw material inventory	_____	
Work-in-process inventory	_____	
Finished goods inventory	_____	
Supplies inventory	_____	
Total current assets	$ _____	$ _____
Funds	_____	$ _____
Fixed Assets:		
Land	$ _____	
Buildings	_____	
Machinery and equipment	_____	
Deferred charges	_____	
Total assets	$ _____	$ _____
Current Liabilities:		
Accounts payable	_____	
Property taxes	_____	
Accrued interests	_____	
Income tax payables	_____	
Total current liabilities	$ _____	$ _____
Fixed Liabilities:		
Long-term notes payable	$ _____	$ _____
Capital:		
Common stock	$ _____	
Premium on stock	_____	
Retained earnings	_____	
Total capital	_____	
Total liabilities and capital		$ _____

FIGURE 9.6 (*continued*)

Show start and completion milestone dates

MANAGEMENT PERFORMANCE OBJECTIVES

No. _____

Statement of objective: _____

State results expected: _____

Key events, tasks or strategies to be executed to achieve objective	Responsible executive	Jan	Feb	Mar	Apr	May	Jun	Jul	Aug	Sep	Oct	Nov	Dec

Executive officially responsible to achieve entire objective _____

	Jan	Feb	Mar	Apr	May	Jun	Jul	Aug	Sep	Oct	Nov	Dec

FIGURE 9.7 Management performance objectives form.

MBO program budget summary	Dept.	Division	Activity	Account no.

Department/division mission statement

Program title	Percent of dept. time	Program resources — Line item accounting				
		Personal services	Supplies, serv. & mtn. repairs	Grants & contr.	Capital outlay	Total
Total	100%					

FIGURE 9.8　MBO program budget summary.

MBO program budget detail	Dept.	Division	Program title	Account No.
Program definition (purpose)				Total program cost

Performance measure	Performance measure	
Performance measure	Performance measure	
Program objective		Cost in addition to program budget request
Program objective		Cost in addition to program budget request
Program objective		Cost in addition to program budget request

Narrative explanation of program or objectives

FIGURE 9.9 MBO program budget detail.

Responsibilities	Days	Jan	Feb	Mar	Apr	May	Jun	Jul	Aug	Sep	Oct	Nov	Dec	Jan	Top mgmt	Planning dept	Total mgmt
Mission meeting	1														x	x	
Strategic planning meeting	2														x	x	
Market analysis & assumptions	10														x	x	
Competitive analysis	5														x	x	
Environmental analysis	3															x	
Preparation of MBO plans	3														x	x	x
Organization analysis	2														x	x	x
Preparation of action plans	3														x	x	x
Preparation of policy changes	1														x		
Primary objectives meeting and collaboration	2														x	x	x
MBO changes	3														x	x	x
Preparation of marketing plan	3														x		
Preparation of facilities plan	3														x		
Profit forecast I	1														x		
Profit forecast II	1														x		
Preparation of detailed plans	10														x	x	x
Completion of all work	2														x	x	x

People involved

FIGURE 9.10 MBO planning calendar.

Evaluator _____   Date _____

Type	Criteria	Description	Evaluation P 1	F 2	G 3	VG 4	E 5	Corrective action
Format	Completeness	All parts of plan included						
	Accountability	Responsibilities assigned						
	Timing	Start-stop sequences clear						
	Brevity	Only essentials included						
	Communicativeness	Meaning easily grasped						
	Coherence	Parts of plan unified						
	Specificity	Detail in adequate						
	Other							
Essentials	Payoff	Yielding greatest results						
	Accurate	Factual and true						
	Measurable	Quantified output						
	Evaluative	Progress milestones						
	Priorities	Needs gives preference						
	Interlocked	All parts connected						
	Challenging	Performance stretched						
	Other							
Confidence factors	Attainability	Expectations reachable						
	Flexibility	Process gives alternatives						
	Participation	Implementees are involved						
	Ease of implementation	Contingencies are ready						
	Oversimplification	Variables overlooked						
	Validation	Potential Problems found						
	Other:							

FIGURE 9.11 MBO plan evaluation.

Organization's Key Measures	Leading the Competitors	One of the Competitors	Struggling to Compete	Grave Concern to Survive
Finance				
Debt-equity structure				
Inventory turnover				
Customer credit				
Capital resources				
Available cash flow				
Breakeven points				
Sales per assets employed				
Ratio fixed to liquid assets				
Performance versus budget				
Return on new investments				
Ownership				
Dividend history				
Production				
Capacity				
Production processes				
Conversion efficiency				
Labor supply				
Labor productivity				
Raw material supply				
Sales per employee				
Sales per fixed investment				
Age of plant equipment				
Quality control				
On-time shipments				
Downtime				
Space for expansion				
Plant location				
Organization and Administration				
Ratio of administrative to production personnel				
Communications				

Clear-cut responsibilities
Management turnover
Management information
Speed of reaction

Marketing

Share of market
Product reputation
Brand acceptance
Selling expense
Customer service
Distribution facilities
Sales organization
Prices
Number of customers
Distribution costs
Market information

Manpower

Hourly labor
Clerical labor
Salespeople
Scientists and engineers
Supervisors
Middle management
Top management
Training costs
Management depth
Turnover

Technology

Product technology
New products
Patent position
R&D organization
Engineering design capability

ACTION STANDARD FOR MAJOR IMPROVEMENTS

FIGURE 9.12 Operations analysis and audit.

TABLE 9.1   Ranking of Alternatives for Guiding Standards

Alternatives	Guiding Standard			Total	Best Rank
	Customer Effects	Costs	Feasibility		
Preventive maintenance program	2	1	2	5	
Improved design	3	2	3	8	← Greatest payoff
More motivated employees	1	3	1	5	

Capacity Planning

In business, capacity is the potential output of or rate at which work can be accomplished with an existing plant, equipment, facilities, and workers. A business or company using all of its resources is said to be working at full capacity. Capacity planning involves anticipation of the facilities and resources that will be needed to meet a higher level of production. Such planning ensures that the necessary resources are ready and in place on time. Capacity requirement planning uses anticipated manufacturing orders from a time-phased materials requirement planning (MRP) system. A capacity schedule relates scheduled work to actual work by machine centers in a time-line system, as illustrated in Figure 9.13.

Input-Output Planning Analysis

Input-output planning analysis is for measuring the ratio of transactions of each item at different stages of development and time, as seen in Figure 9.14. The output of two relationships can often be the input of another relationship.

Validation of Objectives

Validation of objectives is assessment of the confidence that the objectives selected in the MBO plan are likely to be reached. Every objective has a risk factor, since it deals with a futuristic event. Failure to reach an objective affects the success of the MBO plan. All the alternatives available must be identified and the probability of reaching each one assessed through a decision-making analysis (Figures 9.15 and 9.16). The most likely alternative can then be chosen.

Machine Center No. 1		M	T	W	Th	F	S	Weekly Total	M	T	W	Th	F	S	Weekly Total	M	W	
Scheduled capacity																		
Cumulative capacity																		
Orders (capacity utilized)	Co 1 Planned																	
	Co 1 Actual																	
	Co 2 Planned																	
	Co 2 Actual																	
	Co 3 Planned																	
	Co 3 Actual																	
Orders completed (capacity used)																		
Cumulative completed																		
Spare capacity																		
Percent utilization																		

FIGURE 9.13 Capacity scheduling.

347

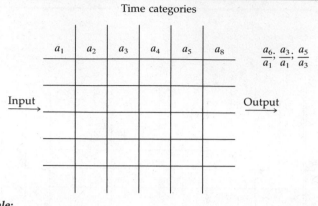

Time categories

| a_1 | a_2 | a_3 | a_4 | a_5 | a_8 | $\dfrac{a_6}{a_1}; \dfrac{a_3}{a_1}; \dfrac{a_5}{a_3}$ |

Input →   Output →

Example:

Output (O)

		1 June 30	2 July 7	3 July 14	4 July 21	$\dfrac{O_3}{a_1}$	$\dfrac{O_4}{a_1}$
	A	30	24	22	18	.73	.60
Planned	B	400	385	375	350	.93	.87
Units	C	90	79	72	65	.80	.72
	D	130	100	80	60	.61	.46

FIGURE 9.14 Input/output planning analysis.

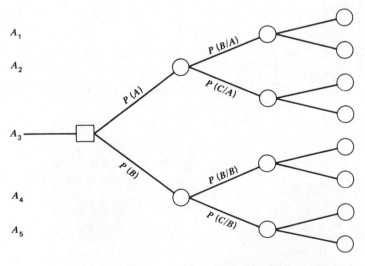

Joint probability $P(AB) = P(A) + P(B)$

FIGURE 9.15 Validating objectives.

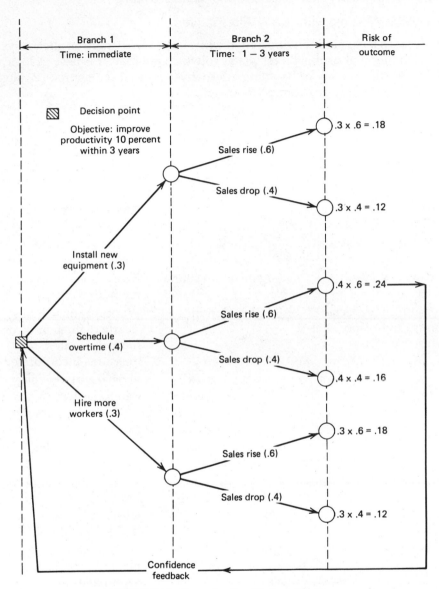

FIGURE 9.16 Example of validating objectives.

Decision-Making with Many Alternatives

A decision maker is often confronted with such a wide variety of alternatives in planning that confusion results as to which alternative is best. A logical and measurable way of handling alternatives is needed. Figure 9.17 illustrates a procedure that can be followed.

Organization

Key Areas of Organization	Typical Practices	Indicators for Tracking and Evaluating
Mission, purpose, goals	MBO documents	Formal statement issued, updated, and signed off
Structure and authority	Organization charts	Charts completed and accountability defined
Spans of control	Organization charts	Expanding or shrinking methods
Job duties, expectations, and responsibilities	Job descriptions	Work responsibilities clearly defined and conflicts eliminated; measures incorporated in each responsibility
Coordination	MBO documents and meetings held	Joint objectives set and written with personnel
Division of labor and jobs	Job specifications and work breakdown structures	Duplications and redundancies controlled
Policies and procedures	Policy and procedure manual written	Formal policies and procedures described in key areas; employees understand, use, and comply
Flexibility	Quarterly reviews and annual appraisals	Structure and strategic planning changes to meet needs and objectives; formal evaluations and corrections
Capacity	MBO documents and financial statements	Used and unused capital and human assets defined in capacity, known, measured, and compared
Key job succession	Replacement planning charts	System of backups of all key jobs for promotion, transfer, firing, and retirement

1) Problems or alternatives	2) Criteria:		Criteria:		Criteria:		6) Sum of rank	Total rank
	3) Tally	4) Rank	Tally	Rank	Tally	Rank		
1.								
2.								
3.								
4.								
5.								
6.								
7.								
8.								
9.								
10.								
11.								
12.								

Objective: Selecting from a series of problems or many alternatives a rank from highest to lowest that is able to satisfy selected criteria.

Procedure: 1. List the problems or alternatives to be ranked.
2. Select criteria to be satisfied when ranking.
3. Judge each problem or alternative as a pair against the selective criteria. 1 with 2, 1 with 3, 1 with 4, 1 with 5, etc., Continue with 2 with 3, 2 with 4, 2 with 5, 2 with 6, etc. Continue until all have been compared as pairs against any and all criteria. For each judgment rendered, enter a tally mark.
4. Count the total tally marks for each problem or alternative received and establish the rank from highest to lowest.
5. Continue the above procedure for any number of desired criteria.
6. Sum across all rank numbers and establish the overall rank.

FIGURE 9.17 Multiproblem decision analysis.

Measures of Total Organizational Efficiency

$$\frac{\text{Revenues}}{\text{Employees}} \qquad \frac{\text{Profits}}{\text{Equity capital}} \qquad \frac{\text{Employees}}{\text{Supervisors}}$$

$$\frac{\text{Revenues this year}}{\text{Revenues last year}} \qquad \frac{\text{Payroll and benefits}}{\text{Employees}} \qquad \frac{\text{Value added}}{\text{Employees}}$$

$$\frac{\text{Programs completed}}{\text{Employees}} \qquad \frac{\text{Total work packages}}{\text{Total time}} \qquad \frac{\text{Profits}}{\text{Payroll and benefit costs}}$$

Quantitative Techniques for Organizational Efficiency

Parkinson's Law. Parkinson was a British economist who said, "Work expands so as to fill the time available for its completion." Work, especially paper work, is elastic in its demands on time. Parkinson established that there is little or no relationship between the work done and the size of the staff that does it. The mathematical expression for Parkinson's law is

$$\text{New staff (NS)} = \frac{2k^m + l}{n}$$

where k is the number of staff seeking promotion, l represents the difference in ages between appointment and retirement, m is the work hours devoted to speaking to subordinates, and n is the number of units being administered. Knowledge of Parkinson's law is crucial for productivity management, as it reveals the high consumption of time by white-collar workers.

Example:

Three supervisors in three sections have an average of 20 years to retirement. Each needs to interview subordinates at least two hours per day.

$$\text{NS} = \frac{2k^m + 1}{n} = \frac{2(3)^2 + 20}{3} = 13$$

Span of Control. Also called the chain of command, this is the number of subordinates a person supervises (Figure 9.18). In practice, work that is highly technical in nature requires a narrow span of control. Work that is highly routine in nature yields a wide span of control. The formula for span of control is

$$NR = 2S + S(S - 1)$$

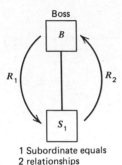

1 Subordinate equals
2 relationships

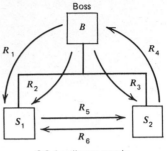

2 Subordinates equals
6 relationships

Boss

3 Subordinates equal
12 relationships

NR = number of relationships that must be managed

FIGURE 9.18   Span of control.

where NR is the number of relationships that must be managed and S is subordinate.

Example:

A supervisor has eight subordinates and wants to know how many relationships he or she must supervise

$$NR = 2(8) + 8(8 - 1) = 72 \text{ relationships}$$

Span of control is a factor that affects the shape and height of an organizational structure.

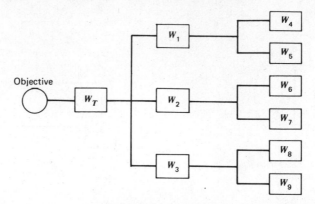

Work packages: end items, method, time element,
accountability, and risk factor

FIGURE 9.19   Work breakdown structure. W, work; W_T, total work.

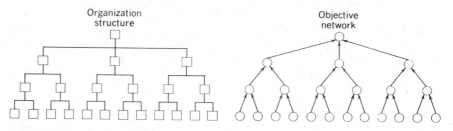

FIGURE 9.20   Objectives for all work packages link all elements of organization.

Objective Networks.   Work breakdown structure is a graphic quantitative tool for linking objectives with resources and activities. The total work to be accomplished is logically broken down into related units. These units are kept in levels and logical divisions and subdivisions of the organization (Figure 9.19). This is how work is grouped. From these work groups often called work packages, objectives are expected to be set. When objectives are stated for all work packages, an objective network emerges that links all elements of the total organization (Figure 9.20).

Marketing

Key Areas of Marketing	Typical Practices	Indicators for Tracking and Evaluating
Customer requirements	Customer profile document	Collections of customer needs and activity for translating into products and services, current and forecasted

Key Areas of Marketing	Typical Practices	Indicators for Tracking and Evaluating
Promotion	Promotion timetable MBO document	Annual plan with effectiveness measures for securing customer orders or services
Customer growth	Customer profiles, marketing statistics	Effectiveness factors and trends in categories, territories, or purchases
Repeat customers	Customer profiles	Frequency of customer repeats and satisfaction
Customer reactions	Customer profiles	Number and types of complaints
Products or services	MBO document	New product development; diversification improvement
Competitive edge	Competitor analysis and MBO document	Developed and maintained annually
Sales performance	MBO document	Formal system for analyzing and improving
Sales staff	MBO document	Annual development programs for improved skills
Image	MBO document	Contributing factors identified, developed, and maintained

Measures of Marketing (Services) Efficiency

$$\frac{Sales}{Marketing\ assets} \qquad \frac{Sales}{Marketing\ costs} \qquad \frac{Sales}{Marketing\ employees}$$

$$\frac{Market\ share\ now}{Market\ share\ in\ base\ year} \qquad \frac{Sales}{Promotion\ costs} \qquad \frac{Sales}{Number\ of\ customers}$$

$$\frac{Sales\ lost}{Customer\ complaints} \qquad \frac{Repeat\ customers}{Total\ customers} \qquad \frac{Customers\ this\ year}{Customers\ last\ year}$$

Quantitative Techniques for Marketing

Advertising Strategies. Advertising performs the function of making people aware, by means of information, reminders, and entertainment, of the value of goods being sold. In many ways it attempts to persuade people to buy by causing changes in attitudes toward a company product or service. Several strategies are used to develop this awareness and to persuade:

- *Product Comparison Strategy.* Advertisements that stress differences between the company brand and a competing brand: "Aspirin A works twice as fast as aspirin B."
- *Use Strategy.* Advertisements that stress the use benefits of the brand if the customer should purchase the product: "Rug cleaner A is easier to apply than is rug cleaner B, and no rubbing or scrubbing is needed."
- *Feature Strategy.* Advertisements that stress a specific feature or characteristic of the brand or service: "Our hotel is the only one that offers a sauna bath."
- *Attitude-Influence Strategy.* Advertisements that stress a message consistent with a consumer attitude or life-style: "Our electric lawnmower does not pollute the environment."
- *Symbolic-Identification Strategy.* Advertisements that stress symbolic attachments and identification to a hero or great person: "Our exercise equipment is used regularly by Johnny Weismuller."
- *Image Strategy.* Advertisements that promote an image or personality around a company or product: "Progress is our only product."

Measuring Ad Effectiveness.   Figure 9.21 shows ways to measure the effectiveness of advertising.

Competitive Edge.   The essence of the business market is rivalry among the sellers. Each seller tries to increase its share of the market, to increase profits. Sellers are continually vying for customers. The seller that offers more than its competitors is likely to gain more customers. The ability to offer more than competitors, as viewed by customers, is the competitive edge. A way of developing and measuring competitive edge is shown in Figure 9.22.

Forecasting Sales.   This means predicting in a quantitative way sales on the basis of past and current conditions. Forecasting sales is different from general forecasting, since the former requires more technical factors than the latter. Good forecasting is a combination of both sales forecasting and general forecasting. General forecasting techniques are described in a subsequent section. A formula for forecasting sales is as follows:

Sales forecast = market share × competitive strength × business conditions

$$\text{where}\quad \text{market share} = \frac{\text{total sales in area}}{\text{No. of competitors} + 1}$$

Competitive strength: <1 = less, 1 = equal, >1 = greater

Business conditions: <1 = recession, 1 = normal, >1 = expansion

Criteria for effectiveness	Methods of measuring effectiveness	
• Awareness	(1.) Send-in coupons	• Tabulate number of coupons that highlight an item
• Favorable impressions	(2.) Write-in letters	• Tabulate number of response letters for information
• Inquiries	(3.) Call by phone	• Tabulate number of telephone response calls
• Information	(4.) Order-form catalog	• Tabulate sales from mail-order catalog
• Persuasive	(5.) Store-traffic survey	• Tabulate from interviews advertised information
• Product purchase	(6.) Make telephone surveys	• Tabulate from statistical simple advertised information
• Repeat Purchases	(7.) Keep sales/ad records	

	Last year				This year			
	Ad Exp.	% of Exp.	Sales	% of Sales	Ad Exp.	% of Exp.	Sales	% of Sales
Jan.								
Feb.								
Mar.								
Apr.								
May								
June								
July								
Aug.								
Sept.								
Oct.								
Nov.								
Dec.								

FIGURE 9.21 Form for measuring advertising effectiveness.

Example:

Four stores in a market each have approximately \$500,000 in sales. A new store will enter the market with less competitive strength and under less than normal business conditions.

$$\text{Market share} = \frac{\$2,000,000}{5 \text{ stores}} = \$400,000/\text{store}$$

$$\text{Sales forecast} = \$400,000 \times 0.8 \times 0.8 = \$256,000$$

Competitors \ Competitive Factors	Price	Quality	Discounts	Inventory	Site Location	Building Area	Delivery	Skilled Employees	Other	Other	Other	Other	
A													
B													
C													
D													
E													
Enterprise													
Enterprise Edge													

FIGURE 9.22   Developing/measuring competitive edge.

Sales Activity Report. Sales improvement planning is nothing more than planning to increase the number of customer orders, the size of orders, and the frequency of repeat orders. Sales activities are a part of this planning. Calculation and tracking of these activities are essential to ensure that needed activities and expenses are properly handled. Figure 9.23 is an example of a sales activity report.

General Forecasting Techniques. Forecasting is the practice of predicting future conditions or activities on the basis of various statistics and data describing past and current conditions. Forecasting may be concerned with the ups and downs of the overall business cycles. Short-term forecasts predict conditions 3 to 18 months ahead. Long-term forecasts predict conditions 5 to 15 years ahead. Medium-term forecasts predict conditions two to three years ahead. The following briefly describes some forecasting methods.

1. *Graphic Extrapolation.* This is extending into the future the average line found by plotting past data patterns. The scatter of points shows the individuality of each point and the general trend (Figure 9.24).

2. *Semiaverage Method.* This is a simple numerical method that makes use of the arithmetic mean for extending into the future a past data pattern. Step 1 is illustrated as follows. Steps 2 and 3 are illustrated in Figure 9.25.

Name:

Area:

Date:

Supervisor:

Date	Sales volume		Travel expenses		Entertainment exp.		Total expenses		Expense/ Sales Ratio	
	Current	To date	Current	To date	Current	To date	Current	To date	Current	To date
Total 19XX										
Total 19XX										
Total 19XX										
Total 19XX										
January										
February										
March										
April										
May										
June										
July										
August										
September										
October										
November										
December										

FIGURE 9.23 Sales activity report.

Step 1   Plot past data pattern to a time series.
(Operational costs in years 1950, 1955, 1960, 1965, 1970 was 20, 24, 23, 26, 25 thousands, respectively.)

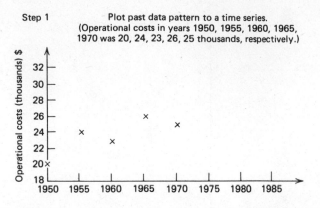

Step 2   Draw a line through the data that represents a visual averaging process.

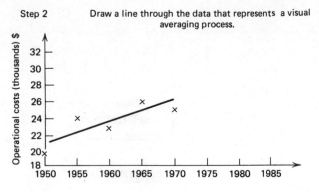

Step 3   Extend the drawn line to the period to be forecasted.
(Operational costs for 1985 estimated at 31 thousand.)

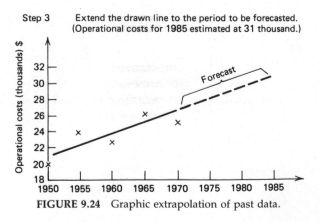

FIGURE 9.24   Graphic extrapolation of past data.

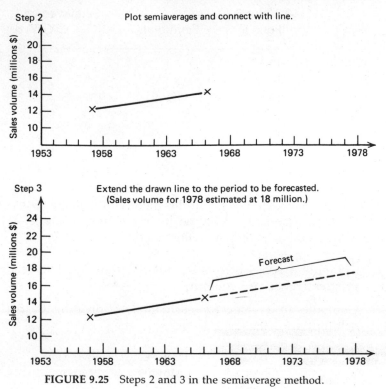

FIGURE 9.25   Steps 2 and 3 in the semiaverage method.

STEP 1.   Split the past data pattern of a time series into two equal parts. Compute totals (Σx) for each half. Divide totals by the number of years (N) in each semiperiod.

Year	Sales Volume (millions $)	Semitotals	Semiaverage ($\bar{x} + \Sigma X/N$)
1953	10.0		
1954	10.5		
1955	11.2		
1956	12.0		
1957	13.4	$\rightarrow$ 110.6	110.6/9 = 12.3
1958	13.5		
1959	12.5		
1960	13.3		
1961	14.2		
1962	14.5		
1963	14.8		

Year	Sales Volume (millions $)	Semitotals	Semiaverage $(\bar{x} + \Sigma X/N)$
1964	15.1		
1965	14.8		
1966	14.8	$\rightarrow$ 137.9	137.9/9 = 15.3
1967	15.2		
1968	16.0		
1969	16.1		
1970	16.6		

3. *Method of Moving Averages.* In this method, the fluctuations of past data patterns are smoothed out by means of a moving average. The first three steps are as follows. Step 4 is illustrated in Figure 9.26.

STEP 1. Compute a series of moving totals by adding five-year spans progressively (third column).

STEP 2. Compute an average for each total by dividing by 5 (fourth column).

Year	Boxes Shipped (Number)	Five-Year Moving Total	Five-Year Moving Average
1950	34	—	—
1951	62	—	—
1952	41	197	39.4
1953	22	207	41.4
1954	38	203	40.6
1955	44	207	41.4
1956	58	220	44.0
1957	45	252	50.4
1958	35	249	49.8
1959	70	276	55.2
1960	41	247	49.4
1961	55	274	54.8
1962	46	279	55.8
1963	62	306	61.2
1964	75	319	63.8
1965	68	331	66.2
1966	68	342	68.4
1967	58	343	68.6
1968	73	353	70.6
1969	76	—	—
1970	78	—	—

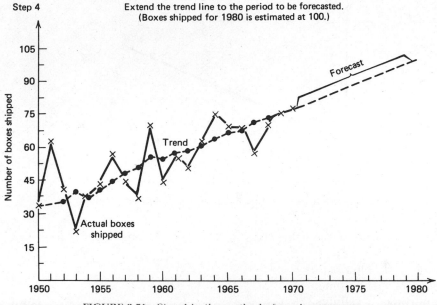

FIGURE 9.26   Step 4 in the method of moving averages.

STEP 3.   Plot the actual data and the five-year average (trend).

4.   *Trend Method of Least Squares.*   This method is used to compute straight trend lines. Estimates of trends are calculated in such a manner that the sum of the squared deviations from actual data is at a minimum. Hence the term "least squares." The method is based on the formula for a straight-line equation (Figure 9.27):

where Y = variable undergoing trend
X = variable causing trend
a = value of Y when X is zero; height of straight line above horizontal axis

$$a = \frac{\Sigma X^2 \Sigma Y - \Sigma X \Sigma XY}{N\Sigma X^2 - (\Sigma X)^2}$$

b = amount of change in Y that occurs with each change in X; slope of line

$$b = \frac{N\Sigma XY - \Sigma X \Sigma Y}{N\Sigma X^2 - (\Sigma X)^2}$$

N = total number of variables

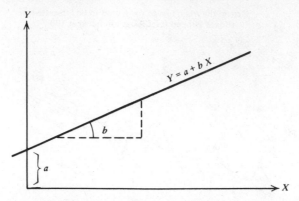

FIGURE 9.27   Formula for straight-line equation.

STEP 1.   Calculate the values of X^2, XY, Y^2 (columns 3, 4, 5).

Field Districts Reporting (X)	Number of Equipment Failures (Y)	X^2	XY	Y^2	Failure Trend
1	1	1	1	1	1.19
3	2	9	6	4	2.47
4	4	16	16	16	3.11
6	4	36	24	16	4.39
8	5	64	40	25	5.67
9	7	81	63	49	6.31
11	8	121	88	64	7.59
14	9	196	126	81	9.51
$\Sigma X = 56$	$\Sigma Y = 40$	$\Sigma X^2 = 524$	$\Sigma XY = 364$	$\Sigma Y^2 = 562$	

STEP 2.   Calculate values for a and b; failures $= a + b$ (districts).

$$a = \frac{(524)(40) - (56)(364)}{(8)(524) - (56)^2} = 0.55$$

$$b = \frac{(8)(364) - (56)40}{(8)(524) - (56)^2} = 0.64$$

STEP 3.   Set up a trend equation and calculate for the failure trend (column 6).

$$\text{Failures} = 0.55 + 0.64 \text{ (districts)}$$

STEP 4.   Forecast using failure trend equation when 20 districts report.

$$\text{Failures} = 0.55 + 0.64(20) = 13$$

5. *Exponential Smoothing.* This forecasting method is a weighted-average approach that allows the forecaster to assign greater or lesser importance to an old forecast relative to current or present values. This method attempts to smooth out fluctuations in a past data pattern by means of the constant alpha (α), which is used to give weight to the time period that appears significant. This method is based on the following exponential-smoothing forecast equation:

$$F_n = F_{n-1} + \alpha(Y_{n-1} - F_{n-1})$$

where
F_n = forecast for next period
F_{n-1} = forecast for previous period; can be calculated by simple average of most recent N observations. Moving average can also be used
Y_{n-1} = actual value for latest period before forecast
α = smoothing constant ($0 \leq \alpha \leq 1$); $\alpha = 0.8$ when more weight given to recent values; $\alpha = 0.2$ when more weight given to past values

STEP 1.   Determine forecast for previous period F_{n-1} by calculating a simple average between 1972 and 1978.

$$F_{1972-1978} = \frac{\Sigma X}{N} = \frac{44 + 48 + 56 + 62}{4} = 52.5$$

STEP 2.   Establish the actual value for the latest period before the forecast (Y_{n-1}).

$$Y_{1980} = 66$$

STEP 3.   Decide on the value for the smoothing constant (α).

$$\alpha = 0.8 \text{ (heavy weight given to recent values)}$$

STEP 4.   Estimate the number of boxes to be shipped for 1982 with the exponential-smoothing forecast equation.

$$F_{1982} = F_{1972-78} + 0.8 (Y_{1970} - F_{1972-68})$$

$$F_{1982} = 52.5 + 0.8 (66 - 52.5)$$

$$F_{1982} = 63 \text{ boxes}$$

Life Cylce of New Products.   The life of a new product in the marketplace undergoes several stages before the product is replaced by additional products. These stages are illustrated in Figure 9.28.

The actual time scale varies with different products and companies, but generally each new product undergoes these phases. The peak in profit as a percentage of sales occurs at a point when acceleration changes to

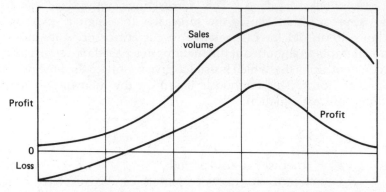

FIGURE 9.28   Life cycle of new products.

deceleration. This is the point at which the effects of competition begin to show.

New Product Value Index.   A helpful tool for selecting from several attractive new product alternatives is the new product value index, calculated as follows:

$$\text{New product value index (NPVI)} = \frac{V \times P \times \text{TF} \times \text{MF} \times \sqrt{\text{LC}}}{\text{TDC}}$$

where V = projected annual volume
          P = profit per unit (price minus cost)
      TF = technical success: 3 = high; 2 = moderate; 1 = low
     MF = marketing success: 3 = high; 2 = moderate; 1 = low
     LC = life cycle of product in years
   TDC = total development costs

Cost of Sales.   This is the cost or expense of all items sold during an accounting period. Each sale made has a cost, either of the sale or of the goods sold. The total cost of sales or cost of goods sold is computed as follows:

$$\text{CS} = \text{BI} + P - \text{EI}$$

where CS = cost of sales
      BI = beginning inventory
       P = purchases
      EI = ending inventory

Example:

The beginning inventory value of 35 items is $93 million, and annual purchases amount to $125 million. The value at the end of the year is $85 million.

$$\text{CS} = \$93 \text{ M} + \$125 \text{ M} - \$85 \text{ M} = \$133 \text{ million}$$

Forecasting Number of Salespersons.   Knowing the sales volume each salesperson should produce is vital, especially when an MBO marketing plan has been set up on a forecasted sales volume.

$$N = \frac{S}{P}(1 + T)$$

where N = number of salespersons needed
S = sales volume forecasted
P = sales productivity of one salesperson
T = sales force turnover rate

Example:

A new product line has a sales forecast of $3 million. The sales productivity of salespeople in a similar line has been $250,000/ person annually. The turnover rate is expected to be 10 percent.

$$N = \frac{3,000,000}{250,000}(1 + 0.10) = 13$$

Sample Size.   This is the number of units in a larger collection of units that needs to be sampled to draw valid conclusions about the larger collection of units. The selection of a sample follows a random process. That is, all units have an equal chance of being selected.

$$N = C^2 \times \frac{F \times U}{E^2}$$

where N = Number of units needed for sample
F = favorable responses, percent
U = unfavorable responses, percent
E = error in the favorable responses, percent
C = 1.96 for being 95% correct
C = 3.00 for being 99.7% correct

Example:

A small survey is made to assess the market. The survey reveals 50 percent favorable responses and 50 percent unfavorable. A manager wants to be accurate within 2.5 percent and to be 99.7 percent confident of the results. The size of the sample to be taken in the market is

$$N = (3.0)^2 \times \frac{50 \times 50}{(2.5)^2} = 3600$$

The size of the sample must be 3600 units.

Budgeting and Controls (Operations and Capital)

Key Areas of Budgeting and Controls	Typical Practices	Indicators for Tracking and Evaluating
Information	Management information system manual	System for collecting and classifying data for organizational and budgetary use
Budget accountability	Zero-based budget documents	All budget managers give accountability for results and variances
Budget formation	MBO, zero-based documents	System for linking and integrating budgets by departments and levels
Budget growth	MBO, zero-based documents	System for validating budget changes
Budget size	Zero-based budget documents	Expansion or shrinkage
Budget components	Zero-based budget documents	Sufficient details for decision making: direct labor, overhead, capital expenditures, benefits, program costs, special projects
Cost avoidance	MBO documents	Annual plan for avoiding future budgeted costs
Cost reduction	MBO documents	Annual plan for reducing existing costs and controlling budget
Cost effectiveness	MBO documents	Annual plan for innovations and capital outlay for reducing costs
Real time decision making on budget priorities	Computerized accounting reports	System to correct variances of control points before accountability

Measures of Budgeting and Controlling Efficiency

$$\frac{\text{Sales}}{\text{Operating costs}} \qquad \frac{\text{Cost reductions}}{\text{Total costs}} \qquad \frac{\text{Budget formation time this year}}{\text{Budget formation time base year}}$$

$$\frac{\text{Program costs this year}}{\text{Program costs base year}} \qquad \frac{\text{Cost reductions}}{\text{Employees}} \qquad \frac{\text{Cost avoidances}}{\text{Employees}}$$

$$\frac{\text{No. of budgets completed}}{\text{Budget employees}} \qquad \frac{\text{Total costs this year}}{\text{Total costs in base year}} \qquad \frac{\text{Budget variances}}{\text{Total budget}}$$

Quantitative Techniques for Budgets and Controls

Audits. This is a process of collecting information and verifying that what is claimed is in fact true. Several types of audits have evolved over the years. They are compared in Table 9.2.

Averages. An average is a value of a distribution that tends to sum up or describe a mass of data. It is a measure of the location of central tendency. For management, it becomes a powerful insight for setting standards, establishing a reference point, or making a decision about a group or distribution of values. Several types of averages are available.

1. *Arithmetic Mean.* This average is the mean of a group of items obtained by adding all the items together and dividing the total by the number of items.

$$\bar{x} = \frac{\Sigma x}{N}$$

where $\bar{x}$ = arithmetic mean
Σ = symbol of sum
x = data expressed as items
N = number of items

Example:

The average cost of four units that cost respectively $60, $63, $70, and $71 will be:

$$\text{Average cost per unit } (\bar{x}) = \frac{\text{total costs for units}}{\text{number of units}}$$

$$= \frac{60 + 63 + 70 + 71}{4} = \$66$$

2. *Median.* This average is an average of position, the value of the middle item when the items are arranged according to magnitude. If there is an even number of items, the median is the midpoint between the two central items. Finding the midpoint requires interpolation. If there is an odd number of items, the central number is the median.

TABLE 9.2 Comparison of Types of Audits

Type of Audit	Scope of Evaluation	Evaluation Focus	Resources to Be Evaluated	Comparison Method
Productivity audit	Organization, functions, departments, programs	Level and amount of productivity in organization	Money, personnel, equipment, space, time, procedures	Objectives and standards
Financial audit	Organization	Verification and certification of financial condition	Money	Standards and ratios
Program audit	Programs	Effectiveness in achieving program results	Money, personnel	Program objectives
Operations audit	Organization, functions, departments	Level and amount of performance effectiveness	Money, personnel, equipment, procedures	Standards and procedures
Compliance audit	Organization	Adherence to legal requirements	Personnel	Policies and standards
Social audit	Organization	Social contributions to individual and community	Money, personnel	Past performance
Management audit	Organization, functions	Quality and effectiveness of management	Management, personnel, policies	Other organizations

Example:

A cost distribution of units is 60, 63, 70, 71. The midpoint or median falls between 63 and 70; it is 66.5.

3.   *Mode.*   This average is the most frequent or most common value, provided there is a sufficiently large number of items available.

Example:

The cost distribution of units is 60, 62, 65, 65, 65, 66, 66, 71, 72, 75. After the numbers are arranged according to magnitude, the most common value, or mode, is 65.

4.   *Geometric Mean.*   This average gives a measure of central tendency for data that change and grow geometrically, such as birth rates or growth of information. It is calculated by getting the nth root of the product of n items.

Example:

Three units have costs that have grown in three years by \$1, \$3, and \$9. The geometric mean is:

$$G_{\bar{x}} = \sqrt[3]{1 \times 3 \times 9} = \$3$$

5.   *Harmonic Mean.*   This average gives a measure of central tendency of a series of changing rates. It is calculated as follows:

$$H_{\bar{x}} = \frac{n}{\Sigma(1/x)}$$

where $H_{\bar{x}}$ = harmonic mean
n = number of items
x = rate

Example:

An auto travels one way at 40 mph and returns at 60 mph. The average rate is 48 mph.

6.   *Quadratic Mean.*   This average gives a measure of central tendency of the average deviations from the arithmetic mean. It is thus the root-mean-square of deviations from the mean.

$$Q_{\bar{x}} = \sqrt{\frac{\Sigma(x - \bar{x})^2}{n}}$$

where $Q_{\bar{x}}$ = quadratic mean
$\quad\quad\quad x$ = deviations from the mean
$\quad\quad\quad \bar{x}$ = arithmetic mean
$\quad\quad\quad n$ = number of items

Example:

The mean price of several products is $12. These same products have been sold in the past for $8, $9, $10, and $14. The quadratic mean is:

$$Q_{\bar{x}} = \sqrt{\frac{(8-12)^2 + (9-12)^2 + (10-12)^2 + (14-12)^2}{4}} = 2.9$$

7. *Weighted Average.* It is often desirable to assign a varying degree of importance to items comprising a distribution. The weighted average accomplishes this by giving proportionate weights to items in the distribution. It is calculated as follows:

$$w_{\bar{x}} = \frac{\Sigma(x)(w)}{\Sigma(w)}$$

where $w_{\bar{x}}$ = weighted average
$\quad\quad\quad x$ = number of items
$\quad\quad\quad w$ = weights

Example:

A book is being sold in three types of stores at three different prices: $1.00 in 10,000 trade stores; $0.80 in 12,000 chain stores; and $0.60 in 15,000 mail-order outlets. The weighted average is

$$w_{\bar{x}} = \frac{\Sigma(1.00 \times 10,000) + (0.80 \times 12,000) + (0.60 \times 15,000)}{\Sigma(10,000 + 12,000 + 15,000)} = \$0.77$$

8. *Moving Average.* The moving average is a series of successive averages calculated from a series of items by dropping the first item in each group averaged and including the next in the series, thus obtaining the next average. A three-item moving average includes three items, a five-item moving average includes five items, and so on. The moving average method is useful in smoothing out fluctuations in data that vary widely. It is illustrated in Table 9.3.

Balance Sheet. The balance sheet is a statement of the financial position of a company at a specific point in time. This sheet lists all assets on the left side or top of the sheet and all liabilities and capital on the right side or

TABLE 9.3   Calculation of Moving Average

Costs	Three-Item Moving Total	Three-Item Moving Average, $\overline{X} = X/n$
3		
5	15	5.00
7	22	7.33
10	29	9.67
12	36	12.00
14	41	13.67

bottom of the sheet. If the total of all numbers on the left side or top is equal to the total of the right side or bottom, the financial analysis is in balance. The equation is

$$A = L + C$$

where A = assets
L = liabilities
C = capital

Base Period.   A base period is a reference period. Index numbers, ratios, and trend series are computed relative to a base period. The base period is assigned the value of 100 percent and should be rather recent. This allows comparisons with the base period to be reasonably relative rather than extreme and unreasonably relative.

Example:

$$PR = \frac{Pn}{Pb} \times 100$$

$$PR = \frac{\$15.65}{\$14.95} \times 100 = 104.7 \, percent$$

where   PR = price relative (index number)
Pb = price during base period
Pn = price during given period

The same general approach can be used with base numbers to calculate quantity relatives, volume relatives, employment relatives, consumer relatives, budget relatives, salary relatives, and inventory relatives.

Cash Flow.   This is the amount of cash remaining in a business operation within a specific period after operating expenses have been subtracted from the revenue generated by the sale of goods or services. The term "flow" reflects the fact that a company's cash position is in a constant state of flux as a result of continuing activity. Cash flow is calculated for any given period as

$$CF = S - OE$$

where   CF = cash flow (before taxes)
        S = sales
        OE = operating expenses

Example:

Sales for the month of April amount to $92,000. Operating expenses are $177,000. Cash flow before taxes is

$$CF = 192,000 - 177,000 = \$15,000$$

A cash flow projection can highlight cash needs for the immediate future (Table 9.4).

Income Statement.   The income statement is a summary of revenues and expenses of a business firm or organization for a particular period of time, generally one year. It is a measured record of operating activities. It serves to document what happened within the period of time. Figures aggregated for each item in the income statement become meaningful when compared with figures from previous years. Additionally, for MBO planning the income statement gives an analysis and sourceness of the operations of the firm and the opportunities for future improvements. Objective setting is facilitated with use of the income statement. Figure 9.29 is an example of an income statement.

Break-Even Analysis.   This is the analysis of variables of a firm to determine whether total revenue equals the total costs of producing and marketing goods or services. When the two are just equal, the firm has neither

TABLE 9.4   Cash Flow Analysis

Item	Jan	Feb	Mar	Apr	May	Jun	Jul	Aug	Sep	Oct
Sales (1000's)	130	150	142	140	130	132	122	128	120	110
Cost of sales	110	132	127	121	115	118	112	116	111	102
Gross margin	20	18	15	19	15	14	10	12	9	8
Selling expense	2	2	2	2	2	2	2	2	2	2
Income before taxes	18	16	13	17	13	12	8	10	7	6

(Present Time: Apr–Jun)

	Last Year	% of Sales	Jan	Feb	Mar	Apr	May	Jun	Jul	Aug	Sept	Oct	Nov	Dec	Year's Total	% of Sales
Net sales																
Cost of goods sold																
Gross profit																
Salaries (owners/mgrs.)																
Wages (office, other)																
Payroll taxes																
Total salaries and taxes																
Nonfixed expenses																
Advertising																
Automobile																
Dues and donations																
Delivery																
Legal and professional																
Office supplies																
Telephone																
Utilities																
Miscellaneous																
Total nonfixed expenses																
Fixed expenses																
Depreciation																
Insurance																
Loan payments																
Rent																
Taxes and licenses																
Total fixed expenses																
Total expenses																
Net profit (loss) (before taxes)																

FIGURE 9.29 Income statement.

made money nor experienced loss; it has just broken even. The firm can be said to have operated at the break-even point. If revenue is greater than costs, the firm shows a profit. If costs are greater than revenue, the firm shows a loss. The basic profit equation is

$$\text{Profits } (P) = \text{total revenue (TR)} - \text{total costs (TC)}$$

Total volume or level of operation (total revenue) can be expressed in three ways. One is the number of units of product made or sold. Another is the dollar volume of sales. The third is the percentage of plant capacity being utilized.

Total costs can be expressed as a combination of total variable costs and total fixed costs; they are measured in dollars. Both variable and fixed costs are further determined by volume or output in units and variable costs per units. The variables involved in break-even analysis are as follows

TR	Total revenues in dollars	X	Volume or output of units
TC	Total cost in dollars	v	Variable cost per unit in dollars
TVC	Total variable costs	P	Selling price per unit in dollars
TFC	Total fixed costs	BEP	Break-even point

To determine BEP in units, in dollars, and in percent of capacity utilized, the following formulas can be used:

In units

$$\text{BEP} = \frac{\text{TFC}}{p - v}$$

In dollars

$$\text{BEP} = \frac{\text{TFC}}{1 - v/p}$$

In % capacity

$$\text{BEP} = \frac{\text{TFC}}{(p - v)(\text{total capacity in units})} \times 100\%$$

Example:

The total fixed costs of a firm are $10,000 for one year, the variable cost per unit is $2, and the selling price of the unit is $4. The break-even point in volume or units is

$$\text{BEP} = \frac{\text{TFC}}{p - v} = \frac{10,000}{4 - 2} = \$20,000$$

A break-even chart (Figure 9.30) is a graphic device helpful for visualizing and making decisions about the relation of (1) changes in sales to changes in profits, (2) changes in costs to changes in profits, and (3) changes in scale of operations to changes in profits. The chart shows the effect of these relationships on profit or loss. With this information a manager may estimate the effects of certain decisions on profits.

In break-even analysis, the following guidelines are important:

1. The analysis is sound if the data from the cost accounting system are valid and accurate.
2. The analysis makes an assumption that cost-volume revenue is a linear relationship. This can only be true in certain ranges. In other ranges the relationship is nonlinear. For example, fixed costs in certain ranges rise with variable costs.
3. The analysis presumes a revenue curve resulting from one selling price. In practice, prices change with changing volume.
4. The analysis cannot be used over the long term but only for the current budget period.
5. The analysis is useful in slow-moving, relatively static situations rather than volatile, erratic ones.

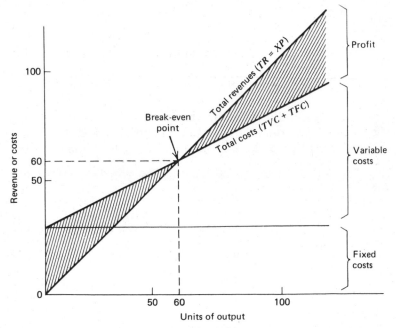

FIGURE 9.30   Break-even chart.

Cost/Benefit Analysis.   This is a systematic technique for judging among alternative ways of optimizing use of resources in achieving objectives. The technique consists of quantifying the expected cost and benefit of each alternative, comparing them, and choosing the best option. The following relationships hold true

$$EB = PB \times PO$$

where   EB = expected benefits
           PB = potential benefits
           PO = probability of occurrence

This is illustrated in Table 9.5.

Cost of Living.   The cost of living is the money cost of maintaining a certain style of living. It is a rough measure of the average price of the basic necessities of life. It is described in comparative terms, such as a rise or fall from one year to the next. It is presently being measured by the consumer price index (CPI). This is a ratio that tracks shifts in prices of items in the typical consumer budget such as housing, food, public transportation, and medical care. The ratio is a price relative that compares total prices in a given period to those in another period, called the base period or reference period.

$$CPI = \frac{\Sigma P_n}{\Sigma P_0}$$

where   CPI = consumer price index
         ΣP_n = sum of prices of commodities in consumer budget for given year
         ΣP_0 = sum of prices of commodities in base year

The consumer price index measures the prices of goods and services purchased by wage earners and clerical worker families in 46 cities. These goods and services constitute a close approximation of the "market basket" of

TABLE 9.5   Cost/Benefit Analysis

Options	Potential Benefits (PB)	Probability of Occurrence (PO)	Expected Benefits (EB)
Sales volume	$10,000	.30	$3000
Cost reduction	6,000	.60	3600
Rework reduction	5,000	.90	4500
Schedule improvement	2,500	.80	2000
Obsolete inventory	1,500	.70	1050
Value improvement	4.000	.40	1600

nearly 40% of the families in the United States. A special caution is that the consumer price index should not be used to measure changes in the standard of living or for regional comparisons; these are misuses of the index.

Payback.   This is the time estimated to be needed for a capital investment to pay for itself. Payback is a calculated measure that aids in making investment decisions. The equation is

$$PBY = \frac{CO}{NCI}$$

where   PBY = payback in years
CO = cash outlay
NCI = net annual cash flow

Example:

A firm has an opportunity to invest $100,000 in a new computer. The investment will result in an annual cash savings of $10,000.

$$PBY = \frac{\$100,000}{\$10,000} = 10 \, years$$

Cost Finding.   Assessment of costs is equal in importance to assessment of sales, since costs and sales drive profits. Several methods can be used to find and track costs for purposes of forecasting, planning, budgeting, and control.

1.   *Average Cost Per Unit (ACU).*

$$ACU = \frac{TC}{TU}$$

where   TC is total product costs for the period and TU is total units produced during the period.

2.   *Overhead Rate (OR).*

$$OR = \frac{TEO}{TEU}$$

where   TEO is total estimated overhead for the coming period and TEU is total estimated units to be produced in the coming period.

3. *Standard Costs Rate (SCR).*

$$SCR = (ACU + OR)EIF$$

where   ACU = average cost per unit
        OR = overhead rate
        EIF = efficiency improvement factor

Example:

A company with $180,000 overhead expects to produce 20,000 units in a coming period. The average cost per unit is $50, and the company wants to improve its efficiency 10 percent. The standard costs rate is

$$SCR = \$50 + \left(\frac{\$180,000}{20,000 \text{ units}} \right) 0.90 = \$53.10$$

Quality

Key Areas of Quality	Typical Practices	Indicators for Tracking and Evaluating
Quality standards	Quality control (Q/C) manual	Lack of standards in work processes
Uncorrected errors	Q/C progress reports	Amount of time required to correct errors
Quality priorities	Q/C manual	Quality control points established, tracked, and evaluated
Prevention of errors	MBO document	Formal system for preventing expected errors with potential problems
Bottlenecks	Q/C progress reports	System for handling speed and accuracy of feedback
Quality and work performance	MBO document	Employees trained and evaluated for self-correcting quality
Rework	Q/C progress reports	Amount and frequency
Quality planning	MBO document	Quality plans for measurement and assurance
Quality assurance	MBO document	Responsibilities for quality assurance
Mediocrity	MBO document	Amount and degree of tolerance for mediocre performance

Measures of Quality Control Efficiency

$$\frac{\text{Number of rejects}}{\text{Costs}} \qquad \frac{\text{Costs of rework}}{\text{Total costs}} \qquad \frac{\text{Time spent on QC activities}}{\text{Number of QC employees}}$$

$$\frac{\text{Sales}}{\text{QC budget}} \qquad \frac{\text{Warranty costs}}{\text{QC budget}} \qquad \frac{\text{Customer complaints}}{\text{QC budget}}$$

$$\frac{\text{Violation of QC standards}}{\substack{\text{Compliance with} \\ \text{QC standards}}} \qquad \frac{\text{Reject work}}{\substack{\text{Standard hours} \\ \text{to produce}}} \qquad \frac{\text{Downtime for QC}}{\text{Total hours}}$$

Quantitative Techniques for Quality

Attribute Process Control. In quality assurance management, there is need for continuous inspection of products to determine how many are defective. Attribute process control allows computation of the percentage defective in a sample. The procedure is as follows:

1. Select samples of work of size n from a work process or production. The sample must be randomly selected, that is, every item has an equal chance of being selected.
2. Determine the number of defective items in the sample.
3. Compute the percent defective in the sample size n:

$$D = \sqrt{\frac{R \times r}{n}}$$

where D = percent defective in entire process
R = minimum percent rejects allowable by standards
r = actual number of defectives in sample
n = size of sample

Example:

Three defective items are found in a sample of 30 items. Only three defectives are allowed by standards (10%). The percent defective in the entire process is

$$D = \sqrt{\frac{(3)(0.1)}{30}} = 0.1 \text{ percent}$$

Quality Level Control. The quality of a given product may be defined as its degree of conformity to given standards or specifications. The need to control prescribed standards is due to the amount of variation in the manu-

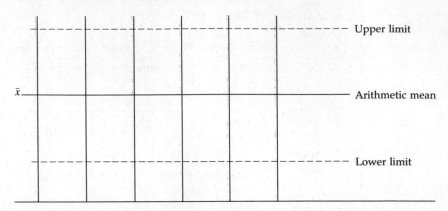

FIGURE 9.31   Graphic content chart.

facturing process despite careful procedures. The aim of quality control is to detect the causes of variation and to keep variations within certain limits. Control of quality level may be achieved as follows:

1. Select samples of size N from production at random.
2. Compute an average (x) of each set of sample measurements.
3. Compute the appropriate standard error of the average used

$$\sigma_x = \frac{\sigma}{\sqrt{N}}$$

4. Prepare a graphic content chart (Figure 9.31) plotting the standard error as lower and upper limits.
5. Plot the averages obtained from the samples. If any of the plotted points fall outside the established control limits, the process is out of control.

Quality Deviation with Standard Deviation.   Standard deviation is a measure of variation, spread, or deviation from a reference point called the mean or quality standard. It is calculated by taking the root-mean-square of the deviations from the arithmetic mean.

$$\text{Standard deviation (SD)} = \sqrt{\frac{\Sigma x^2}{N}}$$

or

$$SD = \sqrt{\frac{\Sigma(x - \bar{x})^2}{N}}$$

where x = deviations from the mean
           N = total number of items
           $\bar{x}$ = arithmetic mean

Example:

The following measures are from a production series of units: 9, 3, 8, 8, 9, 8, 9, 18. The standard deviation is

$$\bar{x} = \frac{9 + 3 + 8 + 8 + 9 + 8 + 9 + 18}{8} = 9$$

$$SD = \sqrt{\frac{(9 - 9)^2 + (3 - 9)^2 + (8 - 9)^2 + (8 - 9)^2 + (9 - 9)^2 + (8 - 9)^2 + (9 - 9)^2 + (18 - 9)^2}{8}}$$

SD = 3.87 units to the left and right of 1 standard deviation

Work Sampling.   Work sampling is detailed analysis of a job to determine how well certain performance standards are met. The procedure requires that the job be broken down into performance categories and that observations be made at statistical prescribed random intervals on how many times each category is performed. Statistical prescribed means a random generation of time periods to infer the total time. The accuracy of results depends on the number of observations made. The greater the number the more accurate. Accuracy of the data can be measured as follows:

$$SD = \sqrt{\frac{P(1 - P)}{n}}$$

where P is the percent of observations and n is the number of observations.

Example:

A worker is observed to operate a particular machine 1000 times out of 10,000 observations.

$$SD = \sqrt{\frac{0.01(1 - 0.10)}{10,000}} = 0.3\%$$

Three standard deviations encompass 99 percent of the normal distribution. This means that it is 99 percent certain that the worker spends 9.1 percent of the time operating the machine.

$$[10\% - (3 \times 0.3\%)] = 9.1\%$$

Standards of Performance.   Quality control can be basically defined as "setting up standards and correcting the difference." Quality performance is performing to standards. Scope, type, level, and intensity are built into the standards and a system is created to measure and correct the deviations (Figure 9.32).

Quality Control Charts.   Quality control charts graphically portray in quantitative fashion the standards to be met and the tolerance allowable in meeting them. The tolerance is specified as upper and lower control limits (Figure 9.33).

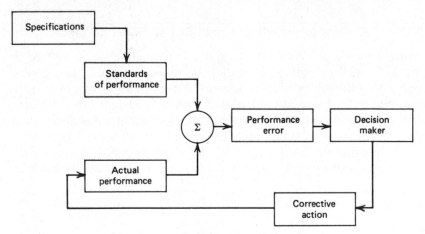

FIGURE 9.32   Standards of performance.

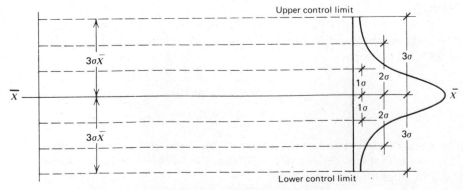

FIGURE 9.33   Quality control chart.

Production

Key Areas of Work Production	Typical Practices	Indicators for Tracking and Evaluating
Work processes	Production procedures manual	Work processes clearly flowcharted for output and in-process measurement
Work methods	MBO documents	Activities for innovations and improvements
Finished product inventory	Inventory reports	Inventory levels and "stock out" frequency
In-process inventory	Inventory reports	Amount and delays
Equipment breakdown	Maintenance reports	Frequency and type
Equipment capacity	MBO documents	Low equipment use
Shipping dates	Shipping reports	Frequency and effects of delays
Work status	Expediting reports	Formal self-correcting status reporting system
Rework	Quality control reports	High scrap/work ratio
Purchases	Expediting reports	Supplies and materials on hand when needed

Measures of Work Production Efficiency

$$\frac{\text{Labor costs/unit}}{\text{Scheduled labor costs/unit}} \qquad \frac{\text{Machines operating}}{\text{Set-up time}} \qquad \frac{\text{Production volume}}{\text{Working days}}$$

$$\frac{\text{Space utilized}}{\text{Space available}} \qquad \frac{\text{Overtime hours}}{\text{Total hours}} \qquad \frac{\text{Man-days lost}}{\text{Man-days worked}}$$

$$\frac{\text{Work processes made efficient}}{\text{Total work processes}} \qquad \frac{\text{Work packages accomplished}}{\text{Work packages expected}} \qquad \frac{\text{Production volume}}{\text{Production overhead costs}}$$

Quantitative Techniques for Work Production Efficiency

ABC Analysis. This is a system of classifying a large number of items into dollar usage and value categories. The items may be inventory, supplies, parts, work in process, raw materials, finished goods, or many others. The analysis is based on Pareto's rule and shows on which items of a

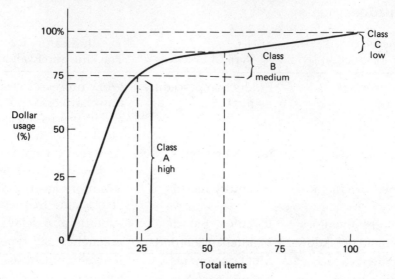

FIGURE 9.34 ABC analysis.

distribution the greatest effort should be made to make the biggest impact on value. The analysis is illustrated in Figure 9.34.

The division of the distribution into three classes (A, B, and C) according to dollar usage provides justification for greater planning and control according to value. In Figure 9.34, "A" items have high value, that is, 15 to 20 percent of the items account for 75 to 80 percent of the total value. Therefore these items should be carefully controlled for order quantities, reorder points, procurement costs, lead time, stock records, and use rates.

"B" items have medium value, that is, 30 to 40 percent of the items account for 15 to 20 percent of total value. Normal controls and good record keeping should be instituted for order quantities and reorder points.

"C" items have low value, that is, 40 to 50 percent of the items account for 5 to 10 percent of total value. No attempt is made to keep a running account of stock level, no formal calculations are made, and only a once-yearly review is needed to check amounts in storage.

The following illustrates ABC analysis of inventory in three steps:

STEP 1.

Item	Annual Usage Units	Unit Cost	Annual Usage Dollars	Rank
Pins	30,000	$0.10	3,000	6
Clips	280,000	0.15	42,000	1
Holders	3,000	0.10	300	9

Item	Annual Usage Units	Unit Cost	Annual Usage Dollars	Rank
Cards	110,000	0.05	5,500	4
Edges	4,000	0.05	200	10
Caps	220,000	0.10	22,000	2
Keys	15,000	0.05	750	8
Rolls	80,000	0.05	4,000	5
Dowels	60,000	0.15	9,000	3
Boxes	8,000	0.10	800	7

STEP 2.

Item	Annual Usage Dollars	Cumulative Annual Usage	Cumulative Percent	Class
Clips	42,000	42,000	48.0	A
Caps	22,000	64,000	73.1	A
Dowels	9,000	73,000	83.4	B
Cards	5,500	78,500	89.6	B
Rolls	4,000	82,500	94.1	B
Pins	3,000	85,500	97.6	C
Boxes	800	86,300	98.6	C
Keys	750	87,050	99.4	C
Holders	300	87,350	99.6	C
Edges	200	87,550	100.0	C

STEP 3.

Classes	Items	Percent of Items	Dollars per Group	Percent of Dollars
A	Clips, caps	20	64,000	73.1
B	Dowels, cards, rolls	30	18,500	21.1
C	Pins, boxes, keys, holders, edges	50	5,050	5.8

Economic Order Quantity. Two basic decisions must be made in inventory management: how much to order at one time and when to order this quantity. There is pressure to order huge lots, minimize ordering costs, and to order small lots, to minimize carrying costs. Ordering costs are the costs of getting an item into inventory; they include costs of issuing purchase orders, expediting, follow-up, receipt of goods, materials handling, placing in inventory, and handling of accounts payable. Carrying costs, also referred to as holding costs, are the costs incurred in owning or maintaining inventories. They include interest on money invested in inventory, obsolescence and spoilage, rent, heat, lights, refrigeration, record keeping, security, taxes, insurance, and depreciations. Extremes in either direction will have unfavorable effects on total costs. The optimum course of action is a compromise or tradeoff between the two extremes. The technique of economic order quantity attempts to find the best compromise (Figure 9.35). The formula for calculation is

Economic order quantity (EOQ) =

$$\sqrt{\frac{2 \times \text{total unit demand/year (UD)} \times \text{cost of placing order (OC)}}{\text{cost of each unit (C)} \times \text{carrying cost as percent of average inventory (CC)}}}$$

Example:

A company uses 10,000 units per year at a cost of $1.00/unit. The ordering cost per order is $25, and the carrying cost is 12.5 percent.

$$\text{EOQ} = \sqrt{\frac{2 \times \text{UD} \times \text{OC}}{\text{C} \times \text{CC}}} = \sqrt{\frac{2 \times 10{,}000 \times 25}{1 \times 0.125}} = 2000 \text{ units per order}$$

The company will optimize its carrying and ordering costs by ordering 2000 units in each order.

   Ideal Index.   The ideal index combines any two indexes whose biases or trends tend to offset one another. Thus it compensates for opposing

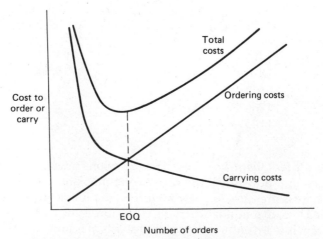

FIGURE 9.35   Economic order quantity (EOQ) technique.

tendencies. It is constructed by taking the geometric average of two indexes, that is, the square root of their product, which is always a slightly lower value than a simple average.

$$\text{Ideal index (II)} = \sqrt{\text{first index (FI)} \times \text{second index (SI)}}$$

Example:

Two productivity indexes were calculated for the operation of a cost center. The first ratio related performance to time ($P_1 = 4.5$), and the second ratio was work packages per week ($P_2 = 3.5$). The ideal index thus is

$$\text{Ideal productivity index} = \sqrt{P_1 \times P_2} = \sqrt{4.5 \times 3.5} = 3.96$$

Index Numbers.   An index number is a device for comparing changes in two or more sets of data; thus it gives relative value compared with a base or a reference. It is used to compare employment, prices, health, productivity, accidents, and many other conditions of business and markets on a weekly, monthly, or annual basis. Several types of index numbers are of national interest and are published, such as the consumer price index, wholesale price index, and national productivity index. The index number, when compiled, gives a strong indication of the behavior of the group as a whole. An index number is simply a relative or ratio

$$\text{Index number (I)} = \frac{\text{Price in year (Py)}}{\text{Price in base year (Pb)}}$$

Thus four kinds of index numbers are generally used:

1. Price indexes, Py/Pb.
2. Quantity indexes, Qy/Qb.
3. Value indexes, Vy/Vb.
4. Special purpose, SPy/SPb.

All index numbers have three features in common. First, each has a base period that is usually assigned the value of 100 and that becomes the reference. Second, each measures representative items of a total group. The items are a sample of the whole. Thus inference of totality can only be made if sampling procedure is valid. Third, each index number is relative to the base period, and therefore index numbers for different periods are comparable.

Inventory Turnover.   This is a control ratio that indicates the amount of inventory a company must sell to realize a given level of sales volume, in other words, the number of times per year inventory investment must revolve. Its calculation is

$$\text{Inventory turnover (IT)} = \frac{\text{Cost of sales (CS)}}{\text{Average inventory value (AI)}}$$

Example:

A company experiences an annual cost of sales of $3.5 million. The average dollar value of inventory is $700,000, between peak and low inventory periods. Turnover thus must be

$$\text{IT} = \frac{\$3,500,000}{\$700,000} = 5$$

Business experiences inventory turnover from 4 to 12 times per year. This is a way of reaching higher sales with a small investment. The primary value of inventory turnover calculation is in evaluating period-to-period performance within a company or division rather than performance compared with that of other companies or other industries.

Learning Curve.   This is a curve showing that workers will increase their efficiency as they perform jobs again and again. For example, the first unit of a product may take 10 hours of labor, the second unit 8 hours of labor, the fourth unit 6.4 hours, and the eighth unit 5.2 hours. An efficiency factor emerges because of repetition. As a result, costs decline as workers gain experience with a new product or process. The curve is illustrated in Figure 9.36.

Materials Utilization.   In the flow of materials through manufacture, certain losses are likely to occur. Errors, shrinkage, scrap, and waste are

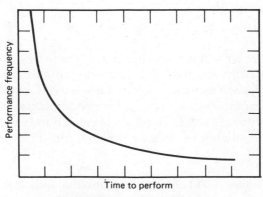

FIGURE 9.36   Learning curve.

more than likely to occur. Materials utilization is a measure of the correctness of estimates of required materials.

$$MU = \frac{O + ES}{I}$$

where   MU = material utilization
   O = output
   ES = expected scrap
   I = input

Example:

It used to take 16 pounds of brass to manufacture a 12-pound valve when utilization of material was 100%. If 18 pounds are now needed to produce the valve, the utilization is

$$MU = \frac{12 + 4}{18} = 88 \text{ percent}$$

   Probability of Meeting Schedules.   A PERT time network provides time relationships among activities and events that have been structured to be completed within a period of time. Critical path analysis reveals slack times and critical times, when the manager should focus attention on tightening or loosening resources to meet schedules. Development of a model and its manipulation is as follows:

$$P_z = \frac{T_s - T_e}{\sigma_{cp}}$$

where T_s = time scheduled for completion of project
   T_e = time estimated by PERT network as expected for completion of project
   P_z = probability that project will be completed
   $\sigma_{cp} = \sqrt{\Sigma(\sigma_1^2 + \sigma_2^2 + \sigma_3^2 + \ldots + \sigma_n^2)}$

   σ_{cp} is the accumulated standard deviation of a series of n activities in the network's critical path. Further, σ equals the variance of optimistic and pessimistic estimates of an actual activity under a normal distribution.

$$\sigma = \frac{t_p - t_o}{6}$$

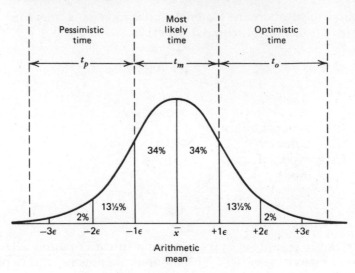

FIGURE 9.37   Probable time estimates.

The PERT network will have many paths. The path that takes the longest time to complete is called the critical path. The time required to complete this path is calculated as follows:

$$\text{Time } (t_e) = \frac{t_o + 4t_m + t_p}{b}$$

In noncritical paths there is time to get work done because there is more time available. These noncritical areas are called slack paths. The estimated times and variances are illustrated in Figure 9.37.

Productivity Measures for Inventory Control. This is given a material focus rather than a labor focus in the measurement of productivity. Some measures are as follows:

1. *Turnover Productivity.* Number of times per year inventory investment turns.

$$\text{Turnover productivity (TP)} = \frac{\text{annual material cost (AMC)}}{\text{average inventory value (AIV)}}$$

2. *Material Productivity.* Ratio of cost of material when converted to manufacturing.

$$\text{Material productivity (MP)} = \frac{\text{annual material cost (AMC)}}{\text{annual manufacturing cost (MC)}}$$

3. *Work-in-Process Productivity.* Ratio of material value in process changes.

$$\text{Work-in-process productivity (WIPP)} = \frac{\text{average material value in process (AMV)}}{\text{average inventory value (AIV)}}$$

4. *Finished Goods Productivity.* Ratio of finished goods value when completed.

$$\text{Finished-goods productivity (FGP)} = \frac{\begin{array}{c}\text{average finished-goods value}\\\text{in inventory (AFGP)}\end{array}}{\text{average inventory value (AIV)}}$$

Quantity Index.   This is a technique for measuring the changes in the sum of the quantities in any given period compared to itself over a given period of time. Calculation is as follows:

$$QI = \frac{\Sigma Q_n}{\Sigma Q_b}$$

where ΣQ_n is the sum of the quantities in any given period and ΣQ_b is the sum of the quantities in the base period.

Example:

Company A produces the following tons of paper in four quality categories: 8, 12, 15, and 17. The same tonnage for the base period was 8, 11, 13, and 15. The quantity index for the current year is

$$QI = \frac{8 + 12 + 15 + 17}{8 + 11 + 13 + 15} = 1.21$$

Cost Standards.   Standards are set up to give performance guidelines to all those who expend in an organization. Standards cover almost every field and discipline. They are primarily set up from past experience and proven practices. The following is an example.

Item	Standards		Standard cost per unit
Materials	Quantity per unit	5 pounds	
	Price per pound	$2.00	$10.00
Labor	Time per unit	10 hours	
	Wage rate	$4.00/hour	$40.00
Overhead	Fixed cost per month	$5000	
	Variable rate	0.45/hour	4.50
	Total standard cost per unit		$54.50

Size Standardization.   When products can be made in a continuous series of sizes from very small to very large, it would be impractical from both a sales and a manufacturing viewpoint to produce all sizes. Concentration on certain sizes permits economical manufacture and sale. An arithmetic progression can be followed, such as 4, 18, 12, 16, and so on, or a geometric progression, such as 4, 16, 64, 256, and so on. A proportionate factor can be used to find the size selection once the largest and smallest sizes have been selected.

$$SR = \sqrt[n-1]{\frac{LS}{SS}}$$

Example:

A chicken feed producer wants to package chicken feed in five different sizes, the smallest being 1 pound and the largest 100 pounds. The size ratio is

$$SR = \sqrt[4]{\frac{100}{1}} = 3.16$$

The size progression using this ratio would be

$$1 \quad 3 \quad 10 \quad 30 \quad 100 \text{ pounds}$$

Time Standards.   A time standard is based on estimates of the time needed to do a particular job. The accuracy of the standard depends largely on the degree of validity of the estimate. The estimate can be made as follows:

$$ET = \frac{OT + 4MLT + PT}{6}$$

where
$$ET = \text{expected time}$$
$$OT = \text{optimistic time}$$
$$MLT = \text{most likely time (average)}$$
$$PT = \text{pessimistic time}$$

Example:

Because the design and manufacture of a pump depends on many different suppliers and manufacturers, several estimates of the time needed are collected. The minimal time is three weeks, the maximum time is ten weeks, and the average time is six weeks.

$$ET = \frac{3 + (4 \times 6) + 10}{6} = 6.17 \text{ weeks}$$

Queueing. Queueing is the analysis and measurement of waiting lines of every conceivable kind, the intent being to measure and reduce bottlenecks and congestion. Queueing techniques deal with capacity of the servicing units to handle the waiting lines. People waiting in line at a bank, cars waiting at toll booths, parts waiting for a machine for an operation are appropriate quantities for queueing techniques. Figure 9.38 illustrates queueing. Equations are

$$\text{Mean number in waiting line } (L_q) = \frac{\lambda^2}{\mu(\mu - \lambda)}$$

$$\text{Mean number in system } (L) = \frac{\lambda}{\mu - \lambda}$$

$$\text{Mean waiting time } (L_t) = \frac{\lambda}{\mu(\mu - \lambda)}$$

$$\text{Probability of } n \text{ units in system } (P_n) = \left(1 - \frac{\lambda}{\mu}\right)\left(\frac{\lambda}{\mu}\right)^n$$

Example:

A toll booth can handle 8 cars/minute (μ) but cars arrive at the rate of 10 cars/minute (λ). The mean number in the waiting line is

$$L_q = \frac{10^2}{8(8 - 10)} = 6.3 \text{ cars}$$

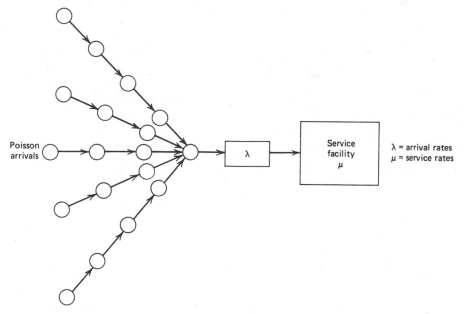

FIGURE 9.38   Queueing.

The mean waiting time is

$$L_t = \frac{10}{8(8 - 10)} = 0.6 \, \text{minutes}$$

The mean number in the system is

$$L = \frac{10}{8 - 10} = 5$$

Time Control Charts.   Time control charts (Figures 9.39a-d) are schedules that relate tasks to be completed to time. The schedules graphically show start-stop of the task, duration of the task, and its relationship to other tasks.

Site Location Analysis.   Site location analysis to appraise new opportunities for improvement in MBO ventures can be made with the format shown in Figure 9.40.

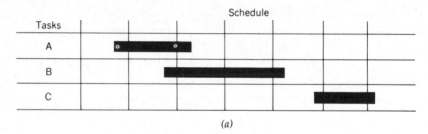

(a)

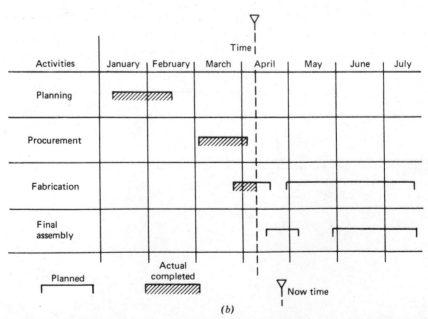

(b)

FIGURE 9.39   Examples of time control charts; (a) Bar chart, (b) Gantt chart, (c) PERT chart, (d) Master chart.

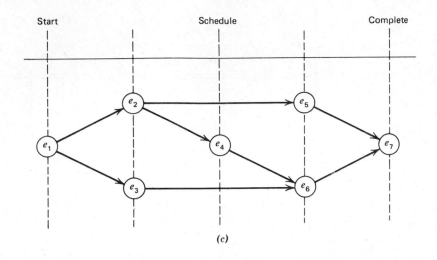

(c)

Schedule of productivity capacity

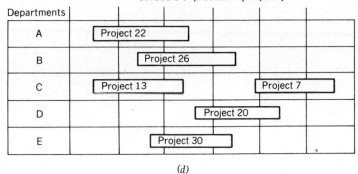

(d)

FIGURE 9.39 *(continued)*

Sites	A	B	C	D	E	F
LOCATION FACTORS						
MARKETING:						
a. Traffic Count						
b. Visibility						
c. Population						
d. Competition						
e. Trading Area						
f. Parking						
g. Per Capital Income						
ECONOMIC:						
a. Transportation						
b. Labor Market						
c. Tax Structure						
d. Insurance						
TECHNICAL:						
a. Raw Materials						
b. Power						
c. Services: water, sewer						
d. Other						
LEGAL:						
a. Zoning						
b. Regulations						
c. Restrictions						
LAND:						
a. Size						
b. Topography						
c. Slope						
d. Value						
MISCELLANEOUS:						
a. Union Activity						
b. Recreation						
c. Community Growth						

Location Selection

Provide location rating from 1 (very poor) to 10 (excellent) for each location

	SITE A	SITE B	SITE C	SITE D
1. Accessibility to customers (including distance)				
2. General appearance				

FIGURE 9.40 Site location analysis.

398

	SITE A	SITE B	SITE C	SITE D
3. Drawing power				
4. Floor space				
5. Available parking				
6. Neighborhood				
7. Competition				
8. Growth potential				
9. Costs (including taxes and utilities)				
10. Site value in ten years				

FIGURE 9.40   *(continued)*

Data Processing

Key Areas of Data Processing	Typical Practices	Indicators for Tracking and Evaluating
User satisfaction	Electronic data processing	Utilization of EDP output
Cost effectiveness	MBO document	Annual plan for cost per program improvement
Quality EDP performance	EDP reports and MBO documents	Amount and type of restarts and rejects
Computerization	Systems reports	Degreee to which inefficient information handling is computerized
Machine capacity	Computer utilization reports	Degree of utilization
Machine downtime	Computer maintenance reports	Frequency of downtime
Programming and processing standards	Systems and procedures manual	Output and flowchart formats
Documentation	Systems and procedures manual	Formal retrieval procedures of valid information
Clerical support	Job descriptions	Over standard or under standard
Staff and user training	MBO documents	Formal programs to improve work output

Measures of EDP Efficiency

$$\frac{\text{Sales}}{\text{Volume of transactions}} \qquad \frac{\text{Volume of transactions}}{\text{EDP costs}} \qquad \frac{\text{EDP costs}}{\text{MIS costs}}$$

$$\frac{\text{Value of EDP reports}}{\text{Report costs}} \qquad \frac{\text{Value of information}}{\text{Total information}} \qquad \frac{\text{User request time}}{\text{Total time}}$$

$$\frac{\text{Transaction errors}}{\text{Total transactions}} \qquad \frac{\text{EDP costs}}{\text{EDP budget}} \qquad \frac{\text{Transaction standards operation}}{\text{Standards required}}$$

Quantitative Techniques for Data Processing

Correlation. Correlation is the relative measure of degree of association or nonassociation between two sets of data, measurements, or trends. The coefficient of correlation is the comparative measure of this association or nonassociation, calculated as follows:

$$r = \sqrt{1 - \frac{(SE)^2}{(SD)^2}}$$

where r = coefficient of correlation

SE = standard error of estimate; measure of deviation about the regression line

$$SE = \sqrt{\frac{\Sigma(d)^2}{n}}$$

SD = standard deviation; measure of deviation about the arithmetic mean

$$SD = \sqrt{\frac{(x - \bar{x})^2}{n}}$$

When the standard error is 2.04 and the standard deviation is 16.74, the correlation coefficient is

$$r = \sqrt{1 - \frac{(2.04)^2}{(16.73)^2}} = .99$$

The magnitude and sign of the correlation coefficient reflect the quality of the relationship between the two variables. The relationship can be interpreted as shown in Figure 9.41.

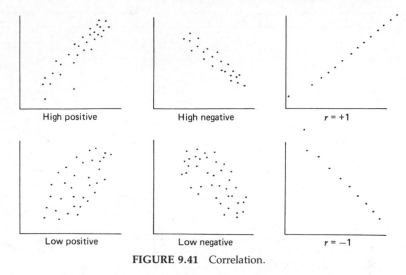

High positive   High negative $r = +1$

Low positive   Low negative $r = -1$

FIGURE 9.41 Correlation.

Flowcharting. A flowchart is a graph or other chart in which symbols are used to represent operations and the movement of decisions, money, work force, design, calculations, or some other element is illustrated through various stages. In manufacturing, a flowchart shows the flow of raw materials through the various stages to the final product. In computer technology, it shows the flow of the steps in the solution of a problem. In a system, it shows the flow of decisions and events to an ultimate use or final decision (Figure 9.42).

Ogives. Ogives are cumulative frequency representations, for example, a cumulation of the data of a histogram so that an upper limit becomes apparent and useful. Ogives or cumulative curves tend to be S-shaped, rising from zero at the lower left to the maximum at the upper right (Figure 9.43). These curves allow interpolation and are useful for objective tracking, scheduling, and simulation.

Computer Simulation. Computer simulation refers to a process that brings in a step-by-step fashion the solution to a problem involving many variables. The process calculates by adding or comparing present values with needed or standard values. Figure 9.44 shows an example.

Information Retrieval Network. Information retrieval is a formal collection of data processing equipment, procedures, software, and people that integrate subsystems into a network in which information is analyzed, classified, distributed, stored, and retrieved in an efficient manner. Figure 9.45 shows an example of a network.

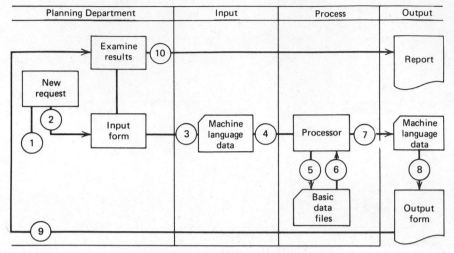

FIGURE 9.42 Example of flowchart.

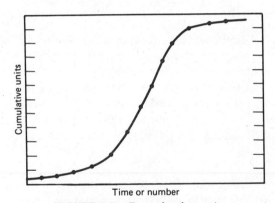

FIGURE 9.43 Example of an ogive.

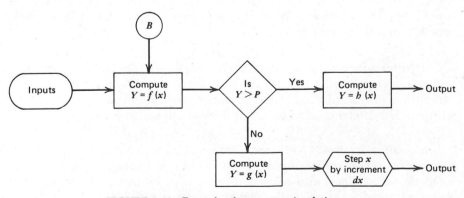

FIGURE 9.44 Example of computer simulation.

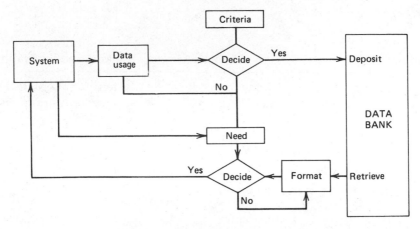

FIGURE 9.45 Example of a network.

Efficiency in a Computer Group

MBO has moved into many departments in organizations. Highly technical groups, such as computer systems personnel and programmers, are vitally interested in becoming more efficient. MBO helps. The following gives examples of how MBO can aid computer groups to be efficient.

Key Responsibility	Key Measure	Accountability	Objective or Performance Standard
User service	Frequency of errors	Data processing manager	Reduce errors 1 percent of documents by end of year
Machine utilization	Amount of lost time	Operations manager	Ensure 95 percent of uptime devoted to productive operations during first quarter
Project testing	Number of reworks	Chief programmer	Ensure no more than 10 percent rework in project testing
Customer file runs	Time of run	Chief programmer	Reduce run time of customer file updating program from 100 minutes to 50 minutes
Work order tickets	Error rate	Operation manager	Achieve a 3 percent reduction in error rejection in next quarter
Program productivity	Processing time	Chief programmer	Achieve file processing time 75 percent of nominal tape speed by August

Staffing

Key Areas of Staffing	Typical Practices	Indicators for Tracking and Evaluating
Job placement	Personnel procedures manual	System for alternatives in selection, hiring, and promotion
Job standards	Personnel procedures manual	Performance expectations known and updated
Job performance	MBO documents	System for evaluating, correcting
Performance improvement	MBO documents	System for stretching annual performance
Skills improvement	MBO document	Formal system of training development and improvement and means of evaluating effectiveness
Employee tenure	Personnel procedures manual	Excessive or insufficient experience
Tolerance for mediocrity and deviant behavior	MBO documents	System for progressive correction and discipline; frequency of discipline
Total employment size	Productivity reports	Too many people in group; too little in group
Employee turnover	MBO documents	Too high; too low
Union contracts	Personnel procedures manual	Contract clauses aiding or inhibiting

Measures of Staffing Efficiency

$$\frac{\text{Staffing costs}}{\text{Employees}} \qquad \frac{\text{Job standards met}}{\text{Total standards}} \qquad \frac{\text{Number of quits}}{\text{Average number of employees}}$$

$$\frac{\text{Productivity clauses}}{\text{Total clauses in union contract}} \qquad \frac{\text{Skills utilized}}{\text{Skills available}} \qquad \frac{\text{Number of recruits on job after three years}}{\text{Number of recruits accepting employment}}$$

$$\frac{\text{Man-days lost in accidents}}{\text{Man-days worked}} \qquad \frac{\text{Man-days lost in absenteeism}}{\text{Man-days worked}} \qquad \frac{\text{Training costs}}{\text{Number of trainees}}$$

Quantitative Techniques for Staffing

Absenteeism. Absenteeism is defined as the absence of employees from work with more than normal frequency. It represents lost time in a company. It is often thought of as part-time termination. Absenteeism has been linked to many causes: (1) dissatisfaction with work; (2) alcoholism; (3) excessive discipline; (4) accidents with work; (5) excessive interference from outside activities; (6) ill-health; and (7) pursuit of personal goals of family and recreation when company policies constrain these pursuits with limited time off. The absentee rate is measured as follows:

$$TAR = \frac{TAD}{TP}$$

where   TAR = total absentee rate
TAD = total absentee drop
TP = total personnel

When causes are known other rates may be set up:

$$SAR = \frac{SD}{TP}$$

where   SAR = sickness absentee rate
SD = sickness drop
TP = total personnel

$$PAR = \frac{PA}{TP}$$

where   PAR = personnel absentee rate
PA = personal days
TP = total personnel

Example:

A company has 3500 employees. A study of absenteeism reveals 600 man-days lost to sickness and 400 man-days lost to personal time off. The total absence rate is thus

$$TAR = \frac{1000}{3500} = 29 \text{ percent}$$

The sickness rate is

$$SAR = \frac{600}{3500} = 17 \text{ percent}$$

The personnel absence rate is

$$PAR = \frac{400}{3500} = 11 \text{ percent}$$

Labor Turnover. Labor turnover in an organization is disruptive to both the job itself and the MBO Plan that involves the plan. Often plan failure can be connected to a high labor turnover rate. Measurement and control of labor turnover are essential.

$$LT = \frac{A + S}{2N} \times 100$$

where   LT = labor turnover, percent
      A = accessions = number of hires and rehires
      S = number of total separations
      N = F + L/2, where F is the number of employees at beginning of period and L is the number of employees at end of period

Example:

In January a company had 1800 employees and in November it had 1650. Fifty quit or retired and 100 were hired.

$$LT = \frac{100 + 50}{2\left(\dfrac{1800 + 1650}{2}\right)} \times 100 = 4 \text{ percent}$$

Intelligence Quotient (IQ). IQ is a measure of mental age, as measured by various intelligence tests, related to chronological age.

$$\text{Intelligence quotient (IQ)} = \frac{\text{mental age (MA)}}{\text{chronological age (CA)}}$$

Educational quotient (EQ), measured by a battery of tests, is related to chronological age.

$$\text{Educational quotient (EQ)} = \frac{\text{educational age (EQ)}}{\text{chronological age (CA)}}$$

Accomplishments in any subject or field can be measured by testing the accomplishment and comparing the result with chronological age.

$$\text{Arithmetic quotients (AQ)} = \frac{\text{arithmetic age (AA)}}{\text{chronological age (CA)}}$$

$$\text{Reading quotients (RQ)} = \frac{\text{reading age (RA)}}{\text{chronological age (CA)}}$$

$$\text{Any subject quotient (SQ)} = \frac{\text{any subject age (SA)}}{\text{chronological age (CA)}}$$

These various quotients suggest that although maturity within each of the areas varies, when related to chronological age a comparative measure profile is established (Figure 9.46).

An accomplishment ratio is obtained by averaging the subject ratios.

Safety Accident Rate.   Frequency and severity rates relate the number of days lost or charged as a result of injuries to the number of hours worked. These calculated rates help eliminate guesswork with regard to managing accident trends and their attendant costs. The rates are calculated as follows:

$$\text{Frequency rate (FR)} = \frac{\text{number of injuries }(I) \times 1 \text{ million}}{\text{number of hours worked }(M)}$$

The number of injuries includes injuries resulting in death, total disability, permanent partial disability, and temporary total disability, all as a result of employment.

$$\text{Severity rate (SR)} = \frac{\text{days charged (DC)} \times 1 \text{ million}}{\text{number of hours worked }(M)}$$

Manpower Forecasting.   Manpower forecasting is the process of looking ahead to the far future for the types of people that will be needed within an organization. The forecast examines types and occupations within product lines, programs, and the overall organization. Figure 9.47 is a manpower forecast form.

Replacement Succession Chart.   An organization's objectives can be attained only through the concerted efforts of all of its people, especially its

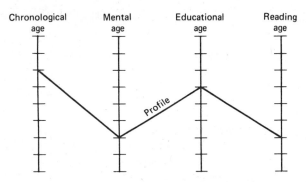

FIGURE 9.46 Comparative measure profile.

Products & Programs:	19__	19__	19__	19__	Current 19__	19__	19__	19__	19__	19__
Product A										
Product B										
Product C										
Product D										
Program A										
Program B										
Project A										
Project B										
Other										
Other										
Totals										
Types & Occupations										
Managers										
Supervisors										
Directors										
Marketing										
Engineers										
Production										
Quality Control										
Accounting										
Administrative										
Other										
Other										
Total No. of Positions										
Retirements										
Unscheduled Terminations										
New Jobs to be filled										
Total positions to be filled										

FIGURE 9.47 Manpower forecast form.

key people. The best MBO plan can experience great difficulty and even default if one or more key individuals leave the organization, get transferred, or retire. Replacement planning is a must—a key person backup system in which every key job in the organization has identified backup to assume the responsibilities in the event of change. The replacement chart aids greatly in setting up replacement succession (Figure 9.48).

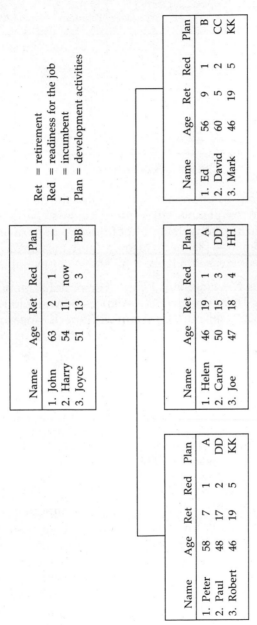

Name	Age	Ret	Red	Plan
1. John	63	2	1	—
2. Harry	54	11	now	—
3. Joyce	51	13	3	BB

Ret = retirement
Red = readiness for the job
I = incumbent
Plan = development activities

Name	Age	Ret	Red	Plan
1. Peter	58	7	1	A
2. Paul	48	17	2	DD
3. Robert	46	19	5	KK

Name	Age	Ret	Red	Plan
1. Helen	46	19	1	A
2. Carol	50	15	3	DD
3. Joe	47	18	4	HH

Name	Age	Ret	Red	Plan
1. Ed	56	9	1	B
2. David	60	5	2	CC
3. Mark	46	19	5	KK

FIGURE 9.48 Replacement succession chart.

Name _____ Position _____ Dept. _____	Schedule				
	January	February	March	April	May

1. Developmental
    Objective _____
        Activities _____					

2. Developmental
    Objective _____
        Activities _____					

FIGURE 9.49   Developmental chart.

Development Chart.   Performance on the job is the most crucial measure of an individual in completing MBO commitments. Next to this is the potential to perform. The conversion of potential to performance is accomplished by development—planned, formed, and measured. This is how performance can be increased. Figure 9.49 shows a development chart.

Human Resources Development Plan.   Personnel seldom meet job requirements exactly. There are always variances between job expectancies and job performance. A plan must be set up with specific measures to ensure personnel development. Figure 9.50 (on page 412) is an example.

Motivating

Key Areas of Motivating	Typical Practices	Indicators for Tracking and Evaluating
Employees not wanting to work	Personnel procedures manual; MBO documents	List indicators: late starts, early quits; slow work pace; low incentives; boring work; unimportant work
Barriers to work effectiveness	Personnel procedures manual; MBO documents	Poor work policies; excessive "waits"; poor work processes and methods
Job matching	Job placement manual	System for matching employee needs and skills with job
Union unrest	Personnel procedures manual; MBO documents	Amount of time spent on grievances, conflicts, and problems

Key Areas of Motivating	Typical Practices	Indicators for Tracking and Evaluating
Leadership	MBO documents	Employees identify and align to objectives of organization
Job recognition	MBO documents	Formal systems for rewarding and recognizing individuality and outstanding performance
Employee treatment	Personnel procedures manual; MBO documents	Indicators of fair and equitable treatment
Compensation	Personnel procedures manual; MBO documents	System for matching responsibility and assuring equities
Wage and salary increases	MBO documents	System for matching increases to contribution
Employee participation	MBO documents	Ways and extent

Measures of Motivational Efficiency

$$\frac{\text{No. of new objectives completed by individual}}{\text{Annual wage increase for individual}} \qquad \frac{\text{No. of grievances this year}}{\text{No. of grievances base year}} \qquad \frac{\text{Performance achievements now}}{\text{Performance achievements last year}}$$

$$\frac{\text{No. of new objectives completed by dept.}}{\text{Annual wage increases by dept.}} \qquad \frac{\text{No. of jobs redesigned}}{\text{Total jobs}} \qquad \frac{\text{Productivity increases}}{\text{Wage and benefit increases}}$$

$$\frac{\text{Recognition practices}}{\text{Total possible list}} \qquad \frac{\text{Employee ideas submitted}}{\text{Total ideas}} \qquad \frac{\text{No. of indicators employee participation}}{\text{No. of depts.}}$$

Quantitative Techniques for Motivating

Adverse Impact.   Adverse impact is a substantially different rate of selection in hiring, promotion, or other employment decision that works to the disadvantage of members of a race, sex, or ethnic group. Adverse impact is determined by the 80 percent rule. A selection rate for any race, ethnic, or sex group that is less than four fifths of the rate for the group with the highest selection rate is generally regarded as evidence of adverse impact.

Development Plan for _____ Present Position _____

Employee Number _____ Location _____

Prepared with (Supervisor) _____ Date _____

What development objectives are you going to achieve to improve your effectiveness in your present position?

No. 1   What? _____
         How? _____
         _____
         By When? _____

No. 2   What? _____
         How? _____
         _____
         By When? _____

No. 3   What? _____
         How? _____
         _____
         By When? _____

What is your next position objective? _____

Why is this a viable choice? _____

What development objectives are you going to achieve to prepare yourself to be considered for this position? _____

No. 1   What? _____
         How? _____
         _____
         By When? _____

No. 2   What? _____
         How? _____
         _____
         By When? _____

No. 3   What? _____
         How? _____
         _____
         By When? _____

Remarks:

Approved: Signed _____ Employee's Signature _____

         Title _____

Distribution: _____

FIGURE 9.50   Example of human resources development plan.

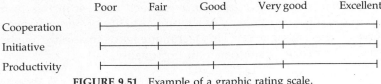

FIGURE 9.51   Example of a graphic rating scale.

As an example, if 70 percent hired applicants for a particular job are men and 60 percent are women, there would be no adverse impact:

$$\frac{60}{70} = 86 \therefore > 80\%$$

On the other hand, if 60 percent of white applicants and 40 percent of black applicants are selected, there would be an adverse impact:

$$\frac{40}{60} = 67 \therefore < 80\%$$

Appraisal Techniques.   Appraisal processes are attempts to assure full utilization of human resources. Appraisal is a deliberate evaluation of an employee's performance geared toward strengthening the total organization. Formal appraisal methods seem to be in a continual state of development. This may be the reason why so many methods are available. The following are descriptive of some of these techniques. In actual practice, features of several of them are combined eclectically to meet the evaluative needs of the organization. Chapter 16 discusses these and other systems in detail.

1.   *Trait Appraisal (Graphic Rating Scale).*   This is the most widely used technique because it is easy, simple, and uncomplicated and concentrates on qualities known to be important in getting results (see Figure 9.51).

2.   *Critical Incident Appraisals.*   This is not often used except in scientific and complex work in which outcomes are not easily seen but incidents are important. The procedure requires listing job elements and recording positive and negative incidents that have been noted in these elements.

Example:

Job Elements	Code	What Happened? (Incidents)	Date
Preparing reports	Medium	10 reports submitted	19xx-19xx
Interpreting research	High	Findings developing new practice	April 19xx
Presenting papers	Low	None presented	19xx-19xx

3. *Standards of Performance.* There is much interest in this technique because it specifies the intensity of action or quality of performance that is acceptable in the organization. This technique tends to apply directly to job performance expectations rather than personality.

Example:

Duties	Rank	Standards of Performance	Evaluation
Work within schedule	1	Overtime less than 4 percent of work week	Actual is 5 percent
Arranges work safety	2	Lost time less than 4.0 per million worker hours	Actual is 3.75

4. *Process Appraisal.* This type of appraisal is just getting started because of "due process" requirements of civil and individual rights. It requires process behavior standards and a way to measure actual behavior with these standards.

Example:

Behavior	Standards	Evaluation
Absenteeism	3 per quarter	5 per quarter
10-minute break violations	3 per year	1 per year
Horseplay	None allowed	None noticed

5. *Forced-Choice Appraisals.* In this type of appraisal, instead of indicating how much or how little of a trait, characteristic, or standard the person possesses, the rater selects from a series of choices the one most applicable to the person.

Example:

Choices	Most	Least
Carries out orders by doing the work	_____	_____
Carries out orders by passing the buck	_____	_____
Temperamental and emotional	_____	_____
Calm, cool, and collected	_____	_____

6. *Appraisal by Results (MBO).* This appraisal process focuses on results or outputs of an employee's effort in an organization. The method requires that supervisor and subordinate agree during a planning period on the results to be achieved during the period.

Example:

Planned Results	Planned Activities	Schedule	Evaluation of Results
Achieve 15 percent volume increase	Add one salesperson Redesign package Expand territory to six	3¼ percent increase each quarter	Reached 17 percent overall increase

7. *Productivity Appraisals (MPBO).* This appraisal process focuses on the productivity of an employee's effort in an organization. The method is similar to appraisal by results but expands the performance measure to productivity measures.

Example:

Planned Productivity	Planned Activities	Schedule	Evaluation of Results
Achieve 15 million sales with no more than 5 percent cost in sales	Add salesperson Expand territory to six Hold expenses to 5 percent	3.75 million increase in each quarter	Reached 14 million with 2 percent cost in sales

Each of the appraisal methods has its own combination of strengths and weaknesses. Yet the purpose of the appraisal, in large part, will shape the appraisal technique, the criteria to be used, and the type of corrective feedback to be employed. In other words, the effectiveness of an appraisal depends on how it is used relative to the purpose it is expected to accomplish.

Attitude Surveys.   An attitude survey is a way of measuring employee views, reactions, feelings, and morale about jobs, work, policies, or the company. The survey allows a participant to share opinions and judgments. These can then be collected and summarized to see if a consensus can be reached. Three general methods are used for attitude surveys: (1) interviewing supervisors of employees; (2) interviewing employees directly; and (3) administering a series of written questions directly to those whose attitudes are sought. The written questionnaire survey is the most popular, as it is easiest to administer and allows the employee to think carefully about the questions. Figure 9.52 shows typical questions that might be found in an attitude survey.

Behavior Modification.   Behavior modification is a process for changing performance-related behavior of personnel in organizations. Its basic principle is that individuals tend to repeat behavior that has favorable conse-

	Definitely Agree	Inclined to Agree	Inclined to Disagree	Definitely Disagree

1. The company is a good place to work.

2. My job enables me to learn new things.

3. My pay and benefits are satisfactory.

4. My supervisor listens to my suggestions.

5. I like to work overtime.

FIGURE 9.52 Sample items in an attitude survey.

quences and to avoid repeating behavior that has unfavorable consequences. To modify behavior, the resulting environment or consequences must be manipulated or controlled. The control or manipulation is done by recognizing or rewarding desirable behavior and punishing or ignoring undesirable behavior. Several steps are followed in behavior modification.

STEP 1.   Identify critical behavior.   Behavior that makes a significant impact on performance, productivity, or organizational goals is identified as either positive or negative. Examples of negative behavior are absenteeism, tardiness, absence from work station, complaining. Examples of positive behavior are meeting work standards, returning from breaks on time, good safety record.

STEP 2.   Measure behavior.   The frequency or number of times that the identified behavior, positive or negative, occurs in the present situation can be measured. A baseline frequency is established to provide the standard below which behavior frequency is acceptable, and above which it is unacceptable. Tally sheets, performance deficiencies, comparisons over time, appraisal forms, number of grievances, charting, and observing are methods of measuring behavior.

STEP 3. Analyze the function of the behavior.   This is accomplished by determining the causes of the behavior and its consequences.

Cause → Behavior → Consequence

This analysis helps identify the type of intervention that can be developed.

STEP 4. Develop an intervention strategy.   This step strengthens and accelerates desirable critical behavior and weakens or decelerates undesirable critical behavior. Several strategies are used:

(a) Positive reinforcement strategy uses rewards that will strengthen the critical behavior. Some reinforcements are money, friendly greetings, personal time off with pay, recognition in newspaper, acknowledgment of achievement, and office with window.

(b) Negative reinforcement strategy uses punishment to weaken the critical behavior. Some reinforcements are cancellation of coffee breaks, quick feedback of complaints, reduction of money benefits, and removal of company car.

STEP 5. Evaluate to assure improved performance.   This is a systematic evaluation to assure that the critical desired behavior reaches the level of frequency need in performance.

Life's Goals.   If there is one single factor that affects a person's motivation, it is personal goals. To find out employees' life goals and to adapt work conditions to help employees reach them is to set up motivators. Figure 9.53 is an example format for a life goals inquiry.

Position Grid.   A position grid is a matrix that allows two or more variables to be plotted in a rectangular display. The degrees of the variables are seen by the positions on the grid. Leadership style can be measured by the degrees of the variables an individual may have (Figure 9.54).

Goal-Seeking Charts.   Goal-seeking charts graphically display three basic features: goal to be reached, planned performance to reach the goal, and actual performance delivered (Figure 9.55). The actual performance curve is the goal-seeking curve. The difference between planned performance and actual performance is the variance.

Attitude Change.   Attitudes are determiners of behavior. They influence behavior, often in undesirable ways. Many MBO plans have been of little use or have failed because of improper or faulty attitudes of management. The MBO practitioner must deal in a formal and significant way with managerial attitudes that need changing, the causes of the attitudes and ways to bring about change. Figure 9.56 suggests how this can be done.

LIFE'S GOALS INQUIRY

Ten attainments I must reach before I die. Be as free as possible in selecting and listing these goals.

Examples: I want a college degree; I want to live what I believe; I want to be a supervisor; I want to fly an airplane; etc.

1. _____ 1. _____

   _____   _____

2. _____ 2. _____

   _____   _____

3. _____ 3. _____

   _____   _____

4. _____ 4. _____

   _____   _____

5. _____ 5. _____

   _____   _____

6. _____ 6. _____

   _____   _____

7. _____ 7. _____

   _____   _____

8. _____ 8. _____

   _____   _____

9. _____ 9. _____

   _____   _____

10. _____ 10. _____

    _____   _____

Priority: Using the 3-point scale assign a value to each of the ten desired attainments.

        1 — of little importance to me

        2 — of moderate importance to me

        3 — of great importance to me

FIGURE 9.53 Example of life goals inquiry.

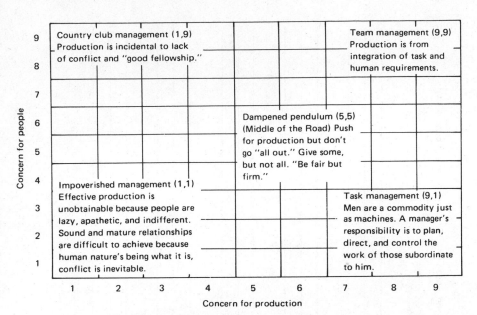

FIGURE 9.54 Example of position grid.

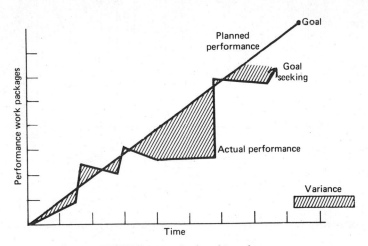

FIGURE 9.55 Goal-seeking chart.

List strong attitudes that need to be changed.

Identify possible source and reason for the attitude.

Suggest ways of controlling or changing the attitude.

Top Management:

Supervision:

Employees:

Union:

Customers:

FIGURE 9.56 Form for addressing attitude change.

420

SUMMARY

This chapter deals with concepts, techniques, and quantitative ways of measuring how well a desired effect is being produced. From an efficiency point of view, MBO is measurement by objectives. This means reaching goals and objectives with the least expenditure possible. The key to evaluating how much or how little lies in the quantitative measures used. "How much is the results" is just as important as "what is the result." Accordingly, measures and quantitative techniques are suggested for all the functions of the organization: planning and profitability; organization; marketing; budgeting and control; quality; production; data processing; staffing; and motivating. The quantitative approaches covered in this chapter should provide a respectable repertoire for moving the MBO process to a high degree of efficiency.

BIBLIOGRAPHY

Follett, Robert, *How to Keep Score in Business*. Chicago: Follett, 1978.

Juran, J. M., *Managerial Breakthrough*. New York: McGraw-Hill, 1964.

Riggs, James L., *Production Systems*. New York: Wiley, 1970.

Sloma, Richard S., *How to Measure Managerial Performance*. New York: Macmillan, 1980.

Westwick, C. A., *How to Use Management Ratios*. New York: Wiley, 1973.

MANAGING
MOTIVATION
WITH MBO

IN THIS CHAPTER

If two people perform the same type of job, one will do it better and faster than the other. This is also true of two groups of people doing the same type of job. Furthermore, if performance of the two people or two groups could be measured, it would probably be found that the better person or group contributes three, five, or perhaps ten times what the poorer contributes. Why? One reason is differences in abilities and skills. Another is differences in experiences and training. Still another is differences in motivation and attitudes. The real reason is probably a combination of all of these factors.

The search is intense for a mystical formula combining these factors that could be followed, cookbook style, to get every employee to work at the highest possible productivity level. With a wave of a wand, masses of employees would act energetically, quickly, and efficiently.

No such formula has yet been found. At best we have discovered factors of the individual, the environment, skills, attitudes, experiences, and the work that both positively and negatively affect the energy to do work. We have gained insight into how these factors can be used to motivate, although human nature is too complex for anyone to be able to turn motivation on and off at will.

Managers cannot wait for a crystal-clear set of attitudes, processes, and practices to guide them to excellence in motivating employees. Getting employees to face and meet the productivity challenge is an immediate need. A primary reason workers do not step up their output or the pace of their work, whether or not they are union members, is the fear that they will work themselves out of a job. This may be unions' single most skeptical attitude toward cooperative efforts for productivity. History verifies the justness of this feeling of insecurity, a feeling that is further nurtured by fluctuating economic cycles.

The purposes of this chapter are (1) to describe why motivating employees is different from and more difficult than in the past, (2) to identify and describe trends that have an impact on management of motivation, (3) to describe three approaches to motivation—economic, behavioral, and managerial—that have developed over the years, and (4) to describe the expectancy alignment process, a practical system managers may use to motivate employees toward greater productivity. Several questions about motivation are answered in this chapter: Does money motivate? Are certain motivators effective for certain groups such as minorities, older employees, women, the affluent, and managers? Is the work ethic dead? The theory of expectancy alignment introduced in this chapter is the foundation for the building of ideas for motivating employees and for developing motivators that are unique and specific to an organization and to employees. The practice of this theory is termed "needs coincidence."

WHY MOTIVATING IS DIFFICULT

Motivating employees is difficult today because motives have become more diffused and complex than they used to be. Motives are defined as needs, wants, drives, or impulses within the individual. Motives are the reasons for behavior. They direct people toward goals. MBO, when handled as a goal participative process, can heighten the motivation of employees. With MBO, employees work to meet the organization's goals but satisfy their own goals in the process.

Motives may be conscious or subconscious. They affect not only the "ability to do" but also the "will to do." The behavior of a person depends on the strength and intensity of his or her motives. Most conceptions of the process of motivation begin with the assumption that behavior or performance is, at least in part, directed toward the attainment of goals or toward the satisfaction of needs. These needs arouse and maintain human energy and activity in certain directions. Motivation, then, is motive strength, the intensity of the "will to do" to meet or satisfy a need. The sequence for developing the "will to do" is (1) a want emerges, (2) the want becomes a need, (3) the need becomes a motive, (4) the motive becomes a purpose or goal, and (5) the purpose or goal becomes the "will to do."

The motives and purposes of workers have changed because workers' needs have changed. Current needs are individualistic, and some are insatiable. They have changed the reasons a worker will work, and how much he or she will respond to the pressures and demands of the organization. Today's worker is better educated, better informed, more independent, more aware, more secure, and more affluent than the worker of the past. Factors operating within organizations are creating this new type of worker. Six factors that greatly affect motive strength—the motivational process— are examined here briefly to give further insight on why present-day motivating is difficult.

Changing View of Authority

The traditional view of authority is breaking down. Employees are less responsive to authority than in the past. Years ago when a supervisor commanded a subordinate to move, the subordinate would merely ask, "When?" Today, when supervisors command subordinates to move, they ask, "Why?" If the answer to the question is unsatisfactory, the subordinate may not move. Supervisors and managers who expect employees to do as they are told, asking a minimum of questions and giving no argument, are experiencing frustrations and reduced performance. Such managers assume that employees are passive and receptive to commands for accomplishing work. The command range of a supervisor and the order acceptance zone of an employee are not coincident (Figure 10.1). The supervisor perceives a large range of orders that an employee should and must accept. The employee perceives a smaller range of acceptable orders. This difference in perception is the cause of the breakdown of the traditional view of authority. Many supervisors look toward motivation to help expand the zone of order acceptance of subordinates, and are disappointed. They discover that employees wish to participate in making decisions that affect the activities within their job. The traditional perception of authority is being replaced by a new perception—authority that relies heavily on how work is assigned and delegated to subordinates. A supervisor may see this as an obstacle to getting employees to work.

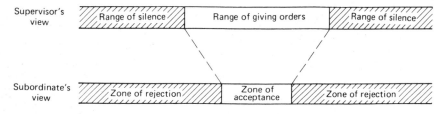

FIGURE 10.1   Authority as perceived by supervisor and subordinates.

Increasing Expectations of Workers

Literacy for all is now moving toward higher education for all. More people are receiving college degrees than ever before. Thirty years ago, approximately 20 percent of high school graduates went to college; today, approximately 70 percent of high school graduates *attend* college. In fact, in some community colleges a high school diploma is not necessary to study for an advanced degree. To be an adult is enough. As a result, the average worker in our society is moving up in the skills spectrum (Figure 10.2).

This move upward has resulted in new levels of awareness that have an impact on employee expectations. Awareness generates new inquiries, into the nature of the organization, the role of employees in it, and how much satisfaction can be derived from day-to-day work, and new expectations. Individuals want more from their job. They want more from their supervisor. They want more from the organization. Their expectations are rising too fast to be met by the organizational system.

The move up the skills spectrum has affected attitudes. For example, a recent survey found a change in the attitude, "Hard work always pays off." In 1968, 69 percent of workers held this attitude. In 1971, 39 percent had it.

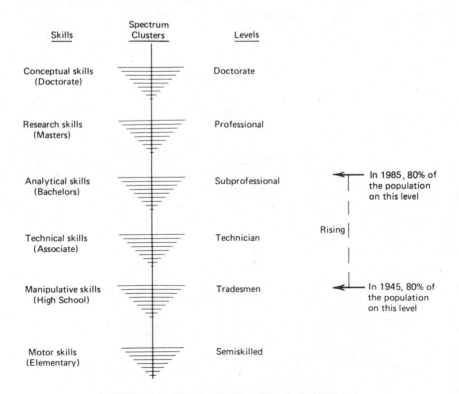

FIGURE 10.2 Rising educational level of employees.

Workers now expect greater quality in their work life. Traditional attitudes are being challenged and often discarded.

Legalized Participative Management

Unions and federal, state, and local governments have intruded into organizations, making demands related to conditions of employment, freedom of association, government codes, unfair practices, benefits of employment, mediation, security, safety, employee activities, picketing, injunctions, health, welfare, and education. Legislative enactments have clarified the rights of workers and introduced new "rights" that were formally prerogatives of management. They have introduced a "system of equal prizes" that does not reward those who build better products or provide better services. Although the ingenious, the inventive, the hard worker should be favored, individual differences are ignored. Legislative enactments have shifted decision making away from management toward collective bargaining. As these enactments increase, more management prerogatives shift into the collective bargaining arena. Union and government intrusions are viewed as "legalized" participative management. Figure 10.3 shows enact-

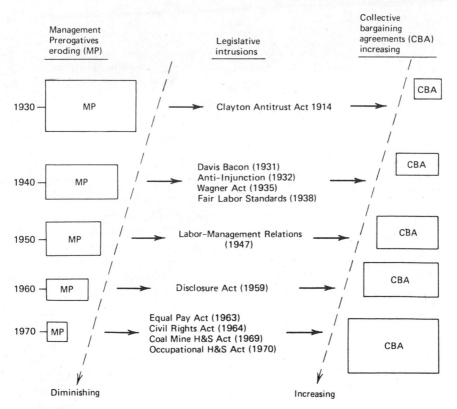

FIGURE 10.3 Laws that have shifted management prerogatives into bargaining agreements.

ments that have forced managerial prerogatives into collective bargaining agreements during the period 1930 to 1970.

In the past, the collective bargaining process, legalized and encouraged by the government, had a positive effect on organizations. Now, however, government intrusions into managerial decision-making processes have reached a point of diminishing returns. Many government decrees are hurting, not helping, organizational productivity. Government has grown bigger and potentially more dangerous as a result of the legislative process. In many instances, government's impact on organizations is oppressive. A review and analysis of bargaining contracts would show that: (1) most contracts emphasize compensation based on time and not productivity; (2) pay scales are based on "putting in" time rather than on productivity; (3) most contracts tend to be the same, ignoring the uniqueness of organizations; and (4) vacation time and grievance handling are detailed but little attention is given to a fair day's work for a fair day's pay. Few firms have been able to get productivity clauses into collective bargaining agreements. In a national survey conducted by the Prentice-Hall Research Staff, to which 600 firms responded, only 10 percent reported such clauses in bargaining agreements. The following are some of these clauses. These clauses are actual extracts without editing.

Subject	Clause
Reasonable productivity	An employee shall perform all assigned work at a reasonable productivity rate which is in accordance with sound time study practices.
Maintenance of high level of productivity	The union recognized that large-scale employment at a fair wage can continue only as long as a high level of productivity is maintained. The parties agree that this result is dependent upon achieving a high quality of individual employee performance and efficiency and the union undertakes to encourage its members in the attainment of this objective. This can be done by reducing scrap and spoilage, good care of tools and equipment, a minimum amount of time wasted, and careful and economical use of supplies, including water, steam, and electricity. Efficiency of production requires cooperative effort toward finding easier, better, and faster ways of performing operations and the ready acceptance of higher production bases due to improvement in operations or methods.

Subject	Clause
Required productivity	The purpose and intent of the parties to this agreement is that the employee will provide a fair day's work for a fair day's pay and that the required productivity and effort of an employee must be consistent with his safety and proper working conditions.
Control over productivity	It is the Company's policy to pay incentive (bonus) wages to hourly paid employees assigned to jobs in which there is opportunity through increased effort and/or attention to turn out additional good production. Jobs must be such that the employee has control over productivity so that he can increase and sustain production over what is normally expected. This increase in productivity must be such that it can be readily measured.
	Individuals should be able to relate increases or decreases in effort and/or attention with proportionate increases or decreases in bonus compensation.
	Accepted industrial engineering practices will be used for measuring the employee's productivity and/or contribution to profit in determining bonus payments. If productivity is limited, the crew size may be adjusted commensurate with work requirements so as to provide bonus opportunity wherever possible.
Productivity of a normal employee	The test which shall be used as a basis for disciplining or discharging an employee for productivity not up to standard shall be the productivity of a normal employee reasonably exercising his working capacity.
Increasing productivity	The Company may, in its discretion, establish production standards and apply wage incentives to jobs where, in the opinion of the Company, sound and proper incentives can be applied with the objective of increasing productivity.
Fair day's work for fair day's pay	The Company and the Union recognize the principle of a fair day's work for a fair day's pay. Each and every employee is expected to meet certain requirements of performance,

Subject	Clause

including quality and quantity of production as determined on the basis of time standards based on the principles mentioned above. Employees who repeatedly fail to meet normally expected production requirements shall be advised of such failure by their supervisors. If the employee still fails to meet such requirements, he will be subject to disciplinary action, including discharge.

Reasonable day's work for reasonable day's wages

The Union hereby recognizes that it is the duty of every employee covered by this agreement to carry out and abide by the provisions thereof, and to promote at all times the efficient progress of the Company's plant, especially in such matters as safety, economy, quality, and quantity of the output of the plant. The Union further agrees that it is the duty of each employee to give a reasonable day's work for a reasonable day's wages. The company agrees that it will not require any employee to give more than a reasonable day's work for a reasonable day's wages.

The parties recognize and acknowledge that increased wages and other benefits guaranteed to the employees by this Agreement will depend to a great extent upon increased productivity resulting from increased employee efficiency; technological progress; better tools; improved methods, processes, and equipment; and a cooperative attitude on the part of the Company and the union. The parties agree to encourage such progress to the end that costs may be reduced and a higher level of productivity maintained so that the competition may be aggressively met and beaten.

Production at no less than standard levels

It is expected that each employee will attain and produce at no less than the standard production levels. If, in the opinion of the company, an employee fails to attain and produce at said standard production levels for reasons other than conditions beyond his control, disciplinary action may be taken by the company.

Subject	Clause
High degree of efficiency in workmanship	The Union agrees to cooperate with the company in all matters pertaining to improving and expanding the company's business and shall assist in every way possible to promote the sale of company products and shall do everything within reason to promote a high degree of efficiency in the workmanship of its members.

Such clauses are contractual commitments by both management and labor. The few firms that have them in their collective bargaining agreements are to be commended, but problems of interpretation may arise as to the intended level of productivity. Additional problems emerge with the lack of measures for evaluating the level and progress of productivity.

Stronger Unions

Collective bargaining in the United States is working, and working well! Union membership exceeds 21 million—an all-time high. "Strike power" has made unions formidable, and contract gains for workers have also hit an all-time high. This growth in strength and effectiveness will continue, because union strategies for organizing new workers are aggressive and negotiating strategies at the bargaining table are at equal power and in many cases above negotiating power with those of management. The following is a sample list of union strategies:

1. Unions have increased their communications about management misuses, abuses, and mistakes.

2. Unions urge employees to submit grievances whenever there is any evidence of contract violations. In some cases they provide financial incentives.

3. Unions train their stewards for effective contract administration. They insist that union leadership know the contract better than supervisors.

4. Unions urge members to communicate all matters, contract and noncontract, through union channels. Unions want to transfer management prerogatives (silent issues) to the negotiating table.

5. Unions urge their leadership to practice the "open door" policy. In this manner, the focal point of leadership moved from supervision to the union ranks.

6. Unions are quick to identify rising, strong leaders. Opportunities are given to potential leaders to rise in the union ranks.

7. Unions are quick to take credit for benefits given to employees. All benefits are derived from the organization, its operations and performance, but unions are quick to exploit their efforts on behalf of employees.

8.   Unions use collective bargaining as a "power tool." Strength and power are deliberately displayed to management by stubbornness, walk-outs, crisis bargaining, job acting, and strikes. Unions want to bargain from strength.

9.   Unions take the initiative to win employee allegiance. Unions seek benefits for employees as a matter of purpose and aim. Management gives benefits to employees as a matter of concession and compromise.

10.   Unions exploit the elusive role of the first-line supervisor. Unions bypass first-line supervisors in the decision process, creating a "weak" first-line level of management.

Labor unions are continually amassing power. In some organizations, management no longer controls the situation. In others, the effect is on motivation. The breakdown of traditional authority means that managers cannot threaten employees into performance. This makes motivation different and more difficult.

Since the number of blue-collar workers is declining and that of white-collar workers is increasing, the future is bright for white-collar unions. White-collar workers are even better educated, more aware, more sensitive to rights, more affluent, and more articulate than blue-collar workers. These qualities will make white-collar unions even stronger in both numbers and strategies for reaching the goals needed and wanted.

VALUES AND ATTITUDES: WHY WORKERS' GOALS CONFLICT WITH EMPLOYERS' OBJECTIVES

Human cooperation has often been portrayed as a peaceful and tranquil scene. More often, organizational life is a "web of tensions" rather than a "network of togetherness." Some give and others take; a few get their way and most compromise their way. A moderate level of conflict may have many constructive effects. In fact, a degree of tension and conflict provides differing viewpoints and alternatives most useful in the decision-making process. When the level of conflict is high and disagreement is frequent, however, the consequences are harmful and disruptive.

Competition for rewards or benefits is one cause of conflict. Division of the pie inevitably leaves some with nothing or with a smaller share. It means satisfaction for one and dissatisfaction for another.

The increasing tempo of participative management is a second cause of conflict. If six people were asked to set their goals independently, they would have no conflict. However, if the six were asked to collaborate for consensus of goals, conflicts would arise.

A third cause of conflict, which is not easily seen as highly deterministic, is attitudes and values. An attitude is a frame of mind created by a combination of one or more beliefs and convictions predisposing to behavior in a certain way. As such, it is a strong "natural" determiner of behavior. It influences an employee to act and react in a preferential manner.

Such expressions as "John has a good attitude even though he has many problems," or "Helen sticks to the job, I like her attitude," are often heard. Managers use the word "attitude" to describe the way a person looks and feels about a situation or job. They use it to describe the frame of mind a person has when faced with a problem. Attitude seems to be a mental perception acquired in the past and now influencing how the present is seen and dealt with. It is an important regulator of behavior, and therefore managers must supervise a person's attitude along with his or her skills. Learning more about attitudes, their characteristics, their formation, and ways of dealing with them becomes an important responsibility for the manager.

Values, on the other hand, are end behaviors to be reached. They act as standards or criteria that guide behavior. When individuals act in exact fulfillment with their values, then their attitudes are their values. However, most people do not act thus, and their attitudes are not coincidence with their values. This is by definition hypocrisy—believing one way and acting in another. For example, most people accept the value that selfishness is wrong and sharing is right. Yet the competitive free enterprise system fosters the behavior of getting as much as possible within legal limits. Unselfish sharing is the value but pursuit of the greatest return for the self and the organization is the attitude. It is under these circumstances that values and attitudes differ. Thus attitudes and values considerably affect whether employees work hard or not. Changing employees' attitudes or values brought about by manager/employee can greatly affect their behavior with regard to productivity. This change is complex and difficult. The most effective method of change is self-behavior modification with self-awareness. Table 10.1 shows the "seeing window" regarding behavior.

Raising questions about one's own behavior is the way to get rid of blind spots and "skeleton" behaviors (this name comes from the expression, "skeletons in the closet"). For example, asking others, "What do you think

TABLE 10.1   Seen and Unseen Self-Behaviors

	How I See Myself ↓	What I Do Not See of Myself ↓
How others see me →	Behaviors visible to all	Blind spots
What others do not see → of me	"Skeleton" behaviors	Behaviors hidden to all

of my proposal?," is a way to find out what others see and thus eliminate blind spots. Another approach is to offer explanations why one behaved in a certain manner in a certain situation and thus get rid of skeleton behavior.

Sample Values

The following are examples of general and specific values that can greatly influence attitudes and behavior:

Classic Values (Accepted by Most)

Life has purpose. Man can reason. A human is more important than the state. Do to others what you wish them to do to you. Man does not live by bread alone. A world at peace is a world free of war and conflict. Nature is beautiful. Children should be raised within a family. Free choice is everyone's endowment. Happiness is everyone's right.

Modern Values (Accepted by Most)

A company is in business to make a profit. All people should be given equal employment opportunities. The government protects person and property. Rewards should go to those who merit them. All people should have the opportunity to reach their highest possible educational level. An active life leads to much satisfaction. Success is what one accomplishes. Wisdom comes from maturity. Productivity goes to those who pursue it intensely. Quality of work life brings satisfaction to employees.

Obsolete Values (Rejected by Most)

The earth is flat. The white race is superior to the black race. When the poor work hard, they will not be poor. Money is the root of all evil. Slavery is an efficient way to get work done. It's who you know and not what you know that counts. Needs of employees are food, shelter, and security. Working hard is the way to earn eternal life.

Recent Values (Controversial)

Corporations should assume social responsibilities. Freedom without limits brings anarchy. Competition results in gain for the consumer. Hard work produces great rewards. Conflicts can be resolved at the conference table. A prosperous life will lead to a comfortable life. Everyone must have an education. Mathematical training develops a logical mind. A job should not be denied on the basis of religion, nationality, race, sex, or age. Corporations that are left alone in markets do better than corporations regulated and aided by government.

New Values (Being Tested)

The world should have one government. There should be one language throughout the world. Populations should be controlled by government. Every employee should be a manager. People should be paid for what they do and not for the time they put in. Everything is beautiful in its own way. Leaders can be developed. Corporations doing business in world markets will prosper. Governments should help corporations avoid bankruptcy if they employ many people. Corporate cultures and subcultures are value centers and greatly affect what the corporation can become.

Why Attitudes Are Important

Very little is known about attitudes, since they are entrenched within the complexity of what we call the human being. We know generally that they deal with experiences, emotions, and values. As we continue to study them we have found out the following:

1. Attitudes travel from one person to another.
2. Attitudes can be learned through rational and logical experiences.
3. People are usually unaware of the origins of their attitudes.
4. Attitudes are difficult to change, since they are entrenched in a person's experience and value system.
5. Attitudes can be changed if the reasons for their development are uncovered and steps taken to deal with them.
6. Attitudes can be changed over time.
7. Attitudes are psychological, that is, they deal with emotions rather than intellect.
8. Attitudes are a form of language that shows and communicates.
9. Attitudes vary even within a person, which can create conflict.
10. Attitudes form barriers in effective use of motivators.
11. Attitudes are significant influences on judgment and behavior.
12. Attitudes can be generally grouped as positive or negative with reference to any situation.

Attitudes, like emotions, can be treacherous masters or useful and reliable servants. The manager should be aware of the importance of attitudes on performance and productivity. If an individual's attitudes are positive to the conditions of the situation, supervision is easier and more effective. Managers should understand the following:

1. Attitudes give an idea of how much supervisory control is needed.

    "The company doesn't care if the parts are wasted." This attitude on the part of an employee alerts the supervisor to the fact that close supervision

will be needed in setting up the employee's work, over, initial performance, and over progress.

2.   Attitudes provide insight into the kind of motivators to be used.

"The pay is lousy here." If the basic physical needs of employees are not met, use of nonfinancial motivators for increased productivity is difficult. Often a motivator does not work because attitudes are barriers.

3.   Attitudes reveal how easily influenced an individual can be in a given situation.

"The unions run this place." A supervisor with this attitude will tend to give up when a union-connected problem emerges. The attitude gives a feeling of defeat before the battle even starts.

4.   Attitudes forecast judgments that may be rendered in given situations.

"I'd rather go skiing than work overtime." The forecast is never precise or completely reliable, but it does give a clue to how a person may behave when given an alternative. From this standpoint, attitudes reveal a posture that is predictive of behavior.

Sample Attitudes Held by People in Organizations

The following is a list of attitudes that influence behavior and performance on the job. These attitudes are both positive and negative.

- I'd rather go skiing than work overtime.
- A woman's place is in the home taking care of children.
- That's all right, I've taken worse.
- It will never work; I've tried it.
- I deserve a raise just to keep even with the cost of living.
- The boss has it in for me.
- We can't do it! It's not in the budget.
- Don't ask me, I just work here.
- Solving problems is part of my job.
- I don't like to waste time.
- This is a lousy place to work.
- Safety rules are for your own good.
- The union runs this place.
- The pay is not too bad and the work is interesting.
- Women complain more than men.

As our society becomes more oriented toward goal setting and value fulfillment as a basis of motivation, conflicts with existing or new goals will increase. The need to align goals with rewards becomes apparent. Harmony of goal expectancies between employees and managers can be greatly influenced by attitudes and values, but can be developed, changed, or controlled through expectancy alignment and needs coincidence. This is discussed further in this chapter in the section on how to motivate for greater productivity.

Worker Affluence Shifting Priorities and Attitudes

Economic achievement in the United States ranges from bare subsistence to incredible riches. Economic levels are not easy to identify; they are on a continuum. Compared with workers in other countries, the U.S. worker is wealthy indeed. American workers have the highest per-capita income and the highest bare subsistence level in the world. Abundance continues to grow in spite of occasional fluctuations due to economic stall or recessions. As workers and families achieve higher incomes and standards of living, they assume life-styles with attitudes and priorities that are characteristic of affluence. This greatly affects views of work and of the remuneration for it.

One view of the continuum from the poor to the superrich is shown in Figure 10.4, where three groups are identified: underaffluent, affluent, and superaffluent. The largest group is the affluent—households with family income in excess of $15,000/year. In 1955, 6 percent of families in the United States were affluent. In 1970, 23 percent were affluent. In 1975, the number reached 34 percent. In 1980, it reached 44 percent. In the affluent group, a larger amount of income is available for optional spending. The definition of affluence is related to the share of income that is available for discretionary spending. The superaffluent group is high in discretionary income and spending. The ratio changes as a family moves up the affluence continuum. This ratio of prescriptive spending to discretionary spending is shown diagrammatically in Figure 10.4.

The problem of motivating the affluent class is difficult and complex. The degree of dissatisfying work people will accept and the degree of satisfying work they already have changes as the ratio of prescriptive and discretionary income changes. Further, what is "satisfying" and "dissatisfying" work varies with each individual. Affluent workers want both pay and satisfying work, regardless of where they are on the affluence scale, but they want these to differing degrees as they change their position on the scale. Affluent "arrivals" want rewards and satisfaction for the most part in the work itself. The upwardly affluent want rewards and satisfaction in both pay and work. The underaffluent want rewards and satisfaction primarily in the one thing they lack most—money. Those engaged in work that can never be satisfying seek more time off with pay or more leisure time. Since satisfaction cannot be found in the work, it is sought in off-job activities that may be started during leisure time or paid time off. For this reason, a shorter work week, early retirement, and more paid holidays are goals that unions actively seek.

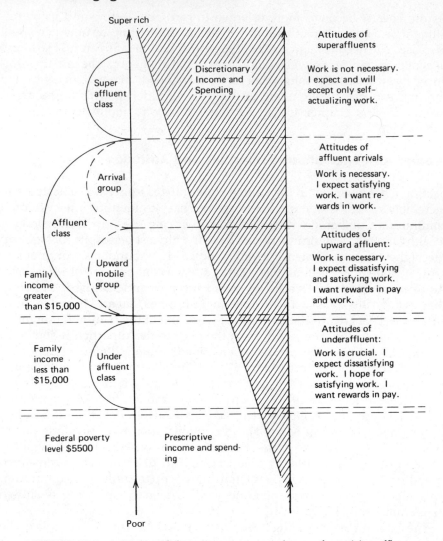

FIGURE 10.4 Attitude and discretionary income changes from rising affluence.

THREE APPROACHES TO MOTIVATION

There are three general approaches to motivating workers toward greater productivity: the economic incentives approach, the behavioral approach, and the management approach. Before each approach is described, a distinction among the three should be made.

1. *Economic Incentive Approach.*
    (a) How to use rewards and work conditions to get good performance on the job.

    (b)   How to use incentives to get people to meet job expectancies.

    (c)   How to urge and persuade people to behave in certain ways.

    (d)   How to help people get what they want by showing them how to get what the organization wants.

2. *Behavioral Approach.*

    (a)   How to meet the needs of people on the job.

    (b)   How individual motives form the basis of the will to work.

    (c)   How organizational behavior can be modified by getting individuals to modify their own behavior.

    (d)   How to improve the quality of organizational life by changing conditions of the job.

3. *Management.*

    (a)   How to meet the needs of both people and the organization.

    (b)   How to set incentives so that people and the organization profit.

    (c)   How to "fit" people and organizational goals into the situation at hand.

    (d)   How to select, from the range of possibilities, the necessary approach that will work for workers and the organization.

The management approach is termed the "eclectic approach." It selects from the economic incentive approach and the behavioral approach the motivational process that best fits the situation at hand. The weaknesses and limitations of the first two approaches are not evaluated here. Only the contribution of each approach is looked at, to give the reader an overview of the variety of motivational methods available as a basis for recommending the method to be used for greater productivity.

Economic Incentive Approaches

The incentive approach to motivating employees is based on the view that workers are eager to maximize their monetary status, power, and prestige. Managers who follow this approach usually "dangle the carrot" to get workers to produce.

Financial Incentives Approach (Adam Smith)

Adam Smith's book *The Wealth of Nations*, published in 1776, had a tremendous influence on economic and political theory. Smith lived in an era in which people struggled for basic material needs. Consequently, Smith insisted that people are oriented toward self-interest. Free people in free markets create the greatest well-being for the greatest number of people. They can be motivated by the carrot-and-stick process. Give them strong enough incentives and they will work. Smith said this approach works because of the following assumptions:

1. Workers want and need monetary gain, hence will do what achieves for them the greatest gain.
2. Workers are only a small element within an organization. The organization controls the monetary gain and therefore can control motivation.
3. Workers do not understand organizational interests and goals and therefore must be prevented from interfering.
4. Workers' feelings must be controlled by the organizational structure. The organization should even encourage and develop workers' feelings and goals to be the same as those of the organization.

To Smith, monetary rewards should be set in steps, with amounts based on the results contributed to the organization. Enormous increases in productivity and output would occur because each person has strong economic self-interests. In a fully free and competitive market, this plan would result in the greatest gain for the individual. How to motivate, according to Smith:

> *Give workers financial incentives strong enough so that they work and experience monetary gain.*

Piece Rate Work Standards Approach (Frederick Taylor)

Taylor developed a systematic approach for accomplishing work with time and motion studies. He advocated dividing the work into "chunks," determining the best time to produce these chunks, establishing these work chunks as standards, assigning pay rates for completing the standards, and giving training and development to workers to perform to the standards. Taylor used this approach because his analysis of work showed a haphazard and random process for its accomplishment. Inefficient, wasteful movements frustrated and demotivated the worker. Taylor pursued these assumptions:

1. Workers can be driven only to a point, and therefore the work situation must change.
2. Workers would work more if their work were made simpler and easier.
3. Workers would get greater results if the work were separated into parts and people were allowed to specialize in these parts.
4. Workers contribute more to the organization when work is defined into chunks and standards of performance are established with pay increases.

Taylor felt people would work to high levels when the job and its processes allowed them to do so. Although Taylor placed great importance on the value of money, he stressed the need for examining the job situation and developing a systematic approach to accomplishing the work. Work must be divided and assigned to those best fitted to do it. Workers need to be scientifically selected, trained, and developed in the jobs best suited to them. How to motivate, according to Taylor:

> *Give workers a job situation in which work is broken up into standards, assign pay to these standards, and give an easy procedure to reach the standards.*

Job Analysis and Wage Structure Approach (Hugo Munsterberg)

Munsterberg classified worker traits, skills, and knowledge in an effort to match worker abilities and skills with job requirements. His work analysis measured worker traits and assigned weights of importance to them for making compensation decisions. Munsterberg used this approach to differentiate jobs and to measure successful performance on the job. Munsterberg pursued these assumptions:

1. Workers see importance in their reward levels in one organization compared with reward levels in another organization.
2. Workers see job satisfaction and wage level as important measures for deciding on one job from among many.
3. Workers see the money rate structure from low to high as a promotional opportunity to go up the organization. The rate structure is a measure of how well they are succeeding.
4. Workers will contribute more if merit recognition allows them to jump steps in the rate structure.

Munsterberg thought that once job classes and levels, with their respective money rates, were established, workers would have a way to compare their achievements in their present job with other jobs in other organizations. How to motivate, according to Munsterberg:

> *Give workers a job structure in steps, assign money rates, and provide merit evaluation when it is recognized jobs have been well achieved.*

Behavioral Approaches

A 1970 survey conducted by the National Industrial Conference Board showed that 241 of 300 American companies (80 percent) reported movement from the incentive approach to the behavioral approach to motivation.

Hierarchy of Needs Approach (Abraham Maslow)

Humans are wanting beings. There is always some need they want to satisfy. Maslow indicated that humans are motivated by needs as they perceive them. These needs urge individuals toward fulfillment and satisfaction. They drive individuals to certain states of behavior. The higher order of needs becomes potent only after basic needs have been satisfied.

NEEDS HIERARCHY, LOWEST TO HIGHEST

Need	Example
Physiological	Food, water, shelter, sex (geared to survival)
Safety	Protection, safety, freedom from fear (concerned with physical and mental well-being)
Love	Belonging, acceptance (geared to social well-being)
Esteem	Respect, recognition, status (geared to self-confidence)
Self-actualization	Fulfillment of potential, growth (geared to ideals for fulfillment)

Maslow emphasized that once a need is satisfied, it is no longer a motivator of behavior. As needs at one level are reasonably well met, people strive to satisfy higher needs. These needs overlap and interact. Workers' need for satisfaction is insatiable. The lower level needs are more demanding, but those higher on the scale are more lasting and effective as motivators. How to motivate, according to Maslow:

Give workers opportunities in a work situation to fulfill their needs.

Theory X and Theory Y Approach (Douglas McGregor)

McGregor developed two sets of contrasting assumptions about humans and their perceptions about work. These assumptions are determinants of leadership styles and motivation of people.

1. *Theory X Assumptions.*
   (a) Workers inherently dislike work and when possible will avoid it.
   (b) Workers have little ambition, shun responsibility, and prefer direction.
   (c) Workers want security.
   (d) Workers have to be coerced, controlled, and threatened to attain organizational objectives.
2. *Theory Y Assumptions.*
   (a) Workers will seek responsibility when conditions are favorable.

(b) Workers want to direct and control their own commitments.

(c) Workers want rewards commensurate with their commitments.

(d) Workers want opportunities to make significant contributions to organizations' objectives.

According to McGregor, managers have trouble motivating their workers because they hold erroneous assumptions about the nature of their people either X or Y. For this reason, a manager should check the assumptions he has made about his subordinates to see if they are interfering. Additionally according to McGregor, it is impossible to motivate people directly. Motivation comes from within. This motivation expresses itself in behavior when conditions allow it. How to motivate, according to McGregor:

> *Give managers a new view and set of attitudes about people and their environment for best advancing the goals of the people and of the organization.*

Motivation-Hygiene Theory Approach (Frederick Herzberg)

Herzberg identified job elements that generate positive feelings as satisfiers and job elements that generate negative feelings as dissatisfiers. Satisfaction and dissatisfaction are separate factors, not end points on a continuum. Satisfiers are also called "motivators," because they are effective in motivating employees to greater productivity. Dissatisfiers are called "hygiene factors," because unless taken care of they would cause dissatisfaction. Five job conditions that stand out as high determinants of satisfaction are:

1. Achievement.
2. Recognition.
3. Work itself.
4. Responsibility.
5. Advancement.

Herzberg claimed that these conditions can motivate individuals to long-term superior performance and effort. He also identified job conditions that stand out as high determinants of dissatisfaction:

1. Organization policies.
2. Administration.
3. Supervision.
4. Salary.
5. Interpersonal relations.
6. Job security.
7. Working conditions.

These may produce short-term changes in attitude and productivity. Herzberg argued that managers tend to create conditions that stress dissatisfiers and ignore the potential value of satisfiers. How to motivate, according to Herzberg:

> *Give workers motivators within the job content that will lead to satisfaction.*

Achievement Motivation Theory Approach (David McClelland)

McClelland stated that high levels of accomplishment at work are due to the fact that a high level of "achievement needs" exists among people. People who accomplish large undertakings are turned on by the accomplishment. Money, position, status, and power are secondary considerations. McClelland noted that patterns of achievement motivation are found with founders of companies (entrepreneurs) and with presidents of small organizations. The high achiever has these characteristics:

1. Assumes responsibility for solving problems.
2. Reaches for goals in spite of high risks.
3. Develops situations that offer frequent feedback of results.

An interesting point with McClelland's achievement motivation is that entrepreneurial behavior can be developed. Once the behavior is learned, entrepreneurial activity usually results. The outstanding characteristic of entrepreneurial behavior (high achievement) is the desire to approach tasks for which there is reasonable chance for success and to avoid tasks that are either too easy or too difficult. How to motivate, according to McClelland:

> *Give workers entrepreneurial development opportunities to experience high levels of achievement.*

Expectancy Theory Approach* (Victor Vroom)

Vroom formulated one of the more popular versions of expectancy theory. It is based on three concepts:

1. *Valence.* The value or importance that a specific outcome has for a worker.

---

*No individual can be cited as a sole proponent to this approach. Many have made contributions. The reader is urged to read the following for more insight into the management approaches: D. Meister and G. Rabidean, *Human Factors Evaluation in System Development.* New York: Wiley, 1965; Howard Carlisle, *Situational Management.* New York: American Management Association, 1973; Gary Dessler, *Organization and Management.* Englewood Cliffs, N.J.: Prentice-Hall, 1976.

2. *Instrumentality.* Worker's view of how high performance will help in getting a promotion.

3. *Expectance.* Worker's feeling of whether his or her efforts will lead to high levels of performance.

Vroom's expectancy theory model assigns mathematical probabilities to predictions about work behavior. In a given situation, human behavior is a joint function of the degree to which that behavior is instrumental (effective) in attaining an outcome and the subjective probability (hunch) that the outcome will be forthcoming. Individuals will choose the behavior—and its needed motivation—that they perceive as leading to the things they want.

Expectancy theory suggests that people tend to expend more effort toward reaching goals when both the probability of receiving a reward and the magnitude of that reward are known in advance.

Magnitude of reward × probability of receiving reward (known in advance)
= high motivation

Magnitude of reward × probability of receiving reward (not known in advance)
= low motivation

How to motivate, according to Vroom:

Give workers opportunities in which rewards are great and the probability of achieving them is high.

Management Approach†

The management approach to motivating workers is based on the view that there is no best way to motivate. Different organizations with different tasks, different competitive environments, and different worker needs require different approaches to motivating. The management approach is therefore an eclectic synthesis of other approaches that will best fit a situation. A few management approaches are described here, although it must be noted that isolating each approach is difficult, since there is a great deal of overlap and similarity.

---

†Many perceptions of the motivational processes are available in the literature. The reader interested in pursuing these ideas will find the following useful: S. W. Gullerman, *Management by Motivation.* New York: American Management Association, 1968; F. Herzberg, B. Mausner, and B. B. Snyderman, *The Motivation To Work.* New York: Wiley, 1965; D. McGregor, *Human Side of Enterprise,* New York: McGraw-Hill, 1960; V. H. Vroom, *Work and Motivation.* New York: Wiley, 1964.

Contingency Approach

There are many contributors to the contingency approach. It recognizes the substantial differences between and among organizations and their constituencies. No one model for motivating will work for all organizations. The appropriate organizational structure, leadership, staffing, planning, motivating, and control are contingent on the organizational environment and the task to be performed. Thus the emphasis in the contingency approach is on researching practices and methods that are appropriate for the situation and adopting those that work. The assumptions underlying the contingency approach are:

1.   Worker situations differ.   These differences affect how managerial knowledge is applied. Different organizations with different tasks and competitive environments require different plans. Just as every human personality and every organization is unique, so every managerial position or situation is unique.

2.   Differences in the working environment, rather than similarities, are the basis of establishing a management practice.

3.   Worker motivational practices cannot be applied across the board. They may be true and useful for a particular problem in a particular situation.

The contingency approach is based on the major idea that there is no one best way to handle all management functions and problems. The best way for a particular situation is developed after careful research and analysis of the situation. How to motivate, according to the contingency approach:

> *Analyze the situation and select elements from the vast array of principles and techniques that would form a model for motivating workers in the situation.*

Systems Approach

In recent years, increasing use has been made of a theory of systematic relationships within organizations. These system constructs provide key tools for diagnosis of human interactions of persons, groups, organizations, and communities. The assumptions of this approach are:

1.   A systems model can be developed that has universal applicability to physical, social, and human relationships, whether the organization be small or large.
2.   A systems model provides "unity" or "coherence" for the wide variety of needs, interests, attitudes, and motives of an organization.

3. A systems model captures the way in which the organization works and predicts what would happen if some new motivational factor were introduced.

A systems model is designed to link the critical parameters of the organization's operations and environment. The model is then used to simulate the effects of human interactions and motivations when changes are introduced or situational factors are removed. How to motivate, according to the systems approach:

> *Develop a systems model for the organization to establish its current motivation process and then find the change agents for its improvement.*

Expectancy Alignment Approach

I recommend the expectancy alignment approach. It recognizes that the complexities of people, situations, goals, and organizational needs are too formidable for simplistic methods. Differences are important, but similarities are important as well! Most important are purposes and expectancies. What do we want? What do we expect? What are we trying to achieve? Literally, this motivational approach requires an assessment of the needs of both the organization and people and a way of creating a situation in which these needs are accommodated within "states of expectancies." Let's make these assumptions:

1. Worker needs are extremely complex and change with changing values, attitudes, interests, and wants. Similarly, organizational needs are extremely complex and change with changing markets, products, services, environment, legislations, and goals. Both of these "packages" of needs are continually changing. A purpose for both groups must be established that provides something to which complex changing needs can be related or made coincident.

2. Workers' needs are in disparity with organizational needs. Both cannot have their needs fully and completely satisfied. A compromise between the two packages of needs is often workable for both.

3. Worker and organizational needs vary not only in number but in the degree of importance assigned to them. The degree of importance changes as the situation changes for both worker and organization.

4. Organizational needs that are aligned or coincident with workers' needs are apt to be pursued intensively, because workers are reaching to satisfy their own needs.

5. The alignment between organizational needs and workers' needs is at best an "accommodating fit" among all of the variables in a given situation at a given time.

How to motivate, according to the expectancy alignment approach:

Plan and obtain the closest possible alignment (needs coincidence) between employee expectancies and organizational objectives.

The author of this book tends to accept the expectancy alignment approach more than the others as most effective for the MBO processes. It is bringing into alignment the expectancies of both supervisor and subordinate. The following is more detail for motivating workers using the expectancy alignment approach.

Motivating with Expectancy Alignment

The basic problem in motivation of employees is neither lack of a framework for thinking about motivation nor lack of insight for understanding people and their needs. Many motivational concepts and principles are useful for understanding human behavior. The big problem is being able to translate these principles and concepts in a manner practical for improving productivity. The complexity of motivational problems suggests that managers should acquire a strategy that works well and use it in delivering results for the organization. But first some preliminary ideas must be described.

· *Needs Coincidence: The Practice for Generating Motivators.* Employees work primarily for themselves and only secondarily for their employer. They work to meet their needs and personal goals. These needs and goals are termed "expectancies." Worker expectancies do not usually fall within the framework of company expectancies. A disparity exists between the two (Figure 10.5). Managers need to align these two packages of expectancies, to reduce the angle of disparity. At the time of employment the disparity is diffused, because both employee and employer role play, that is, they take on roles to try to gain an advantage from each other. During employment the disparity becomes clearer, because role playing ceases. Both parties pursue paths of action that lead to fulfillment of their own package of expectancies, even at the sacrifice of the other party. The result of the struggle is a compromise, which represents the best "coincidence of needs" of a wide array of complex needs by both employee and employer. It is the line of "fit" or "agreement" between two sets of expectancies. This needs coincidence between the two parties forms the basis for managing motivation. Needs coincidence between employee and employer drives both parties to reach their package of expectancies, so that both gain. This concept is illustrated in Figure 10.6. One can see from this concept that the greater the coincidence of needs of both parties, the greater the intensity of drive toward results. This was described earlier as the *principle of expectancy alignment*. The greater the

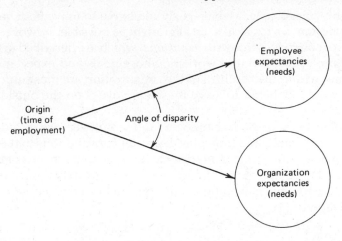

FIGURE 10.5 Disparity between employee expectancies and organizational expectancies.

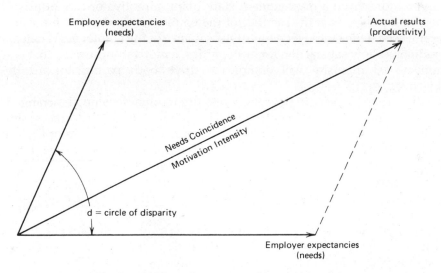

FIGURE 10.6 Needs coincidence between employer and employee expectancies.

alignment of employee expectancies with organizational objectives, the greater the motivation to accomplish both. Therefore, motivational intensity (MI) in an organizational setting is a function of needs coincidence (NC).

$$MI = f(NC)$$

Perfect alignment between organizational expectancies and employee expectancies is virtually unattainable or at best only briefly attainable. The changing nature of both parties makes coincidence of the vectors for a long period highly improbable. Managers should strive to move both vectors or states of expectancies to as close an alignment as possible, however (Figure 10.7). The manager does this with *motivators*, which are described in the next sections. Employers who hire workers whose goals and expectancies can never be met within the confines of the organization are most unfortunate indeed. It would be better to leave these employees on the outside of the door.

When objectives of both employer and employee are brought into alignment in substance and time phase, greater contributions to the organization are made. Motivational intensity is high when the needs of both the employee and the employer are coincident. Therefore managing motivation toward productivity is managing needs coincidence between workers and the organization.

Motivators: Job Conditions That Produce Needs Coincidence. Motivators are job conditions that satisfy the needs of both employees and the organization. From a management standpoint, a motivator cannot exist if the employee gains at the sacrifice of the employer. Similarly, a motivator cannot exist if the employer gains at the sacrifice of the employee. When job conditions allow satisfaction for both parties, a motivator prevails, that is, a motivational intensity will emerge to drive both parties toward the objective.

Job conditions refer to how the work situation is developed, arranged, executed, measured, and controlled. They refer to how both process and procedure are structured with tasks and duties, for example, the organizational need to complete a task within a given period of time. If this need is combined with employee need to control time commitments that affect them on the job, and both the organization and employees agree on a commitment for time, a motivator is developed. In this case, the motivator is participation.

As a motivator, participation implies a process in which both parties can gain. It implies a process in which there is needs coincidence, in which two sets of expectancies are brought into alignment.

> *Motivators are processes for arranging job conditions to enhance needs coincidence and satisfaction for workers and their organization.*

Several nonfinancial motivators that are capable of setting up needs coincidence have been developed over the years. The list that follows shows how the needs of both parties are met. This list is not intended to be definitive. Additional motivators can be developed if needs coincidence can be identified. Financial motivators can also be developed.

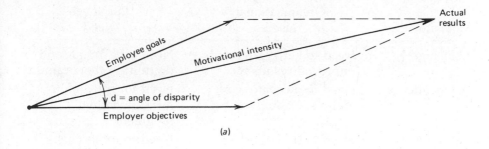

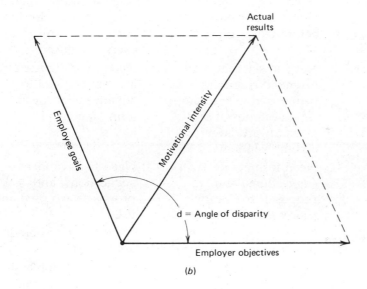

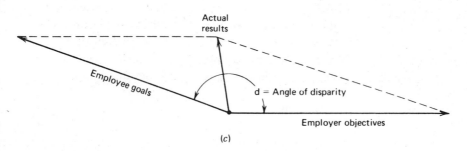

FIGURE 10.7 Motivational intensity caused by employer and employee disparity. (*a*) Case I: Close alignment, strong motivation, high results. (*b*) Case II: Wide alignment, moderate motivation, moderate results. (*c*) Case III: Very wide alignment, weak motivation, poor results.

Motivator	Organizational Need	Employee Need
Challenge	Need to get greater and improved results	Need to be unique and to do things others cannot
Independence	Need to delegate work and responsibilities	Need for freedom to form individual judgment
Recognition	Need to do important and significant work	Need to project self-worth to peers and family
Participation	Need to get commitments to complete work before work commences	Need to know what is going on and why and to have opportunity to exert influence
Achievement	Need to see that extended resources are being used in meaningful milestones of progress toward larger accomplishments	Need to see that efforts and energy lead to advancement toward long-range goal
Innovations	Need for new ideas, suggestions, and proposals to improve processes	Need to have ideas, suggestions, and proposals accepted and used
Enlargement	Need to get maximum use of time as resource	Need to avoid boredom and fatigue
Enrichment	Need to perpetuate organization with management succession	Need to feel job assignments are stepping-stones toward advancement in organization
Overview	Need to have individuals optimize to organization and not to individuals	Need to see where individual contributions fit in overall operations
Learning	Need to have personnel who can handle new and different types of job assignments	Need to have work that generates intense interest

The following are guidelines for using motivators:

1.   Motivators are individualistic. They may work well for one individual but are not so effective for another. Any effectiveness in mass applications is probably due to common conditions affecting many people in a similar way. Each person is like other persons in some ways. But human difference is the rule, not the exception.

2.   Motivators diminish in value over time. Motivators come into existence on the basis of conditions prevailing at a given time. When conditions change, the value of the motivators changes (Figure 10.8).

3.   Multiple motivators may be required. It is naive to think that only single motivators are needed. More often workers need multiple motivators because they want to satisfy a range of needs rather than only one or two.

4.   Motivators have variable effectiveness at different organizational levels. Motivators that are of intense value to top managers are of low value to foremen, and vice versa. Each level in the organization has its effective motivators.

5.   Motivators must be planned for individuals as the job level decreases. Top managers are in a position to plan their own motivators (self-motivation). Lower levels of management are less able to do this (Figure 10.9). Job designs or organizational changes with appropriate conditions must be instituted, or motivation will not be present in the lower levels of the organization.

6.   Motivators are highly effective when they reveal a person's worth. Since we live in an affluent society in which biological and safety needs are generally fulfilled, we look to personal worth and fulfillment needs.

7.   Motivators may be identified through careful assessment of individual and organizational needs. The needs of the individual at a given time are the clue for the development of motivators. Since needs are driven or pulled

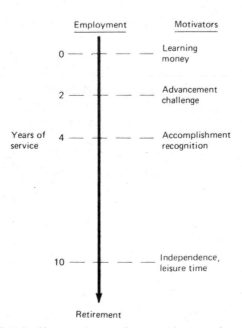

FIGURE 10.8   How motivators change with years of service.

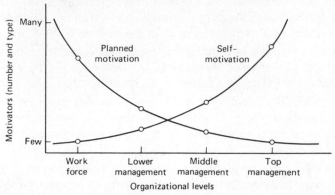

FIGURE 10.9 How motivators change in effectiveness by organizational levels.

by wants, the number of possible motivators is great. When the needs of both organization and individuals are coincident, a motivator is defined.

8. Motivators can become demotivators. Too much or too little of a motivator becomes a demotivator. For example, too much or too little challenge is demotivating.

9. Motivators are effective only in the work process. The nature of organizational life in the United States prevents managers from looking at employees outside the job. The manager must be content with managing motivation within the boundaries of the work.

10. Motivators should be tested. Motivators change with changing needs and wants. Managers must use the experimental approach to check the validity of assumed motivators.

11. Motivators are highly influenced by the style of the boss. Motivators will operate effectively only if they fit the style of the leader. There must be harmony or compatibility between the leadership style of the boss and the type of motivators in a work situation. How different motivators are effective for different leadership styles is illustrated as follows:

Leadership Styles	Effective Motivators
Autocratic "I" style	Provide challenges
	Schedule training and development
	Set up "pride" system for work
Integrative "we" style	Allow participation
	Enlarge job for variety
	Give overview of work
Permissive "you" style	Recognize contributions
	Promote for job opportunities
	Delegate for independence

12.   Motivators vary in effectiveness with different types of workers. Different groups of workers have different sets of needs. This suggests that different motivators will be highly effective for one group but not so effective for another.

Type of Worker	Effective Motivator
Older worker	Sense of independence
Contented employee	Challenging job assignments
Minority employee	Learning and training
Young affluent employee	Job enrichment
First-line supervisor	Recognition
Middle manager	Participation in policy making
Top executive	Opportunity for large scale accomplishment

How to Motivate with Needs Coincidence.   The challenge to managing motivation for greater productivity is not in understanding why people work, in developing models of human behavior, or in conceptualizing motivators that satisfy both the organization and employees. The challenge lies in implementing motivators in a practical way that results in greater productivity. Motivation is closely tied to the participative characteristics of the MBO strategy. In accepting a job with a company, the employee is really entering into a performance contract with the company. The company is doing the same with the employee. Both parties have certain expectations for results from the relationship. The concept of MBO recognizes that exact alignment of these expectations is difficult to attain. There will always be some disparity. However, if the disparity between company and employee objectives is small, the employee will be more motivated. Participation processes that work toward needs coincidence help to reduce this disparity. Five steps are described.

STEP 1.   Establish the productivity objectives to be achieved. Motivation does not begin with people, or with the job. It begins with the organization's purpose, expectations, and objectives. Defining expectations, and objectives. Defining expectations is the first step in bringing about conditions for their fulfillment. Previous chapters described in detail how to determine objectives and to write good statements of objectives. The statement of objectives defines company targets and sets up the entire motivational process.

STEP 2.   Identify organizational needs from productivity objectives. Analyze the statement of objectives for the human requirements needed for completion of the objectives. Completion may also entail non-human requirements, such as technical, financial, procedural.

This step is a difficult one if understanding is lacking about organizations and what mission or goals they intend to accomplish.

STEP 3. Acquire insights into employee needs. These needs represent employee expectations. They are the "whys" of employee behavior. They are the purposes employees seek and obtain employment in the organization. They are motives that establish a person's "will to work."

STEP 4. Decide on the motivator to be used. The list of motivators in the previous section is suggestive only. There is no magic laundry list of motivators. Nor does one motivator have mass applications. Once a manager acquires insight into what motivators are and how they are used, he or she should identify operative ones, such as early time off, flexitime, discretionary decision making, pride system, and personal interest.

STEP 5. Establish an alignment between organizational needs and employee expectancies with motivators. Align the needs of subordinates with productivity goals of the firm with the use of motivators, so that both are accomplished within an expected period of time. When workers see that their performance for the organization also meets their personal needs, drive becomes intense.

The process of motivating with expectancy alignment is illustrated in Figure 10.10. Examples of how the process works follow. Each example is from actual practice in an organization.

Example: *Computer Field Engineering Company.*

1. *Productivity Objective.*   Complete five preventive maintenance procedures per month within the region.
2. *Organizational Need.*   Company needs to keep equipment from failing, since its shutdown has a serious disruptive effect on operation of customer's organization.
3. *Employee Need.*   Employees need to feel their work is important and fulfilling.
4. *Motivators.*   Participation and overview.
5. *Alignment.*   Give employees preventive maintenance responsibility while allowing them to study and participate in the customer's overall operations and how the computer "fits in."

Example: *Town Government.*

1. *Productivity Objective.*   Complete management information systems for ten departments by January 1979.

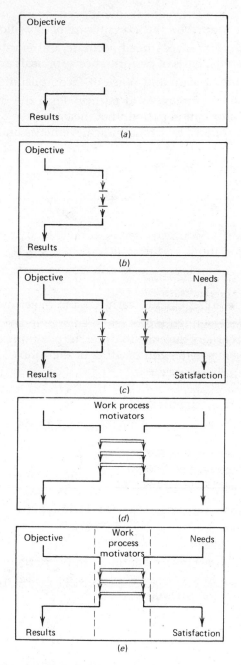

FIGURE 10.10 How to motivate with expectancy alignment. (*a*) Establish productivity objective of the organization. (*b*) Identify organizational needs. (*c*) Acquire insights into employee needs. (*d*) Decide on motivators. (*e*) Align two sets of expectancies.

2. *Organization Need.* Town government needs to give accurate account-ability to town council on the expenditure of city-allocated funds.
3. *Employee Need.* Employees need accurate and equitable information base to establish the basis of performance appraisals and their rewards.
4. *Motivators.* Participation and sense of accomplishment.
5. *Alignment.* Allow employees to participate in the development of a management information system that measures the allocation and ex-penditure of resources by program achievements and individuals.

Example: Cosmetic Manufacturing Company.

1. *Productivity Objective.* Reduce cost of turnover 30 percent within 12 months.
2. *Organization Need.* Company needs workers for a process that requires specialized job stations and in which the work is boring and routine.
3. *Employee Need.* Employees need interesting work with variety and challenge.
4. *Motivators.* Job enlargement, learning, and overview.
5. *Alignment.* Redesign work process to enlarge individual responsibili-ties and train workers to rotate to different positions at different inter-vals. Let workers see the end product of their jobs.

Example: Insurance Company.

1. *Productivity Objective.* Reduce time lag in total work process 50 percent within next budgetary year.
2. *Organization Need.* Company needs to process new subscribers, claims, and accounts receivable faster, since poor cash flow is hurting organization. Time requirements must be increased.
3. *Employee Need.* Employees want more independence and freedom from work, since work routine is boring.
4. *Motivators.* Flexitime.
5. *Alignment.* Set up standards of time productivity for each station and allow employees to set their own hours on a sliding scale as long as standards are met and work is completed.

Example: Health Care Center.

1. *Productivity Objective.* Complete 15 treatment plans with no more than two regressions by start of next budgetary year.
2. *Organization Need.* Center needs to implement therapeutic programs for effective care of resident patients.

3. *Employee Need.* Employees need opportunity to exercise and contribute professional competence in the care of resident patients.
4. *Motivators.* Achievement and recognition.
5. *Alignment.* Allow professional staff to develop treatment plans under schedule and to implement plans with administrative support.

DOES MONEY MOTIVATE?

There are probably many viewpoints on money as a motivator. Two are examined here: behavioral and management.

The Behavioral Viewpoint

Behaviorists are interested in the motives of people, since motives are the basis of motivation. They are interested in how motives develop through wants and needs, and how wants and needs drive people and cause behavior. According to behaviorists, wants and needs are what really cause changes in behavior, since they are internal—they cannot be directed or manipulated from the outside. What a person really wants is to satisfy internal needs. To the behaviorist, money therefore symbolizes purchasing power for meeting present and future needs. Money is worthless in itself but has unique power as a "symbolic motivator," because it aids in acquiring whatever is considered most important in life. People can "keep score" with money. The more they have, the more present and future needs can be fulfilled. Efforts to accumulate money reflect attitudes about present and future levels of need. The compulsive accumulation of money is probably due to the fact that money has become the common denominator for meeting the needs of people everywhere. The amount of money accumulated tells an individual how much progress has been made. If the amount is low, drive is reinforced. *Therefore to the behaviorist, money does not motivate but the satisfaction of individual needs does. Money is the "score" of how well an individual will meet these needs.*

The Management Viewpoint

The manager's view is somewhat different, although not contradictory. The manager must deal with the realities of the situation. People are only one component; the organization is the other. The manager must act and react in such a way that the needs of both are met, if not simultaneously, then in a complementary way. Managers are well aware of the fact that people work to meet their personal needs. But these needs continually change, are very complex, and are often beyond the manager's control. The manager does not have the time to function as a behaviorist. He or she is concerted with behavior on the first level: how to get a person to do a job that also meets the needs of the organization. Money and the way it is dispersed greatly influence behavior. A low salary relative to other salaries tends to demotivate; a high salary motivates. Employees see salary reviews as important feedback regarding their performance. The manager cannot, however, raise or lower salaries at will! At best, the manager tries to find a compromise between the organization and the individual. The manager makes every attempt to find where "needs coincidence" can occur. In nonfinancial areas this is difficult, but where money is concerned it becomes easy, because money is both the universal common denominator for meeting the needs of people and an area where "needs coincidence" between people and the organization can be formed. The more money an organization has or can make, the more of its own needs its employees' needs it can meet. *Therefore to the manager, money does motivate, because it is the means by which a host of present and future needs can be made coincident between the organization and the employees.* Money is a source of pride, security, and satisfaction for both organizations and individuals. The profit a company desperately wants is a way of meeting present and future needs. The chief problem a manager has with money as a motivator is that in many situations *it's the most expensive of all motivators!* To reduce costs in motivating employees is one reason why nonfinancial motivators are sought by managers. The following is a list of financial motivators used by managers in many organizations. They motivate—and motivate well. The biggest problem with them is that they are expensive.

1. Give large increments of money.
2. Set up profit-sharing programs.
3. Give opportunity for ownership.
4. Provide better than average fringe benefits.
5. Give a chance for early retirement.
6. Give tuition rebate for educational courses.
7. Give extra holidays, vacations, and time off.
8. Set up flexitime (leisure or independent time).
9. Provide medical-expense reimbursement.
10. Set up use of company-owned equipment, such as cars.

In short, managers view nonfinancial motivators as adjuncts to financial motivators. Intangible rewards are as important as tangible rewards. Both will cause behavior.

In an informative report on methods of motivating employee productivity (Locke et al., 1979), four methods emerged as the strongest among the financial and nonfinancial motivators: money, goal setting, job enrichment, and participation. The results of this study are as follows:

Method	Number of Studies Conducted	Percent Improvement (Median)	Percent with 10% or More Improvement
Money	10	30.0	90
Goal setting	17	16.0	94
Job enrichment	13	17.0	61
Participation	16	0.5	25

The study revealed that money as an incentive yielded the highest median productivity increase. Goal setting was next. Participation was least effective. The combination of goal setting and money yielded the highest gain—40 percent.

These four methods are part and parcel of the MBO process. For this reason MBO is highly motivational. The seasoned MBO practitioner does not separate these methods but combines them in the overall process.

THE NEW WORK ETHIC AND MOTIVATION

"Work ethic" is the value that people place on work in their lives. To answer the question, "Is the work ethic dead?," is to answer the question, "Is the value of work dead?" The answer is no! But certainly the work ethic and the meaning work has for people have been changing, because work values have been changing. The power organizations previously held over workers was based on how employees valued work in their lives. Since the meaning and value of work for individuals have been changing, the power of the organization or employer to exploit workers is changing. This is measurably and dramatically seen in clashes between authority and self-expression, between how supervisors want to supervise and how employees want to be supervised, between what organizations will give and what unions will take. Several forces in society are feeding trends toward changing the value and meaning of work. They have been covered in detail previously but are given briefly here again.

1. *Increasing Educational Level.* The rising level of educational background of employees brings with it both better skills and a higher level of awareness and expectations.

2. *Travel and Mobility.* Employees travel more than any of their predecessors in history. This ability to travel offers employees more alternatives and options in different labor markets and organizations than at any time in

history. Broader options allow them to select alternatives for the meaning of work in their lives.

3. *Growing Affluence.*   In spite of recessions and inflation, economic affluence continues to grow, greatly reducing emphasis on the necessities of life. More often than not, workers take pay and security for granted. They thus can seek gratification of higher levels of needs. An identifiable self-concept, self-fulfillment, and self-esteem are sought by affluent workers.

4. *Erosion of Traditional Authority.*   Values from school, the family, and the church and self-responsibilities and self-conceived forms of fulfillment conflict drastically with the traditional boss-subordinate structure in business. Employees look for individual fulfillment in the context of work.

5. *Social Commitment.*   Growing appreciation of the role and effects of an organization in a community stresses the need for interdependence and connection with community needs and concerns. Employees are concerned with how their work output affects the community and how work contribution gives them identity, self-concept, and self-esteem.

These forces are shaping a new meaning of work for people everywhere, a new work ethic. This ethic has evolved over many years. The history of man's view of what work means is outlined as follows.

Group	View of Work
Egyptians	Work was a way of accomplishing great projects and programs. Since many people were needed to achieve these programs, people were made slaves. Slavery, the whip, and taskmasters were the way to complete great works.
Hebrews	Work was a way to get ahead. Work was to be pursued intensely to gather the harvest for lean times. "He that tilleth his land shall have plenty of bread" (Proverbs 28:19). Hard work was demanded (Ecclesiastes 9:10), for in all labor there is profit (Proverbs 14:4), but rest was commanded, one day in seven (Exodus 23:12). To the Hebrews, work was necessary not only to meet daily and future needs and thereby avoid poverty and starvation. (Proverbs 10:4).
Greeks	Work was to be avoided. The Greeks relied on slaves to do their work because work was demeaning. The Greek word for work, "ponos," means "suffering" and was to be avoided. The Greeks sought leisure and contemplation. Work was a necessary evil to be delegated to slaves. The aim of business was to gain leisure time.
Romans	Work was needed to build the empire. Leisure was not the ultimate goal of life; leisure was only a relief from work. Everyone had to work to build and maintain the

Group	View of Work
	empire, which provided good for all. Work was not deemed good in itself but was useful and thus was to be pursued.
Christians	Work was to be done and done well. Work was the means to earn leisure time to meditate on God. Individuals should provide for their own necessities and families. Economic pursuit and gain were a means of helping families and others. "If anyone will not work, let him not eat" (II Thessalonians 3:10). The chief usefulness of work was to support oneself for a higher duty and contemplation.
Catholics	Work was a means of glorifying God. To work was to fulfill the mission of life. To work was to pray. The ultimate goal of work was an opportunity for contemplation with God.
Protestants	Work was a moral activity that fulfilled a predestined grace. Hard-earned material success was a sign of heavenly approval of a good and moral life. Idleness was a serious misdemeanor. The ultimate goal of life was to make full use of God's gifts during one's lifetime. Hence a person guilty of idleness or leisure pursuits, poverty, or wastefulness was thought to be committing acts against God. Work was a way of pleasing God. Martin Luther even went further and glorified work, making work sacred and religious.
Americans	Work is a means of fulfilling personal needs. Work provides self-sufficiency and supports society in its many functions and pursuits. It gives humans the means to pursue other activities. Work keeps the economy moving and provides for human power to be used to meet organizational objectives. Full employment is necessary for individuals and for making society work.

The work ethic is alive and well, although it has changed considerably. It is being changed and reshaped by the new desires and demands of workers. People still live to work, but many have now acquired the attitude of working to live. Here is my analysis of how the new work ethic is emerging:

- Work means shaping an identity and individuality.
- Work means doing something important and meaningful.
- Work means reaching for self-fulfillment.
- Work means giving to those who are less fortunate.
- Work means creating leisure time and play.
- Work means developing and subduing the environment for high quality of human living.

SUMMARY

The search for ways to motivate employees toward greater productivity is intense because the problems of motivation are here and now. This chapter describes why motivating employees is different and difficult these days. Six factors are examined briefly:

1. Workers' view of authority is changing.
2. Worker expectations are increasing due to rising educational levels.
3. Worker rights are changing due to legislative intrusions.
4. Worker unions are growing in effectiveness and strength.
5. Worker goals and employer objectives are conflicting.
6. Worker affluence is shifting priorities and attitudes.

Three general approaches to motivating workers toward greater productivity are described. The incentive approach is based on the view that workers are eager to maximize their monetary status, power, and prestige. This is the "dangling the carrot" approach. Three contributors to this approach are:

1. *Adam Smith.* Motivate by giving workers financial incentives strong enough so that they work and experience monetary gain.

2. *Frederick Taylor.* Motivate by giving workers a job situation in which work is broken up into standards, pay is assigned to the standards, and a procedure is developed to reach the standards.

3. *Hugo Munsterberg.* Motivate by giving workers a job structure in steps, assigning money rates, and providing a merit evaluation when the jobs have been achieved.

The behavioral approach is based on the view that people work to meet their needs. They come to the organization to see how many of these needs can be met. Five contributors to this approach are:

1. *Abraham Maslow.* Motivate by giving workers opportunities in a work situation to fulfill their needs.

2. *Douglas McGregor.* Motivate by giving managers a view and set of attitudes about people and their environment for best achieving the goals of the people and of the organization.

3. *Frederick Herzberg.* Motivate by giving workers motivators within the job content that will lead to satisfaction.

4. *David McClelland.* Motivate by giving workers entrepreneurial development opportunities to experience high levels of achievement.

5. *Victor Vroom.* Motivate by giving workers opportunities in which rewards are great and the probability of achieving them is high.

The management approach is based on the view that there is no one best way to motivate. Different organizations with different tasks, different competitive environments, and different worker needs require different approaches. Managerial approaches are, therefore, eclectic approaches. Three techniques are:

1. *Contingency Approach.* Motivate by analyzing the situation, selecting elements from a vast array of possibilities, and forming a model that will work for a given situation.

2. *Systems Approach.* Motivate by developing a systems model for an organization in which the current motivational process is identified and finding the change agents for its improvements.

3. *Expectancy Alignment Approach.* Motivate by planning and obtaining the closest alignment (needs coincidence) possible between employee expectancies and organizational objectives.

I recommend the expectancy alignment approach. It is based on the theory that the greater the alignment of employee expectancies with organizational objectives, the greater the motivation to accomplish both. Motivational intensity (MI) is therefore how well a manager can align or cause needs coincidence (NC) between employee and organization

$$MI = f(NC)$$

Motivators are job conditions that satisfy the needs of both employees and the organization. Where job conditions can be arranged to meet the needs of both parties, a motivator emerges. Several motivators with wide appeal are suggested: challenge, independence, recognition, participation, achievement, innovations, enlargement, enrichment, overview, and learning. Several guidelines are described for using these motivators, but five steps represent a process for motivating employees with expectancy alignment.

1. Establish the productivity objectives to be achieved.
2. Identify organizational needs from productivity objectives.
3. Acquire insights into employee needs.
4. Decide on the motivator to be used.
5. Establish an alignment between organizational needs and employee expectancies with motivators.

Finally, two important questions about motivation are answered: "Does money motivate?" and "Is the work ethic dead?" There are various viewpoints on these questions. I favor the management viewpoint on both: Money does motivate, because it is the common denominator for meeting the present and future needs of people and organizations everywhere. It is the quickest way of getting needs coincidence (but it is the most expensive way). The work ethic is not dead, although it has changed considerably and continues to change. My perception of the new work ethic is as follows:

- Work means shaping an identity and individuality.
- Work means doing something important and meaningful.
- Work means reaching for self-fulfillment.
- Work means giving to those who are less fortunate.
- Work means creating leisure time and play.
- Work means developing and subduing the environment for high quality of human living.

BIBLIOGRAPHY

Guide to Consumer Markets, New York: National Industrial Conference Board, 1973, p. 251.

Herzberg, F., Mausner, B., and Snyderman, D.B., *The Motivation To Work*. New York: Wiley, 1959.

Hodgetts, Richard M., *Management: Theory, Process and Practice*. Philadelphia: W. B. Saunders, 1975, pp. 28–33.

Locke, Edwin A., Feren, Dena D., McCaleb, Vickie M., Shaw, Karyll N., and Deeny, Anne T., *The Relative Effectiveness of Four Methods of Motivating Employee Performance*. Paper presented at NATO International Conference, Thessaloniki, Greece, 1979.

Mali, Paul, *Managing by Objectives*. New York: Wiley, 1972, pp. 55–60.

Maslow, Abraham, "A Theory of Human Motivation." *Psychological Review*, July 1943, pp. 388–389.

McClelland, D. C., *The Achieving Society*. Princeton, NJ: Van Nostrand, 1961.

McGregor, Douglas, *The Human Side of Enterprise*. New York: McGraw-Hill, 1960, pp. 33–38.

Morrison, Donald M., "Is the Work Ethic Going Out of Style?" *Time*, October 30, 1972, p. 96.

Munsterberg, Hugo, *Psychology and Industrial Efficiency*. Boston: Houghton Mifflin, 1913.

Prentice-Hall Research Staff, *Productivity: The Personnel Challenge*. Englewood Cliffs, NJ: New York: Prentice-Hall, 1973, pp. 28–29.

Special Task Force report, *Work in America*. Cambridge, MA: MIT Press, 1971, p. 44.

11

MAKING MBO
WORKABLE

IN THIS CHAPTER

IN THEORY WE CAN; IN PRACTICE WE DON'T—WHY?
MBO TROUBLE SPOTS AND SUGGESTED REMEDIES
COMPENSATION WITH MBO
DEVELOPING MBO PRACTITIONERS THROUGH DOING
SKILLS FOR MBO
MBO DIAGNOSTIC TEST

MBO is not self-taught. Although the strategy seems basically clear and easy to implement, it must be learned, and learning a new skill can be harder than the work itself. For example, the setting of objectives and fitting them into a network of mutually supportive and coordinated efforts require adoption of a whole new outlook and then persuasion of others as to its validity. It is hard to get managers to set targets for results as opposed to activities, since most managers have always used the activity approaches. Getting managers to set and apply measurements to objectives is also difficult. Managers usually sense that their goals are correctly set but they don't know how to measure results. Experience has shown that this difficulty can be overcome by continual practice and application on the job. A manager or supervisor must learn how to develop precise, appropriate, and quantitative measures that define results for goals and control. This skill too comes with continual applications over time.

This chapter deals with some of the issues in making MBO a workable practice in an organization. It suggests why a gap exists between MBO principles and MBO practices, and ways to close the gap between theory and practice, between principles and implementation, between planning and doing. A checklist of trouble spots, pitfalls, and difficulties is included, along with suggested remedies. The issue of linking compensation with MBO is taken up. The skills needed for practicing MBO are discussed, as are ways of encouraging the development of these skills. The perfect management process has not been found; all processes require adaptation and modification. MBO is no different. This chapter suggests ways to adapt and modify it.

IN THEORY WE CAN; IN PRACTICE WE DON'T—WHY?

Good theory is practical. If a theory or principle cannot be implemented, something is wrong with it. A theory or set of principles is a guideline that, if followed, should lead to intended results. The question then arises, "Why is it that in theory we usually can do whatever we want, but in practice we need to make adjustments?" The following are the major reasons for this gap between theory and practice, and some suggestions on how to close it.

Incomplete or Imperfect Assumptions About Future

MBO is a plan for creating a future. To make it work, future variables must be anticipated. This is where the problem lies. We are not good in identifying all the variables that will inhibit or enhance a plan. Our assumptions are not always correct. The assumptions we do make are often fuzzy or incomplete. What can be done? Suggestions:

1. Identify as many variables as possible that can enhance or abort a plan.
2. Assign priorities to the variables as to their importance.
3. Devise an action for each variable both "for" and "against."
4. Try out or test the plan of action in a simulated situation, noting the effects of the variable.
5. Adjust the original plan based on test information.

Risk Factors of Future Plan Unknown

MBO has a risk factor, since it deals with the unknown future. The MBO practitioner must manage this risk as well as the plan. Most MBO plans ignore this risk factor. The higher the uncertainty of the future, the higher the risk, the higher the probability of difficulty, the greater the likelihood of failure. What can be done? Suggestions:

1. Assign risk factors to the plan, for example, 50, 75, 90 percent likelihood of implementing the plan on the basis of information available

when the plan was formulated. When the risk factor is high and confidence is low, revise the plan to build up confidence.

2. Make information collecting a continuous matter. Watch the effects of new information on the risk factor. If the new information affects the plan negatively, that is, if it increases risk, changes are needed.

Lack of Flexibility in Planning

Inflexibility is one chief cause of plan failure. MBO thinking must acknowledge that the future will differ from the present, in many cases radically. The issue then is whether to not plan or to plan and make in-process changes. In-process changes become in-process planning. Suggestions:

1. Set up the MBO plan with milestones of progress. Each milestone allows for adjustments in the plan to handle changes that were not anticipated.
2. In areas in which the potential to abort the plan is high, develop contingency thinking and alternative possibilities.

Imperfect Information Used in Decisions

The number of managers who question the accuracy and completeness of the information they use in making decisions is few indeed! Most managers assume that supplied information is accurate and complete. Obviously, an MBO plan that is based on imperfect information will be imperfect. Decision making on top levels relies heavily on information supplied by lower levels. What can be done? Suggestions:

1. Be far more skeptical about important information. Questioning is an important skill. Third-party reviews will validate whether information needed by decision makers is complete and perfect.
2. Be more formal in certifying information before, during, and after storage. That is, information needs to be formally certified that it is correct and complete before it is used.

MBO Plans Not Validated

From a legal standpoint, valid plans have official approval and confirmation from top management. From a certified standpoint, invalid plans are ill-founded, contain errors and defects, and have low likelihood of producing the intended results. Too often plans are implemented without the benefit of a validation procedure. What can be done? Suggestions:

1. Have third-party scrutiny and objective review to detect flaws, errors, and weak points. (This is similar to quality control for products.)

2. Test the plan before implementation in the areas crucial to the plan. Simulate as closely as possible the future conditions to see what happens to the plan. Multinational corporations have an excellent opportunity to try out a plan in one division before they use it in the entire corporation.

3. Observe and examine other companies who implemented similar plans and learn from their difficulties and failures.

4. Use a miniplan approach in those instances where future variables are unknowable. Reduce the life span of the plan to a period where confidence is attainable. This may mean short-range plans or modified intermediate plans.

Poor Handling of Interface Ripple Effects

MBO plans interact with markets, governments, unions, industry, employees, vendors, competitors, suppliers, money sources, and other companies. Interaction also occurs between departments, sections, functions, and divisions of a corporation. The degree and frequency of interaction, its nature, and its importance will vary in accordance with the intended results of the plans. Too often a job is attempted within a company and the external ripple effects that also affect the company are ignored. Conversely, too often the ripple effects on the company of a job in an external organization are ignored. What can be done? Suggestions:

1. Expect an MBO plan to generate ripples at its interface both internally and externally. This is the nature of creating a future.

2. Trace through with networking who, what, where, and when will be affected by an MBO plan. Describe the nature of this effect.

3. In advance of MBO implementation, contact and consult with affected parties to obtain cooperation, support, and conflict resolution.

Inadequate Training of People

Implementation means skillful managers and workers getting things done as required by the new plan. Too often a plan intended to create new directions and new processes does not include training of people to make it work. Putting it differently, people with old skills must attempt to implement a new future. What can be done? Suggestions:

1. Identify the new skills that are needed once an MBO plan is formulated.

2. Identify individuals who need to acquire these skills once the plan is in operation.

3. Train and develop practitioners for the skills needed. This should be done in advance or during the plan's implementation.

No Built-in Motivators to Implement Plan

It is not enough for managers to know that an MBO plan has been approved by top management as being right and necessary for the company. They must be motivated for the plan. The most common motivational approach is the "carrot and stick" method, that is, giving an incentive to get people to work hard to implement a plan. This is an external method. Chapter 10 described several approaches to motivation, and the reader is urged to review this chapter. A major point must be made of building in motivators in MBO plans, so that plan motivates people. Suggestions:

1. Have the people who will implement the plan participate in plan information.
2. Allow individuals to set levels of challenge and achievement.
3. Permit new ideas and innovations by those who implement the plan.

MBO TROUBLE SPOTS AND SUGGESTED REMEDIES

Despite all of its reported benefits, MBO is not without its problems. Many can be summed up under the headings of hard work and persistent effort. In fact, the work of MBO is so hard that only a long-term commitment to the practice justifies its adoption. Several years are needed for managers to develop the proficiency and skill to make MBO work. Complaints about MBO vary from company to company, but most companies that try it do have complaints. Sometimes there is overshooting of the standards, sometimes undershooting. The quality of performance can be too high as well as too low, as seen in Figure 11.1. Usually it is too low; we all have experience with company products and services that do not meet our expectations. Sometimes the troubles of companies are passed on to the consumer, either

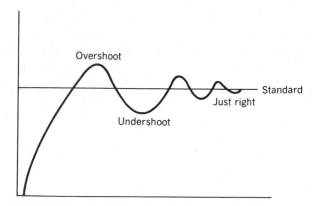

FIGURE 11.1 Controlling the effectiveness of performance.

knowingly or as defects hidden also from the company. The issue of ethics and personal style is immediately apparent when defects must be corrected. Certainly the recall of thousands of automobiles must remind auto managers that quality and cost are items to be reckoned with and that poor quality will come back to haunt them.

The following checklist of trouble spots has been compiled from the many companies that are practicing MBO. Remedies are suggested.

Trouble Spots in Design and Set up of MBO System	Remedies
MBO for only a few. MBO practiced only by some members of the organization, others in the organization may not be convinced of its value. Lack of total system owing to lack of top management support, scattered nature of organization, strong use of traditional management, or omission of staff personnel.	Allow partial practice of MBO, results being shared with others in the organization. Allow for gradual joining together of other parts of organization. Many organizations have started MBO in one area and gradually worked it into total system.
Inadequate top management support for MBO. Tough management with die-hard traditional approach to managing unwilling to experiment with MBO.	Philosophy of MBO must be understood. Distribute among top managers articles, studies, case histories, and books that deal with systems approach to strategy and need for total management involvement and support. Carefully select project that can be set up as objective program. Get agreement from management to implement project using MBO approach. Report results of project and contrast advantages and disadvantages with traditional way. Allow completion of project to be point of influence to persuade others. In most companies that use MBO successfully, chief executive officer and senior managers completely support its use.
MBO inadequately explained. MBO techniques emphasized over philosophy and meaning. Some have gone far to left with techniques, methods, and procedures.	MBO must be properly explained. Some techniques and methods are necessary for practical implementation of concept. Danger lies in using someone else's techniques

Trouble Spots in Design and Set up of MBO System	Remedies
Stress is on working procedures rather than areas of responsibility.	and methods. Good techniques, methods, and procedures are developed for unique factors of organization. MBO philosophy common to all organizations is results planning through participation, doing and appraising, and evaluating for correcting and improving. Stress must be on areas of responsibilities and expectations. Good MBO training is must!
MBO limited in the organization. Supervisors' and subordinates' MBO packages not interlocked with department or with whole enterprise.	General guidelines should start at top with chief executive officer and filter down to bottom. Lower levels of management then create MBO plans for reaching top-level specified guidelines. System is created when agreed MBO package of supervisor and subordinate is moved up to higher levels, each package being integrated to these levels.
MBO is a "paper dragon." MBO involves substantial paperwork and red tape. It can become giant paper-shuffling exercise.	Some paperwork must be tolerated. Keeping number of objectives to critical few necessary for performance stretches and quantum jumps will keep paperwork requirements to minimum. Paperwork shortcuts develop with experience and knowledge of system.
MBO process difficult to start. Deciding on entry points from which to begin MBO process can be difficult.	First enumerate clearly many entry points possible for organization: (a) five-year profit plan; (b) top-down bottom-up system or bottom-up top-down system; (c) common-objective approach, such as cost reduction; (d) performance-appraisal approach; (e) job-descriptions approach. Carefully assess which entry points, either single or in combination, are most likely to set down roots for objective-setting process. Outside consultant can help.

Trouble Spots in Design and Set up of MBO System	Remedies

MBO is as old as management itself. Many say that setting objectives is not new. The technique has been around since the pyramids, so what is it all about now?

Management does in one way or another set goals and attain them. What is particularly important, however, is style of management used in process. Conventional goal-setting approach used in industry for years is someone in higher management position setting certain goals, telling people what these goals are, and then by directing and controlling seeing that they are accomplished. This method is quite different from giving individuals opportunity to use initiative and originality in determining what they themselves consider their responsibilities, measures of fulfillment, and improvements to be attained. Final department objectives will be of better quality when they are synthesis of participation of many individuals.

MBO takes too long to reach organizational effectiveness. Why can't I get results within six months?

Some can, if certain factors of management normally exist in firm. These firms are few. Most have to build climate and process necessary for MBO. This can take anywhere from 1 to 5 years. System never finishes, since changes are continually being made. Designing MBO system for results has two features: creation of system and benefits derived from system. First is usually shortchanged to get benefits of second. Concentrate on first and second will come in time.

MBO is restricted. Difficult to get older persons who have been disillusioned by new programs in the past to become involved, participate in, and accept objective-setting processes.

Reduce resistance and reluctance to participate by: (a) Developing climate: Circulate MBO literature, books, magazines; use company newspaper; circulate successful company cases; hold special presentations on MBO. (b) Provide

Trouble Spots in Design and Set up of MBO System	Remedies
	knowledge and understanding of MBO through training programs, seminars, consultants, company MBO manual, and books. (c) Use certain people to set examples. Have president teach approach to others; hire experienced MBO practitioners as advisors; use managers who show leadership qualities for coaching and persuading. (d) Involve personnel: Allow experimentation and trial of MBO with special projects that pose no great difficulty; allow personnel to try it alone with good coaching.
MBO should be cure for all ills, but it isn't.	MBO is *not* a cure for all organizational problems. It is not simply a "plug it in and it works" process. Thinking that MBO is only process for total organization is oversimplification. MBO centers on planning, doing, and evaluating. But other processes also need to be handled in context of state of the art, such as inventories, hiring, quality control, budgeting, market research, and engineering design.

Trouble Spots in Objective Setting	Remedies
Objectives set too low. Expected results are so low that benefits do not justify expenditure of effort and resources for MBO.	Estimate cost of reaching objectives and compare with benefits to be accrued. If benefits are not greater than costs, objective level must be raised for better results. MBO must exact performance stretch from all employees in its generic emission of improvement.
Objectives set too high. Managers have normal temptation to get as much as they can from subordinates. They force unrealistic performance stretches on subordinates.	Overchallenge and underchallenge are both poor managerial practices. Previous results should be used as basis of start of MBO cycle. Performance standards also help. From

Trouble Spots in Objective Setting	Remedies
	that starting point, levels of contributions can be increased as skill and experience are developed with MBO. Whatever approach is used, subordinate must agree and feel comfortable on challenge agreed to.
Objectives set as activities. Objectives written in terms of work activities rather than in terms of work results.	Set up training programs and workshop seminars for practice in writing objectives as results rather than as activities. Develop manual that illustrates sample objectives similar to company needs. Show how validation procedure can evaluate wording of objective statement.
Objective setting difficult for staff. Staff work is to support line personnel. Their mission is to support doers. Difficult if not impossible to isolate this process.	Set objectives for staff personnel in "line context," and share score of results with them. Line and staff objectives should be jointly set.
Too many objectives. My department has one major objective. Why try for more?	Deciding there is only one major task to be accomplished is not managerial. Besides, no major task is accomplished optimally without maintenance of balance among related responsibilities. Objectives are set for each responsibility to be certain balance is attained. For example, insurance company has for its objective certain volume of insurance. But it also needs objectives to support this—marketing, finance, customer services, hiring and training, and cost control.
Objectives are set in "concrete." Firm fails to switch to more profitable objective and is inflexible when more attractive targets emerge.	MBO is neither inflexible nor flexible. It is what manager wants it to be. Practice of milestones of progress allows for change of objectives when others are preferred. Change must be done formally and carefully.
Objectives are set in writing. Targets to be completed should be	Writing eliminates misunderstanding. A written MBO package be-

Trouble Spots in Objective Setting	Remedies
held in a person's head; they do not need to be written down.	comes document of person's performance and evaluation, allows for future reference, and is indispensable for coordination and control.
Objectives set in a group.	Group objective setting is new practice that is workable. Japanese do it all the time. Once group objective is set, responsibility assignments can be made on individual basis. These individual responsibilities can be put into objectives.
Objectives set with few or wrong priorities. Difficulty in determining priority with a multiplicity of possible objectives, or priorities not set correctly.	Key principles in practice of MBO are those of focus and priority. Practice of MBO demands ability to focus on critical and pursue high priorities. MBO in its conceptual process is priority assessment, decision-making activity. Use decision matrix with payoff to find critical needs with high priority. Try to get consensus.
Objectives are too risky. Desirable objective is too risky and uncertain if pursued.	Objective statement does not normally have risk factor. But there is no reason why it shouldn't. Risk is high when uncertainty and low confidence prevail. Develop risk factor in probability or percentage and assign it to objective statement. Other methods of risk factor determination are decision trees, statistical histories, group consensus, and extrapolation from other sources.
Objectives set without participation. Employee participation is meaningless and not real commitment. Managers refuse to delegate authority or to open up process that allows employees to participate. Managers ignore proposed goals or ideas of subordinates.	Create atmosphere that allows employees to take active role in preliminary phases of decision making. Identify and clarify areas of accountability between objectives set and responsibilities of job. Build motivators into areas of accountability. Allowing employ-

Trouble Spots in Objective Setting	Remedies

ees to participate in decisions that affect their work is central idea in MBO.

Objectives are set without measures. Quantification of targeted objectives difficult. Targets written as traits or duties that merely sound like targets. Indicators difficult to find.

Writing good objectives with measurable indicators is skill developed through training and practice. Performance in every job can and must be measured! Skill can be developed in training programs, workshops, seminars, and staff coaching. Special examples can be formulated as guide for those needing special help. Indicators serve important purposes: (a) clarify job requirements, (b) specify performance standard, (c) indicate when work is completed, (d) basis for controls and evaluation, and (e) point out conditions to be improved. This does not mean that everything must be quantified. In some instances quantification is neither possible nor desirable, such as morale development and improvement.

Objective setting takes too long. Objective setting processes are time consuming and must be done after hours.

Objective setting is not extra work. It is part of person's job to plan ahead, make improvements, and set deadlines. Time must be found during regular hours. Lack of time may be result of practitioner's setting objectives over too wide a range of job responsibilities. Chief value of MBO is focus and concentration on three or four areas most critical to company. Beginner at using strategy should crawl before running.

Objectives set are uncoordinated. Independent objective setting by different departments results in objectives that are overlapping, conflicting, and out of sequence.

Use validation process to bring about coordination. Validity starts with involving individuals who participate in accomplishing objectives. Go through problem co-

Trouble Spots in Objective Setting	Remedies
	ordination analysis to identify difficulties of coordination. Focus on coordination of objectives at interfaces of organization. Sending coordination guidelines to chief executive officer before objectives are set will avoid most problems.
Setting objectives for creative people is difficult. Objective setting does not fit in with highly specialized and creative technical work.	Objective setting fits into any kind of work where "package" of results is expected from work activities. Claims that specialized creative situation cannot be results oriented is not true; situation needs to be reorganized and redefined in terms of getting results. Often redefinition should be shifted to individual rather than department or, conversely, from individual to team or project. Objective-setting process is applicable to areas of responsible creativity. Any R&D effort is intended to support company wide effort to gain new or improved products and services for consumer markets. Responsible creativity is only justification for R&D organizations. Objective-setting process is attainable under these conditions.

Trouble Spots in Implementing MBO	Remedies
Continued implementation when change is needed. Persistent pursuit of targeted objectives when a change or desist is indicated or mandated. Change is probably caused by major problem or major opportunity.	Cease implementing objectives when unexpected changes render existing objectives unfeasible, irrelevant, or impossible. Select alternatives or contingencies from prior analysis and develop "mini MBO" plan for remaining period.
Implementation is at expense of routine work. Overemphasis on achieving targeted objectives at	Targeted objectives must be significant, critical, and high in priority. Keep number of these objectives at

Trouble Spots in Implementing MBO	Remedies
expense of results not specified. Manager ignores very real obstacles which face subordinates, including emergency or routine duties that consume time.	minimum; three to five is normal. Make clear that unanticipated routine work must be completed. Routine work can be set up and written in terms of maintenance objectives or can be handled in traditional way. Manager must allow subordinates time for handling emergency or unexpected time commitments.
Implementation without integration. MBO is a program separate from other management programs.	MBO must be integrated with other management practices of organization. Interwoven with MBO must be planning, budgeting, communicating, productivity, quality, appraising, controlling, and rewarding.
Implementation is too fast. There is unfair acceleration of targeted objectives even to point of unattainability.	Keep to originally set schedule. Performance stretch should be built into performance plan at start of MBO cycle and not during cycle. Hold frequent progress meetings and gear to realistic schedule.
Implementation is difficult with supervisors. Implementation of MBO difficult at lower organizational levels.	Philosophy of MBO must be provided to first-line supervisors before strategy and technique. They must see and understand MBO as managerial way of life. Training programs, seminars, and managerial coaching for first-line supervisor are a must.
Implementation done in ignorance. Objectives have been set and approved. Must there be more? Do we need plans for implementation? Managers fail to think through and act on what they must do to help subordinates succeed.	Setting objectives is laying down navigational course for ship. What is needed next is engine with energy to propel ship to its destination. Implementation of MBO requires action plans, activities, and motivation to get job done. Careful planning and consideration of implementing phase is as important as objective-setting phase. Having objectives but no plans for implementation will lead to failure.

Trouble Spots in Implementing MBO	Remedies
Implementation done without co-ordination. Management people too overloaded with day-to-day production necessities to take time to coordinate with other sections.	Setting objectives is fundamental act of managing. Second to it is establishing necessary coordination needed for reaching objectives. Crisis managing develops when coordination with and confidence in other sections does not exist. Principles for focus, balancing organizations, and interlocking functions should be followed. Ensure that reasonable number of joint objectives exist in every department.
Implementation done without feedback. Achievement-oriented managers need feedback on their performance.	Milestones of progress toward reaching objective should be set up. Variances from progress milestones should be given to managers as feedback targeting.
Implementation done with little motivation. Action toward reaching objectives is at low level, not intensive enough.	Subordinates probably were not involved in objective-setting process and are most likely pursuing manager's personal set of objectives. Get subordinates to feel that commitment of company to MBO is in best interest of individuals. This goes long way in getting them to help with necessary results.
Implementation fails. Formally approved objectives are not attained.	Attaining objectives is important. However, many factors may bring about failure. These factors need to be identified in early phases of MBO installation and eliminated. Those unskilled in MBO will set objectives too high, too risky, uncoordinated, and unsupported. With time, these and other factors will be controlled.

Trouble Spots in Evaluating Results	Remedies
Evaluation reveals MBO failure. Objectives are not attained owing	Failure to attain objectives can provide useful experience and guide-

Trouble Spots in Evaluating Results	Remedies

to circumstances beyond everyone's control.

lines for next round of objective setting. Put greater emphasis on level of attainability and probability of occurrence. Experience with risk factors should provide future guidance. Place greater emphasis on validation of MBO package before pursuing it, if firm is plagued with circumstances beyond everyone's control.

Evaluation with MBO threatens merit appraisal system. Objective performance evaluation will threaten use and value of conventional merit rating system or managerial trait technique or any appraisal system that does not focus on performance contributions.

Objective performance evaluation and merit evaluation serve same purpose. Former emphasizes results, latter emphasizes activities or traits. Merit system will be changed if not eliminated entirely. Some trait evaluation will be retained where it is clearly relevant to manager's ability to get results. Practice of MBO as new strategy will cause impact leading to change in existing practices. Company must be prepared to make these changes.

Evaluation with MBO is fuzzy and delayed. Unable to get feedback of contributions and measurement of progress.

Feedback evaluation under MBO takes five forms. First, expectations are clearly set down in planning period. Individual sees what will be evaluated at some end period. Second, individual observes and knows own performance in relation to what is expected. Third, individual gets periodic reports with evaluations of overall performance from supervisor. Fourth, individual gets coaching, counseling, and appraisal reviews from superiors who have firsthand knowledge from which to assess work. Fifth, individual gets formal annual appraisal that is comprehensive and complete. Any other process is not MBO process.

Trouble Spots in Evaluating Results	Remedies

Evaluation is disjointed. Objectives based on performance appraisal program achiever neither expected results nor management involvement. In most cases there are two evaluation systems: personnel appraisal and company performance.

Most appraisal programs are staff conceived, corporate wide, and personnel oriented. As such, they never become significant part of line managerial process or managerial evaluation of company performance. Instead of administrating MBO program from staff department, decentralize its administration among various line departments. Make it clear MBO evaluation is for all types of evaluating concerns.

Evaluation with MBO is a merit checklist. Listing objectives and results achieved is checklist merit rating form.

Companies that have had merit appraisal systems have difficulty with them. The most recent findings of behavioral science research substantiate this difficulty. Weaknesses of conventional merit rating are: (a) Personality factors and work habits are used, rather than results. Individuals differ considerably in personality and ways of doing things. What is important is end result. This does not mean that factor such as lack of tact is not important. It is, but not only because it interfers with attainment of desired results such as increased productivity, acceptance of change, and low absence and turnover. (b) Merit rating interview is usually held at time far removed from specific incident of work performance. (c) It is negative approach. Weaknesses are emphasized, rather than plan of action to obtain certain results. (d) It doesn't motivate to improved performance because conclusions are too subjective and general. Merit rating is technique for letting people know how they are doing and is guide for determin-

Trouble Spots in Evaluating Results	Remedies
	ing salary increases and promotions. Objectives serve same purpose. Significant difference is they are philosophy of management that emphasizes specific results; they are not a technique.
Evaluation misses potential to perform. Evaluation is for actual performance, but how can we appraise potential in the process?	In analyzing specific accomplishments and contributions, judge whether they were accomplished in shorter time than required or beyond targets or whether many secondary or incidental accomplishments were made along with main targets. Best way to judge potential, however, is to allow individuals to "tackle" new, complex, and challenging responsibilities never before tried.
Evaluation of results too far in future. Time span in which objectives are to be achieved is too long to give feeling of progress and contribution. Manager fails to set intermediate target dates by which to measure progress for subordinates.	Bridge long-range objectives by creating short-range milestones of progress. Each milestone meets target date than contributes toward ultimate set of results. Milestones give important progress feedback. If still shorter periods are needed, practice "mini MBO." These are three- to six-month MBO packages.

Companies that have been successful with the MBO strategy and have overcome trouble spots have done so because their supervisors and managers were not only familiar with the strategy's rationale and procedure, but also were willing to put forth the effort and time needed to make it work.

COMPENSATION WITH MBO

Many elements affect a company's productivity. Two stand out the most: goal setting and compensation. Stated in historic terms, these are "pay for performance" and "performance sets the pay." To link compensation administration with goal setting is to link pay with performance, which links performance to productivity. There are advantages and disadvantages to this linking.

Advantages. Provides incentives for effort; relates results to rewards; provides more objective judgments; provides comparison between people; meets uniform guidelines for Equal Employment Opportunity (EEO); forces communications about effort and compensation; is easily accepted; shows people how they can earn more money; creates a competitive atmosphere; provides a self-evaluation process.

Disadvantages. Uncontrollable factors that affect individuals are difficult to isolate; allows game playing; considers only measurable aspects of job; is costly to install; conflicts with traditional appraisal system; may cloud intrinsic satisfaction; allows people to lose out; reduces risk taking; may create too much competition.

The summing up and "bottom line" of these advantages and disadvantages must be made by each organization. Conditions can be set up to minimize the effects of each of the disadvantages. This does not mean MBO is to be geared up to compensation strictly for results regardless of other factors and influences. MBO practitioners must understand the many factors, internal and external, that can influence compensation. Several were cited earlier, such as competitive conditions, product maturation, cash flow, debt equity, and marketplace pay. However, MBO should be geared closely to compensation. MBO connects results and the rewards for producing results. There is little that demotives managers and employees more than not being rewarded for their contributions. No management system is effective if high levels of performance are expected without rewards or recognition. Rewards must be connected to performance. Higher performance means higher rewards. Lower performance means lower rewards. MBO clarifies and aids the judgment as to who gets the higher rewards and who gets the lower ones. Some5anies that practice MBO and are well aware of this principle find their managers juggling the goals and challenge levels to justify pay increases. The practice of MBO demands documentation of past performance levels and challenges. These written records validate performance stretches and the degree of success in achieving these stretches. "Game players" can be noted by comparing present levels with past levels. It is reasonable to expect that a 5 to 15 percent performance stretch can be reached in each successive MBO cycle.

The MBO process helps to improve productivity in at least four ways. This makes it easier to pay for performance.

1. MBO is highly disciplined and thus forces consideration and evaluation on a time schedule, good and bad performance being determined in terms of results obtained or not obtained.

2. MBO is a reinforcement-of-behavior process. It motivates better employees through reinforcement of high performance. It identifies low performers so that corrective action can be taken.

3.   MBO is an open system and thus assures fairness. The system requires that supervisors manage their subordinates and people openly in matters regarding pay for performance. This eliminates prejudice and other personal discrimination practices.

4.   MBO is a cost controller. This has the highest impact on labor productivity. MBO ensures that compensation dollars are paid for actual results produced.

Many compensation systems are based on the premise that employees who are compensated equally are also compensated equitably. These systems ignore individual differences and contributions. If performance is different, compensation must be different and therefore unequal. The following guidelines help connect compensation to performance vis-a-vis MBO.

1.   *Compensation Starts with Planning.*   Compensation is a subsystem in the total system of an organization. Planning for compensation must be connected with planning for performance. Compatibility between the two starts with compatibility between the plans for the two. Compensation planning must link with the company's business plan. Here is where many compensation systems fail. There is no link between business planning and rewards for the performance that implements the business plan.

2.   *Compensation Must Center on Job Objectives.*   The practice of writing descriptions of jobs in organizations has been a part of compensation administration for many years. The descriptions state the duties and responsibilities the employee is expected to complete. In the MBO process of job performance planning, job descriptions become job objectives. The differences between the two are shown in Table 11.1.

3.   *Compensation Is Equal for Equal Work.*   Compensation ranges are designed and used to clarify and reinforce performance. The top third of the range is reserved for outstanding performance. This level covers the best performance that can possibly be expected of an employee on a job. The

TABLE 11.1   Differences Between Job Descriptions and Job Objectives

Job Descriptions	Job Objectives
Written in general terms	Written in specific terms
Describe activities	Describe performance expectations
List responsibilities	Give performance level (standard) in each responsibility
Closed to employee participation	Open to employee participation
Long term and often obsolete	Annual and kept up to date
Difficult to measure	Measures built in
Linked to pay ranges	Linked to pay ranges, job performance, and business plan implementation

employee goes beyond what is expected by the supervisor. The middle third of the range covers performance that meets job requirements completely satisfactorily to the supervisor. The bottom third is designated for minimally qualified performance expected by the supervisor. Employees at this level are doing the job satisfactorily but need supervision for direction and correction. An employee in this category is barely adequate. If the MBO system takes hold in the organization so that performance improvement is an annual expected event, employees in this third category must either improve or be terminated. The match between job expectations and job performance becomes critical.

Paying for the job while ignoring performance is a cause of great mismatching and results in productivity decline. Paying for performance while ignoring the requirements of the job is another cause of mismatching. On a given job it is not unusual for one employee to produce one quarter more or one half less than another, while both receive the same pay. It is also not unusual for the employer to underpay employees who improve their productivity. Real productivity gains occur when those who do the most get the most pay, when earnings and benefits are directly connected to individual output. Marion Kellogg, in her book on performance appraisals, says of this:

> The problem for the manager lies in the fact that he is expected to get results, to make certain defined contributions to the organization. But he is not expected to do this at all costs. And so his money resources must be carefully and skillfully handled as other resources. But the key to his achieving needed results is the employee who, by his ingenuity and commitment, produces these results. If the employee is to give his best, he must feel he is being fairly treated. If the manager is to live up to his own principles, he also has a need to feel that he is treating the employee fairly.

Table 11.2 illustrates how pay should follow the amount of contribution.

TABLE 11.2   Objectives Completion Pay Rating Scale

	Performance[a] Level in Percent				
	Low	Below Average	Average	Above Average	Outstanding
Percentage of prime objectives completed	60	80	100	Quality point one 150	Quality point two 200
Percentage merit pay increase	0	2	4	6	8
General increase (across the board)	2	2	2	2	2
Total percent pay increase[b]	2	4	6	8	10

[a]Performance that falls between ratings must be interpolated.
[b]Total pay increase in percent = merit pay income in percent + general increase in percentage.

4. *Compensation Increases Vary in Size and Frequency.* Most organizations vary the percentage of increase for performance but keep the frequency of increases constant. The frequency may be annual, on the anniversary date, or during the budget review period. Other organizations keep the percentage of increase constant but vary the frequency. The practice of varying both size and frequency gives the manager the flexibility of rewarding performance in a realistic context. That is, performance level and results both vary, and compensation should be in phase with performance. The supervisor is in the best position to do this effective job of paying for performance.

5. *Compensation Does Affect Behavior.* Subordinates who think or know they are underpaid will behave as if they are underpaid. In many cases, underpaid employees will not reach for performance stretch. The compensation system must be administered to pay people fairly. This may be the basis of leverage for higher levels of contributions. Most employees feel, rightly or wrongly, that success is measured by the annual paycheck. If the paycheck is small, the feeling of success and fulfillment is damaged.

6. *Compensation Should Be Adjusted for Different Performance Leads.* A merit increase is a salary adjustment within a pay range intended to reward performance contributions during the prior evaluation period. A merit increase should be consistent with the definition of the different performance levels. The most important way of determining compliance with these performance levels is examination of evidence. MBO provides the evidence through performance planning and results with its periodic reviews and final evaluation. The evidence is amount of results, level of results, timing of results, problems experienced with results, and novelty of results.

To sum up, MBO is compatible with the standard compensation tools and techniques. It simply needs to be tied into the system. Once this is done, all personnel can be educated on how the system works.

DEVELOPING MBO PRACTITIONERS THROUGH DOING

Training for MBO must focus on the work a manager performs on the job. There may be programs and procedures that contribute to turning out managers who can use the MBO strategy skillfully. At best, these programs only guide the development of this unique skill. A down-to-earth practical approach focuses on the managerial responsibilities carried out from day to day. Individuals who are to be trained must practice the MBO strategy in their own job without external pressures and influences. They can be encouraged to develop themselves through absorption in the strategy and its challenge that calls forth their best effort.

Top management, of course, must encourage this approach by its participation and use of the MBO skill. The emphasis in this approach is on the individual rather than on a group, as in a formal training context. It must be kept in mind that MBO is intended basically to get improvements on the job. Thus on-the-job development and training should be the focus. Marion Kellogg considered this idea as building development into the work itself. Individuals should be allowed to structure delegated assignments in an objective approach. In other words, the individual, when first asked to complete a project, should be allowed to set targets for the project, relate the targets to existing commitments, and proceed to validate and organize precisely for implementation. This process encourages careful analysis of activities, authority, and the work situation to predict accomplishment of the assignment within a specified period of time.

A perfect way to train people to manage by objectives has not yet been found, and probably never will be. Success in many companies, however, seems to result from the following general pattern:

1.   Find the way in which MBO works in the company and do more of it! Focus the strategy on the areas of the company's greatest need. Share with others knowledge of how MBO will fill this need.

2.   Give on-the-job training in the skills with the focus on practicing the strategy at all times to get results. People learn best by doing work and getting results. The methods employed should involve trainees in doing as much of the work themselves as possible.

3.   Develop a guideline manual that sets forth procedures for a systematic approach to the strategy. Include specific examples from within the organization, also include policy guidelines and proven practices.

4.   Do not allow training to be formalized as only a behavioral activity. The soundest approach is to put MBO in a line context for a balanced way of managing. Some departments tend to emphasize the behavioral and human dimensions of the strategy at the expense of the technical, economic, and functional requirements.

5.   Establish through policies and examples that MBO is a way of life. Managers and supervisors develop confidence in its use when they see their supervisor as well as the company's president performing in the same fashion.

6.   Select and hire individuals who have practiced the strategy in other companies successfully and can wield influence and provide information within the natural work setting. These individuals can be demonstrators of the technique and coaches for those who need help.

7.   Key the training of MBO on an individual basis. This means individuals must want to develop the skill. They will ask for needed assistance because they see the value of MBO for themselves and for the company. External pressures and influences should not force them into it.

Without doubt the most effective training for MBO is built into daily on-the-job experience—experience that can vary in type and level to stretch the individual to new levels of achievement. A training program, however, should complement the critical on-the-job implementing experience. Training programs, are most useful in providing simulation, influencing attitudes, and imparting knowledge. Open resistance and antagonism MBO can be brought out into the open. Real understanding of the philosophy of MBO can be acquired during dialogue and discussion. Trainees can be informed about the potential benefits of using MBO, the problems associated with its use, how to overcome these problems, and techniques for applying the strategy. Through open discussion of the difficulties of MBO in the training program, its implementation in the organization can avoid a bad start. Employees can acquire specific skills in the training program or in workshop seminars. The first and most obvious of these skills is the ability to write a formal statement of objectives.

It was pointed out in an earlier chapter that considerable skill is required to set formal statements of objectives. They must undergo several proceses, the last of which is validation. A considerable investment in time is necessary to obtain required commitments of people and resources. Although this investment is advantageous in terms of the potential benefits that can be derived from it, some will not see its worth. These same individuals will attempt to practice MBO informally and individually, thus eliminating the total management approach and management system that needs to be created. *Managing by objectives cannot be carried out in an informal way! To provide the best results and the greatest benefits, it must be carried out with formalized processes of relating, involvement, and commitment.* Extensive training that provides practitioners with a thorough knowledge of MBO processes and that is aligned with on-the-job development and practice will truly give the specific skills necessary to practice MBO as a managerial way of life.

SKILLS FOR MBO

The function of any skill is to make possible application of knowledge and understanding for innovation or solving of problems. Skill is the ability to apply knowledge effectively and readily in the performance of a particular physical or mental task. Knowledge alone does not make the skill; what makes it is how the knowledge is used in a variety of complex applications. The MBO practitioner will apply knowledge with varying degrees of competence and proficiency. Use of the skill is in many ways a measurement of the use of knowledge. For the MBO practitioner, the acquisition of knowledge and understanding about MBO is essential if the skills appropriate for its use are to be developed. Knowledge is defined here as stockpiles of valid information organized from past experiences and applied to specific problems. The following six general categories of skills appear to be the basis from which specific and specialized skills of MBO emerge:

1. *Technical Skill.* This skill involves the proficient use of knowledge in specific disciplines. This is the specialized information, methods, processes,

procedures, and techniques involved in the technology of the product or services of the company or industry.

2. *Behavioral Skill.* This skill is primarily the utilization of knowledge and understanding of people as they conduct themselves with others. Understanding promotes working with others cooperatively and effectively as a natural and continuous activity. It requires awareness of attitudes and beliefs held by individuals and groups and how these govern their goal-reaching processes.

3. *Conceptual Skill.* This skill is the ability to utilize existing knowledge to perceive additional knowledge. It is purposeful risk taking for creating new conditions. Exploration, questioning, and probing are tools that cut across established areas of a business. Conceptual skill is interdisciplinary, since it involves the ways in which various functions of systems depend on other systems as well as the ways changes in any one part affect all the others.

4. *Implementing Skill.* This skill involves the ability to get work done on a day-to-day, program-to-program basis, or the ability to concentrate just enough resources of time, money, and effort to initiate what has to be done, conduct the activity, and bring it to a successful end. Achievement and accomplishments are the measurements of this skill.

5. *Economic-Business Skill.* This skill is the utilization of knowledge and understanding of the business enterprise as a firm operating in a market for the sale of goods and services. It involves the manner in which the enterprise uses scarce and limited resources to meet changing and unpredictable demands. It involves the strategy of production, distribution, and consumption of goods and services with maximization of output and minimization of input.

6. *Managerial Skill.* This skill is the effective utilization of general management information, specific knowledge, and proven practices in the planning, directing, and controlling of a business enterprise toward profit and perpetuation. It involves the organization and strategies of people, facilities, resources, and money for selling products and services within the limits of costs, quality, and time.

The separation of these six broad skill areas is only useful for purposes of analysis and discussion. In practice, these areas are so closely interrelated that it is difficult to determine where one ends and another begins. We receive some benefit from examining each of them separately in spite of their interrelatedness. The capable practitioner of MBO is more a generalist than a specialist, since he or she deals with segments of the skills from each of the six broad areas, as illustrated in Figure 11.2. The practitioner cannot know everything in each of the six areas, yet must have the insight and perception to extract from each the degree of the skill that is needed to achieve results. As defined earlier, a skill is the effective utilization of knowledge. The practitioner must be alert to the generation of new knowledge in each of the

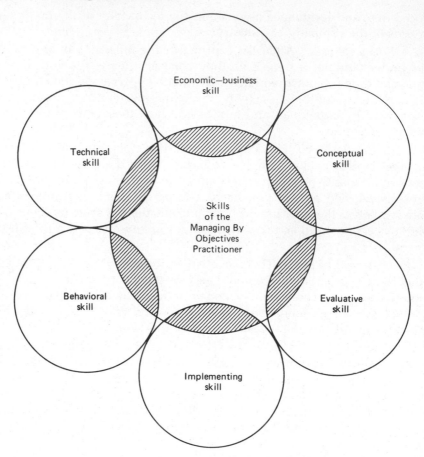

FIGURE 11.2   The MBO practitioner is a generalist.

six categories and assess the manner in which he or she can exploit it to improve the specific nature of the practice of MBO.

The identification of the specific skills of successful MBO practitioners has been difficult because of the extreme complexity of the strategy as a managerial way of life. Tests and measuring techniques have not always been adequate. Different situations call for different managerial life-styles, which in turn require different skills and characteristics. No single set of specific skills exists, since some situations require one set of skills while other situations require another. Thus we cannot expect to generalize from one situation to another. On the other hand, there appears to be a core or common body of specific skills extracted from the six broad areas that, once acquired and developed, can lead to successful practice of MBO. These specific skills are as follows:

1. *Objective-Setting Skills.*
   (a) Ability to generate alternatives or improvements from present and past experiences.
   (b) Ability to estimate likelihoods from present experiences.
   (c) Ability to predict and project concerns and desires.
   (d) Ability to sense and forecast trends.
   (e) Ability to perceive where improvements can be made in everyday experiences, even those not normally in one's province of thinking.
   (f) Ability to predict ends from certain beginnings even without orientation.
   (g) Ability to see the whole from given constituent parts.
   (h) Ability to sense and make use of pace, sequence, and time.
   (i) Ability to sense and forecast an accomplishment at a point in time.
   (j) Ability to shift simple patterns from complex ones.
   (k) Ability to focus on the critical and separate out the trivial.

2. *Implementing Objectives Skills.*
   (a) Ability to work at a task to completion with intensified drive.
   (b) Ability to sense people's needs and drives and relate them to planned accomplishments.
   (c) Ability to foresee barriers and pursue circumventing steps.
   (d) Ability to fit people into proper work assignments.
   (e) Ability to gain rapport and response from people.
   (f) Ability to compromise and gain consensus.
   (g) Ability to articulate and persuade hostile and competing groups.
   (h) Ability to empathize with company life-styles.
   (i) Ability to convey information with clarity.
   (j) Ability to coordinate various "power" groups.
   (k) Ability to move ahead in the face of risk, uncertainty, and unknowns.
   (l) Ability to align, dovetail, and connect two or more directions.

3. *Measuring and Correcting Skills.*
   (a) Ability to measure parts as progression toward wholes.
   (b) Ability to analyze a complex mass of information into numerics and quantification.
   (c) Ability to find measures of central tendencies.

    (d)   Ability to measure deviation, variation, and drift from prescribed directions.

    (e)   Ability to sense progress with sampling indicators on a time spectrum.

    (f)   Ability to initiate feedback corrections or reduce variance.

    (g)   Ability to break down a complex situation into its component parts.

    (h)   Ability to collect relevant information from probing, questioning, and observing.

    (i)   Ability to schedule interwoven and simultaneous projects.

    (j)   Ability to form judgments and determine trends from statistical data.

Formal education is neither an exclusive nor a completely sufficient method for providing these specific skills to the practitioner of MBO. Neither completion of some level of formal education nor work within a specific discipline signifies preparation for MBO practice. At best, this sort of education signifies a breadth and depth of knowledge acquired during a preparatory stage. This forms the basis from which skills can develop. Historically, skills have been acquired and developed through experience on the job. Formal education provides a basis for efficient transmittal of information and knowledge. On-the-job experience is the skill's development process for utilization of knowledge in problem applications.

MBO DIAGNOSTIC TEST

Aptitude testing, in general, is used to assess individuals' natural propensities to develop the skills needed to accomplish a task. Aptitude testing is not a science. Its validity is primarily a statistical correlation between two groups: those known to have the skills and those to be measured for propensity to have the skills.

    The MBO aptitude test has been given to 2200 managers and supervisors known to be successful in the application of MBO in their work processes. In validating the test, a correlation greater than .80 was achieved between performance on the test and a third-party evaluation of successful performance on the job.

    The MBO diagnostic test (Figure 11.3) is for predicting successful use of MBO. It is based on the three fundamental skills described in the previous section: objective-setting skills (OSS); implementing objectives skills (IOS); and measuring and correcting skills (MCS).

OSS 1. "Work fills the time set down for its completion." This means:
1 work is satsifying   2 work is elastic   3 work is controllable
4 work is measurable
_____

IOS 2. Which is the stronger emotion?
1 hope for wealth   2 fear of poverty
_____

MCS 3. Profit is an effect rather than a cause.
1 true   2 false   3 uncertain
_____

OSS 4. Task A has a risk factor of 80 percent. Task B has a risk factor
of 80 percent. What is the combined risk of tasks A and B when done
together?
_____

IOS 5. Greatest results occur in an organization when:
1 supervisor defines goals and delegates to subordinates.
2 subordinate defines goals and supervisor supports him.
3 both define mutual goals, with weight given to supervisor.
4 both define mutual goals, with weight given to subordinate.
_____

MCS 6. A management job to be done was exactly on time at noon
on Monday. At 8 P.M. on Tuesday, it was 32 units behind.
At the same rate, how many units are lost in ½ hour?
_____

OSS 7. Mediocrity is a performance output that is:
1 unacceptable   2 acceptable   3 mostly unacceptable,
partly acceptable   4 mostly acceptable, partly unacceptable
_____

IOS 8. Which pressure is apt to be more urgent?
1 lowering costs   2 raising profits   3 meeting schedules
4 better morale   5 reducing turnover
_____

MCS 9. Count each N in this series that is followed by an O if the
O is not followed by a T.
NONTQMNOTMONOONQMNNOQNOTONMONOM

OSS 10. How may complete squares are
there in the adjacent figure?

_____

IOS 11. Work is routine and even boring at the ABC Automation Company.
What approach would you use to motivate employees:
1 give more breaks and longer lunch hour.
2 offer financial promotion incentives.
3 redesign for job enlargement.
4 give the big picture and show how they fit in.
_____

MCS 12. What events must be completed before event 7 can be completed:

_____

FIGURE 11.3 MBO diagnostic test.

OSS 13. Which group does not belong?
          1 GNFM   2 LKSR   3 WVHG   4 DCYX

IOS 14. Supply the missing step in progressive discipline:
          1 verbal warning   2 _____
          3 layoff   4 discharge

MCS 15. In which of the three companies can improvements most likely
          be made from their record of rejection rates of machined parts?
          A 122331   B 124311   C 212322

OSS 16. Which terminal event is most likely to occur?

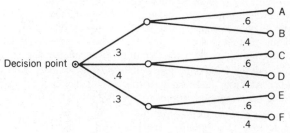

IOS 17. Joe Harris unknowingly contributes to delays in meeting
          schedules. The best approach to reduce delays is:
          1 automate wherever possible.
          2 use modern scheduling techniques such as PERT.
          3 allow participation in scheduling planning.
          4 discuss possible loss of job if delays continue.

MCS 18. A certain inspector has been instructed to keep a tally of the
          color of freezer door panels. After the data were collected, it
          was learned that the inspector is color blind and recognized pink
          as green. The resulting data would lack:
          1 validity   2 reliability   3 accuracy   4 precision

OSS 19. One number in the following series is wrong. What should
          the number be?

                    1 4 2 5 3 6 4 7 5 9 6 9

IOS 20. Which goal-seeking chart will generate the greatest motivational
          intensity toward target T?

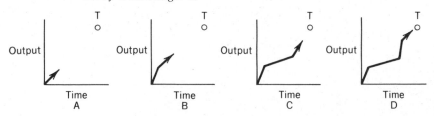

MCS 21. Eighty percent of mass aggregate effects are usually derived
          from ____ percent of smaller dominant causes.

OSS 22. Greatest results occur when coordinated efforts are
          accomplished through:
          1 the president   2 job descriptions   3 a profit plan
          4 contracts

FIGURE 11.3 (continued)

496

IOS 23. The most effective means to align and dovetail management's effort in various levels is by:
1 matching personalities   2 issuing president's directives
3 interlocking objectives   4 selecting people to a team   _____

MCS 24. At what point can managerial improvement most easily be accomplished?

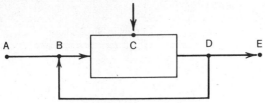

_____

OSS 25. Which group does not belong?
1 KABL   2 MCND   3 DRSE   4 TGHU   _____

IOS 26. To motivate an employee at the top of a pay scale with no prospect of a merit increase, the following can be used:
1 change the merit rating and salary structure.
2 transfer to a higher classification.
3 develop and give experiences for leadership.
4 make up for it with time off.   _____

MCS 27. Where on the matrix does a supervisor fall when his or her decision favors production 75 percent of the time and people 25 percent of the time?

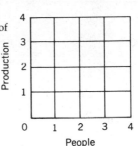

_____

OSS 28. What is the next letter? j k l g h i d e f   _____

IOS 29. A supervisor who is influenced in making a decision by preconceived opinions is said to be:
1 influential   2 impartial   3 stubborn   4 prejudiced   _____

MCS 30. How many of the five pairs are exact doubles?

342	684
1862	3724
25674	51398
100794	201588
4631865	9263730

_____

FIGURE 11.3 (continued)

Name _____ Date _____

Occupation _____

Education (Circle last grade)   7 8 9 10 11 12   13 14 15 16   17 18 19 2X

| | Ele. | H.S. | College | Grad. Sch. |

Degree _____   Major _____

Check One: ____Nonsupervisory   ___Top management

                                                              ___Middle management

              ____Supervisory   Level of Supervision: ___Lower management

---

ANSWER COLUMNS		SCORING

(Write your answers in blank spaces provided)

1.	___ OSS	16.	___ OSS	Total OSS _____
2.	___ IOS	17.	___ IOS	Total IOS _____
3.	___ MCS	18.	___ MCS	Total MCS _____
4.	___ OSS	19.	___ OSS	Total Raw Score OSS ____
5.	___ IOS	20.	___ IOS	NORMS
6.	___ MCS	21.	___ MCS	Total Raw Score Percentile
7.	___ OSS	22.	___ OSS	25−26 99.9
8.	___ IOS	23.	___ IOS	23−24 99
9.	___ MCS	24.	___ MCS	21−22 _____ 98 very high
10.	___ OOS	25.	___ OSS	19−20 95
11.	___ IOS	26.	___ IOS	17−18 _____ 84 high
12.	___ MCS	27.	___ MCS	15−16 70
13.	___ OSS	28.	___ OSS	13−14 60
14.	___ IOS	29.	___ IOS	11−12 50 average
15.	___ MCS	30.	___ MCS	9−10 40
				7−8 30
				5−6 _____ 16 low
				3−4 5
				0−2 _____ 2 very low

Answers to MBO Diagnostic Test

1.	2	OS	16.	C	OS
2.	2	IP	17.	3	IP
3.	1	MF	18.	3	MF
4.	64	OS	19.	8	OS
5.	3	IP	20.	D	IP
6.	½	MF	21.	20	MF

FIGURE 11.3   *(continued)*

7.	4 OS	22.	3 OS
8.	3 IP	23.	3 IP
9.	4 MF	24.	3 MF
10.	40 OS	25.	2 OS
11.	3 IP	26.	3 IP
12.	1,2,3,4,8 MF	27.	MF
13.	1 OS	28.	a OS
14.	written warning IP	29.	4 IP
15.	B MF	30.	4 MF

FIGURE 11.3   *(continued)*

SUMMARY

MBO is not self-taught. The concept seems simple enough to follow, but its complexities and problems emerge when it is to be made workable in an organization. Several reasons are briefly described in this chapter for the gap between theory and practice. They are:

1. Incomplete or imperfect assumptions about the future.
2. Risk factors of future plan unknown.
3. Lack of flexibility in planning.
4. Imperfect information used in decisions.
5. MBO plans not validated.
6. Poor handling of interface ripple effects.
7. Inadequate training of people.
8. No built-in motivators to implement plan.

Several suggestions are made on how to deal with the causes of the gap.

Many companies experience trouble spots, pitfalls, and difficulties as they attempt to make MBO workable. This chapter considers some of these problems and suggests ways to handle them. Each organization must find workable remedies as it develops an MBO system. Issues in making MBO workable are considered, such as linking MBO with compensation and developing the skills most useful to the MBO practitioner. Most MBO failures can be traced directly to ignorance and lack of skills.

BIBLIOGRAPHY

Albrecht, Karl, *Successful Management by Objectives*. Englewood Cliffs, NJ: Prentice-Hall, 1978.

Conley, W. D., and Miller, F. W., "MBO, Pay and Productivity." *Management Review*, May 1980, pp. 26–30.

Drucker, Peter, *Managing in Turbulent Times*. New York: Harper & Row, 1980.

Holsendoph, Ernest, "Think Tanks Have Sprung a Leak." *New York Times*, January 9, 1977.

Kellogg, Marion, S. *Closing the Performance Gap*. New York: American Management Association, 1967.

MacDonald, Charles, R., *MBO Can Work!* New York: McGraw-Hill, 1982.

Porter, Michael E., *Competitive Strategy*. New York: The Free Press, 1980.

"Six Durable Economic Myths." *Wall Street Journal*, September 16, 1975.

PART

4

MBO Applications

A manager who is able to apply MBO in important functions and departments of an organization is a manager who has the MBO philosophy as a lifestyle. Part 4 of this book comprises six chapters. Five deal with the major functions and responsibilities of an enterprise: the business plan; strategic planning; project management; resource management; and performance evaluation. The sixth chapter on Japanese MBO gives the reader insights into contrasts between Japanese and American firms. This potpourri of topics provides a glimpse into how MBO is applied in different areas. The intent here is not depth but rather breadth, to show the total management approach to practicing MBO.

12

THE BUSINESS PLAN WITH MBO

IN THIS CHAPTER

WHAT IS A BUSINESS PLAN?
WHY FORMULATE A BUSINESS PLAN?
ELEMENTS OF THE TOTAL BUSINESS PLAN
HOW IS A BUSINESS PLAN EVALUATED?
WRITING A PERSUASIVE BUSINESS PLAN

There are millions of businesses in the United States. A few are large and most are small, but all are different. Few are extremely successful. Many are profitable; and most are borderline cases. Those that are highly successful work from a business plan of some sort. The business plan may be informal or formal. It may be a direction in the founder's mind alone or it may have a complex set of goals set by the board of directors. It may be an entrepreneur's proposal to a bank for funding and financial help or it may be a comprehensive document of many pages and chapters that took months to formulate. Business plans vary in sophistication. This chapter describes the nature of a business plan, why such a plan should be formulated, and the value it has for the enterprise. "Venturing" is a major understanding in the formulation of a business plan. This chapter explains how MBO defines and gives direction to venturing. A comprehensive outline of a complete business plan is included, with suggested guidelines and formats.

WHAT IS A BUSINESS PLAN?

A business plan is a venture plan, that is, a plan by an enterprise to institute a new project, product, or service, with risk or uncertainty but with the hope of profit. Several terms are synonymous with "business plan." They are "venture plan," "entrepreneurial plan," or simply "business deal." The business plan is the more formal name for this type of document. Business plans are of two types:

1. *Entrepreneurial Type.* The plan is written for outside venture capitalists or for money-lending sources and attempts to convince those moneylenders to invest in or loan money for support of a proposed venture. This type of plan is written by entrepreneurial companies wishing to expand or by entrepreneurs who have an idea or a patent and want to start a new enterprise. This type of plan must be very comprehensive. It must reveal and explain to outsiders the total enterprise—its management, financial position, marketing effort, and any other items necessary to convince that the money lent is a good investment.

Entrepreneurial-type business plans are written for a variety of moneylenders, often called sources of money. Table 12.1 lists some of these.

2. *Intrapreneurial Type.* The plan is written for internal groups, usually top management, to justify budget allocations from limited financial resources for support of a proposed new venture. This type of plan is usually competitive internally. That is, an internal venture group or team competes with other internal venture groups in proposals to top management. The internal business plan is written to persuade top management that the proposed venture should qualify for new venture budgeting, that it will give great profitability to the firm.

TABLE 12.1 Sources of Money

Primary Sources	Secondary Sources
Partner	Pension funds
Family or friends	Customers
Commercial banks	Employees
Savings and loan banks	Equipment manufacturers
Finance companies	Financial consultants
Venture capitalists	Tax-exempt foundations
Small Business Administration	Charitable foundations
Insurance companies	Suppliers
Individual investors	Bank trust departments
Investment syndicates	Veterans Administration
Credit unions	Mutual funds
Corporate financial subsidiaries	Leasing companies
Small business investment corporations	State development commissions

Top management, acting as the money source, will insist that an internal venture group formulate a complete business plan to reveal how the money will be used and the kind of return on investment that can be expected. Internal venture plans are seldom circulated to outside sources. Consequently, they are not as comprehensive as the entrepreneurial plan. They do not have to reveal the total enterprise but merely the elements involved in the proposal.

WHY FORMULATE A BUSINESS PLAN?

There are several reasons for formulating a business plan.

1. To communicate clearly and persuasively to moneylenders and budget allocators the value and attractive return on investment of the proposed venture. Moneylenders and budget allocators are recipients of many business plans. Consequently, the formulated plan must be organized and written to show what the firm or department is trying to accomplish and to convince money sources of the soundness and attractiveness of investment in the enterprise.

2. To enhance the management and leadership of the proposed venture by revealing the quality and sophistication of planning thought and activity. The business plan spells out in detail where the enterprise is currently and, more important, where it is heading. Putting down in a document the products of the enterprise, the innovations, the customer base, its competitive position, its strategies, its organization, and its personnel and financial structure gives outsiders a view of the strengths and weaknesses of the firm. A moneylender or budget allocator wants to know that those given funds know what they are doing, where they are, and where they want to go. MBO aids in this considerably. Incorporation of agreed-on goals, objectives, and strategies into the business plan enhances the thoroughness of the management team that operates in the firm.

3. To provide the basis of performance evaluation. The business plan, once approved, represents expected performance of the venture group or entrepreneurial firm. Measurement of actual performance and its comparison with expected performance gives a basis for managing the venture and working toward its completion. The plan becomes an operating tool from the start of the proposed venture to its completion. Here again MBO aids considerably. The business plan allows for a more careful appraisal of performance for corrective action or for rewards.

4. To provide for coordination of many diverse groups, often needed in a novel, unproven, and uncertain venture. The business plan gives the direction and the results expected with the venture. All support groups view this direction and these results as targets to focus on and complete. Changes, conflicts, inconsistencies, omissions, and incoordination are more readily seen when everyone works with a common plan.

TABLE 12.2 Starting an Enterprise: Overview in Nine Steps

Step	Identify:	What Step Entails
1. Personal analysis	Why—motives Entrepreneurial traits Technical competence Skills and abilities	Persistence Strengths and weaknesses Obligations and commitments Health and energy
2. Opportunity analysis	Identify unfulfilled consumer needs Look for new product development Find business with serious problems to be solved Include:	Examine business that can be managed cheaper Establish business that can advance society and culture Find a business niche in a high-growth area
3. Marketing plan	Marketing potential and demand Forecast sales volume Market test Include:	Competitors' strengths and weaknesses Plan for competitor reactions Plan for competitive edge Promotion and advertisement
4. Financial plan	Fund-raising plan Projected P&L statement Cash-flow analysis Breakeven chart Consider:	Cash budget Expected balance sheet Capital budget Projected ratio analysis
5. Sources of money	Family, friends Commercial banks Savings and loan banks Finance companies Venture capitalists Small Business Administration	Insurance companies Individual buyers or sellers Investment clubs Pension funds Corporate financial subsidiaries Small business investment corporations

6. Management plan — Include:
- Organization and controls — Personnel placement
- Product performance — Equipment and buildings
- Production layout — Compensation
- Site analysis — Training

7. Legal organization — Choose:
- Sole proprietorship — Corporation
- General partnership — Subchapter S corporation
- Limited partnership

8. Timetable — Include:
- Master schedule — Start of operations
- Start of planning — Time of breakeven point
- Start of promotion — Time of expected profit level
- Start of hire and training — Projected peaks and dips

9. Traps that cause failure — Identify:
- Ineffective sales effort — No reserves for lean times
- High operating costs — Low consumer demand
- Unforeseen expenses — Poor location
- Faulty product performance — Competition too strong
- Poor timing — Problems with government regulations
- Undercapitalization — Can't collect receivables

5.   To provide the basis of orientation, education, and development for the many support people needed to implement the plan. These people are seldom involved in the formulation and writing of the plan. They need to be educated on what is happening. Preparation, development of people, and arrangement of resources are needed to implement the plan. The business plan becomes the basis of communicating and educating internally on a new venture that has been launched.

Overall, readers collect impressions from the business plan of how well thought out the proposal is. These readers evaluate if a clear set of steps have been formulated from start to completion of the venture (Table 12.2, on pages 506–507). For example, if the venture is the start of a new enterprise, the business plan must delineate in an overview the start and completion with a timetable (Figure 12.1). This gives the evaluator the overall impression that the formulator of the business plan is competent and knows where he or she is going.

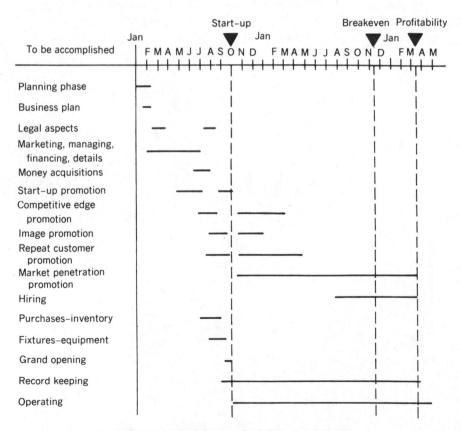

FIGURE 12.1   Start-up schedule for new venture.

ELEMENTS OF THE TOTAL BUSINESS PLAN

The total business plan is a document unique and personal to the enterprise or venture group. Identification of the specific elements and detailed statements of the business plan that would relate effectively and exactly to what is needed by a company is nearly impossible. This section merely provides a comprehensive outline of the elements that make up a total business plan. For a specific venture writers of the plan would select elements that relate to their individual situation.

Section I: Table of Contents

Most business plans are comprehensive. Many require two to four months for formulation and completion. The table of contents gives an overview of the major sections and subsections of the plan. It also gives integration of the entire document for an overall thrust. It affords the reviewer ready access to any part of the proposal for comparative analysis with other plans, which business plan readers and evaluators often do. One of the corporations in the top 25 of the Fortune 500 corporations receives between 50 and 100 business plans per year from companies soliciting acquisition. Here is a typical table of contents for a business plan:

Section I	Table of Contents
Section II	Executive Summary
Section III	Goals and Objectives
Section IV	Organization and Management
Section V	Sales and Marketing
Section VI	Competition
Section VII	Product Research and Development
Section VIII	Operations and Manufacturing
Section IX	Financial
Section X	Conclusions and Statement of Request

Section II: Executive Summary

The executive summary presents, without explanation or descriptions, the highlights of the business plan that are important to those who will evaluate the plan. The highlights presented depend on whether equity is to be sold or long-term debt financing is to be arranged, whether an acquisition is to be made or a new enterprise is to be started. Here are some of the elements possible in an executive summary:

- Brief definition of the business.
- Principal products or services, prices, ranges, and quality.

- Opportunity to be seized and reasons why.
- Diagram, sketch, illustration, or picture of venture innovation.
- Unique features of the opportunity with competition.
- Description of market aimed for or channel to be used.
- Goals and objectives to be reached, financial and nonfinancial, in terms of dollar sales, profit, market share, or growth.
- Anticipated value of selected ratios, such as return on investment, profitability, return on sales, efficiency, value added, or earnings per share.
- Timetable with milestones of progress for starting venture and reaching maturity.
- Factors that favor and that inhibit the venture.
- Strategies to be used in reaching goals and objectives. These include sales, marketing, product development, organization, and financial.
- Checklist of strengths and weaknesses of the firm.
- Statement of what is wanted or needed from the business plan reader and evaluator, such as estimated capital required, new plant facilities, or invitation for merger or acquisition with appropriate schedule.
- Benefits and rewards to be given to investors or supporters of the proposed venture.

A business plan reader and evaluator should be able to get a total perspective for making a decision from the executive summary. Details and supporting data and documents are found in subsequent sections.

Section III: Goals and Objectives

The goals and objectives section presents, with explanation and details, the mission of the company and how the new venture or new opportunity will enhance this mission. It also gives specific objectives that will be achieved within an expected time frame. Here are some of the elements possible in the section on goals and objectives:

- Opportunity assessment analysis and decision.
- Mission of the company, which includes any one or more of the following: Perpetuate the enterprise, increase profit performance, satisfy stockholders, satisfy customers, give directions to the firm for growth, satisfy employees, advance the technology of the firm, and contribute to the community.
- Long-range objectives, which include profitability and growth, market position and penetration, productivity, product leadership, employee morale and development, physical and financial resources and equipment, and public responsibility.

- Short-range objectives, which include annual sales, profit on volume, earnings, return on investment, market share, new product introduction, operating costs, and productivity.
- Goals and objectives related to actual past performance.
- Goals and objectives compared with competitors' positions.
- List of assumptions based on forecasts of industry and trends and market coordination.

The list of assumptions made from both long- and short-range forecasts is essential. Reasons why these assumptions are made should be included in this section, as should data from industry trends, competition growth, and new product information. The goals and objectives section is a key section, as it defines the direction to be taken and the results expected from pursuing this direction. The practice of MBO relates directly to this section, it sets the framework for all the other sections of the total business plan.

Section IV: Organization and Management

This section of the business plan includes a detailed discussion of the organizations, functions, and management policies and procedures to be used in support of the new venture. Here are some of the elements possible in this section:

- Company's major successes or achievements in the market to date.
- Timetable with milestones of progress for start-up of the venture and achievement of maturity.
- Organization chart with management hierarchy.
- Type of management system or style used in the enterprise, such as MBO.
- Managerial competence with measures of value added, profitability and return on investment over the past five years, with a pro forma projection.
- Special policies that have given management a high level of effectiveness.
- Special programs and their success, such as cost reduction, profit improvement, productivity upgrade, executive and managerial development.
- Statement of how innovation and venturing are fostered.
- History of the firm with changes over time of management, policies, and ownership.
- Directors' descriptions and qualifications.
- Key personnel resumés and existing contracts.

- Compensation policies and schedule of existing and proposed compensation including bonuses, fee arrangements, and profit sharing.
- Letters of reference from respected individuals attesting to the business and its management.

The organization and management plan must relate directly to the new venture. This will be the organization and management to be used in the new venture.

Section V: Sales and Marketing

This section of the business plan identifies who will sell which products to which customers at which price with what strategies and why. Here are some of the elements possible in this section:

- Sales and profits for current year and past five years of product line.
- Sales breakdown by industries, markets, seasons, and customers.
- Product line descriptions, price, cost, and historical volume.
- Strategies for customer repeat business.
- Share of market expected, in a timetable from product introduction to maturation.
- Description, size, and history of proposed segment of intended market and product position.
- Sources of estimates and assumptions.
- Selling strategies and tactics to be used to meet goals and objectives.
- Descriptions of customers who will make up 80 percent of sales.
- Pricing policies with respect to all product lines.
- Advertising: budget, media use, and measures of effectiveness.
- Promotion strategies, in a timetable.
- Current inventory and backlog of orders.
- Purchase orders on hand, with dollar amount.
- Warranties on present products.
- Selling ratios as a trend percentage, with revenues, costs, profits, staff, customers, and geographic areas.
- Customers' primary motivation for purchase of product.
- Government regulations that affect market and products.

This section must clearly describe the strategies that will be used for the new venture. Will the product or service be high priced or low priced? Will it be entered into a narrow or wide market? Is the market shrinking or expanding? Will the proposed venture of a new product be at the forefront of product leadership, or a product follower, or some of both? The sales and marketing strategy will describe the firm's policy regarding pricing, product position, advertising, promotion, sales compensation, and the like.

Section VI: Competition

The section on competition describes, with explanation and details, the nature of the competition and how competition will be handled once the new product or service has been introduced into the market. Here are some of the elements possible in this section:

- List of major competitors by location, sales, earnings, percent of market, strengths, and weaknesses.
- Description of competition and financial strength.
- Competition's approaches and strategies and what the enterprise will do to outrival them. This is the intended strategy for meeting the competition.
- Competitive advantages and disadvantages and the development of competitive edge.
- Assumptions about new competitors entering the field.
- Competitive comparisons of price, technological features, reliability, safety, and warranties.
- Competitors' advertising and promotion strategies.
- Competitors' management and skillfulness of employees.
- Extracts of outside evaluations of enterprise compared with competitors.
- Effects of impending regulations on the nature of competition.

The competitive plan clearly shows the strategy that will be used to outmaneuver and outrival the competition once the venture has been launched.

Section VII: Product Research and Development

The product research and development section presents the product line development and improvements over past years. Here are some of the possible elements in this section:

- R & D dollars spent as percentage of sales compared with the competition.
- Percent of current sales generated by past R & D.
- Technical advantages and disadvantages of new product over existing products.
- Summary of tests conducted and test data to support success of new venture in market.

- Statement of follow-on (next generation) products.
- Description of patents, trademarks, and other advantages.
- Description of technological trends and potentialities within the business environment favorable or unfavorable for the new venture.
- Number of professional employees and their unique capabilities.

The product research and development plan must be compatible with the sales and marketing plan. Both plans give the strategy for reaching the stated goals and objectives.

Section VIII: Operations and Manufacturing

This section of the business plan defines the production and operations aspects of the business plan and how these will support the new venture. Here are some of the elements possible in this section:

- Unit costs versus production levels, detailing fixed and variable costs.
- Estimated production capacity and current utilization.
- Kinds of production to be done in-house and to be subcontracted.
- Production scheduling and inventory by product line.
- Description and layout of plant facilities, equipment, location, and value.
- Current operating costs as percentage of sales, profits, payroll, and productivity.
- Description, condition, and value of plant equipment.
- Type of production process and its effect on cost-efficient operations.
- Number of personnel by functions and labor content in cost of goods sold.
- Union affiliation and strike history.
- Labor availability and competition for skills acquisition.
- Turnover, morale, and labor unrest problems.
- Quality control efforts and procedures.
- Degree of formality to improve production methods and costs.

The operations and manufacturing plan describes in detail how facilities, manpower, equipment, materials, and processes will be utilized to support the business plan.

Section IX: Financial

The financial plan section presents with details the financial schedules and pro formas to be used in operating the business plan. As with the executive summary, highlights are distilled from detailed financial disclosures for easy reading, interpretation, and evaluation. Here are some of the elements possible in this section:

- Current financial position with officers' and auditors' statements.
- Pro forma monthly sales projections by product for five years.
- Pro forma monthly income statement for five years.
- Pro forma departmental expense budget for two years.
- Pro forma balance sheet for two years.
- Pro forma monthly cash flow for two years.
- Summary pro forma monthly performance statistics, including sales growth, profit contributions, net income, working capital, accounts receivable, inventory turnover, debt, dividends, and list of shareholders.
- Capitalization equity and description of debt obligation.
- Audited annual reports for past five years.
- Description of accounting procedures operating in firm.
- Description on nonrecurring items of income or expense.
- Summary of tax returns for past five years.
- List of losses from bad debts over past five years.
- Description of firm's profit improvement plan and its success.
- Frequency of IRS audits and their disposition.
- Sources of capital utilized over past five years.

The financial plan integrates all the various subplans and ensures they are reconciled into a harmonious total business plan.

Section X: Conclusions and Statement of Request

This section distills from the previous sections the conclusions to be made from the reported details and the request that is needed for implementing the business plan. Elements in this section depend on what is included in the business plan and what is needed. The following are merely a few sample elements to be included:

- Total capital needed and return to be given to investors.
- Profit expected in a schedule and the confidence of expectation.
- Ownership assurance for present setup and for new investors.
- Entrepreneur's share of initial capital investment.
- Organization chart showing changes to implement the new venture and the new staff additions.
- Research and development facilities required, with estimated costs.
- Equipment, tools, and space required, with estimated costs.
- Training and development required of existing staff.

HOW IS A BUSINESS PLAN EVALUATED?

Anyone who *lends money, invests capital, looks for an acquisition or merger, approves for securities and exchange commissions,* or *allocates for top management* will in the normal course of events evaluate a business plan. In many ways, this evaluator will perceive the business plan as the document that best describes the total performance of the firm. The evaluator will look for supporting statements for the new venture. For this reason, and this reason alone, the business plan must be complete and comprehensive. The evaluator evaluates the total performance of the firm through the information supplied in the business plan. Most evaluators of plans, before beginning their evaluation, establish "averages" from competing companies or the industry at large for comparison. Thus the evaluator of a specific business plan will note whether the performance statistics are below average, average, or above average. Here is a checklist of what an evaluator does in evaluating a business plan:

1. *Evaluates the Venture.*
    (a) Sees if the new product or service is different from competing products.
    (b) Notes if the venture extends the product line or its technological base.
    (c) Determines if the market segment is well defined and appears ready for the venture.
    (d) Checks if the new product is patented, which will give a significant lead over competitors.
    (e) Examines if the venture has the potential to open up a whole new industry or a whole new product line.
    (f) Investigates if present and future competition of the new venture is well understood and strategies exist to handle competitors and the emergence of new competitors.
    (g) Checks if legal restrictions would exist or come to exist with the new venture.
2. *Evaluates Terms of the Venture.*
    (a) Establishes whether the venture gives a return to the investor *greater* than ten times the investment.
    (b) Checks if the company is being sold rather than requesting additional capital.
    (c) Appraises if the debt terms will stress the firm beyond reasonable limits.
    (d) Estimates if the requested capital is a minimum or a comfortable maximum.
    (e) Checks if stock issues for debt are accompanied by stock warrants.

(f)   Investigates subordinated ranking in event of liquidation and the lender's position in the subordination.

(g)   Investigates whether founders of the enterprise are reinvesting in this venture.

(h)   Notes if new funds are to repay old debts or to subsidize new activities of the venture.

3. *Evaluates Total Performance of Company.*

(a)   Examines if net worth from balance sheets is significantly increasing over time.

(b)   Determines if sales and earnings are increasing to new records over time, compared with the industry as a whole.

(c)   Checks if sales growth levels and rates are ahead of or equal to those of leaders in the industry for the future.

(d)   Notes if repeat sales are greater than in previous years.

(e)   Sees if profit has increased over the past several years.

(f)   Assesses if market share has expanded over the past several years.

(g)   Notes if the current ratio, a measure of working capital found in financial balance sheets, is 2 or higher.

(h)   Assesses if the debt/equity ratio is roughly 1:1 over time or less.

(i)   Checks dividend payment record and whether ability to pay future dividends is highly certain and sustainable over time.

(j)   Determines if enterprise has a larger degree of market dominance in the industry.

4. *Evaluates the Company Itself.*

(a)   Checks if company has a broad financial and customer base to support the venture.

(b)   Notes if the image of the company is positive with customers, government, and community.

(c)   Weighs if the number of employees is increasing at a faster rate than sales.

(d)   Judges if the company is in a technological leadership position.

(e)   Assesses if the geographic location of facilities is best for the venture.

(f)   Checks if all assets are real and tangible as opposed to soft assets such as goodwill, trade secrets, and capitalized R & D.

(g)   Sees if the outlook for the industry is above average to exceptional.

(h)   Assures if the competitive position of the firm is stable and unshakeable.

5. *Evaluates the Management.*

(a)   Appraises if the table of contents and the entire document reveal management competence in formulating the plan.

(b)   Weighs whether the managerial staff has skills in all departments to support the venture.

(c)   Checks the track record of the founders and managers; looks carefully at resumés for abilities, depth, and experience.

(d)   Checks if there is a balance among the managerial departments and functions such as marketing, finance, manufacturing, and engineering.

(e)   Notes if management has changed its style as the business grows.

6.   *Evaluates the Caliber of People Involved.*

(a)   Examines if a familiar name is found among founders, directors, current investors, bankers, consultants, and accountants.

(b)   Appraises the reputation and quality of key personnel.

(c)   Investigates if insiders of the enterprise will supply information on key personnel.

(d)   Questions if the internal venture group is highly regarded by corporate management.

(e)   Looks to see if the financial head is reputable, trustworthy, a good caretaker and accurate and has impeccable credentials.

WRITING A PERSUASIVE BUSINESS PLAN

The business plan is a proposal for funds for a new venture. Through the plan, the writer seeks to overcome the evaluator's resistance and skepticism and influence his or her decision to lend support and collaboration to the proposal. Making the business plan persuasive can be the most important effort in the formulation of the plan. Many companies whose ideas have been terrific but poorly described in a document have had their business plans end up in a wastebasket. Conversely, many companies whose ideas have been marginal but persuasively described in their document have had their plan accepted. Every effort should be made to make the business plan persuasive without sacrificing accuracy and truth. If inaccuracy is suspected in the document as well as in the writing, the evaluator will reject the plan no matter how persuasive it may be. Accuracy is a prime concern and should be sustained throughout the entire proposal. Evaluators of business plans read and evaluate many plans. The ones that are accepted are the ones that sell. Writers of business plans must incorporate "selling features" to get their plans accepted. This section briefly describes some guidelines and helpful ideas for writing a persuasive business plan.

1.   Write the plan to meet the needs and expectations of the investor.   The results of the venture should be described in the reader's terms and expectations. Having prior knowledge of investors and their

needs and expectations could be helpful. In fact, identification of venture capitalists and certain top management personnel who will receive the business plan is important for matching the venture with their preferences. Investors are not "welfare agents." They look for a good deal for themselves. The business plan must fully describe the venture but must also show the benefits for all those who join the collaboration. These benefits should not be difficult to find. As suggested in an earlier section of this chapter, benefits to the investor should be highlighted in the executive summary, where they are easily found and clearly seen.

2.   Show superior advantages compared with successful companies.   A performance statistic or ratio by itself tells very little. The evaluator must recollect past performance of other companies to make a judgment which could be unreliable. Plan writers should present important information about the venture and the company relative to leaders in the industry or chief competitors, for example, "average to the industry," "above average of three companies," "20 percent greater than the chief competition," or "growth rate will surpass that of the current leader." Relating the investment opportunity to known and successful companies provides a reference for evaluation. The evaluator makes such a comparison automatically, but it may be inaccurate. Selling is more effective if the writer makes the comparison for the evaluator. The evaluator then only has to spot check to see if everything presented is accurate.

3.   Write the plan using language the evaluator understands.   Use of the reader's language is important. Unfamiliar technical terms should not be used in the business plan. Terms, expressions, and writing style should be slanted to the reader's background, experience, and thinking. Sentences such as: "This new computer will feature a UM × 99 microprocessor with 1000K bytes of RAM. The MMU allows access to the RAM and interfaces between the computer's ROM and the 800K of the RAM that's used for the LOP. Disk drives and a TBS-3 printer allow for processing and storing information" are of little interest. Simple terms make the reader feel the new venture can be easily understood: "This new computer has a keyboard, a video screen, and a central processing unit. The keyboard is like a standard typewriter that any secretary can use. The system allows processing, editing, and filing information that amounts to as much as 600 typewritten pages on one disk alone."

4.   Write the plan using graphics, illustrations, and pictures.   Most business plan evaluators are browsers. They go through the plan casually, picking up bits of information and impressions. The quick look at graphics, exhibits, samples, charts, and letters of recommendation gives them an overall impression of the totality and completeness of the plan. Consequently a well-done diagram, chart, or sketch will create a favorable impression during this leafing-through process. The writer should include in various sections of the document eye-catching enclosures which extend favorable impressions or understanding of the plan. Seldom do unusual

graphs or pictures convince the reader. But they may turn the tide with a half-convinced reader.

5. Write the plan with a style that gives facts in titles and subtitles.   Use of titles and subtitles is now current practice in comprehensive documents. Titles and subtitles separate main ideas and sections from subideas and subsections. Evaluators almost inevitably scan and read titles and subtitles to determine content and content structure. When facts are inserted into titles and subtitles, scanning is made more impressive and persuasive. The following examples illustrate the point:

(a)   Poor subtitle: Costs.
       Good subtitle: Costs are reduced 24 percent.
(b)   Poor subtitle: Computer memory.
       Good subtitle: Computer memory is expandable to 2000K.
(c)   Poor subtitle: Sales growth.
       Good subtitle: Sales growth 18 percent greater than that of chief competitor.

This stylistic approach tends to fit busy readers, scanners, and evaluators of comprehensive documents.

6. Write the plan citing experts and recognized authorities.   There is much uncertainty with a proposed venture, and evaluators are well aware of this. They examine and evaluate the business plan for confidence factors that may offset the uncertainty and even reduce it. Use in the plan of recognized studies and the opinions of experts often reinforces the uncertain points and builds confidence in the plan. Readers tend to accept the validity of claims of support by other experts. The more evidence is cited— facts or examples from reputable authorities or similar ventures—the more likely is reader resistance to be overcome.

7. Write the plan avoiding extreme or sensational claims.   Extreme or sensational statements or words hurt your credibility and turn people off. Expressions such as "results are fantastic," "absolutely no problems are expected," "sales growth of 22 percent is guaranteed" are bound to damage the credibility of the proposed venture.

As another example, if the plan writer has an idea or a proposal for a new fast-operating valve, the plan should not state "the new TB3 valve is vastly superior to any of its predecessors on the market, highly reliable, and considerably cheaper." A statement of the differences is good, but in this way: "The new three-way valve responds 25% faster to controls, is 20 percent more reliable than existing valves known to the company, and will be 10 percent cheaper to manufacture than the leading valve on the market."

Writing a business plan persuasively requires skill and experience. To get the evaluator involved with the issues, problems, and challenges and to decide in favor of the plan requires writing and rewriting the business document to make it a best seller from among many documents that also want to sell.

SUMMARY

A business plan is a way to interest investors and moneylenders in a proposed venture. People who give or lend money want to see a formal proposal. This document is the major negotiation point in the financing of a new venture. This chapter defines the formal business plan as being one of two types: entrepreneurial or intrapreneurial. Business plans are formulated for five reasons:

1. To communicate a proposed venture to moneylenders and venture capitalists.
2. To reveal in the best possible light the management and leadership skills of the venture and the use of loaned funds.
3. To provide the basis of performance evaluation.
4. To explain to support people and staff the venture plan and how they may assist in its completion.
5. To coordinate the many groups necessary for implementing an unproven venture.

Business plans must be comprehensive but also individualistic. Of 100 business plans formulated, 100 must be different and special. No models or standards can be followed. This chapter provides elements of the total plan that can be selected by a business plan writer to fit particular needs. The selected elements should fit the venture, the venture capitalist, and the situation.

A business plan is usually evaluated in six steps:

1. The venture.
2. The terms of the venture.
3. The total performance of the company.
4. The company itself.
5. The management.
6. The caliber of the people involved.

These steps are important to the evaluator in deciding whether or not to fund the venture.

Finally, the business plan is a selling document. The writer must overcome the evaluator's skepticism and influence his or her decision to collaborate and invest. Every effort must be made to make the business plan persuasive, but not at the expense of accuracy and truth. Seven suggestions are made on how to make business plans more persuasive.

BIBLIOGRAPHY

Howell, Robert A., *How To Write a Business Plan*. New York: American Management Association Extension Institute, 1982.

Justis, Robert, *Managing Your Small Business*. Englewood Cliffs, N.J.: Prentice-Hall, 1981.

Lane, Byron, *How To Free Yourself in a Business of Your Own*. Englewood Cliffs, N.J.: Prentice-Hall, 1980.

Lasser, J. K., *How To Run A Small Business*. New York: McGraw-Hill, 1963.

Mali, Paul, *Management Handbook*. New York: Wiley, 1981.

Mancuso, Joseph R., *How To Prepare and Present A Business Plan*. Englewood Cliffs, N.J.: Prentice-Hall, 1983.

Merrill, Lynch, Pierce, Fenner and Smith, *Understanding a Financial Statement*. (booklet) New York, 1983.

13

STRATEGIC AND OPERATIONAL PLANNING WITH MBO

Events in the marketplace determine the success or failure of an enterprise. Most of what happens in the marketplace has been thought out and made ready by businesses long in advance. That is, an enterprise may have taken months and sometimes years to enter or create markets with its products or services.

With these products and services, the company is all right if it enters a market that is growing faster than the economy, if the product or service is significantly different from what competitors are offering, if the technology involved is not very capital intensive, or if the market is so well segmented that the market position is strong. Very little managerial skill is required to make a profit in these types of circumstances. But when a market is either growing slowly or not at all, when the product or service is very similar to that of the competition, when the technology involved is highly capital intensive, or when the market position is shaky, then business, managerial, and marketing strategies are musts. Over 100,000 Packard automobiles were sold in the late 1930s, compared with Cadillac's 10,000 cars. By 1954, Packard disappeared for lack of a strategy as an auto producer, and Cadillac with a new strategy sold over 100,000 cars. Westinghouse and General Electric, giant producers of electrical equipment, stay and grow in the marketplace since they are continually recasting their competitive strategies, objectives, and policies.

This chapter focuses on the nature of strategic planning, and six phases will be described. The strategic thinking process and the factors that should be considered to develop and maintain a competitive edge will also be considered. Customer-oriented strategies, how a strategic plan can be developed with MBO, strategy evaluations, and finally why strategies fail are also covered in this chapter.

STRATEGIC AND OPERATIONAL PLANNING CONTRASTED

The essence of strategic planning is development of a process that enables the chief executive officer and his or her managers to make directions and marketplace decisions today that will produce profitable results over the long range. The essence of strategic planning and managing is to expand the process of decision making by assessing where the company is and establishing where it is to go. This kind of thinking involves the MBO process. In addition, factors of the environment such as competitors, government policies, world issues, and technology are given consideration. These factors are characterized by a high degree of risk and uncertainty.

The essence of operational planning is participation in the strategic planning process in such a way as to support strategic decisions with operating or implementing plans. Operating plans give the details on how the company gets where it is to go. In thought, the two types of planning are different. In practice, they are incorporated into one plan: strategic features and operating procedures. They are both linked and necessary for a complete plan. Table 13.1 differentiates the two.

STRATEGIC THINKING: WHAT IS IT?

Business, like armies, can lose wars and perish for lack of the correct strategy at a given time and place. But where does it all begin, where does a strategic plan start? The right strategy is the outcome of strategic thinking. An overview of the strategic thinking process is shown in Figure 13.1. This kind of overview thinking must be carried on before a plan is finalized. The figure is an extension of the general MBO model found in Chapter 5.

Strategic thinking is outthinking the competition. Strategic thinking is outperforming, outmaneuvering, outsurpassing, and outcircumventing competitors! Strategic thinking is examining the same situation a competitor examines and doing a better job in selecting and integrating critical elements

TABLE 13.1   Strategic Versus Operational Planning

Strategic Planning	Operational Planning
Planning at top management level, CEO taking lead with board of directors	Planning at middle and lower management levels, department heads taking lead
Focus on mission, long-range goals, strategy with competitors, profitability, and future issues	Focus on short-range goals, budgets, costs and productivity, and present-day issues
Information used fragmentary, risky, and subject to change	Information used more complete, confident, and usable for planning period
Small group involved, usually CEO, senior managers, and planning department	Large group involved, usually department heads, key staff, and often all supervisors
Final product a strategic plan with long-term goals and short term objectives	Final product an operations plan with objectives set to implement requirements of the strategic plan
Changes easily made since they are long-term in nature	Changes not easily made, since plan is being implemented

such as trends, events, constraints, customers, government, and competition into a comprehensive set of objectives and plans. It is done in the most advantageous way for the enterprise. The following are companies that are implementing policies to sharpen strategic thinking.

- *Pepsi Cola Corporation.*   Changing its image of being second best by instituting tough competition within management ranks. Sales goals must be met or personnel replacements are sought. Winning is key! This is a reversal of the cultural trend to accept second best.
- *J. C. Penney Company.*   Adding to the paternalistic view of the company; awards employees for stretching for higher levels of performance.
- *Chase Manhattan Bank.*   Once noted for its smugness and impeccable breeding, it is shifting emphasis more to performance and away from appearance. This allows upper managers to participate with lower managers for collaborative decisions.
- *Intel Corporation.*   Constantly striving for new innovations in computer technology, the firm once was run by three individuals. Now management has been opened up to a number of specific committees, which formulate policies and foster direction.

These companies are but a few that are changing their internal operational thinking to external strategic thinking, in order to gain benefits.

Strategic thinking makes little use of past experience, portfolios, or proven practices, since these are also available to competing forces in the

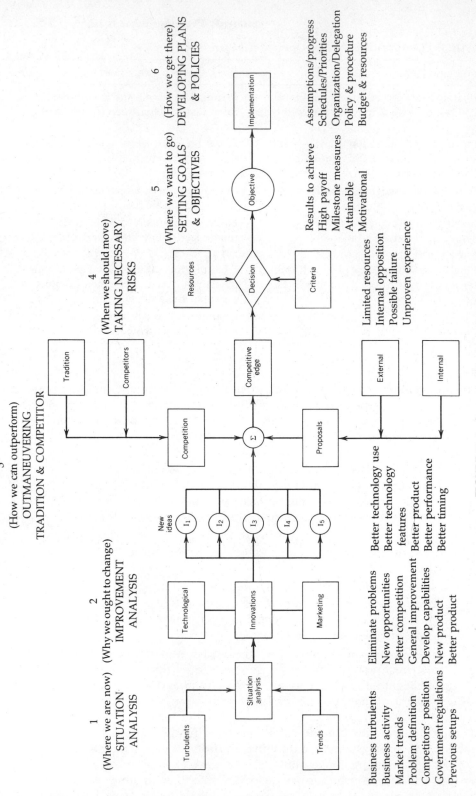

FIGURE 13.1 Strategic thinking process.

market. It isn't that experience is proven wrong. Indeed, experiential logic is usually refined over the years. It is because strategic thinking needs new ideas, new approaches, and new ways of doing things. Experience is being consigned to a much reduced place and used if and when a strategic concept needs it. Thinking in terms of ideas, from initial concept through full implementation, is a difficult intellectual task. It is no assignment for second-rate or narrowly oriented minds. Moreover, it demands the special ability to visualize the translation of an idea with strategies to a controlled operating system.

New ideas are crucial to leaders of their industry. Market leaders, in contrast to their smaller competitors, spend significantly more on research and development relative to sales. Product leaders such as Eastman Kodak, IBM, and Procter & Gamble spend greater than 3.5 percent (ratio of R & D to sales revenues) to be innovative leaders. What strategic thinking means is that all the key elements a competitor will use *plus* how that competitor will act and react to these elements are incorporated into planning. Strategic thinking means cleverly contriving a plan based on the analysis of moves and countermoves of both enterprise and competitors in the environment in which both are located.

Several types of basic conceptual thinking contribute to strategic thinking. These types are briefly described in Table 13.2. Strategic thinking involves all of these forms of thinking in varying degrees.

TABLE 13.2 Types of Thinking: The Basis of Strategic Thinking

Type of Thinking	Process	Description
Intuitive	Insight	Decisions based on "gutsy" feelings and hunches to act and react in certain way; premonition awaited
Experiential	Experience	Decisions based on proven successful experiences of past: Experience is best teacher
Rational	Logic	Decisions based on cause-effect relationships; actions are logical extension of need to act
Creative	Innovative	Decisions based on ideas or alternatives available; ideas never tried before are sought
Flexible	Elastic	Decisions based on changes that have emerged but were not anticipated; adaptive to changing conditions
Imitative	Following	Decisions based on what others have done or are doing: Copy successful leaders and success can be yours
Analytical	Separation	Decisions based on separation of all elements of situation into critical and trivial; essentials separated from nonessentials
Integrative	Synthesis	Decisions based on pulling together needed elements to form strategy

How these various forms of thinking are brought together for maneuvering is shown in Figure 13.2. Five basic stages of strategic maneuvers are outlined: (1) strategic issues; (2) strategic opportunities; (3) strategic advantage; (4) strategic planning; and finally (5) strategic evaluation. These stages are sequential and highly integrative. Strategic maneuvers involve and incorporate whatever thinking is needed to complete a stage. If the purpose of a business unit is to create and keep a customer, the strategic thinker will examine products and product differentiation for values that will induce customers to repeat their business with the firm. This gives strategic advantage. This is the most powerful idea in the strategic maneuvering process— how repeat business can be developed. No enterprise, large or small, can ever maintain repeat business without developing a strategic advantage from a strategic opportunity. Neither can a strategic plan emerge without a clearly defined competitive edge and advantage. Additionally, a strategic plan should not be implemented unless a strategic evaluation has been made to ensure success. The strategic thinker will follow the forms of thinking others use but will recombine, reintegrate, or reinstitute decisions to ingeniously gain some end. The contrived plan gets results in a quick, unexpected, and surprising way. The strategic thinker, in making a move, stating an objective, or marketing a product, expects competitors to make countermoves, state counterobjectives, and market competitive products, and arranges the plan accordingly. This suggests that strategic success cannot be reduced to a formula. Nor can anyone become a strategic thinker by attending a seminar or reading a book. There are, however, habits of thinking, as suggested in Figure 13.1, and ways of relating them to strategic steps, as suggested in Figure 13.2, that can be practiced to help develop the strategic ability, to improve the odds of coming up with a winning strategic plan.

IDENTIFYING STRATEGIC ISSUES

Strategic issues emerge from examination of inputs to the enterprise or its constituent business units that are under the control and influence of other organizations or interest groups and of how the firm responds to these inputs. Inputs may have short or long range, direct or indirect impacts on the firm or the business unit. The firm must list the issues to be examined in carrying out adaptive planning, that is, in responding to short-term environmental changes as they occur. Key questions help in prying these issues loose, for example, "What factors influence our business?," "What impact do these factors have on profitability, productivity, and growth?," "What are the drifts and trends of these factors?," "Is there something I can do to influence or change the uncontrollability of the factors in the business unit?," "What are our strengths and weaknesses in relation to these factors?," "How do these factors create issues for the firm that must be dealt with?" The following are a few sample issues that bear on most enterprises.

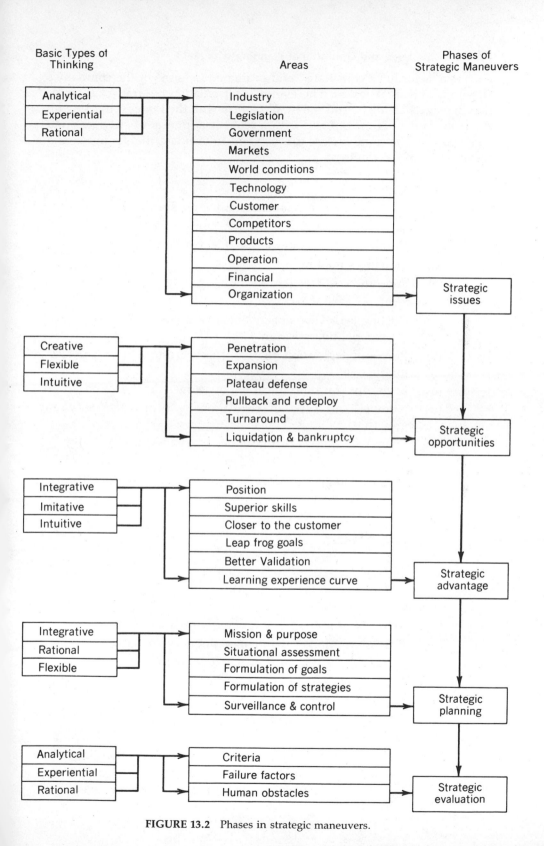

FIGURE 13.2 Phases in strategic maneuvers.

Each is a factor to be considered and evaluated in terms of the company's strengths and weaknesses. The eventual formulation of strategy requires that managers create or find the fit of the firm with the issues impacting on the firm. This fit is determined with a realistic appraisal of strengths and weaknesses. The same factors can be used to evaluate the strengths and weaknesses of competitors.

1. *Industry.*
   (a) Industry leaders' impact on firm's products and services.
   (b) Firm's growth in the same direction as the industry.
   (c) Number of firms entering and leaving industry.
   (d) Industry's maturation.
   (e) Price and cost freedom in industry's regulation.
2. *Legislation.*
   (a) Existing legislative enactments that generate extra cost affecting competitive position.
   (b) Proposed legislation that, if enacted, impacts on operating productivity.
   (c) Legislative taxation of capital investment and growth.
   (d) Number and type of regulations affecting flexibility and growth.
   (e) Business attitudes of legislators and politicians.
3. *Government.*
   (a) Degree of impact government agencies have on growth and expansion of firm.
   (b) Existing regulations that stifle the firm.
   (c) Attitudes and policies of existing leadership toward business.
   (d) Special treatment by or access to government bodies.
   (e) Degree and type of support of business units under emergencies.
4. *Markets.*
   (a) Maturity of market and range of opportunities.
   (b) Position in market with competition.
   (c) Degree and sufficiency of market penetration.
   (d) Market research and new product forecasts.
   (e) Quality and skills of sales force.
   (f) Channel coverage and services.
5. *World Conditions.*
   (a) Number of world collaborations and degree of their impact on resource distribution and use.
   (b) Existing hot and cold wars and their effects on export and import trade.

    (c)   Attitudes and policies of world leaders for or against home country.

    (d)   Overall costs from supply to consumers on global scale.

    (e)   Swiftness of world changes and degree of volatility.

6. *Technology.*

    (a)   Maturity of technological advance and likelihood of break-throughs.

    (b)   Stability of technological base for product development and modifications.

    (c)   Effects of technical growth on capacity and its utilization.

    (d)   Number and quality of firm's patents and copyrights.

    (e)   Degree of firm's exploitation of technological base.

7. *Customers.*

    (a)   Solvency and profitability of existing and potential customers.

    (b)   Number of satisfied customers measured by repeat business.

    (c)   Customer attitudes, habits, and needs.

    (d)   Breadth, depth, and type of customers.

    (e)   Firm's ability to solve customer's problems with products and services.

8. *Competitors.*

    (a)   Leader's impact on existing customers with price, quality, and volume.

    (b)   Number of competitors entering and leaving market.

    (c)   Competitive edge with existing and potential products.

    (d)   Promotional and advertising advantage.

    (e)   Image of competitors with customers.

9. *Products.*

    (a)   Standing of products from user's point of view in each market segment.

    (b)   Degree of product maturity.

    (c)   Breadth and depth of product line.

    (d)   Product seasonableness.

    (e)   Value of product to societal needs.

10. *Operations.*

    (a)   Manufacturing cost position—economies of scale, learning curve, and capacity of equipment.

    (b)   Technological sophistication of production facilities.

    (c)   Labor force unrest and managerial harmony.

    (d)   Access to and cost of raw materials and resources.

    (e)   Site location and accessibility to distributors and suppliers.

11. *Financial.*

(a) Cash flow and pro forma projections.

(b) Short- and long-term borrowing capacity.

(c) Shared costs or shared resources.

(d) Cost position relative to competitors, industry, and customers.

(e) Equity position for owners, raising capital, and inventories.

12. *Organization.*

(a) Unity of values and clarity of purpose in organization.

(b) Responsiveness of organization to strategy.

(c) Leadership qualities of chief executive officer.

(d) Quality, depth, and skills of management.

(e) Flexibility and adaptability of management.

STRATEGIC OPPORTUNITIES

The realization that there is potential for change must be a frame of mind with all managers of an enterprise. Opportunities for change must be pursued and not awaited. Progressive firms even instill this attitude in all employees. Growth and development can be reduced to their simple denominator: improvement through change. The change can be incremental, comprehensive, or a major breakthrough. The decision of what kind of change to pursue depends on the number and type of critical issues the firm faces. At times, incremental changes are needed and nothing more. At other times, the comprehensive approach is necessary. At still other times, major breakthroughs are vital. Progressive firms use all three approaches.

The search for strategic opportunities goes against the normal attitude of managers, which is to maintain the status quo. In fact, the status quo consists of conditions set up by managers, so they tend to defend them. Without a strong push from top management or the chief executive officer, lower level managers are reluctant to adopt new courses of action. This severely limits use of strategic opportunities. The history of bankruptcy is the history of failure to change by taking advantage of a strategic opportunity or to control costs generated from poor strategies. Strategy makers need to keep this fact in mind.

There are a number of strategic opportunities a business unit can take. When such an opportunity is seized, it is called a strategic business unit. Strategy makers should have a segmented view of the marketplace in order to collect the competitive specifics needed for use in the business unit. Strategic opportunities traditionally have centered on products and marketing. This is limiting. They need to be expanded to take into account any and all factors that eventually lead to strategic advantage.

Penetration Strategies

The aim of these strategies is to significantly and progressively increase the market share of the firm. The degree of penetration is a prime target and should be specified as an objective in an MBO strategic plan. A program for penetration should increase market share by up to 50 percent or more. The following are ways to achieve penetration:

1. Expand portfolio through acquisitions of and mergers with competitors.
2. Expand product line through product development and innovations.
3. Improve product quality through product improvement or modification.
4. Increase advertising to target a new market segment with pricing, distribution, and service effectiveness.
5. Innovate with product and service distribution methods for reaching customers.
6. Acquire new and better marketing and management skills for increasing revenues through better competition.
7. Eliminate failure features of past strategies by examining design and implementation.
8. Incorporate successful features of competitors into newly formed approaches.
9. Expand participation in the objective-setting process of MBO for ideas and innovations.
10. Enlarge on practices the firm uses to get and hold good customers.

Expansion Strategies

These strategies allow the business unit to move into rapidly growing market segments that are relevant and connected to the firm's business but have never before been pursued. Market segments are continually changing because technology is changing. Such firms as Digital Equipment Corporation, Coleco Corporation, and Texas Instruments, that enjoyed a position within their own market segment, moved quickly into the new home computer market when it developed. Minicomputer technology was related and connected to the firm but had not been followed to any degree.

There is a danger with expansion strategies, as with any strategy. If the organization has little or no experience with use of these strategies, difficulties will develop. However, these strategies also give an exciting opportunity to experience high sales growth. The following are ways to achieve expansion:

1. Acquire new resources and facilities through capitalization to allow movement into newly expanded technology with R & D projects.
2. Merge with or acquire an existing firm whose business adds a new technology, new facilities, new location, or new skills.
3. Expand existing technology by formal organization and MBO planning of R & D for creation of new customer groups and functions.
4. Hire or develop new strategic and managerial skills that will allow the firm to enter new market segments.
5. Formalize through written annual expectations new product development, modifications of products, and product improvement.
6. Utilize more fully the capacity of the technological base on which the firm rests.
7. Boost sales by increasing advertising in new market segments.
8. Adopt practices of competitors to acquire and hold customers.

Plateau Defense Strategies

Most companies do not experience continuous growth. In most, growth levels off, as on a plateau. Growth-plateau cycles are common, and reveal the nature of the business cycle. Companies need to protect the market share they have captured during the growth stages of their products.

Just as strategies are important for penetration and expansion, they are equally important for maintenance of the position of the firm among competitors. In a firm undergoing transition from a rapidly growing star to a more stable and profitable "cash cow," less emphasis is needed on acquiring assets and developing new markets and more emphasis is needed on quality, efficiency, and service to customers. The following are some plateau defense strategies:

1. Improve productivity and cost control of the firm through formal plans of performance and efficiency upgrading.
2. Reorganize and restructure business units to gain operating efficiencies.
3. Share resources and facilities among business units and departments.
4. Make better use of available total capacity of resources and facilities.
5. Minimize wastes and losses through more efficient use of resources.
6. Eliminate dissatisfactions reported by customers.
7. Introduce the successful features of competitive strategies into the enterprise's strategies.

8. Boost sales by giving price discounts.
9. Establish difficulties or barriers for new company entries into a market through patents, multiple brands, and tying up of distribution and delivery policies.

Pullback and Redeploy Strategies

Companies do overextend themselves in certain markets. Sometimes the market shrinks without warning. Pullback and redeploy strategies allow a firm to redefine its business to a narrow portion of the market segment. This is mainly done to strengthen the position in the market and improve cash flow. Pullback and redeployment mean to reduce sharply the use of resources and expenses and redirect resources. Several reasons make pullback desirable: (1) The firm is weak in competition; (2) the products are maturing; (3) the business environment is declining; and (4) the industry, because of technological changes, is moving in another direction. The following are pullback and redeploy strategies:

1. Cut back advertising and promotion and plan for a new direction.
2. Reduce special services and special customer considerations that have little future value.
3. Reduce business activities in all market segments that are declining and concentrate on those segments that will not decline or are expanding.
4. Cut back major cost factors of the firm such as payroll and materials where the market is shrinking, and redirect them into new and visible markets.

Turnaround Strategies

Companies experiencing heavy losses that would eventually lead to failure require turnaround strategies. This is a serious stage in the operation of a business, and turnaround strategies should be used only if the business is worth saving. Several analyses should be made before a turnaround strategy is adopted. First, future earning capability should be evaluated. Second, future growth possibilities due to a new opportunity should be projected. And third, the possibility that liquidation would not achieve the expected return should be considered. The liquidation value of the firm should be kept as an alternative to turnaround efforts.

Turnaround actions are major and highly disruptive managerial moves. A new course of action is needed to save the firm from default, and time is critical. Near-bankrupt positions demand immediate action. The decision to begin turnaround actions calls for immediate analysis of the causes of declining performance. Poor management, ineffective strategies, insufficient capitalization, poor planning, bad implementation, ineffective problem solving, and poor organization are some causes for failure. The turnaround strategy should focus on the causes. Here are some general ways to achieve turnaround:

1. Cut inventories drastically with attractive price reductions to gain significant cash flow.
2. Replace top management and/or key personnel who lack ability to formulate new course of action.
3. Reduce costs and expenses to the skeletal level needed to keep the business operating.
4. Gain agreement from retained employees and staff for reduction of payroll and benefits.
5. Sell off any assets and resources not directly needed to operate the firm at a low level of activity.
6. Develop a new strategy that will direct the firm to a new business opportunity.
7. Sell off any business units through divestiture.

Liquidation and Bankruptcy Strategies

Turnaround strategies are based on the principle that the firm has weaknesses but can be saved. There are instances, however, when firms will unquestionably fail. In these cases, preservation of the value of the assets and resources is the prime consideration. A decision to liquidate a firm completely is a stressful one by management. The following are ways to liquidate:

1. File bankruptcy under Chapter 11 of the regulation codes to gain time for proper liquidation. Some companies have used this strategy to pull out and redeploy, for example, Continental Airlines and Johns Manville.
2. Sell the firm to a group of customers or to a customer interested in acquiring a supplier.
3. Sell the firm to a competitor who might find advantages to location and distribution.
4. Sell the firm to a noncompetitor interested in a start-up operation in the same market.
5. Sell the resources, facilities, and equipment as a total package to competitors or noncompetitors.

STRATEGIC ADVANTAGE

A company's various moves and activities in the marketplace should be segmented into strategic business units. These units are like small businesses within a business. They are free standing. These units sell one product or a set of related products to a definable, segmented market or customer. In this manner, a company is able to identify competitors precisely and how their performance compares with that of the units. General Motors may manufacture automobiles, refrigerators, diesel engines, appliances, and a host of other products, but each product competes with only one product of another firm. Setting up of strategic business units thus allows a clearer vision of what the business is and who the competitors are. This packaging allows for a better evaluation of competitive edge.

The heart and core of a strategic plan is competitive edge. The planning process of a business unit must result in a plan that gives the unit leverage or advantage over its competitors, whether implicitly or explicitly. Seldom can a firm directly control the actions of competitors without running into the problem of collusion. Yet the actions of competitors in a given year cannot be disregarded. A competitor with a superior product and effective service can cause problems of profitability and survival. Therefore assessment of the business unit's strengths and weaknesses and enhancing of its points of strength are necessary. Study, review, and analysis of competitors are musts for determining whether the business unit is doing better or worse than these competitors. Identification of strategic issues and development of strategic opportunities are done for the purpose of finding strategic advantage as a prelude to the design of a strategic plan. The following are examples of actions a business unit can take to formulate strategic advantage. In every example, knowledge, information, and understanding of competitors are musts.

1. *Positional Advantages.* Rivalry among competitors occurs because one or more feels the pressure of another business unit jockeying for a position in its market or sees the opportunity to shift or improve its own position. Competitive position of the firm among its competitors should be clearly delineated to see if a shift or move could create an advantage (Figure 13.3). Black & Decker's takeover of McCullough, producer of chain saws, gave it a different personality by repositioning it among its rivals.

A shift among rivals is made by examining such competitive factors as price, quality, volume, technical features, delivery, warranties, services, novelty, safety, tax benefits, legislative restraints, and image. Some factors are more stable than others. Price cuts, for example, are quickly and easily matched by rivals; once matched they lower revenues for all. This is a highly unstable condition and likely to leave the industry worse off than before the shift. On the other hand, a new technical feature desired by a customer is not quickly and easily matched. This is a more stable condition, and allows the firm to improve revenues and profitability until competitors catch up.

2. *Superior Managerial Skills.* In the ultimate analysis, competition is between and among people. General Motors is not competing with Ford. Rather the chief engineer, the quality control supervisor, and the auto body painter at General Motors compete with the chief engineer, the quality control supervisor, and the auto body painter at Ford. Rivalry among com-

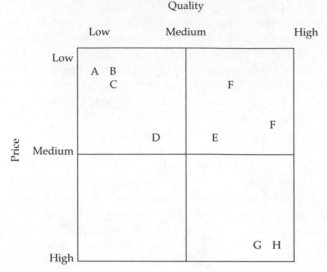

FIGURE 13.3   Positional advantage developed by shift among competitors.

The enterprise

	What we're doing	What we're not doing
What they're doing	Common skills and strategies	Competitor's advantage
What they're not doing	The firm's advantage	Skills and strategies no one's utilizing

The competitors

FIGURE 13.4   Developing skills as competitive advantage.

petitors is skill rivalry as well as product rivalry. Those who gather information about the skills of competitors and then practice these skills better are likely to outrival in the competitors. Competitive advantage is seeing what competitors are doing and doing it better (Figure 13.4).

The function of any skill is to make possible applications of knowledge to innovations and problem solving. Since situations always change and in some cases reverse themselves, having the skills to meet emerging situations is essential. Also since a strategic plan is in reality a design for a new situation, having the skills needed to create a situation in which all competitors will enter gives an advantage to the firm that creates the situation.

3. *Close Customer Orientation.* Firms that are close to their customers are firms that are highly competitive. Being close to customers is no easy task, since customers vary in type, needs, location, relationships, demands, and practices. The effectiveness of any business is measured by the extent to which the firm meets the needs of the customer, that is, to which the firm is customer oriented. Customer-oriented enterprises are ready to help customers solve problems. Customers seldom buy a product or service. What they really buy is an answer to a problem.

Strategic advantage can be developed by formalizing this orientation and making every effort to get closer to the customer than competitors. Here are some ways of getting closer to the customer:

- (a) Meet customer needs. Find out the size of needs, type of needs, growth of needs, permanency, criticality, priority, accuracy, and timing.
- (b) Solve customer problems. Help customers define their problems and then offer them alternative solutions.
- (c) Reduce customer costs. Offer lowest prices, liberal terms, efficient purchasing, minimum freight, little paperwork, minimum errors, lower defects, higher quality, minimum waste.
- (d) Improve customer product performance. Offer easy operation, efficient use, easy training, more safety, longer life, convenient controls, less costs.
- (e) Offer prompt customer deliveries. Give courteous service, correct location, efficient handling, minimum breakage.
- (f) Improve customer communications. Make contacts easy, inexpensive, with a minimum of disruption, and give the right information.
- (g) Enhance customer image. Give customer better appearance, right color, desirable shape.

4. *"Leap Frogging" of Competitors' Goals and Objectives.* Most rivalry among competitors is jockeying for position. A major point made very early in this book and worth repeating is that competition is not a gentleman's or lady's game. It is more an economic war. Tactics such as price competition, advertising conflicts, product introductions, increased customer service, and warranties are more like battlefield tactics. An effective competitive strategy takes defensive actions against the competition but also allows offensive action.

"Leap frogging" competitors' goals means jumping significantly ahead of competitors' positions. To do this, the goals and objectives of competitors must be analyzed. Knowledge of competitors' goals and objectives allows forecasts about whether each competitor is satisfied with its present position and how likely it is to change strategy and vigor in reaction to a move by another firm. For example, a competitor that places high value on sales growth may react very differently to a business downturn than a competitor interested only in rate of return on investment. Knowing a competitor's goals also aids in predicting its reaction to a strategic change such as leap frogging. Strategic changes threaten some competitors more than others. The degree of threat affects the probability of retaliation. A strategic move against a competitor by leap frogging the competitor's goals and objectives will be interpreted as a serious initiative. The competitor may enlist the special aid and support of a corporate parent, or the corporate parent may simply isolate and even divest the losing division. In either case, leap froggiof goals and objectives of competitors is a strategic advantage that could be used to accomplish certain moves in the marketplace.

Another use of the leap-frog approach is for the firm to look for a position in the market where it can meet its own objectives by allowing the competition to leap frog away from the desired position. In this case, competitors leap frog ahead with significant commitments while the firm merely moves over into another segment. In either event, analysis of competitors' goals is crucial. These goals will fall in one or more of the following categories: financial goals; goals and attitudes toward risks; values and beliefs held by the corporate culture; incentive practices; and cost improvement objectives.

5. *Better Validation of Assumptions.* All competitors in the marketplace, in developing their strategies, make certain assumptions about themselves, their customers, their stockholders, their rivals, their industry, and the environment in which they conduct their business. On these assumptions decisions for strategies are made. Decisions based on valid assumptions yield good plans. Decisions based on poor assumptions yield worthless plans. The extent that a firm takes the time and exerts the effort to validate and revalidate its assumptions will be the extent of its advantage over competitors.

More specifically, validation of assumptions about competitors' strategies is critical, since the firm moves and operates on these assumptions. For example, if the firm assumes that a competitor is moving toward becoming a low-cost producer and will be a price cutter, and makes decisions on this assumption but later discovers it was wrong, disaster may be imminent. Assumptions about a situation guide a firm's decisions. It is not possible to be absolutely accurate about assumptions, but improvements in validation do pay off. Improvement can be accomplished through periodic reviews of the information collected about competitors. These reviews can be on the basis of an individual, a group, or both. Outside third-party analysis of the same information can also be helpful in reaching greater objectivity. Intelligence data on competitors can come from many sources: reports given publicly, speeches by a competitor's management, annual corporate

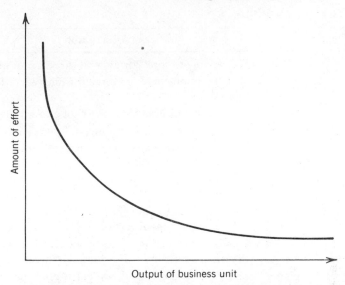

FIGURE 13.5   Learning curve effect in a strategic business unit.

reports, activities of the sales force, customers' statements given publicly, examination of competitors' products, and knowledge of former employees.

6.   *Use of the Learning Experience Curve.*   Every business experiences the learning curve effect. As the business unit does the same job again and again, it gets better and better at it. The amount of effort per business unit output decreases, as seen in Figure 13.5. Business units that build up experience faster than their competitors will achieve a more favorable cost position, since cost goes down with experience. The principle is, the more experience the business unit has, the more efficient it becomes, the less its costs, the less the price need be, the greater the price advantage, and thus the greater the competitiveness. If the experience factor continues with its beneficial effects, the business unit can have a leadership position for some time to come.

STRATEGIC PLANNING AND MBO

Strategic planning is not long-range planning. Nor is it policy planning. Nor is it marketing planning. Long-range planning, policy planning, and marketing planning are components of strategic planning. The terms are not synonymous. Table 13.3 briefly defines the various types of planning.

It is also useful to define the relationships between types of plans and levels in an organization (Table 13.4).

TABLE 13.3   Types of Plans

Type of Plan	Description
Long-term plan	Five years or more, for general direction in industry
Short-term plan	Focused in one area; continued from year to year; called a program
One-time plan	Focused in one area for a one-shot effort; called a project
Progressive plan	Flexible; long- and short-range scopes change with time
Marketing plan	Penetration or expansion into market to improve number of customers or position in market
Operational plan	Annual; coordinates all levels in organization to support strategic plan
Master plan	Five years or more; formulated by wide group of experts to give long-range direction to local planning
Functional or departmental plan	Focused on function or department, such as manpower, financial, or quality control to give direction
Comprehensive plan	Five years or more, with annual supporting plans formulated by all key managers
Policy plan	Long- or short-range standing decisions that guide decision makers in formulating plan

> *Strategic planning is the formulation of long-term objectives and goals for the firm and the selection of strategies to achieve these objectives and goals, which gives direction to the firm for beter competition with rivals and better interaction with uncertain and uncontrollable moves of the customer, the industry, the marketplace, and the government.*

Strategic planning is normally done at the top of the organization. Top management asks, "Where do we want to be three to five years from now? What business do we want to be in five years from now?" The answer is a comprehensive thinking that results in a comprehensive integrated plan. "Comprehensive corporate planning" is another term for strategic planning.

A key feature that separates strategic planning from all other forms of planning is the strong emphasis on dealing with competition. For this reason this chapter has already stressed strategic issues, strategic opportunities, and strategic advantage as these relate to rivals. Another key feature of strategic planning is its emphasis on improvement over past years. A strategic plan that does not incorporate these two key features will become any one or more of the ten previously defined types of plan. Because of these two features, strategic planning and MBO are coordinated processes.

Both Alfred Sloan of General Motors and Julius Rosenwald of Sears and Roebuck, clearly centered on what their company hoped to achieve and to become and setting corporate goals for these, contributed more to the success of their firm than any other single factor. Both parts—achievement (MBO) and becoming (strategic planning)—were very important to Sloan and Rosenwald. It might be useful to list how strategic planning (becoming) resembles MBO (achievement).

TABLE 13.4 Types and Levels of Plans in an Organization

Level	Approach to Planning	Type of Plan				
Top management	Strategic	Strategic plan (integrating all plans)				
Middle management	Tactical	Marketing plan	Financial plan, Profit plan	Engineering plan	Production plan	Human resource plan, Skills development plan
Lower management	Operational	Market research plan, Competitor advantage plan, Sales plan, Customer relations plan, Promotion plan	Cash flow plan, Purchase plan, Investment plan, Budget plan, Capital plan	New product development plan, Product modification plan, Technology development plan, R & D skills plan, Long-range plan	Capacity utilization plan, Cost reduction plan, Q/C plan, Productivity plan	Manpower plan, Incentives plan, Union relations plan, Public relations plan, Retirement plan, Policies plan

1. Both are creative planning.
2. Both entail completely managing with the plan before its implementation.
3. Both are ways of life.
4. Both center on goals and objectives.
5. Both are participative processes.
6. Both create the framework for managing the organization.
7. Both obtain agreement and understanding as to overall direction.
8. Both define priorities.
9. Both require supporting action plans.
10. Both drive the budget.
11. Both are integral to the management process.

This section describes the fundamental processes that, if followed in a certain order, will produce a document termed a strategic plan. The reader is reminded that some of these processes have been covered in Chapter 5 on MBO models. They are repeated here for emphasis and because of their applicability to strategic planning. The ultimate product of strategic thinking, planning, and managing is a document that pulls together individual plans and gives the firm a direction and a competitive edge. The following steps emphasize the written aspects of the strategic plan document.

STEP 1.   *Establish the mission and purpose of the organization.*   Mission or purpose of the firm refers to the scope and nature of the business. Who are we? Where are we? Who are our customers? Where are our customers? What do we do? For example, IBM is in the information-handling and problem-solving business. American Airlines is in the transportation business. Aetna Life and Casualty Insurance is in the security business. This first step results in:

(a)   Statement of the nature of the business and the desire to maintain it or change it.

(b)   Statement of the firm's mission and purpose.

STEP 2.   *Assess the general situation.*   Examine the issues, problems, opportunities, and expectations the firm is likely to encounter in both long-range and short-range time periods. Issues may be economic uncertainty, inflation, shortages, cost of energy, government regulations, supply of skilled labor, political uncertainty in international markets, and health hazards. Opportunities may be financial strength, experience, skilled personnel, and distribution system. This second step results in:

(a)   Statement of forecasts and trends that impact the firm.

(b)   Statement of assumptions that will be guidelines for managers in developing their plans.

(c) Statement of issues and problems that need to be dealt with.

(d) Statement of expectations from customers, stockholders, and top management.

(e) Statement of strengths and weaknesses of the firm.

STEP 3. *Assess the competitive situation.* Examine and understand the issues, problems, and opportunities the firm is likely to face with competitors in the same planning period. Issues may be competitive edge, market saturation, changes in customer purchasing policies, industry shifts, declining product sales, and new competitor entries. Opportunities may be new product development, increasing market share, technical expertise, new patents, and low-cost production. This third step results in:

(a) Statement of competitors' strengths and weaknesses relative to the firm.

(b) Statement of assumptions of the likely behavior and actions of competitors in the proposed planning period.

STEP 4. *Formulate goals.* In the beginning of this book, I defined goals as a general sense of direction over a long period of time and objectives as specific achievements in a short period of time. I recognize that some companies reverse the definitions. This should not be of great concern.

Goals should be selected and formalized in the firm; they should not be assumed or implicit. Their formalization in a written statement becomes important when proposals are considered that will redirect the firm, since goals describe the future state toward which the company is working. Examples of goals remain number 1 in the industry, increase cash flow, avoid merger or acquisition, remain a single-product business, increase sales and profits, and become free of debt. Goals should be written for financing, marketing, productivity, engineering, quality control and personnel. This fourth step results in a state of goals for the firm.

STEP 5. *Formulate objectives.* Objectives, as defined in this book, refer to specific achievements to be realized and contributed within the time period of planning. The writing of objectives is important. Guidelines for writing objectives have been covered in Chapter 4. Objectives are the future contributions each manager will make with his or her individual plan. Objectives follow corporate goals, once these goals have been defined. For every goal there must be one or more objectives. The goal gives the direction to take, the objective is measured by progress in this direction. Objectives should be written for financing, marketing, productivity, engineering personnel, and community goals. The fifth step results in a statement of objectives for the firm.

STEP 6.   *Formulate functional or departmental strategies and operating plans.*   Information obtained in the first five steps enables the development and formulation of strategies. The previous steps define the posture of the organization as it faces environmental reality and the challenge of competition. Top management sets up the goals and objectives of the firm as a pinnacle interaction with these realities and challenges. These are communicated to all key managers, who then formulate an internal or external strategy in support of these goals and objectives. Some examples of functional or departmental strategies, with brief descriptions, follow.

(a)   Marketing. Strategic factors are pricing, advertising and promotion, distribution, selling, growth moves, new customer acquisition, good customer retention, sales training. Strategies are ability to gather needed information about markets, ability to establish a wide customer base, effective sales organization, effective distribution system, imaginative advertising and sales promotion, effective pricing, reduced warrant costs, improved product service, development of new markets for existing products.

(b)   Financial. Strategic factors are cost reduction, cost effectiveness, cost control, purchasing policies, inventory turnover, money sources, debt retirement, capital improvement. Strategies are ability to raise short-term capital, ability to raise long-term capital, ability to achieve satisfactory return on investment, effective cost control, ability to reduce costs, ability to finance new product development.

(c)   Human resources. Strategic factors are skills acquisition and development, performance improvement, reduction of labor unrest and employee dissatisfaction, productivity improvement, improved communications. Strategies are ability to attract competent personnel for management positions, ability to communicate policies to employees, ability to provide effective leadership and to motivate employees, management information system, use of quantitative tools and techniques in decision making, effective organizational structure, effective overall control of company operations, ability to perceive new needs for company's products or services.

(d)   Production.   Strategic factors are productivity improvement, employee training and development, efficiency, waste reduction, cost per unit reduction, maintenance betterment. Strategies are location of production facilities, plant layout, technical efficiency of production facilities, product quality and control, possibilities for cost reduction, ability to achieve economies of scale, flexibility in using production facilities for different products, effective subcontracting of manufacturing.

(e) Research and engineering. Strategic factors are new product development, product design, feasible innovations, product improvement, product reliability, warrantee improvement, operating efficiency. Strategies are improvement of present products, improvement in rate of new product development, improvement of product quality, expansion of existing product line, improvement of product line selection, automation of production facilities.

(f) Quality. Strategic factors are standards development, quality control procedures, managerial and employee error reduction, inspection improvement, reduction of customer dissatisfaction. Strategies are ability to sense and measure error and correct before customer use, operation of standards of performance system, training of employees for error reduction, ability to communicate quickly a new procedure to management and workers, effective customer satisfaction with product.

For each strategy that is developed to support the goals and objectives of the firm, an operating plan must be established to support the strategy. These operating plans are action plans. Operating plans for each functional or departmental strategy deal with subgoals and objectives, schedule, program of activities, resource allocation, manpower, and budgets. The financial front end of a strategic plan for the entire firm is the profit plan. The financial front end of an operating plan is the budget. Strategy approvals for each function and department are approved by the next higher level of management as budgets are approved. This sixth step results in:

(a) Statement of strategy of the department or function to support and implement the firm's overall goals and objectives.

(b) Statement of operating plan of the department or function to support and implement the strategy of the function or department.

STEP 7. *Establish surveillance and control.* This final step requires procedures for comparing actual operating results with the requirements of the strategic plan. The overall strategic plan of the firm is supported by the individual substrategic plans of functional and departmental managers. This is to say, senior and top management pays attention to what is happening in the overall firm's operation, while each line manager pays attention to what is happening to his or her individual area of responsibility.

Four control functions must be fulfilled if strategic planning is to be effective:

(a) Objectives achieved on a quarterly basis for the overall firm.

   (b) Financial results actually achieved on a quarterly basis for the overall firm.

   (c) Subobjectives achieved on a quarterly basis for individual departmental strategies.

   (d) Budgetary results actually achieved on a quarterly basis for the individual departmental strategy.

This seventh and final step results in:

   (a) Statement format that compares planned versus actual objectives and financial performance for the overall company.

   (b) Statement format that compares planned versus actual objectives and budgetary performance for the individual departments.

Example: *Strategic Plan in Brief.*

1. *Business and Mission.*
   (a) Business: Insurance.
   (b) Mission: To provide security to customers and to protect from unexpected emergencies.

2. *General Situation (Critical Assumptions).*
   (a) Prime rate for borrowing will rise to 12 percent in two years and drop to 10 percent thereafter.
   (b) Government policies and administrative procedures will change with new Democratic president and controlled senate.
   (c) Great technological changes can be expected with microcomputers moving into manufacturing.
   (d) No-fault laws will be adopted in ten additional states.
   (e) High mandatory deductibles will be moderate in number for next three years.
   (f) There will be free access to Japanese, German, Italian, and French markets.

3. *Competitive Situation (Critical Assumptions).*
   (a) Price increase of 4 to 6 percent/year by top three.
   (b) Two vice presidents will retire in one year, replaced by more capable assistants, in competitors A and C.
   (c) No new private competitor entering market.
   (d) Competitor B using microcomputers for new selling threat.
   (e) Competitor B targeting overseas sales increase of 10 percent by next year.

4. *Prime Goals and General Strategy.*
   (a) Achieve number 2 position in sales growth in industry.
   (b) Achieve productivity improvement through better customer handling procedures and computerized operations.

5. *Prime Objectives.*
   (a) Increase sales volume by 15 percent for next three years.
   (b) Achieve a minimum ROA of 12.5 percent for next three years.
   (c) Increase overseas sales by 25 percent/year.
   (d) Expand portfolio offerings from 12 to 15 by 19XX.
   (e) Reduce cost of operations by 12 percent for next three years.
   (f) Increase number of prime customers from 3242 to 4000 by end of next fiscal year.
6. *Functional Strategies.*
   (a) Marketing. Objectives:
       (1) Increase sales volume of Group A offerings an average of 20 percent/year with trade association promotion and advertising programs. R. Brown.
       (2) Increase sales volume 28 percent with new portfolio offerings in general market through TV and newspaper campaigns. A. Smith.
       (3) Increase sales volume overseas 25 percent with acquisition of international insurance corporation. Expand offices for 30 percent market coverage. B. Jones.

Critical assumptions: No destructive price competition anticipated; acquisition of multinational insurance company will not be blocked by hosting country; four new portfolio offerings will be ready with promotion campaign by end of year; cooperating trade associations will increase 40 percent.

Plan and schedule:

Activities	Budget	Schedule
Trade promotion	3.6 M	
New offerings	12.5 M	
Acquisitions	32.5 M	

Evaluation:
   (1) Sales volume increase, trade association, 5 percent quarterly.
   (2) Sales volume increase, new offerings, 7 percent quarterly.
   (3) Sales volume increase, overseas, 25 percent annually.
   (b) Financial. Objectives:
       (1) Achieve minimum ROI of 12.5 percent with improved earnings of 15 percent/year for next three years. M. Doe.
       (2) Achieve 16 percent cash flow improvement, through computer aided policy-processing procedures. K. Harry.

(3) Achieve 12 percent cost reduction through productivity improvement effort of all departments and managers. C. Mann.

Critical Assumptions: IBM computer installation completed by end of year; prime rate assumption for general situation holds true for three years; all managers will shrink payroll 10 percent through normal attrition, quits, and retirements.

Plan and schedule:

Activities	Budget	Schedule
Computer processing	600 K	⊢————————⊣
Cost reduction	450 K	⊢————⊣

Evaluation:

(1) ROI quarterly milestones 3.2 percent.
(2) Cash flow improvement 4 percent quarterly.
(3) Cost reduction 4 percent quarterly.

(c) Human resources. Objectives:

(1) Increase productivity operating time from 40 to 60 percent by reducing turnover and sickness time. S. Cast.
(2) Process all sales persons through new behavioral selling program for improving sales per person 16 percent/year.

Critical Assumptions: Design of behavioral selling program with national and foreign selling skills completed by next quarter; special report on turnover and sickness causes and remedies completed by end of year.

Plan and schedule:

Activities	Budget	Schedule
Reducing idle time	135 K	⊢————⊣
Behavioral selling program	250 K	⊢——⊣

Evaluation:

(1) Twenty percent idle time reduction annually.
(2) Sales per person increase 4 percent quarterly.

(d) Operations. Objectives:

(1) Reduce complaints in claims processing through reduction in standard of claims processing time from ten days to six days.
(2) Increase productivity in four major departments with 30-word and data processing terminals.
(3) Improve productivity in all departments through productivity, tracking, and control procedures.

Critical assumptions: All department managers processed through productivity training program.

Plan and schedule:

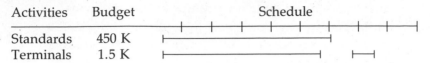

Activities	Budget	Schedule
Standards	450 K	
Terminals	1.5 K	

7. *Overall Surveillance and Control.*   Planned versus actual performance measured, tracked, and reported for corrected action quarterly as follows:

Financial	$\dfrac{Profits}{Assets}$	$\dfrac{Sales}{Costs}$	$\dfrac{Profits}{Sales}$	$\dfrac{Sales}{Employees}$
Marketing	$\dfrac{Sales\ Volume}{Total\ market}$	$\dfrac{Sales}{Costs\ of\ sales}$	$\dfrac{Policies}{Customer}$	$\dfrac{Total\ customers}{Prime\ customers}$
Productivity	$\dfrac{Costs}{Employees}$	$\dfrac{Value\ added}{Employee}$	$\dfrac{Volume}{Costs}$	$\dfrac{Employees}{Supervisors}$

STRATEGIC EVALUATION

Why is it that "in theory we can but in practice we don't"? Why is it that in planning we work out goals, objectives, and policies that meet criteria of effectiveness only to experience a plan that doesn't work. Peter Drucker, in his book *The Effective Executive*, stated that only 40 percent of corporate planning gets implemented. The American Management Association claims 50 percent. This implies that we have the ability to get things done but not necessarily the power. It is probably reasonable to conclude that plans fail at least as often as they succeed. Plan failure means missed targets, disappointed expectations, lowered performance, losses to competitors, shelved programs, declining business position, or possibly bankruptcy.

Strategies fail usually because not enough thought was given to implementation issues during the strategy formulation phase. *Companies have developed the ability to get things done but have lost sight of the power to get things done.* New plans are formulated but traditional power is assumed for their implementation. A new plan calls for a new and different type of power. The power to get things done lies in examining implementation problems during formulation of the plans and answering the following questions:

- Is the strategy workable?
- Is the time scale of opportunities too brief to capture them?

- Is the plan appropriate in the light of available resources?
- Is the risk excessive?
- Is the strategy consistent with and within environmental forces?
- Is the plan based on faulty or imperfect assumptions?
- Is the plan immeasurable and therefore uncontrollable?
- Is the plan a result of good planning thought and skill?
- Does the strategy deal with real situational problems?
- Does the strategy consider the politics and values of the implementers?
- Does the strategy have senior management involvement and support?

Businesses that find themselves in a poor position strategically probably have ignored these questions or not met the criteria effectively. Accurate identification of the failure rate is difficult, since many managers will not disclose failure of their plans. Some go on with an adjusted or altered plan. Some go on with a new mini plan. But most go on with old plans. Failure of strategies can be changed by giving more thought and effort to strategic evaluation, that is, to evaluating both the ability to reach new targets and the power to do it. Figure 13.6 gives guidelines for making this appraisal. Weaknesses call for action to correct them.

Why Strategic Plans Fail and Suggestions for Avoiding Failure

1. *Plans Fail Because of a High Degree of Risk or Because the Risk Factor Is Unknown.* Risk is purposefully allowed in strategic plans to encourage the grasping of strategic opportunity, change, and improvement. There is always risk in expectations. Suggestions: Set realistic and attainable expectations; build confidence through work breakdown clarity; conduct reviews and critiques; develop objective network for visibility and coordination.

2. *Plans Fail Because They Are Inflexible and Have too Much Detail.* There is a happy medium between the need for structure in strategic planning and the threat of rigidity and inflexibility. Most planning includes an excessive amount of detail. This renders the planning document voluminous and makes it difficult to incorporate changes. No one knows the future with certainty, and thus we need to be able to handle changes. Suggestions: Stress that planning thought is more important than plans; develop alternatives and contingency actions; decide on people, equipment, and methods that could be multipurposed; don't wait too long when a change is indicated; keep the details to a minimum.

3. *Plans Fail Because They Are Impractical or Not Useful.* Most plans run the risk of oversimplification or of being not useful to management. The complexity of a plan is often ignored. The integration of functional plans into operating plans is not an elementary procedure. Furthermore, short-term benefits brought about by the plan must be experienced by management. Suggestions: Subdivide a complex plan into manageable units; involve

Division or Program ______ Evaluator ______

Originator ______ Date ______

Criterion	Description	Evaluation P 1	F 2	G 3	VG 4	E 5	Corrective Action
Mission	Business unit defined with goals and objectives						
Decision making	Deliberate, in advance, collaborative, supportive						
Competition	Competitive edge established						
Competitors	Information for winning rivalry						
Environmental forces	Issues and assumptions valid and circumvented						
Gains proposed	Significant for both short and long range						
Timing	Opportunistic practices and practical						
Risk	Known and minimized, contingencies developed						
Other							

(*a*)

FIGURE 13.6 Strategic plan elements and evaluation. *(a)* Strategic factors. *(b)* Essentials. *(c)* Confidence factors. *(d)* Format.

		Division or Program							Evaluator

Division or Program   Evaluator

Originator   Date

Criterion	Description	Evaluation P 1	F 2	G 3	VG 4	E 5	Corrective Action
Payoff	Yields greatest results possible						
Accuracy	Statements factual and true						
Measurability	Quantity of results well defined						
Evaluative	Milestones of progress give feedback and feedforward						
Priorities	Order of preference based on need for results						
Interlocked	Results by levels are connected						
Challenging	Contains performance stretches						
Problem solving	Searches for key alternatives and tracks consequences of choice						
Actions	Selects key factor actions for greatest results						
Resources	Utilizes vital few to an end						
Other							

(b)

FIGURE 13.6 *(continued)*

Criterion	Description	Evaluation P F G VG E 1 2 3 4 5	Corrective Action
Attainability	Expectations realistic and achievable		
Flexibility	Process allows alternatives		
Participation	Implementers are involved with plan		
Ease of implementation	Contingencies are ready for obstacles		
Ease of control	Abilities are ready for variances		
Over-simplification	Critical variables not overlooked		
Validation	Analysis made of potential problems		
Other			
Other			
Other			

Division or Program   Evaluator

Originator   Date

(c)

FIGURE 13.6   (continued)

		Evaluation						
		P	F	G	VG	E		
Criterion	Description	1	2	3	4	5		Corrective Action
Completeness	All elements of plan presented; all actions to be taken noted							
Accountability	Responsibilities assigned and signed off							
Schedule	Schedule gives start-stop sequences and milestones							
Brevity	Only essentials included							
Communicative	Precise meaning clearly grasped							
Coherence	Logical togetherness of all parts							
Specificity	Level of detail adequate							
Clarity	Actions to be taken not ambiguous							
Other								
Other								

Division or Program

Evaluator

Originator

Date

(d)

FIGURE 13.6 (continued)

experienced planners; limit the number of alternatives to a practical few; validate plans in the light of past practical experience; give visibility of results of planning to management often.

4. *Plans Fail Because of Incorrect or Imperfect Assumptions.*   The quality of the plan cannot be any better than the quality or relevance of the assumptions used in developing the plan. Inaccuracy of data, more than any other factor, brings a quick termination to a plan. Suggestions: Validate important information from one source with that from another source; check accuracy of information from origin; test suspect information with sampling; validate interpretation of information with an outsider; continuously check assumptions.

5. *Plans Fail Because They Are Unmeasurable.*   Objectives often consist of platitudes and broad generalities, such as "improve efficiency." Lack of specificity renders a plan unmeasurable. The quantity of results is just as important as the type of results. Suggestions: Use words in the plan that indicate how much; quantify objectives and the progress points in the schedule; build in quantity indicators to activities and programs; build in productivity, financial, and marketing measures for scorekeeping during implementation and control.

6. *Plans Fail Because Insufficient Time Is Given to Their Development.* Planning is not extra work. It is part of the manager's job to plan ahead, make improvements, and set deadlines. Lack of time is often the cause of poor plans. Many managers are very busy people, and finding time for planning is extremely difficult. Suggestions: Use the priority approach in daily assignments; divide a large planning task among several people; allocate a number of hours per day or week for planning.

7. *Plans Fail Because the Planner Has Poor Skills.*   Some managers pretend to know fully and completely how to plan. They are unwilling to enroll in a seminar or workshop on planning, since such enrollment could be interpreted as an indictment of their planning skills. Suggestions: Distribute articles, studies, and books to upgrade skills of managers; hold in-house planning seminars; retain an outside consultant whom the manager can call on without threat when he or she needs help; train for planning skills.

8. *Plans Fail Because There Is No System to Tie Them Together.*   Many overall plans are merely a collection of disjointed individual plans. Individual plans are interlocked and optimized into an overall plan through the iteration process described earlier. Suggestions: Set up the iterative planning process; use committee work for coordination; use a schedule and flow diagram to signal start-stop planning steps.

9. *Plans Fail Because of Ill-Defined Problem Definition.*   It is tragic to work out the solution to a problem to find that only the symptoms have been cured and not the cause. Strategic planning systems should be designed in response to well-defined planning needs and problems. Suggestions: Have third party validate problem definition; use cause-effect diagnosis for problem definition.

10. *Plans Fail Because of Poor Handling of the Politics of Planning.* One of the stickiest obstacles to strategic planning is what has been labeled "the politics of corporate planning." An unwritten image exists about planning: that whoever controls the planning process controls the company. For this reason many want to control planning. Suggestions: Have the CEO support and clearly define, in writing, the role and responsibility of strategic planners; set up the planning process so that all key decision makers participate in it; anticipate who will be allies of the strategic plan and who the enemies, and act accordingly.

11. *Plans Fail Because of Inadequate Documentation.* The users of planning systems are usually executives and managers whose time is also needed for many other things. Without documentation, the planning system remains within the mind of the designer. Furthermore, documentation sets up the basis for improvement of the plan in successive years. Suggestions: Have formal written documentation and computerization of planning process and key procedures; assign responsibility to one individual for maintenance and upkeep; provide training for planning system users.

12. *Plans Fail Because of Inadequate Commitment of Senior Management.* Responsibility for planning falls on all levels of management, since planning is expected of all managers. Many firms, however, assign direction responsibility to a professional planner or planning department. This tends to encourage in senior managers the view that all is organized, delegated, and directed by others. Suggestions: Have an annual two- to three-day strategic planning meeting for senior managers away from the company; include senior managers at the start of the planning phase to guide plan development; have senior managers sign off on and present their plans.

How to Recover After Plan Failure

Managers and supervisors should not assume that, once their individual plan has been processed into the overall annual plan, they can sit back and begin work on the next planning cycle. Usually the ink is hardly dry when an unforecasted trend emerges or event occurs that can cause a serious disruption. It is important that managers take steps to keep planning alive once it is started.

STEP 1. *Monitor.* The assumptions of the plan must be monitored continuously to see if they are still valid. A format must be established to monitor and quickly report any variance between expectations and results. If the direction of actual results is away from expected targets, signals should be given that implementation is out of control.

STEP 2. *Revise.* Assuming an adequate monitoring system has been set up and changes are indicated, the next step is to decide when and where to make revisions. If the plan contains quantitative measures, revision often is a matter of how much. Revisions should be handled systematically by means of a reference number, a date, and reasons for the revision.

STEP 3.   *Recover.*   There comes a time, no matter how careful the planning or how energetic the execution, that unforeseen setbacks occur that can cause the plan to fail. It is senseless to persist in the pursuit of targeted objectives when unexpected changes render objectives unfeasible, irrelevant, or impossible to attain. The number and variety of events large and small that can strike a company in the course of a single year is astonishing. When such a change occurs, several approaches are possible:

(a)   Continue but reduce the existing plan. Plan to recover the losses within the next planning cycle.

(b)   Develop an interim plan. Reactivate the alternatives that were originally used and select another attractive direction. This could be called a miniplan.

(c)   Revert to the previous year's plan. If all alternatives are no longer viable, select a plan that has been proven for the company. Investigate why the plan failed.

The choice is between sailing a ship with no lookout and no navigator or with plotting and navigating toward favorable currents.

Human Obstacles to Planning

The human aspects in planning play a crucial role in plan effectiveness. Planning does not come about without resistance or an uphill struggle. People resist formal planning because it smacks of regimentation, authoritarianism, and excessive control. The following are guidelines that help in overcoming some of the human difficulties in planning.

1.   *Planning Coordinators Must Command the Respect of Other Leaders in the Organization.*   To plan potentially important work, the planner must command the professional respect of colleagues. Informal authority and persuasive cajoling work when the planner is accepted as a professional.

2.   *Planning Coordinators Must Identify Quickly and Prepare Accordingly Who Stands to Gain or Lose From a Proposed Plan or Program.*   A negative reaction is to be expected from those who will lose and a positive reaction from those who will gain. The losers will fight, argue, and may even help to defeat a plan. Noncooperation should be identified early and dealt with.

3.   *Planning Coordinators Should Develop Working Alliances With Other Departments.*   Working alliances are not only protective but invaluable as channels of communication. Valuable support and shared successes can be developed from these working alliances.

4. *Planning Coordinators Should Allocate Their Limited Time in Discussion and Contact Work to the Power Structure of the Organization.* Time will be limited for the planning coordinator and should be devoted to where it counts most. The power structure will provide significant inputs into the planning process in the form of judgments, attitudes, and values.

5. *Planning Coordinators Should Become Consultants to Line Personnel.* Line personnel who are engrossed in everyday operating activities and problems welcome the aid and advice of an internal consultant, especially if the aid helps in completing a required plan.

6. *Planning Coordinators Must Carry Secondary Responsibility for Planning.* An effective tactic of a planning coordinator is to urge managers to come forth with ideas for moving in a desired direction and then swing support to them so that they acquire the prestige that goes with originality and innovation.

7. *Planning Coordinators Should Compromise on Less Important Matters When a More Significant Commitment Can Be Gained.* In many cases, the planning coordinator must practice what might be termed coexistence. He or she must separate out and proceed toward the few but significant gains and compromise on the trivial gains.

8. *Planning Coordinators Should Keep Alert to Unpleasant Problems and Troublesome Trends.* The planning coordinator must watch for disrupting activities, particularly subtle resistance to change. All managers will give "lip" approval to the new planning thrust, but some may rebel privately.

SUMMARY

Strategy is defined as the formulation and implementation of goals and objectives in such a way that the business unit or company outrivals its competitors in the marketplace. This chapter describes six major phases in the process of strategic planning.

The first is strategic thinking. The right strategy starts with strategic thinking, that is, creation of a state of mind in decision makers that will allow outrivaling, outperforming, and outcircumventing competitors. Several basic components of thinking are part of this process, such as intuition, experience, rationality, creativeness, flexibility, imitation, analysis, and integration.

The second is identification of strategic issues that impact on the firm. Impact is analyzed in terms of the strengths and weaknesses of the firm in relation to its competitors. Twelve categories of issues are identified: industry; legislation; government; markets; world conditions; technology; customers; competitors; products; operations; financial; and organization.

The third is recognition of the opportunities available to the firm. A strategic opportunity is an action a firm can take that would give it an advantage over a competing firm. Six strategic opportunities are cited in this chapter:

1. Penetration strategies.
2. Expansion strategies.
3. Plateau defense strategies.
4. Pullback and redeploy strategies.
5. Turnaround strategies.
6. Liquidation and bankruptcy strategies.

The fourth is the development of strategic advantage. This is segmentation of the market in such a manner that the business of the segment can be managed in a superior and advantageous way. The following are competitive advantages:

1. Positional advantage.
2. Superior managerial skills.
3. Close customer orientation.
4. "Leap frogging" of competitors' goals and objectives.
5. Better validation of assumptions.
6. Use of the learning experience curve.

Phase five is strategic planning. This is the actual formulation of goals and objectives on the basis of the opportunities and edge the firm has over its competitors. Development of the plan follows several steps:

1. Establish the mission and purpose of the organization.
2. Assess the general situation.
3. Assess the competitive situation.
4. Formulate goals.
5. Formulate objectives.
6. Formulate functional and departmental strategies and operating plans.
7. Establish surveillance and control.

The sixth is strategic evaluation, that is, a careful look at the factors and problems of implementation that may abort or reduce the value of the plan. The power to get things done is as important or more important than the ability to get things done. Several suggestions are made to develop this power by examining the problems existing during implementation.

BIBLIOGRAPHY

"Corporate Culture." *Business Week*. October 27, 1980, p. 148.

Drucker, Peter F., *The Effective Executive*. New York: Harper & Row, 1967.

Ferrell, Robert W., *Customer-Oriented Planning*. New York: American Management Association, 1964.

Hamermesh, Richard, Ed., *Strategic Management*. New York: Wiley, 1983.

Huse, Edgar F., *The Modern Manager*. St. Paul: West, 1979.

Lorange, Peter, and Vancil, Richard F., *Strategic Planning Systems*. Englewood Cliffs, NJ: Prentice-Hall, 1977.

Lohr, Steve, "Overhauling American Business Management." *New York Times*, January 4, 1981, p. 14.

Naylor, Thomas H., *Strategic Planning Management*. Oxford, Ohio: Planning Executives Institute, 1980.

Ohmae, Kenichi, *The Mind of the Strategist*. New York: McGraw-Hill, 1982.

Paine, Frank T., and Anderson, Carl R., *Strategic Management*. New York: Dryden, 1983.

Porter, Michael E., *Competitive Strategy*. New York: Free Press, 1980.

Rogers, Rolf E., *Corporate Strategy & Planning*. Columbus, Ohio: Grid, 1981.

Steiner, George A., *Strategic Planning*. New York: Free Press, 1979.

"Wanted: A Manager to Fit Each Strategy." *Business Week*. February 25, 1980, p. 166.

14

MANAGING HIGH TECHNOLOGY AND ENGINEERING WITH MBO

IN THIS CHAPTER

One of the many transformations taking place in organizations is the shift from blue-collar workers to white-collar knowledge workers. John Naisbitt, in his book *Megatrends*, identified this as a megashift from an industrial to an information society. The shift has far-reaching social, political, and educational consequences. The biggest impacts will be technological and economic. More specifically, the shift toward more information workers and engineers will alter the way we organize to achieve results. Two major forces among many are causing the shift: high-technology specialization and computerization of work processes.

This chapter describes these forces and the reason for using MBO management techniques. Effective management requires altering old management habits and attitudes and instituting new ways to achieve the objectives of the firm, on time and within the budget. Many aspects of system/project/program/product management are treated in this chapter. Use of the terms "system," "project," "program," and "product" and definitions of subsequent processes varies from company to company,

563

individual to individual. To some extent the terms are confusing. Each firm pursues its own conceptual definition in delivering its products and achieving its profits. This chapter defines these terms as more than just terms. They are conceptual organizational processes for achieving end results. They are highly effective management tools for engineers and high-technology specialists. They are MBO-oriented processes used by managers to handle special situations in engineering, research, and high technology. The terms are briefly defined here and are taken up in greater detail later in the chapter.

System.   A long-term complex undertaking made up of two or more programs. The system has a mission that never ends. The programs give the system structure and meaning. Examples of systems are the federal judicial system and the worldwide telephone system.

Program.   A long-term complex undertaking usually made up of two or more projects. A program has a set of goals that are continuously pursued. Examples are the space shuttle program and productivity programs.

Project.   A short-term usually technical undertaking made up of two or more interrelated tasks. A project has a well-defined set of objectives, a schedule, and a budget.

Product.   A short-term market specific product, usually hardware, produced by a series of one or more projects. A product tends to be consumer oriented and is delivered into the market for sales and profits.

Tasks.   Short-term work efforts needed for completion of a specific work package. Tasks are the work component of a project.

WHAT IS HIGH TECHNOLOGY MANAGEMENT?

A technology is a body of specialized knowledge, methods, materials, and processes that is identifiable and available for practical exploitation for material and service benefits. Technology is the application of science and engineering to the design and production of products. Thus electronic technology is a collection of designs, information, materials, components, products, and systems available for use in electronic product applications. Similarly, food technology pulls together everything that is known about food materials, processing and handling and is used for development of new food products.

Several factors make a technology "high," or advanced:

1.   *New and Developing.*   Technologies have been around for many centuries. But the high technology phenomena of today are the fast-growing

new technologies within systems and programs never before on the scene. Examples are aerospace technology, new energy sources technology, bio-engineering technology, desalinization technology, computer-aided design and manufacturing, optical fiber technology, radiographic technology, software technology, data processing technology, and microprocessor technology.

2. *Highly Complex.* The new high technologies are extremely complex, demanding skills not normally found or available. As a result, technologists from a proximity system or a somewhat related program are borrowed to handle the new technology. Examples are laser technology, nuclear reactor technology, robotic technology, numerically controlled systems technology, genetic technology, automation technology, and geothermal energy technology.

3. *Integrating Several Technologies.* The new high technologies integrate several technologies into one system or program. This poses special problems to the specialist, who must be an expert in several areas, many of which are new and developing. For example, the automated office, a significant and growing trend, incorporates several technologies: computerized systems; software technology; and information management systems technology. Other examples are telemetering technology, word processing technology, and human machine technology.

These new, complex, and integrated technologies are having a competitive impact on existing products and industries. In the early 1950s the United States was clearly a leader in such industries as steel, shipbuilding, automobiles, consumer electronics, farm equipment, and fabric manufacturing. Today the United States has lost its leadership role in these areas. Many factors are responsible, but the outstanding factor is failure to incorporate and keep abreast of high technology changes and the management skills needed for these changes.

Management of high technology is and will become even more a key to successful business growth. It will play a major role in shaping a company's future. With some companies it has already done so. Much time and energy can be spent analyzing market position, market share, market size, product price, volume of sales, product distribution, and sales strategies, but unless management of the technologies on which the firm is based is given equal time, effort and respect, the firm will not remain competitive. Firms that do not manage their future with new technologies will find their competitors have a technological advantage that gives them product superiority in terms of features, quality, costs, and productivity. Management of high technology suggests special managerial attitudes, orientations, and skills not normally found with traditional management. These are as follows:

1. *Ability to Deal With Tasks With a Shorter Life Cycle.* New products or projects emerging from high technologies have short life cycles because the technology is still developing and has not reached maturation (Figure 14.1).

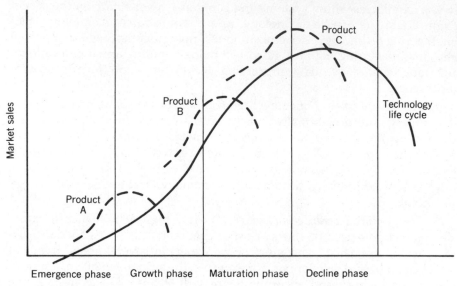

FIGURE 14.1 Product spinoffs with growing technology.

Firms anxious to market products can get caught by important changes. For example, communications delivery technology has been around for the past few thousand years. Much of the time it has had one product—the written message. The first written messages were carried by hand , then by slow conveyance. In the nineteenth century the telegraph was invented. Not too long ago the TWX system became the product for communicating over distances. It was supplanted by the courier dispatch system using high-speed jet airplanes. Now looming on the horizon is a devastating threat— electronic mail. Once electronic mail becomes entrenched, the technology that produced it will produce still newer products.

2. *Possession of Entrepreneurial Skills.* An entrepreneur is one who establishes a new enterprise and takes it from a zero level to an operating profitable level. The skills and attitudes necessary to bring the enterprise to this profitable level are the same skills and attitudes often used to bring an application idea from a developing technology up to generating sales in the open market. Not that innovative genius, hard work, or luck have ever guaranteed new corporate success. The catalytic element is most often the entrepreneurial state of mind. This state is characterized by certain attitudes and skills:

(a) Willingness to pursue an innovation never before found in the marketplace.

(b) Willingness to take a risk with an innovation even when accompanied by uneasiness and personal discomfort.

(c) Ability to see and seize an opportunity for application of the innovation.

(d)   Possession of tough mindedness that stops short of com-
bativeness and discouragement.

(e)   Capacity to solve all kinds of problems, each threatening
survival.

(f)   A mental set of moving ahead with uncertainty.

(g)   Possession of a good set and level of technical and quantitative
skills.

(h)   Astute understanding of business operations and finance in
open markets.

(i)   Adherence to clear set of goals and objectives for taking and
sustaining action.

(j)   Ability to organize with a business plan, goals and objectives,
and a timetable.

3.   *Ability to Manage Technology as a Resource.*   Opportunities and strategic alternatives for a company are often defined by the firm's technological
resources and abilities. The technology itself determines the range of
product and marketing options available. Because of this, managers need to
view technology as a resource along with time, costs, specialized manpower, capital, facilities, and equipment. The firm's technology cannot be
assumed, for this undergoes changes. Keeping up with and exploiting
these changes often means moving existing products to new markets and
applications. From a practical standpoint, managing technology as a resource requires:

(a)   Clear identification and definition of the basic technology and
associated technologies from which products of the firm are
developed.

(b)   Tracing and tracking of the technological advances and changes
that occur within this technology and determination of whether
they are emerging, maturing, or declining.

(c)   Assessment of technological assets in terms of specialized
manpower, facilities, equipment, materials, patents, copy-
rights, and goodwill.

(d)   Determination of the nature, duration, magnitude, segment,
and market size associated with each technology.

(e)   Pinpointing of missing technological assets and resources and
identification of corrective actions needed to ensure success.

(f)   Provision of a focus to coordinate all the efforts needed into an
effective and efficient organization to take advantage of new
product opportunities associated with the technology.

4.   *Ability to Manage by Means of a Matrix.*   On the basis of the foregoing,
management of high technology requires management of technology along
with costs, market options, time, manpower, and facilities. This implies that
a project or program is a business unit and requires a business unit's
direction, a business plan, a strategic program, or a marketing adjustment.

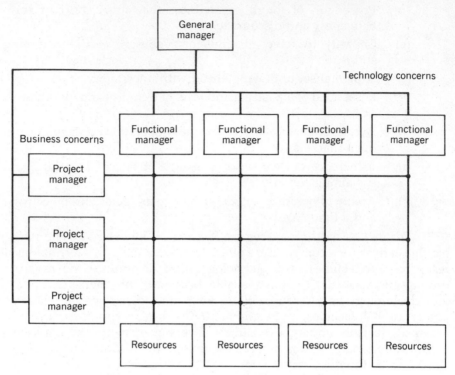

FIGURE 14.2   Matrix organization for business and technology.

The business unit within a high technology project cannot and should not be set up without evaluating the probability of meeting its objectives. The business plan must coordinate all the efforts into an effective and efficient organization. The organization that does this successfully is the "matrix" organization.

The matrix form of organization, sometimes called systems management, divides the organization into two groups: project (or program) managers and department managers, often called functional managers. The second group's emphasis is on technology, equipment, facilities, manpower, and specialized skills (Figure 14.2). Under this scheme, the organization allows some to focus on the business aspects of the project or program and others to focus on technology. This organizational scheme gives high technology the attention and visibility it needs which is often not the case with traditional organizations. Project managers responsible for the completion of their project draw on the functional groups to implement their plans. Functional managers responsible for managing technology and resources draw on project managers to guide and control effective uses of resources for completing the project within time, cost, and expected performance.

Advantages to the matrix organization are:

(a) Focus is given to a project to complete it within limited time and cost.

(b) Customer or market is given a high priority and is not lost in the activities of the project.

(c) Technology specialists' skills are expanded as experience is transferred from one project to another.

(d) Responsiveness to change is faster because project managers provide link between customers and technologists.

(e) Business and technology balance is maintained, since checks and balances are built in between project and functional managers. Project managers are time-cost-profit-oriented people; functional managers are technical equipment-oriented people.

Disadvantages to the matrix organization are:

(a) Time and cost tend to erode technical performance.

(b) Conflicts inevitably emerge due to dual authority over the utilization of resources.

(c) Balance of power between business and technology can shift due to personalities.

(d) Project managers tend to acquire many projects, thus losing the needed focus on a specific project.

HOW MBO ENHANCES HIGH TECHNOLOGY MANAGEMENT

In a major study conducted by the U.S. Department of Defense between 1970 and 1980 in connection with performance by vendor contractors, four areas were cited as failure points:

1. *Cost Overruns.* Contractors' performance lacked a tracking system for cost control in the periods in which correction could be made. In addition, contractors underestimated costs in bidding to win the contract. Contractors lacked an information system that could give up-to-date cost estimates and change the information when needed.

2. *Schedule Slippage.* Over 75 percent of supplying contractors did not deliver their products or services in accordance with the committed schedule. Delays were experienced because of failure to procure long lead items. Programs and projects were disjointed, overlapping, and uncommitted.

3. *Technical Disappointment.* Contractors were unable to meet the technical claims of their proposals. The so-called technical specialists were in reality generalists with a small smattering of technical knowledge. The

contractor's organization was not structured to allow high technology to grow in depth.

4. *Problems at Responsibility Interfaces.* Responsibility for completed work between functions and departments was ambiguous, confused, defused, and vague. Decision making was not clear-cut and top executives often had to step in to solve problems, which caused considerable delay. Problems that could have been solved when "budding" had to be solved when they were "fully in bloom."

In the same study the Department of Defense cited four areas of success: (1) contracts were projectized; (2) contract execution was in an information system; (3) responsibility and accountability were defined in terms of projects and work packages; and (4) the organizations were matrix type with technical and business managers separated. The first three of these are intrinsic in the matrix organization, where projects, programs, products, and technology are allowed to be managed as separate entities. Setting objectives with supporting plans, intrinsic to MBO, is part of the same process. The following describes in greater detail how MBO can aid in the matrix organizational form needed for high technology management.

1. *High Tech Requires Projectizing.* Responsibility, authority, and accountability must be clearly defined in connection with a set of objectives. Most organizations are plagued with a wide variety of responsibilities, which means managers must do many things and spread themselves and their resources thinly. MBO gives definition to a project through a set of objectives with supporting plans. The project's results are defined as objectives and connected with resources of costs, time, and personnel.

2. *High Tech Involves Spiraling Costs.* Because of its complexity, high technology can generate costs not expected or anticipated. Cost overruns are highly likely. MBO is managing packages within controlled periods, that is, in start-achieve-stop cycles. These packages can have short time durations, which can allow for changes in costs, targets, personnel, and resources. From this standpoint, MBO is "mini planning." A "mini-plan" package can be 3 months, 6 months, or 12 months in duration. This MBO discreteness allows for evaluation in shorter periods and more opportunity for changes if needed due to information, costs, or schedule.

3. *High Tech Requires Flexible Time Spans.* The span of time from conceptualization phase to market-readiness phase is getting longer. This is important for procurement of long lead items, and it greatly affects working schedules. The span of time from market introduction to maturation, however, is getting shorter. This is important for profitability. MBO is an organization style that promotes flexibility. MBO processes can be structured for long-range planning and scheduling, to handle long lead item procurement needs, and can be restructured for mini packages of planning and control as needed for short time periods. All organizational forms have

this need for long-range and short-range flexibility. Projects need to be completed in short cycles. Long-range programs need to be continued with short-range progress milestones. Products need to be extended when some of them mature. MBO can be packaged and repackaged with objectives and new objectives for new directions and controls for both long-range and short-range needs.

4. *High Tech Requires Specialized Technical Manpower.* To be knowledge-able about and experienced in a technology requires focus and specialization in the technology. Making generalists out of technical specialists may serve a business responsibility but dilutes the effort to continue the expert specialization. MBO gives a management framework within the matrix organization that allows coexistence of the generalist with one set of objec-tives and the technologist with another. Both use the same managerial process but have different objectives. The integrity of both technology and business is maintained and even enhanced.

5. *High Tech Fosters Collection of Details.* High technology generates an incredible number of details that must be stored easily, retrieved, developed, and even changed. Handling of information involves time and money. In fact, information is now seen as a costly resource. MBO as a process allows for information generation, storage, and retrieval. MBO is an information generator but it provides for information visibility, participa-tion, decision making, and accountability. MBO as an information package collects the details needed to pursue objectives and makes these details available to whoever needs them.

6. *High Tech Capital Commitments Need Visibility.* There is nothing more devastating than to start a project or program with an assumed capital requirement and later find that more capital is needed to continue or com-plete the program. MBO gives the needed visibility to capital requirements in a project, program, or product in the planning phase—long before the actual need. This promotes capital-use decisions in the planning phase where they belong.

7. *High Tech Corporations Need "Mini" Planning and Control.* Large, highly specialized high tech organizations have difficulty in focusing needed planning and control in specific areas. Problems of high perfor-mance under conditions of advanced technology demand unique project or program planning and control. The MBO concept allows for large, small, broad, or narrow planning and control as needed. The setting of goals and objectives is like a telescopic directional site for use where specifically needed.

8. *High Tech Requires Accountability.* High technology demands high-cost assets, resources, and capital. Pinpointing of missing or misused assets and resources and identification of corrective actions are needed to ensure continued success. MBO places and gives visibility of accountability to one person or group for the overall results of the project. It permits preemptive

actions and decisions to capitalize on technological opportunity, while identifying accountability for these decisions.

9. *High Tech Requires Unique Coordination.* One aspect of high technology described earlier is its integration of several technologies into a whole. Integration requires the assurance that decisions are made on the basis of overall good of the project or program and are balanced among and between the technologies. MBO provides for coordination of all functional and business-type contributions to the project. It assures decisions for the good of the whole rather than for the good of one or the other contributors to the project.

10. *High Tech Requires Early Identification of Problems.* Problems that are not identified early in high technology not only generate high costs but may jeopardize the success of a project or program. MBO demands much thinking and planning in advance. Intrinsic to the process is the spotting of problems in the planning phase. This early identification of problems allows for resolutions and corrective action in the planning phase, when costs are minimum and corrective action can be maximum.

11. *High Tech Means Handling Innovations, Opportunities, and Risks.* High technology is by its nature a process of innovation and integration. Its complexities require "packaging" a set of results on an ascending curve. This packaging of start-develop-achieve-stop is best handled with the MBO process of setting objectives (start), preparing for what must be done (develop), reaching a set of results (achieve), and evaluating results (stop).

PROJECT MANAGEMENT WITH MBO

A project is an organizational process whose mission is completion of a set of objectives. Achievement of these objectives represents completion of the project and a milestone achievement in the program. The project is a targeting process, as seen in Figure 14.3.

Targeted objectives often involve research, development, design, manufacture, construction, and installation. They may also include completion of a study, development of computer software, or processing of a package of data as required by users. A project has a finite and fairly well-defined life span, usually short. It is not an activity that will go on and on as a part of the organization's existence.

Each project has a project manager or project engineer with a team of people committed to completion of the work. Authority for making project decisions is defined by top management in the remaining organization. Most firms who practice project management have a matrix form of organization, which was described in an earlier section. The project manager has the top management view of the project—its completion within a certain budget and time and according to the objectives. Responsibility for the profitability of the project is indirect. That is, when the project manager

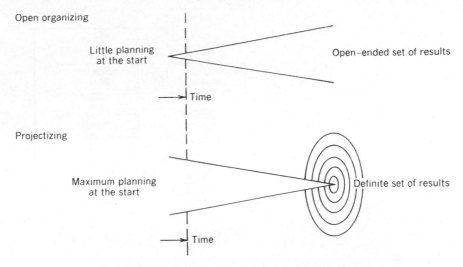

Open organizing

Little planning
at the start

Open–ended set of results

Time

Projectizing

Maximum planning
at the start

Definite set of results

Time

FIGURE 14.3   Project management is a targeting process.

completes the project within the planned budget, a profit contribution is made.

In the organization and management of a project, it is useful to think in terms of project phases. That is, the project is broken down into a series of discrete steps or phases which are sequentially related. MBO objective setting and follow-through fall in many of these phases. The steps are illustrated in Figure 14.4 and briefly described in the following.

1. *Project Proposal Phase.*
    (a)   Communicate with customer and user as to needs.
    (b)   Establish liaison with customer to reach clear agreement on requirements.
    (c)   Analyze for technical, quality, and cost needs; include feasibility studies; cost benefit studies, and operating and maintenance requirements.
    (d)   Define technical approach and scope of work with matrix organization.
    (e)   Set tentative objectives and goals to be met.
    (f)   Identify resources to be used—staff, equipment, facilities, and materials.
    (g)   Participate and negotiate with others in matrix organization for agreement.
    (h)   Negotiate and control for work package completion and performance attainment.
    (i)   Write proposal for customer or user adaptation.

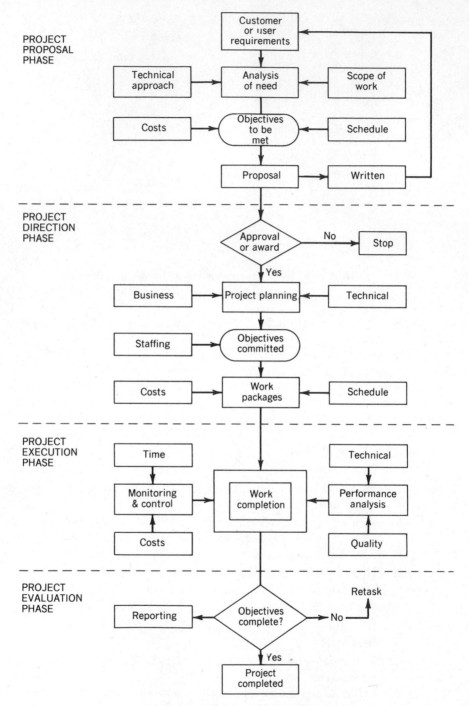

FIGURE 14.4 Phases of project management.

(j)   Renegotiate and finalize into commitments.

(k)   Sign the contract or statement of approval.

2.   *Project Direction Phase.*

(a)   Confirm project manager and establish project organization.

(b)   Translate contract requirement to planning and task elements.

(c)   Separate business elements from technical elements to fit matrix organization.

(d)   Commit manpower loading and key personnel assignments.

(e)   Formulate number, type, and priority of tasks into work packages including engineering design, testing, development, manufacture, installation, and operation.

(f)   Establish for each work package, end items or task goals, technical requirements, schedule, accountability, cost, quality standards, engineering drawings, bill of materials, and purchasing requirements.

(g)   Identify constraints and limitations of project work and cautions to be taken.

(h)   Establish event and time sequences for master schedule and progress milestones.

(i)   Organize for use of equipment, tools, instruments, facilities, and buildings.

(j)   Complete make or buy decisions (internal manufacture or vendor supply).

(k)   Organize project team for performance and budgeting reporting.

(l)   Orient key managers and department heads to project.

(m)   Establish documentation checklists for all participants.

3.   *Project Execution Phase.*

(a)   Approve scope and direction of project to entire organization.

(b)   Assign work packages and project tasks, with priorities, to all managers.

(c)   Commence work in departments and sections.

(d)   Consult and aid where problems emerge or confusion exists.

(e)   Motivate personnel working on project to achieve commitments.

(f)   Resolve conflicts and frustrations over constraints.

(g)   Make technical and business tradeoffs and compromises for good of the project.

(h)   Monitor and control for work package completion and performance attainment.

(i)   Renegotiate priorities where needed to complete project.

(j)   Handle emergencies as contingency decisions to complete work.

(k)   Conduct progress milestone meetings for feedback and correction.

(l)   Assemble, test, and operate hardware and final product of project.

(m)   Place and store product in inventory for customer delivery and use.

4.   *Project Evaluation Phase.*

(a)   Gather formal progress milestone variance reports for costs, time, and budgets.

(b)   Schedule meetings for communications, control, and conflict resolution.

(c)   Sign off for acceptance documentation checklists.

(d)   Ensure work package completion meets stated project objectives.

(e)   Ensure project products meet customer and contract standards.

(f)   Provide special reports to external and internal management.

(g)   Follow through on corrective actions specified in progress reports.

(h)   Assure that quality standards of final product are met.

(i)   Evaluate performance and behavior of project personnel.

(j)   Conduct final evaluation of project to meet customer's contractual needs and organization's budgetary and profitability needs.

(k)   Terminate project with records closure and documentation filing.

In the early stages of a project, technology predominates. Rough estimates of profits, costs, and time are deemphasized, since these elements all depend on the technical approach. After the project progresses into engineering, design, and development and the technical approach is well cast, the emphasis shifts to the business concerns of costs, time, and execution. Both technical and business factors exist side by side from beginning to end, but the emphasis on them shifts as the project is completed.

PROGRAM MANAGEMENT WITH MBO

A program is an organizational process whose mission is completion of a set of goals or subgoals. A program may consist of several projects. Completing a project means attaining a progress milestone in a program. Programs tend to be long-term undertakings which usually consist of more than one project and sometimes deliver products. The projects come to an end but the program continues; often it never ends. Programs contain the goals for long-term directions, projects contain the objectives for short-term results. Table 14.1 illustrates this definition.

A major difficulty in the management of a program is failure to define the projects to be completed within the mission of the program. The program sets the major direction, but the projects establish the achievements along the way. From an MBO standpoint, the program is the goal, the projects are the objectives. Some programs are so vast and complex that subprograms and subgoals are needed. The man-on-the-moon space program is such an example. This was a ten-year program for landing a man on the moon. The program continues with the space shuttle. The man-on-the-moon program involved more than 150,000 individual contractors, who participated with subprograms and an awesome number of projects and products. In the history of managerial achievements, few if any will rival the scope and complexity of the man-on-the-moon program. Its complexity is the management of vast systems, many programs, a huge number of projects, and an unbelievable number of tasks yielding a specific set of well-defined products.

Program management assures, first, that program goals are well defined, are communicated to the program team, and are integrated with specific projects and products to be achieved. A single point of integrated responsibility is the program manager, who is responsible for the entire program. Since programs seldom end, the program manager directs the program from

TABLE 14.1 Program Definition

Program	Duration	Program Projects	Duration
Welding program	Continuous	Electrode moisture control project	6 months
		Automation of subassembly project	24 months
		Recertification training project	10 months
Crime reduction program	Continuous	Street relighting project	6 months
		Crime neighborhood watch project	2 years
		Patrol car surveillance project	6 weeks
Productivity improvement program	Continuous	Engineering measurement project	10 weeks
		Activity value-analysis project	24 weeks
		Productivity performance appraisal project	2 years
Office automation program	Continuous	Word processor project	4 weeks
		Telemetering system project	1½ years
		Model office project	6 months

its inception to points in time at which major achievements have been made and reported. The program team includes all persons needed to execute the phases of the program. Programs, like projects, undergo phases, as illustrated in Figure 14.5. These phases are briefly described as follows.

1. *Program Proposal Phase.*
    (a) Establish communications with a needy or demanding constituency such as customers, taxpayers, stockholders, employees, or citizenry.
    (b) Define needs or demands in terms of goals to be pursued.
    (c) Agree on nature of goals and the direction they specify.
    (d) Identify benefits gained from pursuit of goals.
    (e) Formulate program or programs needed to attain goals.
    (f) Propose program or programs to constituency for approval.
    (g) Estimate resources needed to execute program.
2. *Program Direction Phase.*
    (a) Establish program management, organization, and staffing.
    (b) Identify number, type, and priorities of projects or products for program results.
    (c) Appoint project or product managers to handle responsibility.
    (d) Complete for each project an entire plan including objectives, costs, schedule, staff, technical requirements, accountability, work packages, and productivity.
    (e) Complete for each product development an entire plan including objectives, costs, schedule, staff, technical requirements, work packages, design, text, prototype development, manufacture, and installation.
    (f) Establish budget for entire program, with master schedule.
    (g) Organize and make available resources, equipment, staff, and facilities.
    (h) Establish documentation checklists and reporting procedures.
3. *Program Execution Phase.*
    (a) Approve scope and direction of program to entire organization.
    (b) Commence work on all projects and products according to schedule.
    (c) Resolve conflicts and frustrations over constraints.
    (d) Consult and aid where problems emerge or confusion exists.
    (e) Conduct progress milestone meetings for feedback and correction.
    (f) Renegotiate priorities where needed to complete program projects.
    (g) Institute budgetary and performance controls in program.

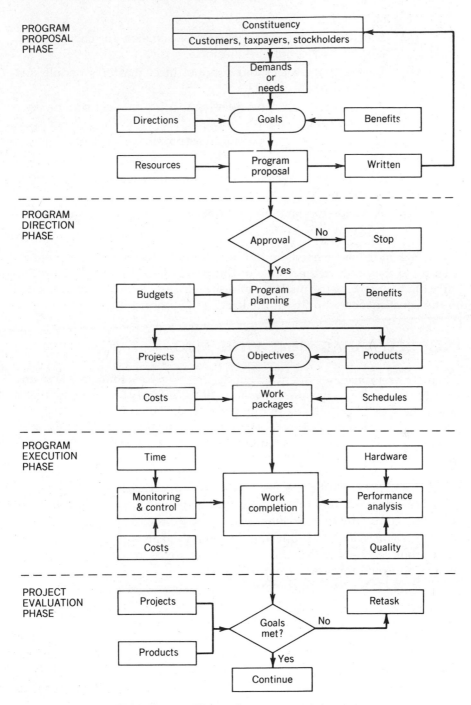

FIGURE 14.5 Phases of program management.

4. *Program Evaluation Phase.*

   (a) Schedule meetings for program evaluation for coordination, control, and conflict resolution.

   (b) Ensure that project and product meet master schedule and technical requirements.

   (c) Ensure project and product completion to meet constituency expectations, standards of quality, and goals.

   (d) Conduct quarterly milestones of progress meetings.

   (e) Evaluate performance and behavior of program personnel.

   (f) Conduct final evaluation of work in program and report to constituency.

   (g) Advance preparation of projects for new budgeting year of program.

The program manager needs to pull together all elements of the program relating to the products or results of the program, to the time required to carry out the work, to the final cost of resources, and to the benefits accrued to the constituency who first formalized and authorized the program.

PRODUCT MANAGEMENT WITH MBO

Products are consumer-oriented goods and services that are sold and bought in a market. They are the results of the efforts of management and labor, the specific outputs of an organization delivered for sale and profit. Product management is a way of organizing to make product delivery efficient and effective while maximizing profits. Several features make product management unique:

1. *Delegation.*   Profit and loss and other concerns of general management are delegated from top management to a lower level of management, for direct control by one person, termed the product manager.

2. *Accountability.*   A profit center is organized around a single product. This profit center is within a department or division. Controls, accountability, and reporting issue from this center.

3. *Entrepreneurial.*   The product manager assumes total responsibility for the product, as in a small business. The product manager is a venture manager. He or she starts, organizes, and manages a small business within the corporation, dealing with strategy, marketing, risk taking, operations, and profits as if he or she were in a separate and functioning small business.

4. *Single Product Line Segment.*   The product manager in many ways functions like a project manager, with high focus on one product or project. This means the product manager has the mission of achieving a set of objectives centered on one product. The marketability and profitability of this single product become the life-style and existence of the product manager.

5. *Customer Orientation.* The product manager has close customer relations. His or her mission is to attract and cultivate customers and then give them high product use satisfaction.

6. *Future Oriented.* Since the product manager is entrepreneurial, he or she strives to continue the venture. This is accomplished with planning, setting of objectives, performance measurement, quality attainment, and growth.

Product management does not exist as a single organizational function. It is part of a general organizational matrix (Figure 14.6). In practice there are all sorts of variations on the fundamental theme exhibited in Figure 14.6. But the basic idea of product management, irrespective of other organizational features, is the breakup of a large, cumbersome, and complex organization into an assemblage of individual small but autonomous businesses, each headed by a product manager.

Not all organizations can benefit from the concept of product management. Enterprises that find this organizational scheme useful are those with diverse, multiple, and unrelated product lines with a high degree of technological sophistication. Additionally, the firm believes in decentralization. The concept of product management continues the historic trend of "pushing downward" top management responsibility for profits, strategies, and controls. A firm whose philosophy is more for centralization will find the product management concept difficult to practice. A comparison of the major organizational concepts described in this section is shown in Table 14.2.

SCHEDULING AND CONTROLLED TARGETING

Whatever organizational approach is used for getting a set of results, scheduling and control are musts. In fact, planning, decision making, and results in program management, project management, product management, functional management, and executive management cannot take place without controls.

Control begins with planning. Planning and controlling are inseparable. The purpose of any control scheme is to keep activities, jobs or work packages, tasks, projects, and products on a prescribed course that will lead to expected results. Building milestones of progress into a plan allows assessment and regulation of work to make sure that what is happening is what should be happening in accordance with the plan. Four boundaries ensure that what is intended to be accomplished is accomplished:

1. Quantity (how much?).
2. Quality (how good?).
3. Cost (what expense?).
4. Time (when accomplished?).

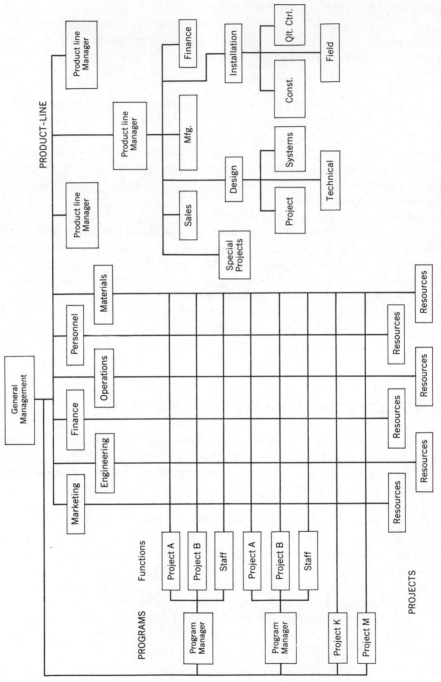

FIGURE 14.6 General matrix organization with programs, projects, and product management.

TABLE 14.2 Comparison of Managerial Concepts

Type of Manager	Targeted Emphasis	General Responsibilities	Type of Skills	MBO
Program managers	Program results	Continue program with greater success	Business, managerial, and technical	Short-range and operational planning
Project managers	Project completed	Complete project within schedule and budget	Business and technical	Operational planning
Product managers	Product line growth	Extend product line and profits	Business and entrepreneurial	Strategic and operational planning
Functional managers	Technological expertise	Provide resources needed	Technical and experiential	Operational planning
Executive managers	Company growth and profits	Extend growth and profits	Business, managerial, and economic	Long- and short-range planning

Tasks and activities are kept in perspective within these boundaries when they are directed toward the objectives of a program or project. Performance standards or program estimates become guidelines for comparing actual performance with expected performance. Sometimes there is overshooting of program estimates; sometimes there is undershooting. This overshoot or undershoot can make the difference between cost overruns and time delays. The overshoot or undershoot concept is illustrated in Figure 14.7. Controlled targeting means controlling program performance to keep quantity, quality, costs, and time to the requirements of the program. Hence the purpose of scheduling is to develop a structure for controlled targeting toward program or project objectives.

Definition and Development of a Schedule

Scheduling is a common time management practice found in almost every organization. Simply and briefly, *a schedule is a timetable for signaling when things should get done.* We use and are a part of many types of schedules—train schedules, airline schedules, work week schedules, compensation schedules, production schedules, material usage schedules, and others. A more formal definition is: *A schedule is a time-negotiated agreement on how allocated resources will be committed to achieving an objective.*

Organizations that use schedules effectively experience the following advantages:

1. Delegation and spreading of responsibilities to many groups.
2. Time baseline for coordinating starts and stops of various projects and programs.
3. Surveillance of work progress toward completion.
4. Signaling to a variety of groups when they are to start coordinating their actions toward project completion.
5. Formation of the basis of a negotiated agreement on how resources will be deployed to organizational programs.
6. Less dependence on personal relationships and "politics" and more on formal organizational links to gain commitments.
7. Reduced costs because of formalization of time-cost functions.
8. Enhanced managerial worth, since the greatest measure of successful management is achievement of a project within cost and on time.

To achievement-oriented managers, time presents an opportunity to achieve programs or objectives, but also provides limitations that constrain them. Time flows at a uniform, constant speed, every minute being like any other, yet to managers time seems uneven, fast or slow depending on how a program is progressing. There is no question about it—a measure of the effectiveness of managers is their ability to manage time to get the job done within the limited time committed to it.

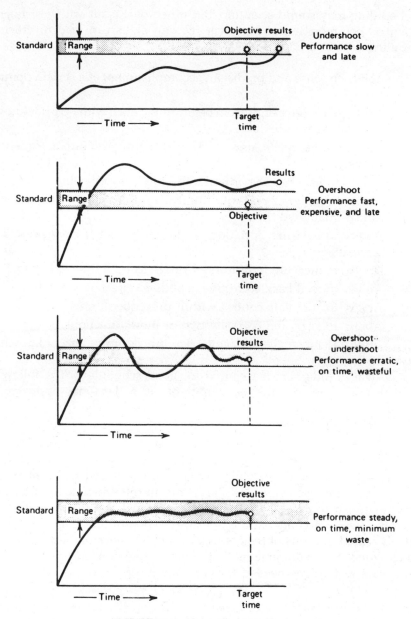

FIGURE 14.7 Controlled targeting.

Scheduling may sound scientific, but much of it is an art. Its strongest element is common sense. However, certain skills can lead to efficient scheduling:

1. Ability to sense and predict an accomplishment at a certain point in time.
2. Ability to perceive ends from beginnings, even with no prior knowledge or experience.
3. Ability to see, relate, and pace constituent parts into a sequenced whole.
4. Ability to focus on the critical and ignore the trivial.
5. Ability to analyze a mass of complexity into numbers and parts that can be quantified.
6. Ability to measure deviation, variance, and drift from prescribed directions.
7. Ability to measure indicators of progress on a time spectrum.
8. Ability to feed back corrective actions to effective variables.
9. Ability to stimulate control within prescribed limits.
10. Ability to align and correlate two or more directions.
11. Ability to move ahead despite risk, uncertainty, and unknowns.

A great deal of judgment is required for good scheduling. The following guidelines are aids in the development of a personal approach to scheduling.

1. *A Schedule Must Start With Well-Defined Objectives.* A schedule is a plan-ahead process that has a series of deliberate phases, events, and work processes from start to finish. Objectives provide the perspective for setting and structuring the schedule. All the details in the schedule are timed for start and finish to coordinate their interrelationship with the clock and calendar so as to accomplish the objective. Therefore objectives must be formally stated in terms of results, quantified for measurement purposes, and assigned time requirements that cover a single-ended result, and the resources and facilities needed for completion of the objectives must be clearly stated.

2. *A Schedule Must Be a Combination of Backward and Forward Planning.* Backward scheduling starts with a deadline and calculates the events necessary to reach the deadline. Forward scheduling starts with the present and calculates the events necessary to complete the project as soon as possible. Both have delivery dates. In the backward method, the customer dictates delivery. In the forward method, the events, resource allocations, or work processes dictate delivery. Good scheduling requires a combination of the two (Figure 14.8). Although the customer may not dictate, the customer should always be kept in mind.

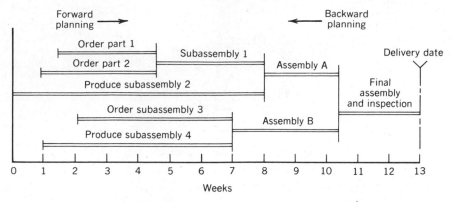

FIGURE 14.8 Good scheduling requires both backward and forward planning.

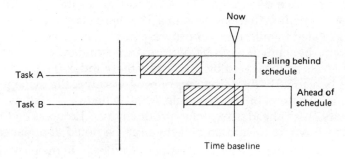

FIGURE 14.9 Good scheduling requires "now" time baseline.

3. *A Schedule Must Provide Readouts for Real-Time Reporting.* After-the-fact information helps only in future actions. It cannot control present activities. Real-time reporting means that progress variances are identified in sufficient time for the manager to make a useful correction before the target deadline. It may require day-to-day, week-to-week, or month-to-month surveillance. Real-time reporting puts the manager in position to make changes in the work processes or resource allocation in order to meet deadlines. Real-time reporting is infused into the schedule with the inclusion of the "now" time baseline (Figure 14.9).

4. *A Schedule Must "Play The Clock" With All Critical Items.* A schedule has "pace" as a theme. This means that work elements are arranged sequentially under a time tension. Not all items can be included in a schedule. All critical items, however, especially those with short lead times, must be included to signal the start and finish of the less significant items in the program. A schedule may include work phases, work centers, work packages, cost centers, machines, departments, workers, orders, operations, and assemblies. Efficient managers know that their entire performance is pitted against time. They have no choice but to "run the race." They can only assure that critical results are accomplished as they run along.

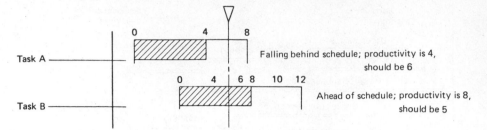

FIGURE 14.10   Productivity performance as benchmarks in a schedule.

5.   *A Schedule Must Give an Overview of Progress at a Glance.*   A graphic display of the entire program gives a manager the whole picture of progress at a glance. But more than this, variances between the progress expected and the progress experienced can be noted for special attention. Thus status reports on a schedule that has benchmarks where start and finish commitments are related to milestones of progress put the manager "in control" of the program. Benchmarks can be performance standards or expected productivity levels as measured by the productivity index (Figure 14.10). Setting these benchmarks for milestones of progress gives the manager a guide for spotting instances of "on schedule," "off schedule," "falling down on productivity," or "ahead of expected productivity." Progress on the overall program as it works toward an objective can be noted at a glance.

6.   *A Schedule Must Follow "Progressive" Planning.*   In the past, fixed time schedules were undisturbed until the work was completed. Today, flexible time schedules are the only workable kind. Conditions that may have a major impact on the completion of a program or project are changing continuously. The scheduler should be prepared and willing to take a "progressive" attitude and revise the schedule when a change is indicated. Progressive planning as a technique for flexible schedules calls for short-range results in the context of long-range expectancies. Suppose the short-range is one year and the long range five years. In progressive planning this means that at the end of the first year, short-range results are evaluated and long-range expectancies are revised in light of this evaluation. This continues each year for the five years.

7.   *A Schedule Must Be Analyzed for "Potential Failure" Points.*   Many indicators are "potential failure" points that can render a schedule useless. The scheduler should be alert to these indicators:

(a)   Confused or undefined work allocations.

(b)   Incorrect or unreliable information used in development of the schedule.

(c)   Loading of the schedule without coordination with other schedules and consultation with those who will implement the schedule.

(d)   Contingencies not built in to make the schedule flexible.

(e) Results expected by the scheduler not measurable.

(f) Control points not built in for implementation of the schedule.

(g) No analysis made of what could go wrong.

(h) High risk and impossible dates in schedule.

(i) Oversimplified schedule that ignores complexity of work.

Gantt Productivity Schedule

A Gantt productivity schedule is a graph of work activities plotted as bars on a linear time line that is scaled with productivity measures. Usually the work activities or programs are indicated vertically and future time is shown horizontally. Work activities are the variables, that is, the scheduler can increase or decrease them in terms of project needs. Time is the constant, that is, work is pitted against an even, uniform flow of time. Time divisions can be hours, days, months, weeks, or years. Productivity measures are plotted along the time line to give standards that must be met in a completed work package. The productivity index is used as this measure. Typical symbols and descriptions used in Gantt schedules are shown in Figure 14.11.

The Gantt productivity schedule is easy to construct and understand. The graphic display presents, at a glance, the total project on a time grid with time and productivity standards. It shows the time estimated for completion of each phase and the work that has been accomplished thus far. The Gantt productivity schedule is a moving picture of the work planned and the work completed. There isn't a great deal of detail in the schedule because it is intended as an overview of how the project or program is planned, the sequences of activities, and the work progress to date. From this standpoint, the schedule facilitates communication and coordination among many groups in the programs and projects. To develop a Gantt productivity schedule the following steps are suggested.

STEP 1.   List the work packages or work phases needed to complete the entire project.

STEP 2.   Arrange the list in a sequence of how the work packages will actually be completed from start to finish.

STEP 3.   Estimate the amount of time needed for each work package.

STEP 4.   Estimate the productivity expected for each work package. Use the productivity index.

STEP 5.   Using forward scheduling, plot each work package on a time grid as a bar indicating when each is to start and to finish.

STEP 6.   Project on the time grid any special requirements, such as overtime or contingency for delays.

Term	Symbol	Comments
Gantt		Henry L Gantt, originator of the scheduling technique in 1916
Inverted L left-hand		Start of a planned work activity
Inverted L right-hand		End of a planned work activity
Bar		Line connecting two inverted L's-estimated time for a complete work activity
Carot		Indicates present date on time scale
Bar with half crosshatching		Work activity half completed at the present date
Bar with full crosshatching		Work activity fully completed at the present date
Bar with a productivity index scale, partially crosshatched		Work activity falling behind-productivity index is 4. It should be 5 at present time
Circle with letters	(M)	Explanatory notes: In this case delay due to material (M) shortage
Long flat "X"		Reserved time for anticipated delays (contingency)

FIGURE 14.11 Symbols used in Gantt productivity schedules.

STEP 7. Indicate with a caret the date on which work progress is to be reported.

STEP 8. Identify in each work package the degree of work completion, that is, the variance from the "now" time line. Draw a progress line or crosshatch. This line shows actual progress to date.

STEP 9. Project on the schedule a note when a work package is falling behind and corrective action is to be taken.

The steps for developing a Gantt productivity schedule are illustrated in Figure 14.12.

The Gantt productivity schedule can be quantified to give a percentage completion approach for controlled targeting. "How much" is just as essential as "when accomplished." This requires calculation of a ratio of actual work packages completed, to the number of work packages required which gives the percentage of the project or program completed. A table or curve can be developed as a reference to the amount of lead time required for each work package before final project completion. A cumulative frequency distribution is developed that gives a measure of rise or fall in relation to a total. The productivity scheduler thus has an effective visual display of progress of actual work and productivity relative to expected work and

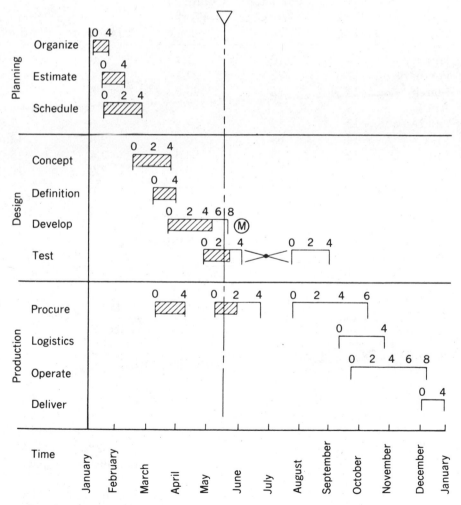

FIGURE 14.12   Gantt productivity schedule. *Note:* Manpower shortage Ⓜ. Completed in one week. Productivity is 5.2, should be 7.

productivity. These scheduling ideas are illustrated in the following example and also in Figure 14.13.

Example:

A program contains 90 work packages to be completed by five staff members within seven months. Halfway through the program, 30 work packages are completed. Determine the percentage completion and percentage productivity at the halfway mark. Show actual progress relative to scheduled progress in a cumulative productivity progress chart (Figure 14.14).

			Planned Schedule		
Time	Work Package	Cumulative Work Package	Percent Cumulative Work Package	Productivity	Cumulative Productivity
January	10	10	11.1	2.0	2.0
February	12	22	24.1	2.4	4.4
March	14	36	40.0	2.8	7.2
April, midway	13	49	54.4	2.6	9.8
May	14	63	70.0	2.8	12.6
June	12	75	83.3	2.4	15.0
July	15	90	100.0	3.0	18.0
Total	90			18.0	

$$\text{Percent work completed} = \frac{\text{work packages completed}}{\text{total work packages}} \times 100$$

$$= \frac{30}{90} \times 100 = 33.3$$

$$\text{Percent work completed} = \frac{\text{productivity completed}}{\text{productivity expected}} \times 100$$

$$= \frac{30/5}{9.8} \times 100 = 61.2$$

Schedules are inevitably affected by changes. In addition, information at the time of scheduling is usually partial and imperfect, so schedules must be changed when information becomes complete and precise. Managers should not hesitate to change a schedule if the schedule is to be a realistic control tool. The advantages of Gantt productivity schedules are as follows.

1. They are easy to understand for people outside the program.
2. They give an overview of the entire program.

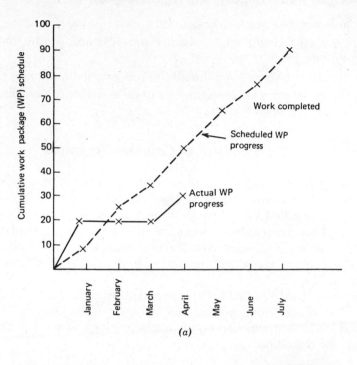

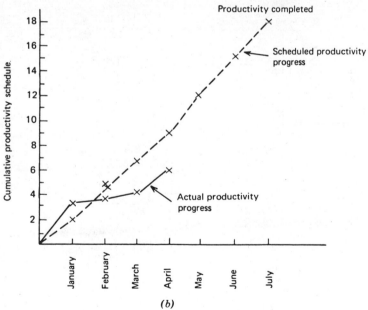

FIGURE 14.13 Cumulative progress charting: (*a*) Work package progress, (*b*) productivity progress.

3. They are easy and quick to construct.

4. Status readouts give a sense of work progress and productivity achievements.

5. They require little space for the amount of information given.

6. Changes in the form of corrections or improvements can be made with ease and dispatch.

PERT Schedules for Time Control of Complex Programs

A time-control technique that has gained wide acceptability as a network scheduling device and a network for the scheduling of nonrecurring projects within programs is called PERT (program evaluation review technique). Like Gantt, PERT is a visual graph of work activities and events spread out in a network to show clearly the interrelations between and among the work packages. The concept deals with planning and control problems of a nonrepetitive nature.

Unlike in Gantt schedules, in PERT there are no linear time scales. Time is assigned and controlled within the work package itself. Overall time is computed to provide a sense of accomplishment through all work packages in a network. By definition:

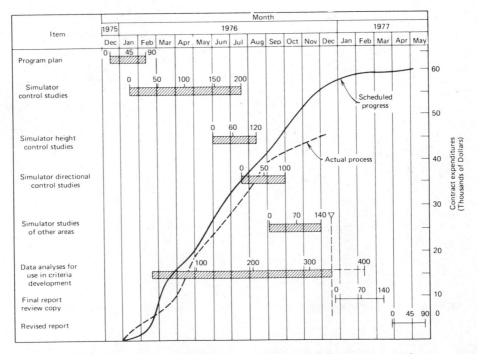

FIGURE 14.14   Cost accomplishment progress schedule: A case example.

PERT is a visual network that time controls the individual work events and activities to give progress toward a deadline of completion.

The purpose of PERT scheduling is to put a complex and uncertain plan into a structure and then to analyze what is to be done, when it is to be done, and what the probability is of getting there. PERT permits a program manager to "play the clock" in such a way that a job is accomplished in the shortest period of time with well-organized resources and activities. Typical symbols and descriptions used in PERT are shown in Figure 14.15.

PERT as a scheduling technique has several characteristics that make it valuable for certain applications.

1. *PERT Develops Planning and Controlling Skills for Program Management.* PERT skills are a development of a logical discipline in the defining, planning, scheduling, and control of projects. Seventy-five percent of the value of PERT for program managers is that it gives them a sense of mission, direction, start, finish, scope, interconnections, coordination, progress, and overview. It contributes greatly toward defining what is to be accomplished but not how it is to be accomplished.

2. *PERT Is Efficient for "One-Shot" Programs.* A PERT schedule gives a high degree of controlled targeting for one-of-a-kind programs that must meet deadlines. Repetitive programs usually have developed standards, in which case Gantt schedules are more efficient. PERT is superior to Gantt when standards are not available but only estimates.

3. *Program or Project "at a Glance" Communicates Interrelationships.* The network approach for connecting and interconnecting events and activities gives not only an overview of the project but the relationships in terms of input and output of all participating groups. In addition, the network serves to monitor or control the work program as it proceeds to its destination. The overview shows the best possible use of resources to achieve a goal within overall time and cost. It provides a means of documenting and communicating to all groups the commitments of time and cost performance.

4. *Schedule Can Be Structured Despite Uncertainties.* A schedule is no better than the information used for its development. When information is uncertain, schedules are weak. PERT allows for dealing with uncertainties so that risk factors are identified and carefully watched. Each PERT schedule has a probability factor for reaching a deadline.

5. *PERT Schedule Provides Control Where It Is Critical.* In each PERT schedule the work package that is significant to the project is identified as the critical path. This identification allows special surveillance and control for the scheduler and program manager. The critical element of the plan, usually 20 to 30 percent of the project, is brought into focus as it constrains the whole project. Potential trouble spots can also be identified through simulation and network manipulation. Debugging is made easier because program errors are visible.

Term	Symbol	Comments
PERT		Abbreviation for program evaluation and review technique
Event		Events shown as squares or circles, indicate what has gone before. Therefore events are phrased in the past tense. Events are "checkpoints" and show that work has been accomplished up to this point
Activity	$\xrightarrow{\;5\;}$	Lines represent work needed to accomplish an event. Event is completed when activity is accomplished. No work can start on next activity until preceding event is completed. Activity lines are not scaled, but numbers over the line indicate time required
Network (sequential flow diagram)		Web of events and activities with one starting event and one objective event
Time estimates		Discussed more fully in text
Optimistic time	t_o	Chance that activity can be done in less time than t_o is small
Most likely time	t_m	Best guess of time required. If only one time were available, this would be it. This is the "mode" of the distribution
Pessimistic time	T_p	Chance that the task will take longer than t_p is small
Expected time	t_e	Probability is 50% that activity completion will take less or more time $$t_e = \left[\frac{t_o + 4t_m + t_p}{6} \right]$$
Earliest expected time	T_e	Summation of all times, t_e, up to an event, staying with single path from start to finish. When two paths lead to an event, use the one with the greatest time. For example:
Latest allowable time	T_L	Latest time an activity can start and stay on schedule
Completion time		Instant in time that the project is scheduled for completion
Critical path	$\xrightarrow{T_c}$	Longest time path through the network. Any delay in the critical path will cause delay in the final event
Slack	T_s	Difference between latest allowable time and earliest expected time: $T_L - T_e$

FIGURE 14.15 Symbols use in PERT (program evalaution and review technique) schedules.

6. *Complex Number of Parts Are Planned on an Orderly Basis.*   PERT is efficient for handling large numbers of detailed events that must be brought together at the right time to produce an extremely complex project or product. The conception, development, design, procurement, testing, and assembly of projects in which work-time execution is critical are handled on an orderly and consistent basis by PERT. PERT allows preplanning of involved work packages and early signaling of special actions that should be taken by the manager.

Use of PERT for a Project or Program

The use of PERT for a project or program consists of five steps: (1) Define the work to be done for the entire project; (2) use backward planning and sequence the work definition from finish to start; (3) sequence into a network on a flowchart; (4) assign time estimates for each major activity or milestone of progress in the network; and (5) calculate the risk factor for meeting the deadlines. These steps are discussed here and illustrated with an example.

STEP 1.   Define the work to be done for the entire project.   Work should be thought of as a "package," that is, as made up of an event with its associated activity. This could also mean an objective with its action plan, an end item with its tasks, or a phase with its processes. All events arc paths leading to the terminating event. Defining the work is the first step in a PERT network. The most important analytical tool for definition of work is "work breakdown structure." It is a planning tool for linking objectives with resources in a framework in which other planning activities can be correlated. The work breakdown concept is a logical separation into related units of the total work required to do a job or reach an objective. It breaks the work down into logical divisions and subdivisions. Work breakdown structure is in principle an expanded definition of work in logical subunits. The concept of work breakdown into levels with logical divisions and subdivisions is not new to the average person. It is part and parcel of life. Many examples come to mind of this grouping into logical functions, departments, or branches. The organization chart is a graphic display of the division of labor, showing how work is grouped by specialties and hierarchy levels. A book such as this one, or a dictionary, or the Bible, is divided into smaller and smaller sections: chapters, sections, paragraphs, sentences, and words. These subordinate parts are tied logically into a framework to give meaning to the whole. Geographic location has the following breakdown structure: country, state, town, street, and number. The finished automobile is another illustration of work breakdown: We can trace engine level, carburetor level in the engine, float level in the carburetor, and aluminum material level of the float, each level depicting, respectively, an assembly, a subassembly, a component, a part, and a new material.

The manufacturing process offers another example of grouping by levels and functions: (1) concept feasibility and design level create the product; (2) development, testing, and feasibility checkout assure the product concept; (3) process planning, material ordering, and production control set the stage for hardware; (4) implementing and operating produce the hardware; (5) packaging, shipping, and distributing get the product into the hands of the consumer. From initial concept to consumer utilization, work breakdown provides a logical framework of divisions from system to subsystem, through task, subtask, level 1, level 2, level 3, and so on.

Figures 14.16 through 14.19 show examples of four general types of work breakdown structures: hardware, functional, process, and questioning. These structures give a number of important organizational uses to a project or a program. These uses are:

(a)   Overview of the work provided for the work team.

(b)   Structure of the work, showing how work packages are logically divided into work units and how they differ from one another.

(c)   Definition of the work, revealing omissions and overlapping.

(d)   Focus of the work, in pyramid fashion toward an objective.

(e)   Number of work packages, giving clarity, definition, and scope of the work of the total project.

(f)   Levels of the work, providing the basis for a time schedule.

(g)   Clear indication of the objective to be achieved; its measurability, starting point, and ending time; and its estimated cost and accountability.

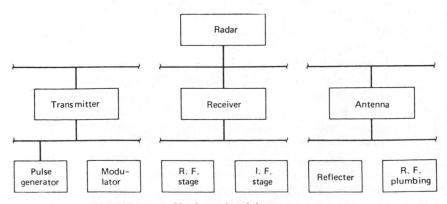

FIGURE 14.16   Hardware breakdown structure.

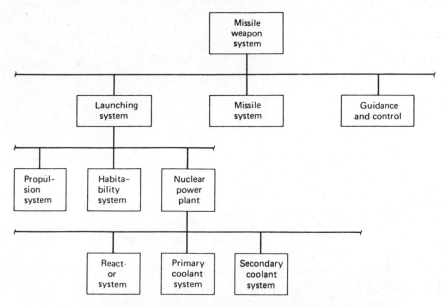

FIGURE 14.17 Functional breakdown structure.

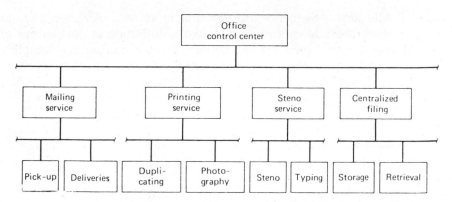

FIGURE 14.18 Process breakdown structure.

The use of the concept of work breakdown as a scheduling procedure starts with the objective to be reached. The practitioner relates all elements of the breakdown structure to this objective. He or she begins the breakdown by identifying the total effort required at the top level to support the first level. The second level contains work that must be completed to support the objectives. The third level contains more detail and a finer division of the work necessary to support the second level.

This work breakdown continues until the last level of work that can be delegated is identified. The subdivisions of the work at each

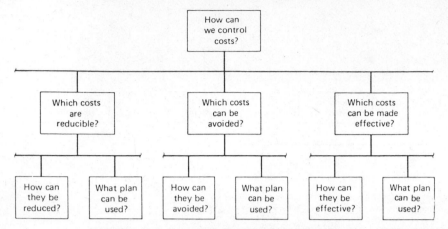

FIGURE 14.19 Questioning breakdown structure.

level are verified by examining the whole to be sure that the whole equals the sum of its parts. The subdivisions under a particular item must define completely all considerations making up that item.

STEP 1. Alternate. Sequence input/output modules. An alternative to work breakdown structure for work definition is the concept of input/output modules in a tandem flow. A module is a complete work package but conveys the idea that completion of the package feeds into an overall plan of work. When connected, the individual modules "flow" or "add" to form a total contribution. But more than this, a view of work packages for measuring productivity emerges, since productivity is the ratio of ouput to input. When total work can be seen as a series of connected work packages, a clarity of work definition and productivity emerges. Using the missile weapon system application shown in Figure 14.17, the total work flow using input/output modules is illustrated in Figure 14.20.

STEP 2. Sequence the work packages on a time grid. Each unit of a work breakdown structure can be considered as making up one or more events with an associated activity. The event is the end item to be accomplished at a recognizable point in time. If each subunit of a work breakdown structure can be regarded as an event, the structure contains starting events, terminating events, interface events, and feeder events. All events are milestones connected along paths leading to the terminating event, which is the ultimate completion of the work. The symbols for events and activities are shown in Figure 14.15. Circles are events, and arrows are their supporting activities. Figure 14.21 shows how events are connected on a start-finish grid. Since events are end items, they take up no time,

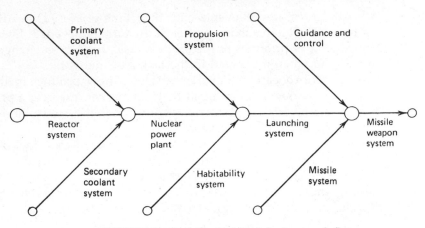

FIGURE 14.20   Input/output modules in a work flow.

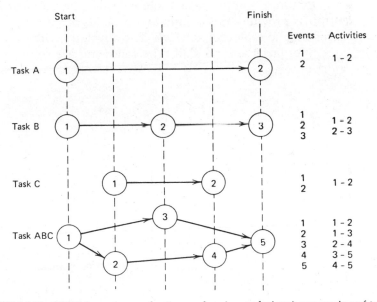

FIGURE 14.21   PERT (program evaluation and review technique) sequencing of tasks.

money, or resources in themselves. Activities, however, require time, money, and resources. Sequencing event activities on a time grid sets the stage for flow charting.

Suppose a market research program is to be the first step in the development of a new product. Event 1 would be described as market research begun; event 2 would be described as market research finished (Figure 14.21). The arrow between these two events is described as the activity necessary to conduct market research. Task A is seen as two events and one activity; task B is seen as three events and one activity, but shifted in time phase;

task ABC integrates all events with their time phases. Task ABC ties together all items that must reach the terminal event 5. Event sequences and priorities of the original tasks have been changed and shifted when integrated in the task ABC network.

As described earlier, development of a new product in the network may now require, in addition to market research, a production status analysis, an engineering feasibility study, and a state-of-the-art technological forecast.

The work breakdown structure can be a useful tool for sequencing and interrelating the work packages. By rotating the structure 90 degrees clockwise, placing it on a time grid, and shifting the events forward or backward, the stage is set for flowcharting into a network. This is illustrated in Figure 14.22.

STEP 3.   Flowchart sequence into a PERT network.   The term "network" indicates that several events and activities are combined in such a way that input-output relationships lead to an ultimate end. No formulas provide a precise and logical series of steps leading to an excellent and foolproof network. The development of meaningful networks takes art and skill. The following are some suggested guidelines.

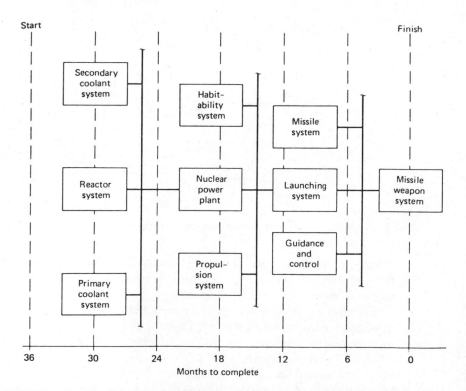

FIGURE 14.22   Rotation of work breakdown structure shown in Figure 14.17 to a time grid.

(a) The network should be developed by the individuals familiar with and committed to the objectives and requirements of the program.

(b) The work breakdown structure, which includes the logical sequence of end items and activities, must be agreed on by those developing the network.

(c) Development of the network should start with the ultimate targeted objective and move backward to the beginning event. The end objective is constantly and clearly in view, and the network is developed in direct relation to it.

(d) As the network is developed, the question is asked about each end item, "What activities must be completed before this event is completed?"

(e) An activity cannot begin until the event or end item preceding it has been completed.

(f) Wherever possible, two or more end items and associated activities that can be accomplished concurrently should be set up in parallel paths. This allows a high degree of delegation because of the related parallel efforts.

(g) A critical path should be identified to discover the longest time needed to accomplish end items and their associated activities. It is called "critical" because there is little time to do many things. Increased paralleling will decrease critical path time. Increased sequencing will increase critical path time.

(h) A slack path should be identified to discover the shortest time needed to accomplish end items and their associated activities. It is called "slack" because there is a great deal of time to do the few things. Decreased paralleling will increase slack path time. Decreased sequencing will decrease slack path time.

(i) When an event or an end item keeps two or more activities from starting, there is an even constraint. The event should be broken down into smaller events.

(j) When two or more activities hold back the completion of an end item, there is an activity constraint. The activities should be combined to lead to the end item. Figure 14.23 illustrates the development of a network.

STEP 4. Assign time estimates for each activity in the network. Once the tasks to be performed have been developed into a PERT network, a definite schedule of when each end item will be completed and the approximate date each activity will be started must be established. By including a schedule as a part of the program for implementation, the PERT plan not only helps keep actions in the proper phase but also sets target dates for those who are assigned the

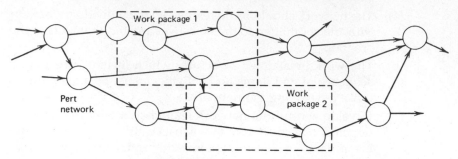

FIGURE 14.23 Work packages in a PERT (program evaluation and review technique) network.

responsibility for completion. These target dates go a long way toward ensuring that committed individuals execute their work before others commence theirs. This automatically forces coordination in starting and completing activities among several committed individuals. Time is clearly the basic variable in the PERT network, since it measures how long parts of the project will take. PERT time is expressed in days or weeks and is estimated on a probability projection of most likely time (t_m), most optimistic time (t_o), and most pessimistic time (t_p). Most likely time is an estimate of the time an activity would take if the same activity were repeated an independent number of times under identical conditions. It coincides with the central interval of a probability distribution curve encompassing 68 percent of the area on each side of the arithmetic mean (Figure 14.24).

The most likely time is the time estimate at the mean. The most optimistic time indicates work completed under better than normal conditions. It is an estimate of the minimum time an activity would take if unusually good circumstances and favorable conditions were experienced. It coincides with the interval segment of the probability curve encompassing approximately 16 percent of the area to the right of the first standard deviation.

The most pessimistic time concerns work completed under conditions less favorable than normal. It is an estimate of the maximum time an activity would take if unusually bad circumstances and unfavorable conditions were experienced. It coincides with the interval segment of the probability distribution curve encompassing approximately 16 percent of the area to the left of the first standard deviation.

An estimate of expected time, considering the effects of favorable and unfavorable conditions, can be calculated with the formula of expected time (t_e), as shown in Figure 14.24. Time estimates in a PERT network can now be assigned in terms of most likely time (t_m), most pessimistic time (t_p), most optimistic time (t_o), expected time (t_e), and the variance (t_e) measured in the calculation of expected time.

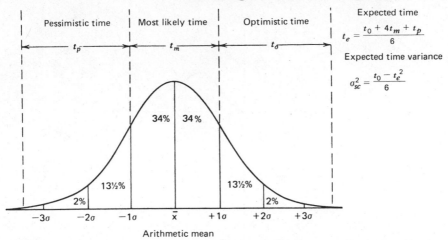

Pessimistic time | Most likely time | Optimistic time

t_p | t_m | t_o

Expected time

$$t_e = \frac{t_0 + 4t_m + t_p}{6}$$

Expected time variance

$$\sigma_{sc}^2 = \frac{t_0 - t_e^2}{6}$$

34% 34%

13½% 13½%

2% 2%

-3σ -2σ -1σ $\bar{x}$ $+1\sigma$ $+2\sigma$ $+3\sigma$

Arithmetic mean

FIGURE 14.24 Estimating time for PERT (program evaluation and review technique) activities.

STEP 5. Calculate the risk factor for meeting schedules. The opportunity to determine the probability that a project will be completed by a certain time is a unique feature of PERT. This probability is called the risk factor. Its calculation requires a knowledge of the mean time and variance for each activity. The accuracy of t_o, t_p, and t_m largely determines the shapes of the distribution curves (Figure 14.25). In calculating the risk factor of a PERT network, the distribution is assumed to be unimodal and the peak at t_m substantially normal.

Once the three time estimates are obtained and assigned to activities of the PERT network, the total time required for the entire network to reach the terminal event can be analyzed. Each activity time of a specific event is cumulated along the path of the network so that cumulated expected time and cumulated variance to expected time can be estimated for the objective to be reached. A PERT network that has several paths will have different cumulated time estimates. Paths that have the longest cumulated time are called critical paths because the entire project or program will be held up because of them. Paths that have the shortest cumulated time are called slack paths because a great deal of slack time occurs in completing their chain of events. To estimate the probability of meeting the schedule of events or work packages in the completion of an objective, the critical path must be calculated. Time estimates from this path are used as a basis for entering the normal probability distribution tables. The following illustrates this calculation.

Example: *Developing a PERT Time Network*

A research lab has tentatively decided to construct a new lab facility in Florida. An objective—completion of the facility in 18 months—has been

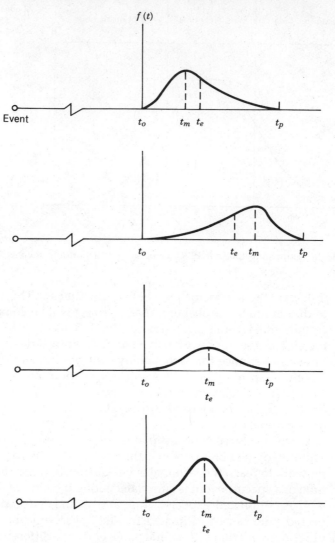

FIGURE 14.25   Time estimates affect PERT (program evaluation and review technique) distributions.

tentatively set. The management of the lab would like to know the probability of this objective being met.

STEP 1.   Define the work packages with work breakdown structure (Figure 14.26).

STEP 2.   Sequence work packages on a time grid (rotate work breakdown structure 90° clockwise)(Figure 14.27).

STEP 3.   Flowchart sequence into a PERT network (Figure 14.28).

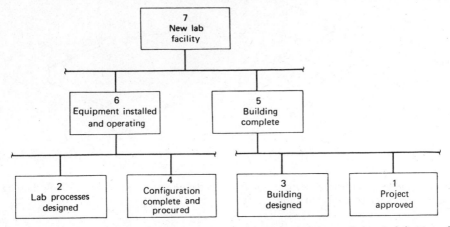

FIGURE 14.26 Step 1 in use of PERT (program evaluation and review technique): definition of work packages with work breakdown structures.

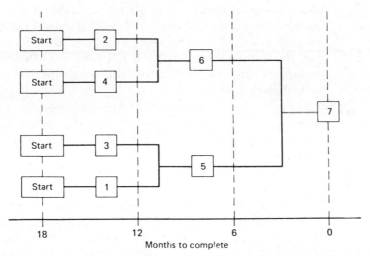

FIGURE 14.27 Step 2 in use of PERT (program evaluation and review technique): sequencing of work packages on a time grid.

STEP 4. Assign time estimates for each activity and calculate expected time (t_e), expected time variance (t_e^2), total earliest expected time (T_E), and total latest allowable time (T_L). Determine the slack $(T_L - T_E)$. A step-by-step calculation follows.

(a) Estimate, on the basis of past data, the time required to complete each of the events and enter these estimates in three columns: t_o, t_m, t_p (Figure 14.29)

(b) Calculate, using the formulas from Figure 14.24, the expected time and the expected time variance, and enter those values in two columns: t_e, σ_{te}^2 (Figure 14.29).

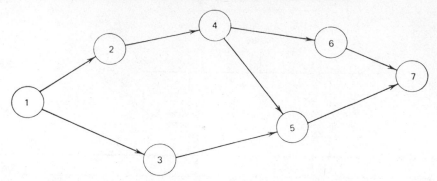

FIGURE 14.28   Step 3 in use of PERT (program evaluation and review technique):flowcharting of work package sequence into a network.

(c)   Calculate for each branch the total earliest expected time, which is the cumulation of t_e along a path, and enter those values in the column T_e. It should be noted that this results in three paths: 1-2-4-6-7; 1-2-4-5-7; 1-3-5-7 (Figure 14.29). Since the path 1-2-4-5-7 has the longest expected time for completion, it is termed the critical path. Completion of the events in the longest time can hold up the entire program. It is the path of least slack time.

(d)   Calculate, using the 18-month constraint, the latest allowable time (T_L) by working backward through the paths. Tabulate this in the column T_L. The latest allowable time (T_L), which represents the scheduled constraint of 18 months, is the maximum allowable time in which an event can be completed without affecting the completion of the network.

(e)   Calculate slack time (S_L) by getting the difference between the latest allowable time (T_L) and the earliest expected time (T_E). The slack of each event and the branches are illustrated in the flowchart in Figure 14.29. Critical path 1-2-4-5-7 has the least slack time because the cumulated slack time of events is at a minimum. Enter the values calculated in this procedure in the column for slack time (Figure 14.29).

(f)   Calculate the risk factor for meeting the schedule. The calculation for risk factor (probability) is

$$\text{Probability factor } (PF) = \frac{T_L - T_E}{\sigma_{T_E}}$$

A low PF indicates the schedule is not feasible. A high PF indicates the schedule is feasible. The standard deviation of the timed activities (T_E) of the critical path is 1.48 (determined

Event Number	PERT Events	Successor Events	Past Estimates			Calculations				Slack Time (S_L) $(T_L - T_E)$
			t_o	t_m	t_p	t_e	$\sigma_{t_e}^2$	T_E	T_L	
1	Project approval	2	1	2	9	3	1.28	3	5	2
		3	3	4	5	4	.112	4	8	4
2	Laboratory process designed	4	2	4	6	4	.448	7	9	2
3	Building designed	5	3	5	13	6	2.78	10	14	4
4	Configuration complete and procured	5	4	45	8	5	.448	12	14	4
		6	1	2	3	2	.112	9	15	6
5	Building completed	7	4	4	4	4	.0	14	18	2
6	Equipment installed and operable	7	2.5	3.0	3.5	3	.278	12	18	6
7	Laboratory facilities completed	—	—	—	—	—	—	—	—	—

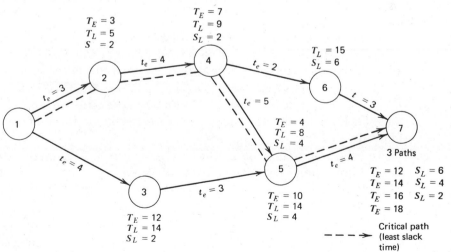

FIGURE 14.29 Calculating the critical path in a schedule.

by adding the variances of $\sigma_{T_E}^2$ of critical path 1-2-4-5-6 and extracting the square root). The PF calculation for our example is

$$PF = \frac{T_L - T_E}{\sigma_{T_E}} = \frac{18 - 16}{1.48} = 1.35 \ (one \ half \ the \ normal \ curve)$$

A PF of 1.35 corresponds to a probability of .4115 (Table 14.3). For the full normal distribution curve, this value is added to .5000, to equal .9115, or 91.2 percent. This means the probability of meeting the 18-month schedule for completion of the new lab facility is 91.2 percent.

PERT/Cost Time Schedules

"PERT/cost" is an extension of "PERT/time." The PERT/time network (which is PERT applied to a schedule) surveils time as the PERT/cost network surveils cost. The PERT network becomes the basis for analysis of cost alternatives and deciding on the best plan of action. PERT/cost analysis is done to find the best mix of time and cost for the project or program. The traditional approach follows a single line-cost estimate for each work package, but this prevents study of the amount of time that might be saved if more money were spent or, conversely, the amount of money that might be saved if deadlines were extended. Research and experience have verified the inverse relationship between costs and time (Figure 14.30).

Implementation of a PERT/cost network follows three general approaches.

1. *Single-Point Cost Estimates of Expected Actual Cost.* Estimates are made for the total direct costs of each work package. Indirect costs are added either to each work package or to the total cost of the project.
2. *Three-Cost Estimate of Expected Actual Cost.* Three estimates are made: C_P, pessimistic cost estimate; C_o, optimistic cost estimate; and C_L, most likely cost estimate. The expected cost estimate formula combines the three.
3. *Variable Estimates Based on a Known Cost Function.* Estimates are made from a time-cost curve. Differential costing with time is the variable. This approach assumes a direct relationship between time and cost.

An example of time-cost tradeoffs is shown in Figure 14.31. Time-cost tradeoffs give the cost priority for reducing the project time. Several patterns suggest how much flexibility is possible in a tradeoff (Figure 14.32). The program manager must determine which function may apply to the project.

TABLE 14.3 Probability of Meeting Schedules

PF	.00	.01	.02	.03	.04	.05	.06	.07	.08	.09
0.0	.0000	.0040	.0080	.0120	.0160	.0199	.0239	.0279	.0319	.0359
0.1	.0398	.0438	.0478	.0517	.0557	.0596	.0636	.0675	.0714	.0753
0.2	.0793	.0832	.0871	.0910	.0948	.0987	.1026	.1064	.1103	.1141
0.3	.1179	.1217	.1255	.1293	.1331	.1368	.1406	.1443	.1480	.1517
0.4	.1554	.1591	.1628	.1664	.1700	.1736	.1772	.1808	.1844	.1879
0.5	.1915	.1950	.1985	.2019	.2054	.2088	.2123	.2157	.2190	.2224
0.6	.2257	.2291	.2324	.2357	.2389	.2422	.2454	.2486	.2518	.2549
0.7	.2580	.2612	.2642	.2673	.2704	.2734	.2764	.2794	.2823	.2852
0.8	.2881	.2910	.2939	.2967	.2995	.3023	.3051	.3078	.3106	.3133
0.9	.3159	.3186	.3212	.3238	.3264	.3289	.3315	.3340	.3365	.3389
1.0	.3413	.3438	.3461	.3485	.3508	.3531	.3554	.3577	.3599	.3621
1.1	.3643	.3665	.3686	.3708	.3729	.3749	.3770	.3790	.3810	.3830
1.2	.3849	.3869	.3888	.3907	.3925	.3944	.3962	.3980	.3997	.4015
1.3	.4032	.4049	.4066	.4082	.4099	.4115	.4131	.4147	.4162	.4177
1.4	.4192	.4207	.4222	.4236	.4251	.4265	.4279	.4292	.4306	.4319
1.5	.4332	.4345	.4357	.4370	.4382	.4394	.4406	.4418	.4429	.4441
1.6	.4452	.4463	.4474	.4484	.4495	.4505	.4515	.4525	.4535	.4545

(Continued)

TABLE 14.3 (Continued)

PF	.00	.01	.02	.03	.04	.05	.06	.07	.08	.09
1.7	.4554	.4564	.4573	.4582	.4591	.4599	.4608	.4616	.4625	.4633
1.8	.4641	.4649	.4656	.4664	.4671	.4678	.4686	.4693	.4699	.4706
1.9	.4713	.4719	.4726	.4732	.4738	.4744	.4750	.4756	.4761	.4767
2.0	.4772	.4778	.4783	.4788	.4793	.4798	.4803	.4808	.4812	.4817
2.1	.4821	.4826	.4830	.4834	.4838	.4842	.4846	.4850	.4854	.4857
2.2	.4861	.4864	.4868	.4871	.4875	.4878	.4881	.4884	.4887	.4890
2.3	.4893	.4896	.4898	.4901	.4904	.4906	.4909	.4911	.4913	.4916
2.4	.4918	.4920	.4922	.4925	.4927	.4929	.4931	.4932	.4934	.4936
2.5	.4938	.4940	.4941	.4943	.4945	.4946	.4948	.4949	.4951	.4952
2.6	.4953	.4955	.4956	.4957	.4959	.4960	.4961	.4962	.4963	.4964
2.7	.4965	.4966	.4967	.4968	.4969	.4970	.4971	.4972	.4973	.4974
2.8	.4974	.4975	.4976	.4977	.4977	.4978	.4979	.4979	.4980	.4981
2.9	.4981	.4982	.4982	.4983	.4984	.4984	.4985	.4985	.4986	.4986
3.0	.49865	.4987	.4987	.4988	.4988	.4989	.4989	.4989	.4990	.4990
4.0	.4999683									

$$C_e = \frac{C_p + 4\,C_L + C_o}{6}$$

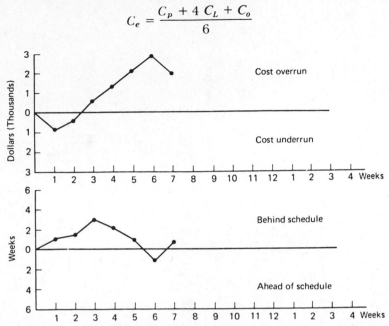

FIGURE 14.30 Cost−time performance relationship. C_e, expected cost; C_p, pessimistic cost estimate; C_L, most likely cost estimate; C_o, optimistic cost estimate.

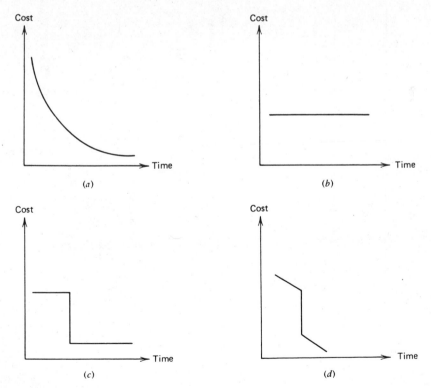

FIGURE 14.31 Cost-function tradeoffs. (a) Marginal cost function. (b) Constant cost function. (c) Step-increase constant cost function. (d) Step-increase increasing cost function.

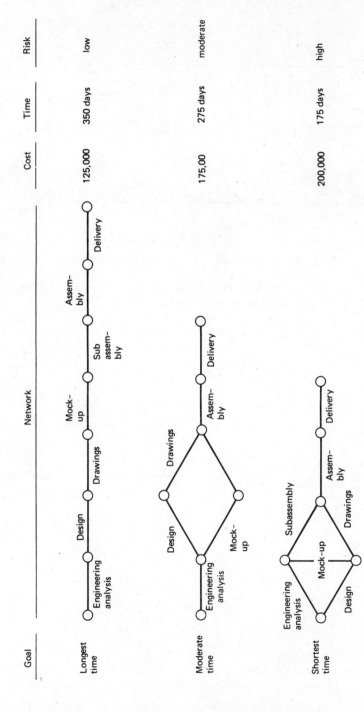

FIGURE 14.32 Cost-time tradeoffs.

PERT Productivity Time Schedules

PERT productivity is an extension of PERT time. PERT networks control time; PERT cost networks control costs with time, and PERT productivity networks control productivity with time. A PERT productivity network becomes the basis for analyzing productivity alternatives for deciding the best plan of action. The analysis develops time options in order to find the best mix of time and productivity for a project or program. A PERT productivity network is developed to estimate the probable productivity within a probable delivery date with that figure, decisions can be made to accept or trade off productivity with time or accept or trade off time with productivity.

The example of the research lab used previously will be used again to illusrate how PERT productivity schedules are developed. The most recent allowable productivity for the program is 6.5. The formula for expected productivity (P_e) combines the three productivity estimates made of each work package:

$$P_e = \frac{P_o + 4P_m + P_p}{6}$$

$$\sigma_{P_e}^2 = \left(\frac{P_p - P_o}{6}\right)^2$$

where
P = productivity as estimated from the productivity index (PI)
P_e = expected productivity in the network
P_o = productivity when work package (wp) conditions are optimistic (PI = wp/t_o)
P_p = productivity when work package (wp) conditions are pessimistic (PI = wp/t_p)
P_m = most likely productivity (PI = wp/t_m)
σ_{p_c} = expected productivity variance
P_E = total expected productivity
P_L = most recent allowable productivity (6.5 for the entire program)
$P_L - P_E$ = slack productivity

Productivity figures for the previous example are now calculated. The results are shown in Figure 14.33. The critical path 1-2-4-6-7, where estimated slack is minimal is the path that should be of major concern in the completion of the laboratory facilities design and construction. An option is always available to the manager who is to make the decision to trade off productivity with cost or time. Alternatives in this option would necessitate recalculations of alternate time and cost estimates.

Event Number	PERT Events	Successor Events	Work Packages	Productivity Estimates			Calculations				Slack Productivity (S_L) ($P_L - P_E$)
				P_o	P_M	P_p	P_e	$\sigma^2_{P_e}$	P_E	P_L	
1	Specs and approval	2	8	8	4	.88	4.2	1.44	4.2	2.2	2.0
		3	5	1.6	1.3	1	1.3	.01	1.3	.5	0.8
2	Laboratory process designed	4	4	2	1	.67	1.1	.05	5.3	3.3	2.0
3	Building designed	5	10	3.3	5	.77	4.0	.187	5.3	4.5	0.8
4	Configuration complete and procured	5	6	1.5	1.3	.75	1.2	.02	6.5	4.5	2.0
		6	2	2	1	.65	1.1	.05	6.4	5.8	0.6
5	Building completed	7	8	2	2	2	2	0	7.1	6.5	0.6
6	Equipment installed and operable	7	2	.8	.67	.57	.7	.001	7.3	6.5	0.8
7	Laboratory facilities completed	—	—	—	—	—	—	—	—	—	—

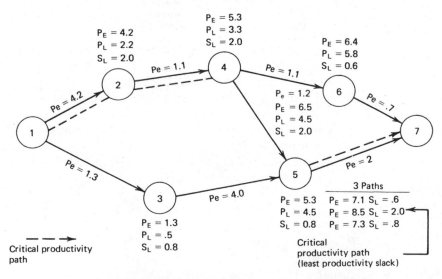

FIGURE 14.33 Calculating the critical productivity path.

Critical Ratio Scheduling for Developing Priorities

Program managers who are responsible for the completion and delivery of many often-conflicting programs will find critical ratio scheduling a useful technique for resolving these time conflicts. This technique attempts to organize, surveil, and control the priorities of the many programs that need to be completed. The critical ratio relates the time relationship between service needs and the organization's capacity to supply these needs. The ratio is

$$\text{Critical ratio (CR)} = \frac{\text{service demand time (DT)}}{\text{organization's supply time (ST)}}$$

$$\text{CR} = \frac{15 \text{ weeks}}{20 \text{ weeks}} = .75$$

The critical ratio indicates how fast or how slow a program should be completed in relation to normal time. In the example just given, the program should be accelerated and completed in three quarters of the normal time. When this program and its critical ratio are compared with other programs and their critical ratios, priorities can be established. Priorities are determined primarily by the customer. The critical ratio is used for the following reasons.

1. *It Gives an Overview of the Relative Priorities of Several Programs.* A matrix can be set up that provides the relative priorities of the respective programs at a given date. At that date all programs are directly comparable regardless of when they are needed or why they will be completed (Table 14.4).

In complex organizations, these relative priorities signal where special attention is needed and where resources are critically required.

2. *Senses Trends in Which a Delivery May Be Faulted.* Tracing through the reporting periods on a program matrix gives the drift that may prevail for each program. Action may be required to change the drift.

TABLE 14.4   Critical Ratios of Different Programs on Reporting Dates

Programs	January	February	March	April
A	1.26	1.25	1.25	1.25
B	1.00	1.00	0.75	0.50
C	1.50	1.50	1.50	1.50
D	2.00	2.00	2.00	2.00
E	0.50	0.75	1.00	1.00

(a)   When CR = 1.00, the program is on time and delivery will be as expected.

(b)   When CR > 1.00, the program is ahead of schedule and delivery will be in advance.

(c)   When CR < 1.00, the program is behind schedule and delivery may be faulted (critical).

Note program B will be in trouble in March and April. Program E will improve by March and April. Spare capacity in other programs can be shifted to help Program B.

3.   *It Relates Service Demands to the Capacity to Fulfill Them.*   A procedure is created that relates the capacity to provide customer services with the time demands of the system. This procedure utilizes frequent feedback information of the demand and supply placed on the capacity system. Programs with low delivery demands are "set aside" so that the critical programs can move faster. In this way a master schedule can be set up and made dynamic for the organization.

Setting Up a Critical Ratio Schedule

STEP 1.   Establish a centralized cost, or productivity, center.   This center records programs in the order of their arrival. It identifies the oldest job based on start date and finish dates. It records and centralizes all information for program expediting. In most cases, the productivity center is not a place but rather the program manager.

STEP 2.   Formalize the capacity system.   In complex organizations the functional groups are the operating resources that provide the capacity system. A master schedule should be set up to show, *in general, the total capacity available and the capacity being utilized*. When the system is placed on a time grid, supply time readouts are readily available.

STEP 3.   Establish the critical ratio for the program.   Use the generalized formula for the supply-demand time relationship:

$$CR = \frac{\text{date required} - \text{present date}}{\text{time required to complete job}} = \frac{\text{demand}}{\text{supply}}$$

STEP 4.   Establish program queues in tabular form.   After calculating all critical ratios for the programs within a work center, sort and display them in a tabular sequence and arrange the sequence in a priority queue.

Program Productivity

Programs	Man-Hours	Cumulative	Critical Ratio	Critical Programs
C	300	—	.55	*
A	250	550	.75	*
D	570	1120	1.00	
E	1300	2420	1.21	
B	450	2870	1.35	

Advantages of Critical Ratio Scheduling

The advantages of using the critical ratio scheduling approach for time management are as follows:

1. Gives status of a specific job relative to the capacity system.
2. Shows where the program manager should focus attention.
3. Provides a basis for adjusting priorities.
4. Permits tracking program progress to completion.

Master Scheduling for Tracking Total Capacity

Most organizations have to schedule many programs and projects that utilize the same resources. Rarely are resources developed for and used solely in one program or project. Management of several programs during the same time using the same resources is the order of the day, no change seems likely in the near future.

Master scheduling is a centralized scheduling concept that tracks the total capacity of the system and how the system is being utilized. It is especially useful when many items must be sequenced for accomplishment and the capacity system is limited. Program work loads are apportioned so that individual work requirements are subordinated to the master scheduling program. Due dates for customer orders and completion times for delivery are critical in master scheduling formats.

Master scheduling procedures are developed within the conditions prevailing for a capacity system; no one "model" fits the master scheduling needs of all organizations. The following are some of the essentials that each model should contain.

1. *Sales or Service Demand Forecast.* This is a projection of the future work to be placed on the capacity system. The projection should be both short and long range over a variety of customers or those requiring service.

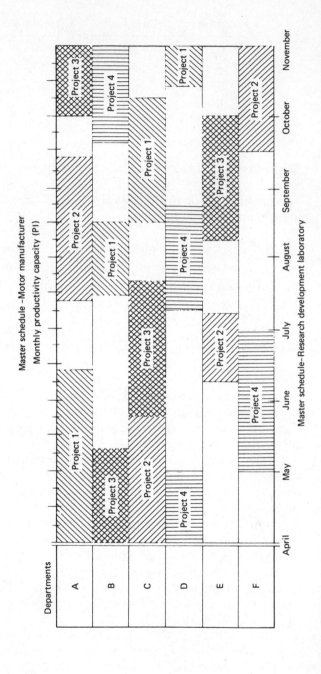

Master schedule –Motor manufacturer
Monthly productivity capacity (PI)

Master schedule– Research development laboratory

Master Schedule—Motor Manufacturer

	January	February	March	April	May	June	July	August	September	October	November	December
AC Model												
Units scheduled	500	400	500	400	400	400	500	400	500	400	400	400
Actual units	500	900	1,400	1,800	2,200	2,600	3,100	3,500	4,000	4,400	4,000	5,200
Monthly hours	6,000	5,000	6,000	5,000	5,000	5,000	6,000	5,000	6,000	5,000	5,000	5,000
Actual hours	6,000	11,000	17,000	22,000	27,000	22,000	38,000	43,000	49,000	54,000	59,000	64,000
DC Model												
Units scheduled	1,000	1,000	1,000	1,000	1,000	1,000	1,000	1,000	1,000	1,000	1,000	1,000
Actual units	1,000	2,000	3,000	4,000	5,000	6,000	7,000	8,000	9,000	10,000	11,000	12,000
Monthly hours	10,000	10,000	10,000	10,000	10,000	10,000	10,000	10,000	10,000	10,000	10,000	10,000
Actual hours	10,000	20,000	30,000	40,000	50,000	60,000	70,000	80,000	90,000	100,000	110,000	120,000
AC/DC Model												
Units scheduled	30	20	20	30	30	20	20	30	30	20	20	20
Actual units	30	50	70	100	130	150	170	200	230	250	270	290
Monthly hours	5,000	3,000	3,000	5,000	5,000	3,000	3,000	5,000	5,000	3,000	3,000	3,000
Actual hours	5,000	9,000	11,000	16,000	21,000	24,000	27,000	32,000	31,000	40,000	43,000	46,000
Total units	1,530	1,420	1,520	1,430	1,430	1,420	1,520	1,430	1,530	1,420	1,420	1,420
Total hours	21,000	18,000	19,000	20,000	20,000	18,000	19,000	20,000	21,000	18,000	18,000	18,000

FIGURE 14.34 Examples of master schedules.

2. *Customer Completion or Delivery Service Requirements.* Customer demands or specific delivery service requirements must be made specific to a time baseline in a context of all programs and projects of the organization.

3. *Total Capacity of the System.* Total capacity in quantitative terms such as man-hours per month or productivity per month should be displayed on a time grid (Figure 14.34). Spaces that are not used represent open capacity still available.

4. *Operating Department Capacities and Loads.* The effectiveness of a master schedule is directly related to how well surveillance can be conducted of the utilization of resource departments, how well "spare" capacity can be identified during different periods of time. An example of surveillance of total forecasted work in relation to available capacity is shown in the following.

5. *Project Status Details That Indicate Action Needed.* A need develops from time to time in master scheduling practices to collect the status of several projects or programs. A project or program status board should be developed that lists the projects and programs on a time matrix. The status of each project or program is also indicated on this matrix for an overview (Figure 14.35). Action required to correct the status may also be indicated on the status board.

					Forecasted Work			
Month	Week	Total Capacity	Program A	Program B	Program C	Miscellaneous Programs	Total Forecasted Work	Available Capacity
January	1	9,600	1200	1000	500	200	2,900	6700
	2	9,600	6500	3000	1000	500	11,000	(1400)
	3	9,600	4600	3800	2500	1000	11,900	(2300)
	4	9,600	5000	2500	1800	200	9,500	100
		38,400					35,300	3100

SUMMARY

High technology and computerization of work processes are two major forces causing shifts in the work force and in how organizations operate. The information and knowledge worker is a product of these forces. Old-style managerial processes need to be adjusted to accommodate these major shifts.

"High technology" is a term that describes new, complex, and developing technologies that are changing how products are produced. The unique feature of high technology is its integration of several technologies. Management must keep abreast of these integrated technologies and develop the ability to deal with tasks or products that have short life cycles, to use

1976   1977

Programs		J	F	M	A	M	J	J	A	S	O	N	D	J	F	M	A	M	J	J	A	S
	A		○																			
	T			○	○	○	○	○	○	○	○	○	○	○	○	○						
A	S			○	○	○	○	●	●	●	†	†	*	*	●	●	○					
	Q			●	●	●	●	○	○	○	○	○	○	○	○	○	○					
	C			†	†	†	†	†	†	●	●	○	○	○	○	○	○					
	F			*	*	†	†	●	●	○	○	○	○	○	○	○	○					
	A				○																	
	T						○	○	○	○	○	○										
B	S						○	●	●	○	○											
	Q						○	●	†	*	†											
	C						○	○	○	○	○											
	F						○	○	○	○	○											
	A									○	●	●	○									
	T											○	†	†	●							
C	S											●	●	○	○							
	Q											○	○	○	○							
	C											○	○	○	○							
	F											○	○	○	○							
	A			†																		
	T			●	●																	
D	S			*	*																	
	Q			○	○																	
	C					†																
	F			†	†																	
	A					○																
	T							○	○	○	○	●	●	●	●	○	○					
E	S							†	†	*	*	*	*	*	†	†	●					
	Q							●	●	●	●	●	○	○	○	○	○					
	C							○	○	○	○	○	○	○	○	○	○					
	F							○	○	○	○	○	○	○	○	○	○					

A = Program plan approved
T = Technical status
S = Schedule status
Q = Quality status
C = Cost status
F = Funding status

○ = Work OK
● = Work OK but be alert
   to conditions that
   could cause trouble.
† = Warning, action needed
   to avert trouble.
* = In trouble-out of
   control.

FIGURE 14.35   Programs status board.

entrepreneurial skills, to view technology as a resource itself, and to manage decision making more as a matrix type of activity than a linear type.

Three major types of organizational processes for getting results are described in this chapter: project, program, and product. Each of these processes is useful for managing high technology developments. The selection of one over another depends on the complexity of the process and the circumstances of the organization. This chapter describes in detail how each of these processes can be instituted and managed.

Whatever approach is selected, scheduling and controlled targeting are needed to ensure progress toward results. Controlled targeting ensures that quantity, quality, cost, and time are achieved according to the organization's process and expectation. This chapter provides considerable detail on the following topics:

1. What a schedule is and how it is developed.
2. Gantt productivity schedules.
3. PERT schedules.
4. PERT/cost time schedules.
5. PERT productivity time schedules.
6. Critical ratio scheduling.
7. Master scheduling.

The essential principle is that most organizations seldom have all the resources they need to achieve their results. Scheduling is a way of sharing and matching resources to needs to certain points in time.

BIBLIOGRAPHY

Arai, Joji, "U.S. and Japanese Technology. A Comparison." *National Productivity Review*, Summer 1982.

Archibald, Russell, D., *Managing High Technology Programs and Projects*. New York: Wiley, 1976.

Breeding, Robert E., and Morris, Frederick K., "Product Management." In P. Mali, Ed., *Management Handbook*. New York: Wiley, 1981.

Levine, Susan J., and Yalowitz, Michael S., "Managing Technology: Key to Successful Business Growth." *Management Review*, September 1983.

Naisbitt, John, *Megatrends*. New York: Warner, 1982.

O'Brien, J. J., *Scheduling Handbook*. New York: McGraw-Hill, 1969.

15

RESOURCE MANAGEMENT WITH MBO

IN THIS CHAPTER

WHAT IS RESOURCE MANAGEMENT?
CAUSES OF THE NEW SCARCITY
WHY RESOURCE MANAGEMENT IS NEEDED
RESOURCE USE STRATEGIES WITH MBO
MAXIMIZING RESOURCE USE
EXAMPLE OF CAPACITY UTILIZATION WITH MBO

Resources are scarce! They will always be scarce. The managerial practitioner must prepare for continual material shortages on the road to the twenty-first century. Every company's goal is to obtain scarce resources from suppliers at the lowest possible cost while maintaining competitive position. The first chapter of this book gave statistics and trends that indicated that scarcity of resources will become more and more critical. During the oil shortage of the early 1970s, people talked of this shortage and little else. A resource shortage consumes our time and attention. However, as soon as the emergency passes, we seem to forget the shortage and behave as though it never existed. Companies are no different. They develop ingenious strategies during the crisis and later forget them when the crisis is over. Savvy companies, however, devise strategies for the long term so they do not have to struggle from crisis to crisis. A special need exists for companies to keep watch over their sources of supply and levels of consumption.

This chapter provides some well-thought-out strategies for surviving the short-range shortages while making long-range conservation efforts. More specifically, the chapter covers (1) what resource management is and why it is important for all managers regardless of their position and responsibility, (2) the causes of the new scarcity, (3) strategies for maximizing resource use, (4) MBO for resource-use management, and (5) guidelines for effective resource managing. An example is given showing maximization of capacity use by a manufacturing resource.

WHAT IS RESOURCE MANAGEMENT?

Resource management is a formal effort and responsibility designed to identify savings and efficiencies relative to the use of operational, human, marketing, and financial resources in the achievement of company objectives. Therefore resource management is a responsibility of all managers who deal with and consume resources. The deployment of limited resources for organizational objectives does not automatically assure their efficient use. Since the supply of resources tends to change, usually becoming scarcer, productivity is affected greatly by how resources are handled. This should give some insight into why productivity can decline even though resource use has not exceeded the allocation. Changes make the gap between demand and resource use grow wider (Figure 15.1). Scarcity increases as a result of upward changes in demand and obsolescence in resource use. Resource management means organizing to identify and manage these changes. It is an effort, particularly in multidivisional corporations, to integrate resource use in the face of increasing demand. Managerial efficiency is defined in terms of resource utilization in relation to organizational goal attainment. If organizations are using their resources well to attain their goals, their managers are efficient. In reality, there are degrees of managerial efficiency. The closer organizations come to achieving

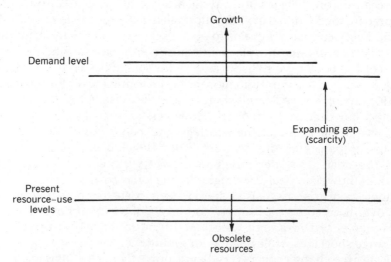

FIGURE 15.1   Scarcity is the gap between demand and resource use.

their goals with expected or less than expected resource use, the more efficient the managers are said to be.

In the role of resource allocator, a manager tends to allocate according to some historic pattern. The manager decides who will get what resources on the basis of how the resources were allocated in the past. It might be well at this point to define resource.

Resources are

- Buildings, plants, tools, equipment (fixed asset resources).
- Inventories (material resources).
- Time (opportunity resources).
- Skilled and semiskilled employees (human resources).
- Supplies, paper, and sundries (support resources).
- Budgetary allocations (developmental resources).
- Money (cash resources).
- Energy (overhead resources).
- Information (knowledge resources).

The manager often focuses with magnificent skill on the objectives to be achieved but does little with the choices that are available for how resources are allocated. Since allocation of a resource to one area automatically deprives another area of that resource, the manager must employ effective resource-use strategy. In other words, if two roads lead to the same destination, the road on which the least resources are expended should be selected.

CAUSES OF THE NEW SCARCITY

Shortages are everywhere. There hasn't been a time in the history of mankind that shortages did not prevail. Philosophically, that is what it means to be poor. Poor people, poor companies, poor nations are people, companies, and nations with shortages. Causes of the shortages fall into two categories, the general and the specific.

General Causes of Shortages	Specific Causes of Shortages
Wars (hot and cold)	Consumer overhead
Political shifts and upheavals	Price hikes
Bankruptcy of companies	Consumption of nonrenewable materials
New alliances	Curtailed services
Government policies	Substituted materials
Taxation and regulations	Long-lead procurement
Inefficient stockpiling	Shelved plans

General Causes of Shortages	Specific Causes of Shortages
Changed leadership	Depleted materials
Resource obsolescence	Military buildup
Climatic upheavals	Delivery delays
Accidents	Product maturation
Fluctuating currencies	Limited capacities
Inflation	Changed priorities
Depression	Changed personnel
Environmental disruptions	High wastes
Fire	Unavailable space
	Higher quality standards

Scarcity is often the result of rumors. A poor season for coffee growers gives rise to the rumor that coffee will be scarce. This prompts the consumer to buy, stock, and even hoard coffee. Prices rise and scarcity results. Looking ahead toward the twenty-first century, three major causes can be forecasted as the culprits of the new scarcity. They are:

1. *Technology Expansion into Adjoining Interfaces.* Technology is becoming multitechnical. Several technologies now act as one (the definition of high technology). Complex growth at the interfaces of all these technologies needs to be defined and its impact on existing resources described. Present skills will become old skills for the emerging super complexities. Computer applications, for example, will demand not only an understanding of computer technology but also of information technology, design technology, and even manufacturing technology.

2. *Quality Demands Are Increasing.* The catchup of quality by competitors is already here. But a new gap has developed between multitechnology and warranted existing performance. Performance is certified and warranties are issued to support expected quality levels. Quality management skills need to be given to all who influence the quality of the product. Foreign competitors are using quality as their chief competitive edge. This, combined with low price, makes them formidable competitors.

3. *Refusal to Accept Resource Scarcity as a Life-Style.* Assumptions about the ready availability of resources are stumbling blocks to dealing with the new challenges. Some managers continue to behave as if all resources needed will always be available. New attitudes are needed to accept resource managing as a life-style.

Whatever the cause of a shortage, each company and each manager will react different to it, the reaction ranging from complete indifference to panic obsession with stockpiling. A dangerous aspect of the problem is that material deficiencies often appear suddenly, and they are almost impossible to predict.

WHY RESOURCE MANAGEMENT IS NEEDED

Since shortages will continue to be a way of life, the need to formalize resource-use and skills has sharpened. Some specific reasons are:

1. *Global Competitors Are More Effective in Resource Management.*   If there is any one managerial strength or skill foreign competitors have over their American counterparts , it is their ability to be more efficient in resource use. For example, the Japanese have a life-style of resource-use curtailment. This is probably due to the fact that the Japanese have no natural resources on their islands. They have created an artificial resource, productivity, with great emphasis on efficiency and avoidance of waste. Global competitors are offering customers attractive prices based on better resource use, allocations, and maximizations.

2. *Vital, High-Growth New Divisions Are Starving.*   Resource allocations follow a historic procedure. Large divisions of a multidivisional corporation tend to dominate resource allocations, such as in budgeting. They are often overfed. New divisions or young divisions or departments with new ventures, new ideas, or new products with high growth possibilities find they must struggle to get the resources they need. These new divisions are often acquisitions and mergers. They are profit integrated with the corporation but seldom resource-use integrated. These young, vital, and high-growth divisions or departments are starved while they watch the old, low-growth divisions being overfed.

3. *Discoordinated Divisions Generate a Ripple Effect.*   All divisions or departments in a corporation do not perform equally. Some perform well, some perform poorly. This disparity in performance generates resource-use ripples in which inefficiencies of one division or department must be made up by others. For example, a delay in one department must be made up in the next. If not made up, the delay is passed on like a ripple until it reaches the end, usually the customer.

4. *Resource Discoordination Increases Costs.*   Poor communication of resource needs often causes duplication of resource use. Some divisions or departments are not aware of resources located internally. They will procure outside what is already available inside. This duplication of resources blocks the pursuit of attractive and needed opportunities.

5. *Resource Use Is a Determiner in Strategic Plans.*   Too often well-laid strategic plans are shelved because of their disconnection with efficient use of internal resources. Human resources, for example, are managed in a historic and habitual way, while strategic plans are changed continuously. This makes human resources a loose commitment to support actual plans. Productivity declines when resource use is inefficiently connected with strategic plans.

6. *Accountability for Resource Use Is Often Diffuse and Unclear.*   A common practice of corporations is to account for resource use after the fact. Budget

reporting, for example, accounts for what was used during a past period. Accountability must shift to the planning phase, so that how, when, where, and why resources will be used can be appraised before the plan is approved. Casual and mediocre performance on all levels occurs when accountability for resource consumption is diffused, unclear, and difficult to trace.

7. *Procurement Is Preferred Over Resource Sharing.* There are several reasons for this. Lack of a resource-sharing policy is one. The prestige connected with equipment possession and control is another. Avoidance of the discouraging and conflicting problems of having to share resources is still another. Ignorance of resource availability finally is another. These reasons hardly justify expenditures for duplication of resources. Operating and capital expenses increase excessively when procurement is given priority over resource allocation and sharing.

8. *Capacity Is Unused and Idle.* The capacity of plants, equipment, and people is seldom utilized 100 percent. An across-the-board figure would be difficult to state, since every company varies as to its utilization rate. The rate probably falls between 50 and 100 percent, which suggests the presence of unused capacity. There is a need to identify and fully use the capacity of equipment, departments, sections, manpower and time.

RESOURCE USE STRATEGIES WITH MBO

The conventional approach to management of resources is to follow historic patterns. This assumes that conditions of a situation have not changed, which is seldom the case. If we identify the new changes, it becomes obvious that strategic approaches must follow predicted future patterns. The impulsive, habitual in-process decision making usually found in formal and advanced planning is no longer adequate. Decisions should be made in advance on selected key actions. Formal and advanced planning utilizing strategic MBO approaches specifies the resources to be used in the achievement of objectives. Here are some examples:

Poor   Increase market position from 15 to 20 percent.

Good   Increase market position from 15 to 20 percent with present budget allocation.

Poor   Achieve net profit average of 7 percent of sales.

Good   Achieve net profit average of 7 percent of sales with present level of payroll.

Poor   Increase merchandise turnover from four to six times.

Good   Increase merchandise turnover from four to six times while reducing promotional ad expenses 10 percent.

Poor   Deliver 16 units/day to shipping point B.

Good   Deliver 16 units/day to shipping point B at less cost than $4500/unit.

Poor   Reduce equipment handling costs by $55,000/month.
Good   Reduce equipment handling costs by $55,000/month while uti-
            lizing idle equipment availability with division B.

Resource management is a formal approach, using strategies, for better use of resources in the achievement of objectives. Ten strategies are briefly described here.

Resource Surveillance

Resources that are critical to an enterprise require careful surveillance as to their sources, their availability at the sources, their rate of consumption, and transportation problems from source to company. The first step, however, is identification of the resources that are critical for the operations of the company. The next step is identification of suppliers, their capacities, and the risks associated with each supplier. A third step is estimation of total resources available for all, the rate of depletion of the resources, and the resource consumption position of the company. Finally, strategies need to be developed for both internal use of the resources and for getting the resource to the enterprise. Resource surveillance requires well-thought-out planning and managing as a major responsibility.

Resource Conservation

Resource conservation is a formal effort to conserve resources on all fronts. Wherever resources are consumed and wastes are generated, resource conservation efforts are applied to cut down on the amount of the resources needed and on the wastes. MBO practitioners set resource conservation into their MBO plans by specifying the amount of resources to be used within the objective itself. This conservation effort is started with planning and achieved when results are completed. This makes a tight connection between performance to be achieved and the amount of resources to be consumed. With this approach, resources can greatly influence the achievement of objectives, while productivity is managed in the process.

Resource Buildup

Almost all companies experience at one time or another critical shortages of a vital resource, but they experience more frequently normal shortages of most resources. This is a major justification for inventories. An inventory is built up to avoid the resource being in short supply when needed. Material inventories are now clearly viewed for this purpose, as are inventories of oil and energy. What are not clearly viewed as inventories are skills, money supplies, and information and related high technology tooling. As we move more and more into world markets and use of international vendors, we need to deal with these resources on a long-term basis. We need to pinpoint supply problems in advance and assess the criticality of the resource and the supply, then proceed to prebuild inventories to safeguard against the uncertainty and risk. Resource management can be likened to marketing management. As market managers study and manage the customers within their market, resource managers study and manage the resources within their supply community.

Resource Sharing

Resource sharing means the communication of resource needs between and among departments and divisions in a company. This is accomplished formally with written requests or with regularly scheduled meetings. One corporation in the northeastern United States communicated in a technical newsletter information about newly acquired capital and other equipment to those who regularly rent used outside services for this equipment to those who regularly rent used outside services for this equipment. One division of this corporation saved $60,000 by sharing a test pile with another division that did not have a test pile. To make this strategy work, policies for sharing unused internal capacities and external suppliers must be instituted and communicated to those in need. Sometimes simple engineering and design standardizations and organizational procedures can make sharing between departments and divisions workable, thus reaping great savings for the firm.

Resource Allocations

Multidivision corporations follow policies in which each division must live within its own cash flow. Although this approach is simple to follow, its effect is to stifle young and promising divisions from getting the cash needed to pursue a new venture. As large divisions level off with their matured products, the high-growth young divisions with new products must take an increasingly greater role in keeping the corporation surviving and profitable. Resource allocations must give some weight to the prospects of new ventures. This requires formalizing through business plans the promising possibilities of a new venture.

Resource Maximization

Idle capacity is every company's nemesis. The cost of setting up capacity runs high, whether the capacity is an operating plant, a computerized robot, or a skilled engineer. Time, effort, and money are needed to bring the capacity to the level of performance needed. The accountant's use of return on investment is in practical terms the return expected on the utilization of capital asset capacity. Thus utilized capital asset influences greatly return on investment. Resource management formally identifies the capacity available and its utilization rate. From this standpoint, resource management can be thought of as capacity management.

Resource Use Priorities

Resources are and always will be limited and scarce. Decision makers in the allocation of resources are most anxious to have these limited resources used where they best profit the company. Business plan formulation provides a way that internal venture groups can compete for limited resources. Resource allocators can evaluate each business plan as to its risk and benefits and then compare it with others. They can also assign priorities in the allocation of resources. This is another way of saying that resource use should be matched with the highest payoff possibilities. Assignment of priorities among competing business plans is a practice of resource management.

Resource Substitutes

Substitutes for resources have often been made to reduce costs. This is highly justified. We now need to consider substitutes for resources in limited supply or fast undergoing depletion. Resource substitution in recent times is a major practice for many progressive companies. Plastics for steel, word processors for typewriters and filing cabinets, automated machinery for manual labor, and electricity for oil are but a few of the dramatic examples. As resource surveillance identifies resource suppliers and vendors that are unstable and limited in capacity, the firm needs to step up its R&D for seeking substitutes and alternatives for critical items. Purchasing personnel have a major responsibility for tracking substitutes for materials used in a firm. The more the American economy moves into a worldwide market, the more competition it will encounter for nonrenewable and limited supplies.

Resource Use Accountability in Planning

Accountability for resource use is seldom included at the planning phase. Planning tends to be oriented toward performance and not toward resource use. Decisions for resource allocation and use should be made during this period. This is the time when goals and objectives are formulated, when a direction is taken and commitments are made. It should be the time for a special focus on the resources needed to implement plans. It is also the time in which consequences for taking or not taking an action are noted. Accountability is made clear when resources are allocated and committed to an individual or department for follow through. This is especially true when the consequences for not taking action have been clearly identified. In other words, accountability for resource use should be made before resources are consumed, during the planning phase when commitments are formulated.

Resource Recycling

Resources, when used, are not always totally consumed. Much of them remains, such as waste paper, steel, wood, old typewriters, water, glass, garbage, and so forth. People long away from their jobs and careers have not lost their skills. Recycling of an incomplete or partial resource is an attractive strategy for coping with shortages, especially if the resource is nonrenewable. This strategy is workable if the cost of recycling is equal to or less than the cost of the original resource. There may be other advantages to recycling, however, such as shorter lead times, less reliance on unreliable workers, better surveillance of capacity of resource sources, and in some cases more economy. But the chief advantage is recapturing a resource which in the long run is nonrenewable.

MAXIMIZING RESOURCE USE

Resource use is maximized:

1. When resource maximization objectives are set in planning.
2. When all resources are allocated with limits.
3. When resource allocations in a multiindustry corporation are based on zero-based decisions of today and of the immediate future rather than on traditional historical patterns.
4. When all who use resources are aware of the inefficiencies possible and of how these inefficiencies can be eliminated.
5. When priorities and timing and allocations for resource use are shifted to new and critical objectives as part of a strategic planning process.
6. When objectives, benefits, and resources have priorities resulting from tradeoffs or balancing among competing demands.
7. When functions of an organization act and react in unison in resource use toward achievement of objectives.
8. When resource sharing matches unused capacity with needed capacity within and between divisions.
9. When decisions for procurement are made after the benefits of resource sharing, allocation, and capacity are considered.
10. When information about suppliers of good resources is shared with others in the company.
11. When procurement and sharing are done collectively to gain economies of size and time.
12. Across divisions when there is information flow on and sharing of opportunities for improving resource conservation and efficiency.
13. When managers formalize their efforts for savings and efficiency through skillful resource use.

14. When accountability for resource use is given visibility and commitment at the planning phase, with agreed-to priorities.
15. When funding decisions are made in favor of attractive entrepreneurial prospects for growth in smaller and newer units with less political clout rather than the larger prestigious units with small prospects for growth.
16. When managers stir up motivation for resource conservation among all personnel in the organization.
17. When productivity set points establish the integration of operations, human resources, marketing, and financing.
18. When formal communications for resource sharing and utilization are made on a continuous basis.
19. When managers seek out the right kind of resource suppliers and develop good working relations with them, to give the company high strategic advantage.
20. When equipment procurement decisions are made after resource sharing and allocations with sister divisions or departments have been considered.
21. When resource use is given accountability in performance appraisal systems.
22. When work and productivity policies are aimed at maximization.
23. When incentive rewards and benefits are allocated on the basis of efficient resource use.
24. When resource conservation-mindedness is developed through communications and coaching.
25. When consumers of time are all given time management training.
26. When productivity is managed by MBO.
27. When resource use leadership is demonstrated with action research.
28. When management skills for resource maximization are effective and kept up to date.
29. When capital purchases are made for productivity improvement.
30. When operations audits are conducted.
31. When equipment purchase and use are justified with productivity data beforehand.
32. When union-management agreements enhance maximization.
33. When procurement value analysis is practiced.
34. When the organization is committed to resource conservation with top management support and personal involvement.

EXAMPLE OF CAPACITY UTILIZATION WITH MBO

North American Metallizing Corporation is a small manufacturing company producing metallized paper, vinyl laminated paper, mylar laminations, and mylar vinyl laminations. The corporate purpose or general mission is defined as sale of the roll-goods process technology. This defined mission has more meaning for special customers than for general market appeal. North American Metallizing Corporation sells roll-goods process capacity for a variety of applications to a variety of customers. This selling of capacity is a major determiner of the business. New products, product improvement, and product development by customers inevitably bring in manufacturing requests for new capacity utilization and process improvement. Capacity is the chief resource to be managed in the firm. The following is a brief description of how North American Metallizing identifies capacity, how capacity is set up as a target, and how capacity is maximized with MBO plans.

1. *Capacity Identification and Utilization.*   This is a schedule of the total capacity of plant machinery and the existing utilization of this capacity. From this, space capacity available is identified for sale to existing or new customers. From the schedule shown in Table 15.1, in 1984 North American Metallizing was utilizing 55 percent capacity and thus had 45 percent available for new sales.

2. *Capcity to Be Sold, 1984.*   This is a forecast of total sales capacity available and both minimum and desirable sales for 1984 (Table 15.2 and Figure 15.2). Table 15.3 shows sales targets for 1984.

3. *Capacity Maximization with MBO.*
    (a)   Sales plan.   The mission of the sales function is:
        (1)   To book sales orders to meet committed sales targets at planned profit levels.
        (2)   To ensure progressive and expanding sales for the growth of the firm through an effective sales force.
        (3)   To provide effective customer services to ensure retention of existing customers and acquisition of new customers.

Figure 15.3 and Table 15.4 show the organization of the sales function and sales objectives respectively.

    (b)   Marketing plan.   The mission of the marketing function is:
        (1)   To develop a market research effort for yielding needed information for the sales growth and expansion of the firm.
        (2)   To project North American Metallizing's image in existing and potential markets.
        (3)   To create or discover customer markets for the company's existing or newly developed products.

Figure 15.4 shows the organization of the marketing function. Table 15.5 shows marketing objectives.

TABLE 15.1 Capacity Management at North American Metallizing

Machines	Total Capacity (Yards)	Utilization Yards	Utilization Percent	Spare Capacity Yards	Spare Capacity Percent
Metallizer no. 1	26,000,000	26,000,000	100	0	0
Metallizer no. 2	16,250,000	16,250,000	100	0	0
Metallizer no. 3	13,000,000	13,000,000	100	0	0
Metallizer no. 4	2,400,000	1,200,000	50	1,200,000	50
Metallizer no. 5	10,000,000	0	0	10,000,000	100
Total	67,650,000	56,450,000	83	11,200,000	17
Coater no. 1	12,500,000	6,250,000	50	6,250,000	50
Coater no. 2	12,500,000	6,250,000	50	6,250,000	50
Coater no. 3	7,500,000	3,000,000	40	4,500,000	60
Coater no. 4	2,500,000	750,000	30	1,750,000	70
Coater no. 5	2,500,000	750,000	30	1,750,000	70
Total	37,500,000	17,000,000	45	20,500,000	55
Extruder	1,250,000	312,500	25	937,500	75
Coater-laminator	12,500,000	6,250,000	50	6,250,000	50
3-ply laminate	1,750,000	700,000	40	1,050,000	60
Lembo laminator	2,500,000	0	0	2,500,000	100
Water-based coater	24,000,000	0	0	24,000,000	100
Total	42,000,000	7,262,500	18	34,737,500	82
Grand Total	147,150,000	80,712,500	55	66,437,500	45
Minimum capacity to be sold	47,088,000				
Desirable capacity to be sold	85,337,000				

[a] Number of rolls for 2 shifts × yards per roll × 5 days per week × 50 weeks per year.

TABLE 15.2 Total Sales Capacity, Minimum Sales, and Desirable Sales (in Millions of Yards)

Month	Capacity Available (Total Sales) Monthly	Capacity Available (Total Sales) Cumulative	Capacity to Be Sold (Minimum Sales) Monthly	Capacity to Be Sold (Minimum Sales) Cumulative	Targets to Be Reached (Desirable Sales) Monthly	Targets to Be Reached (Desirable Sales) Cumulative
January	12.3	12.3	3.9	3.9	7.1	7.1
February	12.3	24.6	3.9	7.8	7.1	14.2
March	12.3	36.9	3.9	11.7	7.1	21.3
April	12.3	49.2	3.9	15.6	7.1	28.4
May	12.3	61.5	3.9	19.5	7.1	35.5
June	12.3	73.8	3.9	23.4	7.1	49.7
July	12.3	86.1	3.9	27.3	7.1	49.7
August	12.3	98.4	3.9	31.2	7.1	56.8
September	12.3	110.7	3.9	35.1	7.1	63.9
October	12.3	123.0	3.9	39.0	7.1	71.0
November	12.3	135.3	3.9	42.9	7.1	78.1
December	12.3	147.6	3.9	46.8	7.1	85.2
Totals	147.6		46.8		85.2	

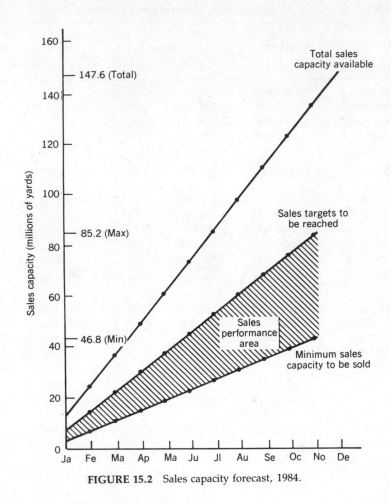

FIGURE 15.2 Sales capacity forecast, 1984.

TABLE 15.3 Sales Targets for 1984 in Millions of Yards and in Dollars

| | Existing Customers | | New Customers | | | | | |
| | Existing Products and Services | | Existing Products and Services | | New Products and Services | | Totals | |
Projections	Yards[a]	Dollars	Yards	Dollars	Yards	Dollars	Yards	Dollars
Valid	42.5	$4,500,000	—	—	—	—	42.5	$4,500,000
Nonvalid	4.7	$500,000	9.5	$1,000,000	28.5	$3,000,000	42.7	$4,500,000
Totals	47.2	$5,000,000	9.5	$1,000,000	28.5	$3,000,000	85.2	$9,000,000

[a] Millions of yards.

638

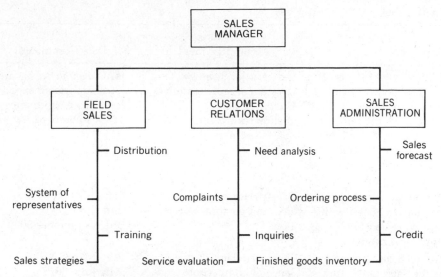

FIGURE 15.3   Organization of the sales function.

    (c)   Research and development plan.   The mission of the research and development function is:

    (1)   To produce new products and services for diversifying products.

    (2)   To find new uses for existing products and services.

    (3)   To provide R&D services and tests to other functions of the organization as the need arises.

    (4)   To assure product quality and validity to meet customers' expectations.

Figure 15.5 shows the organization of the research and development function. Table 15.6 shows the objectives.

    (d)   Production plan.   The mission of the production function is:

    (1)   To operate plant capacity with deliveries that effectively meet sales demand and customer expectations.

    (2)   To provide materials managing processes that ensure customer deliveries at a required cost performance level for meeting the firm's profitability objectives.

    (3)   To operate a centralized time frame for the entire company that coordinates sales capacity demand, materials purchasing, and customer deliveries.

Figure 15.6 shows the organization of the production operations function. Table 15.7 shows objectives.

TABLE 15.4. Sales Objectives

Objectives	Methods of Accomplishment	Date Completed
Achieve sales targets of 47.2 million yards, existing customers 9.5 million yards, new customers 28.5 million yards, new products Issue monthly sales variance reports	Set up sales strategy System of representatives Customer lists Selling campaign Sales training	Issue *monthly* sales variance reports on expected sales performance of 7.1 million yd
Revalidate sales targets on quarterly basis with reports issued to all functional heads	Sales performance information and customer projections	1st: May 30 2nd: June 30 3rd: September 30
Submit 6 improvements in the sales of existing or potential products 2 cost reductions 2 quality improvements 2 new uses for existing products	Increased sales surveillance of competitors Customer needs analysis Customer complaint analysis	2 by March 30 2 by June 30 2 by September 20
Develop and have ready sales training program for six sales representatives in six territories	Set up training objectives Establish selling strategies Adopt training methods Establish training budget Gain approval	January 30
Complete "customer service evaluation" program for all existing customers	Develop survey form Collect "service" strengths and weaknesses- Corrective program Develop complaint-handling procedure Recommend company policies for changes and improvements Issue report	Study: April 30 Changes implemented: June 1
Complete 1984 sales plan	Sales analysis and planning President's approval	November 15

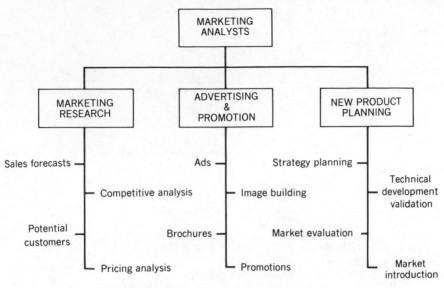

FIGURE 15.4 Organization of the marketing function.

TABLE 15.5 Marketing Objectives

Objectives	Method of Accomplishment	Date Completed
Complete 1985 sales capacity forecast and guidelines for company	Projections from validated 1974 quarterly reports President's guidelines Capacity utilization analysis	October 15
Recommend three improvements to company's competitive edge	Develop competitive edge: List competitors and reasons customers buy from them List customers and reasons customers buy Establish competitive edge Recommend improvements	May 30
Communicate services and products to all potential customers from newly identified markets. Follow up on all inquiries.	Develop potential customer list Complete brochure Design sales letter Develop samples Mail sales packet First followup Second followup for orders	First step by January 30 Second through fifth steps by March 30 Potential customers: 50% April 30, 50% May 30

(Continued)

641

TABLE 15.5 *(Continued)*

Objectives	Method of Accomplishment	Date Completed
Recommend and issue report on enhancing North American Metallizing in market	Logo for North American Names for products Description of services	February 30
Issue major report on marketing analysis for roll-goods processing industries	Checklist of indicators that influence roll-goods industries Checklist on a time-line of indicators that affect company	August 30
Complete-product marketing strategy for market introduction	Technical development validation Make list of potential customers Make list of existing customers Develop brochure Develop sales letter Samples developed Set up ads First followup with samples; handle telephone inquiries Second followup for orders	March 30
Complete 1984 marketing plan	Marketing analysis and planning	November 15

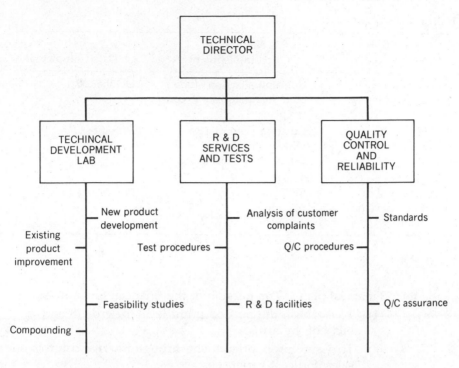

FIGURE 15.5 Organization of the research and development function.

TABLE 15.6 Research and Development Objectives

Objectives	Method of Accomplishment	Date Completed
Develop three marketable products whose total predicted sales volume is no less than 27 million yards/year	R&D feasibility development Sales and marketing surveillance Staff "brainstorming" conferences	One by March 30 One by June 30 One by September 30
Submit three each improvements on existing products: Cost reduction improvement Quality improvement New uses for existing products	R&D feasibility development Sales and marketing surveillance Staff "brainstorming" conferences Analysis of customer complaints	by February 30 by April 30 by July 30

(Continued)

TABLE 15.6   *(Continued)*

Objectives	Method of Accomplishment	Date Completed
Conceptualize 100 ideas for long-range feasibility analysis	Conceptualization studies Staff "brainstorming" conferences	October 30
Establish ten Q/C standards for production	Customer complaints History analysis Customer requirements Q/C policies and manual	December 30
Complete 1984 research and development plan	R&D analysis and planning	November 15

(e)   Financial plan.   The mission of the financial function is:

(1)   To establish the needed profit level for growth and visibility of the firm.

(2)   To assure profit attainment through internal controls on sales and cost variances.

(3)   To provide a system of reporting on the utilization and accountability of North American Metallizing assets and investments.

(4)   To assure policy communication and effective administrative support to all functions of the firm.

Figure 15.7 shows the organization of the financial function. Table 15.8 shows objectives.

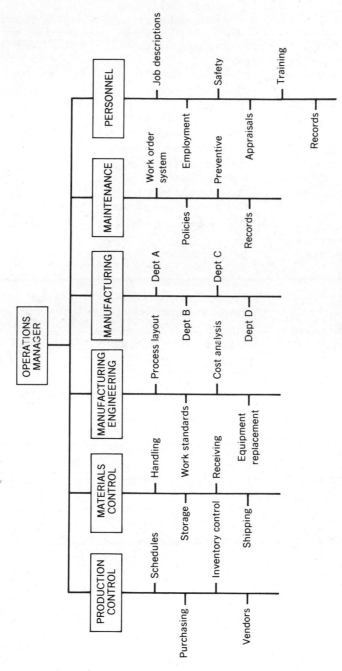

FIGURE 15.6 Organization of the production function.

TABLE 15.7 Production Objectives

Objectives	Methods of Accomplishment	Date Completed
Achieve production readiness and performance as forecasted in sales targets: 47.2 million yards, existing customers, 9.5 million yards, new customers, 28.5 million yards, new products Issue monthly variances on operating performance	Set up production control system: Master schedules Inventory position tracking Progress position on customers' orders Cost projections of direct material and labor Optimization of production runs and lot sizes Raw material inventories	March 30
Set up employee performance appraisal system and implement	Set up system and formalize: Job descriptions Supervisory training System of backup Compensation schedule Employee improvement	February 30
Complete formalized safety program	Establish safety rules Printed information to all employees Safety surveillance	April 30
Complete capital equipment and facility acquisition plan	Capital equipment inventory Replacement value analysis Capital acquisition procedure	June 30
Complete purchasing system for reducing costs of materials purchasing	Set up purchasing procedure: Purchase specifications Make/buy procedures Vendor quotations Vendor selection and controls Quantity purchasing	January 30
Set up and maintain employee record system to comply with EEOC, OSHA, and Department of Labor requirements	Establish regulations Gather information Develop plan Make corrections Maintain records	December 30
Complete production plan	Production analysis and planning President's approval	November 15

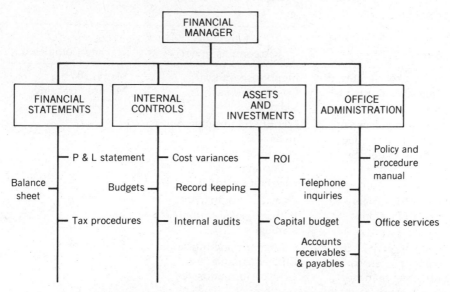

FIGURE 15.7   Organization of the financial function.

TABLE 15.8   Financial Objectives

Objectives	Method of Accomplishment	Date Completed

Complete and issue monthly performance variance reports:
  Sales
  Capacity utilization
  Costs
	Develop format
	Identify controlled items
	Hold monthly meetings for corrective action
		Monthly report to all functional heads

Achieve 10 percent cost reduction throughout company	Materials cost Expense costs Labor costs	December 30
Complete customer complaint handling system	Develop format Set up procedure Action steps Followup	January 30
Complete sales inquiry handling system	Develop procedure Telephone training Follow through	January 30
Complete system of internal controls of assets, purchases, staff, and inventory	Review internal control questionnaire Develop internal control procedure Institute internal control procedure	June 30

(Continued)

TABLE 15.8 *(Continued)*

Objectives	Method of Accomplishment	Date Completed
Develop six significant financial ratios in a time chart control	Identify six ratios Develop format Validate	March 30 Monthly tracking
Write five policies for administrative effectiveness and efficiency of firm	Identify five troublesome areas Write policies Set up manual Distribute manual	
Issue P&L variance reports to President	Quarterly comparison with projected annual P&L statement	March 30 June 30 September 30
Complete plan for instituting cost centers and budgeting management for all department heads	Cost center identification Budget formulation Cost performance reporting	September 30
Complete 1984 financial plan with P&L projection	Financial analysis President's approval	November 15

SUMMARY

Resource management is a formal effort to identify savings and efficiencies relative to the use of resources in the achievement of objectives. Resource management is a responsibility of all managers who consume resources. Scarcity results from gaps between demand and resource use; as the gap increases the need to manage resources more formally and deliberately becomes critical. The causes of the growing gap are many, but three are most important: technology expansion, quality demands, and refusal to accept scarcity as a life-style. Since shortages are becoming a way of life, the development of skills for resource managing is a critical issue.

The resource manager uses strategies for better use of resources. This chapter identifies and briefly describes ten strategies:

1. Resource surveillance.
2. Resource conservation.
3. Resource buildup.
4. Resource sharing.
5. Resource allocations.

6. Resource maximization.
7. Resource use priorities.
8. Resource substitutes.
9. Resource use accountability in planning.
10. Resource recycling.

Guidelines on how to maximize resource use are presented with an example of a company whose annual effort is to utilize idle capacity with MBO.

BIBLIOGRAPHY

Aggarwal, Sumer C., "Prepare for Continual Material Shortages." *Harvard Business Review*, May-June, 1982, pp. 68–75.

Gottlieb, Daniel W., "Shortage Causes: Price Controls, Panic Buying." *Purchasing*, November 23, 1976, p. 32.

Meitz, A. A., and Castleman, B. B., "How to Cope with Supply Shortages." *Harvard Business Review*, January-February, 1975, p. 45.

Osell, Roger, R., and Wright, Robert V., "Allocating Resources." *Handbook of Business Problem Solving*, Kenneth T. Albert, Editor in Chief. New York: McGraw-Hill, 1980, pp. 1–89.

16

PERFORMANCE APPRAISAL SYSTEMS

IN THIS CHAPTER

PURPOSES OF APPRAISAL SYSTEMS
ASSUMPTIONS MADE IN APPRAISAL SYSTEMS
TYPES OF APPRAISAL SYSTEMS
SETTING UP A COMPANY APPRAISAL PROCESS
EVALUATING POTENTIAL FOR NEW PERFORMANCE
PERFORMANCE APPRAISAL INTERVIEWS
MBO PERFORMANCE APPRAISAL GUIDE

Almost everyone will agree that current performance appraisal methods need a great deal of improvement! Winstanley of the Xerox Corporation goes even further, to say most organizations would do better without them. He urges that we make an effort to clean up the "mess." He is not the only one who has a low regard for performance appraisals; others have voiced similar reactions. The reason for the low value placed on appraisal methods is their wide range between two extremes: (1) informal, random, slipshod, and highly opinionated judgments of one individual, usually a supervisor, of another, usually a subordinate; and (2) formal, well-organized written judgments with objective criteria, used in systems for precise assessment of results. No matter where on the continuum the appraisal method lies, it seems to fail in its purpose. Some managers even play games with the appraisal process. Managers who dislike confronting employees with their inadequacies because of lack of proof may resort to approaches such as "peer evaluation." Peer evaluation is an ill-conceived practice in an organization in which competitive pressure is high. In other cases, managers go

651

through the appraisal process but do little or nothing at all with the results. If the appraisal effort is not going to affect decisions, practices, or development, it is a futile exercise.

Nonetheless, despite imperfections, inconsistencies, and variations in application, appraisal systems seem to be here to stay. But they do need considerable improvement. Formal appraisal systems, adopted by many organizations, are a commendable attempt to evaluate precisely the contributions made by individuals. This evaluation forms the information base for decisions about rewards, promotions, and remuneration. Formal appraisal methods seem to be in a continual stage of development. Perhaps we're merely sampling an evolutionary process.

This chapter describes the varying purposes for appraisals. It includes the various types of appraisal systems being practiced in corporate life, the assumptions managers make about appraisal of subordinates, and how to set up a company appraisal system. This chapter also contains special guidelines, such as collecting indications of performance potential and getting more from appraisal interviews. Finally, a complete performance appraisal guide with MBO guidelines is given.

PURPOSES OF APPRAISAL SYSTEMS

"Appraisal" is an elastic word that stretches to cover evaluations of many kinds and types. If an appraisal does not affect decision making or change, it is an exercise in futility. Each of the appraisal methods described in this chapter has its own combination of strengths and weaknesses. Yet the purpose of the appraisal, in large part, shapes the criteria, method, measures, and type of corrective feedback to be employed. The effectiveness of the appraisal depends on how it is used relative to its intended purpose. Perhaps the reason for the development of several methods is the varying uses for and intended purposes of appraisal procedures. Let's examine briefly some of these appraisal purposes.

1. *Validation of Employee Job Placement.*   Performance appraisals provide planned periods of time for both supervisor and subordinate to evaluate whether the job is right for the subordinate and the subordinate is right for the job. It can be a check on hiring practices. The latest estimate is that 50 percent of people are mismatched with their job. A need exists to evaluate the propriety of job placement. Hiring a person is a prediction. Performance appraisal helps to validate the prediction.

2. *Justification of Pay Increases.*   Performance appraisals produce the framework and procedure for comparing and evaluating employees' performance in levels and categories of equity for increasing wages or salaries. This is commonly known as "merit rating." Acceptable performance on the job is the sole basis for compensation. This is not to infer that an excellent performance appraisal means an excellent increase in pay. Pay increases are based on formulas that include many factors, only one of them being

performance appraisals. However, an employee who performs the job outstandingly is more likely to get a larger pay increase than an employee just barely meeting minimum requirements.

3. *Evaluation of Results.* Performance appraisals provide a procedure for assessing the results contributed by an employee. The stress is on *actual* results. Important as activities may be, results are the ultimate criterion. Appraisal periods allow for agreement of what actually was contributed by the employee.

4. *Accounting for Productivity.* Performance appraisals provide an evaluative procedure for review of employee accomplishments and contributions in relation to the resources consumed in the process. Accountability for productivity must link results and resources. The appraisal process evaluates both in the same context and time. When productivity goals are specified in a quantitative way, accountability of resources use is sharpened.

5. *Setting up of Conditions for Achievement Motivation.* When properly developed, performance appraisals provide the basis for feedback to staff and employees so that they can reach higher levels of performance through a plan-do-achievement cycle. Communicating in a climate of openness and participation engenders a meeting of the minds before work commences. Most employees want to know where they stand. They can guess, but guessing worries them unnecessarily. Feelings, uncertainty, lack of confidence, worry—all damage motivation. Feedback removes guessing and can be the basis of motivation.

6. *Setting up of Feedback for Organizational Change.* Performance appraisals provide feedback on how well managerial processes are operating with the staff and what changes are required. What may appear to be weaknesses in the individual often may be weaknesses in the organization. The organization that is growing and becoming is the organization that has its people growing and becoming. Appraisals help to make this process deliberate.

7. *Development of Personnel for Positional Changes.* Performance appraisals provide data for making decisions on promotions, transfers, retentions, or demotions. They help in the long-range planning for development of employees to occupy higher levels in the organization. This suggests that the primary emphasis of performance appraisal is development of people. Appraisal time is not a time for firing someone. It is a time for correction, development, and improvement.

8. *Identification of Employees with Hidden Potential.* Performance appraisals provide a formal way to identify high-potential employees who are assigned jobs that do not utilize their potential. This is the problem of mismatch. People are placed in jobs for a variety of reasons, but usually not because the job will release and develop their potential. Appraisals when properly designed aid in the identification and development of performance potential.

9. *Counseling of Employees with Problems.* Performance appraisals aid managers in understanding the actions and behavior of subordinates. The appraisal interview raises all kinds of questions about how subordinates feel

about their work, what their expectations are, and what problems they are experiencing. The responses provide the basis of counseling and improvement for managers. Appraisal periods provide much of the substance of counseling discussions.

10.   *Helping People Improve.*   Performance appraisals are aimed at helping managers understand subordinates' abilities and goals. Helping people improve means knowing their abilities and goals and then helping them progress toward their goals. Helping people achieve their goals nurtures their "growing process."

ASSUMPTIONS MADE IN APPRAISAL SYSTEMS

A common attitude with managers in many operations is that their performance appraisal system has problems, but that they will have new and larger problems without the appraisal process. They feel that the appraisal system they have is better than nothing at all. This section identifies some of the basic assumptions underlying use of the appraisal process and usually opposite reality. In my opinion, the gap between assumptions and reality is a matter of the changing state of the art and the poor design and operation of appraisal systems.

Assumptions	Reality
Performance can be measured accurately and objectively.	Performance measures are both subjective and objective and are often inaccurate. One important reason is conflicting multiple uses of the appraisal system. Another is that system design was not validated for the intended uses.
Performance pay increases can be clearly established with merit.	Performance pay increases depend on factors such as cash flow of the firm, profitability, salary inequities, salary compression levels, salary scales, and labor market conditions.
Performance appraisal is a useful tool for a supervisor.	Performance appraisals are useful to a wide variety of people: supervisor, subordinate, salary administrators, department heads, and human resource managers. Some supervisors, however, find little or no utility to such appraisals, especially when a union contract is involved. Compa-

Assumptions	Reality
	nies that make the appraisal process part of the plan-do-evaluation of work are more likely to have supervisors that use appraisal as a tool. When this connection is made well, a conceptual justification for the appraisal system emerges.
Everyone wants a performance appraisal.	Performance appraisals do not appeal to all, especially the mediocre, the immature, the emotionally unstable, and the worrier. These make up a large group in any organization.
Performance appraisals result in behavior changes.	Performance appraisals sometimes lead people to higher productivity, but not always. There are no guarantees. Quite often where such an effect is most needed, it does not happen. Frequently, goal setting has no impact on performance.
Managerial training is the key to effective appraisals.	Managerial training is important but not always conclusive. Appraisal differences exist with one effectively trained manager and two or more subordinates. Additionally, managers are ill trained to administer appraisals even though they have been to many training programs. Some appraisal systems need professional psychologists or sociologists.
Performance appraisal systems are used for the appraisal of employees.	Performance ratings are often biased for pay considerations. Supervisors play games to get more money for their subordinates. They use the system for personal needs.
Performance criteria are available and equitably applied to all employees.	Performance criteria are not always available or clear. When they are, they change so much that often general criteria are used. This lowers the value of the use of criteria.
Potential-to-perform ratings can be	Separating potential from perfor-

Assumptions	Reality
separated from ratings for actual performers.	mance is very difficult. Often the rater includes both. Many firms separate these two evaluations.
The "halo" effect can be controlled and even ignored.	The halo effect, which is a favorable impression by others of the subordinate, can cause errors in the evaluation of employees. Also favorable evaluations in strong areas have a spillage effect in weak areas. To control this can be very difficult.
Managers like to give feedback information to employees on their performance.	Managers frequently find themselves defending their judgments with subordinates. Defense is often stressful. Managers seek ways to avoid this stressful experience. Many dislike giving feedback that will cause them distress.
Performance appraisals relate to business goals.	Managers view appraisals of employees as an administrative task not related to business goals. Many view the activity as taking them away from the pursuit of business goals. Additionally, business goals are not always clear to them.
Managers as raters give the same degree of leniency to all subordinates.	Rating errors are many. The most common is leniency with some employees and not with others. Lenient and nonlenient ratings generate unfairness and inequities. Another error is common evaluations, that is, all employees are given the same rating, usually average. Raters are usually not aware of these influences.

These assumptions are only a few of the many that are made in using performance appraisal systems. How they can be overcome is a problem for vigorous research and development of the appraisal state of the art. There needs to be less emphasis on forms, scales, and criteria and more on the objectives to be achieved with the appraisal process, that is, determination of what the organization wants to accomplish with the appraisal system and design of a system to meet these objectives. A closer connection is needed between the results of the appraisal process and the human resource and business system of the organization. Nothing destroys confidence in an appraisal system more than filing away the results and keeping them separate from the heart and core of the firm. Finally, both the supervisor and the appraised subordinate need more understanding about the appraisal system and skill in its use.

TYPES OF APPRAISAL SYSTEMS

At the risk of oversimplification, ten appraisal methods are described here. For purposes of description, these methods are treated as if they are used singly. In actual practice, their features are combined eclectically to meet the evaluative needs of the organization. This brief analysis of methods currently in use may help readers decide on one or more of the methods for the task of evaluating employee contributions.

Appraisals That Focus on Behavior and Personality

Trait Appraisal (Graphic Rating Scale)

The most widely used performance evaluation technique is the trait appraisal, or graphic rating scale. The evaluator is presented with a series of traits or behavior-related characteristics on a scale and asked to rate employees on each of these. Examples of traits are leadership, communications, initiative, dependability, cooperation, and personality. The advantages of this method are that it is uncomplicated, it reaches for human qualities that are known to be important in getting results, and it recognizes that all organizations require certain characteristics to make them work. Its disadvantages are that supervisors are reluctant to label deficiencies and criticism without foolproof evidence, it is unilateral—the employee is not involved, supervisors have a tendency to remember recent or negative incidents; and definitions of traits are not always clear.

Essay Appraisals

Not so widely used as the trait appraisal, the essay appraisal is one or more paragraphs about the employee's strengths, weaknesses, and behavior on the job. The information, as complete as is deemed necessary by the evaluator, is used to decide pay increases, promotion, or termination. The fact that the evaluation is written makes it a formal entry for the employee. The advantages of this method are that it allows in-depth evaluation of job factors that are vital for the employer, it is easy to use for jobs that are changing, and it eliminates a fixed set of expectancies and allows a broad focus to meet individual differences. Its disadvantages are that its variability in length and content prevents meaningful comparisons among employees, it is unilateral, and the evaluator must possess communication skills for the description to be accurate.

Process Appraisals

Interest in process appraisals has recently been high because of "due process" requirements of civil and individual rights. The method requires a series of descriptive and quantitative statements that represent standards of effective behavior on the job. The difference between process behavior standards and actual behavior is the strength or weakness of the behavior. Examples of process behavior standards are absenteeism, tardiness, alcoholism, and violation of rules covering, for example, coffee breaks, safety, and insubordination. The advantages of this method are that it controls behavioral activities directly needed for the job, it specifies the human behavior that will lead to job effectiveness, and it provides data that are critically needed for "due process" procedures. Its disadvantages are that human behavior is too broad to be described by levels of effectiveness, not all behavior can be externally controlled, and employees with terrible behavior patterns can perform well.

Behavioral Anchoring

A technique that can minimize several of the previously discussed disadvantages is the technique of behavioral anchoring. Behavioral anchoring means replacement of the words "excellent" or "average" in performance grades with short descriptions of actual job behaviors. For example, in the rating of compatibility, the grades of "excellent" and "poor" might be replaced with the behavioral anchors "inspires others to work with and assist co-workers" and "does not work well with or assist others." The advantage of this technique is that it breaks up certain types of rater errors, such as leniency and overgenerosity. It forces the insecure rater to avoid rating everyone "average." Very little is gained when all employees have the same rating. This technique also reduces the halo effect. Its disadvantage is that not all behaviors have a cause-effect relationship; identification of one behavior may not identify the single cause. Another disadvantage is the poor and oversimplified descriptions of complex behaviors. Human phenomena are very difficult to describe.

Appraisals That Focus on Work Activities

Critical-Incident Appraisals

Not often used, critical-incident appraisals attempt to observe and record both positive and negative factual incidents or behaviors of an employee. The incidents or behaviors are recorded in a log of some type, often daily, so that they are not forgotten. These incidents or behaviors are recorded as outstandingly good or outstandingly poor. This record is often termed the "little black book." For example, an employee has a disastrous experience with a client and hostilities are exchanged; the supervisor records the incident. The advantages of this method are that it relates closely to performance elements of the job, it records work incidents that are never known with any degree of specificity, and it overcomes partial remembering or later incident remembering. This approach is particularly good when the only purpose of the evaluation is to counsel the employee. This system can be helpful when a chart system is used, to give visibility to behaviors toward jobs at certain times. Its disadvantages are that the log tends to have a "police" adjudication image, there is a tendency to identify more negative than positive incidents, and employees are not usually involved in this appraisal method.

Standards of Performance Appraisal

Many organizations are greatly interested in standards of performance appraisals. Use of the method requires a series of descriptive and quantitative statements that represent standards of effective performance on jobs. For example, a performance standard for a supervisor is that overtime hours are controlled to less than 4 percent of scheduled hours. The advantages of this method are that it directly relates to the requirements of the job, it specifies the level and consistency of effort necessary for job effectiveness, and subjective judgments are minimal. Its disadvantages are that there is little or no participation by the employee in the standards or the evaluation, not all important areas can be quantified, and it can be used only when work does not change frequently.

Appraisals That Focus on Comparisons

Ranking Appraisals

This approach recognizes that an individual must at some point be compared with other individuals, especially when limited wage increases are to be given to a few employees and not to all. The method involves an employee ranking technique. Supervisors are asked to choose the "most valuable" and "least valuable." Paired-comparison rankings or normal distribution ranks are two popular methods for this procedure. Its advantages are that it provides a way to compare people who work for different departments and supervisors, it allows an overall judgment that includes additional facts and impressions, and pooled judgments are possible, that is, an overall ranking may be developed from the rankings of several supervisors. Its disadvantages are that there is no standard form or way to replicate the judgment that was executed, minor and insignificant impressions may take a strong priority in the evaluation, and it lacks the focus that is needed for important job elements.

Forced-Choice Appraisal

Designed to reduce the bias and prejudices of the evaluator, forced-choice appraisals set up standards of comparison among individuals. The evaluator is asked to choose from categories of statements those that accurately fit the individual being rated. Also the evaluator is forced to select statements that least fit the "evaluatee." The statements are then weighted or scored. Employees with high scores are, by definition, the better employees. The advantages of this method are that a high degree of reliability is possible, that is, the evaluator can repeat the appraisal and compare the results over a period of time; it tends to be more objective, since the evaluator does not know the scoring; and the designer of the statements can incorporate almost any element required for the job. Its disadvantages are that evaluators are forced to select one or another statement with no choice between; the "halo" effect may operate, in which the evaluator may be appraising a model employee and not the actual employee; the method is unilateral—the employee does not participate in either the statements or the evaluation; and the method is expensive to formulate, validate, and execute.

Training Simulation Appraisal

Training techniques that have recently shown some promise are simulation and conference. In the simulation technique, videotapes showing a rater making errors have been employed. In the conference technique, conferees are asked to provide examples of their own that illustrate evaluation errors. Other conferees then identify the type of error and discuss it. In addition to skills training, some attitude development is desirable. The rater who feels that evaluation is a silly waste of time—a meaningless, routine chore—will most likely do a poor job. Training simulation is a recent technique for rating a performance under a job situation. An individual is given, under simulated conditions, the tasks he or she is expected to accomplish in a real situation. The appraisee is compared with others who undergo the training simulation. The advantage of this approach is a closer evaluation of real performance even under simulated conditions. Also counseling and correction can be done in a training experience. Video feedback tapes give the appraisee a better understanding of the problem. The disadvantage with this technique is the "distance factor" of the real world. Everyone knows simulation and training are not for real. Also many aspects are required to make this work. The supervisor-subordinate relationship is enlarged to include others. Finally, the learning value in training and simulation is not always transferred to the job.

Appraisals That Focus on Results

MBO Appraisal

Because MBO focuses on outputs or results of the employee's efforts in the organization, there is a great deal of interest in it by organizations. The method requires a supervisor and subordinate to agree during a planning period on the results to be achieved during the period. The results are written as objectives. At the end of the period both evaluate the output, or results. An example of an objective for an educational administrator is achievement of an admission acceptance level of 1500 students (60 percent of applicants) by April 1 of an admitting year. The advantages of this method are that it is future oriented and does not have to follow past practices; it is not passive, that is, it involves supervisor and subordinate; the role of the evaluator changes from being a defensive one to being a supportive one; it is highly connected to results needed and expected by the organization; and when used properly it motivates the staff. Its disadvantages are that targeted results can be influenced and changed by uncontrollable factors; it ignores personal traits, activities, and work habits that are deemed important; and it does not purposely and precisely connect inputs, or resources, with the output, or results (productivity), with feedback and feedforward progress controls.

How to Appraise Using MBO.   Performance appraisal is not an isolated personnel technique divorced from the mainstream of management decision making of a company. It is part and parcel of the total management process. MBO as a results-oriented appraisal process is, in essence, an appraisal of how well the management process is taking place within the operations of the organization. Commitments to objectives not only serve as a meaningful basis for evaluation of company performance but also give significant advantages to individual performance appraisals. The strategy of MBO, when used accurately and meaningfully, can provide the basis for enlightened periodic review of an individual manager's or employee's performance. The rater enjoys the opportunity to use the resultant accurate data as the basis for the appraisal, while the ratee enjoys participation in and commitment to the performance requirements of the job. A strong and impartial attitude toward the appraisal process generally prevails between the two. Performance appraisals, as part and parcel of the entire managing process, can include virtually all elements of managing: organizational planning, delegation, evaluation, control, communications, development, motivation, and coordination. MBO as a performance appraisal system provides results-oriented job descriptions and clearcut company objectives from which accountability and measurability are clarified. From this standpoint, *a performance appraisal program that uses MBO is both a "rating" device for evaluating individual performance and a "managing" procedure to ensure the processes of management.* Previous chapters in this book have centered on the latter, but a few words need to be said about the former. The MBO performance appraisal system should be tailored to the unique requirements of the company, department, and individual. To make the MBO system a rating device for individual performance, the following steps need to be taken:

STEP 1.   Prepare performance commitments.   The individual prepares a *preliminary* list of the most important objectives to be achieved in a given year for the company, department, and individual. These objectives are intended to solve a problem or take advantage of a new opportunity. They are developed with careful regard for an analysis of responsibilities, needs, challenges, or problems. *The superior participates in this development!* The final commitments are written as objectives, and not as activities. Practice and skill are needed to set objectives in the right nomenclature. Areas of responsibility that give rise to objectives might be the following: volume output; quality level; cost performance; methods improvement; housekeeping; sales; skills development; and time control. The objectives developed from these areas form the basis for discussion and subsequent joint agreement between subordinate and supervisor. Each objective must be written according to guidelines that make objectives measurable. A most important guideline is to build the performance measurement or indicator into the statement of objective. Without this quantitative indicator, progress toward results becomes merely a matter of interpretation. Performance standards for the activities are developed to indicate the level or intensity of effort needed to achieve the objectives. From this standpoint, standards of performance are used with objective statements. Prior agreement is obtained on these performance standards, and evaluation is made on this basis. The job or position descriptions can be useful if they are written to incorporate both objectives and standards. If not, new appraisal forms should be developed. Figure 16.1 shows sample formats for MBO appraisals.

STEP 2. Plan and schedule activities. Supervisor and subordinate agree on the methods and activities necessary to reach the stated objectives. Outside departments and personnel may be involved as resources to pull together all necessary work for the objective program. There must be a meeting of the minds between supervisor and subordinate in this step so that they have confidence in reaching the stated objectives. The value of working toward a targeted date must also be discussed. Feeder objectives can be set into a time schedule on which both supervisor and subordinate agree.

STEP 3. Implement scheduled activities. The subordinate proceeds to implement the planned objectives. The individual applies his or her skills, ingenuity, effort, time, and energy to getting done what has to be done. The supervisor provides day-to-day coaching and help to the individual. Managing by exception is not the rule in this case. The supervisor does not sit back and wait for exceptions to arise before acting. Instead he or she looks for progress in implementation, both positive and negative, and is informed not only about what is wrong but also about what is right.

Name _____

Date _____

Location _____

MBO Planning Guide

☐ Job description agreed upon
☐ Time expectation settled
☐ Participation by support depts

Responsibilities (area of contribution)	Measurement indicators (ways of evaluating)	Objectives 19 — (problem-solving innovations)	Priority	Action plan (methods settled)	Progress review (milestones)	Date	Accomplishment review (results)	Date

Summary of accomplishments

Completed items _____

Percent completed _____

Type of completion _____

FIGURE 16.1 Sample formats for MBO appraisals.

Performance Objectives Appraisal

Name		Date
Position	Dept	Division

Step 1.   Priority   List objectives   Start date   Complete date   Give performance standards

Step 2.   Comment on results achieved for each objective listed in step 1:

Step 3.   Improve individual's performance:

Where performance is strongest	Where performance is weakest

Step 4.   Specific plans to improve:

   Actions and activities   Responsibilities   Dates

Supervisor	Date	Next higher supervisor	Date

FIGURE 16.1 *(continued)*

CONTROLLING AND REPORTING STATUS OF OBJECTIVES

Cost Reduction
Performance Appraisal

Objective: _____

_____

_____

_____

_____

Target: $ _____

Activities: _____

_____

_____

_____

_____

_____

Results: _____

_____

_____

_____

Percent of Objective	Jan	Feb	Mar		Apr	May	Jun		Jul	Aug	Sep		Oct	Nov	Dec
150%															
125%															
100%															
80%															
60%															
40%															
20%															
0%															

Status review · Theoretical · Status review · Progress · Status review · Commitment reached

FIGURE 16.1 *(continued)*

Results Planning and Appraisal Report

Name _____   Department _____   Date _____

Results expected: Performance standards:

1. _____   1. _____
   _____   _____

2. _____   2. _____
   _____   _____

3. _____   3. _____
   _____   _____

Approved: _____ Date _____   Coordinated with _____ Date _____

Planned activities: Schedule:

1. _____   Start   Complete

   _____ |—+—+—+—+—+—+—+—+—+—+—|

2. _____

   _____ |—+—+—+—+—+—+—+—+—+—+—|

3. _____

   _____ |—+—+—+—+—+—+—+—+—+—+—|

4. _____

   _____ |—+—+—+—+—+—+—+—+—+—+—|

Evaluation of results: Tentative objectives for next year:

_____   _____

_____   _____

_____   _____

_____   _____

_____   _____

Evaluation approved:

_____ _____   _____ _____
Reporting Manager   Date   Coordinating Manager   Date

FIGURE 16.1 *(continued)*

STEP 4. Conduct progress reviews. Periodically during the ensuing months there are formal discussions relating to the objectives that were set. These can be quarterly progress reviews. The purpose of such reviews is to keep a large part of management informed about progress so that objectives may be revised if necessary. New objectives may be introduced, old ones eliminated, or priorities reorganized. Reviews are not intended to be performance appraisals with formal interviews to discover individual performance. The aim is to determine work progression toward targeted objectives. The atmosphere is one of mutual help, progress assessment, and problem solving.

STEP 5. Prepare annual progress review. The underlying value of annual performance review is the opportunity it affords to gain feedback about results achieved and about progress toward results expected. The annual cycle is convenient because of other annual instruments, such as budgets, profit statements, and forecasts. The manager prepares, in advance, this annual review, summarizing individual achievements and suggesting ways to improve in subsequent years. The principal purpose of the formal annual performance review is to determine what was actually accomplished and what improvements can be made. Causes for lack of progress or lack of achievement are brought out at this time. There is a meaningful exchange between supervisor and subordinate.

Benefits and Values of MBO Appraisals.

1. *MBO Appraisals Relate Closely to the Job and to the Management System.* An MBO appraisal is oriented toward job requirements and work results rather than toward personality traits or general descriptors. Specified objectives are highly related to results needed and expected by the company. Evaluation is tailored to an already well-structured situation. Job clarification and responsibility definition from the practice of MBO make appraising more accurate.

2. *MBO Appraisals Focus on Results.* An MBO appraisal evaluates what was accomplished in terms of what was expected. This is the ratio of goals to accomplishment. When objectives are set for the company, the department, and the individual, evaluation can be made in terms of the needs of both the enterprise and the individual.

3. *MBO Appraisals Are Future Directed.* An MBO statement of goals and objectives can be set for any future need or any problem to be satisfied or solved. It is these goals and objectives that set the future direction to be taken. Once a need or problem is satisfied, new needs and new problems can be pursued. This is a key point. Most appraisal systems are concerned with the past. MBO is connected with the future. Setting a goal or objective sets a future direction for company, department, or individual.

4. *MBO Appraisals Are Objective.* Supervisors are usually reluctant to cite employee deficiencies without outstanding evidence. Having reliable

and accurate information on performance helps the supervisor to be objective. The role of the appraiser changes. He or she does not have to defend the position. The supervisor is on solid ground during a confrontation with employees. He or she is armed with information with which the employee is acquainted and understands.

5. *MBO Appraisals Are Active and Positive.*   The appraisal involves both the supervisor and the subordinate, and thus is not passive. Each is active in assessing job performance. There are no unilateral actions, as found in other appraisal systems. This enhances a meeting of the minds, communications, job expectations, and motivation.

6. *MBO Appraisals Are Opportunistic.*   Appraisals do not have to follow past practices or procedures. New opportunities or new challenges are easily handled within the objective-setting process. The performance appraisal approach avoids slavish following of preconceived ideas and methods. It encourages an employee to innovate because it is future oriented.

7. *MBO Appraisals Encourage Performance Stretches.*   Appraisal has many purposes. Chief among them is the stimulation it gives to improving individual performance. The mission of improvement is generic to the practice of MBO. Level and consistency of effort can be readily evaluated for individuals in the system.

8. *MBO Appraisals Sharpen Accountability.*   MBO is a highly structured process that identifies the resource be used in an action plan and those responsible for the results. *MBO provides good accountability of both resources and results!* This gives more precision to the appraisal process and makes it more objective. Evidence is available to supervisors about deficiencies and for assistance in the elimination of these deficiencies.

9. *MBO Heightens Motivation for Productivity.*   When practiced as a participative form of management, MBO "sharpens" the personal role in commitment formulation, and this tends to motivate employees. The sense of participation, feeling of accomplishment, and recognition of worth form a potent motivational base on which the organization can rely to help it reach its goals. Unlike other appraisal systems, with MBO there are no unilateral actions. This enhances agreement, communication, and commmitments.

10. *MBO Encourages "Preventive" Rather Than "Corrective" Managerial Work.*   MBO demands a high degree of planning and anticipating skills. This allows the shifting of operational problems to the planning phase of a manager's or supervisor's job. In this manner many problems are solved during the planning rather than the operational phase.

11. *MBO Has Great Flexibility to Meet Appraisal Purposes.*   An appraisal system is used for a variety of purposes. MBO has the flexibility to meet a variety of purposes. It needs only the proper design. A comparison of appraisal methods in relation to purposes is seen in Figure 16.2.

12. *MBO Tends to Be Acceptable to Employees.*   Employees tend to accept a system that allows them to participate in performance planning and to influence the measures that will be used for evaluation, that gives them

Appraisal Purposes

Appraisal Methods	Validation of Job Placement	Justification of Pay Increases	Delivery of Results	Accountability for Productivity	Achievement Motivation	Organizational Development	Individual Development	Assessment of Potential	Counseling	Aid in Improvement
Traits						X	X		X	X
Essay							X		X	X
Process									X	
Behavior Anchoring						X	X		X	
Critical Incidents			X				X			X
Standards of Performance	X	X	X	X		X		X		
Ranking	X					X			X	X
Forced Choice						X	X		X	X
Training Simulation					X		X		X	X
MBO	X	X	X	X	X	X	X	X	X	X

FIGURE 16.2 Comparison of how appraisal methods meet appraisl purposes.

counsel and help during the implementation phase, and that allows them to evaluate how well the plan was completed much more readily than they accept a system that allows them no participation.

13. *MBO Contributes to Employee Development.* The setting of goals and high levels of performance demands behavioral changes. Behavioral change is the core of development. An MBO system that is designed with continuity will contribute to a continuous series of behavioral changes. This is development.

Case Illustrations.

1. *IBM Performance Planning, Counseling, and Evaluation.* IBM's performance appraisal system is MBO oriented, since measurements of accomplishment are both objective and subjective. The IBM system has three phases: performance planning, counseling, and evaluation. Figure 16.3 shows the form used.

PERFORMANCE PLANNING			PERFORMANCE EVALUATION							
Responsibilities (key words to describe major elements of employee's job)	Performance Factors and/or Results to be Achieved (key responsibilities and/or goals employee can reasonably be expected to achieve in coming period)	Relative Importance	Actual Achievements	Level of Achievement	Far Exceeded	Consistently Exceeded	Exceeded	Consistently Met	Did Not Meet	

Changes in Performance Plan
(may be recorded any time during appraisal period)

Optional Additional Plans

Additional Significant Accomplishments

FIGURE 16.3 Form used by IBM for performance appraisal and evaluation.

(a) Performance planning. Manager and subordinate meet to discuss the job to be done and what is expected of the subordinate. They reach a mutual understanding of responsibilities. In this phase, objectives to be achieved are developed. The performance plan is the primary basis for appraisal. The manager encourages subordinates to take on additional responsibilities, but only when these would not interfere with prime responsibilities.

(b) Counseling. Manager gets together with subordinate periodically to review how subordinate is doing. Changes are discussed on how they affect the original performance plan. These reviews give an opportunity for the manager to give his or her view of performance to date and to counsel, if necessary. Reviews are held whether or not the manager or subordinate thinks there's a need. This enhances communication.

(c) Evaluation. Manager makes an evaluation of job performance on the basis of the employee's achievements in carrying out the performance plan and responsibilities. Highest ratings are given to achievements of the plan, but responsibilities not defined in the plan are also covered. Evaluation interviews are

held every six months or sooner, if needed. During the interviews, the subordinate has a chance to discuss details of the
evaluation. At the conclusion of the interview, the manager
records the significant items discussed, the employee having a
chance to react pro or con to any of the items.

(d) Higher Level Reviews. All performance plans and evaluations
involve the next higher level of management to ensure consistency, equity, and the overall quality of the program. This
higher level review assures fairness of the plan and the evaluation made by the manager with the subordinate. Finally, the
completed evaluation form is filed in a personnel folder and is
available to the subordinate for his review.

(e) Merit pay. The performance planning, counseling, and evaluation program identifies the contribution made by the employee in the job. The rating is used in the administration of
salary. Salary is based on proper pay for sustained performance.
Salary increases, however, depend on any one of three factors:
(1) improved performance; (2) promotion to a new job; (3) upward movement of the value of the job.

2. *University of Tennessee MBO Evaluation.* Three essential documents
are to be completed in the MBO evaluation process by faculty members.

(a) Statement of objectives. This is arrived at through the MBO
goal-setting conference between the faculty member and his or
her department head or director. Each faculty member is expected to prepare a summary of goals and objectives for the
coming academic year. The objectives are set within the framework of the overall objectives of the college or department. The
overall objectives are written and supplied to each faculty member prior to the goal-setting conference. This statement of objectives is issued between September 15 and October 15 of each
year.

(b) Faculty MBO activities report. This is a summary of the activities of the individual faculty member that are related to his or
her performance at the university. This report summarizes four
factors necessary for each faculty member:

(1) Classroom instruction and related activities.

(2) Institutional and departmental contributions.

(3) Professional activities and public service.

(4) Research, publications, and other scholarly activities.

(c) Faculty MBO evaluation form (Figure 16.4). This is used in a
formal evaluation of the faculty member's efforts and activities.
It documents an evaluation conference held between February 1
and March 1 of each year. The department head or director
evaluates the faculty member's performance in view of the objectives that were established earlier. An optional self-evaluation

Name _____   Department _____
Academic Rank _____   Date of Appointment _____
Years of Service _____   Tenured _____

Rating Scale   Outstanding 5
                                       More than satisfactory 4
                                       Satisfactory 3
                                       Less than satisfactory 2
                                       Unsatisfactory 1
                                       Not applicable .... NA

I.   Classroom instruction and related activities
       A.   Classroom instruction .... _____
             (preparation, presentation, interaction)
       B.   Classroom related activities .... _____
             (advising, independent study, thesis)
       C.   Student evaluations .... _____

II.   Institutional and departmental contributions .... _____

III.   Professional activities and public service .... _____

IV.   Research, publications, and other scholarly activities .... _____

V.   Personal attributes
       A.   Relationship with colleagues .... _____
       B.   Initiative .... _____
       C.   Adaptability .... _____
       D.   Institutional commitment .... _____

Overall MBO performance rating .... _____

Reviewed by:

Signature of department head:

Signature of individual evaluated:

FIGURE 16.4   MBO evaluation form used by University of Tennessee at Chattanooga.

may be included. This self-evaluation may be in narrative form, it may be quantitative, or it may be on the MBO evaluation form (Figure 16.4).

The results of the performance evaluation, whether it is self-made or made by the department head or director, is available to the faculty member and is also placed in a permanent University file for future reference. The results are used for consideration of teaching assignments, promotion, tenure, and salary adjustments.

Requirements for Use of MBO Approval.   MBO as an appraisal process has advantages and disadvantages. An organization experiencing productivity problems will find that its advantages far outweigh its disadvantages. However, certain features must prevail to make MBO an effective appraisal system: The system must have management support at all levels and must be applicable to all levels. The system should allow evaluation based on the employee's overall contribution during the entire rating period. This does not preclude day-to-day informal observations of performance, timely feedback, and constructive suggestions for improvement. It means the supervisor should look for the large, significant accomplishments made by the employee.

Finally, use of MBO appraisal requires that supervisor and employee work together to establish the productivity goals that must be pursued and the degree of priority they have in relation to other organizational concerns. A sample guide on practicing MBO is described at the end of this chapter.

Getting Accountability from MBO Appraisals.   The demand for accountability in business, education, human service institutions, and government has sharpened. It derives from a democratic society that holds that those who are entrusted with public resources, who sell to a consumer market, who give returns to stockholders, who extract a fee for educating, curing, or developing people have the responsibility for giving a full account of what they did and how well they did it. This demand for accountability is not coming from supervisors, managers, top management, or boards who direct organizations. The sharpened demand is coming from consumers who cannot understand why prices continually change, from funding sources that want to know exactly what was accomplished from given support, from taxpayers who see an ever-expanding budget to meet, from retirees whose fixed incomes are dwarfed by the cost of living, and from stockholders whose dividends are eroded by the high costs of operating a company.

The new demand for accountability is raising fundamental questions. Has the huge amount of money and support given to our educational system failed to accomplish its mission in education? America's public education budget in 1948 was $6.5 billion; it rose to $68 billion in 1969, just a little more than 20 years later. Can we account for how that money was spent in results? At its present growth rate, spending on education will eventually equal the U.S. gross national product. Has the huge amount of money and support given to welfare, social action, and poverty programs helped individuals to become responsible citizens in society? Has the huge amount of money and support given to our government brought about the quality and efficiency that government must have? Has the huge amount of money extracted by big business and industry in the form of increased prices and products been used for capital expansion and increased employment, or has it been used to line the coffers and pockets of the greedy? Has the huge amount of money and support given to our penal systems reformed prisoners? There is a demand to know what has been accomplished, who accomplished it, what resources were consumed in the process, and if fewer resources could do the same job. Hundreds of billions of dollars are being spent, yet do conditions improve in proportion? What are we getting for our money?

Accountability as a concept has always been with us. Traditionally, it has meant explaining what, how, and why responsibilities are discharged or executed in the manner they are. This traditional concept means that educators explain and justify the expenditure of funds for education, legislators explain and justify the expenditure of budgets for government and social action, and businessmen explain and justify the reinvestment of money for capitalization and expansion.

This traditional view of accountability of controlling and reporting is only partially adequate for today. New dimensions have been added. *They are expectancy and achievement. The new concept of accountability is evaluation based on agreed-on expectations.* This new concept of accountability is seen as reporting achievements at a needed and expected level. It involves funding and budgeting at agreed-on levels of expected results. The traditional concept of accountability depended on authoritarian styles, with crude coercion and threats. This style is no longer legal or effective. A new style of managing is needed.

The process of making all managers and employees accountable for productivity and results continues through all phases of work life. (Accountability itself begins early, with education in understanding how and why our economy operates.) Guidelines for establishing accountability with management and employees follow.

1. Broad, nebulous, and elusive goals of the organization must be replaced with definable, specific, and measurable objectives. This gives definition to expectancy!

2. Loosely assigned responsibilities assumed by departments, agencies, and organizations must give way to well-defined commitments from individuals by name and position. Job descriptions must be written so that each responsibility has a measurable evaluator to indicate effectiveness in completing the responsibility. This relates individual commitments to levels of expectancy.

3. Subjective and highly opinionated judgments must be replaced by evaluations based on measurable achievements that are agreed to by those responsible for the achievements. This incorporates evaluative measures into participative planning.

4. "Pointing the finger at the other person" is not appropriate; individuals must hold themselves accountable. Productivity should be a personal goal rather than an organizational goal imposed on employees. The attitude that the person who plans the action, creates the action, and follows through on the action is accountable is developed.

5. Nebulous and unrelated incentives must be replaced with "motivators" that encourage employee commitment to personal accountability. The conditions of the organization should motivate employees to honor their commitments.

There can never be accountability for results unless there are commitments to purpose. There can never be commitments to purpose unless there is clear understanding of and competence in the process of transforming resources into expected levels of performance. MBO provides a model for this process. MBO is a meaningful way to meet the demands of accountability.

SETTING UP A COMPANY APPRAISAL PROCESS

The ultimate objective of an appraisal process is to improve organizational effectiveness through better use of human resources. Too often appraisal systems fail from the weaknesses of the organization itself, while the appraisal system takes the blame. Building a quality performance appraisal system takes planning, involvement, and evaluation. But it begins with assuring that the basics of the organization are operating adequately. It may be useful to make an assessment of the organization itself. Figure 16.5 can help. It is reproduced here by permission of the U.S. Office of Personnel Management. Each item in the figure evaluates the organization. The item also suggests what can be done to move the organization to a higher level of effectiveness.

An organization that is effective must be maintained in its effectiveness. The appraisal process is a major way to do this. Appraisals assure the proper connection of human resources with the organization. Steps for setting up an appraisal process are outlined here and flowcharted in Figure 16.6.

STEP 1. Form an appraisal development committee. This committee consists of representatives from administration (raters), subordinates (ratees), and personnel staff and a knowledgeable consultant. It is practical to involve all those who will be affected by the appraisals with those who must make or administer the appraisals.

STEP 2. In committee, decide on the purpose(s) of the appraisal system. The committee identifies what the appraisal system is intended to do. If several purposes are adopted, a priority ranking must be made, since it is difficult for a single appraisal system to serve equally.

STEP 3. Select the appraisal process best suited for the purposes. The committee examines all appraisal techniques available and with the organization's climate and conditions in mind, selects the process best suited for the organization.

STEP 4. Develop an evaluative measurement form. This form incorporates the performance criteria and measures that will be used to evaluate personnel. The performance criteria and rating must clearly and accurately assess the individual as he or she relates to the purpose of the appraisal.

For "outstanding" give 3 points.
For "satisfactory" give 2 points.
For "minimally satisfactory" give 1 point.
For "unacceptable" give 0.

Points

Points

1. The mission, goals, and objectives of your organization are clear.

2. There are carefully developed priorities for the organization.

3. The organization and its resources are aligned with the priorities and objectives.

4. The necessary authority and discretion to accomplish the objectives are available.

5. The necessary resources (manpower, funds, capital) to accomplish the objectives are available.

6. The necessary time and stability to accomplish the objectives are provided.

7. There is understanding and good will on the part of those who provide resource and policy support for the organization.

8. There is quality leadership, management, and supervision.

9. There are good processes and techniques for new program development.

10. There is commitment of employees to the organization's goals.

11. Clear and challenging performance objectives are specified for each employee.

12. Employees believe that results and performance are the real basis for the rewards provided by the organization.

13. There is opportunity for employees to fully utilize their ideas and skills and develop themselves in their work.

14. There is measurement and evaluation of individual performance.

15. There is measurement and evaluation of organizational performance.

16. There is measurement of program and mission performance (including client satisfaction).

17. There is quick and accurate feedback to both employees and management concerning performance.

18. There are tangible recognitions and rewards for good performance.

19. Corrective action is taken in the case of poor performance (individual and organizational).

20. Selection and development of staff are arranged so that people are in jobs that fully utilize their individual strengths and abilities.

21. Communication within the organization and between the organization and its clients is full and open.

22. There is a sense of trust and security among employees.

23. There is healthy competition within the organization.

24. Staff and support service functions are kept small relative to line functions.

25. Staff and support service functions are held accountable for providing services and support to line functions.

26. The organization takes special steps to reduce unnecessary or conflicting procedures, processes, or policies.

27. Employees are provided attractive, safe, and healthy working conditions.

28. There is an organization environment which is conducive to constructive change and utilization of new technology.

29. Research or analysis is conducted to support the future operations of the organization.

30. The leadership of the organization generates high expectations of accomplishments.

Evaluation: 0–34   Need new leadership and complete change in management.
35–54   Need major improvements in organization and management.
55–74   Need to fine tune a good organization and management.
75–90   Need to maintain an outstanding organization.

FIGURE 16.5 Form for rating an organization. Reproduced by permission of the U.S. Office of Personnel Management.

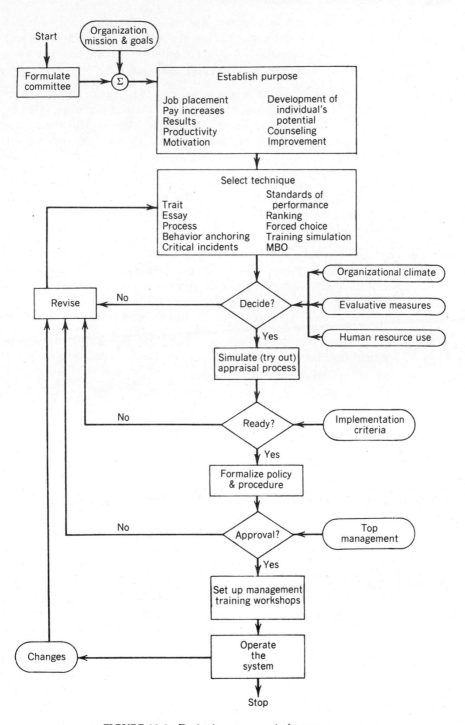

FIGURE 16.6 Designing an appraisal process.

STEP 5.   Simulate the newly adopted appraisal procedures in selected areas.   Areas in the organization are selected in which to try out the appraisal procedure. A good simulation is one that incorporates the best, worst, and average situation.

STEP 6.   Revise and formalize the appraisal process.   Examine the difficulties and areas needing change and revise procedure, criteria, and evaluative measurement. Formally write up the entire appraisal process as a policy, accompanied by a set of instructions for the raters.

STEP 7.   Gain official approval of the appraisal process.   Submit the policy, the procedure process, and the evaluative measures to the governing boards of the organization for official adoption in the organization.

STEP 8.   Set up workshops for training the raters.   These workshops give raters complete information on the policy and procedures as well as skills for conducting an unbiased rating, holding an appraisal interview, agreeing on future actions to be taken, and recording essential information for future reference.

STEP 9.   Operate the appraisal system.   Take the five steps of the appraisal process:
   (a)   Preparation of commitments.
   (b)   Planning and scheduling of activities.
   (c)   Implementation of the planned activities.
   (d)   Progress reviews.
   (e)   Annual reviews and feedback.

EVALUATING POTENTIAL FOR NEW PERFORMANCE

There is a difference between actual performance and potential to perform. Most appraisal systems are designed to evaluate actual performance. However, some appraisal systems are being revised to incorporate indications of potential to perform. Potential is important in the assignment of new work, transfer of employees to other jobs, and promotion. The following is a checklist of what can be done to assess unused potential in personnel. No method can ever be accurate in measuring human potential; the checklist is for *indicators* of potential.

1.   *Use Versus Nonuse Skills.*   This is a description of skills gained from experience, abilities, and accomplishments of the past. For each of these skills, a use and nonuse evaluation is made. The nonuse skills are a defined potential of the individual.

2. *Performance Stretches.* These are deliberate and planned stretches of the MBO goals to accomplishment ratio. Supervisor and subordinate set goals and objectives to higher levels of achievement. For each cycle of "plan-do-evaluate," new levels of performance are expected. As these levels are attained, potential is released and evaluated. Stretches are done with existing abilities and skills.

3. *Vertical Job Loading.* This is delegating work assignments and responsibilities from higher positions and levels of management to lower positions and levels of management. The delegation must be challenging, novel, and problematic. The degree of response and effectiveness of the delegatee is a measure of hidden and unused potential.

4. *Designed New Experiences.* This is a planned series of new experiences for subordinates to force the emergence of new skills and abilities. This is not a performance stretch, which is an extension of an existing ability. The supervisor plans as part of a new cycle of results, new experiences to release hidden potential.

5. *Competitive Comparisons.* This is the placement of an individual in a group in which each member competes for one or more targets. All members are aware that top management is watching the performance of the group members. Rewards and benefits go to the individual who outperforms other members of the group.

PERFORMANCE APPRAISAL INTERVIEWS

There are many reasons why managers do not hold appraisal interviews. First, managers experience fear, discomfort, and unpleasantness in openly discussing personal difficulties, disagreements, and goals. Managers may even be embarrassed, especially those who have never conducted interviews before or have not been trained in the process. Subordinates often ask questions that the supervisor is not able to answer. This heightens the embarrassment.

Second, many supervisors avoid facing subordinates over subjective judgments that must be defended. Supervisors record their judgmental impressions without significant data or measures. Defense of subjective impressions often ends in argument and hostility. Instead of the relationship between supervisor and subordinate being strengthened, it is weakened or broken. In subsequent appraisals, the supervisor usually does two things: rates the subordinates as average, a rating that seldom needs to be defended, and avoids an appraisal interview, since such an interview is not needed for average employees.

A third reason for managers not holding interviews is lack of time and perceived lack of reason. Supervisors claim that they inform and speak to their subordinates daily. Consequently there is no need for the formal, once-a-year, in-depth interview. Usually, however, these daily discussions are unilateral. Seldom are employees allowed to "open up" and say what is on their mind. Seldom are they encouraged to state their feelings about management, problems, personal goals, and whatever else may be inhibiting their work, their productivity, and their satisfaction.

Employees need encouragement to ask questions and express their thoughts, and to do so in an atmosphere that is nonthreatening. Most employees want to do a good job and even improve. They need their supervisors to tell and explain to them where they stand and how they can improve. If this climate of trust and openness is not created, a game ensues between supervisor and subordinate and the principal value of the appraisal is lost. This value is how the subordinate can correct, change, or improve on performance once an appraisal is made.

Several steps can be taken to make appraisal interviews more open and responsive to the needs of both supervisor and subordinate.

STEP 1.   Prepare for the interview.

    (a)   Review performance appraisal.

    (b)   Collect facts, information, and examples of behavior on performance.

    (c)   Anticipate where disagreements may emerge and prepare notes on substantiating evaluations.

    (d)   Evaluate progress made since the last interview and prepare notes on how the employee can improve.

    (e)   Ignore trivial or insignificant items and concentrate on important result areas.

    (f)   Consult with higher management and other supervisors to collect data, information, and views as they may relate to the issues of the interview.

    (g)   Select the day, time, and location carefully for both parties with minimal interruption.

STEP 2.   Conduct the interview.   Suggested questions for discussion are: feelings about the job (How do you feel about your job? Where are your duties and responsibilities not clear to you? What parts of your job do you consider most important? What suggestions do you have for improving your area? What aspects of your job do you find most challenging? What questions do you have about company plans for this department? What company policies are you interested in knowing more about?); performance of the work (What parts of your job do you find most enjoyable and rewarding? What parts of your job do you feel you do particularly well? Where do you feel there is greatest room for improvement in your work? How can I help you do a better job?); the future (What job would you like to be doing two years from now? Three years? Five years?

What are your plans for reaching those goals? How can I help you?).

(a) Cover one item at a time; gain agreement before going on to another item.

(b) Examine how each performance result compares with established targets. Search for causes that inhibited or prevented complete results.

(c) List actions that can be taken to avoid future disruptive causes. Open new doorways to improvement.

(d) Take notes if the interview is long.

(e) Summarize the parts of the interview on which agreement has been made.

STEP 3.   Mutually develop a plan of action.

(a) Take the areas of mutual concern and write them as targets or goals to be achieved in the future.

(b) Agree on each target or goal and how accomplishments toward the targets will be measured for the next appraisal period.

(c) Outline in a complete plan how the performance is to be accomplished. Wherever possible let the employee write the plan in his or her own words.

(d) Assure the employee that the plan can be discussed anytime in the future, especially when problems are experienced.

Appraisal interviews are important followups to performance appraisal. They can mean success or failure of the appraisal itself. The appraisal is the supervisor's view of the employee; the interview is the opportunity to get the employee to agree on this evaluation and to do something about improving weak points. In the interview, two-way communication is stressed. This is a period of a meeting of the minds and an agreement on joint action.

MBO PERFORMANCE APPRAISAL GUIDE

The following are suggestions for use in performance appraisal forms.

Foreword to Supervisors

This form is intended to assist you in appraising the performance of your employees. It is similar to performance appraisals that have been used in the past except it focuses specifically on productivity. This does not mean all other important performance expectancies are ignored. It means you must give careful attention to the requirements of productivity when you plan, delegate, implement, control, and evaluate work. Every time you plan and assign work, you must think of the most productive way it can be accomplished! *Productivity is defined as reaching the highest level of performance with the least expenditure of resources.*

Policy Statement

Every manager and supervisor is responsible and held accountable for ensuring that every employee understands the specific criteria that will be used to evaluate his or her effectiveness of performance and his or her efficiency of resource utilization. Every manager and supervisor will conduct:

1. Planning sessions annually with employees to agree on objectives for the year.
2. Verbal appraisals quarterly to evaluate employees' progress toward objectives and performance on the job.
3. Written formal appraisals annually to evaluate achievements of objectives and performance on the job.

The Appraisal Process in Steps (Figure 16.7)

STEP 1. Look for ways to improve productivity.   Examine ongoing day-to-day work that needs to be improved. Review large-scale projects that need to be accomplished. Analyze what needs to be done to accomplish the organization's annual plan.

STEP 2. Meet with individual employees.   Review with employees future work projects and work procedures. Collect suggestions, get participation in the areas of responsibilities, and agree on commitments to be pursued in the coming year.

STEP 3. Write formal statements of objectives.   Write clear, concise targets to be reached as formal commitments by individuals and the group. Keep the number of these commitments to a minimum. They must be significant.

STEP 4. Specify evaluative measures within objectives.   Include in objective statements evaluative measures for appraising progress toward or achievement of the objective. Productivity measures should include ratios that connect performance to resources. Establish how progress will be monitored.

STEP 5. Develop action plans.   Each statement of an objective should have an action plan or a set of activities that, when completed, will achieve the objective. Action plans are developed when objectives are being formulated. They validate the statements of commitments.

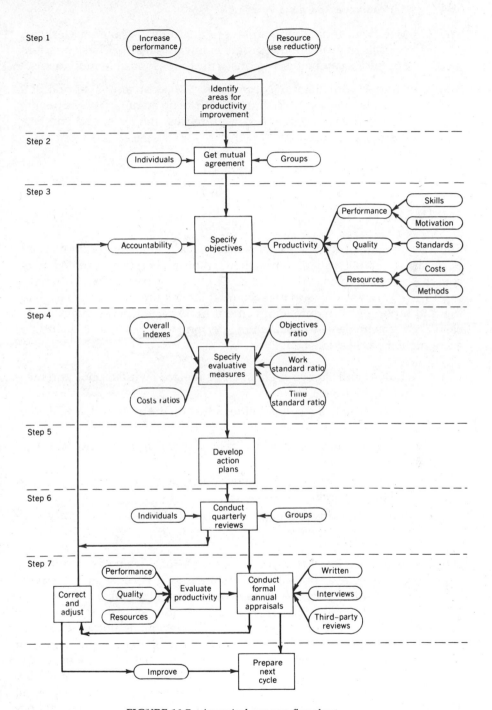

FIGURE 16.7 Appraisal process flowchart.

683

STEP 6.   Meet with individual employees quarterly.   Make quarterly appraisals to evaluate the progress toward targets. These quarterly appraisals can be discussions with the responsible individuals.

STEP 7.   Conduct formal annual appraisals.   Make an annual appraisal to evaluate total accomplishments. Write up summary of the results. Review areas of agreement, differences, interests, and conflicts. Formulate future plans.

Figure 16.8 shows an example of appraisal of an individual.

SUMMARY

The new demand of accountability is raising many kinds of questions about performance. What was accomplished? Who accomplished it? What resources were consumed in the process? Could it be accomplished with fewer resources? This new demand for accountability requires more than explaining and reporting. It requires agreement on expected performance and a clear and measurable way of evaluating performance. Several guidelines for accountability are established:

1.   Nebulous and elusive goals must be replaced with specific and measurable objectives.
2.   Loosely assigned responsibilities must give way to individual commitments.
3.   Opinionated judgment must be replaced by evaluation based on measurable achievements.
4.   Dependence on others as being accountable must give way to personal accountability.
5.   Nebulous incentives must be replaced with motivators for accountability.

Accountability requires an appraisal process that evaluates results and productivity. Several appraisal methods are in use, because of the varying uses for and intended purposes of such methods: validation of employee job placement; justification of pay increases; evaluation of results; accounting for productivity; setting up of conditions for achievement motivation; provision of feedback for organizational change; development of personnel for positional changes; identification of hidden potential of employees; and counseling of employees with problems. The ten appraisal methods described in this chapter—trait appraisal, essay appraisal, process appraisal, behavior anchoring, critical-incident appraisal, standards of performance appraisal, ranking appraisal, forced-choice appraisal, training simulation appraisal, and MBO appraisal—are practiced in companies today.

Name   *John Smith*   Date *Jan. 15*   Beginning   *Jan.*   Ending *Dec.*

Position   *Foreman of Electrical Distribution*

Productivity Expected—Objectives and Evaluative measures. List the major results expected for the section, group, or department. Include evaluative measures and relative priority of each item. This plan should be revised to reflect changes as they occur during the year.

Priority	Objectives To Be Achieved (Performance Expected with Resources to Be Used)	Evaluative Measures (Indicators)	Target Date
1	Complete 1400 commercial electrical installations with no more than two personnel	$PI = \dfrac{1400\ installations}{2\ workers}$	Oct. 30
2	Install 150,000 feet of three #4 wire for less than $2500 per foot	$PI = \dfrac{150,000\ feet\ of\ wire}{\$2500}$	Feb. 10
3	Total rework is less than 10% of total installations	No more than 10%	Dec. 30
6	Supervise transportation system to keep incidents to five or fewer	Checklist of incidents: (a) Complaints by customers (b) Unable to start work by schedule (c) Vehicle breakdown (d) Vehicle accidents	Dec. 30
5	Assist superintendent in certifying 300 installations with no more than 5% recertifications	$PI = \dfrac{285\ certifications}{300\ total}$	25 per month
4	Complete four departmental budget checklist items within required planning time	Budget checklist: (a) Estimates of all costs (b) Completion of all forms (c) Validation in the field (d) All approvals	July 1

FIGURE 16.8   Example of individual appraisal.

4. Evaluation and Summary of Performance Appraisal

Name _John Smith_   Date _Jan. 15_

Department _Electrical Distribution_   Location _Field Engineering_

Position Title _Foreman_   Supervisor _____

Time in Position _17 years_   Last Appraisal Date _Jan. 22_

Performance Results   List objectives expected and the actual results achieved for each of the major commitments agreed upon on the planning phase. Include comments on the quality of attainment and circumstances affecting results.

	Target Date	Priority
1. Objective expected Complete 1400 commercial installations with no more than two personnel	Oct 30	1
Results Achieved Completed 1200 installations with no more than two personnel $PI = \dfrac{Actual}{Planned} = \dfrac{1200}{1400} = 86\%$		
2. Objective expected Install 150,000 feet of three #4 wire for less than $2500 per foot	Feb. 10	2
Results Achieved Installed 160,000 feet for $2200 per foot $PI = \dfrac{Actual\ PI}{Planned\ PI} = 120\%$		
3. Objective expected Total rework is less than 10% of total installations	Dec. 30	3
Results Achieved 1200 installations completed, 60 reworked installations $PI = \dfrac{1200\ completed}{1400\ planned} = 86\%$		
4. Objective expected Complete budget within expected time	Dec. 30	4
Results achieved Budget preparations completed $PI = \dfrac{4\ checklist\ items}{4\ expected\ items} = 100\%$		
5. Objective expected Assist in certifying 300 installations	Dec. 30	5
Results Achieved 250 certifications were completed $PI = \dfrac{250\ certifications}{300\ expected} = 83\%$		

FIGURE 16.8 *(continued)*

<u>Job Performance Factors</u>   Check the appropriate block to indicate the employee's degree of effectiveness in looking for and actually contributing to performance improvement. Cite examples of observed performance improvement where applicable.

		Strong	Satis-factory	Needs Improve-ment	Comments
1.	Problem analysis – finds critical factors and arrives at sound solutions.	☐	☑	☐	_____ _____ _____
2.	Organizer – plans and completes own work by target dates.	☐	☐	☑	*Suggest he learn scheduling techniques*
3	Quality – work quality meets expected standards of job and profession.	☐	☑	☐	_____ _____
4.	Amount of work – produces volume of work on a day-to-day basis.	☐	☑	☐	_____ _____
5.	Controls—understands standards, measures results, and corrects.	☑	☐	☐	*Sets up standards even where they do not exist.*
6.	Motivation – motivated to complete work to a successful end.	☐	☑	☐	_____ _____ _____
7.	_____	☐	☐	☐	_____
8.	_____	☐	☐	☐	_____

FIGURE 16.8   *(continued)*

<u>Resources Use Factors</u>   Check the appropriate block to indicate the
employee's degree of efficiency in following methods and responsibilities
for best utilization of resources. Cite examples of observed efficiency in
resource use.

		Strong	Satis-factory	Needs Improve-ment	Comments
1.	Cost—mindedness — does work with best cost judgment.	☐	☐	☑	*Needs to make cost benefit analysis before proceeding*
2.	Budget use — completes work within prescribed limits.	☐	☑	☐	
3.	Time use — utilizes time efficiently and eliminates unnecessary activities.	☐	☐	☑	*Personal activities excessive*
4.	Space — makes best use of space allocated for completing work.	☐	☑	☐	
5.	Supplies — uses only supplies needed to accomplish work.	☐	☑	☐	
6.	Fellow workers — does not waste efforts and time of colleagues	☐	☑	☐	
7.	_____	☐	☐	☐	
8.	_____	☐	☐	☐	

FIGURE 16.8   *(continued)*

688

Personal Factors   Ch.:ck the appropriate block to indicate the employee's
degree of acceptable behavior in interpersonal relations and personal
conduct in job responsibilities. Cite examples of observed personal qualities.

	Strong	Satis—factory	Needs Improve—ment	Comments
1. Learning — learns quickly and effectively applies skills to job.	☐	✓	☐	
2. Self—development — aware of strengths and weaknesses and plans development.	☐	☐	✓	Needs to be reminded continuously
3. Communication — selects proper media and effectively writes, listens, and speaks.	☐	✓	☐	
4. Team relations — works well as a member of a team.	☐	✓	☐	
5. Adaptability — ability to react to changes in job requirements or expectancies.	☐	✓	☐	
6. Self—starter — does not have to be told to start and works with limited supervision.	☐	☐	✓	Tends to forget
7. _____	☐	☐	☐	

FIGURE 16.8   *(continued)*

689

Development Plans   Indicate plan for further development of employee in
the next appraisal period. Relate plans to the strengths and improvements
cited earlier.

1. Should enroll in course on scheduling techniques
2. Would like him to visit another department to see cost
   control practices
3. Suggest the development of a personal planner and
   time log for recording deadlines

Summary and Recommendations   Record any additional comments and
make whatever recommendation deemed necessary to other individuals in
the organization such as merit increase, promotion, transfer, development,
or termination.

No significant change is presently recommended

Employee's acknowledgment
and Agreement   _____John Smith_____   Date _Jan 12_

Employee's Acknowledgment
and Disagreement   _____   Date _____

Appraised by   _____Bob Doe_____   Date _Jan. 12_

Reviewed by   _____   Date _Jan. 30_

FIGURE 16.8   (continued)

690

MBO appraisal is a multipurpose performance appraisal process. It has a variety of objectives. The practice of MBO in appraisal has several advantages:

1.   It relates closely to the job.
2.   It focuses on results.
3.   It clarifies directions.
4.   It gives information objectively.
5.   It involves supervisor and subordinate.
6.   It seeks opportunities for improvement.
7.   It encourages performance stretches.
8.   It sharpens accountability.
9.   It heightens motivation for productivity.
10.   It encourages preventive rather than corrective managerial work.
11.   It gives flexibility in meeting several appraisal purposes.

This chapter describes how to set up a company appraisal process. Assessment of the organization itself is the first step, since a solid managerial foundation is a must before the appraisal process can be set up. Several other steps are suggested. The appraisal interview is an important part of the appraisal process. Suggestions are made on how such interviews might be conducted with greater effectiveness. Methods for evaluating employees' potential for new performance are also given. Finally, an MBO performance appraisal guide is given.

BIBLIOGRAPHY

Kekom, Anton K., "The Internal Consultant." *American Management Association Special Report*, New York, 1969, pp. 41–73.

Mali, Paul, *Managing By Objectives*. New York: Wiley, 1972, pp. 237–243.

United States Office of Personnel Management, *Performance*. Washington, DC, January 1980.

Upjohn Institute for Employment Research, *Work in America*. Cambridge, MA: MIT Press, 1972, p. 106.

Winstanley, N. B., "Performance Appraisal: Another Pollution Problem?" New York: *National Industrial Conference Board*, September 1972, pp. 59–63.

17

JAPANESE MBO

IN THIS CHAPTER

WHAT'S BEHIND JAPANESE SUCCESS?
JAPANESE MANAGERIAL PRACTICES
JAPANESE MBO SYSTEMS
MBO COMPARISONS: JAPANESE VERSUS UNITED STATES

A managerial revolution is taking place throughout the world. Germany, Italy, France, Israel, Korea, and China are but a few of the countries in which business management is catching up to American business management. In some cases, it is surpassing it. This is true of Japanese management. Japan's outstanding performance is particularly remarkable when traced from the World War II military, political, and economic defeat of Japan to the present-day supereconomy that encompasses global managerial skills that rival those of any other country with or without a major war defeat. Table 17.1 shows how the productivity ranking of Japan against other industrial countries rose between 1976 and 1980. It shows that American productivity declined while Japan experienced a growth rate unparalleled by any other industrial country.

Despite its rapid growth rate, Japan is still influenced by traditional values. This chapter examines the business style that has lead to Japan's present-day global position. The Japanese phenomenon is still in the making. Consequently, it is difficult to describe the changing scenario. Nonetheless, some factors and practices are explained, especially as they relate to the practice of MBO. To begin with, the chapter identifies what's behind Japanese success. Everyone wants to know how they did it. Japanese managerial practices are identified. Included also is a brief description of a Japanese MBO system. Finally, a comparison is made between Japanese MBO and American MBO.

TABLE 17.1   Comparison of
Ranking in Productivity Growth
Rate in 1976 and 1980 of Eleven
Developed Nations

Country	1976	1980
United States	1	11
Belgium	2	2
Norway	3	5
Sweden	4	8
Canada	5	9
Denmark	6	7
France	7	6
West Germany	8	3
Japan	9	1
Great Britain	10	10
Italy	11	4

WHAT'S BEHIND JAPANESE SUCCESS?

The reasons for the success of Japanese management in world markets probably need volumes to describe. The literature is replete with accounts of how a fallen nation got up and underwent the most spectacular economic and business growth the world has ever seen. Here we will identify only the management practices that have brought about significant changes. It is not likely that duplication of these practices by non Japanese organizations would bring about the same positive changes. But there may be lessons to be learned.

Good Planning

The Japanese are good planners because they are good detailers. They are good detailers because they take the time needed for decision making. That is, they think in advance of all the details needed for implementation of a plan and reflect this thinking into the planning phase. They think in advance of all the details that could abort a plan and make whatever adjustments are needed to make the plan effective and workable. There is an old saying in management circles: "The British walk before they think, the Americans think while they walk, and the Japanese think before they walk." Plan validation means thinking through the implementation phase of the plan sufficiently to perceive what problems will emerge and then modifying the plan to avoid the problems. In many ways this reduces the risk factor for the plan. A good plan has low risk, brought about by anticipation and solving of the difficulties involved in making the plan work. This unerring attention to details in the planning phase for workable implementation serves as an effective base for MBO.

Hard Work

The Japanese work hard. They are industrious and diligent. There seems to be two reasons for this. First, the Japanese put national interest first. They have a deep sense of national purpose and achievement of clearcut national goals. Personal interviews with several Japanese analysts have conveyed to me the concern the Japanese have over their lack of natural resources. As one put it, "We have no natural resources except one—productivity." Consequently, the Japanese see hard work and high productivity as the few options available to them for achieving national goals and personal gain. As William Ouchi reported in his book, *Theory Z*, "On an assembly line of a U. S. company in Atlanta, Georgia, 35 American women assemble transistor panels in a prescribed set of steps. In Tokyo, at another plant of this company, 35 Japanese assemblers use the same technology and the same procedure to manufacture the same part. The only real difference between the two lines is their productivity: the Japanese workers turn out 15% more panels than their American counterparts 7,000 miles away."

The Japanese are near obsessed with finding new ways to increase personal and company productivity. They come very close to "worshipping" productivity. The lack of natural resources forces Japan to depend greatly on foreign sources. This becomes a driving force behind Japan's need to maintain good relations with potential suppliers while at the same time exporting aggressively to pay for these needed supplies.

High productivity in Japan results from a national esprit de corps in addition to company esprit de corps. The productivity effort is not segmented, sporadic, or localized but a national effort involving the total work force and even the entire Japanese people. The Japanese are regaining their pride and standing through this national esprit de corps, they are showing the world that they can stand tall. For the Japanese, the productivity race is more than a livelihood and a means of employment. It is an opportunity to make Japan again into a world power.

The second reason is mutual employee-employer loyalty. This loyalty is a bond. As Ouchi argued in his book, *Theory Z*, Japanese managers get more out of their employees than American bosses do because the whole structure of business organizations encourages mutual trust and cooperation. A powerful bonding exists between workers and their firm from such practices as lifetime employment, participation, and collective decision making. More will be said about these practices in the next section.

Stable Societal Character

Ask any sociologist for the factors involved in a secure and stable society. Among the many, four will be identified: crime rate, prison population, number of divorces, and mental clinic activity. In a special comparison of Japan with England, France, ~nd West Germany, Japan ranked first for the fewest policemen, first for the fewest people in prison, second for the fewest divorces, and first for the fewest admissions to mental clinics. These rankings may not be conclusive, but they do give an indication of fewer community problems that local, state, and national governments must handle. In the United States there are 400,000 lawyers, compared with 15,000 in Japan. The most important reading from these statistics is the character of the Japanese people. They indicate such personality traits as trust, loyalty, sincerity, honesty and conformity. These help to reduce worker alienation, productivity decline, job turnover, disobedience, waste, and pilferage.

Pursuit of Quality and Service

The Japanese fiercely pursue quality and service, and this factor probably ranks highest as a reason for Japan's high performance and success. The "made in Japan" image for quality has changed. Prior to World War II, "made in USA" was a distinct asset to product salability and long use. "Made in Japan," however, was a signal that quality was poor and use would be short. Repeat sales were not even expected with products "made in Japan." However, the Japanese, both government and business management, experienced through the loss of World War II how low quality and poor service could have a devastating and defeating effect. The Japanese have adopted the victorious American style of quality and service to such a degree that they have even refined and surpassed American quality control procedures. Japanese quality planning begins with market research design review, model construction and tests, environmental and life testing, and innumerable inspection checks. This process is carried out by virtually all manufacturers.

High Priority on Technology

Japanese management encourages through its policies, organizational structure, and R & D budgets technological ventures and innovations. Japanese high technology dominates global markets in such areas as semiconductors, communications, information processing, and automation. This dominance is seen as a national goal. These industries have been selected for dominance because of their low energy use and low natural resource requirements. Government and companies are pouring unprecedented amounts of money, time, and talent into high-technology areas. If the top ten Fortune 500 corporations were compared with the top ten German and top ten Japanese with regard to percentage of gross profits plowed back into R & D, the figure for American firms would be 11 percent, for German 22 percent, and for Japanese 25 percent. The Japanese spend more money on R & D as a percentage of GNP. Between 1966 and 1976, Japan's capital investment as a percentage of GNP was almost double that of the United States. One of the most effective Japanese strategies is the willingness to accept lower profits initially in efforts to penetrate an emerging market. The Japanese will sacrifice return on investment today for a larger share of the market tomorrow. This reinvestment into their own firms allows them to take advantage of opportunities in high technology.

Formally, the Japanese strategy in high technology has been to buy technology from overseas; produce it first for the home market, which in many areas is shut off from foreign producers; and then, when volumes get high, sell it to foreign markets with low prices. The pressure by foreign competitors to enter Japanese local markets, however, is high, and thus Japan's high technology strategy is changing in two important respects: Japan will develop its own high technology ability and will compete internationally in the technology race.

Natural "Organizational" Behavior

Any organization can be seen as people within groups. If the people work in these groups, they exemplify group behavior, that is, individuals functioning within a group accepting group goals and responsibilities over individual goals and priorities. Teamwork is defined in this fashion. A team is a collection of individuals whose mission, objectives, and orientation require the working cooperation and contribution of each member of the team. Individuals exist for the team. They must often compromise and forfeit individual gain, preferences, and priorities for the sake of the team. The Japanese are world famous for teamwork. Cooperation, collaboration, and participation, basic components of organizational behavior, are bywords among the Japanese. Even corporations and businesses share and exchange the latest technical data and skillful procedures of manufacturing. In the United States much of this sharing would be illegal.

The main reason that the Japanese follow a natural group behavior, in which harmony is important, is their love for the family. Historically and socially, family life is important. The Japanese believe in shared values. They expect lifetime membership in their family. They see security within the family. They accept an authoritative and paternalistic father. Japanese management uses paternalistic treatment of labor as a style. This is in contrast to the impersonal approach used by American management. It is because of these natural groups working within business organizations that a cooperative relationship develops. Presidents of companies are often perceived as paternalistic and authoritative fathers.

"Big Think" Approach

Japanese managers, in addition to their concern for people and their commitment to shared values, are bold thinkers with an extraordinary sense of competitive urgency. They overwhelm the big problems. In the normal course of business, big problems are not handled in a routine way. Big problems require big approaches. The Japanese solve them by overwhelming them with "big time," "big numbers of participants," and "big thinking." Americans may view this approach as overdone, overreacting, and out of proportion. For example, the zaibatsu group—the financial and industrial Japanese conglomerates—are the powerful drives for "thinking big" while maintaining a paternalistic ideology in labor management. These zaibatsu groups were once small family affairs. By thinking big they have become big.

Unique Government-Business Collaboration

The Japanese have a tight working combine of government and business that is unique in world governments. This combine also involves banks and labor organizations. The expression, "Japan, Inc.," is not farfetched, as the nation is one large enterprise, with economic, business, social, and political collaboration. The Japanese government develops and maintains an effective cooperative relationship with existing businesses and "bends backward" to help new ventures and enterprising entrepreneurs. This cooperation between government and business gives the businesses major competitive advantages in the marketplace with regard to technology, investments, regulations, loans, taxes, and protective tariffs. Some American firms have not been able to enter and compete in Japanese markets. This is markedly different from other countries, in which the government constrains business or even has adversarial relationships with the business community. Japanese businesses, in turn, give Japan employment, expanding economy and high cash flow, reduced crime, needed consumer products, pension programs, and world image.

In spite of this close combine, the Japanese economy operates in a highly competitive environment. While the government established national priorities and goals, intervention by government in business is minimal compared with other developed countries. The policies of government are to encourage competition within Japan. The companies that are winning in the local Japanese market have become formidable in world markets.

JAPANESE MANAGERIAL PRACTICES

MBO works well when an organization is practicing good basic management. Here is a summary of the basic management practices that, for the most part, are found in Japanese organizations. These practices are contrasted with American practices in Table 17.2.

Each of these managerial practices is briefly described here.

Collective Responsibilities (Quality Circles)

Quality circles are small groups of employees in the same work area who meet on a voluntary basis to discuss their problems, investigate causes, recommend solutions, and take corrective action. Participants are taught elementary techniques of problem solving, including statistical methods. They concentrate on job-related quality problems.

The principal concern in the circles is quality, and such circles have been the primary vehicle for high quality in Japan. But other concerns and

TABLE 17.2 Comparison of Managerial Practices in Japanese and American Organizations

Japanese Organizations	American Organizations
Collective responsibilities (quality circles)	Individual responsibility
Lifetime and permanent employment	Short-term and changing employment
Cluster/satellite centralization (zaibatsu)	Cluster/satellite decentralization
Strike behavior with continued productivity	Strike behavior with interrupted productivity
Multiple group membership	Limited group membership
Ringi: Collective decision making	Individual decision making
Holistic concern for people	Concern for people only at work
Kanban: "just-in-time" production	"Be ready" production
Japanese MBO emphasizes "doing"	American MBO emphasizes "planning"

investigations are considered. A typical breakdown of time in a quality circle is:

Quality	22%	Process control	9%
Efficiency	12%	Absenteeism	8%
Costs	11%	Safety	4%
Equipment	10%	Learning	3%
Morale	10%	Miscellaneous	11%

If efficiency, costs, process control, and equipment are viewed as components of productivity, productivity concerns total 42 percent. The argument can thus be made that productivity is the major effort in circle work.

Nine steps are used in a quality circle process:

- Choose a problem. Why that problem?
- Gather specifics about the problem
- Analyze it for causes.
- Decide on a solution.
- Plan the "how" of the solution.
- Do it! Take action.
- Check—did it fix the problem?
- Be sure it stays fixed.
- Move on to the next specific problem.

Four factors in the practice of quality circles are reasons for their success.

1. *Employees Who Accept Supervisory Responsibilities as Their Own.*   Responsibility for quality, productivity, safety, costs, absenteeism, morale, equipment, learning, and methods has traditionally been in the domain of supervisors. Workers' willingness to accept these responsibilities is a unique form of participation of ordinary workers in the everyday decision-making managerial process. It is exercising the principle, "every employee a manager." Involvement of workers in these key areas is seen as the major factor for increased productivity.

2. *Formal Pursuit of Ideas and Innovations and Ways of Implementation.*   An idea is the substance by means of which product and process development is improved. It is good to have professional employees work formally and deliberately in product and process development. It is much better when ordinary workers who build the product and operate the processes are added to the professional employees. Improvement is more likely when both groups, professionals and workers, focus on how new ideas can be implemented. The basic thrust of quality circles is the collection of ideas for change and improvement and how these ideas can be implemented.

3. *Formal and Effective Training for All Employees.*   Before quality circles are organized and operating, massive training is given to employees on problem solving, quality control, group processes, and communications. Training increases quality awareness and provides the skills for interfacing effectively in groups. This training makes employee participation in responsibilities more effective and efficient.

4. *Annual Program of Quality and Productivity Improvement.*   Quality and productivity improvement is annualized. Each year a strong expectation of doing better than the previous year is imposed on every employee, including managers. Annual programs of "doing better" have been institutions in Japan, for some time, creating a climate and encouraging a life-style. Rewards and recognition are signaled with these improvements. This explains the progressive stance that Japan has enjoyed since World War II.

One of the approximately 300 U. S. companies that have picked up the quality control circle concept from Japan is Westinghouse. It formed its first circles in September 1978 and at this writing has established more than 400 circles in 50 locations, with an estimated 40 new ones being created each month. Ultimately it expects to have well over 2000 circles. Westinghouse takes precautions to avoid making the quality circles a dictate from the top. Members are not assigned; they are volunteers, and the facilitator rather than the supervisor is the main link between the circle and management. It is essential for the members to feel that the circle is theirs, not Westinghouse's.

In contrast to the circles in Japan, U. S. circles meet on company time. It is felt in America that meeting on company time makes participation more acceptable to workers, thus maximizing the talents of the labor force. This also helps prevent union problems, because unions may consider meetings held outside working hours as overtime.

Morale in the circles is sustained as long as members feel that they provide a useful function. Westinghouse assists its circles by providing tools (problem-solving techniques) and the environment (time and meeting places). The facilitators ensure that the time is spent effectively and communicate the experiences of other circles.

Managers are willing to take the circles seriously. They sit down and listen to ideas, implement the good ones, and explain why the others are rejected. To provide recognition, Westinghouse holds an annual conference at which outstanding projects are noted and prizes awarded.

Westinghouse emphasizes that its quality circles are not cost-cutting programs but rather a people-oriented management policy aimed toward providing opportunities for workers to make group efforts, promote a sense of belonging, and having employees participate in problem solving. The intangible effects are better work morale, initiative, and communications and more pride in the job.

Lifetime Employment

Lifetime employment is more than a company or work policy. It is a fabric under which many facets of Japanese work, culture, and life-styles are integrated. Only 35 to 40 percent of Japan's work force has lifetime employment. But this employment is with significant and powerful large corporations and government bureaus, which have caused the great change in Japan's product quality and productivity. Those who have lifetime employment enjoy a unique status and reward system. They "work hard" to remain lifetime employees, since discharge means turning to a small company, lower wages, and little security. Japanese workers thus are more likely to identify themselves with their company than with their profession. The principal features of lifetime employment are:

1. *Skill Proficiencies Are Reached.* Lifetime employment perpetuates good, skilled workers to the time of retirement (55 years old). Under this system, skill proficiency is not only developed but realized long before a person retires.

2. *Workers Are Motivated in Job and in Work.* A large part of an employee's motivation is accomplished and maintained before actual placement in the work. To be a member of the 35 percent also means working hard to not be a member of the 65 percent nonlifetimers. Termination is hard punishment, since a person who is fired has no hope of finding employment in a comparable firm. An argument can be made that as 35 percent lifetime expands to 90 or 95 percent of the workforce, lifetime employment will cease to be a motivator.

3. *Training Is Accomplished at One Time.* Hiring by lifetime employment organizations is done once a year, in the spring when graduates complete their studies. Thus many new employees join the company all at once.

Hiring is done whether work is available or not. (In the American system, hiring is done piecemeal when work is available or an opening occurs.) ifetime hiring also allows massive, consistent, and total training for all employees. Training under this system tends to be formal and rigorous.

4. *Retirement Fund Is Attractive.*   Japan does not have pension or social security systems for retirees. Those who maintain their lifetime employment to age 55 are severed with five to six years' worth of salary. Thus a person earning $20,000/year will be given $100,000 to $120,000 at the time of retirement. This is enough for the rest of the employee's life. Thus lifetime employment is a powerful motivator to the point of retirement.

5. *Compensation Is a Combination of Salary and Bonus.*   Every six months each employee is paid a bonus equivalent to six months of salary. The amount is not contingent on individual performance but on the performance of the firm. Bonuses give employees an incentive to feel a part of the firm and motivate them to cooperate in any way they can. During bad times, a company can cut the payroll without laying anyone off. The loss is made up during good times when salary is restored and bonuses are added.

6. *Women Are Employed Part-Time.*   Women comprise a large category of temporary employees who serve as a buffer against the temporary ups and downs of sales and costs of the firm. This buffer protects the hard-core job stability of lifetimer men. Rarely are women hired into lifetime jobs in professional or managerial work.

Cluster/Satellite Centralization (Zaibatsu)

Major firms in Japan are organized into small groups called *zaibatsu*. Each group consists of 20 to 30 firms, all clustered around a powerful bank. Each firm is representative of a major industry (steel, insurance, shipping, auto, etc.). Around each of the major firms are a host of satellite small companies (100 or more) which provide technical services, subassembled parts, materials, and so on, sold only to their one major customer in the cluster. The small companies range from family size to up to 100 employees. Figure 17.1 illustrates the *zaibatsu*.

Zaibatsu were legally dissolved after World War II, but the relationships still continue. Here are the principal features of the *zaibatsu*:

1. *Bilateral Monopoly and Cooperation.*   The satellite suppliers have only one customer for their products and the major firm has only one supplier for each of its inputs. Exceptions are made by the major firm when a mutual advantage is to be maintained in the market.

2. *Three-Hour In-Process Inventories.*   The working relationship between cluster and satellite is so close and cooperative that the supplier delivers parts right to work stations on the assembly line. The supplier will deliver only the amount of parts that will be needed for two to three hours of production and will redeliver when more parts are needed. Thus a large firm does not need large in-process inventories, saving money and space.

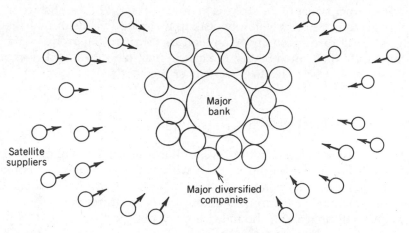

FIGURE 17.1   Japanese cluster/satellite (*zaibatsu*) form of business organization.

3. *Cooperation Resulting in Great Productivity.* A high dependence develops among the closely knit firms in the zaibatsu with each other and with the major bank. This working team needs productivity of the highest order to compete with other zaibatsus or foreign competitors. The teamwork, along with lifetime employment, results in great productivity.

4. *Part-Time Employment by Satellite Companies for Retirees of Major Firms.* A retiree from lifetime employment (55 years old), who is given $120,000 severance retirement pay, is also placed for 10 to 15 years in a satellite company in a part-time position. Thus severance pay and part-time employment within the zaibatsu allow the person to retire in comfort.

Japanese "Strike" Behavior

Japanese unions are unique. Their practice of the strike is unique. Traditionally, a strike is the weapon a union uses to hurt the company and management so it can get its issues and problems resolved. When Japanese workers strike, they separate hurting the company from hurting management. They do not want to hurt their company, since they have a lifetime job and they are not disloyal. They strike more to hurt management. Features of the Japanese "strike" are:

1.   Labor unions are organized by companies, that is, labor unions are company unions. This makes the negotiation and administration of labor contracts a family affair, and there is little or no interference from internationals. Disputes and difficulties are settled internally.

2.   Many companies have strikes in which work continues as productively as ever. Black bands and wall signs are the only outward signs of the strike.

3.   Some workers who strike for the day will make up the loss in productivity the following day, even if this means personal overtime.

4.   The principal use of the strike is to send a message of dissatisfaction to top management. Strikers will not speak to their supervisors or managers, which is great disrespect and humiliation. Meanwhile productivity is maintained. (In the United States, the loss in man-days from strikes in one year was over 100,000. This loss was never recovered.)

Multiple Group Membership

Every employee from top to bottom is simultaneously a member of as many as eight to a dozen work groups, each with a different task to complete (Figure 17.2). Membership in the groups changes, but for the most part an employee remains in a group throughout his or her career.

Under this arrangement, the following are noticed:

1.   Group memberships influence attitudes, motivation, and behavior. Individuals are greatly concerned about what group peers think of them.

2.   Individuals attempt to adhere to the norms of the group. Failure to adhere to norms can bring about loss of group support or approval or even group rejection. Group interaction has a great deal of influence on behavior.

3.   Young people are admitted into groups when openings occur. This gives the group a chance to inculcate its norms and behavior into the young person in the formative stage. Over the years, individual behavior blends into group behavior, if group norms are high and rigorous.

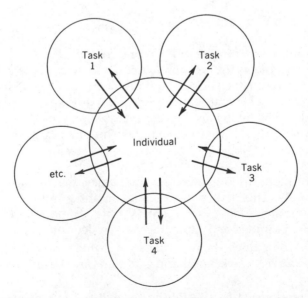

FIGURE 17.2   Multiple group membership of Japanese worker.

MBO: Japanese Style

MBO is practiced by Japanese management but in a style that fits the culture and traits of Japan. Differences between the American and Japanese practice of MBO are as follows:

| American MBO | Provide reports to President; give information on competitors; recommend role of company | President sets objectives; others follow and support |
| Japanese MBO | Learn customers' needs; find out about competitors; determine role of company | Individual sets own objectives |

The Japanese system creates a basis for self-evaluation rather than evaluation of what the boss does for the worker. It encourages individuals to figure out for themselves what an appropriate objective would be for any situation, no matter how unusual or new. The president never has to set the objectives, never has to give them targets. More will be said later about Japanese MBO.

Ringi: Collective Decision Making

A well-known feature of Japanese organizations is their participative approach to decision making. Active participation by everyone tends to close status gaps and facilitates creativity in the workplace. In the typical American organization, "the buck stops here" is typical. That is, each level takes responsibility for making decisions. The *ringi* system is a collective decision-making system in which a proposed decision, document, or need for approval passes from manager to manager on level to level for official approval. This decision-by-consensus technique, called *ringi* from the words *ri*, meaning "ask from below," and *gi*, meaning "deliberate," allows for debate and argument until the essence of a solution is committed on paper. Several advantages are likely under this system:

1. It yields more creative decisions, more alternatives, and more anticipated problems.
2. It yields more effective implementation than does individual decision making.
3. It yields better control over errors or unforeseen disruptions.
4. It yields better opportunity for development of neophytes in the decision-making process.
5. It normally would take more time, but if members of the group are in the same room, time is expedited.

6. It yields better understanding of why the alternative selected is the decision to be made. There is no need to inform all, since all have participated.

At the end of the *ringi* process, a proposal or document will be literally covered with the stamps of approval of 60 to 80 people.

The *ringi* method requires a long time for the decision but implementation is then short (Figure 17.3).

The typical Japanese "office" helps make the *ringi* system work. It is a large room with desks and tables arranged in much the same way as the people are arranged in the organization chart. This layout is essentially a decision-making factory designed to provide widespread communication and to promote consensus. Superiors, subordinates, assistants, and secretaries sit side by side. Superiors are highly accessible and do little that their associates do not see and hear. In such a highly verbal environment, many important messages are spoken rather than written. Subordinates are thus kept up to date not only on the workings of their own department but also of related departments.

The need for a decision through the *ringi* process finds the proposal or problem shuttled from position to position, desk to desk, at each of which it is debated, modified, and confirmed until the manager agrees with it and fixes his seal of approval to the document. The *ringi* process is essentially an authorization-confirmation process designed to spread, not individually pinpoint, the responsibility for a decision—the opposite of the American decision ethic. Therefore the more seals of approval, the more confident is a senior manager that sufficient bargaining, discussion, and compromise have occurred to permit successful and rapid implementation of a decision. At the end of the process, a *ringi* document may have 60 to 80 stamps of approval.

Holistic Management of People

Japanese management does not ignore relationships and commitments that exist outside the firm. Examples of interest in the whole person are training program graduation ceremonies at which families and friends of graduates hear the message given to trainees by the president. Families hear what is expected of their children. Zaibatsu retirees, even though severed with retirement pay, are assisted in getting a part-time job in a satellite company so that they may extend their working life. In the American sys-

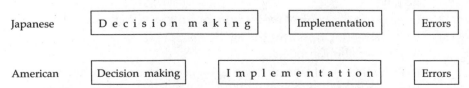

FIGURE 17.3 Comparison of Japanese *ringi* decision-making process and American process.

tem, family life and social concerns are not considerations of management. Its focus is on the work life.

Just-in-Time Production

The kanban system is a control system for the "just-in-time" production method. Kanban is a "pull" inventory system, in contrast to the American "push" system in which a production run is made and finished parts are pushed to the next production process. The kanban system pulls from the previous process, thus eliminating buffer stock and inventory buildup. Kanban thoroughly eliminates wastes and minimizes costs by assuming that anything other than the minimum amounts of equipment, materials, parts, and workers needed for production are merely surpluses that raise costs. Kanban can best be understood by comparing it with the American production system (Figure 17.4).

In the kanban system, two kinds of cards are used: production kanban cards used to order production from the subsequent process and conveyance kanban cards used to order production from the preceding process. These two types of cards are attached to containers holding parts.

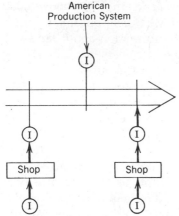

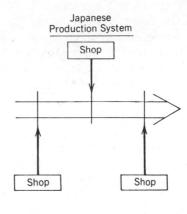

"Be-ready" type of production using lead time deliveries.	"Just-in-time" type production using exact timing.
Inventories give buffer for high reliability if part in error.	High reliability achieved through elimination of errors; no need for inventories.
Inventories sustain production when suppliers are distant.	Zaibatsu cluster permits deliveries of supplies in matter of minutes.
Waste of non-depleted inventories if product changes or rework not complete.	No waste if product changes, since no inventories.
Inventories are money piled up, in some cases debt equity with high interest.	Lack of inventories eliminates investment capital with debt interest rates.
(a)	(b)

FIGURE 17.4 Comparison of American ("be ready") (a) and Japanese ("just in time") (b) production systems. I, inventory.

There are two major reasons for the use of the kanban system. First, as mentioned in an earlier section, Japan has few natural resources. Consequently, companies use methods that deal with scarce resources. They act and react in a manner that treats all resources carefully and efficiently. Japanese managers are excellent resource-use managers—few world managers can compete on this basis. Second, the Japanese target cost reduction in a fierce way. These cost reductions take the form of reducing in-process handling costs, wastes and surpluses, and in-process inventories.

JAPANESE MBO SYSTEMS

Japanese MBO systems adapted from American models have variations, as do American MBO systems. The principles are roughly the same, but implementation varies in accordance with products, industry, and managerial experience. This section reports primarily the ten-year experience and practice of the Toshiba Corporation as described by Takanobu Hongo and translated by Hiroyoshi Umezu and Keinosuke One. Written permission to reproduce charts (Figures 17.7, 17.8, 17.9) has been granted by the Asian Productivity Organization. The Toshiba Corporation, a private electrical manufacturing firm, has annual sales of $1 billion and employs about 70,000 people. The Toshiba Corporation's practice of MBO is applicable to other Japanese industrial enterprises. I have added information about Japanese practices and processes that I have acquired over the years from consulting experience to give the reader a fundamental view of Japanese MBO.

A Japanese MBO management cycle consists of three basic phases: Plan, do, see. These correspond roughly to the three American steps of goal setting, goal accomplishment, and goal performance evaluation. These steps are taken in order. Nobody jumps to the "do" step without examination of consequences, or neglects the "see" step after the job is done. Initially these three phases were based on the management concepts and style of "order, control, and evaluation," but these concepts have had difficulty at the Toshiba Corporation because they subtracted human participation and contribution. Today, the plan-do-see style is based on the managerial concepts of "recommendation, support, and appreciation." These phases and concepts are illustrated in Figure 17.5.

The MBO system uses a combination of "top-down" and "bottom-up" between superiors and subordinates. Superiors often recommend and subordinates participate. Likewise, subordinates recommend and superiors participate. The ringi pattern of decision making and communicating described in the previous section provides some details of the dynamics of this interchange. Few Japanese MBO systems operate with an extreme form of either pattern. When they do, problems emerge. Both top-down and bottom-up exist simultaneously, even though there is varying emphasis depending on company, style, and experience. The integration of both

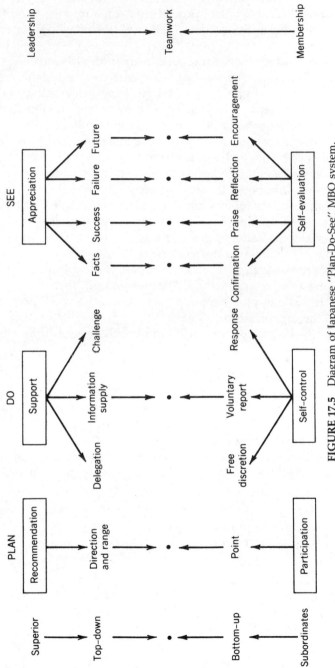

FIGURE 17.5 Diagram of Japanese "Plan-Do-See" MBO system.

patterns is not easy, and authoritative, unilateral decision making tends to emerge. This practice alone requires Japanese managers to promote changes in their own behavior from the traditional "order giving" to the new "recommending," from "control procedures" to "support," and from the traditional "one-sided evaluation" to "self-evaluation" within the context of teamwork.

The coexistence of top-down and bottom-up under the recommendation-participation managerial style is the heart and core of Japanese MBO. It develops teamwork and group effort by allowing leadership to take place from both superiors and subordinates. The traditional notion that leadership exclusively belongs to the manager and followship belongs to subordinates is rapidly changing in Japanese management. Leadership and followship are not by hierarchy or position but rather by innovation, drive, timing, and commitment. Everyone has some capacity to lead others. Some people may even have better leadership capability than their manager. The same thing can be said of followship. This concept of leadership recognition allows innovations to flow from all facets of an organization. Practice, however, finds more leadership actions are initiated from superiors than from subordinates. Wherever the leadership is initiated, both superiors and subordinates are expected to be good members of the group. The managers are the linking pins between the upper levels and lower levels, but the groups are the linking pins between and among the work processes and functions of the organization.

The three phases of Japanese MBO are briefly described as follows:

1. *Plan Phase (Goal Setting).*
    (a) Manager holds meetings with subordinates as a group to identify problems, difficulties, and opportunities in the business unit or section as they relate to proposed budget or futuristic planning.
    (b) Manager supplies information and background so that each member of the group can understand and get involved in problem solving and decision making.
    (c) Manager allows discussions in the group so that problems are identified and categorized.
    (d) Manager and group come to a consensus as to the urgency and importance of the problems.
    (e) Manager conveys recommendations of the goals that should be pursued in each of the problem categories. Unit recommended goals are agreed on by the manager's superior and are explained in the form of recommendations.
    (f) Manager and group identify goals as strategic, tactical, and operational. These goals are set up as work unit goals or individual goals. The challenge of the goals is arranged according to the following formula:

Degree of Attainment	×	Difficulty	×	Efforts Made	=	Overall Evaluation
100%	×	100%	×	100%	=	100% (good)
100%	×	120%	×	100%	=	120% (very good)
100%	×	120%	×	130%	=	150% (excellent)

(g) Subordinates prepare their own goals for both job accomplishment of the group and personal development.

(h) Manager reviews in joint discussion goals of each subordinate and recommends changes.

(i) Manager provides support needed for each subordinate to reach his or her goals. Support is either additional budgeting or extra help.

(j) Manager holds goal presentation meetings in which each subordinate presents his or her goals for the coming period. This tends to strengthen participation in the group and engenders healthy competition among members.

2. *Do Phase (Goal Accomplishment).*

(a) Manager delegates whatever authority is needed to subordinates for subordinates to use their own judgment in getting their goals accomplished.

(b) Manager aids and supports subordinates with problems and encourages them in the process of resolution.

(c) Manager provides timely information for the subordinate to do the job through meetings and personal interviews.

(d) Manager meets each subordinate for periodic progress reports, both negative and positive.

(e) Manager maintains challenge-response communication relationships with subordinates.

(f) Manager resolves exceptional problems jointly with subordinates.

(g) Manager revises goals jointly with subordinates in the event there are two major changes in the business environment.

(h) Manager sets up goal progress chart (Figure 17.6) and shows graphically the degree of attainment and completion of goals.

3. *See Phase (Goal Evaluation).*

(a) Manager requests subordinates to prepare self-evaluation of their accomplishment. The evaluation falls within three standards of expectations: above the expected level, as expected, and below the expected level.

(b) Manager discusses group goals with all members of the group and individual goals personally with each individual.

	Goal Progress Chart			Group Name:		
		Degree of Goal Attainment (%)				
Name of Individual	Goals	60	80	100	120	140
Isshikowa	1. _____
	2. _____
	3. _____
	4. _____
	5. _____
Oni	1. _____
	2. _____
	3. _____
	4. _____
	5. _____
Jogi	1. _____
	2. _____
	3. _____
	4. _____
	5. _____

FIGURE 17.6   Goal progress chart.

(c)   Manager finalizes and accepts self-evaluations of subordinates.

(d)   Manager holds results presentation meeting, inviting all the members of the unit to hear accomplishments of the past cycle and the goals for the coming cycle.

(e)   Manager uses evaluation results as a reference point for promotions and salary increases.

(f)   Manager summarizes all information in a Goal Summary Statement as described in Figures 17.7, 17.8, and 17.9.

MBO COMPARISONS: JAPANESE VERSUS UNITED STATES

Japan and the countries of the west exhibit a good deal of commonality in their approach to MBO. This common approach can be traced to common managerial principles, experiences, and practices. Important differences do exist, however, traceable to culture, history, values, and experiences. This section contrasts some of the thinking and methods used by MBO practitioners in Japan and in the United States. This does not imply that there is unified homogeneity within each country. The facts indicate a wide variety of philosophies and applications within each. The contrast is made only with some of the major issues. The differences do not imply advantages or merits. They can be both deficiencies and strengths.

1.   *Japan's Goal Setting Is Bottom-Up; the United States' Is Top-Down.*
Japanese MBO is highly decentralized and is affected by worker groups at
the bottom of the pyramidal hierarchy. Both countries encourage employee
participation. In Japan, employees are encouraged to initiate goals with
management approval. In the United States, management initiates goals
with employees' participation for support: Top management people in a
business meeting can discuss major problems of the firm, select alternatives
for action, and decide. The decision is implemented by lower levels.

2.   *Japan Uses MBO for Motivating; the United States Uses It for Strategy
Planning and Control.*   Japanese corporate management is adroit at inspiring
a sense of purpose in workers. This is intended to get higher productivity
from employees. The practice of MBO in the United States does reach for
motivation, but MBO is primarily for strategy, plans, and control. Japanese
managers are succeeding and becoming famous for inspiring loyalty,
willingness to work long hours, and high quality production in their
workers. This is accomplished by the high value given to achieving goals of
productivity as the way to benefits for individuals, the group, the company,
and the country. Yoichi Takalashi, labor union leader of 70,000, once said,
"What is good for the company is good for the union and what is good for
the union is good for the country."

3.   *Japan Uses MBO as a Tool for Managers and Employees; the United States
Uses It as a Tool Exclusively for Managers and Executives.*   Japan uses MBO
procedures with white-collar and blue-collar employees to get them involved in their own commitments as well as those of the corporation. This
has promoted worker productivity and has made lifetime employment
workable. It has engendered company loyalty. In the United States, only
managers are involved with company concerns. Techniques and processes
other than MBO are used to heighten employee productivity. There is much
less class and status distinction between executives and workers in Japan
than in the United States.

4.   *The Japanese Use MBO in Practicing Innovations Among All Employees and
All Departments; Americans Use MBO Where Feasible for R & D.*   In the United
States, innovations are associated with R & D personnel, product develop-
ers, and other types of specialists. But in Japan the drive for innovations is in
all departments and functions of the organization. The Japanese attitude
does not confine innovations to product development or improvement.
Innovations are generated in sales, marketing, distribution, quality, cost,
manufacturing, and administration. Consequently, goals for innovations
are expected in Japan in all departments of an organization. In the United
States, goals for innovations are expected and demanded in selected departments and only encouraged in all departments.

5.   *Japan Practices MBO With Groups of People; the United States Practices It
Primarily With Individuals.*   A work ethic of the Japanese that separates
them from Americans is working and interacting in groups. This stems from

Goal Administration Card

Term:

Manager, Sales Department, Household Electric Appliances Department

Area	Weight (which to start with)	Goal (what)	Measurement of goal attainment (how much)	Means for goal attainment (how)	Schedule (by when)	Related dept. (with whom) Individual | Group	Performance evaluation (what happened) Self-evaluation	Performance evaluation (what happened) Evaluation by superior
Job performance goals	35	Planning of small product	Minimum of three models	Hand-made oriented One unit with multi-functions Low price	Planning Trial manufacture Testing Mass Production	Electrical Appliance Engineering Dept. Electric App. Plant	Ⓐ B C Well received in the market	Ⓐ B C Big success
	20	Promotion of grouping retail stores	5 stores in A area 3 in B area 2 in C area	4 stores to be newly installed 6 to be converted expenses: xxx mil. yen	Selection Negotiation Implementation	Sales Promotion Section	A Ⓑ C 7 stores covered	A Ⓑ C Not yet attained, efforts appreciated
	20	Strengthening the retail stores	Education tour covering 50 stores Training of store owner and employees: 15 times	Education tour in quantitative management Training of storeowner and employees	In Tokyo In Kanto area 2.5 per month on average	Accounting Section Training Section	Ⓐ B C All consumed	Ⓐ B C Effects of education to be followed
	15	Reduction of sales expenses	5% of the budget	To assign the controllable expense items to each group	Check at the end of every month	Accounting Section	Ⓐ B C Accomplished	A Ⓑ C It is regrettable that the sales has not attained the goal

Personal development growth goals			Planning　Preparation　Employment	Personnel Section	A　B　C	A　B　C
10	Introduction of female companion system	5 companions	Recruiting junior college graduates. Personnel required for demonstration of new products	←—x———x———→		Ⓐ　B　C Approved　—	Ⓐ　B　C
60	Implementation of family training	In the middle of the term	Purpose: to enhance the morale Training of KJ method given to the leaders in advance	←——→	Training Section	A　Ⓑ　C Considerable results attained	A　Ⓑ　C To be promoted in the future
40	Training of the newly transferred people	3 people for 3 months	Chief in charge of product knowledge training Business talk exercise done by accompanying salesmen	Product Training with knowledge salesmen ←——→	(Training Section)	A　Ⓑ　C They seem to gain confidence	A　Ⓑ　C Well done
						A　B　C	A　B　C

FIGURE 17.7　Sales goals statement.

Goal Administration Card

Manager, Sales Department, Household Electric Applicances Department

Term:

Area	Weight (which to start with)	Goal (what)	Measurement of goal attainment (how much)	Means for goal attainment (how)	Schedule (by when)	Individual ¦ Group — Related dept. (with whom)	Performance evaluation (what happened)	
							Self-evaluation	Evaluation by superior
Job performance goals	25	Cost reduction of designings & drawings	By 30%	Automatic designing (partly) by computer / Abolition of subcontracted desiging	Examination —x— Test run —x— Implementation; Preparation —x— Implementation	Business Machine Section / Procurement Section	A Ⓑ C Reduction by 20% achieved	A Ⓑ C Not enough appeal made made for the subcontractors
	25	Development of new product	New direct current motor with the performance improved by 20%	Coordination with the Research Laboratory	Planning —x— Trial manufacture —x— Appraisal	Research Laboratory / Manufacturing Sections	A Ⓑ C Though performance improved, the cost is questionable	A Ⓑ C To be further improved at the stage of mass production-
	20	Cooperation extended to receive more orders for plant	A company (cement plant) / B company (metal melting plant)	Cooperation with the Sales Department	Contact once a week —→ Order received	Sales Department	Ⓐ B C Both of them successful	A Ⓑ C Low margin

716

					A B C	A B C
15	Standardiza-tion of parts and compo-nents	Registration of 12 models / Subcommit-tee for stan-dardization	(arrow)	—	A B © Results: 7 models	A B © To be carried over to the next term
15	Renewal of cost estima-tion system	Form to be im-proved: 50 forms / Common use of data base: 20 items / Cooperation with Engin-eering Con-trol Section	Examination Preparation Implemenation (× ×)	Engineering Control Department	Ⓐ B C	Ⓐ B C Efforts appreciated
50	To attend the creativity de-velopment program	NM method: 3 persons / Seminar held by As-sociation	(arrow)	X Association	Ⓐ B C Two people attended	A Ⓑ C What effects?
50	To hold the reading meet-ing	8 persons (the chief assistant class or up) "Development of Creativity" written by Fanjie / Two chap-ters as-signed to one person	Every Saturday (arrow)	(Training Section)	A Ⓑ C Attendance rate: 60%	A Ⓑ C Initiative of the section manager needed
					A B C	A B C

Personal development growth goals

FIGURE 17.8 Engineering goals statement.

Goal Administration Card

Term:

Foreman, Manufacturing Section

Area	Weight (which to start with)	Goal (what)	Measurement of goal attainment (how much)	Means for goal attainment (how)	Schedule (by when)	Related dept. (with whom) Individual ¦ Group	Performance evaluation (what happened) Self-evaluation	Evaluation by superior
Job performance goals	30	Improvement of work efficiency	Standard product: 120% Special product on order: 105%	Preparation of operation standards Process improvement by PERT	Investigation Preparation Planning ✕ Implementation ✕	Engineering Control Section	A ⒷB C Standard product: 115% Special product on order: 102%	A ⒷB C Modification of PERT needed
	25	Cost down by VA	By 2%	To set CD ratio for each model To assign a person to be responsible for each model	CD rate set. The chief assigned Implementation	Materials Section	Ⓐ B C 26 out of 30 models OK'd Average CD rate: 1%	Ⓐ B C CD of profitable models needed
	20	Elimination of late delivery of subcontracted parts	Late delivery rate: 40 → 20%	A joint project team formed with the Material Section	Training of subcontractors ✕ Implementation	Materials Section	A B Ⓒ The ability of subcontractors questionable	A ⒷB C Efforts appreciated

					A B C	A B C
15	Reduction of the loss caused by the defective products	Decrease from 10 mil. yen to 5 mil. yen a month	Analysis of accidents, proper countermeasures taken; Training of unskilled workers	Analysis, planning → Training →	Training Schools	A B Ⓒ 6 mil. yen a month. Check in process unsufficient	A Ⓑ C To be discussed at the meeting
10	Promotion of the suggestion system	Increase of the number of suggestions from 0.5 to 2.0 per worker	Preparation of samples list; Distribution of suggestion cards in advance	Preparation of sample list → Implementation	Training Section	Ⓐ B C 2.3 proposals/worker	Ⓐ B C Sample list well made
70	To hold the meeting in the shop regularly	Once a month	Preparation of materials; To master the bridge method	← →	Training Section	Ⓐ B C Better results attained than expected	Ⓐ B C Myself to attend once in half a term
30	Reading of technical literature	Once a month (6 books in half a year)	One hour a day	← →		A B C 3 books completed in half a term	A Ⓑ C Quality rather than quantity?
						A B C	A B C

Personal development growth goals

FIGURE 17.9 Manufacturing goals statement.

the strong cultural connection with family. The quality circle is an illustration of the group approach to commitments. Consensus and achievement are standards to be reached in groups. The United States, on the other hand, has, through culture, emphasized the individual. Individuals often compete with individuals. Teamwork does not come naturally. It must be developed. Quality circle work groups have been operating in the United States. The groups tend to be competitive. In Japan, the work groups are somewhat competitive for management's attention but are cooperative and supportive. Japanese workers seek more individuality in a work group style than outside the group.

6.   *Japanese Success With MBO Is Not at the Expense of Employee Satisfaction; in the United States MBO Compromises Employee Satisfaction.*   American management as a whole is not as concerned with its workers' welfare as its Japanese counterpart. Unneeded American workers are "laid off," whereas unneeded Japanese workers may be transferred to other jobs and they maintain their lifetime employment. The uncaring attitude of the American worker leads often to mistrust of management practices. This leads American workers to be more mobile, jumping from one job to another for more money. They take their skills and work experience with them. A Japanese worker's skills are retained in the company and even enhanced.

7.   *Japan's MBO Is a Life-Style Approach; American MBO Is a Management Tool.*   The life-style approach of Japanese business encourages all subordinates at work, at home, at recreation, or at school to concentrate on achieving goals and objectives agreed on in the company. Achievement of management objectives in Japan is not just an 8-to-5, five-days-a-week approach but a total life-style involvement and approach to completing commitments. The family is often involved. The United States does not have this total life-style approach. Achievement of goals is confined primarily to work life. Americans do not regard work as the most important part of their lives. The Japanese do.

8.   *Japan's MBO Is Revolutionary in Management Practices; American MBO Is Evolutionary.*   Japan's MBO is a substitute for dissatisfaction with its traditional management practices. This is especially true with quality. Therefore MBO has become a program of revolution. Most managers are highly trained in the process. Training programs for managers are massive. American MBO is another of the many managerial processes that are used in corporate life. Therefore MBO is a program of evolution. Many managers in America do not follow the MBO process. Many who do are not highly trained in its effectiveness.

9.   *Japanese MBO Emphasizes Long Range as Well as Short Range; American MBO Aims More at the Short Range.*   Japanese MBO is practiced not for the quick payoff or big quarterly jumps in shareholder dividends. It is practiced in a forward-looking manner that emphasizes the long range and future benefits. It aims at solid market position rewarded over the long term, rather than at quick return on investment needed for the next stockholder meeting.

This tends to give the Japanese an edge in handling complicated, more challenging projects and products that need a long-range effort for break-throughs and improvements. This willingness to defer maximum profits forces a stronger MBO process for research and development of new products. Japan has already matched the United States and Western Europe's level of R & D, the greatest emphasis being placed on programs and products with the most economical future potential. This long-term view is paying off for the Japanese. Their insistence on strengthening the company's financial position over time rather than increasing present earnings helps them to satisfy the basic cost of capital. It took eight years for Toyota to become profitable in the United States.

SUMMARY

Japan's rapid revolution into a major industrial power is awesome. There is no secret to its success. The Japanese do what Americans and Europeans do but with more effort, more seriousness, and more productivity. Japanese MBO conceptually is an American product. The Japanese have "picked up" this product, like other products, and have introduced innovations. This chapter describes Japanese MBO.

Some factors behind Japanese success are good planning, hard work, stable societal character, fierce pursuit of quality, high priority on technology, natural "organizational" behavior, the "big think" approach, and harmonious government−business collaboration. The joining of these factors in the MBO process has brought about spectacular economic and business growth for Japan.

The Japanese managerial practices that aid MBO are identified in this chapter. They are collective responsibilities and consensus decision making in groups, lifetime and permanent employment, cluster/satellite centralization, strike behavior with continued productivity, multiple group membership, collective (ringi) decision making, holistic concern for people, and the "just-in-time" production system.

The Japanese MBO system as typified by the Toshiba Corporation is described. The system has three phases: plan (goal setting), do (goal accomplishment), and see (goal performance evaluation). There are many similarities and differences between Japanese and American MBO systems. This chapter describes a few of them. They are bottom-up rather than top-down goal setting, MBO for motivation rather than for strategy planning, MBO as a tool for managers and employees rather than just for managers, MBO for groups rather than for individuals, MBO that meets employee satisfaction rather than compromises it, MBO as a life-style rather than a company process, MBO that is revolutionary rather than evolutionary, and MBO for both the long range and the short range, rather than only the short range.

BIBLIOGRAPHY

Christopher, Robert C., *The Japanese Mind*. New York: Simon & Schuster, 1983.

Hongo, Takanobu, *Management By Objectives: A Japanese Experience*. Tokyo: Asian Productivity Organization, 1980.

Kobayashi, Shigeru, *Creative Management*. New York: Simon & Schuster, 1980.

Langer, Paul F., *Japan—Yesterday and Today*. New York: Holt, Rinehart, and Winston, 1966.

Mitsyzurki, Masatsuzu, *The Modern Samurai Society*. New York: American Management Association, 1982.

O'Connor, Mary S., *Report on Japanese Employee Relation Practices and Their Relationship to Worker Productivity*. Hartford, CT: Lowengard & Brotherhood, 1980.

Ouchi, William, *Theory Z*. Reading, MA: Addison-Wesley, 1981, p. 35.

Prindl, Andreas R., *Japanese Finance: A Guide to Banking in Japan*. New York: Wiley, 1981.

Thompson, Philip C., *Quality Circles*. New York: American Management Association, 1982.

18

U.S. CASE HISTORIES

IN THIS CHAPTER

UNITED TECHNOLOGIES CORPORATION
ALCAN ALUMINUM CORPORATION
PEOPLE'S BANK
NEW YORK CITY TRANSIT AUTHORITY
CITY OF PHOENIX

MBO is not an all-purpose program for all organizations. Some firms have tried to do too much with their MBO program only to find themselves in a curtailment process. Indeed firms that have several years' experience with MBO tend to relate the process to areas of critical need and areas where it works and works well. Important as it is for managers to reach objectives they have set, some managers become too obsessive about reaching them. Objectives should be set for major goals, but other work always must be done even though such work is routine and administrative in character.

The few firms discussed in this chapter reflect this general use of MBO. They concentrate on reaching results, but not at the exclusion of other work. These firms have been selected to provide the reader with a broad spectrum of organizations from private to public. All the firms are practicing MBO successfully. They are all doing it differently. The firms' managers see the forest as well as the trees.

UNITED TECHNOLOGIES CORPORATION*

Sales	$14.7 billion
Fortune 500 rank	18
Rank in commercial aircraft engine production	First
Rank in helicopter production	First
Rank in air conditioning	First
Rank in defense contracting	Third
Founded	1925
Employees	193,700
Management personnel	4600
Headquarters	Hartford, Connecticut

United Technologies Corporation (UTC) is a growth company. Sales in 1971 were less than $2 billion. In 1983, sales were $14.7 billion and still growing. Harry Gray, UTC Chairman and prime mover, has transformed the company into a firm six times as large as the one he inherited. If this growth rate is sustained up to 1995, UTC will become one of the largest corporations in the world, similar to Exxon, General Electric, General Motors, and IBM. This growth has many implications. The strongest is that managing at UTC now and for the next several years means managing for results, growth, and complexity. The Management Resource Development Program (MRDP) is the process UTC uses for handling these three vital company requirements. MRDP is designed for UTC's unique requirements for human resource development. As Gray said, "To grow as a corporation, we invest in technology. To ensure we have the human resources needed by the corporation, we invest in the development of each manager."

Growth, Organization, and Products

When Gray came to UTC from Litton Industries in 1971, the company was called United Aircraft. It was a highly centralized, high technology organization with product emphasis on jet engines, helicopters, and aerospace systems. After 1971 the corporation embarked on a huge expansion program, highly decentralized, with movements into commercial markets. Gray has assembled a strong assortment of companies, a move that has leveraged UTC into a mainstream of growth. In 1972, sales to the U. S. Government were 51 percent of total sales. In 1980, government sales dropped to 22 percent and there was a 600-percent increase in commercial sales. Because the company designs and builds a broad range of technological products in the leading areas of scientific and technical know-how, the

* I am especially grateful to Harry Gray, UTC Chairman and Chief Executive Officer for permission to write this brief glimpse of UTC. Also for the support and help given to me by Paul A. Farnham, Director of Management Development at UTC.

organization of the company centers on managing technologies within groups. This emphasis on technologies is reflected in research and development activities. Only five U. S. corporations, each of them much larger than UTC, spend more on research and development annually. Of the ten largest spenders in this area, UTC ranks first for R&D expenditures as a percentage of sales.

Productivity: Effective Use of Human Resources

UTC, like most American enterprises, finds that human resource management impacts heavily on productivity. The underlying philosophy of the Management Resource Development Program is to assure that executives work as effectively as possible. Careful assessment and evaluation are made to eliminate activities that have little direct impact on productivity. All such activities may be useful and even necessary, but the essence of human resource management is to fully use human resources in achieving UTC's goals and objectives.

Efficient use of human resources requires a formal and elaborate management process that gives focus and direction toward needed productivity. Seldom does a simple activity, technique, or method provide the basis for a meaningful improvement in productivity. Firms that have looked for simple answers or guiding organized programs for productivity improvement have always been disappointed. Copying what some other company does seldom works. The most effective approach is to consider all possible activities and techniques; analyze their adaptivity to the needs and unique characteristics of the business; and select, try, and modify until the approach works and works effectively. This is what UTC does. A look at UTC's productivity performance using human resource measures reveals that productivity has increased over many years but has soared over the past several years (Figure 18.1). The following are indicators of productivity in human resource management.

1. *Organizational Efficiency (Figure 18.1a).*   This is the amount of sales per employee. It measures the performance of the total corporation in the marketplace and how well employees are utilized in delivering products and services to customers.
2. *Production Efficiency (Figure 18.1a).*   This is the amount of costs per employee. It measures the "productiveness" of human resources in manufacturing.
3. *Profit Contribution (Figure 18.1b).*   This is net income per employee. This ratio measures the bottom-line results for the firm on how well each employee is managed for profitability.
4. *Productivity (Figure 18.1c).*   This is profits per dollar assets. This ratio measures output of the corporation (profits) with its input (capital assets). This is the traditional return on investment (ROI). This is the return to investors for capital investments.

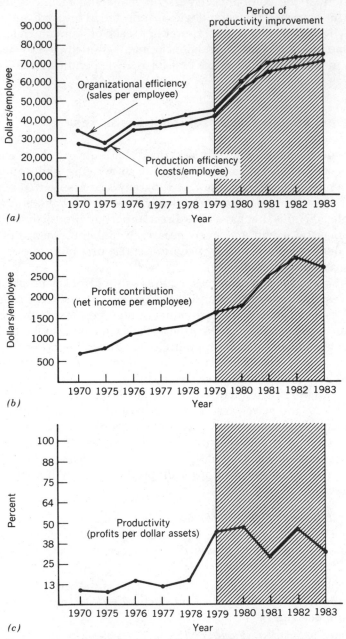

FIGURE 18.1 Recent productivity indicators for United Technologies Corporation. (*a*) Organizational efficiency and production efficiency. (*b*) Profit contribution. (*c*) Productivity.

Purpose and Overview of MRDP

The Management Resource Development Program, UTC's management process for utilizing and developing human resources, is a process for relating executive-level human resources and their development needs to the current and long-term business plans of the company. It covers primarily upper levels of management. The program has a five-fold purpose:

1. *Utilization of Human Resources.* To match human resources to requirements by evaluating the present organization in relation to the requirements of strategic planning and overall business plans.
2. *Performance Evaluation.* To evaluate the contribution made by each executive in order to make compensation decisions.
3. *Performance Improvement.* To enhance improvement by highlighting managerial strengths and weaknesses through objectives assessment and performance appraisal.
4. *Succession Placement.* To plan career development action programs for correcting weaknesses, strengthening the managerial group, and supporting the business plan by ensuring succession for every key job.
5. *Objective Treatment.* To identify and develop managers consistent with Equal Employment Opportunity policy and Affirmative Action goals.

MRDP is a management development process in two segments: organizational planning and individual planning. The nature, content, and requirements of these segments are determined and driven by business and strategic planning. These two segments, when completed and implemented, are responsive to and supportive of the company plan. Each segment contains a series of efforts, analyses, and decisions that, when completed, result in a series of documents that support human resource management at the executive level. The segments and elements and their interrelations are illustrated in Figure 18.2.

Elements of MRDP

The overall design and development of MRDP issue from the Corporate Personnel Resources Department, which prepares an annual implementation schedule to be followed by all divisions and subsidiaries. Senior corporate officers review all the evaluations and assessments appropriate to their functional areas of responsibility. But the responsibilities for MRDP fall on operations management. MRDP is a tool for human resource management for operations personnel.

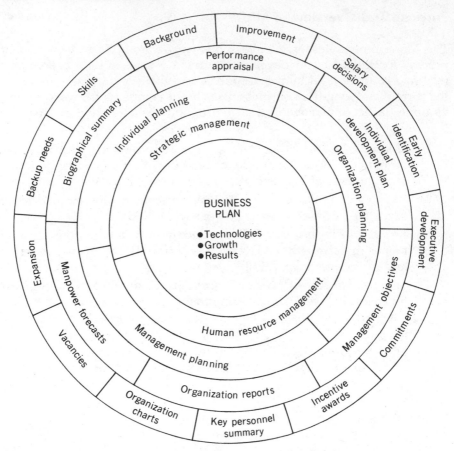

FIGURE 18.2   Human resource management: segments, elements, and interrelations.

Management Resource Forecast

The management resource forecast summarizes anticipated changes in a specific management organization and includes size, talent mix, structure, needs, and changes over the next five years with special emphasis on the next two years, to meet requirements of long-range plans, strategic plans, and the business plan. The forecast is summarized in a document that includes five major sections:

1. Changes in management organizational structure.
2. Major expansion or reduction of management personnel.
3. Filling of key management vacancies.
4. Development of backup candidates for key management positions.
5. Programs to improve performance.

Organization Reports

Two major reports are required for each division or subsidiary: an organization chart and a key personnel summary. The organization chart is the typical chart identifying incumbents in key functions by name and the reporting relationships. The key personnel document summarizes important information about key personnel—who they are, their present position, and their career directions. More specifically, the key personnel document contains the following for each individual:

1. Name, title, code grade, and reporting relationship.
2. Total years of service and years in current position.
3. Annual salary and grade penetration.
4. Assessment factors for performance appraisal of management skills and assessment of completed MBOs.
5. Current status indication and potential for next job.
6. Nearest next job defined by title and grade.
7. Replacement for individual indicated with codes.
8. Backup identification.

Biographical Summary

The biographical summary contains information relevant to the education and experience of individuals in upper management as well as replacement candidates not part of UTC's employment. The summary is updated periodically. It highlights background and unique skills, allowing recognition of these factors by senior staff even though such talents and skills may not be currently used on the job. This enhances the opportunity for individuals to use all of their skills in some position in the future. The summary contains key information such as name, hire date, birth date, place of birth, social security number, salary number, photograph, educational degrees, schools attended, special skills and affiliations, previous experience with dates, position, employer, and UTC experience—dates, positions occupied, divisions, and grade.

Performance Appraisal

Performance appraisal at the managerial level provides a method by which individuals are measured and counseled to assure continuation of the same high degree of technical skills and competence. Therefore the appraisal focuses on the managerial skills needed at the same grade levels. The primary emphasis of appraisal is how skills are used in performance of the complete job. Attainment of specific objectives during the current year is also considered. The complete appraisal along with other data serves as a basis for salary increase decisions. It also serves as a vehicle for discussion regarding skills, strengths, and development needs. The appraisal form is illustrated in Figure 18.3.

Management Objectives Assessment

Management objectives assessment emphasizes the commitment of the individual to achieving certain specific results and executing certain duties and responsibilities. Consistent achievement of these results over time and the effective handling of ongoing duties and responsibilities are the best measure of a manager's development and growth. Since the objectives do not represent all the work for which an individual is primarily responsible, the total assessment considers the objectives results and, to a lesser degree, the results of the regular job responsibilities. This assessment (Figure 18.4) serves as a basis for annual incentive compensation awards. The following are guidelines used in practicing management objectives assessment:

1. Objectives are limited to six to eight and are those with the highest impact/payoff potential for the company.
2. Objectives must represent a "stretch" in difficulty but must be attainable.
3. Objectives are stated in a top-down approach related to the business plan, to nonquantified quality and technical factors, and to R&D expectations. The top-down approach starts with a key group of executives and results in a bottom-up reaction.
4. Objectives must be quantifiable.
5. Objectives are set as a part of the annual planning cycle.
6. Objectives are assigned weights to indicate their value to an operating unit. The total of all weights must be 100.
7. Objective weights can be changed if unforeseen circumstances change the values of objectives or if new situations substantially limit the possibility of achieving an objective.
8. Objectives that are unplanned in the initial planning cycle are allowed and superiors will give appropriate weights to their accomplishment.
9. Objectives assessment is based on degree of achievement of key objectives and degree of completion or neglect of other ongoing duties and responsibilities while objectives are being met.

Individual Development Plan: Executive Development

Judgments reached through performance appraisals and management objectives assessments are useful in defining the longer-term potential of each individual. Career planning is concerned with recognizing future potential, tracking progress, and planning development action. The objectives of executive development are identification of the future potential level for

MANAGERIAL PERFORMANCE APPRAISAL

Name: _Bob Ames_

Title: _Vice President — Marketing_

Unit: _Baker Division_

DIRECTIONS: Indicate present performance in the context of the skill requirements of the position, achievement of key objectives and execution of other duties and responsibilities, assuming that your evaluation is based only on job related aspects of performance. Effectiveness in carrying out the Corporation's Equal Employment Opportunity/Affirmative Action policies is to be considered in the appraisal.

NOTE: Use reverse side if necessary.

WGT.	SKILL	Out	Exc	Good	Sat	Unsat	COMMENTS IN SUPPORT OF ASSESSMENT
10	**PLANNING** Ability to set objectives and adapt strategies, policies and procedures for achieving them.		X				Ames has improved his performance because of coaching and attendance at a seminar devoted to planning skills.
10	**ORGANIZING/STAFFING/DEVELOPING** Ability to staff and develop an effective technical/management team, recognizing subordinates' strengths and potential and providing developmental opportunities.	X→X					Adam Sloan is retiring next year and Ames has identified and is taking meaningful action to develop Susan Smith as his replacement.
15	**DIRECTING** Ability to delegate and lead subordinates in accomplishment of objectives.			X			While concentrating on new market areas, he should have delegated responsibility to ensure protection of market share.
10	**CONTROLLING** Ability to measure against planned performance standards and to take corrective action to assure that events coincide with plans.			X			Should have projected a revised market share after competitor was lost and then planned action to reach higher share of market. Needs to improve his skill in controlling.
10	**PROBLEM SOLVING** Ability to solve broad, strategic, unstructured problems and to apply existing knowledge in new and different ways.		X				No comment
20	**COMMUNICATING** Ability to inform and influence others by clear and concise expression of ideas and information in verbal and written form.		X				No comment
10	**WORK COMMITMENT** Ability to affirm and demonstrate a dedication of resources and time to the job.	X					At times may overextend himself physically — may affect efficiency.
15	**WORKING WITH OTHERS** Ability to motivate, to develop a rapport, and to earn the respect and trust of others.		X				No comment

SUMMARY APPRAISAL:

☐ **Outstanding**   ☒⁺ **Excellent**   ☐ **Good**   ☐ **Satisfactory**   ☐ **Unsatisfactory**

COMMENTS:

Overall is doing a better than excellent job. Although he did not take advantage of a lack of competition to expand the market share for the Baker Division, he has more than compensated for this by entry into new markets in the international arena.

Needs to improve ability to control. Will attend the Advanced Management Seminar to improve this functional management skill.

Recommended by Date	Employee Review Date	Approved by Date

FIGURE 18.3 Example of managerial performance appraisal, United Technologies Corporation.

MANAGERIAL OBJECTIVES ASSESSMENT

Name: *Bob Ames*

Title: *Vice President — Marketing*

Unit: *Baker Division*

DIRECTIONS: Objectives should be reasonably demanding but attainable and should clearly specify how performance will be measured, quantified where possible in terms of how many, when, what quality, etc.

At year end, assess actual results achieved, checking appropriate box for each objective. Add major unplanned objectives and assess results against the same standards.

NOTE: Continue on reverse side of form if necessary.

Wgt'ng Factor	1. KEY OBJECTIVES _____ Year	Out	Exc	Good	Sat	Unsat
30	Develop and implement a business strategy which will achieve this division's first entry into new markets in the international arena. Accomplish sales of $10 million in 1980.	X				
15	Improve the quality and effectiveness of the regional offices to enhance the image of the division, reinforce customer relations, and both protect and expand our market share. Specifically:		X			
	• Sell a major trade publication on featuring our regional office network in an article during 1980.					
	• Reduce customer warranty response time by an average of 2 days from the current level of 18.					
	• Maintain overall market share of 22%. Improve market position in Alpha Division from 5 to 4 by year-end.					
25	Increase Baker Division's share of the market by five points over 1979.				X	
15	Establish a fully staffed and operating regional office by April 1, 1980, to handle a substantial amount of new and potential business from the Mideast and Africa.		X			
15	Either identify and develop or recruit a Manager of International Marketing to replace Adam Sloan who is retiring.	X				

_____   _____   _____   _____
Employee   Date   Approved By   Date

FIGURE 18.4 Example of managerial objectives assessment, United Technologies Corporation.

MANAGEMENT OBJECTIVES ASSESSMENT

Wgt'ng Factor	1. KEY OBJECTIVES	2.	Out	Exc	Good	Sat	Unsat

3. SUMMARY ASSESSMENT

DIRECTIONS: The summary assessment should be based on your overall perspective of the individual's performance and should not be an average. While most of the weight of your assessment should be concerned with the achievement of key objectives, some of your judgment should reflect the individual's performance of ongoing responsibilities. You should take note of the degree of difficulty of each objective, its value to the unit and the effort put forth by the individual. In addition, you should consider whether objectives changed during the period and if so why and how; the individual's performance of ongoing responsibilities in relation to the achievement of objectives and any circumstances that may serve to enhance or detract from the overall rating. Comment below.

COMMENTS:

Although Mr. Ames attained a larger increase in market share than called for by his objective, his performance is regarded as only satisfactory because the increase was not due to his effort primarily, but rather to the loss of a competitor in the market which should have made an opportunity for an even larger increase in market share. However, he has worked tirelessly to establish a regional office and is well ahead of schedule. He has also identified, and is developing rapidly, a replacement for the Manager of International Marketing. In addition, Mr. Ames did an outstanding job in opening a new market for us in the international arena.

DIRECTIONS: Insert in the box your summary assessment of results. Use this schedule:

SUMMARY ASSESSMENT	RATING RANGE	1.10
Unsatisfactory	Below 0.70	
Satisfactory	0.70 — 0.89	
Good	0.90 — 1.09	
Excellent	1.10 — 1.19	
Outstanding	1.20 and above	

Prepared By   Date   Approved By   Date   Employee Review Date

FIGURE 18.4   *(continued)*

each individual, definition of a backup candidate for each executive-level position, determination of the personal career goals of each individual, and outlining of a development plan for each individual (Figure 18.5). These are the actions taken to assure these objectives:

1. *Backup.* All upper-management positions are classified by level. Executives have the responsibility of identifying probable backup candidates for their position level. Candidates are identified as to current level status and an indication is given of the potential level they could assume within the next five years.

2. *Career Goals.* Individuals are expected to define their career drives and motivations and how assumption of greater responsibilities will help them as well as the company.

3. *Development Plan.* Executives with their subordinates develop a 12-month action program in which inadequate performance of subordinates on the present job is corrected, satisfactory or good performance is increased, and new skills are developed in preparation for greater responsibilities or advancement.

4. *Action Program.* Executives plan learning experiences for their subordinates to help them meet the objectives of their individual plan. This may involve on-the-job experiences, educational experiences, job assignments, or job rotation. These experiences are implemented as assignments.

Early Identification Program

Executives early identify professional and supervisory employees they believe have the potential to attain an executive-level position. Six factors are used to measure or indicate potential for upper-level advancement:

1. Creativity.
2. Supervisory ability.
3. Communications ability.
4. Problem-solving ability.
5. Initiative and drive.
6. Educational background and previous experience.

The early identification program report contains the names of all employees identified as backups for upper levels of management, plus those of employees whom management believes have longer-term potential to attain higher levels. The report includes the following:

1. Names and current grade level of all high-potential individuals within an operating or functional unit.
2. Description of experiences within certain functions and the number of years, for each person.

INDIVIDUAL DEVELOPMENT PROGRAM

Name: *Bob Ames*

Title: *Vice President — Marketing*

Unit: *Baker Division*

NOTE: The information on this page is for Division/Subsidiary Corporate management planning use only. As such it is inappropriate for discussion with the subject employee until firm decisions have been made for status change.

POTENTIAL: Identify below the individual's current level and your assessment of potential level within the next 5 years. If you can be more specific with respect to future responsibilities and time frames, do so. Comment as necessary.

STATUS:

Current Level *II*

Potential Level *II L*

Time Frame *2 Yrs*

Division/Subsidiary President and Above	LEVEL I	Corporate Vice President and Above
Division/Subsidiary Vice President	LEVEL II	Corporate Director
Division/Subsidiary Manager of Major Function	LEVEL III	Corporate Manager of Major Function
Division/Subsidiary Program Managers or Staff Specialists	LEVEL IV	Other Corporate Managers or Staff Specialists
Expand responsibilities on present job	E	Expand responsibilities on present job
Move to larger unit with same responsibilities	L	Move to larger unit with same responsibilities
Under review	R	Under review

COMMENTS: Include identification of what function candidate is backup to, if any.

Substantial potential to assume position of marketing vice president in a larger unit, for example, the Beta Division. Ames works very hard, but has become too comfortable in his present job. Need to prod him to assume position that can challenge his full potential. Ames is currently backup for Bob Baker, Director of Marketing, Alpha Division.

PROPOSED NEAR-TERM ACTION: Check probable status change *in next 12 months only.*

1. ☒ No change
2. ☐ Promote

3. ☐ Transfer laterally
4. ☐ Expand responsibilities on present job

5. ☐ Demote
6. ☐ Outplacement

PERSONAL CAREER GOALS: Describe this individual's career aspirations. If they differ from your assessment of potential, explain.

He indicates that he is satisfied and proud that he has attained vice presidency of marketing. His strong work commitment and success in the international marketing area indicates his capacity to grow further by either expanding his responsibilities in this division or moving to a larger division with a larger marketing department.

BACKUP CANDIDATES: List backups to this position. Indicate when qualified, place asterisk by most likely candidate. Note "None Required" if appropriate.

NAME	PRESENT POSITION	AVAILABILITY (Q, Q1, Q2, etc.)
Susan Smith	*Director — Int'l Mktg.*	*Q1+*

Prepared by	Date	Reviewed by	Date

FIGURE 18.5 Individual development program, United Technologies Corporation.

INDIVIDUAL DEVELOPMENT PROGRAM

Career planning for each individual is essential to meet both the resource needs of the organization's business plan and the career aspirations of the individual; therefore, both requirements should be considered when completing this form.

DIRECTIONS: Review the individual's managerial skills and experience in the context of the requirements of his/her present position and/or the position he/she would most likely be assigned next. Indicate for each objective whether it is to correct inadequate performance, improve good performance, or enhance skills and experience in anticipation of new responsibilities. Then describe the specific action program (what, when, where, who) to be completed to achieve each development objective.

NOTE: Developmental programs are above and beyond normal job assignments, duties and responsibilities. Coaching is to be considered to be a part of a manager's normal job responsibilities and, therefore, is not to be considered as a development objective for a new assignment.

Correct	Improve	Enhance	DEVELOPMENT OBJECTIVES	ACTION PROGRAM
	X		Improve organizational and communication skills to increase potential for larger span of control.	Implement, with assistance of Training branch, programs to improve marketing skills of subordinates. Reorganize domestic marketing branch along product lines instead of by geographical areas.
		X	Be prepared to adapt marketing techniques to specific international markets.	Attend seminar on International Marketing. Implement program to prepare marketing representative for social and business environment in newly assigned areas.

Employee _____   Review Date _____

FIGURE 18.5   *(continued)*

3. Total years of experience and years of UTC service for each.
4. Degree(s) earned and year degree awarded for each.

Manpower Planning at UTC

No one person or group can possibly have sufficient information about the full range of factors involved in manpower planning. Isolation of the factors and assumptions that affect the manpower needs of each unit of the organization permits greater accuracy in planning. Manpower plans cannot be more accurate than the data that go into them. In the final analysis, the success of manpower planning depends on the skills and judgment of the management that does the planning. Consequently, UTC practices manpower planning as:

1. *Simplistic.* Manpower planning is conducted in as uncomplicated a manner as possible. It is a simple process of identifying, communicating, and addressing the two or three most critical manpower issues as early as possible with concentration on the qualitative aspects. Quantitative backup information can then be developed as the need arises. The process is intended to be used by the operating units, as opposed to a corporate requirement and paper activity. The emphasis is on the plan as a catalyst to cause management to address both existing and potential manpower problems, which have an impact on the bottom line of the business, as efficiently as it does capital, technical, and financial issues.

2. *Integrated with Strategic Plan.* Just as each of the other functional plans is integrated with and driven by the strategic plan, so too is manpower planning. Accordingly, it is addressed in conjunction with business planning and individual business unit strategies for three- to five-year periods. The formal medium for addressing manpower planning and displaying its quantitative aspects is the Corporate Planning and Measurement Guide. There is no separate manpower section in the guide, but each operating unit builds critical manpower issues into the Technical Plan; into the operating requirements in the Capital Plan; into clerical and administrative needs and concerns in the Financial Plan; and into employee mix requirements in the Strategic Plan. This formal process is streamlined by experience and the improvements introduced each year.

3. *Related to MRDP.* The means of addressing manpower plans and organization plans is presently the MRDP (Management Resource Development Program). Every attempt is made to integrate formal manpower planning, as defined here, into the existing MRDP process. It is the responsibility of the operating units to address their own manpower problems, plans, and issues. However, to the extent that these involve the executive population, become common among business units, or require attention at the corporate level, corporate and group senior managers and the senior corporate personnel officer are made aware of them. The most appropriate forum for this is through MRDP review with the Chairman of the Board.

Consequently, the more qualitative and confidential aspects or key issues are introduced through the existing MRDP documents with particular emphasis on an expanded management resource forecast, which deals with both organization and strategic manpower subjects.

Sample Objectives of Manpower Planning

1. Assist the company in achieving overall profit, growth, and balance in strategic goals.
2. Provide manpower information to facilitate overall planning and decision making in relation to short-range and long-range goals. Estimate the possible effect on the size and nature of the employee force of any proposed changes in objectives, markets, products, technology, internal organization, or available labor supply. These possible manpower effects, in turn, are factors to be considered in determining the feasibility of the changes.
3. Identify possible manpower problems of the future and actions that can be taken to avoid or minimize the problems.
4. Assure adequate manpower capacity now and in the future.
5. Achieve more effective utilization and development of human resources employed in the business.

Factors Considered in Manpower Planning

One of the most difficult aspects of manpower planning is the determination, for analysis, of the factors that have significance for a particular unit, plant, division, region, or department. Some factors to be considered for the purpose of manpower planning are: job requirements (present and future); present manpower levels and mixes, planned manpower levels (numbers); company policies; corporate, departmental, and unit objectives; capital budgets; secret projects; market research results; lead time for development of personnel; product mix changes; product changes—new products, new services; labor supply, unemployment, availability of skills (geographic, skill, numbers); internal organization, organization structure, decentralization, reorganization; future skill requirements (experience, background, education); attrition—normal and early retirements, deaths, resignations, releases; changes in personnel practices, compensation, or other conditions of employment (vacations, retirement plan, etc.); economic conditions—national, state, regional; industry economics; production methods; work-scheduling techniques; work load—time schedules; internal recruitment requirements, external requirements; projected growth rate; balance of company employees in community; increases in productivity, efficiencies, advancements in automation/robotics; long-term operating plans, forecasts, schedules; employee group peculiarities, such as overaged, underskilled, promotable; manpower versatility, mobility, flexibility; employment standards and objectives; employee transfer plans; new studies, research, and programs; medical problem cases, problem employees; organizational replacement requirements; discontinuance, consolidation, revision, or expansion of activities—markets, products, services, operations, projects, specific jobs, plants, and so on; extent of employee developmental and training activities and needs; employee mix requirements (ratio among categories of manpower); attendance statistics—by skill level, location, reason; use of temporary employees; effect of labor contract negotiations; federal wage and hour legislation.

Experiences with MBO

UTC executives are convinced that technological growth, decentralization, and management resource development with MBO is the direction to take. Even though the program has only recently been instituted, evaluations at this writing indicate the effort and payoff have been and will continue to be worthwhile. These executives do not consider the elements of the program as gimmicks that the company is tacking on and calling their management style. They really are using the MBO process into their overall management system for growth and performance. MBO is viewed by UTC as a whole process of skills, development, and experiences and not just a technique. Since UTC is large and has a variety of needs and emphases, MBO is allowed to be practiced with flexibility within the great range of managerial styles in the company. For example, some managers participate more in the objective-setting process than do other managers. The UTC policy is to have objectives with encouragement toward participation. The company insists on written objectives, but managers and subordinates are only encouraged to participate. This allows them to use their own style. Also some managers are comfortable with risk taking, while others are more cautious. Some managers seem naturally attuned to planning and control, while others have yet to learn the value of and skills for planning.

Because of these styles and the newness of the program at UTC, it is not surprising that there are a wide variety of reactions to and practices and values of MBO. Managers and executives have learned to apply MBO with more or less success, making new discoveries as to its value. For instance, a major value of MBO not originally expected has been as a communications tool. Reaching consensus with each subordinate and with staff on the nature of responsibilities, accountability, priorities, and payoff for a future period brings great clarity to the process and direction of decision making.

As far as UTC is concerned, MBO is not only here to stay but will be used as a contributing process in its system for managing results, growth, and technical complexity. UTC treats its management system as a matter of serious concern. The system is continually evaluated and changes are made when needed to maintain the system's compatibility with the corporation's growth and evaluation.

Objectives Tied to Management Bonus

Top management ties accomplishment of objectives to a bonus incentive program. This exerts pressure for both setting of high-payoff objectives and their accomplishment. Only upper levels of management qualify for the bonus awards. For those executives and managers who are eligible to participate, careful planning and review are carried out.

The actual bonus a person receives depends on results, both what is achieved personally and what is achieved by the larger unit of which the manager is a part. These larger units are major parts of the company, such as an operating division or an administrative service unit. The performance of these major units is analyzed and a determination is made if an award is to be advocated. Since performance appraisal provides the data for base salary decisions, total compensation for the manager depends on the total of the two: performance appraisal and management objectives assessment.

The company's intent with the incentive awards is to stimulate managers to view their objectives as a part of a larger effort toward achievement of corporate goals. Thus achievement of a set of objectives contributes to the company and to the individual—both win.

Bibliography

Ehrban, A. F., "United Technologies Master Plan," *Fortune*, September 22, 1980.

Gray, H. J., "Eras and Evolution: Story of United Technologies Corporation." Presented before Newcomer Society of North America, Mystic, Conn., August 23, 1979.

United Technologies Corporation, *Annual Reports*, 1971–1980.

United Technologies Corporation, *Who We Are; What We Do*. Public relations brochure, undated.

"What Makes Harry Gray Run?" *Business Week*, December 10, 1979.

ALCAN ALUMINUM CORPORATION*

Sales	$1.54 billion
Profits	$3.39 million
Rank in aluminum production	Second
Founded	1928
Employees	4819
Corporate headquarters	Montreal, Canada
U. S. headquarters	Cleveland, Ohio

Alcan Aluminum Limited, the corporate Canadian giant, produces with all its subsidiaries 1.9 million metric tons of aluminum, representing 20 percent

* Special thanks to Roy A. Gentles, President and Chief Executive Officer, for sharing information about the management system being used by Alcan Aluminum Corporation.

of the noncommunist world's aluminum supply. This results in total sales of $5.2 billion. The Alcan Aluminum subsidiary, the subject of this case history, accounts for approximately 30 percent of the total revenues of Alcan Aluminum Limited. The process for making aluminum requires enormous amounts of electricity. Alcan generates most of its own from hydroelectric dams. It is now the world's largest nonutility producer of electricity. It produces so much electricity that it often sells the excess to public utilities for consumer use. These factors of high-volume aluminum production, keen competition in the marketplace, widely scattered divisions and subsidiaries, and high use of energy provide a unique managerial challenge for Alcan. As Roy Gentles, president of Alcan Aluminum, said, "The companies that survive will be those that recognize the new competition and develop strategies to adapt. Some will be better positioned than others, not only to encounter changes taking place but also to exploit them as opportunities. In the aluminum industry, Alcan is in such a position." Alcan intends to grow by exploiting opportunities through strategies and the MBO process.

Productivity Program to Improve Efficiency

Alcan Aluminum Corporation has launched a formal productivity program to improve the company's business efficiency. The program has five goals:

- Stimulate awareness of the need for improved productivity.
- Involve employees and recognize their efforts.
- Measure effectiveness of productivity efforts.
- Promote new technology and innovative thinking.
- Conserve energy.

The main channel for productivity efforts is employee involvement groups, such as circles and teams, which demonstrate how individuals working together can contribute significantly to increases in overall productivity. Members of the various groups include production, maintenance, secretarial, clerical, managerial, and administrative employees. These productivity groups are making important contributions to the company's operating efficiency at locations throughout the United States.

There are 85 organized productivity groups within Alcan Aluminum Corporation, operating at 30 locations throughout the country. They consider ways of improving work surroundings, production methods, material flow, safety practices, and any other procedures that will make jobs more productive and fulfilling. Employees have suggested solutions to problems ranging from small hindrances to major operations, and the results have included zero defects records, less downtime and maintenance for production machines, and significant savings from improved salvage and scrap recovery. Approximately 900 employees participated in productivity groups in 1983.

Studies conducted in 1983 indicated that Alcan Corporation is above the industry average in productivity, both in terms of value added per employee and output per employee. Alcan's comprehensive productivity program includes a total productivity measurement index applied across the corporation, broken down by division and by major work centers that include both blue-collar and white-collar workers. Thirty percent of employees are involved in quality circles and teams and this percentage is expected to increase. In addition, Alcan instituted statistical process control groups in each of five divisions.

Even though saving money is a secondary goal of Alcan's productivity program, the financial results are beginning to be substantial. The company projects that by 1990 productivity efforts will save Alcan Aluminum Corporation $70 million in operating costs through better use of raw materials and equipment and increasing product quality and metal recovery. In addition, productivity circles and teams are making important contributions to improved supervisor/employee communications, work procedures, safety practices, and the quality of work life.

Computer and Communications Systems for Information

Last year, Alcan Aluminum Corporation invested more than $11 million in computer and communications systems to bring the latest technology to office operations and customer service. The backbone of Alcan's multimillion dollar network is Alcan Electronic Mail System (AEMS), composed of more than 450 pieces of electronic equipment, including display terminals, printers, and a host of office automation units and computers interconnected by 18 telephone lines nationwide. Using AEMS, Alcan employees can send and receive messages at the speed of 240 words per second, 100 times faster than possible with other automated wire systems.

In 1983, Alcan completed the installation of its Distribution Control System (DCS) to provide the Metal Goods Division with the most advanced customer-information network of any U. S. metals distributor. More than $1.2 million was spent to link Metal Goods' service centers via DCS. This high technology system allows employees instant access to inventory, order/entry, invoicing, and purchasing information at any one of the division's service centers. Employees need only to retrieve the necessary information on their display terminals to ship metal from one location to another or directly to any one of Metal Goods' customers nationwide.

Alcan's biggest thrust in electronic data processing and communications is to link customers and vendors to AEMS so that orders can be entered directly into the system, eliminating countless hours of processing and mountains of paperwork.

Another major program Alcan is developing is the Manufacturing Resource Planning System (MRPII), which Alcan Sheet and Plate is scheduled to have operational in 1986. MRPII will enable the division more precisely to schedule customer orders and loads on production equipment, and to track metal from one department to another during the fabricating process. This will let Alcan Sheet and Plate tailor its production runs to cyclical changes in the markets it serves and also to prune inventories while providing just-in-time deliveries.

Alcan is currently at the forefront of the U. S. aluminum industry in its program to accelerate information exchange between the company and its customers. Alcan invested about $13 million in 1984 to maintain its lead in customer-oriented service.

At Alcan, these investments in computer and communications systems are synonymous with increased productivity.

Employee Recognition for Outstanding Achievements

In late 1983, Alcan Aluminum Corporation introduced "A+," a new company-wide program to recognize the efforts and achievements of employees. Designed to encourage superior performance, the A+ program covers six areas: general job performance, productivity, innovation, quality, customer service, and safety.

The need for a program such as A+ became evident following the company's survey of employee communications in 1981. It revealed that a major source of employee dissatisfaction was lack of recognition for job performance. The A+ program is designed to demonstrate that as a company Alcan does emphasize and recognize individual excellence.

Evaluation and selection of A+ employee are done by a committee of one—the employee's immediate supervisor—who has the authority to make an on-the-spot award for outstanding performance. The awards process has been designed to be as simple as possible: The paperwork is minimum and there is no lengthy evaluation process or set of rules to follow. Groups of employees—a team, department, plant, or even an entire division—can also win A+ awards for the excellence of their combined efforts, for reasons ranging from achieving sales, production, or safety records to innovative product development or accomplishment of a difficult task in record time.

No cash prizes are given for receiving an A+. Winners receive special aluminum replicas of the A+ symbol and are honored at special events at each location annually. During the first quarter of 1984, more than 650 employees received A+ awards, either as individuals or as members of award-winning groups.

Integrated Communications System for Managing

Alcan Aluminum Corporation has devoted much time and effort over several years to developing its Integrated Communications System for Managing, which coordinates and integrates five well-known and established management processes. The qualitative benefits derived by managers, as well as the quantitative benefits, are reflected from high performance of this system.

Since establishing the system, Alcan Aluminum has expanded its overall market share in fabricating at more than twice the average of the aluminum industry. At the same time, profits have been comparable to those of the best of its competitors. The Integrated Communications System for Managing has made a crucial contribution to this achievement. The five parts of the system are:

1. The job description, particularly the accountability section.
2. An "organalysis" process, which is a technique for plotting and charting the key responsibilities of a job in relation to the job's interfaces.
3. A modified MBO process.
4. A zero-based budgeting (ZBB) process.
5. Short- and long-term planning (the most critical of all).

There is nothing novel about any of these processes. Many companies use some or all of them but fail to derive their full potential because the processes are not properly coordinated and integrated into the management process. Roy Gentles believes that the effectiveness of a system taken as a whole is derived from the integration of the parts and not from the action of the individual parts. Managers must arrange for coordination of the system. The heart and core of this coordination is getting everyone in the system going in the same direction at the same time to accomplish a common and well-defined goal.

For a management process to be effective, certain prerequisites must be met. A clear and precise understanding must be developed, well before implementation, of what the process is expected to achieve. Top management, the CEO in particular, must be completely committed to making the process work. And top management must have the patience and determination to make it work. The following is a description of the five parts of the Integrated Communications System for Managing at Alcan Aluminum Corporation.

Job Descriptions.   Most companies use some form of job descriptions. But in many companies they are little more than window dressing. Often they are not properly developed to serve their purpose, which is to indicate an individual's main responsibilities and accountabilities. Otherwise the individual's role is confused and the authority vested in him or her may not be compatible with the delegated responsibilities. Frequently it is left to the employees or prospective employees to draft their own job descriptions, which managers simply approve. This procedure in Alcan resulted in individuals with essentially the same level and type of job having markedly different job descriptions.

At Alcan the job description now forms the basis of an evaluation system that determines job grade and compensation. This greatly complicates the equitable application of the system, particularly in line and staff relationships.

Finally, the accountabilities of the job description provide both the basis from which the key responsibilities are identified and the foundation for needs analysis, from which annual objectives are developed. Figure 18.6 shows the job description format.

In Alcan, objectives are derived by each division president and corporate vice president working through the needs analysis exercise. Each person's accountabilities (per job description) are the key to identifying areas of concern or need for the coming year. An objective is then identified that will satisfy the need. Criteria are developed to measure performance against the objective. After all division presidents and corporate vice presidents develop their objectives, the major objectives for Alcan Aluminum Corporation are developed and "cascaded" to the appropriate members to ensure that each objective has someone with ultimate responsibility for its implementation and that each supporting member accepts and understands the supporting role and responsibilities.

Alcan likes to identify where two or more individuals have a significant role in the outcome and attainment of any one objective, so that even though one individual is given the ultimate responsibility for its attainment, the other participants "sign on" to make their contribution toward its achievement. This, then, completes the needs analysis, objectives setting, cascading, and sharing process.

To maximize the effectiveness of individuals as well as the subsequent processes in the system, job descriptions must reflect a high degree of accuracy and consistency in defining managers' roles. For these reasons, Alcan has developed a disciplined and well-defined process to ensure that job descriptions for similar jobs are comparable, particularly with respect to the major accountabilities. For instance, why should the key accountabilities of one division head, and hence the authority vested in him or her, differ from those of another? Similarly, why should the principal broad accountabilities of the vice president, Human Resources, differ in scope from those of the vice president, Operations?

Needs Analysis

Division/Dept.　————————————

President/Corp. VP　————————————

Accountability*	Need	Objective	Criteria

* Each accountability as per job description

FIGURE 18.6　Job description format at Alcan Corporation.

No matter how precise a job description might be, it is an impersonal document that cannot reflect the employee's particular management characteristic or style, or how that person will interact with others in fulfilling responsibilities. This last point is significant, because it must be recognized that others in the corporate hierarchy may not interpret an individual manager's role exactly the way he or she sees it.

Organalysis. The key responsibilities in a job description should be consistent with the key accountabilities, which is a vital element of the "integrative" aspect of Alcan's management communications system. Key responsibilities form the vertical axis of a matrix used in organalysis. The horizontal axis consists of the names of the superiors for each of the two levels above the individual for whom the matrix is designed. The matrix also includes the individual's peers, both line and staff, and the individuals reporting directly to him or her, with whom the manager may be involved in fulfilling each specific responsibility. Using a prescribed code in the appropriate boxes, the individuals indicate the type of organizational relationship they see existing between themselves and each of those with whom they interface, plus what kind of authority they believe they have to get the job done.

Alcan divides the principal responsibilities for managers into two basic categories—management responsibilities and technical responsibilities. The former is subdivided into the basic management functions of planning, leading, organizing, and controlling, and the organalysis matrices reflect these divisions.

The organalysis process is carried out within management groups in three distinct steps. The first step is for each individual to complete his or her own matrix. Once all the initial matrices have been done, they are individually presented by the manager to the management group for discussion. The second step has somewhat of a functional "T" group aspect to it, because it should be conducted in a way that encourages open and frank discussion. In effect, each person presents his or her perception of key responsibilities and defines the type of boundaries, accountabilities, and authorities he or she perceives in relation to others with whom each interfaces. If the organalysis sessions are properly conducted, they can be highly effective in minimizing the two most constant organizational irritants: the frictions inherent in the line-versus-staff interface and the confusion that often arises from the delegation of responsibility and authority.

By the time the dialogues between all segments of the management group are completed, a consensus develops about who is responsible for what and how each individual should go about the job and interface with others in performing the tasks. The process quickly identifies organizational aberrations and is effective in defining workable boundaries between jobs that, by nature, tend to have substantial overlap.

The third and final stage is reworking the individual matrices to reflect the results of the dialogue, which, apart from the benefits already described, also ensures that the authority delegated to each manager is consistent and compatible with the responsibilities vested in him or her. In effect, this element of the system deals with communicating the nature of the organizational relationship that should prevail in the management group.

MBO.   There are two pitfalls in the implementation of MBO. The first is overemphasis on technicalities. In the early stages of MBO program development, it is easy to become mesmerized by the complex technicalities of measurement. How do you set objectives so that an individual's performance in achieving them can be fairly measured? How do you differentiate between providential factors and those over which an individual has some influence? And how do you account for an individual's performance in achieving an objective when the ability to do so is partially dependent on others?

Alcan's experience indicates that it is critical to limit the number of objectives. In *In Search of Excellence*, Thomas J. Peters and Robert H. Waterman contended that the number of objectives should be only three or four. Alcan's experience suggests that an MBO system, if properly designed, can cope with up to ten. Also, from the top down, a rigorous effort is made to assure a satisfactory balance between long- and short-term objectives. At Alcan, management compensates for the ramifications of longer-term objectives in an individual's annual performance evaluation by limiting attainment of these objectives to 50 percent of a person's annual rating. The other half depends on how the person has carried out his or her principal accountabilities or performed overall.

An even more treacherous pitfall encountered in MBO programs involves trying to develop a program without ensuring that a formal linkage exists between everyone who has a role related to the accomplishment of a particular corporate or individual objective. At Alcan, the corporate objectives are developed by the CEO in conjunction with a management group, each year. The process begins with all divisional and functional heads, using the "integrative link" of the backdrop of their accountabilities plus the principal strategies with which they are directly involved, doing a needs analysis that results in a draft of no more than ten potential objectives. From the draft, the two or three objectives deemed the most important from a corporate standpoint are selected, and a composite list for the corporation is developed. In the past, the list generally contained between 30 and 35 objectives. The eight to ten most important objectives are chosen in a management meeting, the need for balance from both functional and time standpoints being kept in mind. The corporate objectives selected then become the basis for the CEO's objectives.

The critical process then begins to "cascade" the CEO's objectives down through the appropriate divisional and/or functional heads. When the attainment of an objective is equally dependent on the efforts of two or more managers, such as a functional head and the president of a division, or two division presidents, management ensures that the shared responsibility is understood and accepted by each of the individuals involved.

The success and vigor of an MBO program are almost directly proportionate to the effectiveness with which the cascading and "shared" process is carried out. For certain key objectives, it is not uncommon for the CEO's objectives to cascade in one form or another through several layers of management, both in the divisions and one or more of the functional departments.

To have a successful MBO program, not only must objectives be set so they can be fairly measured and thoroughly cascaded, but performance evaluation must be effective and constructive. The importance of good periodic performance evaluations was emphatically brought home to Alcan by a survey of a cross-section of employees, which indicated that evaluations were considered the most important form of feedback by all groups of employees.

Zero-Based Budgeting. The ZBB process, which is applied to all of Alcan's sales, research, and administrative expenses excluding plant overhead, is the only component not essential to the Integrated Communications System for Managing. Alcan includes it because, by its very nature, it is an important channel of communication involving an important and high volume of expenses, now totaling about $80 million a year. The whole ZBB process is based on a clear and precise definition of corporate and divisional objectives, including key strategies and tactics, which once again provide an "integrative link." Despite all the publicity given to ZBB since former President Carter first implemented the concept in Georgia, Alcan has found very few companies that actually use ZBB today. ZBB's greatest drawback is the awesome amount of work it requires. In a two-year period, when Alcan ZBB'd all of the corporation's sales, research, and administrative expenses (SR&AE) (excluding plant overhead), Alcan produced 487 packages. (A package is a description of a department's activity, including costs and benefits). Approximately half of these were reviewed at the divisional level and the rest at the corporate level.

Because of the extensive work involved in the ZBB program, management scheduled its application to the total corporate budget over two years. After the second year, a complete ZBB of each major unit every three years is adequate, individual units updating only significant changes in the interim.

This process is the only means available that provides a proactive and meaningful evaluation of this large mass of indirect expenses, much of which is for qualitative, rather than quantitative, ends. For example, 1982 was a recession year for the economy and certainly a depressed year for the aluminum industry. But one of the principal strategies at Alcan's cable division was to promote a proprietary aluminum alloy for building wire to exploit its economic advantage over copper wire. Though there was great pressure to minimize all expenses, Alcan recognized that it had to fund the alloy's promotional and other ancillary programs if it were to implement this strategy and hold the division responsible for its implementation. Then Alcan had to evaluate this strategy and its costs (including advertising) versus other alternatives for exclusion. The ZBB process, therefore, is the means by which both compatibility and linkage can be established between what is wanted and the sales, research, and administrative expense funds that are committed to get the job done.

Conversely, if circumstances dictate that sufficient funds are not available for everything needed to support the overall programs, the ZBB process allows inverse priority to portions of the intended programs not to be funded. The ZBB process also puts the whole block of SR&AE expenses under a microscope, providing detailed knowledge and understanding of the expenditures throughout the organization. Further, it provides an excellent opportunity to expose nonfinancial employees to the rigorous discipline of quantitative analysis.

Planning. The planning process, both short and long term, is the most crucial component of the whole system. It is both the foundation and the bond for the other elements, because it is through the planning process that Alcan determines what it's going to do, how it will do it, and who is going to do it. It operates as the brain center of the organization, and, like the brain, it both reasons and communicates. Good planning must be creative, credible and doable, and good execution is 50 percent of the battle. Alcan devotes great effort and resources to planning. Alcan is well aware that if resulting plans are not implemented, even though modified as circumstances dictate, efforts will have been wasted. The plans are truly the working documents by which a business is managed.

Alcan periodically monitors its progress in implementing both long-term and short-term tactics. Equally important, management guarantees there is an adequate degree of linkage between the strategies in long-term plans and the tactics in annual plans. It is from strategies and tactics that candidates are drawn for corporate objectives each year, against the backdrop of the job descriptions and key responsibilities of all the individuals involved. An outline of the annual plan followed by Alcan is shown in Figure 18.7. This last step is the incorporation of objectives into the annual and strategic planning cycles with high assurance of linkages between the two.

Bibliography

Alcan Aluminum Limited, *Annual Report*, 1983.

Alcan Aluminum Corporation, *Alcan Facts USA 83/84*.

American Management Association, "Alcan's Integration of Management Techniques." *Management Review*, two-part series, April 1984.

Peters, Thomas J., and Waterman, Robert H., *In Search of Excellence*. New York: Warner Books, 1979.

I. CEO'S SUMMARY

II. EXTERNAL ENVIRONMENT

    A. Economic environment
    B. Aluminum industry environment

        1. Metal balance and industry shipments
        2. The smelter scene
        3. Acid rain

    C. Competitor environment

        1. Group analysis
        2. Competitor strategies

    D. Competing materials

III. BUSINESS THRUST

    A. Corporate objectives
    B. Alcancorp objectives related to Alcan Aluminum themes
    C. Linkage between 1984 plan and 1983–90 strategic plan objectives

IV. FUNCTIONAL THRUST

    A. New products
    B. Marketing/pricing
    C. Operations
        1. Capital expenditures
        2. Productivity
        3. Quality
        4. Metal flow

    D. Technology and the environment
    E. PIMS
    F. Human resources
    G. Systems
    H. Government affairs

V. FINANCIAL COMMENTARY

    A. Net income
    B. Returns
    C. Financing
    D. Credit

VI. APPENDICES

    A. Financial schedules
    B. Capital expenditure rankings
    C. ROCE charts

FIGURE 18.7 Outline of 1984 annual plan of Alcan Aluminum Corporation.

PEOPLE'S BANK*

Total deposits	$3.39 billion
Total assets	$3.98 billion
Total reserves	$250 million
Rank in U. S. largest savings banks	Eleventh
Rank in New England largest residential mortgage lenders	First
Founded	1842
Employees	1700
Headquarters	Bridgeport, Connecticut

There's plenty of anguish and challenge behind the serene facades of banks around the world. This is probably the most difficult time for banking ever seen. There are many reasons for this: deregulation, rate competition, interstate and intrastate mergers, consolidations, unpredictable international financial markets, international currency swings, defaults by large borrowers, large portfolios of loans to leverage buyouts, and the introduction and use of new technology for productivity and service. As Norwick R. Goodspeed, Chairman and Chief Executive Officer of PEOPLE'S BANK, said, "Deregulation, rate competition, new technology have all completely reshaped the way we do things."

Banks have become more and more business oriented in their markets, dealing with managerial challenges of growth, strategies, mergers, acquisitions, cost control, quality of service, and productivity. Even competition has changed. "It used to be other savings banks that formed our competition," Mr. Goodspeed declared, "but now we have keen competition among commercial banks, Merrill Lynch, Sears, American Express, Prudential/Bache, Citibank, and Bank of America."

Services of the Bank

PEOPLE'S BANK has had steady growth since its inception in 1842. A variety of factors are responsible—innovativeness, mergers, aggressive lending, publicity, community involvement, high morale among employees, and a growing economy. Some of these factors have been historical, but most are recent. Since top management is "new market driven," the bank pursues opportunities as they arise. Most of these opportunities are in entirely new fields from those in which the bank started. Today, PEOPLE'S BANK is known as a "progressive and innovative financial institution oriented toward the consumer."

* Special gratitude and thanks to Dr. David J. Walker, Vice President and Chief Economist, Corporate Planning and Economics, for his assistance in sharing the MBO process at PEOPLE'S BANK.

Two basic reasons are offered for this reputation. The first is that broad range of financial services offered to customers, which include savings accounts, money market accounts, investment certificate accounts, club accounts, retirement investment accounts, checking accounts, commercial loans, mortgage loans, student loans, brokerage services, real estate management services, savings bank life insurance, repurchase agreements, on-the-job banking, treasury tax and loan payments, safe deposit boxes, wire transfers, and retirement services. These services reveal a management team that is business oriented toward new markets, a team that might be regarded as visionary with organizational flexibility.

The second reason for the reputation is the quality and convenience of service offered to customers. The bank has 63 offices in five Connecticut counties, 23 24-hour automatic teller machines at 21 locations, quick cash machines, supermarket minibranches for serving customers grocery shopping, and master services for the State of Connecticut's Yankee Mac mortgage program. From the number, type, and quality of services at PEOPLE'S BANK, it seems there are a multitude of businesses under one corporate roof, each with its own methods of doing business, and each growing and expanding in terms of opportunities available. This is the heart and core of the growth and expansion of a corporate entity. The growth of the component business units makes up for the growth of the whole. Growth heightens the need for coordinated effort to prevent conflicts and to share resources. This is one reason for the existence of the MBO corporate planning process at PEOPLE'S BANK—to coordinate all business units into a corporate entity. Thus PEOPLE'S BANK follows a decentralized form of management but uses MBO to make decentralization work.

The Organization

The company and its subsidiaries employ around 1700 people. It has gone through a series of changes and mergers since its inception. Its development can be summarized as follows:

- Founded in 1842 as Bridgeport Savings Bank.
- Became Bridgeport People's Savings Bank in 1927.
- Opened first branch in 1953.
- Merged with Southport Savings Bank in 1955.
- Acquired First Stamford Bank & Trust Company in August 1981.
- Purchased Heritage Mortgage Finance Corporation in December 1982.
- Acquired Guardian Federal Savings & Loan Association in December 1982.
- Formed People's Real Estate Services, Inc., in November 1982.
- Merged with National Savings Bank of New Haven in March 1983.
- Merged with State Bank for Savings in Hartford in September 1983.

- Merged with People's Bank of Vernon in September 1983.
- Changed name to PEOPLE'S BANK in September 1983.
- Formed People's Securities, Inc., a discount brokerage subsidiary, in September 1983.
- People's Securities, Inc., gained membership in the New York Stock Exchange in February 1984.

The bank's organizational structure at the present time is depicted in Figure 18.8. Although business is conducted through eight major divisions, the functions, responsibilities, activities, and operations of the bank are carried through many departments. Twenty-four departments have MBO planning submission responsibilities. Strategic planning is formulated by a special committee of key executives interacting with the Corporate Planning Department. These executives, through a series of meetings, analyses, discussions, and conclusions, formulate a five-year strategic plan to be implemented by 24 department heads on a two-year cycle basis.

Planning and Performance in Challenging Environments

PEOPLE'S BANK is active in assessing the environments affecting its strategies and its operations. Economic forecasts and trend evaluations are made on a regular basis. The forecasts bring up the concerns and impacts that should be brought to the attention of key individuals in the management ranks. For example, a recent economic analysis to 1990 of five trends, made by the Corporate Planning Department, centered on deficits and international factors, recovery in the business cycle, inflation increases, direction of interest rates, and increasing unemployment level. Here are examples of the concerns revealed in this study:

1. Any interruption to world oil reserves, for whatever reasons, would produce an immediate and negative jolt to the U. S. economy in the form of higher inflation and higher interest rates.
2. Debt levels of other countries and unstable political atmospheres in the international "global economy" could severely test the U. S. economy. Monitoring of international economics is now essential.
3. Since the advent and practice of adjustable rate mortgages, changes in the financial positions of mortgagees could affect their commitments. For the bank the potential for increased loan delinquencies is substantially heightened.
4. Increasing money market interest rates will mean shrinking margins and lower profits. The development of fee income looms high in importance.
5. Shrinking margins, which lower profitability, require immediate cost containment and higher productivity at the bank.

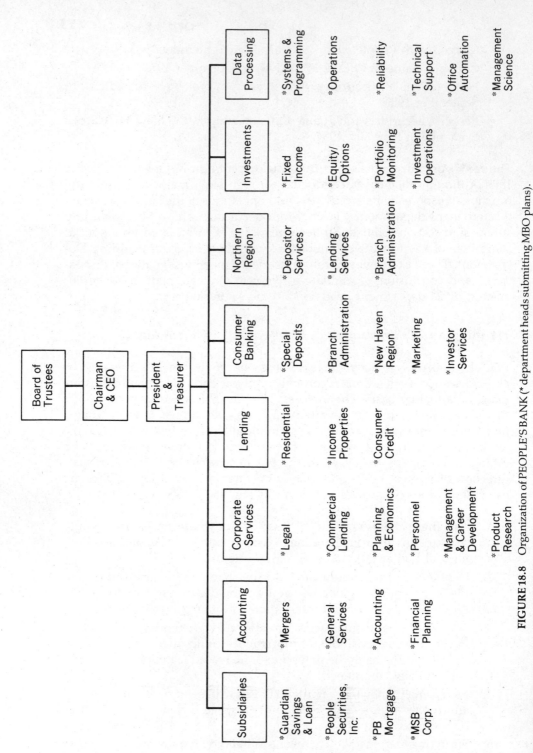

FIGURE 18.8 Organization of PEOPLE'S BANK (* department heads submitting MBO plans).

754

These and other implications and concerns are communicated to key management personnel as guidelines for their MBO planning within corporate planning cycles.

There is no question that other banks face similar concerns. The common trend running through all strategies of banks is the maintenance of the old-fashioned bankerly traits of caution, confidence, and conservation. These traits are perhaps even stronger.

Comparing the performance of banks, both national and international, is difficult and often tricky. Accounting procedures, regulatory practices, and tax policies vary so widely that financial reports mean entirely different things for different places. Some banks hide their true profits and capital strength, while others are required by government regulators to disclose their complete financial picture. Inflation can cause distortions as well. Nonetheless, a comparison can be made among PEOPLE'S BANK, Mutual Savings Banks, and Savings and Loan Associations here in the United States. Over the turbulent and fast-changing period from 1974 to 1983, with deregulation and high competitive rate changes, the PEOPLE'S BANK performance still remained high compared with these institutions (Figure 18.9).

The MBO Process at PEOPLE'S BANK

PEOPLE'S BANK seeks to become a more effective enterprise. Thus it emphasizes forward planning by requiring all key managers to make their function and responsibilities more effective through planning. Individuals

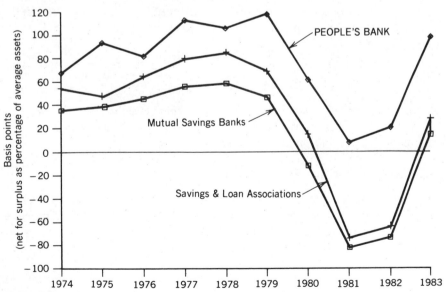

FIGURE 18.9   Performance of PEOPLE'S BANK compared with that of other financial institutions.

and their bosses at all levels determine, agree on, and precisely state the specific results that are to be accomplished by some designated future date, either by the individual or by the units he or she manages. These managers go to work to achieve their objectives, presumably fired up with enthusiasm because in the process of developing an objective of its supporting plan they become sincerely committed to achieving it. Selected times are designated for reviewing performance. Managers are measured against the objectives that were set previously. This emphasizes the principle stated earlier in this book—to accomplish anything, you must know what it is you are trying to accomplish.

The entire MBO planning process starts with a committee of key executives who set and continuously review the corporate mission and the objectives to be reached by the bank. The process is illustrated in Figure 18.10 and is known as the strategic planning process by levels of management within the context of a time scale. It is the function and expectation of all key managers at each level to become involved, follow guidelines, and develop specific operational plans to ensure the implementation of the strategic plan. Department heads need some idea about the direction of the people above them if they are to develop supportive objectives and operational plans. The strategic plan is a document of expectations from above. While fairly firm, it is still subject to rethinking and negotiations in the planning and goal-setting process. Department heads below can then come up with more realistic suggestions, ideas, and possibly breakthrough innovations. In this interaction of ideas from below and the expectation from above, sound and meaningful objectives and supportive plans are developed.

Examples of the corporate mission, objective setting in a five-year plan, and supportive operational plan by a department head are described in the following. Figure 18.11 shows a project status report and Figure 18.12 is the corporate planning calendar for 1984.

PEOPLE'S BANK Corporate Mission

> *To be the primary financial services organization in Connecticut, providing a broad range of services to chosen consumer and commercial markets in an effective and profitable manner.*

Objective-Setting in a Five-Year Plan

Objective I. To attain a level of profitability that would produce a return on average equity of 12.5 percent, a return on average assets of 0.75 percent, and a minimum surplus to deposits of 8.0 percent.

Supportive operational plan:

1. Maximize the net interest margin through product pricing that will recover all associated costs plus the desired profit factor for all diversified products.

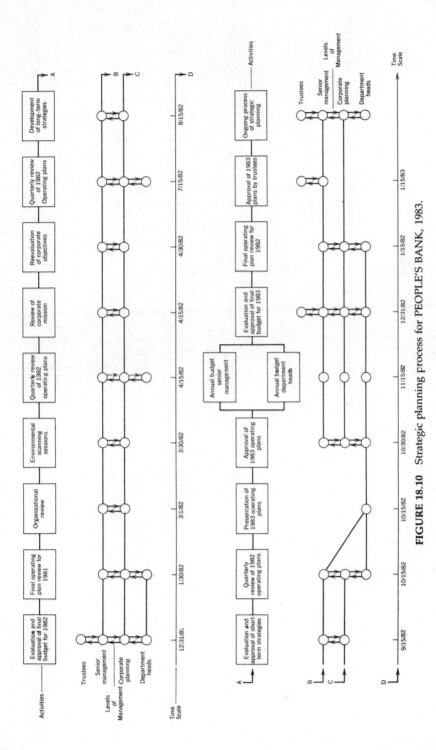

FIGURE 18.10 Strategic planning process for PEOPLE'S BANK, 1983.

PEOPLE'S BANK

PROJECT STATUS REPORT

1984 OBJECTIVES

DATE _____ JUNE, 1984 _____

PREPARED BY _____

PAGE _____ 3 _____ OF _____ 3 _____

DIVISION _____ ADMINISTRATIVE SERVICES _____

DEPARTMENT _____ PERSONNEL _____

SECTION _____

Project	Corporate Objective Satisfied	Assigned to	Priority			Scheduled Quarter				*	Delete Added	On Added	Delay Time Added	Date Complted	Comments
			H	M	L	1	2	3	4						
11. State Merger	II	Dept													• Completed on schedule in March.
• 6 Month Review															
12. Vernon Merger	II	Dept													• Completed on schedule in March.
• 6 Month Review															
13. PB Mortgage Co.	II	Dept													• All VP's and above are written and will be evaluated by Hay by end of 3rd quarter.
• Hay Installation															• All others will be written and evaluated by the end of the year.

758

No.	Project			Status
14.	Job Posting Enhancements	IV	MLG	• Survey completed. • Preliminary proposal drafted.
15.	Mini computer			
	• Manpower Planning Module	IV	CH	• To start up on completion of Human Resource Planning Project.
	• Benefits Administration			• Delayed due to personnel changes. To be completed in October.
	• MIS Enhancements/Micro graphics			• Ongoing.
	• Second Generation System			• In process.
16.	Interviewing Skill Training Program	IV		• On hold.
17.	Climate Survey	IV	CH	• Scheduled for 4th quarter.
18.	Predictive Index Project	IV	CH	• Scheduled to start 3rd quarter. • NE evaluation committee members being trained.

*ATP = As time permits

FIGURE 18.11 PEOPLE'S BANK Project Status Report.

Apr 23 – May 4	• First quarter reviews
May 11	• Presentation of environmental updates to senior management
	• Group setting of objectives
	• Critiques to senior management of:
	- Mission statement
	- Corporate objectives
	- Major strengths
	- Major vulnerabilities
	• Presentation of four strategic direction statements:
	- Financial
	- Corporate/commercial services
	- Systems
	- Retail services
May 17	• Approval by senior management of May 11 agenda items
May 25	• Environmental updates to department heads
Jun 1	• Presentation of "refined" (if applicable) mission statement, corporate objectives, and major strengths and vulnerabilities to department heads. (Dept. head luncheon)
	• In light of strategic plan, ask department heads to prepare a one- to two-page general departmental plan for next two years (1985 and 1986)
Jul 6	• Departmental two-year action plans due
Jul 9–13	• Senior management review of departmental action plans
Jul 16–27	• Second quarter reviews
	• Feedback to departments (during second quarter reviews) of any suggestions regarding departmental two-year action plans (prioritize, eliminate, etc.)
	• Ask department heads to prepare 1985 action plans and 1985 staffing plans
Aug 17	• 1985 action plans (include staffing) due
Sep 6–8	• Senior management planning retreat to review/approve 1985 plans
Sep 21	• Budget process begins (budget process calendar to come from J. Adams)
Oct 22–26	• Third quarter reviews
Dec 13	• 1985 presentation to Board of Trustees
Dec 14	• 1985 presentation to department heads (dept. head luncheon)

FIGURE 18.12 PEOPLE'S BANK corporate planning calendar.

2. Increase fee revenue 20 percent per year through the pricing of new and existing services.

3. Achieve established asset/liability targets.

4. Attain subsidiary profit goals.

5. Seek through merger or acquisition, finance-related entities that would enhance the profitability of the Bank.

6. Improve cost-effective production of services through utilization of "technology-driven" systems.

Objective II.   To market products to chosen consumer and commercial segments at a profit.
Supportive operational plan:

1. Identify and target defined consumer and commercial market segments.
2. Expand customer relationships within these segments through the packaging, sales, pricing, and servicing of products.
3. Generate increases in revenues from new and existing fee-based services.
4. Achieve market-share targets for all product and business lines in Hartford, Stamford, New Haven, and Bridgeport.

Objective III.   To develop, maintain, and utilize a full qualified staff capable of innovation and high productivity, while assuring a high level of employee morale and job satisfaction.
Supportive operational plan:

1. Integrate human resources planning into the overall corporate strategies of the Bank.
2. Develop and manage a system that effectively recruits, selects, develops, measures, and rewards human resources.
3. Develop goals and objectives that measure accurately and fairly productivity and achievement within the Bank.
4. Develop and implement specific programs of recruitment, selection, development, and employee growth without regard to race, color, religion, marital status, sex, age, or national origin and with the objective of matching individual needs and abilities with organizational purpose.
5. Develop and manage a continuity plan that meets all human resource needs in timely fashion.

Key Features of the Corporate MBO Planning Process

1. MBO is started as a top-down process commencing with a strategic five-year plan.
2. MBO mission, objectives, and activities are committed to all levels of management in a top-down bottom-up participative process including trustees, senior management, corporate planning department, and department heads. PEOPLE'S BANK has discovered that the process cannot be exclusively top-down or bottom-up if it is to be an effective way of managing the company. The communications and planning effort must go in both directions.
3. MBO is unique by the absence of complicated and comprehensive reporting forms and documents.

4. MBO works in an easy communications environment when all managers, regardless of level and reporting relationship, have easy access to senior and top management.

5. MBO as a process of participation is set in a corporate planning calendar.

6. MBO progress and attainments are regularly monitored and reviewed in quarterly meetings between senior management and department heads.

7. MBO is not regarded as a program but rather as an approach to corporate planning, coordination, and individual managing. It is a significant part of the management process for most managers.

Bibliography

Connecticut Business Journal, Vol. 13, No. 28, July 26-August 1, 1983.
PEOPLE'S BANK Fact Sheet.
PEOPLE'S BANK, newsletters, 1981 to 1984.
"The Best of the Biggest Banks." *Fortune*, Aug. 20, 1984, p. 193.

NEW YORK CITY TRANSIT AUTHORITY*

Budget	$1.75 billion
World rank in biggest	First
Rank in route miles	First
Rank in number of cars	First
Rank in number of stations	First
Rank in passengers moved	Second
Rank in car miles	Second
Founded	1953
Employees	46,742
Headquarters	Brooklyn, New York

New York City Transit Authority has undergone many changes since its inception in 1953. The Transit Authority's original investment capital was $2.5 billion. Capital replacement costs today would be over $55 billion. The Authority negotiates with 19 union and supervisory organizations and administers annually agreed-on union contracts representing 45,864 employees. Transit services are coordinated in a 12-county region of commuter rail services, bus services, and feeder routes offering unitickets for approximately 4.5 million passengers per day. This combination and coordination

* I am grateful for the special contribution, help, and support given to me by Len Armon, Manager of Management Development at the Transit Authority.

of bus-rail ticketing and services, along with union and investment efforts, gives to the Authority the most challenging set of managerial problems one can find in public administration. MBO is being used for this challenge. MBO is raising confidence in the ability of government to produce needed and useful results. MBO is merging limited resources and budget crunches with performance improvement and problem solving. The New York City Transit Authority is an illustration of how a government agency is managed for results.

Rapid Transit Systems

New York City Transit Authority, compared with foreign and other city subway systems, is the biggest and most complicated transit system in the world. There are many ways of measuring the size and complexity of subway systems. For this summary, the number of miles of routes, number of stations, number of cars, car miles, and number of passengers are used for comparison (Table 18.1).

Many historic steps and decisions were made to arrive at the size and level of complexity that prevails today. The demand for new and greater coordinated services is still high. As the Transit Authority meets these demands, the system will grow to even greater complexity.

Organization of the Transit Authority

New York City Transit Authority was created by the New York City Legislature in 1953 to operate all city-owned subways and bus lines. The Operating Board has 14 members, including the chairman. All are appointed by the Governor of the State of New York with the advice and consent of the State Senate. Of this number, four come from suburban areas and four are recommended by the Mayor of New York City. The organization chart

TABLE 18.1 Comparison of Transit Systems in Selected Cities

City	Miles of Routes	Number of Stations	Number of Cars	Car Miles (millions/yr)	Passengers (millions/yr)	Total Rank
New York	137	458	6424	230	1055	1
Paris	105	353	3485	116	1050	3
London	98	248	4434	213	546	2
Moscow	91	103	2392	239	2083	4
Tokyo	86	159	1829	117	1779	5
Stockholm	27	89	883	35	185	6
Toronto	25	49	494	34	198	8
Montreal	21	35	363	22	148	9
Mexico City	19	48	690	38	605	7

shown in Figure 18.13 depicts the major departments of the Authority and the lines of communication.

The two major operating units of the Authority are Rapid Transit, with 26,021 employees, and Surface Transit with 14,100 employees. The work force of 45,864 employees makes the Authority the largest blue-collar employer in New York City. Supervisory unions represent the first three levels of supervision in the organization. Managing the organization means managing and controlling a coordinated series of interwoven transit services among subways, bus lines, tunnels, commuter rail services, bridges, and airport express carriers. Managing the organization also means managing and controlling the needed support services in maintenance, energy, traffic control, enforcement, and new construction. This type of managing delves heavily into decision making and problem solving. Rapid Transit at this writing is the only division of the Authority that has applied MBO in its managerial ranks.

Starting MBO in the Transit Authority

MBO was selected by Transit Authority managers to generate significant performance improvements and give direction and progress with the corporate mission statement. Several consultants were used to start the program and conduct executive workshops for assuring the implementation of MBO systemwide. MBO started at the executive officer level in Rapid Transit and was carried down to the supervisory level of management. The MBO process is a team-centered system. That is, a manager and his or her team are the focal point of the system. Thus the MBO process at the Rapid Transit Department is group MBO. Transit personnel are convinced that group MBO can work effectively without necessarily having a total organizational commitment. Group MBO was implemented in three phases, to avoid

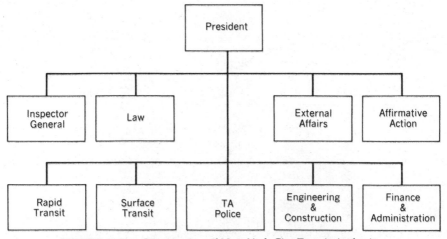

FIGURE 18.13 Organization of New York City Transit Authority.

disruptions, frustrations, and loss of time from the sudden use of a new management system. These phases were as follows:

1. *Phase I, Learning and Development.* Workshops were conducted to teach MBO as a group process, emphasizing team building, group problem solving, and the development of a team's own practices of group MBO. Each team constructed its own group process emphasizing participation and sharing of responsibility by the team. In this manner there would be less organizational resistance and individual competitiveness, and this would avoid the problem of managers who relate to each of their subordinates as individuals and encourage them to strive to achieve their own objectives while disregarding whether their colleagues achieve theirs. With group MBO, managers and subordinates act as teams reaching for team objectives and not for individual objectives. This phase gave an opportunity for managers to learn the MBO language and answer questions that might arise. These workshops required six full days over a four-month period.

2. *Phase II, Implementation.* After the completion of the MBO workshops, each team or group came together, developed its MBO package, and committed it to a schedule.

3. *Phase III, Evaluation.* One year after group MBO was implemented and operating, it was evaluated. Each team evaluated its own performance against its objectives. Within a 12-month period, 155 evaluation workshops were held with 350 managers attending.

How Group MBO Was Established

A typical Phase I workshop was attended by a manager and his or her staff. Groups smaller than five often lack diversity; groups larger than 15 may become impersonal. In most cases Rapid Transit was fortunate to have 12-to-15 member teams. A management development specialist acted as a group process facilitator. Each workshop focused on a single step of a six-step group MBO process:

Day 1	Development of mission statement
Day 2	Identification of key result areas
Day 3	Identification of indicators
Day 4	Agreement on objectives
Day 5	Development of action plan
Day 6	Setting of MBO system controls

One full day of workshop sessions and group discussion was required for a good team-building session. Subsequent workshops were held at two- to three-week intervals over a four-month period.

How the Group MBO Process Works

The following is an example of a typical workshop session. Assume the team is coming into its second workshop session, the "identification of key result areas" session. The team is guided during the workshop through the following developmental stages of identifying key result areas:

Stage 1	Issue identification
Stage 2	Subgroup problem solving
Stage 3	Group problem solving
Stage 4	Group consensus

1. *Issue Identification.* This is extremely important, to get total group involvement and to resolve any issues before process building takes place.

2. *Subgroup Problem Solving.* This is the first task- or problem-solving session held during a workshop. Subgroups often work on an MBO process-related issue prior to coming into a workshop or during a workshop session. Each subgroup is asked to present its recommendation for consideration by the total team.

3. *Group Problem Solving.* This takes place after all subgroups have made their presentation.

4. *Group Consensus.* This is reached by synthesizing all the desirable problem-solving elements of presentations by the subgroups and the team as a whole. Group consensus provides a forum in which the team develops a part of a new system or plan. Generally after the second workshop a climate has been established in which lines of communication are more open, issues are more clearly defined, and group problem solving has become more fluid.

Key Features of Group MBO at Rapid Transit

1. Each manager and his or her team jointly negotiate all steps of the MBO process.
2. MBO is adapted to meet group needs by the members of the group.
3. Resources and information are shared by all members of the group.
4. Facilitators are used to help the group reach consensus in negotiations.
5. Group MBO is not imposed by edict or power of position but by participative interaction and contributions by all team members.
6. Training and orientation are required to get the group MBO process working.
7. Six operational objectives is a typical number for a group.
8. Group MBO can be implemented on all levels of management.
9. Group MBO should be monitored on a periodic basis.

10. Workshop activities play an important role in the group process.
11. Top management holds at least two major formal reviews with department heads in the division prior to submission of budgets.
12. Group MBO coincides with the fiscal calendar.
13. The success of group MBO is judged by the number of objectives achieved.
14. MBO coordinators prepare and issue progress and performance reports.
15. Group MBO focuses on seven target areas: safety, reliability of service, cost control, productivity, staff improvement, passenger environment, and security.
16. Group MBO indicators are formalized into seven result areas.

Making Group MBO Work at Rapid Transit

The most important single practice that keeps MBO alive and well at Rapid Transit is the periodic formal reviews of MBO progress. The review is done quarterly. Paperwork is kept at a minimum. Reports are made on a single sheet of paper, and they specify the following:

1. Rationale for an objective.
2. Statement of the objective.
3. Trend chart showing control of the objective.
4. Managerial accountability.
5. Schedule showing action items to complete an objective.

A second practice is the use of MBO coordinators trained and knowledgeable in the theory and operation of MBO. They are valuable in administering and counseling managers in the procedures of the group MBO process. Coordinators are kept up to date through seminars and conferences.

A third practice is the commitment of the top executive to the program. MBO was started in other departments but was canceled when top administrators resigned or were transferred. The program can only get started and move along when top officials are behind it. There is a strong correlation between "boss support" and how effectively MBO will be implemented.

A fourth practice that keeps MBO moving is the allowance of qualitative performance indicators for staff departments. Qualitative judgments and measurements have been acceptable standards for measuring performance where quantitative indicators are not feasible.

Benefits of Group MBO at Rapid Transit

1. MBO has provided the Transit Authority with a management process.

2. MBO has given the organization a base from which all practitioners can begin to plan for improvements. The seven performance areas cited in this summary are only beginnings.
3. MBO has improved communications throughout the entire system.
4. MBO has forced the organization to use more precise performance indicators than in the past.
5. MBO has made it possible for budgeting and planning to be congruent processes.

Thus the benefits of MBO at Rapid Transit are significant. As Len Armon from Rapid Transit said, "MBO is still very much alive. It's difficult to install and difficult to sustain. Most practitioners agree that MBO is a most relevant and formal discipline that is not too far removed from what managers should be doing."

Bibliography

Kreitner, Robert, *Management: A Problem-Solving Process*. Boston: Houghton Mifflin, 1980.

Likert, Reusis, *The Human Organization: Its Management and Value*. New York: McGraw-Hill, 1967.

New York City Transit Authority, *Facts & Figures, 1981–1982*. Brooklyn, New York.

CITY OF PHOENIX*

Budget	$630 million
Total assets	$3.4 billion
Rank in U. S. cities population	Ninth
Rank in U. S. cities area	Twelfth
Rank in four performance factors in top ten U. S. cities	First
Total employees	8605

Since World War II, Phoenix has grown from a small desert community of 106,818 to a major community of 790,000, becoming the ninth largest city in the United States. This is 738 percent growth between 1950 and 1980. This meteoric growth has been based on many factors: climate, industries, people, environment, and resources. But the largest contributing factor is the distinguished history dating back to 1950 of management innovations and productivity improvements in city government, which has managed growth effectively and efficiently.

Phoenix provides how a municipality can perform its functions and

---

* Special thanks to Edward Schlar, Operations Analysis Administrator, who gave his time and efforts in sharing information about the management system used by the City of Phoenix.

discharge its duties toward its citizenry by integrating sound industrial engineering practices with behavioral management to get a total involve-ment of all people from the City Council to white- and blue-collar workers in a common commitment. The public sector of the United States is as con-cerned about productivity issues as is the private sector. Many people just assume that low productivity is endemic to the public sector. This may have been true in the past, when officials and workers were nonprofessional and nonbusiness oriented. It is no longer true today. Personnel of the City of Phoenix exemplify the professional staff and its professional approach to improving productivity. Phoenix has introduced productivity innovations as a matter of practical necessity to meet increasing demands for urban goods and services while containing costs to prevent rising taxes. Its effort rivals that of many good private organizations. The MBO process works well in Phoenix's management system.

Brief History of Management Innovations in Phoenix

In the late 1940s, as World War II servicemen began to return to Phoenix, a population boom commenced. City government was neither organized nor prepared to cope with new municipal demands. A citizen's charter revision committee was appointed in 1947 to revitalize city government, and a council-manager form of government was instituted. From that point to the present, a series of management innovations has been inaugurated to bring the City of Phoenix to a high level of organizational effectiveness and efficiency. Here are the major highlights of this history of management innovations.

1950	City manager appointed and professional management in-fused in all administrative affairs. City government com-pletely reorganized and professional appointments made on merit.
1954–1955	Modern budgeting, accounting, planning, and research in-troduced. Annual budget includes work program statistics to measure performance.
1950–1960	City of Phoenix receives 70 national awards for municipal excellence, including two All-American City awards.
1958–1962	Policies instituted for solidifying local tax base and prevent-ing proliferation of satellite communities on city periphery. Budget review procedures improved. City programs im-prove productivity.
1969–1970	Businesspeople on City Council propose private sector business approaches to organization and work methods to reduce future tax increases. (The presence of businesspeo-ple on the council should not be dismissed lightly. This City Council decision brought into the public sector the

successful practices employed in the private sector. Because of this the City of Phoenix was becoming an organization in which improved productivity was a way of corporate life.)

1970   MBO approach started with a pilot planning-programming-budgeting system with program analysis reviews. Municipal objectives set and work planning and control established in City Manager and budget departments.

1973   Overall municipal goals and objectives developed and used for 1973–1974 budget preparations.

1975   Performance auditing commences by city auditor.

1977   Revitalization and redirection of productivity effort and program with citizen participation, advisory committee, and employee involvement.

1977–1979   Revisions and refinements of zero-based budgeting system. Performance achievement program commences. Management salaries connected to achievement of job responsibilities. Nine productivity improvement tools identified and a program developed. The tools are (1) effective supervision, (2) automation, (3) work simplification, (4) work measurement, (5) job enlargement and job redesign, (6) systems analysis and design, (7) improved staffing programs, (8) incentives, (9) training.

1980–1982   Value management resource office set up. This group functions as a team of internal consultants who combine industrial engineering with behavioral science methods. The staff assists city departments with diagnostic, behavioral, and analytical reviews. Services within each of these three approaches available to all members of city administration are as follows:

1. *Diagnostic Services.*   Employee and/or client surveys, work load distribution, problem diagnosis, work output measures.

2. *Behavioral Services.*   Team building, work group development, management consultation, conflict resolution, customized training.

3. *Analytical Services.*   Work measurement/standards, methods improvement, work flow and scheduling, office systems and procedures, productivity training, decision-making assistance.

Prior to the organization of a value management group, analysts would go into a department to solve a technical problem, only to discover it was really a people problem. Conversely, they would go into a department to solve a people problem, to discover a technical problem.

With the establishment of the value management resource office, a total approach, technical and behavioral, is applied to a needed service.

1982–1983   Competitive bidding process established. (Since the city continues to search for ways to contain costs, maintain services, and raise productivity, a competitive bidding process is opened up between outside contractors and inside city departments. The inside city department bids on the job as a private company does. This is a businesslike approach.)

The Phoenix productivity effort has been evolutionary in its approach. Changes have been instituted to fit prevailing economic conditions, public attitudes, and the nature of the work force. These changes are thought of as management innovations. The innovations by themselves do not result in specific productivity improvements, but they create the climate and the processes in the organization for helping people find better ways to improve productivity. The emphasis is on people, goals, cooperation, attitudes, skills, and quality of work life along with work methods, techniques, and procedures for making work efficient and effective.

Ten Central Productivity Program Elements

Phoenix has taken the idea that productivity is the efficiency and effectiveness with which a business is operated and has applied it to the city with managerial strategies, behavioral techniques, innovations, and MBO. Here are the objectives of the work improvement and productivity plan:

1. Create an atmosphere of cooperation and coordination among all city employees.
2. Harmonize the goals of the individual and the goals of the organization.
3. Develop a positive, challenging attitude toward existing methods and procedures.
4. Develop skills for effectively identifying and evaluating opportunities for productivity improvement.
5. Improve city operations to reduce costs and improve the quality of work life.

From these objectives came the ten central elements of the Phoenix Productivity Program:

1. Top management support.
2. Organizational development.
3. MBO.

4. Central staff assistance.
5. Employee suggestion program.
6. Productivity training.
7. Technology transfer.
8. Employee training.
9. Citizens' Productivity Advisory Committee.
10. Productivity organization.

Top Management Participation and Commitment

The City Council, the city manager, department heads, and supervisors are all involved and committed to productivity improvement. Frequent meetings are held with the focus, "How can we improve?" The attitude in top management is one of openness to criticism along with a positive view of change.

Organizational Development

Organizational development has been instituted to improve communications and feedback regarding employee perceptions, attitudes, and behavior. Styles have been adjusted to accommodate new conditions. Frequent surveys are conducted to assess attitudes. The emphasis is on the human factors of productivity.

MBO

The performance achievement program closely follows the MBO process. Much of the Phoenix productivity plan is based on MBO. Employees set job accomplishment objectives with their supervisors to be measured over a period of time; later an evaluation is made on how well the objectives were met. The MBO effort includes performance, achievement, compensation for managers, zero-based budgeting, performance auditing, and organizational objectives.

Central Staff Assistance

While it is important that top management support any productivity effort, it is also important that assistance be given to managers further down the line so the wishes of top management can be implemented. It is the assistance given to lower-level managers that determines whether productivity will really improve or simply be a subject for discussion.

The Phoenix Productivity Program offers managers assistance through operational or managerial studies. These studies aid managers in identifying the major areas for productivity improvement and the most likely avenues for success in achieving those improvements. This type of assistance saves managers a great deal of time, as it gives them a structured way to look at their departments, provides the knowledge of experts in the field, and gives them confidence that they are focusing on issues that can truly lead to improvement in the operation of their departments. In sum, this type of guidance provides both incentive and direction to a manager's productivity improvement efforts.

Employee Suggestion Program

The employee suggestion program was revitalized. The program gives employees additional incentives in the form of monetary awards and personal recognition for suggestions made and proposals submitted. This has been a huge success at Phoenix. The city has won national awards for tallying the largest savings per employee. The reasons for success in this program are timely handling of ideas, fair and objective evaluations, recognition, and cash awards.

Productivity Training

Phoenix has instituted a special program to give employees skills for productivity improvement. For a given department, specific training topics are provided in a wide range of areas. Customized training is set up for operating departments. Frequent meetings are held with departments to share and cross-fertilize improvements. A variety of activities has been instituted to provide the recognition necessary to maintain the visibility and importance of productivity to the City of Phoenix.

The following list indicates the topics available for inclusion in a department productivity training program; additional topics may be added on request.

1. Orientation to the Phoenix Productivity Program.
2. Work improvement workshop.
3. Process flow charting.
4. Work distribution analysis.
5. Forms and records management.
6. Work measurement tools and techniques.
7. Layout and location of equipment.
8. Work sampling procedures.
9. Te management.
10. Project management.
11. Cost analysis procedures (equipment and labor).

Training in the Phoenix Productivity Program has played a vital role in improving productivity. Not only has it prepared key staff members to perform their jobs efficiently, but it has also helped to create a sense of pride among employees toward developing better work methods within their departments.

Technology Transfer

Phoenix has set up a technology-sharing network involving other cities in the southwest region as well as Federal Research Laboratories. This allows the city to keep abreast of the latest in technological improvements in a wide variety of fields. The city wants to keep abreast of what's new and latest and how it can apply for productivity improvement.

Employee Training

Employee development and training are a continuing part of productivity improvement within the City of Phoenix. Skills and abilities acquired by employees either to do their current job better or in preparation for a future job contribute to a more effective workplace. To encourage employee development, the City of Phoenix offers a tuition reimbursement plan for job-related courses. In addition, many in-house training programs beyond those specifically dealing with productivity are available to employees.

Citizens' Productivity Advisory Committee

A Citizens' Productivity Advisory Committee was established by the mayor and city manager to review, from an independent perspective, the performance of the city's productivity improvement program. The committee includes management personnel representing a cross-section of community interests as well as individuals administering the productivity program. The committee is charged with recommending changes to strengthen and improve the program. These recommendations are now incorporated into the overall objectives and emphasis of the program.

Productivity Organization

The city places great emphasis on keeping productivity improvement foremost in the minds of its employees and managers. Each department has a productivity coordinator to implement efforts in his or her own department. These coordinators then join together to mesh their programs with the programs from other departments to reach the overall objectives of the entire program. To assist in this effort, productivity/organizational development teams have been formed to focus on specific productivity problems and to search for solutions.

Performance Achievement Program With MBO

The Performance Achievement Program allows managers to work closely as a team in city operations. The process allows communications in setting targets for continuously improving performance. Improving performance is a central goal of management at Phoenix. The overall approach of the program is to define the quality and quantity of work desired and then produce it. Performance achievement is technically an MBO system for setting objectives and evaluating performance in meeting objectives. The City Manager is in the best position to reward good performance and work to improve poor performance. The performance achievement program has several steps, as seen in Figure 18.14 and described in the following.

Define Major Job Responsibilities (What's My Job?)

The manager and supervisor use this step to develop a better understanding of the employee's responsibilities. In this way, the employee can target work time and energy in accomplishing the goals of the organization. Although managers assume that there is a full understanding of each party's expectations, studies have shown that this frequently is not the case.

Job responsibilities describe the overall services, products, or outputs of the employee and the organizational unit the employee supervises. Basi-

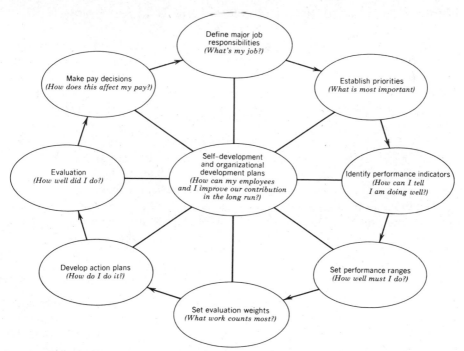

FIGURE 18.14   Performance Achievement Program of the City of Phoenix.

cally then, the job responsibilities definition capsulizes the reasons for the existence of a particular manager's position. In many ways it serves as a brief description of the job. In the Approved Performance Program (Figure 18.15), responsibilities are listed in order of the priority points assigned, the job responsibility with the highest priority being listed first. The Approved Performance Program form has columns for job responsibilities, priority, performance indicators, performance range, weight, and data source.

Establish Priorities (What Is Most Important?)

Clearly job responsibilities are of greatly differing importance. By establishing relative priorities, the manager and supervisor can come to an understanding of the importance of various job elements. This understanding helps to prevent a common problem in management communications in which a subordinate focuses attention and becomes successful in a job element that the supervisor thinks is unimportant, while neglecting job areas that the supervisor regards as critical. The priority column in the Performance Program form indicates the importance of each job responsibility. Priority is based on the importance of the responsibility to the department or the organization. The most important responsibilities get more points, the least important get less. The sum of the points in the priority column must total 100.

Identify Performance Indicators (How Can I Tell I Am Doing Well?)

Performance indicators are the measurement standards used to determine the quality of performance. Performance indicators should describe the end products of the employee's work and should be as concrete as possible. They should avoid describing activities that are intermediate steps in obtaining final results. Indicators should be designed for all major results for which the employee is responsible.

Performance indicators must be measurable and quantifiable. They should begin with a measuring criterion. Managers are responsible for maintaining records on every indicator list.

Unfortunately, plans can be developed with indicators based on data that are unavailable or impossible to collect. Managers therefore are asked to state, on the final plan, the source of data for evaluating each indicator. This assures the manager that the plan is in fact concrete and measurable.

Set Performance Range (How Well Must I Do?)

The performance range sets standards for how well the employee must do. The range is the basis for evaluation in that it establishes minimum, acceptable, target, and maximum practical performance. Targeted performance is a matter of negotiation between supervisor and subordinate. The range is stated in numbers, percentages, dates, ratios, or any other quantifi-

PERFORMANCE ACHIEVEMENT PROGRAM

APPROVED PERFORMANCE PROGRAM 78-79 **FY**

CITY OF PHOENIX

Signature of employee: Lou Kwarm

Signature of supervisor

FOR INSTRUCTIONS SEE SECTION A OF THE PERFORMANCE ACHIEVEMENT GUIDE BOOK

JOB RESPONSIBILITIES	PRIORITY	PERFORMANCE INDICATORS	PERFORMANCE RANGE MIN/TARGET/MAX	WEIGHT	DATA SOURCE RESPONSIBLE PERSON
1. Manage Livestock Sanitation Division	29	a. No. of significant program deficiencies identified by federal auditors.	6/4/2	8	Dept. of Ag. Report 72 (Smith)
		b. No. of animals destroyed due to poor sanitation	120/180/240	5	Sanitation Division Stats. (Jones)
		c. No. of federal inspection citations issued to owners.	100/75/50	7	Dept. of Ag. Report 58 (Smith)
		d. No. of sanitation inspections made	360/480/540	4	New data (Jones)
		e. No. of tons of manure moved.	100/150/200	5	Sanitation Division Stats. (Jones)
2. Manage Livestock Extension Services	23	a. No. of livestock owners adopting department suggested practices.	300/350/400	7	New data (Brown)
		b. Ratio of cost of Phx cattle to statewide cattle cost.	100%/99%/96%	4	New data (Me)
		c. Ratio of price of Phx cattle to statewide cattle price.	103%/105%/107%	5	New data (Me)
		d. No. of new practices pamphlets prepared and printed.	3/5/7	4	By count (Brown)
		e. No. of extension service visits made.	600/650/700	3	Extension Div. Data (Brown)

FIGURE 18.15   Performance Achievement Program, Approved Performance Program form, City of Phoenix.

able term. There are three items to the range: minimum, target, and maximum. Employee performance at minimum level is competent and acceptable. Target performance is set high enough to require the employee to "stretch" but low enough to be clearly achievable. Maximum performance is the highest level possible. This is for the truly exceptional employee. Supervisor and employee negotiate target performance anyplace between minimum acceptable and maximum possible.

Set Evaluation Weight (What Work Counts Most?)

Weights are assigned in accordance with the importance of each indicator under a responsibility. The greater the importance, the higher the number of points assigned. The sum of the weights for all the indicators in each job responsibility must equal the responsibility's priority. In this way, the supervisor incorporates into the evaluation process his or her own priorities along with the employee's priorities.

Develop Action Plans (How Do I Do It?)

Action plans are excellent tools for accomplishing difficult objectives and assuring high performance. They are especially useful in work environments that are crisis oriented, because they are a method of looking beyond the "brush fires" toward longer-term goals. The Action Plan form (Figure 18.16) has columns for result areas, performance indicators, what will be done, when, and what preparatory action is needed.

Evaluation (How Well Did I Do?)

The evaluation phase is the key link in the development of the manager, in improving objectives, and in improving performance. During the evaluation phase, the manager provides information on actual performance and discusses with the supervisor the conditions under which performance was achieved. The two working together look for ways to improve work conditions; the methods being used; and the knowledge, skill, and abilities of the manager.

The evaluation provides the supervisor an opportunity to compliment the manager for superior performance. Frequently this opportunity does not present itself in day-to-day work activities as energies are devoted to accomplishing a wide variety of goals. During the evaluation phase, data are presented and accomplishments are compared with the goals. At this time, good performance can and should receive appropriate praise.

During the discussion of accomplishments, every opportunity should be made to discover items that interfere with higher achievement. Bottlenecks in work flow should be explored and corrective actions discussed. Frequently, items requiring further exploration will be discovered. These items may very well be subjects for productivity studies.

FY	77-78
NAME	Lou Kwarm
POSITION	Director of Livestock Services
DATE	5/1/78

PERFORMANCE ACHIEVEMENT PROGRAM

ACTION PLAN

CITY OF PHOENIX

FOR INSTRUCTIONS
SEE SECTION H
OF THE PERFORMANCE
ACHIEVEMENT GUIDE BOOK

RESULT AREAS	PERFORMANCE INDICATORS	ACTION PLAN		
		WHAT WILL BE DONE	WHEN	WHAT PREPARATORY ACTION IS NEEDED
1. Sanitation	a. Program Deficiencies	Review federal standards with	6/1/80	Obtain copy of
		Division Heads		Federal Regulations
		Conduct in-house inspection	8/1/80	
		using Federal Rules		
	b. Animals destroyed	Identify specific sanitary problems	7/15/80	Assign Bill Smith to
		which can lead to death of animals		do thorough study
		Determine how these specific	8/15/80	
		problems can be overcome		
		Instruct inspectors to concentrate	9/1/80	
		on prevention measures		
	c. Federal citations to livestock	Write a pamphlet explaining	10/20/80	Assign Bob Jones to
	owners	Federal regs. in layman's language		this
		Obtain federal approval for	1/15/81	
		pamphlet		

FIGURE 18.16 Performance Achievement Program, Action Plan form, City of Phoenix.

During the discussion, both parties will be able to identify areas where more knowledge or skill would be helpful toward the accomplishment of the goals. This information should be used to refine the employee's self-development plan.

The discussion of accomplishments and performance targets provides an opportunity for both parties to build a trusting atmosphere and an interpersonal relationship useful in communications throughout the year. As the manager finds the supervisor assisting in the solving of problems and suggesting ways to accomplish the goals, the manager can better identify with the need for open, trusting communications.

The evaluation phase is also useful in discovering objectives that are poorly written. When it is found to be hard or impossible to measure the performance identified in the indicator, performance indicators should be revised. Frequently, when performance is far above or far below the target level, it is because the original targets were not realistically set, and they should be reestablished. As each job responsibility and indicator is discussed, careful attention should be given to the evaluation weights to see if the priorities are still proper for the job under the present conditions. This evaluation discussion is extremely important to manager, supervisor, and employee in defining the conditions under which the performance was achieved. The supervisor must know if the conditions surrounding the performance were an asset or a liability toward performance. The supervisor must know if work conditions were under the control of the manager and how the manager attempted to influence them. These conditions are considered in the establishment of an evaluation score.

An evaluation of performance is conducted at least semiannually, but a quarterly or monthly review is more desirable to identify areas of concern and explore ways to reach all goals. The final evaluation, which is conducted at the close of the fiscal year, serves as an aid in developing the plans for the next year and as a basis for setting salaries. New responsibilities and performance indicators can be designed in response to new issues and problem areas. However, once a practical plan is developed, responsibilities and performance indicators are unlikely to change. On the other hand, performance ranges should change almost every year. Managers should be challenged through the ranges to improve their performance annually.

The evaluation step, using the Evaluation Data Worksheet (Figure 18.17), involves the comparison of actual results with the performance range. Superior, satisfactory, or poor performance is identified for the employee's job as a whole and for individual job responsibilities, on an objective basis.

However, the more important work of the evaluation occurs at another level. The heart of the evaluation is a cooperative discussion by subordinate and supervisor about how they can work together to improve performance. This discussion is important regardless of whether performance is judged superior, good, or poor. The tone of the meeting should combine elements of problem solving and brainstorming and should avoid a guilt-setting or

FY 78-79 **NAME** Lou Kwarm

Director of Livestock Services **POSITION**

DATE 8/1/79

PERFORMANCE ACHIEVEMENT PROGRAM
EVALUATION DATA WORKSHEET

CITY OF PHOENIX

FOR INSTRUCTIONS
SEE SECTION B
OF THE PERFORMANCE
ACHIEVEMENT GUIDE BOOK

PERFORMANCE INDICATOR (NO. AND ABBREVIATION)	RANGE	ACTUAL RESULTS	CAUSES OF UNUSUAL PERFORMANCE	A EVALUATION SCORE	B EVALUATION WEIGHT	WEIGHED SCORE A · B
1.a. Federal audit defic.	6/4/2	5		6	8	48
1.b. Animals destroyed	120/180/240	173		7	5	35
1.c. Fed. citations to owners	100/75/50	87		5.5	7	38.5
1.d. Sanitation inspections	360/480/540	393		5	4	20
1.e. Manure moved	100/150/200	145	Moved too slow – big stink	4.5	5	22.5
2.a. Suggestions used	300/350/400	391		10	7	70
2.b. Phoenix cost/AZ cost	100/99/96	95.7		10	4	40
2.c. Phoenix cost/AZ cost	103/105/107	106.2		9	5	45
2.d. New pamphlets	3/5/7	6		8.5	4	34
2.e. Visits·made	600/650/700	674		8.5	3	26
3.a. Meat citations	50/35/20	23		9.5	9	85.5
3.b. Meat spoiled	1.5/1.2/1.1	1.15		8	6	48
3.c. Meat rejected	.5/.3/.1	.2		8.5	3	25.5
4.a. Slaughter forecast/Act	2/1/0	.4		9	5	45
4.b. Price forecast/Act	2/1/0	2.1	Market very volatile/OK	8	3	24
4.c. Loans forecast/Act	4/1.5/0	.4		9	3	27
5.a. Complete EEO plan	6/15-4/15-2/15	3/1		9	2	18
5.b. % A.A. letters OK	85/95/98	97.7		10	1	10
5.c. Productivity improve	2/4/6	6		10	3	30
6.a. Revise OD plan	4/15-2/15-1/1	3/1		6	1	6
6.b. Labor Relations obj.	3.5/4.5/5.5	5		8	3	24
6.c. Self dev. goals	2/3/5	3		7	1	7
6.d. Obj. for safety	2/1-1/1-1/1	11/20		9	2	18
7.a. % Policy items on time	85/92/97	98		10	1	10

FIGURE 18.17 Performance Achievement Program, Evaluation Data Worksheet, City of Phoenix.

blaming atmosphere. Judgments on the quality of work can be made in a simple, straightforward fashion on the basis of the data.

Salaries are established by combining the factors of current salary level, actual performance, and the evaluation by the supervisor of the subordinate's intangible performance.

When evaluation is complete, a new cycle is started. The evaluation provides information for improving job definition and performance indicators.

Make Pay Decisions (How Does This Affect My Pay?)

A point/salary basis is used to calculate the employee's salary.* The total weighted score points rating, the supervisor's point rating (Figure 18.18), and the City Manager's point rating (Figure 18.19) are added to develop a total point rating. The maximum possible point rating is 1500 points, as follows:

Weighted score rating	1000
Supervisor's rating	300
Management rating	200
Total	1500

The salary-setting system begins with the Evaluation Data Worksheet (Figure 18.17). The employee reports performance on this form. The employee is evaluated at year end on the basis of the performance indicators and ranges agreed to by the employee and supervisor in this plan. The evaluation weights establish priorities for these indicators. By using the employee's plan as the evaluation tool, the supervisor and employee can rate the employee on how well the employee provided service to the public and/or other departments. The supervisor notes any causes of unusual performance and rates the performance on a 1-to-10 scale. Actual results are measured against the minimum, target, and maximum performance levels set in the performance range and an evaluation score is made by the supervisor. The scores are then multiplied by the evaluation weight from the Approved Performance Program to develop the weighted scores. Finally, the weighted scores are added to arrive at the total weighted score.

Supervisory Rating Guideline. The supervisor uses this form (Figure 18.18) to make his or her intangible rating and to explain it to the employee. This explanation is critical, as it must direct the employee to those specific actions or inactions on which the rating is based. Each manager's supervisor performs the supervisory rating. With the exception of a supervisor who is

---

* Readers interested in the salary-setting mechanism used by the City of Phoenix should write directly to the city for details.

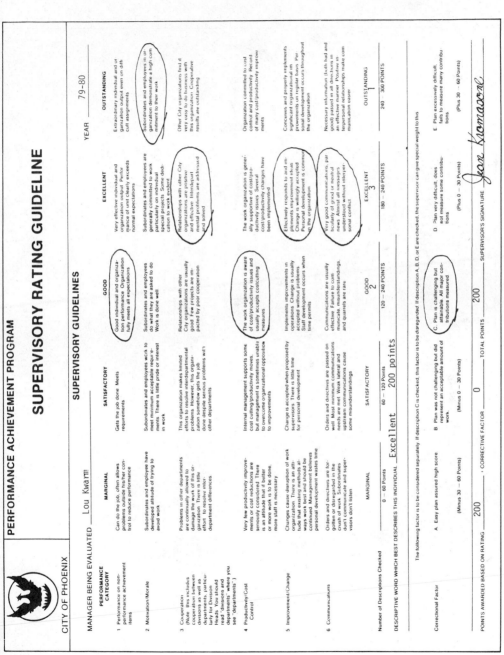

FIGURE 18.18 Performance Achievement Program, Supervisory Rating Guideline, City of Phoenix.

CITY OF PHOENIX

FY 79 J NAME Lou Kvarm

POSITION Director of Livestock Services

DATE 9/13/80

PERFORMANCE ACHIEVEMENT PROGRAM

MANAGEMENT RATING

DIFFICULTY OF PLAN
Reason for Rating: Good plan, challenging but attainable   Possible Points 60   Points Assigned 30

COMPARIBILITY OF SUPERVISOR'S RATING
Reason for Rating: Strong, effective evaluation by supervisor.   Possible Points 50   Points Assigned 40
25 + 15 points

OPENNESS TO CHANGE/IMPROVEMENT
Reason for Rating: Lou has worked to find ways to improve his operation   Possible Points 30   Points Assigned 20
+ 5 points

COMMITMENT TO REDUCE COSTS/INCREASE PRODUCTION
Reason for Rating: Costs need more attention -5 points   Possible Points 30   Points Assigned 10

OTHER Special contributions   Possible Points 30   Points Assigned 15
Reason for Rating: Lou has contributed time and energy to a key task force on work outside his department. He has spoken publicly on several occasions with good results.

TOTAL POINTS 115

COMMENTS: Lou is a positive manager who is working to improve his department
and the public's perception of it.

I. M. Bigg.

MANAGER'S INITIALS OR SIGNATURE

FIGURE 18.19   Performance Achievement Program, Management Rating, City of Phoenix.

an assistant department head or above, the supervisor must obtain the department head's approval before finalizing the rating and informing the management employee about the rating.

The supervisor's point rating of up to 300 points is based on this intangible rating. The scoring system is:

Outstanding	240 – 300
Excellent	160 – 240
Good	120 – 160
Satisfactory	60 – 120
Improvement necessary	0 – 60

Management Rating. The management rating (Figure 18.19) involves the allocation of up to 200 points. Urban Service managers perform the management rating for middle managers reporting to them through department heads. The City Manager performs the management rating for executives and middle managers reporting directly to Urban Service managers. In performing the rating, the various managers utilize the latest management rating form which categorizes the 200 points. In each area the appropriate manager assigns points in the middle of the point range for normal *good* performance. For extraordinary, good, or poor performance, points are added to or subtracted from this middle point. For example, "openness to change/improvement" is allocated a total of 30 points. Most managers with good approaches to change and improvement would earn half of these 30 points, or 15 points. The extraordinary manager who very actively implements appropriate improvements might merit 25 points, while the manager who fights change might be assigned 5 points.

Results of Phoenix Productivity Management

The productivity improvement results in the City of Phoenix have been outstanding over the years. Here is a summary of the highlights.

1. From 1970 to 1979, Phoenix achieved savings or cost avoidances of over $2 million/year and cumulative savings of over $23 million. The improvement in service and higher morale are impossible to measure.

2. Productivity results during 1979–1984:

Improvements	1979–1980	1980–1981	1981–1982	1982–1983	1983–1984
No. of significant improvements	156	268	295	272	280
Value of improvements (millions)	$4.2	$7.4	$8.6	$11.7	$14.2

TABLE 18.2 Comparison of Ten U. S. Cities With Highest Population for Four City Parameters

Rank	City	Population (1000s) 1980	1950	% Change	Labor Force (1000s) 1980	1970	% Change	General Expenditures (millions) 1980	1970	% Change	Taxes Collected (millions) 1980	1970	% Change	Total Employment (Government) 1980
1	New York	7071	7892	(10.5)	3064	3191	(4)	$14,399	$6619	217	$7446	$2504	297	326,281
2	Chicago	3005	3621	(17.1)	1498	1388	7.9	1,832	690	265	792	333	238	42,495
3	Los Angeles	2967	1970	(50.6)	1538	1151	33.6	1,339	477	280	756	267	282	40,602
4	Philadelphia	1688	2072	(18.6)	798	767	4.4	1,631	58	280	844	114	738	33,508
5	Houston	1594	596	267	989	516	91.6	767	138	555	404	99	410	18,226
6	Detroit	1203	1850	(35)	504	561	(11)	1,174	354	332	361	126	287	20,397
7	Dallas	904	434	208	514	374	36.5	453	166	273	235	88	267	13,350
8	San Diego	876	334	262	397	244	62.7	325	96	339	136	41	335	6,602
9	Phoenix	790	107	738	447	49	912	414	76	547	123	40	309	8,605
10	Baltimore	787	950	(17.2)	395	353	11.8	1,150	579	198	348	159	218	33,489

TABLE 18.3 Comparison of Ten U. S. Cities With Highest Population for Four Performance Ratios

City	Expenses/Total Employees	Best Rank	Labor Force/Total Employees	Best Rank	Population Served/Taxes Collected	Best Rank	Taxes Collected/Expenses	Best Rank	Total Rank Score	Total Best Rank
New York	2036	1	9387	10	0.949	10	51.711	6	27	7
Chicago	0.6	5	35.25	6	3.79	6	43	5	22	5
Los Angeles	0.451	9	37.87	5	3.92	4	56.4	10	28	8
Philadelphia	0.966	4	23.81	8	2	9	51.74	7	28	8
Houston	0.481	8	54.26	2	3.94	3	52.6	9	22	5
Detroit	0.975	3	24.7	7	3.33	7	30.7	3	20	3
Dallas	0.501	7	38.5	4	3.84	5	51.9	8	24	6
San Diego	0.371	10	60.13	1	6.44	1	41.7	4	16	2
Phoenix	0.524	6	51.94	3	6.42	2	29.7	1	12	1
Baltimore	1.46	2	11.79	9	2.26	8	30.2	2	21	4

3. Special awards and recognition:

   (a) National award by the National Association of Suggestion Systems for highest savings per employee among all units of local and state government (the fifth year in a row the City has won this award).

   (b) National award by the Municipal Finance Officers Association for best municipal budgeting system in the United States.

   (c) National award by the Urban and Regional Information Systems Association for the Phoenix Fire Department computer-aided dispatch system.

   (d) Selection of the Phoenix Energy Conservation Specialist as "Energy Manager of the Year" in competition with public and private sector organizations.

   (e) Selection of the Fire Department as the National Photographic Department of the Year by the Professional Photographers Association (in competition with public and private sectors).

   (f) Selection of the word-processing operation as number 1 in the country by *Office Magazine* (in competition with public and private sectors).

To compare the performance of the City of Phoenix with that of other major cities is a difficult exercise. The oversimplification of complex and interwoven activities may render the results meaningless. Nonetheless, a "hint" of comparative performance can be made with basic parameters of a municipal government (Table 18.2). The information used for this comparison was extracted from the U. S. Department of Commerce, *Statistical Abstracts of the United States*. Phoenix has experienced 638 percent growth in population from 1950 to 1980, representing among the top ten cities in population the fastest growing city in the United States. Despite this growth it has achieved a per-capita performance profile among the same top ten cities of number 1 with respect to the four performance ratios seen in Table 18.3. These ratios define productivity in terms of output (performance) and input (resources). This gives the City of Phoenix the best rank among the top ten largest populated cities in the United States.

These and other comparative factors indicate Phoenix is enjoying one of the most outstanding productivity effects in the country. MBO has been extremely useful in achieving this end.

Bibliography

City of Phoenix, *Performance Achievement Program Guidebook*. 3rd ed., October 1, 1980.

County and City Data Book of United States, 1983.

Phoenix Productivity Program, publication financed by Federal Intergovernmental Personnel Act Grant, July 1979.

U. S. Department of Commerce, *Statistical Abstracts, 1950–1983*.

PART

5

Future
of MBO

The last section of this handbook contains only one chapter, on the future of MBO. I have projected current trends several decades into the future to create a vision of where MBO is heading. My purpose, first, is to make clear that MBO has a future. Second, I want to provoke readers to look ahead themselves and create a vision for their own journey into the managerial future.

19

PREDICTIONS AND DIRECTIONS FOR MBO

IN THIS CHAPTER

A LOOK AT MANAGEMENT OF THE PAST
A LOOK INTO THE FUTURE
WHERE IS MBO GOING?
WHAT MAKES AN EXCELLENT MBO MANAGER?

Does MBO have a future? Will it disappear by the twenty-first century? Has it emerged as a personal technique that's unique to the individual? I once received an interesting telephone call from the president of a company in the top 25 of the Fortune 500 corporations. He was concerned over the low level of technological innovations and diminishing productivity in his company. This prompted his request for development and installation of the MBO process for his entire company. My reaction was amazement over this eleventh-hour interest in MBO. "Why, after all these years, the sudden interest in MBO?" His reply: "In the early fifties, we started MBO but abandoned it. We thought and judged it to be a short-lived fad. But over the years we've been drifting back in almost a natural way to its philosophy and its process. We want to formalize this and get the most from it."

This is not an isolated case. Many have made the same discovery. The basic process of participative planning, doing, and progressive evaluation has now become a worldwide managerial process. MBO has a bright future down to the twenty-first century. It will not disappear. This book has identified many areas of applications that will flourish with MBO. This last chapter considers four additional topics: (1) managerial achievements of the past; (2) predictions for the future (I have taken some liberties in suggesting what may appear from a managerial standpoint down to 2025 AD); (3) where

791

MBO is going; and finally (4) the model of an excellent MBO manager. The chapter intends to relate the past to the present and the future of MBO. This is not the last chapter of MBO—only the last chapter of this book. Since MBO is not a viable part of the managerial process, it has no end; it will only change.

A LOOK AT MANAGEMENT OF THE PAST

Management is not a recent phenomenon. It goes back as far as recorded history. This is not to suggest that MBO appeared at the dawn of history. But its elements were there! Wherever there was a leader and group, or a new technology produced a product or service, or a new project or innovation was completed, management was there and the elements of MBO were there. In the pyramids of Giza, the Diocletian control schemes, or men landing on the moon—management was there. Even though the word "management" was not in early records, its function and operation were present. In early days, disciplines such as science, architecture, economics, mathematics, religion, politics, and the military overshadowed management. Only in recent times has the management discipline formally emerged.

Management over the years has not always been successful, but identification of failed organizations or accomplishment is difficult. Analysts are more inclined to record and report successes. Thus it is difficult to catalog failed organizations. But the history of successful achievements over the years has learning value. Santayana once said, "Those who do not learn from their own history are condemned to relive it." The converse is also true: Those who learn from their own history can expect their accomplishments to expand to new plateaus of achievement and satisfaction.

This section presents a brief overview of outstanding management accomplishments throughout history. A good way to view the present and the future is from the solid basis of the past. Here events are identified with their approximate dates and contributions to managerial state of the art. The reader should note the workings of MBO attitude, thought, and practices. The MBO elements of planning, goal setting, participation, achievement of results, motivation, and total involvements are present in these achievements.

Date	Group or Individual	Managerial Accomplishment	Managerial Contribution
In the beginning	God	Created heavens and earth	Planned and implemented with no errors super macro and exacting micro celestial and terrestrial systems and

Date	Group or Individual	Managerial Accomplishment	Managerial Contribution
			subsystems in feedback self-correcting cycles; created organisms with extraordinary capabilities; set down standards for directing, controlling, and evaluating states and quality of existence, growth, development, and maturation
4000 BC	Mesopotamians, Mesopotamia	Domesticated plants and animals	Started food inventories to reduce hunting time, which brought about settled existence and genesis of small villages or towns; developed concept of city for gregarious and collaborative undertakings; raised survival standards and longevity; started farm work processes with efficient and effective tools; created labor markets for use in work
3200 BC	Sumerians, Sumeria	Devised money for value and exchange	Devised divisional metal units in weights and sizes as standards of value for measurement and exchange; started use of coined money as easy, efficient, and convenient way of handling value exchange among buyer, seller, and arranger; developed system for storing and accumulating value for delayed and long-range gratification

Date	Group or Individual	Managerial Accomplishment	Managerial Contribution
2700 BC	Egyptians, Egypt	Developed written form for communications	Developed alphabetic form of written communications; established written numerics and measurements for planning, devising, and control; first to write job descriptions, instruction manuals, and work procedures; instituted consultancy as a prelude to staff management; formalized principles and practices of management for communications and development
2170 BC	King Cheops, Egypt	Ordered great pyramid at Giza	Started project management with sophisticated measurements for planning, precutting, erecting, and assembling huge objects; developed materials, scheduling, and transportation system; used organizational hierarchy for putting diverse groups to single task; set up quality control procedures both off site and on site
1650 BC	Hammurabi, Babylonia	Established codes, laws, and standards	Set up laws to control responsibilities and commitments in all business transactions such as sales, loans, contracts, agreements, promissory notes, and real estate; first record of establishing supervisory responsibilities; introduced written standards and documenta-

Date	Group or Individual	Managerial Accomplishment	Managerial Contribution
			tion for control purposes; started formal hiring procedures and organized labor markets
1491 BC	Moses the Hebrew	Directed exodus and established laws of conduct for 2 million people traveling to unknown land	Established laws, codes, and principles of justice, morality, and behavior; set up processes of delegation, authority, span of control, and representation; developed pyramidal form of organization; established personnel selection, training, and reporting; set up procedures for participation and group conflict resolution; first known to start managing by exception
1100 BC	Chow, China	Implemented vast civil service system	Developed directory listings of services available to public; established duties of effective civil administrator; enforced standards of performance to control administrators in system; eight major regulations were developed and practiced to control government and public
600 BC	Nebuchadnezzar, Babylonia	Set up production control systems for granaries and textile mills	Developed production run processes and materials requirements planning; established methods for in-process inventories and inventory storage systems; set up inventory management for stock reporting, spoilage, pilferage, and reordering

Date	Group or Individual	Managerial Accomplishment	Managerial Contribution
387 BC	Plato, Greece	Devised process for chief executive selection	Introduced participation process of popular will for selecting best person to lead and manage an organization on basis of merit; developed symposia for group dialogues for agreements, which started conference method; established universality of management in various disciplines
342 BC	Aristotle, Greece	Applied scientific logic and method to management	Used scientific and systematic inquiry and analysis for comparisons, logical predictions, and conclusive decision making; emphasized how results are product of cause-effects working as laws; first to receive government funding for private research
300 BC	Chow Dynasty, China	Constructed Great Wall of China, 1684 miles	Largest constructed project with largest conscripted labor pool with largest volume of material ever deployed and managed in single project; developed materials transportation and handling system for diverse multilayout terrain; devised, set up, and maintained 40,000 watchtowers for surveillance and control
45 BC	Julius Caesar, Rome	Developed logistics management	Established strategies for deployment and sustaining of forces using strategic planning, procurement, storage

Date	Group or Individual	Managerial Accomplishment	Managerial Contribution
			transportation, distribution of personnel supplies, equipment, and facility construction; set up procedures for managing from distance; developed use of time and calendar in managerial decision making
33 AD	Jesus of Nazareth	Developed and demonstrated models of excellence in managerial leadership	Established leadership style in getting results from people; set down principles and standards for human behavior; formalized methods of resolving and handling conflicts, hostilities, and aggression; gave examples of attitudes and leadership skills for development of new leaders; established guidelines for moral code in managerial decision making
64 AD	Paul of Tarsus	Developed strategies for marketing in new territories	Developed persuasive approaches for introducing new thinking and new services in hostile and reactionary territories; established goal-setting processes and principles of priorities for growth and development; set up followup procedures in establishing growth penetration in new territories
284 AD	Diocletian, Rome	Reorganized empire to highly centralized	Developed tight unity of command with 100 dioceses geographically

Date	Group or Individual	Managerial Accomplishment	Managerial Contribution
		administrative management process	divided and two levels of managerial delegation in far-flung Roman empire; centralized power by delegating civil government authority to local dioceses but retained centralized reporting of military forces under centralized authority
1449 AD	Venetian merchants, Italy	Formally developed international commerce	Set up international trade and business ventures, commissioning and paying agents profit sharing in foreign countries; developed two types of business organizations—partnership and joint venture; started financial methods and cost-accounting procedures for control and accounting
1454 AD	Johann Gutenberg, Germany	Developed mass production printing process	Set up complete manufacturing process for mass production of printing, which initiated books and publications for large general masses; started information documentation, storage, distribution, and retrieval; provided process of exchange of information and experience for general masses
1512 AD	Niccolo Machiavelli, Italy	Developed power strategies for organizational control	Set up tactical principles for use in behavioral inducement and control; started role-playing strategies for managers

Date	Group or Individual	Managerial Accomplishment	Managerial Contribution
			and leaders to gain certain results; wrote first handbook of practical consultancy to heads of state
1759 AD	Richard Arkwright, England	Operated successful factory system	Developed and operated power-driven machinery in highly centralized large-scale under-one-roof factory system for cotton textiles; introduced division of labor and specialized skills training to operate factory system; introduced capital costs, capital requirements as investments; stimulated invention of capital equipment and its substitution for labor costs
1776 AD	Adam Smith, Scotland	Formalized private enterprise system	Identified that seemingly chaotic free market can actually be self-regulating mechanism if it is free to meet needs of community; stimulated entrepreneurial private ownership to general masses; enhanced competitiveness based on self-interest, which leads to great benefits to individual and society; introduced formal arguments against government restrictions and regulations for hampering expansion
1793 AD	Government, Republic of	Elevated educational level of	Set up compulsory education in France from the

Date	Group or Individual	Managerial Accomplishment	Managerial Contribution
	France	masses of workers	age of 6 and opened up mass education for workers
1800 AD	SOHO Engineering Foundry of Boulton, Watt & Co., England	Applied scientific methods to factory system	Laid out, built, and operated factory system whose output was planned, expected, and arranged on basis of forecasting and production planning for steam engines; initiated wage-payment system approach based on work standards established by motion and time study for each job classification; first to set up piece-rate incentive systems for foremen and workers to increase output of working groups
1810 AD	Robert Owen, New Lenark Mills, Scotland	Started modern personnel management	Instituted human relations reforms to advance quality of work life for employees, such as open-door policy for grievance handling, performance evaluation, feedback for employees, minimum working age, minimum wage rates, effective but not punitive discipline, working conditions that enhanced productivity
1832 AD	Charles Babbage, England	Inaugurated research and development in organizations	Introduced scientific approach in use of machinery and manufacturing process by doing R&D work and time and motion studies; developed first digital computer; set up opti-

Date	Group or Individual	Managerial Accomplishment	Managerial Contribution
			mum size of manufacturing unit for each class of product development
1863 AD	Singer Sewing Machine Co., United States	Developed franchising system	Created selective distribution system for manufactured products under brand name through outlets owned by independent entrepreneurs; designed high-quality standardized products and services sold as chain identity throughout all outlets; formalized continuing relationship among corporate franchisor, risk-taking franchisees, and local capital investor
1867 AD	Alexander Bell, American Telephone & Telegraph Co., United States	Devised largest and most comprehensive communications network in world	Devised communications network that quickly processes 500 million messages per day to any destination for over 200 million network hookups; created biggest monopoly in world, whose assets exceed $600 billion; 19-member board directs organization of over 1 million employees
1888 AD	George Eastman, United States	Perfected coated photographic paper	Started process for documenting and certifying visual events, documents, and communications
1903 AD	Frederick Taylor, United States	Applied scientific methods to management practices	Applied scientific methods to management practices in worker selection, job

Date	Group or Individual	Managerial Accomplishment	Managerial Contribution
			determination, work environment, and task assignments; shifted responsibility of work methods and output from labor to management; advanced scientific management movement
1903 AD	Wright Brothers, United States	Successfully flew aircraft that could transport people	Established new form of transportation to move people quickly from one place to another
1908 AD	Henry L. Gantt, United States	Devised Gantt system of time control	Devised system of time-control charting by portraying time required to complete task with actual time used to complete it; developed task-and-bonus plan for enumerating workers in differential piece-rate system
1908 AD	Henry Ford, United States	Devised mass production	Set up low-cost high-volume production processes for assembling uniform, standardized, and interchangeable parts; formalized subcontracting system for manufacture of component parts from national vendors to supply mass assembly system; developed sophisticated inventory control systems
1910 AD	Hugo Münsterberg, Germany	Applied psychology to management	Founded industrial psychology (forerunner of behavioral management) by applying psychological principles and conditions for fitting employees to assigned jobs;

Date	Group or Individual	Managerial Accomplishment	Managerial Contribution
			developed and applied tests for personnel selection and placement suitability
1914 AD	Theodore Roosevelt, United States	Ordered building of Panama Canal	Completed, after two major attempts by other countries, 50 miles of canal with largest number of locks in world, providing efficient waterway transportation system between two major oceans, effecting a mileage reduction from 7000 to 50 miles; construction and completion of canal that passes 35 ships daily was made with 43,000 workers and at unbelievable odds, including political revolution, lethal diseases, lack of money, spiraling costs, and lack of equipment
1915 AD	Guglielmo Marconi, Italy	Developed wireless for managerial communications	Developed processes for wireless communications used for transmission of news, entertainment, military messages, scientific data, police work, and other requirements; set down fundamentals that gave rise to radio, television, and satellite communications; provided basis for television networks that send programming to hundreds of affiliate stations
1916 AD	Henri Fayol, France	Developed first comprehensive	Recognized that management activity com-

Date	Group or Individual	Managerial Accomplishment	Managerial Contribution
		theory of management	prises five components: planning, organizing, commanding, coordinating, and controlling; enunciated 14 principles for effective managerial performance; stressed that management was separate body of knowledge but applicable to all forms of disciplines, thus supported universality of management
1922 AD	Robert K. Wood, Sears, Roebuck & Co., United States	Combined mail order with retail distribution	Reorganized company to decentralized operation combining mail-order distribution through chains of retail stores for growing urban markets; used novel incentive systems of profit sharing and ownership to attain high performance from employees
1923 AD	Alfred P. Sloan, General Motors Corp., United States	Devised coordinated decentralization	Devised decentralization plan giving full authority to operating managers while making them accountable for central policies to corporation; formalized progressive planning for all operating managers as medium of coordination, control, and accountability; set down basic ideas of MBO
1924 AD	American Management Association, United States	Advanced formalization of management as profession	Created opportunities for management development through seminars, workshops, courses, conferences, books, and library; formed forum of

Date	Group or Individual	Managerial Accomplishment	Managerial Contribution
			information and experience exchange by management practitioners to spread effective management throughout American industry; operates "business school for managers," enrolling 75,000 students annually without formal faculty; institutionalized curriculum or granting of degrees
1927 AD	Charles Lindbergh, United States	Opened up long-distance air transportation	Opened up vast opportunities for long-distance air transportation for air mail, equipment, and passenger service; planned, organized, and implemented solo non-stop flight from New York to Paris inaugurating long-distance commercial air transportation and communications to all parts of world
1928 AD	Elton Mayo, United States	Started behavioral management movement	Found that workers in factory had subculture of their own, separate from factory, and that participation in this subculture enhances productive output; formalized sociological concept of group interactions in work setting
1930 AD	Independent American Food Retailers, United States	Devised supermarket	Devised high volume, wide variety, and low-priced food items sold on a self-service basis; initiated consumer-

Date	Group or Individual	Managerial Accomplishment	Managerial Contribution
			oriented discount stores, which spurred mass production for low-priced goods; responsible for development of corporate chain organizations to meet consumer mobility
1942 AD	Bell Aircraft, United States	Successfully test flew first jet airplane	Devised technical means for making available world markets and world community
1942 AD	J. Robert Oppenheimer, Manhattan Project, United States	Directed project for harnessing nuclear energy	Assembled, organized, and directed most formidable collections of scientists, engineers, and technicians ever gathered for single project for development and release of nuclear energy requiring thousands of tedious, time-consuming, trial-and-error, dangerous experiments; set down processes and procedures for generating electricity
1951 AD	Ralph Cordiner, General Electric Co., United States	Devised decentralized profit centers	Devised multinational corporation with decentralized authority in profit centers that operate with considerable autonomy; developed workable organizational format of many independent companies operating under corporate coordinating "umbrella"
1954 AD	Jay Hopkins, General Dynamics Corp., United States	Devised single-customer marketing strategy	Devised organization to supply technological products and services to single customer—the

Date	Group or Individual	Managerial Accomplishment	Managerial Contribution
			government; developed high concentration of scientists and engineers with capabilities and skills to solve wide variety of problems faced by its single customer
1955 AD	Dwight D. Eisenhower, United States	Advanced development of highway network to reach all sections of country	Advanced development of highway system and network of roads to reach efficiently all sections of country, resulting in tremendous economic, social, and political changes in country; established easy conveyance of materials, equipment, food, and supplies for rapidly growing and mobile population
1955 AD	Computer industry, United States	Applied computer chip-studded equipment to data processing	Established computers to process data, words, and numerics in mass production, communications, offices, and entertainment
1956 AD	Thomas J. Watson, IBM Corp., United States	Created customer-oriented corporation	Established tenets for managerial practices and decision making; required superior effort— more than accountability but a way of life; gave emphasis to service to customers by helping customers solve their problems; spurred development of human resources through education, development, and retraining
1960 AD	U. S. Government	Developed nuclear ship that	Developed nuclear-propelled submarine

Date	Group or Individual	Managerial Accomplishment	Managerial Contribution
		circumnavigates globe underwater	that circumnavigates globe without ever surfacing for air, food, or energy; demonstrated effective systems management for coordinating technical and managerial requirements of hydrodynamics, nuclear power, and habitability
1964 AD	"Colonel" Harland Sanders, Kentucky Fried Chicken Corp., United States	Devised fast food franchising to owner/operators	Devised aggressive promotion of fried chicken to franchising owner/operators conveniently located around corner in growing suburbia; standardized product image and quality using prescribed ingredients for mass distribution in outlets; used flexible site location plan to move with moving consumers
1964 AD	U. S. Congress	Enacted Civil Rights Act of 1964, prohibiting discrimination in employment	Instituted federal laws prohibiting discrimination and preferential treatment of workers on basis of race, sex, age, religion, ethnic, national, or union background
1969 AD	General Motors, United States	Commitment to quality control with product sold to customers	General Motors recalled 5 million cars at great expense for adjustment of mechanical defects and supports product warranties and reliabilities
1969 AD	John F. Kennedy and U. S. Apollo expeditions	Achieved man walking on moon	Coordinated decision-making process to gain agreements and collaboration among political,

Date	Group or Individual	Managerial Accomplishment	Managerial Contribution
			scientific, technological, and managerial groups to undertake and complete $24 billion project never before attempted; established and implemented PERT time control network of 150,000 individual contractors to complete project; applied latest R&D technologies to solve multiple new problems never before experienced in human endeavor
1970 AD	Japanese Managerial Practices, Japan	Devised *ringi* system of decision making	Devised decision-making process (*ringi*) for collecting and knitting together subdecisions on lower levels of management in such a way that all levels of management are responsible for carrying out requirements; fostered lifeline employment which results in loyalty, cooperation, and commitments
1970 AD	U. S. Congress	Enacted Postal Reorganization Act, reorganizing postal system	Developed 100-billion-item automated sorting and interchange system, greatest in the world, for dispatching written communications; devised and maintains macro operating network to reach multimillion home units; operates large fleet of vehicles and delivery personnel to provide six-day, 52-week uninterrupted service

Date	Group or Individual	Managerial Accomplishment	Managerial Contribution
1971 AD	Japanese ship-builders, Japan	Devised largest movable cargo and inventory conveyance vehicle ever built	Designed and built 372,400-ton oil tanker Nisseki Maru, largest ship built to date
1975 AD	Yugoslavian Managerial Practices	Developed self-management	Developed decentralization schemes to allow local communities, through communes, to plan and implement their own development; self-management integrates elements from both communistic (highly centralized) and capitalistic (highly decentralized) countries
1977 AD	Alaskan pipe-line, United States	Devised and built major oil pipeline	Devised and built major 800-mile oil pipeline delivering 1.2 million barrels per day in record time of research, planning, organizing, and implementing; effort required coordinated decision-making process among federal groups, state and local governments, and host of private contractors
1979 AD	Members of OPEC (Organization of Petroleum Exporting Countries), Middle East	Developed world's most effective cartel	Thirteen nations developed world's most effective price cartel to manipulate prices at will; demonstrated how international belligerents as market competitors can combine and cooperate in common venture to ensure gain by all its members

Date	Group or Individual	Managerial Accomplishment	Managerial Contribution
1980 AD	Wall Street, United States	Operation of vast financial network	Financial network connecting and coordinating banks, investment firms, stock markets, accountants, lawyers, stockholders, venture capitalists, and government agencies to complete on daily basis financial transactions for United States and foreign countries on vast scale that exceeds gross national products of countries it services
1981 AD	City planners, United States	Direction of city growth and urban megalopolises	Planners direct city and urban megalopolis growth to accommodate population growth shifts from country to city; orderly handling of technical and economic interfaces between and among expanding super cities in spite of inflexible political structures and discontinuities
1982 AD	Thomas Schlier, Foundation for Product Testing, Germany	Devised product-testing process for consumer enlightenment	Devised product-testing process to give feedback information on safety, reliability, and misleading advertisements to general masses of consumers; created organization that operates 150 consumer counseling centers around country to provide information needed for decision making; succeeded in giving consumers a basis for return of money spent on poor goods

A LOOK INTO THE FUTURE

Futurism—the art of predicting tomorrow on the basis of what we know today—is at best a primitive process. It is like looking through a dark glass. At its greatest, it is "grasping for visions" of what might be. The process can never be accurate. It can never produce details on how future outcomes may result from options or choices that are available today. This speculative process, however, can give us a sense of the challenges, the opportunities, and the prospects realizable if managerial breakthroughs are to occur, breakthroughs that are the painstaking work of many people over long periods of time.

This section is on predictions for the future. In many ways it is a listing of conjectures. But conjectures are often needed to start processes of self-reinforcement, self-fulfillment, and self-direction. Self-fulfilling prophesy often starts with conjecture. Conjecture sets in motion subconscious forces for making the conjecture realizable. In this chapter I look ahead as far as 2025 AD. It is my wish that these predictions give the reader a sense of progress as this book comes to an end.

1990 AD Predictions

1. People's motivations shift from money, career, and status to leisure, independence, and rights.
2. Electric automobiles are used for short-distance driving.
3. There is electronic mail delivery to businesses, corporations, and some governments.
4. Salary increases for employees or other forms of compensation increases are given only with supporting productivity data that assure its justification.
5. Job benefits such as vacations, time off, and insurance are reported weekly and taxed along with job income.
6. Self-MBO for personal goals is practiced along with MBO in companies and groups.
7. Physical-fitness programs for management personnel are required. Most corporations sponsor internal programs.
8. Video is used for simultaneous conferences with managers in several different locations.
9. Devaluation is common and emerging expedient used by most countries to cope with continuing stagflation.
10. Electronic boards are used to transmit messages in conference rooms anywhere where there is a telephone and an outlet.

1995 AD Predictions

1. Time employment for professional employees, the 40-hour work week, is displaced by performance contracting, work packages per

week. Employment is a business arrangement with a formal contract in which both sides negotiate.

2. Performance appraisals of employees by supervisors are replaced by employee self-appraisals. Employees are sufficiently skilled to execute their own corrections and take their own actions.

3. Age 55 is common retirement age after person has had three minicareers.

4. Interests, attitudes, and self-will are prime requisites for placement and work assignments.

5. Megalopolis managers integrate into their working systems the political and budgetary discontinuities of many autonomous towns and cities.

6. Product and professional services are legally certified before being sold.

7. Home offices with all the communication devices, conveniences, and equipment found in corporate offices will be a second office for many management personnel.

8. Canada, the United States, and Mexico have a unique common market concept and a tightly knit economic system.

9. All written material is printed on thin paper-like plastic from which the writing can be removed efficiently and the plastic sheets recycled.

10. Ninety percent of the corporations in existence began existence within the past ten years and have major products that came into existence within the past ten years.

2000 AD Predictions

1. Employees are sufficiently skilled to practice self-management. General management is concerned with providing alternatives, resources, and coordination.

2. Employees teach themselves any subject with self-teaching publications, computerized teaching devices and books.

3. Great or nearly impossible projects are accomplished more from the "collective will" of employees than from rigidly structured organizations and systems.

4. Information retrieval systems in libraries provide access to any information collected in the past.

5. A monetary system is in operation throughout the world in which value rather than money is transferred. The economy is a computerized credit card economy.

6. Many factories are automated from design to manufacturing with computerized, electronic robots.

7. Accurate predictor models are available for selecting executives to lead gigantic work centers that assign people work.

8. Air transportation of 12,000 miles/hour delivers passengers anywhere in the world within two hours of takeoff.

9. Quality and accuracy are multiplied: watches are accurate to one 100th of a second; solar converters are 99 percent efficient; greeting cards are recycled and used thousands of times; adhesives last a lifetime.

10. Information technology sufficiently sophisticated with statistical indices to track: public happiness by race and geography; individual fulfilled by work assignments and interest; character development toward a super model of expectations.

2025 AD Predictions

1. Private corporations become work centers and professional workers have the freedom to move in and out of any center on a prearranged and preselected basis.

2. Air-conditioned dome settlements on the moon begin in which heat and food are derived from solar radiation. Moon manufacturing commences.

3. The seas are farmed with domestication of marine life such as lobsters and fish. Large-scale ocean mining is in progress. There are several land farming seasons to ripen crops three to four times per year with artificial light and growth chemicals.

4. Humans are able to speak several languages fluently, to remember most of what they read, and to complete their personal work from any location on the globe.

5. The life span has accelerated, greatly owing to environmental and nutritional breakthroughs; average life expectancy is 100 years.

6. Warfare is internationally banned and controlled. Disputes are handled and resolved with a world centralized intelligence group in Jerusalem.

7. The population of the earth is housed in self-contained apartment minicities, 1000 stories high, incorporating food stores, shops, restaurants, swimming pools, and leisure activities.

8. Swift automated transportation systems are able to move masses of people great distances within a matter of minutes.

9. Zero population growth has been achieved throughout the world, since most nations have signed population stabilization agreements.

10. Science, technology, politics, economics, and religion are integrated so that decisions in one area are not to be made until the impact in other areas is well known.

WHERE IS MBO GOING?

MBO is going where management is going! MBO is not management. Nor does it lead or follow management. It is a style of thinking, planning, directing, behaving, and evaluating for results that is needed for managing. It is the framework for the management process. If we can see the direction that management is taking, we can get a glimpse of where MBO is going. Based on our look into the past and a speculative look into the future, here are some of the future directions for MBO.

1. *MBO Is Moving Down to Workers, Especially Professional Workers.* It is moving down to workers because management is moving down to workers. The ethic of participation in decision making is crumbling centralized structures and authoritarian decision making. As decision making is decentralized to lower levels, the line of demarcation between management and workers becomes nebulous. In many cases such as engineering, it is hard to find where management ends and workers begin. Workers are invited by management to participate in decisions affecting quality, innovations, safety, costs, and productivity. Subordinates welcome this opportunity! Subordinates whose lives are affected by a decision in management want to be a part of the process of arriving at that decision. As the United States becomes more and more a service economy with more and more professional workers, decision making is moving to lower levels and to workers. The separation of managers as a group from workers and workers as a group from managers is breaking down to new groups comprising both managers and workers. As a result, every worker becomes a manager and every manager becomes a worker. These new managerial workers need fundamental skills of planning, preparing, doing, and evaluating. MBO fits effectively for this situation.

2. *MBO Is Becoming a Group Process.* It is moving into a group interaction process because management is moving more formally into a collective body of groups. Group MBO has started and is here to stay. This is not to imply that supervisor and subordinate participation is on its way out. It only means a new goal-setting process has been established. This has been described earlier in the sections on group MBO and Japanese quality circles. Involving workers in job improvements, innovations, change, and problems is smart! The assumption that all wisdom resides in the minds of the managerial elite is ridiculous. The Japanese have shown us that participation in decision making works and works well, not because many heads are better than one but because better definitions of problems come from their being viewed from all possible angles. Once problems have been clearly defined and everyone in the group has participated in the definition, implementation of the decisions reached comes easier and faster. The people within the group already know their roles and how to perform them, since they were involved in their identification.

Effectiveness of an organization is giving way to effectiveness of groups. Each group is different and each decides on its own criteria of effectiveness. With this concept, effectiveness is measured by a different set of criteria for each group involved. Traditionally, the process of defining the goals of an organization has been to attune these goals to the needs and requirements of a relevant group of stockholders. Now it is to attune the goals to the stockholder group, executive group, functional group, staff group, special assignment group, and worker group. Effectiveness of an organization is becoming defined in terms of the goals, structures, and operations of groups. MBO is a fundamental process for group interaction, decision making, and goal setting.

3. *MBO Is Moving Toward Entrepreneurship.*   It is moving to an entrepreneurial life-style because management is moving toward becoming more entrepreneurial. Innovations have always been and will continue to be the major way an economy is enhanced or moved. Historically, technological innovations created economies! Success in breakthroughs can put one company far ahead of another. Failure in experiencing a reasonable number of breakthroughs can mean total failure. The management of breakthroughs is the management of technical problems. Translating problem formulation into understandable opportunities is a sure way to move toward breakthroughs. Too often a technical problem is seen as simply needing a solution. Technical problems should be seen as attractive opportunities for changing the conditions that produced the problems. These could be opportunities to solve the problem in such a way as to give a competitive edge to the problem solver. Many companies are experiencing product maturation. That is, their products have been on the market for extensive periods of time with little product differentiation. Differentiation will not take place until companies pursue a reasonable number of technological goals. MBO is moving more and more into scientific and engineering uses. MBO for engineers is a growing practice.

4. *MBO Is Moving to Include Risk Factors, Productivity, and Quality.*   It is moving to include these three factors more formally and deliberately because management is formalizing intensely their efforts in these areas. MBO plans contain risk factors, which suggest the confidence level for a set of plans in achieving a set of results. MBO plans contain productivity data, in order to compare the planned year with previous years. A plan when approved must reveal a productivity implementation strategy better than those of the past. MBO plans also state the quality levels that must be reached in achieving a set of results. The new MBO practitioner needs the skills of risk taking, productivity improvement, and quality assurance.

5. *MBO Is Moving Toward Large-Scale Accomplishments.*   It is moving toward such accomplishments because management is facing the largest problems in its history. The bumpy road to the twenty-first century will encompass gigantic aggregates—the largest population ever, the widest world markets ever, the biggest population of ''have nots'' ever, the greatest

technological and economic complexities ever, the largest scarcity of resources ever, and the greatest transnational ventures ever. Any given goal has a strategy; the larger the goal, the larger the strategy. Any large-scale globular goal can be broken down into a number of small subgoals that will be less overwhelming and more manageable. MBO allows for goal hierarchies from macro levels to micro levels. MBO fits effectively as management moves toward handling globular aggregates.

6. *MBO Is Moving Toward Performance Contracting.* It is moving toward such contracting because management of professional employees and services is moving toward performance contracting. Traditionally, employees have been hired on a time basis. That is, they are hired for so many hours a day, so many days a week. Compensation is allocated when the agreed-on units of time have been consumed. Wages are dollars per hour or dollars per week: salaries are dollars per month or dollars per year. In return for compensation per unit of time, the employee agrees to do what the employer requires during the pay period. This traditional basis of employment might be termed "time contracting." It is contractual because an employee agrees to put in time and the employer agrees to pay for this time. The contract is broken when either party fails to uphold the commitment.

Over the years, management has had to assume responsibility for ensuring that pay is connected to performance and productivity. Managers have had to be skillful enough to get a fair day's work for a fair day's pay. Management has obtained a high degree of success for both organization and the individual employee.

The traditional time-contracting form of employment is gradually being replaced—in a small way, to be sure—by a new form of employment—"performance contracting." This type of employee-employer agreement is relatively new and ties compensation to the performance contribution of productivity improvement. Some employees are being hired on the basis of performance rather than time. They are hired to do a particular job, a specific project, or a definable task. Compensation is agreed to during the planning and contractual phase and allocated when performance is complete and productivity is delivered. Thus fees or wages are dollars per job, dollars per project, dollars per production output, or dollars per assignment. In return for the compensation per project or assignment, the employee agrees to do the work without using time as the basis. This gives the employee a great deal of independence and discretionary prerogatives of when work must be completed. Salespeople, contractors, consultants, lawyers, teachers, and other professionals practice performance contracting.

A comparison of time contracting with performance contracting follows.

Time Contracting	Performance Contracting
Pay for time worked	Pay for jobs completed
Pay not held up if work not completed	Pay held up if work not completed

Time Contracting	Performance Contracting
Continuous availability of workers	Discontinuous availability of workers
Close process supervision required	Little or no process supervision required
Supervisor and evaluator are one	Evaluators required
Employee works for the organization	Employee works for self
Projects or tasks ongoing and routine, often never ending	Projects or tasks are "chunked"; each has start and stop time
Work stretched to fill time allocated	Work compressed to get it done
Wage and salary increases are annual projects	Fee increases are negotiated on basis of productivity improvement
Benefits automatically paid regardless of actual productivity	Benefits not paid; individual arranges individualized benefits
Unemployment benefits assured	Unemployment benefits are not assured
Escalators are triggered on basis of time and other indirect factors	Escalators do not exist
Organization develops employees to avoid obsolescence	Individual uses "free time" to develop self
Jobbers not required for third-party intervention	Jobbers for third-party intervention add their fees
Accountability centers on being at place within period of time	Accountability clauses can be written for wide range of requirements
Money a weak base for motivation	Money a strong base for motivation
Idle time exists and is expensive	Idle time is eliminated
All jobs can be time contracted	Not all jobs can be performance contracted

This partial list of differences between time contracting and performance contracting shows that there are advantages and disadvantages to each approach. But as the proportion of white-collar workers grows in relation to blue-collar workers, the need for flexible compensation system linked to productivity will increase. Performance contracting appears to satisfy the conditions for compensation for productivity. Highly successful internal consultants in companies such as General Electric, Gulf and Western Industries, and Stanley Works are showing that performance contracting can work.

The question remains whether performance contracting can work for nonprofessional workers as it does for professional workers. One possibility that could make it practical for both groups of workers is use of both performance and time contracting. A third-party intervenor could help determine in which situations each type of contracting would be feasible and agreeable. Unions already act as third-party intervenors for time contracting, and jobbers are available to act as such intervenors for performance contracting.

7. *MBO Is Moving Toward Transnational Collaboration.* It is moving toward transnational collaboration because management is moving in this direction. As the world economy becomes more integrative, participative management with mutually agreed-on goals and objectives will be between multinational corporations and host countries. The huge multinational corporations need world markets to survive and grow. They will confront world problems and solve them with the political entities. This will enhance competition from political-business collaborations as well as from business-business collaborations. A comparison between the old multinationals and the new transnationals is shown in Table 19.1.

MBO will be interwoven between government goals and objectives of service for its constituency and multinational corporations' goals and objectives of profits and growth for their stockholders.

8. *MBO Is Moving Information as a Strategic Resource.* It is moving information as a strategic resource because management is moving in the direction of managed information for corporate use. We are moving more and more into the age of information. Most workers are and will become information workers, because we are moving into an information economy in which knowledge and know-how will create new values. The emerging manager will be viewed as an information processor. That is, he or she will generate, analyze, store, retrieve, and communicate information in such a way as to perceive alternatives in decision making. The new emerging manager will conceptualize change and new directions through his or her role as purveyor and utilizer of information. The key elements of an information economy are knowledge workers, performance packages, service responses, time capsules, brainpower contributions, and computer productivities. MBO precedes the process of systematizing these elements into strategic goal setting.

TABLE 19.1 Comparison of Old Multinationals and New Transnationals

Old Multinationals	New Transnationals
Large management with affiliates, subsidiaries, and branches	Small management with host governmental collaboration
Capital investment from corporation	Capital investment from host national
Technology, marketing, and manufacturing	Technology and marketing
Taxes on earnings plus profits	Profit sharing with government taxes on company profits
Conspicuous giants with political overtones	Invisible giants with few political overtones
Pyramid-type oganization	Systems-type organization

9. *MBO Is Moving into "Collective-Will' Groups.*   It is moving into such groups because management is moving into large-scale projects that are complex and unwieldy. The traditional structure of functions and specialties will prove ineffective with these complexities. Technical and economic disappointments will be experienced. Groups will be formed with the will and motivation to complete a project in spite of disappointments, frustrations, and opposition. Those who create a "mental map" of what they want to do and how to do it are more likely to get it done than those who cannot. MBO will provide the process for this collective will to operate.

10. *MBO Is Moving to Integrate Multidisciplines into Super Goals.*   It is moving toward super goals and super objectives because management is moving in this direction. The purity and the narrowness of a field are breaking down. Historically, a discipline such as economics was maintained relatively narrow. Today the intrusions and assimiliations of many disciplines have expanded the field to enormous proportions. Economics, to be understood and practiced properly, now includes elements of science, technology, politics, history, cultural anthropology, and religion. MBO will provide the process for integrating elements of various disciplines into strategic planning and operating for a set of results.

WHAT MAKES AN EXCELLENT MBO MANAGER?

Is it special organizational structures, such as matrix management of functions and projects? Is it the use of sophisticated techniques, such as computer-aided decision making, behavior modeling, or zero-based budgeting? Is it having a set of policies and rules in a book, which guide and direct the management group? Most well-run companies use a fair sampling of these tools. However, these tools alone will not result in MBO excellence. Nor will any amount of technique or structure produce MBO excellence. Excellence comes about with a strength of thinking, preparing, and doing that can never be captured from a book. In fact, we can no longer "go by the book" in these days of turbulent change. If we are going to accommodate more people than ever before, more older people than ever before, less traditions than ever before, we need a new leverage of competence to take the needed jump upward, for we are losing the simple life. No book will help! Keeping an organization vital and strong is no job for the complacent, slovenly, or inaccurate. *To be a good MBO manager, one must be competent! To be an excellent MBO manager, one must be competent regularly!*

> *Self-development is this simple. If you never try anything new, you never learn. If you never learn anything, you'll never change. If you never change, you'll never transcend the old self. If you never take a risk or "stick your neck out," you'll stay right where you are—you won't move. You hold yourself back. If you trade appearances, personal comforts, and security for opportunity and innovations, you'll find what you really like*

as your real potential unfolds. Self-development is doing new things, learning, changing, transcending, while experiencing stress, discomfort, and insecurity. Strive for comfort, security, and ease and you'll be the old self. Strive for innovations, learning, and challenges and you'll experience self-reward, self-improvement, and self-development.

Self-excellence is this simple. If you never develop a personal model of excellence, you never have expectations. If you never have expectations, you'll never strive. If you never strive, you never experience new records of achievements. Expectations of excellence produce excellence, because they are self-reinforcing. They become self-fulfilling prophecies. Excellence is striving to do better than others or than oneself by rising above the past. The future is always clear with this one point. Reaching for new achievements is to never let up. It is to never compromise standards or ideals. We care to think the best of everything. We care to expect the best of everything. We care to make the best of everything. Excellence is leaving this world better than we found it!

But MBO excellence is not a skill, or a technique, or a condition. In answer to the questions, "What does it mean to be an excellent MBO manager?," "How do I know that I have become an excellent MBO manager?," "What do I need to become an excellent MBO manager?"—MBO excellence is a process. It is not a destination. It is moving from measurable ignorance to unmeasurable enlightenment, from clear individual authority to vague collaborative participation, from comfortable expectations and routines to stressful innovations. MBO excellence moves from small milestones to larger milestones, low plateaus to high plateaus, small achievements to great achievements in a never-ending journey of being better. MBO excellence, then, is becoming!

This section describes 20 standards or attributes of the excellent MBO manager. Each is a *detail for creating a definition* to answer the question, "What does it mean to be an excellent MBO manager?" Each is also a *dimension for measurement* to answer the question, "How do I know I have become an excellent manager?" And each is a *goal to pursue* to answer the question, "What do I need to do to become an excellent manager?"

Attribute	Standard of Excellence	MBO Excellence
Practices entrepreneurship	Knows there's always better way to do just about everything; searches for product and service innovations to further enterprise as business venture in competitive market; venturing is normal and natural	Excellence is starting leadership rather than emulating past leaders

Attribute	Standard of Excellence	MBO Excellence
Is proactive for accomplishments	Confidently active to bring successful and timely end planned set of expectations pursued and needed by customer, business enterprise, and manager; accomplishments are needed, pursued, and experienced on regular basis	Excellence is necessity rather than luxury
Thinks strategically	Sees competitiveness as positive force; plans new maneuvers with all existing factors in business process for creating and maintaining the competitive edge; strategically outrivals competitors	Excellence is outthinking, outknowing, and outdoing rivals
Sets objectives	Consistently exceeds goals and expectations by stretching profitability and productivity performance with formal strategic plans and activities that are attainable; objectives are mental targets always in focus	Excellence has much in common with quality
Improves productivity	Avoids wasting time on trivia and unimportant things; makes decisions with people to consume minimal resources and costs while reaching for highest level of performance; productivity is increased each year	Excellence is knowing what the productivity level is and getting angry over it
Uses knowledge and fundamentals	Develops concepts and makes judgments based on relevant, complete, and current understanding of company, product, information, technology, and job responsibilities; knowledge is current, relevant, and useful	Excellence starts with transcending idea
Tolerates uncertainty	Job is not made up of guarantees; moves toward significant accomplishments while handling new unknowns, new ways, new risks, and new	Excellence is doing it, fixing it, and avoiding it happening again

Attribute	Standard of Excellence	MBO Excellence
	probabilities; uncertainty is life-style as innovations are pursued	
Meets with customers	Maintains time, energy, and service with customer as investment with short- and long-range return; customers treated as most important persons in enterprise	Excellence is getting customer to come back for more, more, and more
Judges accurately	Possess needed skills to weigh, evaluate, and separate relevant from irrelevant, trivial from critical, needed from unneeded, important from unimportant; judgments are seen as strokes of wisdom	Excellence is preventing fixes, errors, and faults from happening in the first place
Is skillful problem solver	Goes beyond easy and quick solutions to needed and lasting solutions; problems get solved as fast as they emerge	Excellence is finding ways to prevent problems as part of problem-solving process
Establishes priorities	Separates and pursues critical, high-payoff results from low-payoff demands from the trivia; priorities are established and maintained	Excellence is getting results way they are planned rather than by accident
Wills to excel	Has driving urge to exert extra effort and strength that are different between good and great performance and super performance; will to do is strong, persevering, and unrelenting	Excellence originates with people rather than departments, standards, or organizations
Completes work in time frame	"Plays clock; never plays it by ear"; analysis, decisions, actions, activity, and results are made now, within time opportunity; time is seen as resource not to be wasted, as signal to start and move ahead, and as milestone to evaluate what happened	Excellence is accepting pressures and life as synonymous

Attribute	Standard of Excellence	MBO Excellence
Handles costs discriminately	Tradeoffs in decision making are made to favor cost reduction, cost avoidance, cost control, and cost effectiveness; decisions are seldom made without asking cost and how it can be kept minimal	Excellence is doing job right the first time
Communicates persuasively	Presents oral and written communications for people to grasp quickly, understand decisively, and move convincingly; communicates to listeners and readers with conviction and movement	Excellence is preventing disturbing word disrupting entire sentence
Maintains tough-mindedness	Winning and losing are everyone's legacy, but not quitting while facing rigorous challenge belongs to few; tough-mindedness means never to be discouraged or dissuaded in achievements	Excellence is expecting more and more from oneself and less and less from others
Unfold human potential	Advances perception, attitudes, talents, and skills of people through performance stretches and innovative thinking; potential is released with annual increases in performance	Excellence does not start at top, middle, or bottom but from "within"; it is internal
Builds teamwork	Leads collection of workers into cohesive group and frequently helps them to solve their problems and reach their goals; team is formed on the basis of goals to be reached	Excellence is getting others to execute their role in script
Adapts to changes	Moves to go over, around, and occasionally under obstacles, but never halts when obstacles appear; unwanted changes are expected and dealt with, and adjustments are made; wanted changes are identified, assimilated, and managed	Excellence is dealing with complex in simple way

Attribute	Standard of Excellence	MBO Excellence
Receives satisfaction	Real enjoyment is in work, work life, work challenges, and fellow workers; satisfiers emerge with contributions made to company, to work life, and to fellow workers	Excellence finds rewards of work; it is not end of working but increased capacity to perform work

SUMMARY

This last chapter focuses on the future of MBO. Many have thought MBO was fading out, because they failed to see its conceptual elements in the managerial process. A look at the managerial achievements of the past helps to see that these elements existed throughout history. What has been happening in recent times is the identification of these elements and their formalization into a way of thinking and managing.

This chapter also looks into the future, and predictions are made about the next 40 years. From these two perspectives, past and future, ten directions for MBO are identified.

1. MBO is moving down to workers, especially professional workers.
2. MBO is moving into a group process.
3. MBO is moving toward entrepreneurship.
4. MBO is moving to include risk factors, productivity, and quality.
5. MBO is moving toward large-scale accomplishments.
6. MBO is moving to performance contracting.
7. MBO is moving toward transnational collaboration.
8. MBO is moving information as a strategic resource.
9. MBO is moving into "collective-will" groups.
10. MBO is moving to integrate multidisciplines to super goals.

The chapter also includes factors that make an excellent MBO manager. These are not techniques, skills, structures, or policies, even though excellent managers use these tools. What makes an excellent MBO manager is being part of a process that allows for improvement. Attributes, standards, and a style of thinking are the active agents in the process.

BIBLIOGRAPHY

Cleveland, Harlan, *The Future Executive*. New York: Harper & Row, 1972.
Crosby, Phillip B., *Quality Is Free*. New York: McGraw-Hill, 1980.

Flaherty, John E., *Managing Change: Today's Challenge to Management*. New York: Morrow, 1976.

George, Claude S., *History of Management Thought*. Englewood Cliffs, NJ: Prentice-Hall, 1968.

Mali, Paul, *Improving Total Productivity*. New York: Wiley, 1978.

Manual of Excellent Managements. New York: American Institute of Management, 1970.

Naisbitt, John, *Megatrends*. New York: Warner, 1982.

Peters, Thomas J., and Waterman, Robert H., *In Search of Excellence*. New York, Warner, 1979.

Toffler, Alvin, *The Third Wave*. New York: Bantam, 1980.

Index